FALL IN

'The other day I came across an ancient school notebook. It was one of those with weights, measures and multiplication tables printed on the back cover. In it were the first notes I made for *Dad's Army*. I'd written them on the train on my way from Victoria to Stratford East where I was working as an actor in the legendary Joan Littlewood's famous Theatre Workshop company.

'The idea for a comedy series about the Home Guard had come to me a few days earlier. I'd served in the original Dad's Army at the age of 16 and remembered it very well, but I thought I'd brush up my facts as, even in 1967, it was a long time ago. I went to the Westminster public library and asked if they had any reference books about it. "Never heard of it!" said the girl behind the desk. My next visit was to the library at the Imperial War Museum. They produced several Home Guard training pamphlets and a couple of memoirs from Spanish Civil War veterans who had served in the Home Guard; there was no reference to it anywhere else – the Home Guard had been completely forgotten.

'The story of how David Croft and I got together, and how the series became a national institution has been written so often; there have been so many books, articles and TV programmes about the series that legends have grown up around it, some of them are completely untrue. One that persists is that David and I changed the parts of Captain Mainwaring and Sergeant Wilson around, and that John Le Mesurier was originally going to play the officer – this is completely incorrect. The true story is very simple: we cast Arthur Lowe as the officer long before casting the part of the sergeant. The then head of comedy [at the BBC] was Michael Mills who, incidentally, thought up the title, *Dad's Army*. Michael had been a lieutenant-commander in the navy during the war and always behaved as though he was on the quarterdeck in a force ten gale. "I got you Sergeant Wilson!" he shouted. "It's John Le Mesurier." And that was it.

'I know it's a sign of dotage to keep harping on the good old days, but working in BBC television in the late sixties and seventies was a wonderful experience. The creative freedom and encouragement were amazing: David and I were having lunch in the canteen one day when Huw Wheldon, the then managing director of BBC television, stopped at our table and asked: "What are you boys doing now?" We told him. "Well done," he said. "Cleared it with Michael Mills have you?" We nodded. "Excellent. Good luck." And that was it. He moved on. No committees to argue with, no heads of department to convince, the BBC had complete confidence in our work. They were indeed the golden days of television.'

JIMMY PERRY

INTRODUCTION

We may have entered a new millennium offering hope and expectation, but it's comforting to know that at the dawning of this new era we bring with us treasures and heirlooms of days gone by, including the jewel in the crown of British sitcoms, *Dad's Army*. Some people believe the new millennium is good enough reason to focus on the adage, 'Out with the old, in with the new', to look forward instead of clinging hold of the past. Thankfully, not everyone feels the same, and we can still sit back and wallow in the delights of yesteryear with the adventures of Walmington-on-Sea's Home Guard.

The success story from the pens of the estimable team of Jimmy Perry and David Croft keeps rolling on and on. It's over 32 years since the crisp, freshly-typed scripts of the first episode, 'The Man and the Hour', were opened and brought to life by a bunch of, largely, veteran character actors, whose experience and abilities had been founded on years of slogging away in repertory theatres up and down the country. In what is arguably the star of British sitcoms, the brilliant cast of regulars was often joined by guest artists, dropping in for a perfectly crafted vignette. Who can forget Robert Dorning's Mr West, the stuffy official from Swallow Bank's head office and the eccentric Captain Rogers in 'Something Nasty in the Vault' played by Norman Mitchell, or Philip Madoc as the memorable U-boat captain in 'The Deadly Attachment'?

Every one of Perry and Croft's characters were finely drawn, never a weak link in sight, which helps partly to explain the show's longevity. But the writers were just as adept at creating characters who didn't even appear in the show, like the irascible Mrs Mainwaring. We heard her heavy footsteps on the stairs and her moans while sleeping in the Anderson shelter, but she never honoured us with her presence. One of the many delights about watching *Dad's Army* was eavesdropping on Captain Mainwaring's private phone conversations with his wife, which were usually brought to an abrupt end when Elizabeth dropped the receiver in anger. In his wife's eyes, Captain Mainwaring could do nothing right, and for a brief moment one could afford the bank manager a little sympathy: his was not a marriage to crave!

Like any small-screen masterpiece, *Dad's Army* was built on solid foundations, including a perfect cast and fine scripts, essential for long-term success in the world of television. It became the strongest comedy team on TV, a quality ensemble that also enabled individuals within it to grow.

Other factors which played their part in the show's appeal and subsequent success were the gentle, harmless humour, so beautifully played by Messrs Lowe and Co, making for ideal family viewing, and also Perry and Croft's attention to detail and authenticity. For those like me, too young to have experienced life during the Second World War, *Dad's Army* can act as a revealing social document. Sure, it's comedy at the end of the day, and can be enjoyed as such, but through its exploration of attitudes towards various wartime issues, including conscientious objection, the threat of fifth columnists, the American influence on the war, call-up, rationing and the blackout, it's ideal material for anyone wanting to gain an appreciation of what life was really like in Blighty during the war years.

Jimmy Perry and David Croft, who experienced the period first-hand, were able to generate an atmosphere which reflected accurately a period of history when the citizens of Britain stood united against the evils of Hitler's ideologies. Nowadays, *Dad's Army* is devoured by millions of people, partly because of its nostalgic feel; for its many fans the adventures at Walmington-on-Sea provide a form of escapism to a place where life seemed more gentle and relaxed. Sure, the home nations were embroiled in the traumas of war, but the pace of life in the coastal town was relatively relaxed and slow, with everyone working together towards a common goal. People in Walmington carried on with their business as best they could, but the workplace was a much simpler environment. Nowadays the Swallow Bank would exist via e-mails, computers, banking cash machines and aggravating call centres, whereas in Mainwaring's day, face-to-face contact was the name of the game. Although life was harsh during the 1940s in many ways, Perry and Croft's *Dad's Army* is synonymous with the

THE COMPLETE A–Z OF

DAD'S ARMY

THE MEN OF
"DAD'S ARMY"

BECK.

THE COMPLETE A–Z OF
DAD'S ARMY

BY RICHARD WEBBER

BASED ON THE TELEVISION SERIES *DAD'S ARMY*

BY JIMMY PERRY AND DAVID CROFT

ORION

CONTENTS

To HILARY JOHNSON, THANKS FOR
ALL THE HELP AND ADVICE OVER THE YEARS.

First published in hardback in 2000 by Orion
An imprint of Orion Books Ltd.
First published in paperback in 2001 by Orion
Orion House, 5 Upper St. Martin's Lane
London WC2H 9EA

Text Copyright © Richard Webber, Jimmy Perry
and David Croft
Script Copyright © Jimmy Perry, David Croft
and Arthur Julian for *The Rear Guard*
Documents reproduced in book: BBC, Jimmy Perry,
David Croft and Herman Rush
Song on page 196: the Estate of the late Edward Sinclair
Pictures supplied by: *Radio Times*, Hugh Cecil, Bill Pertwee,
Paul Joel, David Davies, Mr B Woods, *Eastern Daily Press*.
Walmington map: Paul Carpenter
Locations list: Tony Pritchard
Paintings on pages 1 and 2: © Keith Turley
and the estate of the late James Beck respectively.

A CIP catalogue record for this book is available
from the British Library.

ISBN 0-75284-637-X

Printed and bound in Italy by Trento S.r.l.

Dad's Army Television Programmes

(Original transmission dates shown in brackets)

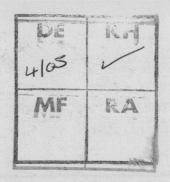

SERIES ONE
The Man and the Hour (31/7/68)
Museum Piece (7/8/68)
Command Decision (14/8/68)
The Enemy Within the Gates (28/8/68)
The Showing up of Corporal Jones (4/9/68)
Shooting Pains (11/9/68)

SERIES TWO
Operation Kilt (1/3/69)
The Battle of Godfrey's Cottage (8/3/69)
The Loneliness of the Long-distance Walker (15/3/69)
Sgt Wilson's Little Secret (22/3/69)
A Stripe for Frazer (29/3/69)
Under Fire (5/4/69)

SERIES THREE
The Armoured Might of Lance Corporal Jones (11/9/69)
Battle School (18/9/69)
The Lion has 'Phones (25/9/69)
The Bullet is Not for Firing (2/10/69)
Something Nasty in the Vault (9/10/69)
Room at the Bottom (16/10/69)
Big Guns (23/10/69)
The Day the Balloon Went Up (30/10/69)
War Dance (6/11/69)
Menace from the Deep (13/11/69)
Branded (20/11/69)
Man Hunt (27/11/69)
No Spring for Frazer (4/12/69)
Sons of the Sea (11/12/69)

SERIES FOUR
The Big Parade (25/9/70)
Don't Forget the Diver (2/10/70)
Boots, Boots, Boots (9/10/70)
Sgt – Save My Boy! (16/10/70)
Don't Fence Me In (23/10/70)
Absent Friends (30/10/70)
Put That Light Out! (6/11/70)
The Two and a Half Feathers (13/11/70)
Mum's Army (20/11/70)
The Test (27/11/70)
A Wilson (Manager)? (4/12/70)
Uninvited Guests (11/12/70)
Fallen Idol (18/12/70)

CHRISTMAS SPECIAL
Battle of the Giants (27/12/71)

SERIES FIVE
Asleep in the Deep (6/10/72)
Keep Young and Beautiful (13/10/72)
A Soldier's Farewell (20/10/72)
Getting the Bird (27/10/72)
The Desperate Drive of Corporal Jones (3/11/72)
If the Cap Fits… (10/11/72)
The King was in his Counting House (17/11/72)
All is Safely Gathered In (24/11/72)
When Did You Last See Your Money? (1/12/72)
Brain versus Brawn (8/12/72)
A Brush with the Law (15/12/72)
Round and Round Went the Great Big Wheel (22/12/72)
Time On My Hands (29/12/72)

SERIES SIX
The Deadly Attachment (31/10/73)
My British Buddy (7/11/73)
The Royal Train (14/11/73)
We Know Our Onions (21/11/73)
The Honourable Man (28/11/73)
Things That Go Bump in the Night (5/12/73)
The Recruit (12/12/73)

SERIES SEVEN
Everybody's Trucking (15/11/74)
A Man of Action (22/11/74)
Gorilla Warfare (29/11/74)
The Godiva Affair (6/12/74)
The Captain's Car (13/12/74)
Turkey Dinner (23/12/74)

SERIES EIGHT
Ring Dem Bells (5/9/75)
When You've Got to Go (12/9/75)
Is There Honey Still For Tea? (19/9/75)
Come In, Your Time is Up (26/9/75)
High Finance (3/10/75)
The Face on the Poster (10/10/75)

CHRISTMAS SPECIAL
My Brother and I (26/12/75)

CHRISTMAS SPECIAL
The Love of Three Oranges (26/12/76)

SERIES NINE
Wake-up Walmington (2/10/77)
The Making of Private Pike (9/10/77)
Knights of Madness (16/10/77)
The Miser's Hoard (23/10/77)
Number Engaged (6/11/77)
Never Too Old (13/11/77)

ACKNOWLEDGEMENTS

Many people help when it comes to writing a book, especially one of this nature. First and foremost I want to thank Jimmy Perry and David Croft for letting me write my second book about what is, in my opinion, their greatest situation comedy. In addition to granting permission, they have given up much of their time to talk, answer questions and write contributions for the book.

Next, I'd like to pass on my gratitude to all the actors, members of the production team and relatives of those who have sadly died, for allowing me the chance to interview them or borrow some of their photos. In particular, thanks go to Ian Lavender, Clive Dunn, Bill Pertwee, Frank Williams, Gladys Sinclair, Joan Le Mesurier, Althea Ridley, Kay Beck, Veronica Laurie, Mary Husband, Alan Hunter-Craig, Colin Whitaker and Bob Spiers.

As well as being interviewed, some people have contributed pieces to the book, which have added much interest. Thank you to Harold Snoad, Michael Knowles, Eric Longworth, Paul Joel, Sandra Exelby, Peter Chapman, Stuart Sherwin, Gordon Peters, Desmond Cullum-Jones, John Ringham, David Davies, Tim Ball, Peter Day, John Gatland, Caroline Dowdeswell, Brian Fisher, Jean Gilpin, Alec Coleman, Tony Harding, Hugh Cecil (who also took some of the location shots used in the book) and Jo Austin.

Some people helped in other ways, so I'd like to thank Jack Wheeler, for checking for any factual slip-ups, Hilary Johnson for her expert editorial advice when the rush was on, David Hamilton for providing data regarding the radio episodes, Paul Carpenter and Tony Pritchard for allowing me to use the Walmington-on-Sea street plan and location guide respectively, Dave Homewood, John Simpson, Herman Rush for letting me reproduce *The Rear Guard* script, Deborah Wyatt, Susan Pound, Simon Hall, John Barrett, Victoria Jones and Chris Dancy at the BBC, Neil Somerville at BBC Written Archives, Gordon Brodie, Iain Wilson, Ray Moore and Keith Eldred.

I'm grateful to Keith Turley for letting me reproduce his excellent painting of the *Dad's Army* cast. Keith can be contacted on 01384 270143 regarding the painting.

Thanks also to Don Smith (who took many of the photos in this book and whose enthusiasm for his job has resulted in the creation of a photographic *Dad's Army* archive), David Porter (for his photos), my agent Jeffrey Simmons, Pandora White and Trevor Dolby at Orion and Harry Green. And love as always to my wife, Paula, for maintaining her sanity when every second of the day was being taken up with *Dad's Army*!

RICHARD WEBBER

The team played their cards right and became a national institution.

human desire to wallow in nostalgia, to hold on to a belief that life was simpler in days gone by.

It's hard to imagine a time when *Dad's Army* is finally pensioned off to the dusty vaults at the BBC. While more contemporary shows struggle even to tread water in today's tough media market, it must be reassuring for executives at the Beeb to know that the antics of Captain Mainwaring and the rest of the bungling Walmington-on-Sea Home Guard can be relied upon to pull in sizeable audiences. The continuing success of *Dad's Army* is remarkable, and there is surely nothing to match it in the annals of British comedy. It has endured the test of time

because it has a timeless appeal, enabling it to transcend boundaries that weaker programmes struggle to cross. The strong characterisations and well-tuned humour is accessible to all ages, which partly explains why the show is enjoyed by young and old alike.

I hope, just like the entire population it would seem, that Perry and Croft's tales from sleepy Walmington-on-Sea enjoy a life of eternity, allowing future generations to experience and relish this feast of televisual comedy.

RICHARD WEBBER
Clevedon, March 2000

ABOUT THE BOOK

Writing this book has been a mammoth task. One of the biggest problems faced by anyone contemplating penning an A–Z of any description is knowing where to draw the line. A manageable task can quickly become an uncontrollable monster if you're not careful; usually time constraints provide the final discipline, but it's no easy feat deciding what qualifies for inclusion in an A–Z of any TV show. Since setting out to compile a definitive reference book exploring, hopefully, every aspect of *Dad's Army* I have been faced with just such issues.

One of the most difficult and time-consuming tasks has been tracking down some of the actors, actresses and crew members associated with the sitcom, stage show or film, many of whom have long since left the profession or died. Often, agents held no contact address or records, which made it virtually impossible, in some cases, to obtain sufficient material to write a profile for the book. Occasionally I have resorted to telephone directories in the hope of locating some of the more elusive people. I have included as many profiles as possible, which I hope will help fans of the sitcom know a little more about the careers of thespians who appeared in supporting or minor roles, or those who helped behind the scenes. Inevitably, given the enormity of the task, it's not been possible to include career details on everyone. If I had another two years to write the book, no doubt I could cover many more.

Although I've included plenty of details regarding the stage, radio and film adaptations of *Dad's Army*, I make no excuses in focusing primarily on the television series that over the years

has brought much welcome relief to some tired and, otherwise, mundane television schedules. Obviously I enjoy watching the movie on its regular outings, have wondered for some time why the BBC don't repeat the very entertaining radio series and would loved to have caught sight of the stage show on its nationwide tour but, for me, the television series will always be the pre-eminent facet behind the *Dad's Army* legend.

As mentioned earlier, I've tried to make this book as comprehensive as possible, cramming in as much information as time and the final word count would allow, but there are bound to be some details or areas that have not made their way in. However, I hope you find what is included informative, entertaining and helpful in answering all those nagging questions you have about the sitcom. As well as actor profiles I've included character profiles, too. Even those unseen characters who were mentioned in the scripts have been given their rightful place in this publication, together with details of who mentioned them, in which episode and the context in which their name/s were used. If during my research I have been unsure about the spelling of a particular place or character, I have referred to Perry and Croft's original scripts.

Locations, such as the many cafés in the town of Walmington, have been detailed, together with the incidental music used throughout, the names of the extras whose names never appeared on the closing credits, the scenes that were cut prior to recording and much, much more.

Enjoy your read.

'Absent Friends'

AA MAN, The

Played by Dervis Ward (film)

The AA patrolman refuses to help Mainwaring when he pulls up on his motorbike. As soon as he notices the platoon's broken-down van is gas-fuelled, he suggests calling the gas board and rides off.

ABSENT FRIENDS

Recorded: Friday 7/8/70

Original transmission: Friday 30/10/70, 8.00–8.30pm

Original viewing figures: 13.9 million

Repeated: 4/7/71

CAST

Arthur Lowe	Captain Mainwaring
John Le Mesurier	Sergeant Wilson
Clive Dunn	Lance Corporal Jones
John Laurie	Private Frazer
James Beck	Private Walker
Arnold Ridley	Private Godfrey
Ian Lavender	Private Pike
Bill Pertwee	ARP Warden
Janet Davies	Mrs Pike
Edward Sinclair	Verger
J G Devlin	Regan
Arthur English	Policeman
Patrick Connor	Shamus
Verne Morgan	Landlord
Michael Lomax	2nd ARP Warden

Platoon: Hugh Hastings, Colin Bean, Freddie Wiles, Vic Taylor, Leslie Noyes, Frank Godfrey, Desmond Cullum-Jones, Freddie White, George Hancock, Emmett Hennessy

ATS Girls: Diana Holt and Betty Goulding

ARP Wardens: Victor Croxford and Ron Gregory

Irishmen: Ray Emmins and Fred Davies

PRODUCTION TEAM

Script: Jimmy Perry and David Croft

Producer/Director: David Croft

Production Assistants: Harold Snoad and Donald Clive

Sound Supervisor: Michael McCarthy

Lighting: Howard King

Design: Paul Joel

Assistant Floor Manager: David Taylor

Vision Mixer: Dave Hanks

Costume Supervisor: Barbara Kronig

Make-Up Supervisor: Cynthia Goodwin

Mainwaring arrives at the church hall unexpectedly: he has decided not to attend the Lodge meeting in London because his wife hates being left alone during air raids. Jones, Wilson and Pike are the only people on parade, the rest are down the pub playing darts with the ARP wardens, even though Wilson would rather they didn't! Mainwaring turns a blind eye so long as Wilson gets them back within ten minutes: but he fails.

Mainwaring decides to go with Wilson and Jones to the pub. He talks to his men but they're still not prepared to return. If they're back in five minutes, he'll say nothing about it, but Godfrey is the only one who returns.

Back at the church hall someone from GHQ phones: an armed IRA suspect has been found in Ivy Crescent, and the police require the Home Guard's help. With the rest of the platoon AWOL, it's up to the intrepid Mainwaring, Wilson, Jones and Pike to apprehend the suspect. They arrest an Irishman and take him to the church hall, but when his brother, Shamus, arrives later to try and free Patrick, a fracas ensues. Mainwaring's attempt to resolve matters ends in failure, and it's down to Wilson to sort them out single handed.

ACCIDENTS

Inevitably filming a TV programme carries a risk of accidents, especially if scenes involve any degree of physical exercise or effort, and *Dad's Army* wasn't without the odd injury. For insurance purposes, details of such incidents had to be recorded on an 'Accident and Industrial Disease Report Form', some of which are retained in the production files of the BBC archives.

5.5.69: John Le Mesurier strained a ligament in his left leg at the Stanford Practical Training Area near Thetford, Norfolk. Le Mesurier told the production assistant that the accident probably happened 'during the action shooting when he – along with the other members of the platoon – had to fall flat on the ground on cue.'

16.6.70: While filming a scene for 'Boots, Boots, Boots' on the beach at Winterton-on-Sea, Norfolk, Desmond Cullum-Jones was drilling in the sea in bare feet. He suffered a nasty cut under the toes on his left foot, which was cleaned in disinfectant and dressed by Harold Snoad.

18.10.70: Colin Bean cut his hand and was treated by a first-aid attendant from British Industrial Sand Ltd, Leziate, Kings Lynn. The accident took place in the sand dunes above the quarry, during a scene in which he had to 'rush to the shelter of a sand dune, throw himself down for cover and fire at an imaginary enemy. An explosive charge which had been laid in the sand to represent enemy fire hitting the sand dune, exploded underneath Mr Bean's left hand. Mr Bean in the excitement of the moment had thrown himself down in a different spot to that rehearsed.'

18.10.70: Bill Pertwee had sand in his eyes resulting in mild conjunctivitis, while filming at the British Industrial Sand Quarry, Leziate, Kings Lynn. He was given eye baths to relieve the discomfort. The report form states: 'During a filmed fight scene between John Laurie and Bill Pertwee, a considerable amount of sand entered Mr Pertwee's eyes and although he bathed his eyes immediately, the accident gave him some discomfort for the next three days.'

20.10.70: Clive Dunn cut the inside of his mouth on the sports ground at the Stanford Training Area. The incident occurred during a film scene in which Clive, playing a wicket keeper, 'had to catch a ball bowled by Andy Luckhurst. Clive missed the ball and was struck in the mouth.'

20.10.70: Arthur Lowe suffered bruising to the left side of his head when a ball hit him while filming the episode 'The Test' on the sports ground at the Stanford Training Area. 'During a film scene in which Arthur Lowe – playing a batsman – had to duck a bumper, a soft ball thrown as part of the action by Phil Bishop, the PA [production assistant], struck Mr Lowe on the head. The accident resulted from a combination of the batsman not ducking quickly enough and the thrower throwing too low.'

28.8.71: On a bridge over River Little Ouse, within the Stanford Practical Training Area, Arnold Ridley was required to 'clear the way of a lorry backing towards him'. While making this movement, he twisted his knee, and was taken to Thetford's Cottage Hospital, where he was found to have pulled a cartilage in his leg.

6.10.72: Freddie Wiles had his right eye scratched by the branch of a tree, and was seen by the pharmacist at Boots in Thetford. The incident occurred in a field at Walnut Tree Farm, when he 'walked into a tree and a branch brushed across his right eye'.

6.10.72: Ian Lavender suffered a small cut and bruising to his right hand and wrist while filming in the same field as Freddie Wiles at Walnut Tree Farm. 'During action in the filming, Ian Lavender slipped on the grass and fell on to the trigger of a Tommy gun, sustaining a cut and bruising to his right hand thumb and wrist.'

10.10.72: A contractor, Rodney Simpson, a Kirby Wire specialist, hurt himself while preparing a stuntman for a scene at the Railway Bridge, Fornsett St Peter, Norfolk. 'While assisting with Kirby Wires which were being attached to a stunt artist, Simpson slipped down the railway embankment causing shin scuffing to his left leg – on a previous operation scar.'

23.5.73: Bill Pertwee bruised the top of his thigh while filming at The Grange Farm, Sapiston, Norfolk. The report says the 'artist moving across van caught his left leg on trailer attachment.'

26.5.73: John Laurie took 'the top layer of skin off the top of his head' while working at the Honington Church Hall School. He was treated with Savlon and an antiseptic dressing by Gordon Pert, the production assistant, after grazing his head on a low shed for cycles.

22.6.73: While rehearsing at Television Centre for 'The Deadly Attachment', Philip Madoc suffered an abrasion to his left temple. As the report form explains, during a 'special effect sequence the artist lowered his head to avoid special effect jabolite falling from the ceiling, and hit his head on a dummy revolver lying on the floor.'

ACOCK WOOD

When Jones, Walker and Pike are out on patrol in the early hours of the morning in the episode 'The Enemy Within the Gates', the air raid siren sounds. A bomb drops nearby and Jones comments that it fell in Acock Wood, situated on the outskirts of Walmington.

ADAMS, BERNICE

Born: London

Roles: ATS Girl (S9, episode 5: 'Number Engaged') (TV); Mrs Pike, Carmen Caramba, an Andrews Sister and Girl on the Beach (stage show)

At the age of 13, Bernice studied at a full-time dancing school in London for three years, after which she started getting work in pantomimes, variety shows and cabaret around the country.

In the late 1950s, she was successful in getting a part in her first West End musical, *Most Happy Fella*, followed by a succession of West End productions, including *Gentlemen Prefer Blondes*; *Promises, Promises*; *Gypsy*; *Sweet Charity*; *Bordello*; *Jack the Ripper* and, of course, *Dad's Army*. She also appeared in stage plays, summer shows and the occasional TV production, such as *Are You Being Served?* and *It Ain't Half Hot, Mum*, before moving into directing. For a time she worked in Holland.

In the 1980s she gave up acting and worked as a production manager for a dance and theatre company, before relocating to France and working in the Cannes office. Other than a brief spell working on a cruise ship, Bernice has remained in France, and is now an office manager for a company in Monte Carlo.

ADAMS, MR

He owns a music shop in Walmington and, although not seen in the episode 'Command Decision', his bank account is drawn to Mainwaring's attention when he issues a cheque while having no funds. Wilson points out that Mr Adams is inclined to over-order; he asked for 400 copies of the record, 'We're Gonna Hang Out the Washing on the Siegfried Line'. Admiring his spirit, Mainwaring agrees to honour his cheque.

ADAMSON, REG

Played by Stuart Sherwin (TV); Michael Segal (radio, although called '2nd Warden')

Reg is the junior warden in 'A Brush With the Law'. The eagle-eyed warden spots a light burning in the church hall office, leading to Mainwaring being summoned to court. Unlike his superior, Reg is a level-headed sort of guy who points out that it could have been anyone in the office that night, not necessarily Mainwaring.

AGNEW, PRIVATE

Not seen in the sitcom, Agnew is a member of the Walmington Home Guard. Jones calls his name in 'Absent Friends'.

AILES-STEVENSON, ANN

Make-up supervisor on the sixth series (TV)

Ann, who was born in Ipswich, trained as a hairdresser while working for Fortnum and Mason's. Talking to someone who worked in Australian TV fanned her ambition to move into television make-up, something she achieved by joining the BBC in 1964, at the age of 19. After completing three months training at the Beeb's make-up school she became a trainee make-up artist, assisting on shows including *The Black and White Minstrel Show*. After eight years with the BBC she was promoted to make-up designer and went on to work on some popular shows, such as *Softly, Softly*; *Barlow at Large*; *The Liver Birds*; *Only Fools and Horses*; *Steptoe and Son*; *The Day of the Triffids*; *Dear John*; *Lorna Doone*; *Last of the Summer Wine*; *Bergerac*; *Grange Hill*; *That's Life*; *Anna Karenina*; *EastEnders*; *Blankety Blank* and four series of *Keeping Up Appearances*. Ann left the BBC in 1992 and now works freelance, mainly for Anglia and the BBC.

AIR RAID WARDENS

The experiences of bombing during the Great War ultimately led to the formation of Air Raid Precautions (ARP) in 1924. When Hitler appeared on the scene and began building up his air force, Parliament introduced the 1937 Air Raid Precautions Act forcing local authorities to plan how they could reduce the impact of enemy action against the population.

A year later, a nationwide appeal for at least one million men and women to become air raid wardens was launched, but recruitment was slow, until the Munich crisis in 1938 and the subsequent issuing of an official pamphlet titled 'The Protection of Your Home Against Air Raids' focused people's minds on the dangers facing the nation. Soon the ARP was inundated with volunteers.

The wardens played a vital role in the war

LIFE AS AN ARP WARDEN

'I was rather young – 18 to be precise. The Home Guard, or Local Defence Volunteers as they were then called, wouldn't accept me because I was sure to be called up before I could be trained.

'We were staying with my grandmother in Poole, Dorset, where I had organised the street fire watchers and pressganged them into buying a stirrup pump. This impressed the chief warden so I was asked to join the Air Raid Wardens. A bit of training was involved: I did a first aid course and learned how to put a broken arm in a sling and to stop arterial bleeding. I was taught a little about poisoned gases and how they smelled, and I was shown how to deal with droplets of mustard gas should they fall on me.

'Another memorable event was the technique for dealing with incendiary bombs. This entailed crawling through a smoke-filled hut, nose to ground, with the business end of a stirrup pump hose, shouting: "Water On!" when near the bomb and knowing when to use jet or spray, something we did in an episode of *Dad's Army*. My mother and I then moved to a posher part of Bournemouth where I shared a tiny warden's hut with Sir Robert Ropner and was deputed to check the fitting of gas masks to various old ladies in large houses.

'All this had very little to do with the formation of the character of Hodges. The programme needed an aggressive character who could get right up the nose of Mainwaring. I had cast Bill Pertwee in like roles in *Hugh and I* and *Beggar My Neighbour* so I had no hesitation in asking him to join us.'

DAVID CROFT

effort and were trained in all manner of duties, including identifying poisonous gases. But they were never the most popular people, as shown by Mainwaring and his men's disdain for Hodges. In *Dad's Army*, the wardens have lectures in the church hall every Wednesday evening. These interfere with Mainwaring's plans to defend the homeland, adding further tension to an already strained relationship between Hodges and Mainwaring – although the rest of the platoon don't take too kindly to the greengrocer's constant snide comments either.

Hodges becomes Chief Warden in 'The Armoured Might of Lance Corporal Jones', swapping the obligatory black helmet for the coveted white version. He's the bane of Mainwaring's life, as are the rest of Hodges' wardens, including Mrs Cole, Mr Cole, Mr Yeldan, Mr Alberts and Mr Adamson.

ALBERT

Never seen, Albert is mentioned by Walker in 'No Spring for Frazer'. He's a friend of Joe's who from time to time has helped make spare parts; how-

ever, he's unable to help when it comes to a butterfly spring for the platoon's Lewis gun because he's in jail after making a spare part for a safe!

ALBERTS, MR
Played by Stuart Sherwin (TV)
A junior air-raid warden reporting to Hodges, Mr Alberts is responsible for the immediate vicinity surrounding the Jolly Roger Ice Cream Parlour, with his base situated on Walmington's sea front. He is seen in 'Put That Light Out!'.

ALDOUS, ROBERT (1934–)
Born: Mansfield
Role: German Pilot (S3, episode 12: 'Man Hunt' and 1969 *Christmas Night with the Stars* insert) (TV)
Robert studied at RADA between 1953 and '55 and has been a professional actor for over four decades, during which time he's appeared on stage – his preferred medium – and TV, including appearances in *'Allo, 'Allo*, *Softly, Softly* and *Jeeves and Wooster*. He's been busy ever since leaving drama school, and received two offers of work the day he graduated. In the West End he's played Sir Toby Bumper in *The School For Scandal* and Chief Weasel in *The Wind in the Willows*, among other things.

His first professional part was in the BBC production of *She Stoops to Conquer*, after which he secured a job in Aberdeen, followed by two years as Assistant Stage Manager (ASM) at London's Royal Court Theatre. Over 21 years, Robert has become one of the country's leading pantomime villains, performing alongside most of the famous variety actors, including seven productions with Danny La Rue.

On TV, he's been seen in *Probation Officer*, *The Golden Spur*, *Captain Moonlight*, *The First Churchills*, *Special Branch*, *Doctor Who*, *Warship*, *Crossroads*, *The Bill*, *The Face of the Enemy* and *Z Cars*.

His recent credits include a 13-month period with the National Theatre in *Enemy of the People* and *Peter Pan*, and the film *Extremely Dangerous*, with Sean Bean.

ALEXANDER PARK

In the original script it was called Alexander Gardens, but the park is near the library in Walmington. It was here that Godfrey spotted Wilson with his arm around a young lady – who turns out to be his daughter – in 'Getting the Bird'.

ALL IS SAFELY GATHERED IN

Recorded: Friday 3/11/72

Original transmission: Friday 24/11/72, 8.30–9.00pm

Original viewing figures: 16.5 million

Repeated: 18/8/73, 8/3/77, 24/10/89, 20/7/90 (N Ireland), 27/8/93, 24/1/97

CAST

Arthur Lowe . . . . .Captain Mainwaring
John Le Mesurier . . . . .Sergeant Wilson
Clive Dunn . . . . .Lance Corporal Jones
John Laurie . . . . .Private Frazer
James Beck . . . . .Private Walker
Arnold Ridley . . . . .Private Godfrey
Ian Lavender . . . . .Private Pike
Bill Pertwee . . . . .ARP Warden
Brenda Cowling . . . . .Mrs Prentice
Frank Williams . . . . .Vicar
Edward Sinclair . . . . .Verger
Colin Bean . . . . .Private Sponge
April Walker . . . . .Judy, a Land Girl
Tina Cornioli . . . . .Olive, a Land Girl
Platoon: Hugh Hastings, Michael Moore, Freddie Wiles, George Hancock, Leslie Noyes, Evan Ross, Hugh Cecil, Freddie White, Desmond Cullum-Jones
Extras: (Non-speaking Land Girl) Amanda Bishop, (Harmonium Player) Vera Palmer
Note: In the original script Mrs Yeatman was the harmonium player, but it's a different character in the televised version.

PRODUCTION TEAM

Script: Jimmy Perry and David Croft
Producer/Director: David Croft
Production Assistant: Gordon Pert
Film Cameraman: James Balfour
Sound Recordist: Les Collins
Film Editor: Bob Rymer
Lighting: Howard King
Studio Sound: John Delany
Design: Paul Joel
Assistant Floor Manager: Peter Fitton
Vision Mixer: Dave Hanks
Costume Supervisor: Susan Wheal
Make-Up Supervisor: Anna Chesterman

Godfrey requests three days holiday, so Mainwaring calls him to the office to explain why he wants a break when Hitler's troops are ready to pounce at any minute. Godfrey tells how before the Boer War he fell for a beautiful woman who lived nearby. The lady eventually married a farmer, but now she's widowed and has a large farm to look after; with her foreman in hospital with a hernia problem, and only three land girls to manage 100 acres of wheat, she needs help with the harvest. Understanding her plight, Mainwaring suggests the whole platoon helps Mrs Prentice.

Hodges, meanwhile, experiences a near miss: when a bomb knocks a beer glass from his hand, he's so shocked he examines his life and decides to turn over a new leaf and like all his enemies, including Captain Mainwaring. His new approach to life sees him helping the Home Guard bring in the harvest.

At the farm, Mrs Prentice says she has a problem: her neighbour, Mr Yates, hasn't supplied his thresher because he's behind with his own harvest, and no one knows how to work hers. Mainwaring isn't worried because Sponge is a farmer, but he's a sheep farmer and hasn't a clue about threshing machines. Jones eventually saves the day in his usual long-winded way, and the men get to work.

It isn't long before the problems start with Jones falling in the hopper, shredding his trousers in the process. But the harvesting continues and everyone works hard, except Walker who spends his time chatting up the land girls.

After three days' graft the harvest is complete, and the men celebrate with potato wine and home-made pasties. By the time the Vicar arrives to bless the harvest, nearly everyone is drunk, including Hodges and his fellow wardens, and it's not long before there is trouble among the congregation.

ALLEN, JOY

Born: Werrington

Roles: Clippie (S5, episode 3: 'A Soldier's Farewell') and Lady with the Pram (S7, episode 3: 'Gorilla Warfare') (TV)

Joy always wanted to become an actress and upon leaving school took elocution lessons before joining RADA. After drama school she was offered the chance to join a production of *King's Rhapsody* in two capacities: as an understudy and as a member of the chorus. Later,

In 'A Soldier's Farewell' Joy Allen played a leading role in Mainwaring's dreams.

when the principal girl in a Peterborough panto was taken ill, Joy took over, gaining valuable stage experience in the process.

Shortly after, Joy got married, raised a family and left the acting profession. But in the early 1970s, a director of a theatrical company in Corby, Northants, spotted her in an amateur production and invited her to join his company. She stayed three years, by which time she'd made the first of two appearances in *Dad's Army*.

Joy has been seen in other TV shows, including *Are You Being Served?*, and has taken on several non-speaking roles. Nowadays she works mostly as an extra.

ALLEN, JUDY
Costume designer on the Christmas special, 'Battle of the Giants'

AMERICAN VERSION
A pilot programme for an American version of *Dad's Army*, titled *The Rear Guard*, was recorded in 1976. Based on the British episode 'The Deadly Attachment', the American version was penned by Arthur Julian, who also produced the one-off. However, the pilot wasn't strong enough to convince executives to commission a complete series. (See 'Rear Guard, The' for information on the script Perry and Croft wrote for the American market.)

ANCHOR, THE
A pub in Walmington where Frazer meets George Clarke, who was in the same regiment as Jones. While the hostelry was mentioned in 'The Two and a Half Feathers', it had been seen earlier in the fourth series, when Wilson and Mainwaring attempt to have a pint after parade in 'Don't Forget the Diver'. Sadly, their post-parade ritual is ruined because they find Captain Square and a couple of his men also in the pub.

ANCHOR HOTEL, THE
Situated in Bridge Street, Thetford, the hotel, along with The Bell, was used by the cast and production team whilst filming on location. The 18th century former coach house is now a family-run, 16-bedroomed hotel, just a few minutes walk from the town centre.

ANDERSON SHELTER
Originally named after its designer, Dr David A Anderson, the shelter, which could provide protection for up to six people, sprang up in many gardens during the Second World War. As the threat of air strikes turned into reality, the Chamberlain government feared that hordes of people gathering in large, public shelters might produce huge casualties. They felt it best that people were dispersed in small groups, and so launched the Anderson shelter – which was originally intended for use indoors before technical objections saw it become an outdoor shelter.

Free to anyone earning below £250 per annum, the corrugated steel construction was simple, cheap and largely effective, protecting against almost anything except a direct hit. By the start of the Blitz, over two million had been issued by the government.

The shelter was sunk into the ground (approximately four feet down) and covered with earth; but it had its problems: not everyone in the areas most prone to air attacks had a garden in which to erect the shelter. For those fortunate enough to have the land, the shelters were prone to flooding and were extremely uncomfortable. The shelter's life came to an end in 1940, when steel shortages saw production lines cease.

In *Dad's Army*, the Anderson shelter plays a big part in Elizabeth Mainwaring's life, partly because she spends so much time there. In 'The Recruit', while her husband recovers in hospital from an operation to remove ingrowing toenails, she sends him a solitary apple with a note explaining the shelter is leaking again.

ANGERS, AVRIL
Born: Liverpool
Roles: Telephone Operator (S3, episode 3: 'The Lion has 'Phones' and S4, episode 7: 'Put That Light Out!') (TV); Mrs Keen ('Under Fire'), Operator ('Sorry, Wrong Number' and 'Put That Light Out!'), Waitress ('Brain versus Brawn') and Edna ('The Two and a Half Feathers') (radio)

Avril, born of theatrical parents, never felt stage struck but pursued a career in the entertainment world because it seemed the logical thing to do. She made her debut as a dancer at the age of 14.

She went on to write her own material for a stand-up comedy routine before moving into TV, where she's had her own series, *Dear Dotty*, and appeared in a string of shows, including *All Creatures Great and Small*, *Coronation Street* (in two different roles), *The Dustbinmen*, *Just Liz*, Granada's *Victoria and Albert* and the 1970 series, *The More We Are Together*. Avril is still busy in TV.

Her extensive theatrical performances include many West End appearances in *Oklahoma!*

ANGRY MAN, THE
Played by Nigel Hawthorne (TV)
During the air raid exercise in 'The Armoured Might of Lance Corporal Jones', this character isn't amused when Lance Corporal Jones borrows his bike.

ANN'S PANTRY
Seen in the episode 'Mum's Army', Ann's Pantry is one of Walmington-on-Sea's quaint cafés. Frequented by Mainwaring from time to time, it holds a special place in his heart for two reasons: it's where he met up with Mrs Gray for a quiet little chat, only to find half the platoon there, and it's where, before the war, he used to indulge himself in the Pantry's famous Devonshire cream teas.

It's easy to understand why Ann's Pantry is so popular: little round tables are dressed with crisp, frilly lace tablecloths, while the lightly patterned wallpaper is adorned with pictures on every wall, helping promote the homely feel the customers treasure.

ANSTRUTHER-STEVENS, MAJOR GENERAL
Played by Arnold Diamond (TV)
The highly decorated Major General is seen in the episode 'My Brother and I', attending the sherry party at St Aldhelm's church hall, which was organised by Home Guard officers in and around the area of Walmington.

APRIL HAIRDRESSER'S
(Film only)
A shop in Walmington's High Street, the hairdresser's is next door to Frazer's establishment.

ARCHARD, BERNARD (1916–)
Born: London
Role: Major General Fullard (film)
A veteran actor of stage and screen, Bernard learnt his trade in rep before branching out into films and TV. He was planning to emigrate to Canada when the offer to play Colonel Oreste Pinto in the long-running TV series, *Spycatcher*, which gave him his greatest success on the small screen, came along. From that moment he never looked back.

His extensive list of small-screen credits include appearances in *Night of Talavera*, *Dracula*, *The Suicide Club*, *Robin Hood*, *Sister Dora*, *World of Wodehouse*, *Lytton's Diary*, *Emmerdale* and ten episodes of *The Sound Recordist* in 1990. His film work includes over 30 pictures, such as *The Shadow Line* in 1975, *Sea Wolves*, *God's Outlaw* and *Hidden Agenda* in 1990.

Mainwaring enjoyed frequenting Ann's Pantry in Walmington-on Sea.

ARMOURED MIGHT OF LANCE CORPORAL JONES, THE

Originally titled, 'The Armoured Might of Jack Jones'

Recorded: Sunday 25/5/69

Original transmission: Thursday 11/9/69, 7.30–8.00pm

Original viewing figures: 10.5 million

Repeated: 4/4/70, 18/8/71, 4/1/77, 21/6/92, 25/5/96, 7/6/99

CAST

Arthur Lowe . . . . .Captain Mainwaring
John Le Mesurier . . . . .Sergeant Wilson
Clive Dunn . . . . .Lance Corporal Jones
John Laurie . . . . .Private Frazer
James Beck . . . . .Private Walker
Arnold Ridley . . . . .Private Godfrey
Ian Lavender . . . . .Private Pike
Janet Davies . . . . .Mrs Pike
Bill Pertwee . . . . .ARP Warden
Frank Williams . . . . .Vicar
Queenie Watts . . . . .Mrs Peters
Pamela Cundell . . . . .Mrs Fox
Jean St Clair . . . . .Miss Meadows
Olive Mercer . . . . .Mrs Casson
Nigel Hawthorne . . . . .Angry Man
Harold Bennett . . . . .Old Man
Dick Haydon . . . . .Raymond
Platoon: Colin Bean, Frank Godfrey, Richard Jacques, Hugh Cecil, Derek Chaffer, Richard Kitteridge, George Hancock, Michael Moore, Vic Taylor, Freddie Wiles
ATS Girl: Coreen Reed
Sailor: Brian Justice
Ladies in Shop and in Street: Patricia Matthews, Anne Evans and Mary Power

PRODUCTION TEAM

Script: Jimmy Perry and David Croft
Producer/Director: David Croft
Production Assistant: Harold Snoad
Film Cameraman: James Balfour
Film Editor: Bob Rymer
Lighting: Howard King
Studio Sound: Michael McCarthy
Design: Paul Joel
Assistant Floor Manager: Bill Harman
Vision Mixer: Dave Hanks
Costume Supervisor: Odette Barrow
Make-Up Supervisor: Cecile Hay-Arthur
Visual Effects: Peter Day

GHQ send a communiqué saying there isn't enough co-operation between the Home Guard and the ARP and the new chief warden – the dirty-finger-nailed Hodges – will be seeing Mainwaring to discuss ideas for co-operation.

Later, at Jones' shop, Walker has a quiet word with Jones and suggests he loans the delivery van as platoon transport. Walker confesses it will help his black market activities, and Jones will get petrol coupons in return so they'll both win. Jones agrees, and after the van is converted for military use, the platoon practise embarking and disembarking. Although it's primarily used as a troop carrier, its versatility sees it doubling as an ambulance. When Hodges, who's been working inside the church hall, comes out into the yard and hears it will be used as an ambulance as well, he commandeers the vehicle and the men for Saturday's air raid practice as stretcher-bearers.

Just when Walker and Jones think they'll be getting some petrol coupons, Mainwaring tells them the van will be converted to gas, but it's not long before Walker puts a bayonet into the gas supply pipe and the vehicle runs out of juice. Thanks to the Vicar's gas fire, the vehicle is refuelled, but before the day is out disaster looms for Mainwaring's platoon.

ARMSTRONG, MR

Mr Armstrong is not seen in the series, but Jones talks about him in 'Keep Young and Beautiful', by which time he's been dead a month. He was a Walmington-on-Sea resident, who died at the grand age of 96. When Jones and Godfrey are worried about being kicked out of the Home Guard due to their age, they butter up Frazer by claiming his embalming skills meant Mr Armstrong didn't look a day over 60.

ARMY CAPTAIN, THE

Played by Robert Mill (TV)

A member of the regular troops whose responsibilities in guarding an important stretch of telephone wires are taken on by Mainwaring and his men in 'Number Engaged'.

ARMY SERGEANT, THE

Played by Kenneth MacDonald (TV)

A sergeant in the regular army who hands over responsibility for guarding the stretch of phone lines to Mainwaring and his mob in 'Number Engaged'.

ARTILLERY OFFICER, THE

Played by James Taylor (TV)

In 'The Desperate Drive of Corporal Jones', the artillery officer is responsible for issuing the co-ordinates and orders during the divisional scheme attended by the Walmington Home Guard.

ASH, JOHN (1954–)

Born: London

Role: Raymond (S4, episode 8: 'The Two and a Half Feathers') (TV)

As a child actor, John trained at the Barbara Speake Stage School, and appeared in the original 1962 stage production of Oliver! He also appeared in shows like Nicholas Nickleby, and Out of the Unknown for BBC2, and worked a lot for the Children's Film Foundation.

John's mother was a Tiller Girl and he'd always wanted to enter the world of showbusiness. He joined stage school at the age of 11, and appeared in five West End shows whilst a student, including Dancing Years, Flint and My Little Boy, My Big Girl. He toured in a production of Peter Pan and played the title role in Oliver! at Northampton Rep. During his years at the school he also worked on the screen, appearing in many films. On television he played a boy scout in an episode of Father, Dear Father and was a regular in the series The Flaxton Boys.

After leaving the school in 1970 he trained with the Royal Shakespeare Company for a while, and appeared in a Hammer film, but eventually decided to leave the profession. He's since become a qualified electrician and works behind the scenes on commercials and television, whilst retaining his Equity membership.

ASHLEY-JONES, CAPTAIN

Played by Rex Garner (TV)

Ashley-Jones captains the Dymwhich Home Guard platoon and attends the School of Explosives at the same time as Mainwaring and his men in 'Fallen Idol'.

ASLEEP IN THE DEEP

Recorded: Friday 26/5/72

Original transmission: Friday 6/10/72, 8.30–9.00pm

Original viewing figures: 17 million

Repeated: 30/6/73, 10/10/89, 14/2/90 (N Ireland), 30/7/93, 20/12/96

CAST

Arthur Lowe . . . . .Captain Mainwaring
John Le Mesurier . . . . .Sergeant Wilson
Clive Dunn . . . . .Lance Corporal Jones
John Laurie . . . . .Private Frazer
James Beck . . . . .Private Walker
Arnold Ridley . . . . .Private Godfrey
Ian Lavender . . . . .Private Pike
Bill Pertwee . . . . .ARP Warden
Colin Bean . . . . .Private Sponge
Platoon: Vic Taylor, Freddie White, Hugh Cecil, George Hancock, Leslie Noyes, Freddie Wiles, Desmond Cullum-Jones, Hugh Hastings, Michael Moore

PRODUCTION TEAM

Script: Jimmy Perry and David Croft
Producer/Director: David Croft
Production Assistant: Gordon Pert
Lighting: Howard King
Studio Sound: Michael McCarthy
Design: Paul Joel
Assistant Floor Manager: Peter Fitton
Vision Mixer: Dave Hanks
Costume Supervisor: Susan Wheal
Make-Up Supervisor: Cynthia Goodwin
Visual Effects: Peter Day

While the Home Guard keep an eye out for Nazi parachutists from the pavilion, Hodges appears and announces two bombs were dropped in the recent raid, one landing in the woods and the other on the pumping station, where Walker and Godfrey are on patrol.

At the pumping station the bomb causes sub-

'Asleep in the Deep'

Even back then it was felt the show was ideal family viewing, and not just accessible to those who remembered, or even belonged to the Home Guard.

Authenticity was another key factor in the show's appeal. The author of the Audience Research Report for 'The Man and the Hour' wrote that many people felt that it was a 'true picture of village and small town preparations

stantial damage, trapping Walker and Godfrey in the process. To make matters worse, Walker thinks Godfrey's dead. Mainwaring and Hodges – having drawn lots – form the head of a chain removing rubble in order to free their two compatriots, and eventually get through. Godfrey finally wakes up, but when Jones closes the door and brings the ceiling down, everyone is trapped.

To add to the chaos, the water pipes burst and the underground room starts flooding; it's a race against time, especially as Jones can't turn off the stopcock. The water continues rising and ideas regarding their escape route are slow in coming, but when Godfrey notices a man-hole cover, there's hope for Mainwaring and his men yet.

ATS GIRL, THE
Seen in 'Number Engaged'. (See 'Doreen'.)

AUDIENCE FIGURES
There is no doubting that *Dad's Army* is a sure-fire ratings winner. Even now, over three decades since its debut, the sitcom pulls in remarkable audiences, leaving most of its pallid modern rivals in its wake. Back in its infancy, the TV series quickly attracted a strong, loyal following and by the second season was pulling in audiences of over 12 million. *Dad's Army* reached its peak – in audience terms – during the fifth season, by which time it was averaging over 16 million viewers per episode.

Average viewers per series

Series 1: 8.2 million	Series 6: 12.3 million
Series 2: 12.2 million	Series 7: 14.8 million
Series 3: 12.1 million	Series 8: 13.5 million
Series 4: 14.4 million	Series 9: 10.5 million
Series 5: 16.3 million	

Most watched TV episodes (on first showing)
'Battle of the Giants'
'Brain versus Brawn'
'A Soldier's Farewell'
Least watched TV episodes (on first showing)
'Museum Piece'
'The Man and the Hour'
'The Enemy Within the Gates'
By the time the first episode was broadcast on the radio in 1974, its big brother on TV had been running six years and was firmly established, which explains why the audience figures remained fairly constant throughout the 67-episode run on the radio.
Most listened to radio episode (on original broadcast)
'A Soldier's Farewell' (1,414,000 people)
Least listened to radio episode (on original broadcast)
'A Question of Reference' (454,500 people)

AUDIENCE REPORTS
One method the BBC employed to monitor public opinion towards the Corporation's shows was to conduct an audience survey after every, or selected, episodes. Such reports were completed for *Dad's Army* and make interesting reading. Those who took part in the survey became known as members of the BBC1 viewing panel and, after watching all, or part, of the selected episodes, expressed their views about the show via the questionnaire.

The opening episode, 'The Man and the Hour', received a favourable response, with the majority of the panel agreeing that the series had made a promising start, exploring a theme that had 'considerable potentialities for comedy'.

against Hitler', while many said they could 'almost see the people of my own small village at that time in the characters.' It was generally felt that 'if the following instalments are as well acted and true to life as this one, it should be a very good series.' Settings, costumes and make-up were all spot on, as the opening episode caught the wartime atmosphere well.

However, not everyone felt as positive towards the sitcom, although disgruntled viewers were certainly in the minority. Some people felt that the episode was too exaggerated and the treatment 'too farcical', perhaps even 'lampooning the LDV'.

By the time an Audience Research Report was completed for 'The Showing Up of Corporal Jones', the report's author pointed out that *Dad's Army* was 'clearly a popular show', with the fifth instalment being more favourably received than any of the previous four. One of the qualities of Perry and Croft's writing is the ability to blend and interweave pathos with comedy, and many viewers felt the comedy element within this particular episode was 'heightened by this touch of pathos'.

Perhaps the show's greatest appeal was its gentle humour and, as the series progressed, a smaller minority suggested the series took the mickey out of the real-life Home Guard. By the end of the second series, most people were saying the sitcom's greatest strength lay in the 'gentle humour, stemming from accurate observation of human nature in general and the personal traits of a mixed bunch of men in particular.'

By the start of series four, viewers, in response to the screening of the episode 'The Big Parade', were rating the sitcom as 'head and shoulders above most comedy programmes' around at that time: a view still echoed today.

When 'Never Too Old', the final episode, hit the screens in 1977, the viewing panel's opinions hadn't wavered from those voiced nine years earlier. In response to the closing instalment, the author of the Audience Research Report wrote: 'It was also widely agreed that the programme had been one of the most consistently amusing on television'. Simply expressed by one viewer, there was nothing to dislike about *Dad's Army*, and its outstanding feature was felt to be 'the relationships between all the major characters, especially as these had been particularly well developed and were portrayed in such a convincing manner'.

The quality of the storylines was also highlighted as a major attraction, and they were regarded as, 'generally humorous yet plausible'. The report signs off with the most laudatory of comments. The author writes: 'Altogether, it was generally agreed that the programme had always been magnificent, that the cast could not have been better chosen and that it was sad to see the series come to an end.'

AUDIENCE REPORT EXTRACTS

'THE MAN AND THE HOUR'
(Series 1, episode 1, transmitted 31/7/68)

'"What memories it brought back! I really enjoyed it. We chuckled all the way through." These comments are characteristic of the response of over half the reporting sample who thought this a very promising start to a series whose basic theme had considerable potentialities for comedy. Its nostalgic appeal for the older generation goes without saying, but there were also comments to the effect that its entertainment value was not restricted to those who remembered the Home Guard, and that in many cases it made excellent family viewing.'

'Authenticity was vouched for by many. "Such a true picture of village and small-town preparations against Hitler; I could almost see the people of my own small village at that time in the characters", is a comment echoed by others who confirmed that this first chapter ... was "typical of what went on in those days". Among viewers who could speak from experience, an ex-officer in the Home Guard commented: "I found this very good. Although an awful lot of good fun was poked at the Home Guard, a great deal of it was really true. I look forward to the following episodes."'

'Roughly one in three were more guarded in their opinions. Although some of them enjoyed the episode up to a point, even finding it "quite funny in parts", there was a feeling that the picture was rather exaggerated and the treatment "too farcical", with more than a hint of "taking the mickey out of the Home Guard". The following are two examples of this:
• "I enjoyed it, but wondered how those actually in the LDV would feel about this send-up. We can laugh now, but it was anything but laughable then." (Housewife / Schoolgirl during the war)
• "Very true to life, but I didn't care for the lampooning of the LDV. Everything in the early days of the war had its funny side, but not buffoonery like this." (Book-keeper / former ATS)'

'Settings, costumes and make-up were also exactly right, many noted, and the episode caught the 1940 atmosphere well, with many "authentic touches" and careful attention to detail. As one delighted viewer remarked: "This play forgot nothing."'

'THE SHOWING UP OF CORPORAL JONES'
(Series 1, episode 5, transmitted 4/9/68)

'This episode ... was even more favourably received than the previous four. *Dad's Army* was clearly a popular show, and a number of regular viewers expressed their regrets that it was coming to an end and hoped for a further series.'

'The episode was considered particularly funny by the majority of viewers in the sample, with the comedy element heightened by the touch of pathos. Viewers who could remember the war years obviously felt that it captured the spirit of wartime Britain, with endearingly recognizable characters "only slightly larger than life". But it appealed also to younger viewers, it was often added, who could apparently believe in the situations and join their elders in "one long laugh". Several older viewers summed it up as "inoffensive" and "good clean fun", eminently suitable for family consumption.'

'The actors were highly praised, Arthur Lowe, Clive Dunn and John Le Mesurier having established themselves well in the leading parts, it was said, and the whole team giving convincing characterisations. There were a few complaints of such points as "forced acting", "artificial sets", and the contrast between film inserts and studio scenes being too noticeable, but the production as a whole was gener-

ally considered satisfactory. Attention to detail and the inclusion of excerpts from wartime songs, it was remarked, added greatly to the atmosphere of authenticity.'

'OPERATION KILT'
(Series 2, episode 1, transmitted 1/3/69)

'There was a generally warm welcome for the return of the show. Indeed, if this was a sample of what was to come, they were in for a real treat, viewers often observed. As always with this series, it seemed, part of its appeal lay in its nostalgia, its reflection of wartime Britain and the early days of the Home Guard being only a little exaggerated. The platoon had developed, each member having become a real personality it was said and, in spite of the slapstick, there was always the feeling that such situations might just have occurred.'

'Although only a few of those reporting actually disliked the programme (considering it dated, "corny" and idiotic) some were only mildly amused by the antics of Captain Mainwaring and Co. It was all rather silly and childish, they thought, and too far-fetched to be really funny. For the most part, however, reporting viewers responded cordially to both the script and the performance. The members of the platoon had been very well played, they thought, with particular mention for Clive Dunn, John Le Mesurier (whose facial expressions in the part of Sergeant Wilson were, apparently, "a joy") and James Beck as the spiv, Walker – "as an old Home Guard sergeant myself, I can vouch that we had a James Beck in every platoon". The production, too, was considered excellent, the filmed inserts being particularly well handled.'

'UNDER FIRE'
(Series 2, episode 6, transmitted 5/4/69)

'Over two-thirds of those reporting again found themselves laughing "immoderately and out loud" at these characters and their antics which, although larger than life, were basically so true to the spirit of the Home Guard. The chaos surrounding their efforts at fire-watching resulted in a hilarious half-hour's viewing which achieved its comic effect without recourse to either malice or vulgarity, many declared, and therefore made excellent family entertainment. Indeed, it was not only those who remembered the war who enjoyed *Dad's Army*; several reporting viewers said that their youngsters "wouldn't miss it for anything!"'.

'For a few the joke was apparently beginning to wear a bit thin, but, on the whole, the minority (about one in ten) who expressed disappointment were viewers who usually enjoyed the series but found this episode rather below standard. This was usually attributed to the "slapstick and childish fooling about" with buckets of water in the fire-fighting sequence which, a number felt, spoilt the natural humour of the characters, some adding that they were also disappointed by the overacting of artists whose performances up to now had contributed so much to the success of the series.'

'For most of the sample, the main appeal lay in its gentle humour, stemming from accurate observation of human nature in general and personal traits of a mixed bunch of men in particular.'

'THE ARMOURED MIGHT OF LANCE CORPORAL JONES'
(Series 3, episode 1, transmitted 11/9/69)

'According to the majority of the sample audience this edition of *Dad's Army* had been all they had expected – a hilarious romp, deliciously amusing and delightfully nostalgic. Certainly the chaos resulting from the well meaning efforts of "our heroes" of the Home Guard brought vividly to mind some of the lighter moments of the last war – the incident in the butcher's shop, for instance ("I did laugh at the scene in the butcher's shop. This was so very true during rationing, people trying to get a bit more than their share").'

'SONS OF THE SEA'
(Series 3, episode 14, transmitted 11/12/69)

'This had been one of the most amusing series they had seen for a long time, viewers in the sample often remarked, and their only regret was that it had come to an end – for good, according to current press reports. The platoon's final adventure ... rounded off the series quite hilariously, as far as most reporting viewers were concerned.'

'THE BIG PARADE'
(Series 4, episode 1, transmitted 25/9/70)

'The return of *Dad's Army* was warmly welcomed and this first programme in the series agreed to be extremely funny. According to a small group, it is true, it was not one of the better episodes. Nevertheless, even if the humour was somewhat "muted" on this occasion, they seemed to feel, it was still head and shoulders above most comedy programmes.'

'The performance, it seemed, left nothing to be desired. By now, of course, the various personalities were so well established that viewers found it difficult to separate the actors from the characters they played ... the whole team always worked well together – and Bill Pertwee gave a good performance as the aggressive ARP Warden.'

'FALLEN IDOL'
(Series 4, episode 13, transmitted 18/12/70)

'This had been one of the funniest, if not the most hilarious, of the series, a number of viewers declared. The script had been "cleverly devised", giving "plenty of laughs" and seeming "true to life". Even if the humour was predictable, it had been nonetheless enjoyable. The cast were "all in good form", but "Arthur Lowe had excelled himself", many singling him out and mentioning his "drunk scene" in particular. Production and settings had been highly satisfactory in all respects, according to the majority, a fast pace and an authentic atmosphere of the period having been maintained, some said.'

'ASLEEP IN THE DEEP'
(Series 5, episode 1, transmitted 6/10/72)

'Considered by many as one of the funniest series on television, its "far-fetched, yet just possible" situations were said to be handled so skilfully as to seem quite credible: "My husband was in the Home Guard and says this hardly exaggerates at all".'

'Widespread praise was recorded for a really "polished" production. Costumes, make-up and pace were all considered excellent. The realistic flood sequence was often singled out for special mention: "It was all extremely convincing. It looked as if the scene was real when the water was rising". Furthermore, some viewers were undoubtedly impressed by the close attention to detail, adding that "the facts are always so correct", and it was obvious to many that a great deal of thought had been required to "create such an air of authenticity".'

'THE DEADLY ATTACHMENT'
(Series 6, episode 1, transmitted 31/10/73)

'There had been "some remarkably fresh ideas" in this episode – "it was a change and good fun to see them with a real job to tackle" – "the job of guarding the U-boat crew brought a freshness and was so funny".'

'Nevertheless, though still amusing, it had seemed "not one of the most enjoyable episodes" for some reporting viewers. It was said, the theme had been a bit stretched, unrealistic, dragging in places, and the humour too exaggerated, for instance, "the naïveté of

some characters was overdone" and "the U-boat captain rather overdrawn".'

'But only a third of the sample were at all half-hearted, and most seemed well satisfied with every aspect of production and settings. There was, of course, plenty of praise for the acting team, some favourites – Mainwaring, Pike and Jones – being especially mentioned, while Philip Madoc's contribution as "the malicious U-boat captain" was particularly commended. The only regret of some was that the programme was so early in the evening that they missed the beginning ("on the way home" – "having a meal" – "clashed with *Crossroads*").'

'THE RECRUIT'
(Series 6, episode 7, transmitted 12/12/73)

'Most of the sample greatly enjoyed the Vicar's recruitment into the Home Guard. It was an excellent script, they said ("clean and good humoured"), and the idiosyncrasies of this "rather earnest" group were "not over-exaggerated", just "cleverly emphasised" so as to make each episode "superbly funny", and 'The Recruit' was, evidently, no exception. However, a minority, responding more moderately, thought it less funny than usual. It seems they were often unimpressed by its "very thin" storyline, the new recruits and "cheeky" schoolboy being "too weak a focal point" on which to centre, in their opinion. But, as has been said, for most it was undoubtedly "first-class" entertainment: both relaxing and amusing.'

'EVERYBODY'S TRUCKING'
(Series 7, episode 1, transmitted 15/11/74)

'One if its strengths, some suggested, was that the characters remained "human" and consistent no matter how ridiculous the situations they got themselves into. The performance was generally commended – the well-tried cast seemed to be "in their element" – and the episode was said to be fast-moving and well produced. There was a fair amount of visual humour, convincingly done (for example, the scene where the steamroller demolished a telephone kiosk), and the settings seemed authentic; the old vehicles were said to be particularly evocative.'

'A few people had expected more of *Dad's Army*. Others felt it was too predictable in plot and in characterisation: "the actors are beginning to resemble puppets who can only repeat the same actions over and over again". Nevertheless, very few would appear to suggest that the potentiality for humour has been exhausted.'

'TURKEY DINNER'
(Series 7, episode 6, transmitted 23/12/74)

'In the opinion of just under two-thirds of the sample audience, the last show in the present series had a very funny, well-written script, which, as always, made the best of the characters' individual reactions to any situation ... the seasonal story was well up to standard, the "committee meeting", especially, being "almost horribly true to rural life!", according to one or two. Arthur Lowe was most often singled out for special mention, but it was generally felt that excellent teamwork by the whole cast was largely responsible for the success of the series, several reporting viewers speaking with affection of James Beck, whom they very much missed.'

'RING DEM BELLS'
(Series 8, episode 1, transmitted 5/9/75)

'"A splendid start" was made to this new series with a script that was "fresh and original" and "as funny as ever" if not, in some opinions, one of the most amusing of the series: the idea of a switch of uniforms was unusual and produced some hilarious situations, viewers said. Though the humour was simple, constant and obvious, this was part of the comedy's appeal as was its near credibility ("I can believe it happened which makes it all the more funny"). Private Pike's "transformation to film-version Nazi officer and upstaging of Mainwaring" made a great impression, having given Ian Lavender "his best

chance to display his versatility and comedy talent"; he had "surpassed himself", many declared – his portrayal was "the highlight". But all the regulars had been "as impeccable as ever" – "how could they be improved?", Arthur Lowe and John Le Mesurier most frequently singled out among "a tremendous cast" for their well-judged performances.'

'A small minority feared the danger of familiarity and over-exposure, wondering if the show had been "running too long": plots seemed to be "wearing a bit thin" and characters, such as Corporal Jones ("his routines are too repetitive") were too "predictable". One or two of the minor characters "could be improved". However, none appeared to be seriously discontented.'

'THE FACE ON THE POSTER'
(Series 8, episode 6, transmitted 10/10/75)

'In the main, reporting viewers continued to enjoy the hilarious comedy ... finding the "crazy" theme of this edition most amusing. A few said they felt they had "seen it all before", or that they regretted seeing little of Ian Lavender this week.'

'The response to the series as a whole was mainly most favourable; several reporting viewers remarking on how it seemed to have retained its original freshness, with perhaps a tendency in this series to focus more on individual characters. Though a small group said it had deteriorated somewhat nowadays or appeared to have run out of ideas ("could do with a rest"), the vast majority evidently agreed that it was "first class fun and well acted". In fact, for a sizeable number of fans it seems that "anything these lads do appeals"; "always buck me up"; "something I try and stay in for".'

'NEVER TOO OLD'
(Series 9, episode 6, transmitted 13/11/77)

'The majority of reporting viewers greeted this, the last ever episode of *Dad's Army*, warmly. It was generally felt to have been a very enjoyable story which provided an excellent, if somewhat final ending to the series. It was also widely agreed that the programme had been one of the most consistently amusing on television and that this episode had been no exception. There were a few who thought the story too contrived or who felt it had been rather melancholy and sentimental but, despite this, the overwhelming majority found it a pleasant and appropriate finish to what many regarded as a very good series.'

'For many members of the sample the outstanding features of the programme had been the relationships between all the major characters, especially as these had been particularly well developed and were portrayed in such a convincing manner. The stories themselves were felt to have been successful as well, for they were thought to be generally humorous yet plausible, and, though some disagreed on this count, the majority would appear to share the opinion of the viewer who said of the programme: "I cannot think of anything to dislike".'

'The acting and production were almost universally commended, as it was felt that both had been of a consistently high standard ("acting very good and production always very smooth"). It was felt that all the characters had been beautifully portrayed ("a superb performance from all") and special mention was made of Arthur Lowe as Captain Mainwaring and Ian Lavender as Private Pike. The production, too, was highly praised for bringing out a convincing sense of period and for paying great attention to detail. Altogether, it was generally agreed that the programme had always been magnificent, that the cast could not have been better chosen and that it was sad to see the series come to an end.'

AUDIO CASSETTES

Over the years, ten volumes of audio cassettes have been released by the BBC. They are listed below in respect of cumulative sales up to December 1999.

- **Volume 5 / BBC ref: 1687 / Sales: 37,822**
Episodes included: 'Something Nasty in the Vault', 'The Showing Up of Corporal Jones', 'The Loneliness of the Long-Distance Walker' and 'Sorry Wrong Number'
- **Volume 4 / BBC ref: 1533 / Sales: 25,700**
Episodes included: 'The Armoured Might of Lance Corporal Jones', 'Sergeant Wilson's Little Secret', 'Operation Kilt' and 'Battle School'
- **Volume 6 / BBC ref: 1812 / Sales: 25,193**
Episodes included: 'Under Fire', 'The Bullet is Not for Firing', 'Room at the Bottom' and 'The Menace from the Deep'
- **Volume 1 / BBC ref: 1140 / Sales: 24, 824**
Episodes included: 'When Did You Last See Your Money?', 'A Jumbo-Sized Problem', 'Time On My Hands' and 'Ten Seconds From Now'
- **Volume 7 / BBC ref: 1977 / Sales: 18,464**
Episodes included: 'Don't Forget the Diver', 'If the Cap Fits…', 'A Brush with the Law' and 'Getting the Bird'
- **Volume 3 / BBC ref: 1455 / Sales: 16,234**
Episodes included: 'The Honourable Man', 'High Finance', 'The Battle of Godfrey's Cottage' and 'A Stripe for Frazer'
- **Volume 8 / BBC ref: 2128 / Sales: 13, 740**
Episodes included: 'My British Buddy', 'The King was in his Counting House', 'The Deadly Attachment' and 'The Godiva Affair'
- **Volume 2 / BBC ref: 1272 / Sales: 12,503**
Episodes included: 'The Man and the Hour', 'Museum Piece', 'Command Decision' and 'The Enemy Within the Gates'
- **Volume 9 / BBC ref: 0563 / Sales: 7,482**
Episodes included: 'The Day the Balloon Went Up', 'Branded', 'Round and Round Went the Great Big Wheel' and 'A Man of Action'
- **Volume 10 / BBC ref: 0563553472**
Episodes included: 'A Soldier's Farewell', 'All is Safely Gathered In', 'The Big Parade', 'Asleep in the Deep' (Released February 2000)

AUNT ELSIE

Played by Nellie Griffiths (TV)
Aunt Elsie doesn't have any lines, but she can be relied upon in a crisis as Mainwaring and his men discover in 'Everybody's Trucking' when Godfrey's elderly aunt stands on a ladder, holds a sign and helps divert a military convoy. She lives in a cottage beside a crossroads just outside Walmington.

Note: Known as Aunt Ethel in original script.

AUNT LAVINIA

One of Godfrey's relatives, Aunt Lavinia doesn't appear in the series. In 'No Spring for Frazer', Godfrey's fruit knife, which his aunt had given him, is ruined by Frazer while trying to unscrew the late Horace Blewitt's coffin.

AUNT LETTICE

Not seen in the sitcom, Wilson's aunt is mentioned in the episode 'The Captain's Car'. When the haughty Lady Maltby arrives at the church hall to donate her Rolls Royce to the Home Guard, she strikes up a conversation with her old friend, Sergeant Wilson, who tells her that he heard about Lady Maltby's son's wedding through his Aunt Lettice.

AUSTIN, JO

Production assistant on seven episodes: S6 and production manager on eight episodes: S8; 'My Brother and I'; 'The Love of Three Oranges'
Born in Wolverhampton, Jo Austin studied at a business college in London before returning to her home town and working in an estate agents. She eventually moved back to London and, after temping for a while, joined a market research company. Always interested in working within the television industry, Jo applied to the BBC when BBC2 was launched, and was offered a position in 1962. After working as Bill Cotton's secretary for a time, she completed a production course and transferred to the production department at the end of 1963, initially as a production assistant on shows like *It's A Square World*, *The Beat Room* (an early music show), *The Likely Lads*, *'Till Death Us Do Part* and *Top of the Pops*. While working for David Croft, she also helped on *Are You Being Served?* and *It Ain't Half Hot, Mum*.

Jo took early retirement in 1989 after 27 years service with the Beeb.

AUXILIARY TERRITORIAL SERVICE (ATS)

In 'War Dance' we learn that Pikey's sweetheart, Violet Gibbons, is a member of the ATS, which was formed in 1938 and ran until 1948. Women between 18 and 43 were eligible to join the women's branch of the army, and were trained in all duties not involving direct combat. Duties included cooking, driving, cleaning, clerical work, mechanics and operating anti-aircraft guns, although the act of firing remained the responsibility of men. Ernest Bevin suspended recruitment in 1943, when a shortage of workers in aircraft production meant women were asked to join the factories.

AVON, ROGER (1914–1998)

Born: Jarrow
Role: Doctor (S3, episode 11: 'Branded') (TV)
Roger, who spent over six decades in the business, worked in all mediums. His vast list of TV credits include appearances as a maintenance man in *Department S*, *Doctor Who* and a policeman in *Randall & Hopkirk (Deceased)*. His film work saw him appear in titles such as *Fun at St Fanny's*, *Stars in Your Eyes*, police sergeants in *The Scamp* and *Kill Her Gently* and *The Ugly Duckling* during the 1950s, *A Hard Day's Night*, *Dead End Creek*, *Daleks Invasion Earth 2150 AD*,

Cuckoo Patrol, an electrician in *Quatermass and the Pit* as well as Sergeant Tyson in *Curse of the Crimson Altar* during the 1960s, and a host of pictures since, including *George and Mildred* as a commissionaire, *Mutiny on the Buses*, *The Likely Lads* and Charles in *The Dresser*. More recent credits include playing George Field in *The Black Candle* (1991), the Duke of Cheapside in *Blackadder the Third* and a chauffeur in an episode of *Ripping Yarns*. Roger died in 1998.

AWARDS

Dad's Army and the show's writers, Jimmy Perry and David Croft, have been the recipients of many awards over the years. In 1971 alone, they were decorated with four accolades. Jimmy Perry won the treasured Ivor Novello Award for the best theme from any film, television or stage

show with his evocative title song, 'Who Do You Think You Are Kidding, Mr Hitler?' Other awards given that year included one from the Society of Film and Television Arts for the production of the best sitcom. The Writers' Guild of Great Britain, meanwhile, chose *Dad's Army* for the best comedy script for the third time (it had previously won in 1969 and 1970), while the Variety Club of Great Britain chose the entire team for an award.

A WILSON (MANAGER)?

Recorded: Friday 27/11/70

Original transmission: Friday 4/12/70, 8.00–8.30pm

Original viewing figures: 15.4 million

Repeated: 8/8/71, 23/11/83, 8/1/91, 23/7/93, 31/8/96, 15/1/97 (Wales)

CAST

Arthur Lowe . . . . .Captain Mainwaring
John Le Mesurier . . . . .Sergeant Wilson
Clive Dunn . . . . .Lance Corporal Jones
John Laurie . . . . .Private Frazer
James Beck . . . . .Private Walker
Arnold Ridley . . . . .Private Godfrey
Ian Lavender . . . . .Private Pike
Frank Williams . . . . .Vicar
Edward Sinclair . . . . .Verger
Janet Davies . . . . .Mrs Pike
Blake Butler . . . . .Mr West
Robert Raglan . . . . .Captain Pritchard
Arthur Brough . . . . .Mr Boyle
Colin Bean . . . . .Private Sponge
Hugh Hastings . . . . .Private Hastings
Platoon: Vic Taylor, Hugh Cecil, Freddie Wiles,
Desmond Cullum-Jones, Leslie Noyes, George Hancock,
Frank Godfrey, Freddie White
Middle-aged Bank Clerks: Richard Sheekey,
John Cleavedon, Bob Hooper
Two Pretty Girl Bank Clerks: Hilary Martin, Jeanette
Clarke

PRODUCTION TEAM

Script: Jimmy Perry and David Croft
Producer/Director: David Croft
Production Assistant: Phil Bishop
Lighting: George Summers
Studio Sound: Michael McCarthy
Design: Paul Joel
Assistant Floor Manager: Roger Singleton-Turner
Vision Mixer: Dave Hanks
Costume Supervisor: George Ward
Make-Up Supervisor: Cynthia Goodwin
Visual Effects: Peter Day

It's 9.15 at the bank and Wilson is late. When the phone rings, it's head office on the line: Mr West announces that no one will be sent to replace Wilson when he takes over as manager of the Eastgate branch. The news shocks Mainwaring because he didn't even know he'd been promoted! More bad news follows when Captain Pritchard from HQ calls to confirm Wilson's commission has come through, and Captain Square wants him to take up his duties as 2nd lieutenant with the Eastgate platoon as soon as possible. Mainwaring can't believe what he's hearing.

When Wilson finally arrives at 9.40, after buying his officer's hat, Mainwaring brands him a Judas. He's so infuriated he jumps the gun and promotes Pike to chief clerk and Jones to sergeant of the platoon, resulting in mayhem when a memo to Jones confirming his promotion is wrongly circulated to the rest of the platoon, bar

Pike, and everyone turns up wearing three stripes.

As Wilson bids farewell to Mainwaring the atmosphere is tense, and Mainwaring, refusing to shake hands, declares their friendship over. Wilson starts his first day at the bank after receiving a few days training from head office's Mr West, which Mainwaring classes as a privi-lege, but an air raid forces Wilson to abandon his first staff meeting. The raid also puts paid to Wilson's job: the bank takes a direct hit and head office decides to transfer all business to Hastings. Once again, Wilson finds himself back under Mainwaring's thumb as chief clerk and sergeant – will he ever break free?

MY MEMORIES OF DAD'S ARMY

'Working on *Dad's Army* was a wonderful experience. 'The Royal Train', which was filmed on the North Norfolk Railway, was a memorable episode. Everyone had a marvellous day riding on the train and generally pretending to be train drivers. John Laurie loved it so much that it was difficult to persuade him to get out of the cab. Although Bill, Teddy and Frank weren't quite as enthusiastic; as they pointed out that they were pumping the little trolley along the line in blazing heat all day!

'During the haunted house filming ('Things That Go Bump in the Night') we needed some "savage army dogs" to chase the platoon. The dogs we had, although well-trained and ferocious looking, were complete "softies" and preferred to lick everyone to death. However, in the end the handler managed to make them "smile" which passed for snarling for a brief moment. Naturally any animal filming takes time and patience, and we were some while on this sequence. None of this impressed Jimmy Beck, who was stuck up a tree for a very long time with an imminent thunderstorm getting closer. He was not too keen on dogs anyway.

'Finding a suitable property to act as Godfrey's cottage in 'Is There Honey Still For Tea?' was an absolute nightmare. The original brief: thatch roof, pink wash walls, quiet lane, beautiful garden, easy reach of our base, seemed a doddle in Norfolk. Not so. After several fruitless searches I was told about the place we eventually used. When I went to check it out I took the designer, Bob Berk, with me as we were getting very close to filming dates. Although the situation was perfect, from the front the place was useless; we trailed round to the back which had a lovely big garden and was more promising. Bob reckoned that with a lot of dressing to cut off the front shape of the house we could do it. Later I took David to see it – his face when he first saw the frontage was a picture of horror – but we hurried him round to the back which he passed as OK.

'Any mishaps during filming had to be reported on a form. We were on the Stanford Training Area by the river for 'Come In, Your Time is Up', the episode where the German aircrew were on the lake; the weather was absolutely roasting and we had a troop of sea scouts with Teddy Sinclair (the Verger) as their senior. He, of course, had to wear the uniform of shorts and his knees (and those of several of the children) got quite scorched. So I had to continually coat his knees with sun-cream – which led to a lot of merriment to all and a very strange report form. In fact the recipient of the form actually asked me if it was a wind-up!

'Filming in the training area was an interesting experience. While filming one episode in the early morning mist, there was a pretend war going on. The army liked having us there because it enabled them to use our presence to change orders at the last minute and test their communications systems. A junior officer was seconded to us so that disturbance and out-of-period noises, etc, could be stopped while we were shooting. I have never had so much power in my life – rushing round in a jeep shouting "stop the helicopters" and "stop the tanks". Bill Pertwee said all I lacked were the jackboots and whip.

'During my time on the series Jimmy Beck died, which was totally traumatic for all of us, all the more so because this was the one unit where we got to know all the wives of the actors as most of them used to join us at weekends. We felt so much sympathy for Kay Beck. While Jimmy was still alive but on life-support machines, we had two more studio recordings and naturally the audiences wanted news. We could hardly tell them the truth that it was just a matter of time so had to keep up a façade of "slight improvements" in his condition. It was very difficult for the cast – particularly for Arthur Lowe who was very close to Jimmy.

'When it came to recording "The Recruit" David phoned me Saturday evening, the night before the recording, to say Jimmy wouldn't be able to make it. That evening him and Jimmy Perry had to rewrite the script, reallocating the lines they had written for Walker. David asked if I could arrive at Television Centre early on the Sunday because he wanted me to retype the scripts. It was very sad.'

JO AUSTIN

BAILEY, CAPTAIN

Played by John Ringham (TV); Michael Knowles (radio)

Captain Bailey meets Mainwaring in 'A Stripe for Frazer' to hand him standing orders from the Assistant Adjutant Quartermaster General, confirming he can promote a member of his platoon to corporal. He reappears in 'Room at the Bottom' with the embarrassing news that Mainwaring has been demoted and must join the ranks. Bailey is back on the scene in 'Don't Fence Me In', when he visits the Italian POW camp with some MPs.

BAILEY, MR

A character not seen in the series, but mentioned in 'Museum Piece'. A member of the Walmington Home Guard and, it would seem, one of Jones' employees, because Jones tells Mainwaring that the reason Bailey is absent from parade is because he's counting coupons at the shop, a task undertaken every Monday.

BAILEY'S CIRCUS

During the war the circus closed down and its animals were farmed out to people willing to look after them for the duration, such as Colonel Square, who took in horses at Marsham Hall.

BAKER, INSPECTOR

Played by Jay Denyer (TV); Fraser Kerr (radio)

Walmington's police inspector is seen in 'A Man of Action'. He discusses the town's plight when a mine brings chaos, cutting off water and gas supplies, bringing down phone lines and damaging over 100 yards of railway track. But a lack of manpower leaves the town's police force toothless, as demonstrated when Baker is powerless in preventing Mainwaring declaring martial law.

BAKER, MISS

Played by Joan Cooper (TV and radio)

The antiquated receptionist at the funeral directors, H E Drury, in Walmington, appears in 'No Spring for Frazer', when Mainwaring, Frazer and others from the Home Guard are trying to track down the coffin that could hold the missing spring as well as the late Mr Blewitt!

BALFOUR, JAMES

Film cameraman on 19 episodes (TV): S3, episodes 1, 2, 3, 4, 6, 7, 8, 10, 13 & 14; S5, episodes 8, 10, 12 & 13; S6, episodes 1, 3, 4, 5 & 6

Born in Aberdeen in 1917, James wanted to work in the film industry from the age of six, but pressure from his father saw him leave school and undertake an apprenticeship in marine engineering, a job he hated. To escape, he joined the merchant navy, sailing the world on cruise liners.

At the age of 21, the Second World War broke out and he returned home before joining the navy as an officer, initially on the North Atlantic, later on the Indian patrols.

Upon demob he set about achieving his goal of working in the film industry, and was briefly employed by a new film company in Aberdeen, until the operation folded. He moved between jobs, before applying to an advert in the *Radio Times* for assistant cameramen in the newsreel section at Alexandra Palace.

After several years in newsreel, he moved into the film department, working on countless series and documentaries. Increasingly, he was allocated light entertainment shows, including *Monty Python's Flying Circus*, *My Wife Next Door* and *Some Mothers Do 'Ave 'Em*.

James had been working on a series with Derek Nimmo when he collapsed and died of a heart attack in 1976, at the age of 58.

BALL, RALPH

Born: London

Role: Man on the Station (S3, episode 14: 'Sons of the Sea') (TV)

Before serving with the RAF during the war, Ralph had a variety of jobs, including a spell with the Post Office. After being demobbed, he decided to follow a different career path and joined an acting company at Hornchurch while in his late twenties. During his career, as well as plenty of theatre work, Ralph made a handful of films, and appeared many times on television, including parts in *Softly, Softly, Spycatcher, No Hiding Place, Barlow at Large* and a leading role in the BBC production *Man from the Sun*.

Ralph retired from acting in 1981 and set up a theatrical agency, which he runs with his wife.

BALLOON AMY

The code name given to the stray barrage balloon in 'The Day the Balloon Went Up'.

BARDON, JOHN (1939–)

Born: London

Roles: Harold Forster (S8, episode 1:'Ring Dem Bells') (TV); Private Walker (stage show)

John originally trained as an industrial designer before turning to acting. His theatrical career includes many West End performances, such as *The Good Companions*, and *Kiss Me Kate*, for which he won a Laurence Olivier Award. He also toured with his successful one-man show, *Here's a Funny Thing*, dedicated to Max Miller. He has completed seasons in rep at Exeter and Oxford, and worked with both the Royal Shakespeare Company and the National Theatre.

He has appeared regularly on TV, earlier in his career in *General Hospital*, *The Sweeney* as Doc Boyd, *Antony and Cleopatra* and BBC2's *Joey*. More recent credits include *Seconds Out*, Ron Armitage in *Hi-De-Hi!*, *After Henry*, *Birds of a Feather*, *The Paradise Club*, Jack Morris in *Casualty*, *The Bill*, Eric Lumsden in *Coronation Street*, *The Darling Buds of May*, *Goodnight Sweetheart* and two series of *Get Back*. Currently he's appearing as Jim Branning in *EastEnders*.

John has also appeared in several films, such as *S P Y S* with Donald Sutherland, *Khaki Doesn't Suit Me*, *One of Our Dinosaurs is Missing*, *The Keeper*, *84 Charing Cross Road*, *Ordeal by Innocence* and *Clockwise*, playing a ticket collector.

BARMAID, THE

For the barmaid in 'Ring Dem Bells', see 'Doris'.

BARMAID, THE

For the barmaid in 'Battle of the Giants!', see 'Shirley'.

BARMY ARMY FILM CLUB

Based in Kent, the Barmy Army Film Club consists of over 35 people, all of whom are interested in the Second World War and amateur dramatics. After carefully researching uniforms, vehicles, historical events and many other aspects of life during the war years, the club members have spent much of their spare time over the last decade making feature-length films, based on Perry and Croft's *Dad's Army*, and other more original projects.

The idea for the club was conceived in 1987 by John Simpson, who has had a lifelong interest in the Second World War, and in particular the British Home Front. Because John, like millions of others, enjoyed watching *Dad's Army* and

other World War Two dramas he decided, along with like-minded people who shared his passion, to try his hand at producing his own movies set during the war years. The relative ease of collecting household and military props of the 1940s encouraged them to use the Home Guard as a subject to explore.

Although the club's first film, *The Exercise*, was influenced by the BBC sitcom, it didn't follow any particular *Dad's Army* storyline. Some of the characters seen in Perry and Croft's programme were recognisable in the Barmy Army's film, but new characters were introduced too. While the Captain and the Sergeant resembled

Mainwaring and Wilson, and an air raid warden and a Pike-style character were involved, other people they created bore no resemblance to anyone in *Dad's Army*.

By the time the film club, whose patron is Colin Bean, was ready to make a second film, people had offered to loan all sorts of equipment, including vehicles, machinery and even a plane. The second film, *Recruitment Drive*, was released in 1991 and became the club's best-selling video, with over 500 sold to date. It also generated plenty of media interest with London Weekend Television, TVS and newspapers all eager to find out more about John and his friends. Interest reached such a peak that several TV, radio and press requests had to be declined. To date, members of the Barmy Army have taken part in seven television appearances and four radio interviews.

With one film awaiting editing and another ready for shooting, life remains busy for members of the club, who receive a regular newsletter, and hold monthly meetings at a Maidstone pub.

Films/Videos produced to date

The Exercise (Duration: 40 mins, released 1988)
Recruitment Drive (Duration: 60 minutes, released 1991)
Something's Going On (Duration: 75 minutes, released 1997. Colin Bean makes a cameo appearance as Private Sponge.)
Out of the Blue (Duration: 25 minutes, released 2000)

Awaiting shooting

Something's Going On Again (Duration: 60 minutes)

All titles written by John Simpson, except *Out of the Blue*, which was written by Jeff Tucker.

Dad's Army interviews

Colin Bean (Duration: 97 minutes, released 1997)
Jimmy Perry (Awaiting editing. Duration: 90 minutes, released 2000)
For more information about the Barmy Army Film Club, write with an sae to John Simpson, Three Trees, Stone Street, Lympne, nr Hythe, Kent CT21 4JY.

BARRAGE BALLOONS

In 'The Day the Balloon Went Up', Mainwaring and the Verger both get lifted up while trying to hold down a stray barrage balloon. The use of such balloons over potential bomb targets, like cities, forced enemy pilots to fly their aircraft higher which meant they lost accuracy when trying to pinpoint potential bomb targets; it was also easier for the anti-aircraft batteries to spot them. Barrage balloons became a vital component in Britain's air defences. Being attached to the ground by a steel cable prevented aircraft flying below them because such attempts could result in wings being ripped off.

The balloons were inflated with hydrogen and could be winched to the required height within minutes by members of the Royal Auxillary Air Force, who were tasked with looking after them.

BARRETT, TIM (1933–1990)
Born: London

Roles: Captain Pringle (S3, episode 4: 'The Bullet is Not for Firing') and Doctor (S8, episode 2: 'When You've Got to Go') (TV)

Originally known as Arthur Barrett, Tim worked extensively in rep before entering TV, the medium for which he's best known. He quickly established himself as a popular, reliable character actor who was always in work, appearing in programmes such as *The Dick Emery Show*, *Terry and June*, *Are You Being Served?*, *The Janet Brown Show*, *The Fall and Rise of Reginald Perrin*, *That's My Boy*, *Kelly Monteith*, *Life Begins At Forty* and *To the Manor Born*, playing a car salesman. He never reached leading status, but his familiar face led to a fruitful small-screen career.

Tim hadn't been well for some time when, upon returning from a Greek holiday, he died at the home he shared with his mother.

BARRON, JOHN (1920–)
Roles: Mr West ('Something Nasty in the Vault'), Colonel Pierce ('Round and Round Went the Great Big Wheel') and Captain Cadbury ('Things That Go Bump in the Night') (radio)

John, whose mother was an actress, couldn't decide how he wanted his future to pan out, so his mother reluctantly suggested he became an actor. She persuaded his godfather to pay the tuition fees at RADA, which he joined in 1938.

Before he'd had any chance of establishing himself in the profession, he was called up into the navy. As soon as he was demobbed he didn't waste any time in resuming his career, beginning many years of acting in repertory theatres around the country, before getting involved in directing various rep companies, and being offered meatier roles in the West End. By 1948, he had moved into television work, thanks to a live performance from Palmers Green.

After cameos in various programmes, John was lucky enough to get a part in ATV's twice-weekly soap, *Emergency – Ward 10*, which led to almost constant employment on the box, usually playing upright citizens like chief constables, lawyers, judges and vicars.

During a busy career spanning the whole profession, John spent three years playing a chief constable in *Softly, Softly*, and has also been the minister in *Doomwatch*, the vicar in *Potter*, the dean in *All Gas and Gaiters*, and a host of other characters in shows such as *Whoops Apocalypse!*, *To the Manor Born*, *The Foundation*, *Yes, Minister*, *Department S*, *The Saint*, *No Hiding Place*, *No Place Like Home*, *Don't Wait Up* and *The Fall and Rise of Reginald Perrin*, playing the tyrannical CJ.

John has also made several films, including *The Day the Earth Caught Fire* in 1961, *Jigsaw* and *The Italian Secret Service*. In recent years he's been living in Sussex and has dedicated his time to working in the theatre.

BARROW, ODETTE
Costume designer on seven episodes (TV): S3, episodes 1, 2, 3, 4, 5, 6 & 7

After five years at art college, Odette learnt her trade while working for costumiers, Bermans. After three years, she joined a fashion house as a sketcher, before moving on to Lyon's designing window displays for their famous cornerhouses. In 1959 she began a three-year spell with The Royal Opera House, employed as a costume assistant and, later, costume director. She worked abroad for five months and was engaged by the Royal Shakespeare Theatre, before joining the BBC in 1963 as a costume designer.

After two years based at BBC Wales in Cardiff, Odette – who specialised in period dramas – moved to London and stayed until 1987, when she left to look after her bed-ridden father. She has now retired from the business.

BASKCOMB, JOHN (1916–)
Born: Purley

Role: Mayor (film)

After leaving school, John worked as a wine waiter at London's Carlton Hotel, before taking a series of jobs, including working in an office at a drinks company, at Imperial Airways and at Croydon aerodrome. Then he joined the Bank of England where he stayed until the Second World War broke out.

During the war years he served in the Royal Navy, and was lucky to survive when his ship was sunk in 1941. After demob, John – who had always been a keen amateur actor – returned to the bank, but in 1949 took the plunge by giving up his job and turning to acting professionally. His first engagement was as principal comedian of a small concert party at Lyme Regis.

His career progressed and he began working in all mediums. He has made over 20 films, including *Battle of Britain*, *Chitty Chitty Bang Bang*, *No Trees in the Street*, *Work is a Four-Letter Word*, *Oliver!*, *Diamonds for Breakfast*, *Zeppelin* and *The Final Conflict*.

On stage, he was busy in variety and pantomime, and among his theatre credits is the role of Alfred Doolittle in *My Fair Lady*, which he played for five years, performing in Australia, New Zealand and South Africa.

On TV, he's appeared in numerous productions, including *The Forsyte Saga*, *A Month in the Country*, an episode of *The Railway Children* in 1957, *Counterstrike*, *The Harry Worth Show*, *Softly, Softly*, *Doctor Who*, *My Wife Next Door*, *The Dick Emery Show*, *Z Cars*, *Shades of Green*, *Crown Court*, *The Onedin Line* and *Poldark*.

John, who lives in Cornwall, has now retired from the business.

BATES, MICHAEL (1920–1978)
Born: Jhansi, India

Role: Private Clarke ('The Two and a Half Feathers') (radio)

Michael is, perhaps, best known for his performances in two of the UK's most popular sitcoms. He was part of the original trio in *Last of the Summer Wine*, playing Cyril Blamire, before ill health forced him to quit the role after the second series, and was also seen in five series of Perry and Croft's *It Ain't Half Hot, Mum*.

Although in his final years he was seen as a television actor, particularly in sitcoms, his career encompassed theatre and film, too. His movie credits include playing Major Brooke-Smith in the 1955 picture, *Carrington VC*; *Dunkirk*; *I'm All Right, Jack*; *Battle of Britain*; a drunk lance-corporal in *Oh, What a Lovely War!* and *Frenzy*.

Michael died of cancer shortly after filming his last series of *It Ain't Half Hot, Mum*.

BATESON, TIMOTHY (1926–)
Born: London

Roles: Elliott ('The Man and the Hour'), Captain Marsh ('The Bullet is not for Firing'), Mr Blewitt ('No Spring for Frazer' and 'When Did You Last See Your Money?'), Captain Turner ('No Spring for Frazer') and Mr Maxwell ('Sons of the Sea') (radio)

Timothy, who was originally considered for the part of Corporal Jones, began studying history at Oxford but failed his finals because by that time he'd become engrossed with acting. He had appeared in several university plays and was spotted and subsequently offered a part in a film version of *Nicholas Nickleby*. Just before his finals he'd completed a small part in a film with Peter Ustinov, so there had been little time for revision.

Abandoning plans to become a teacher, Timothy focused on acting and spent over five years at the Old Vic. His career has covered all areas of the profession. As well as stage work, he's made over 50 films, including *The Guinea Pig*, *Carrington VC*, *Our Man in Havana*, *What a Carve Up!*, *Doctor in Distress*, *White Corridors*, *Father Came Too*, *Danger Route*, *The Italian Job* and *A Christmas Carol*.

On television his face has become familiar for appearing in many top shows, such as *Barnaby Rudge*, *The Saint*, *The Avengers*, *Paul Temple*, *Going Straight*, *Don't Wait Up* and, more recently, the 1996 production, *The Sculptress*. He is still busy in the profession.

BATHURST, MR
A member of the Walmington golf club who's seen at the Rotarian Dinner in 'Brain versus Brawn'. He ignores Mainwaring when he tries striking up a conversation.

BATTLE OF GODFREY'S COTTAGE, THE

Recorded: Sunday 20/10/68 (made in black and white)

Original transmission: Saturday 8/3/69, 7.00–7.30pm

Original viewing figures: 11.3 million

Repeated: 22/8/69

CAST

Arthur Lowe . . . . .Captain Mainwaring
John Le Mesurier . . . . .Sergeant Wilson
Clive Dunn . . . . .Lance Corporal Jones
John Laurie . . . . .Private Frazer
James Beck . . . . .Private Walker
Arnold Ridley . . . . .Private Godfrey
Ian Lavender . . . . .Private Pike
Janet Davies . . . . .Mrs Pike
Amy Dalby . . . . .Dolly
Nan Braunton . . . . .Cissy
Bill Pertwee . . . . .ARP Warden
Colin Bean . . . . .Private Sponge
Platoon: Richard Jacques, Frank Godfrey, Alec Coleman, Hugh Cecil, Jimmy Mac, Desmond Cullum-Jones, Vic Taylor, David Seaforth, Richard Kitteridge
(Originally titled 'The Battle of Mon Repos')

PRODUCTION TEAM

Script: Jimmy Perry and David Croft
Producer/Director: David Croft
Production Assistant: Harold Snoad
Lighting: George Summers
Sound: Buster Cole
Design: Oliver Bayldon
Assistant Floor Manager: Tony George
Vision Mixer: Dave Hanks
Costume Supervisor: Marjorie Lewis
Make-Up Supervisor: Sheila Cassidy

GHQ confirms that in the event of an invasion the Novelty Rock Emporium will become the Home Guard's command post, and with newspaper headlines warning, '50 Nazi Divisions Poised Across Channel', conflict is imminent. Wilson is supposed to be taking the men to the pictures at Eastgate to watch *The Next of Kin*, a film which emphasises the fact that 'careless talk cost lives'. As the bank closes for the day, however, Mainwaring sends him after Mrs Pike who's just left her gloves behind at the bank. In the meantime, Mainwaring puts Mrs Pike's deed box back in the vault and fails to hear the church bells ringing. Do the ringing bells indicate an invasion? Wilson thinks they do and so he and Pike abandon plans for the pictures and rush off to the Novelty Rock Emporium. Mainwaring is shocked when Frazer and Jones tell him about the bells when he arrives at the church hall office. Mainwaring is also concerned because if Hitler decides to invade, there will only be three of them to try and defend the town because he thinks the rest of his men are at the pictures.

With decisions to make, Mainwaring opts to defend the crossroads leading into the town and

'Battle of the Giants!'

heads for their second command post, Godfrey's Cottage, with the Lewis gun. When they arrive, Charles – whose visit to the clinic meant he wasn't able to go to the pictures – is just finishing tea with his sisters. The men set up the Lewis gun and move the furniture around, but still Cissy and Dolly sip their tea and offer the men a cuppa, oblivious to the danger an invasion could bring. As they await the Germans, Jones realises in all the panic he's forgotten his helmet, so borrows an old German one Godfrey had collected as a souvenir from the last war.

At the Novelty Rock Emporium, meanwhile, Wilson and the others wait, concerned as to Mr Mainwaring's whereabouts. After two hours, Wilson decides it's time for action. Accompanied by Walker and Pike, he heads for the second command post, the Cottage, while Sponge is left in charge at the Emporium.

With Mainwaring, Frazer, Godfrey and Jones based inside the cottage and Wilson, Pike and Walker in the revolving summer house at the bottom of the garden, trouble looms when three shots are fired at Jones as he dashes to the outside toilet wearing his German helmet. As he staggers through the cottage door, Frazer opens fire at the summer house.

Not wanting to disturb the men while they're busy playing soldiers, Dolly shakes the crumbs off the white tablecloth from the bedroom window; Wilson mistakes this as a sign of submission. But Mainwaring thinks the same when he spots them approaching the cottage with handkerchiefs tied to their rifles. There's a shock in store when Mainwaring meets the so-called enemy, and the warden arrives to book them for disregarding blackout regulations, and also to tell them that the sounding of the church bells was a false alarm.

BATTLE OF THE GIANTS!

Recorded: Sunday 19/9/71

Original transmission: Monday 27/12/71, 7.00–8.00pm

Original viewing figures: 18.7 million

Repeated: 26/8/72, 10/1/83, 8/1/86, 26/12/92, 18/12/93, 19/12/93 (Wales), 27/12/96, 20/1/01

CAST

Arthur Lowe . . . . .Captain Mainwaring
John Le Mesurier . . . . .Sergeant Wilson
Clive Dunn . . . . .Lance Corporal Jones
John Laurie . . . . .Private Frazer
James Beck . . . . .Private Walker
Arnold Ridley . . . . .Private Godfrey
Ian Lavender . . . . .Private Pike
Bill Pertwee . . . . .ARP Warden
Frank Williams . . . . .Vicar
Edward Sinclair . . . . .Verger
Geoffrey Lumsden . . . . .Captain Square
Robert Raglan . . . . .Colonel
Charles Hill . . . . .Sergeant Parkins
Colin Bean . . . . .Private Sponge
Rosemary Faith . . . . .Shirley, the Barmaid
Platoon: George Hancock, Emmett Hennessy, Lindsay Hooper, Michael Moore, Leslie Noyes, Vic Taylor, Freddie White, Freddie Wiles, Hugh Hastings.
Messenger Boy: Paul Huckin
Other Extras: Douglas Bartin, Bill Lodge, Fred Gambia, William Curran, Jonathan Keys, John Belsey

PRODUCTION TEAM

Script: Jimmy Perry and David Croft
Producer/Director: David Croft
Production Assistant: Phil Bishop
Film Cameraman: Stewart A Farnell
Film Sound: Les Collins
Film Editor: Bob Rymer
Lighting: Howard King
Studio Sound: Michael McCarthy

Design: Paul Joel
Assistant Floor Manager: Bob Spiers
Vision Mixer: Dave Hanks
Costume Supervisor: Judy Allen
Make-Up Supervisor: Penny Bell
Visual Effects: Len Hutton

There's a ceremonial church parade on Sunday and Mainwaring's new hat has arrived just in time, but during bayonet practice Pike puts his bayonet straight through it. Just as Mainwaring has gone home, Captain Square and Sergeant Parkins arrive. Square wanted to check that his memo arrived confirming all medals should be worn on parade. But Mainwaring had discarded the memo because he didn't want to be shown up as not having any medals himself, so Captain Square tells Wilson to order the rest of the platoon to wear theirs.

At the next parade, when Mainwaring inspects the platoon, he's embarrassed to find everyone wearing medals, except Pikey, of course, who's displaying his scout badges! The platoon is dismissed and Mainwaring confronts Wilson in his office, angry at him for going against his orders.

On the morning of the parade, with the men proudly wearing their medals, Mainwaring arrives in his business suit and bowler hat. He says he won't be able to parade with them because his wife sent his uniform to the cleaners. But when Pike turns up carrying the uniform, Mainwaring knows he can't wriggle out of it.

After the parade everyone has a drink at a pub where Captain Square jokes about the Walmington-on-Sea platoon's inept drilling; he also thinks some of them had trouble marching. Mainwaring is annoyed and says that his men are better led, better trained and fitter than the Eastgate platoon. With the Vicar, Verger and Hodges as umpires, the Eastgate and Walmington platoon challenge each other to a series of initiative and shooting tests, including bursting balloons, carrying feathers to barrels and a water exercise.

At the firing range the men from Walmington finish first and sprint to a nearby tower to raise their flag and be judged the winners, but they experience difficulties with the flagpole, allowing Captain Square's platoon to nip in and fly their flag first; but Mainwaring's men get a pleasant surprise thanks to Private Walker.

BATTLE SCHOOL

Recorded: Sunday 1/6/69

Original transmission: Thursday 18/9/69, 7.30–8.00pm

Original viewing figures: 11.4 million

Repeated: 11/7/70, 22/10/82, 21/7/92, 7/9/96, 18/1/97, 4/9/99

CAST

Arthur Lowe . . . . Captain Mainwaring
John Le Mesurier . . . . Sergeant Wilson
Clive Dunn . . . . Lance Corporal Jones
John Laurie . . . . Private Frazer
James Beck . . . . Private Walker
Arnold Ridley . . . . Private Godfrey
Ian Lavender . . . . Private Pike
Alan Tilvern . . . . Captain Rodrigues
Alan Haines . . . . Major Smith
Colin Bean . . . . Private Sponge
Platoon: Frank Godfrey, Richard Jacques, Hugh Cecil, Richard Kitteridge, Desmond Cullum-Jones, George Hancock, Michael Moore, Vic Taylor, Freddie Wiles
Stuntman: Johnny Scripps
Extras: Ron Hickey, Derek Chaffer, Anthony Powell, Pat Gorman, Jay Neil

PRODUCTION TEAM

Script: Jimmy Perry and David Croft
Producer/Director: David Croft
Production Assistant: Jim Franklin
Film Cameraman: James Balfour
Film Editor: Bob Rymer
Lighting: Howard King
Studio Sound: Michael McCarthy
Design: Paul Joel
Assistant Floor Manager: Bill Harman
Vision Mixer: Dave Hanks
Costume Supervisor: Odette Barrow
Make-Up Supervisor: Cecile Hay-Arthur

The platoon is travelling by train to a battle school for the weekend. When they arrive at the railway station, Mainwaring opens the sealed orders and finds directions to the school. He plans getting there by tea time, which is just as well because everyone is famished, but he's not the best map reader and after marching for hours they find themselves back where they started.

Eventually they reach their destination only to discover they've missed dinner. The school is a special Home Guard Battle School where the Walmington platoon will be initiated into the intricacies of guerrilla warfare. Captain Rodrigues, who's in charge, fought in the Spanish Civil War and knows all the tricks. He hates the arm-waving associated with military discipline, and tells Mainwaring and his men that they'll be roughing it with raw carrots and onion to eat, and just a blanket to keep them warm.

Next morning, Rodrigues wakes Mainwaring's men with the aid of a fire cracker, only for the men, who by now are starving, to be told they have missed breakfast. He tells them that during their stay at the school, they are to be given the opportunity to capture his HQ, something no one has yet achieved. The HQ is in a former POW camp and with barbed wire, electric fences and vicious alsatians everywhere, it makes for a real fortress.

Rodrigues certainly puts the Walmington platoon through its paces, but when Mainwaring has another mishap and tumbles down a bank he discovers a tunnel leading straight into the HQ. He collects his men and ends up in the stores, adjacent to the base. Mainwaring takes pleasure in catching Rodrigues' men unawares, and it's a happy platoon that heads back to Walmington.

BAXTER, SERGEANT

Played by Michael Middleton (radio)
In the radio episode, 'We Know Our Onions', Baxter helps Captain Ramsey during the efficiency tests.

BAYLDON, OLIVER

BBC designer on one episode (TV): S2, episode 2
'The Battle of Godfrey's Cottage'
After leaving Stamford School in Lincolnshire, Oliver studied Fine Art and Design at Leicester, gaining a diploma as well as winning several awards. He began his professional career at the Theatre Royal in Nottingham. He moved on to design sets and costumes for the Royal Academy of Music, and designed TV commercials. He joined the BBC as a design assistant, rapidly rising to director and senior director on many award-winning films, serials and documentaries, including *Richard III*, *Marks* and *Never Come*

'Ring Dem Bells'

Back. He's won four BAFTA nominations and one BAFTA production design award.

Since leaving the BBC he's been working freelance, and has had several scripts published. He is currently finishing a novel.

BEAL, QUEENIE
Played by Hilda Fenemore (TV)

Queenie arrives in Walmington with Harold Forster to make a picture for the Crown Film Unit. She's a costume designer who insults Mainwaring in 'Ring Dem Bells' by claiming he has girl's feet.

BEAN, COLIN (1926–)
Born: Wigan
Roles: Private Sponge (28 episodes), member of the platoon (48 episodes) (TV)

Colin wanted to act from childhood and started his career at an early age as a shepherd in a nativity play. After leaving school in 1944 he gained some professional experience before being called up for national service in the army for four years; while serving in Japan he had opportunities for some part-time acting with the BCOF.

He graduated from drama school in 1952, but stayed on to teach for a year before joining Sheffield Rep as ASM. Colin's early career was dominated by the theatre: he spent four years with the Court Players and five with the Victor Graham Players.

His first speaking role on TV was playing a yeoman in 1961's *Richard the Lionheart* with Richard Greene, but he was also seen as an antiques dealer in *Z Cars* and a policeman in *No Hiding Place* before joining *Dad's Army*. Other small-screen credits include being a customer in *Are You Being Served?*, a policeman and a soap box orator in *The Liver Birds*, policemen in *The Goodies* and *The Harry Worth Show*, appearances in 13 episodes of *Michael Bentine Time* in 1973, several roles in *The Gnomes of Dulwich*, a loud supporter in *Fallen Hero* and the Verger alongside Frank Williams (as the Vicar) at Gladys' wedding in the penultimate episode of *Hi-De-Hi!* in 1988.

Working for Jimmy Perry at Watford's Palace Theatre in 1962 led to the start of almost 20 years playing a pantomime dame, and the role of Sponge in *Dad's Army*. Colin, who gained a master's degree in Speech and Projection during the 1980s via a correspondence course, is now restricted to radio work due to arthritis. He has also turned his hand to writing, completing his autobiography, *Who Do You Think YOU ARE KIDDING!*, in 1998.

BECK, JIMMY (1929–1973)
Born: Islington, London
Role: Private Joe Walker (all TV episodes and *Christmas Night with the Stars* inserts up to the seventh series; the film and seven episodes of the radio series)

Jimmy, who was educated at Popham Elementary School, endured a tough childhood. He

'Gorilla Warfare'

grew up in Islington, London, and while his mother made artificial flowers for a meagre fee, his father spent long periods unemployed.

From the age of 14, Jimmy attended art school for three years. After graduating he worked as a commercial artist until being called up for national service, working as a PT (Physical Training) instructor in the army. Upon leaving military life, he pursued a career not in art but in the theatre. While travelling on the top deck of a bus he noticed a man reading some scripts and proclaimed his interest in becoming an actor. By coincidence the man was Alec Mason, who ran a little repertory company at Ramsgate; he offered Jimmy his theatrical break as a student actor earning £1 a week. Stints at various reps, including Hornchurch, Ipswich and Scarborough, followed before he joined York, first as ASM, then progressing to leading roles in productions like *The Long, the Short and the Tall*, *The Entertainer* and *The Merchant of Venice*.

Jimmy began receiving rave reviews for his performances in rep and realised that if he wanted to progress in the business, London was the place to be, so he moved to the capital with his wife, Kay. Although he was a true cockney, the first few years of his career were spent playing northerners, with *Dad's Army* being his first cockney role.

The exposure gained from appearing in a top comedy series like *Dad's Army* was immense and it wasn't long before offers for more TV roles began arriving.

Jimmy died in 1973, aged just 44. While opening a fête in aid of dogs for the blind he suddenly felt ill. He returned home and within an hour was being rushed to hospital. He lived a further three weeks.

TV credits include: *Fabian of the Yard*, *Coronation Street* (playing Sergeant Bowden in 1964), *Romany Jones* (playing the lead role, the workshy Bert Jones in two series of the programme), *Z Cars*, *Softly, Softly*, *The Troubleshooters*, *Counterstrike*, *Beggar My Neighbour*, *Sword of Honour*, *Born Every Minute*, *Scoop*, *The Motorway Men*, *Dr Finlay's Casebook*, *The Bishop Rides Again* (playing a policeman in this BBC Comedy Playhouse), *Give Me Your Word, Here's Harry, Taxi, Not in Front of the Children, Never a Cross Word, Jackanory.*

Theatre credits include many years in various repertory companies, such as the Theatre Royal in York, Ramsgate, Ipswich, Bromley, Watford, Paignton, Nottingham, Hornchurch, Harrogate, Bridgwater. Also *The Mating Game* at Bournemouth and *Staircase.*

Film credits include: *Dad's Army* and *Star.*

BECKWORTH, MISS

Not seen in the sitcom, but referred to by Captain Mainwaring in 'Command Decision'. She helps Mrs Samways run the local guides troop, and has cause to complain, via Mrs Samways, after being followed home by a member of the Home Guard shining an unobscured light on her legs. It turns out the offender is Jones.

Miss Beckworth is a young, local school teacher, and is mentioned again in 'Operation Kilt'. While the platoon start their 15-minute PT session, some local boys in the churchyard shout rude comments, so Mainwaring promises to have a word with Miss Beckworth about the children. She's also Frank Pike's former teacher and was responsible for telling him everything he needed to know about girls, or so he claims in 'War Dance'.

A helpful woman, Miss Beckworth loans Captain Mainwaring a book, *How to Handle Your Oars,* which is issued to the Sea Scouts, when the platoon take charge of a boat in the episode, 'Sons of the Sea'.

BEDWELL, GRAHAM

Film sound recordist on four episodes (TV): S9, episodes 1, 2, 3 & 5

Ever since childhood, Graham wanted to work in television, but after finishing national service in the RAF he began working life as an apprentice in the grocery trade. He moved jobs and worked in Switzerland for a year, prior to joining the BBC as a trainee assistant sound recordist in 1963, just as BBC2 was being launched. Early productions he worked on included Harold Pinter's play, *Tea Party, The Great War* and the *Tonight* programme.

In 1968, Graham was promoted to sound recordist and worked on programmes such as *Nationwide, Wheelbase, The Expert, The Survivors, The Money Programme, Horizon, The Secret War, Z Cars, Poldark, Dixon of Dock Green* and *The Onedin Line.* The last major project he worked on was *Going Live,* which he was involved in for five years before being made redundant in 1995. He now works freelance.

BELBIN, SUSIE

Assistant floor manager on seven episodes (TV): 'The Love of Three Oranges', S9

Born in Glasgow, Susie wanted to work in the the-

atre from childhood. At nine she attended part-time drama classes, but by the time she left school she knew that stage management was where her true interest lay, and enrolled on a full-time course for a year. Upon graduating she worked at Glasgow's Citizens' Theatre for 12 months before turning freelance and working at several venues, including the Opera House in Harrogate.

When the opportunity to help at BBC Scotland came along, she snapped it up, and before long was offered a permanent contract and was promoted to assistant floor manager. During her 28-year career in the Beeb, she spent four years based at Television Centre in Scotland, and the rest in London, where she moved in 1973 and began a three-year spell on *The Morecambe and Wise Show.*

By 1976 she was working for David Croft, and during the seven years she was assigned to his office, she worked on shows like *Come Back, Mrs Noah, It Ain't Half Hot, Mum, Are You Being Served?* and *'Allo, 'Allo,* which she helped direct.

During her career she has directed *Bread* and *Only Fools and Horses,* and produced and directed *One Foot in the Grave* and *Life Without George,* which was scripted by Penny Croft, David's daughter.

Susie took a break from the television business in 1997, but is now back in the industry.

BELL HOTEL, THE

This 46-bedroomed hotel was used by members of the cast and production team whilst they were on location in Norfolk. Situated in King Street, Thetford, just a stone's throw from the town centre, the hotel, which is supposed to have a resident ghost, was formerly a coaching inn, dating back to the 15th century. It's now part of the Old English chain of hotels.

BELL, PENNY

Make-up artist on one episode: 'Battle of the Giants'

Penny, who was born in West Kirby, left school wanting to become a BBC make-up artist, so she qualified in hair and make-up via the London College of Fashion, majoring in hairdressing. She achieved her goal when she joined the Beeb

in 1963. Early shows she worked on included *Juke Box Jury* and *The Black and White Minstrel Show.* She was promoted to make-up supervisor after two and a half years, and the first job in her new position was *The Frost Report.* She also worked on *'Till Death Us Do Part.*

Penny left the BBC to have a baby in 1972, but when people began offering her work, she accepted the occasional freelance assignment, initially on commercials and corporate videos. Nowadays, she works chiefly in TV, and recent credits include *The Sculptress, Gone to the Dogs, A Sense of History* and *Midsomer Murders.*

BENNETT, HAROLD (1899–1981)

Born: Hastings

Roles: Old Man (S3, episode 1), Mr Blewitt, also spelt Mr Bluett (S3, episodes 4, 8 & 13; S4, episode 10; S5, episodes 9 & 13; S7, episodes 1 & 2; S8, episodes 4 & 6; S9, episode 1) (TV); Mr Blewitt ('Turkey Dinner') (radio)

Harold's packed life resembled a colourful montage. He left school at 12 and became a jeweller's

apprentice, but during his lifetime also taught English during the evenings at the Working Men's College, London, studied and painted in Paris and worked as a circus clown.

After acting as an amateur he turned professional and embarked on a career involving plenty of theatre work, including a tour with Donald Wolfit and numerous West End appearances.

While his three children grew up, he took a break from the unstable acting world and worked for an electric light company, but retained his interest in the stage with various amateur companies. After retiring at 65, Harold returned to acting professionally and earned the success he deserved appearing in various TV productions, among them Mr Halliforth in BBC's sitcom *Whack-O!*, but most notably as Young Mr Grace in *Are You Being Served?*, after David Croft spotted him in a theatre production of *The Rose and the Ring*.

Harold, who always looked older than his age, died in 1981, aged 82, after suffering a heart attack. He left behind a career that boasted more than 200 stage and TV credits.

BENNETT, MR
Played by Roy Denton (TV)

In 'Big Guns', Mr Bennett, the borough engineer, goes along with Mr Rees and other members of Walmington's town council to watch a demonstration of how Mainwaring and his men would use their new large naval gun in an emergency. Mainwaring has requested that the bandstand in the park be demolished because it's in the new gun's line of fire, but the demonstration fails to impress and the request is refused.

BERK, ROBERT
Designer on seven episodes (TV): S8 and 'My Brother and I'

Robert trained as a furniture designer, graduating from the Royal College of Art. After working in the industry for a while, he changed direction and joined the BBC as a design assistant in 1965. Early programmes he was assigned to included *Sykes*, *Softly, Softly* and *The Expert* but, other than *Dad's Army*, the most famous show he worked on was *Monty Python's Flying Circus*.

In 1968, Robert left the Beeb and spent time out of the profession, renovating an old farmhouse in rural Essex. But he returned to the industry on a freelance basis, working for Channel 4, the Children's Film Foundation and TV-am, in 1983. For the last few years he's been working for Rag Doll Productions.

BERT
Played by Alister Williamson (TV)

A merchant seaman in 'Wake-Up Walmington', he drinks at The Six Bells before heading off to a port. *En route* he bumps into Mainwaring and his men and finds the bank manager dressed in identical attire to himself.

BERTHA
A traction engine seen in the TV episode, 'All is Safely Gathered In', which is now housed at the Bressingham Steam Museum. (See 'Vehicles'.)

BERWICK ROAD
A road in Walmington mentioned in 'Mum's Army'. Edith Parish, one of Joe's many girlfriends, lives at number 25 with her father.

BETTY
Played by Linda James (TV)

A cashier at Walmington's Plaza Cinema, the 25 year old pops up in 'The Lion has 'Phones'. She also works lunchtimes at the town's British Restaurant, and can be seen serving in 'The Two and a Half Feathers'.

BEVIS, MICHAEL
Born: Bournemouth

Roles: Police Sergeant (S8, episode 6: 'The Face on the Poster') (TV); Private Staines, BBC Announcer, General Gordon and Ramsbotton (stage show)

After completing his national service in the RAF, Michael joined RADA. Upon graduating he spent years on the stage, including a period at the Palace Theatre, Watford, then run by Jimmy Perry, before making his TV debut during the 1960s. Although the lion's share of his career has been spent in the theatre, his TV work includes *It Ain't Half Hot, Mum*, *Wentworth* and *Terry and June*.

Michael appeared in 'The Face On The Poster' as a consequence of being recruited for the stage show, primarily to understudy John Le Mesurier. Most of his time now is taken up writing and presenting music features for Radio 2, as well as appearing in pantomime.

BIG GUNS
Recorded: Sunday 6/7/69

Original transmission: Thursday 23/10/69, 7.30–8.00pm

Original viewing figures: 13.2 million

Repeated: 16/5/70, 29/8/92, 20/7/96, 18/9/99

CAST

Arthur Lowe	Captain Mainwaring
John Le Mesurier	Sergeant Wilson
Clive Dunn	Lance Corporal Jones
John Laurie	Private Frazer
James Beck	Private Walker
Arnold Ridley	Private Godfrey
Ian Lavender	Private Pike
Edward Evans	Mr Rees
Edward Sinclair	Verger
Don Estelle	Man from Pickfords
Roy Denton	Mr Bennett

Platoon: Colin Bean, Richard Jacques, Frank Godfrey, Hugh Cecil, Vic Taylor, Richard Kitteridge, Michael Moore, George Hancock, Freddie Wiles, Leslie Noyes
Removal Men: Edward Western, Charles Adey-Gray, Colin Cunningham

Committee Members: Eileen Winterton and David J Grahame

Note: In the original script, the town clerk was a small, sharp Yorkshireman with glasses called Mr Pendleton.

PRODUCTION TEAM
Script: Jimmy Perry and David Croft
Producer/Director: David Croft
Production Assistant: Harold Snoad
Film Cameraman: James Balfour
Film Editor: Bob Rymer
Lighting: Howard King
Studio Sound: Michael McCarthy
Design: Paul Joel
Assistant Floor Manager: Bill Harman
Vision Mixer: Dave Hanks
Costume Supervisor: Odette Barrow
Make-Up Supervisor: Cecile Hay-Arthur

The platoon is excited when a delivery arrives in the shape of a naval gun, but unfortunately no one knows how to use it, not even Frazer who'd been a jack-tar during the Great War. A manual comes with the gun and the platoon set about familiarising themselves with its operation.

If the gun is to be any use in the defence of Walmington, Mainwaring decrees that everything in its firing line must be demolished, including the bandstand, so he writes to the town clerk telling him it must come down within 48 hours.

Mr Rees (the town clerk) and Mr Bennett (the borough engineer) visit Mainwaring, complain about his ultimatum and state they're not prepared to dismantle the bandstand. To convince Rees, Bennett and the other officials, Mainwaring lays on a full-scale presentation on Sunday morning, but the demonstration is a complete shambles, and does nothing to convince Mr Rees.

BIG PARADE, THE
Recorded: Friday 17/7/70

Original transmission: Friday 25/9/70, 8.00–8.30pm

Original viewing figures: 14 million

Repeated: 30/5/71, 12/9/89, 10/1/90 (N Ireland), 16/7/93, 17/2/96, 7/3/96 (Wales), 4/8/00

CAST

Arthur Lowe	Captain Mainwaring
John Le Mesurier	Sergeant Wilson
Clive Dunn	Lance Corporal Jones
John Laurie	Private Frazer
James Beck	Private Walker
Arnold Ridley	Private Godfrey
Ian Lavender	Private Pike
Bill Pertwee	ARP Warden
Janet Davies	Mrs Pike
Edward Sinclair	Verger
Colin Bean	Private Sponge
Pamela Cundell	Mrs Fox

Platoon: Hugh Hastings, Vic Taylor, Leslie Noyes, Freddie Wiles, Desmond Cullum-Jones, Freddie White, George Hancock, Frank Godfrey, Ken Wade

Extras in Cinema: Civilians: David Melbourne, Bill Leonard, Nina West, Ellison Kempe, Leslie Goldie, Jean Woolland, Julia Stretton. Army: David Pike, Lloyd Goode. RAF: Ronnie Laughlin, Roger Tolliday. Sailor: Tim O'Sullivan. ATS: Maureen Neil, Anna Hilton. Usherette: Gypsy Kempe

Other Extras: Anthony Hamilton and John Holmes

PRODUCTION TEAM
Script: Jimmy Perry and David Croft
Producer/Director: David Croft
Production Assistants: Harold Snoad, Donald Clive
Film Cameraman: Stewart Farnell
Film Sound: Les Collins
Film Editor: Bill Harris
Lighting: Howard King
Studio Sound: John Holmes
Design: Paul Joel
Assistant Floor Manager: David Taylor
Vision Mixer: David Hillier
Costume Supervisor: Barbara Kronig
Make-Up Supervisor: Cynthia Goodwin

When Mainwaring, Wilson, Mrs Pike and Frank go to the pictures, Mainwaring gets an idea while watching the newsreel. He wants to get a regimental mascot for the platoon in time for Sunday's big parade of all the civil defence units and the Home Guard units marking the start of the Spitfire Fund Week. Jones' idea for a painted lady, Pike's little white mouse and Godfrey's suggestion of a cat are all turned down, but Mainwaring's quick to agree when he hears Sponge has a ram on his farm, even though Sponge warns it will be difficult to catch.

Before the evening is out, Hodges arrives and tells Mainwaring the Home Guard will be at the back of the procession for the big parade. They argue about this, but then agree to disagree and nothing is resolved.

The following day, Number 1 section head for Sponge's farm to catch their mascot, but it's not easy and before long their efforts are diverted towards saving Pike when he falls in a bog. Wilson's first on the scene but gets stuck on barbed wire, so it's left to the rest of the platoon to pull him out.

It looks as if the Walmington platoon will have to make do with a goat for their mascot, but Mainwaring isn't happy and abandons the idea. At the parade the argument between Hodges and Mainwaring over who'll lead the parade escalates and they end up racing each other down the road.

BILL
Played by Stuart Sherwin (TV); Michael Segal (radio)
As one of the air raid wardens working for Hodges in Walmington, Bill helps run the civil defence exercise in 'Branded'. He could also be the same warden who's talking to Hodges in 'Menace from the Deep' when they spot a light at the end of the pier, although his name isn't mentioned.

BILLINGS, DICK
Played by Tony Hughes (TV); Timothy Bateson (radio)
Chairman of the Serviceman's Canteen Appeal and a local shopkeeper, Dick Billings appears in 'When Did You Last See Your Money?' as the saviour of Jones' sanity. When Jack Jones thinks he's lost the £500 local shopkeepers have collected in aid of the appeal, he decides the only answer is to use his life savings to fill up the kitty. But Mr Billings saves the day when he enters the bank and tells Jones, who happens to be there, that instead of wrapping up sausages the other day, he wrapped up the money.

Note: In the original script, the character was called Dick Humphreys.

BILTON, MICHAEL (1919–1993)
Born: Hull
Role: Mr Maxwell (S3, episode 14: 'Sons of the Sea') (TV)
After completing his education at a prep school in Scarborough and Nymers College, Hull, Michael joined the navy at the outbreak of war. As a second lieutenant, he was wounded in the stomach on the first day of the Battle of Alamein. A long spell of recuperation followed, before he began his career as an actor, beginning in rep at Worthing.

He gradually built up a solid career and became a familiar character on TV and radio, latterly seen as Basil in *Waiting for God*, and Ned, the chauffeur, in the BBC's *To the Manor Born*. However, many people remember Michael for those well-loved adverts for Yellow Pages, in which he played a gardener. Other appearances on the small screen include playing Dan, a villager, in *The Night People*, an episode of the '60s series, *The Champions*, a butler in *Brideshead Revisited*, Mr Macey in BBC's *Silas Marner*, *Terry and June*, *Don't Wait Up*, *One Foot in the Grave* and *The Fall and Rise of Reginald Perrin*.

Although he rarely appeared on the big screen, Michael was cast in *A Taste of Honey*, the Norman Wisdom picture, *The Early Bird*, *Frenzy* and as Kim Philby in *The Fourth Protocol*.

BINNS, MRS
Played by Wendy Johnson (TV)
Although she never appeared in the credits of 'When Did You Last See Your Money?', Mrs Binns utters a line in the bank saying she's very well when Mainwaring enquires. A dark-haired customer, wearing a lime green dress, Mrs Binns is a very smart resident of Walmington.

BIRD, NORMAN (1926–)
Born: Coalville
Role: Bert Postlethwaite ('Present Arms') (radio)
Norman has extensive experience in all areas of the profession, and frequently found himself being cast as hen-pecked, friendly men or small-minded officials. On TV, he's been seen in shows such as *Worzel Gummidge*, *To Serve Them All My Days*, *Yes Minister*, *One By One*, *Lytton's Diary*, *Ever Decreasing Circles* and *Boon*.

His film career has been just as busy, especially during the 1960s, when he appeared in numerous productions, including *The Man in the Moon*, *Very Important Person*, *Whistle Down the Wind*, *Hot Enough for June* and *All at Sea*. In recent years, he was seen in *Shadowlands*.

BIRKETT, JENNIE
Producer's assistant on the seventh series (TV)
Jennie shared the job with Diane Taylor.

BISHOP, DIANA
Roles: Miss Meadows ('The Armoured Might of Lance Corporal Jones'), Sergeant Wilson's daughter ('Getting the Bird') (radio)
Diana's acting career has included many appearances on television, including *Coronation Street*, playing Mrs Anderton, *Juliet Bravo*, Mrs Rogers in *London's Burning*, *The Troublemakers*, *This Office Life* in 1984, and two *Play for Today*s during the 1970s.

BISHOP, PHIL
Production assistant on eight episodes (TV): S4, episodes: 'Put That Light Out!', 'The Two and a Half Feathers', 'Mum's Army', 'The Test', 'A Wilson (Manager)?', 'Uninvited Guests' and 'Fallen Idol'. Also worked on 'Battle of the Giants'
London-born Phil Bishop left school at 14 and joined the Royal Navy. When he left the forces, he got a job helping paint the Clifton Suspension Bridge and re-studied for his O- and A-levels. While he awaited his results, he applied for a job as a summer relief scene shifter at the BBC, and although unsuccessful, he was offered another position in the department at Bristol.

Phil eventually transferred to Television Centre in London, where he worked as an assistant floor manager in the drama department for a temporary period. Just when it looked as if he'd be returning to his previous role as scene shifter, he was offered a position as AFM in Belfast. While working for the Beeb in Northern Ireland he was promoted to floor manager (1967) and gained his first taste of producing and directing shows.

In 1969, he was back in London working as a production assistant in Light Entertainment, before moving permanently into producing and directing. Some of the shows he worked on include the original *Cilla* show, *Seaside Special*, *It Ain't Half Hot, Mum* and *Top of the Pops*.

Phil left the BBC in 1980 and worked for an Australian television station for a while, before joining LWT on his return, where he produced and directed *Game For a Laugh*. He also worked for other ITV stations and Sky. For six years (1991–1997) he helped launch new television channels around the world, including Australia, America, Hong Kong and Norway.

Nowadays Phil works for Anglia Television as well as running his own aviation company.

BISHOP, SUE
Role: Ticket Collector (S6, episode 3: 'The Royal Train') (TV)
Sue has made several appearances on TV, including an episode of *The Benny Hill Show*, a 1973 BBC production of *Jane Eyre* playing Louisa, Hilary in *The Brothers*, a dancer in *Yeoman of the Guard*, and *Are You Being Served?*, in which she had a regular non-speaking part as a lift girl at Grace Brothers' department store. She was also seen in the 1982 BBC series *Nancy Astor* as Mrs Keppel, and in the film, *Legend of the Werewolf*, playing Tania. Sue now works outside the profession.

BISMARCK
In 'Room at the Bottom', the Verger rushes into the churchyard shouting the news of the *Bismarck*'s sinking. The battleship was the biggest vessel in the German fleet and responsible for sinking *HMS Hood*, the world's largest battle cruiser. The *Bismarck* was sunk in May, 1941, while sailing in the Atlantic.

BLACKETT, DEBBIE
Born: London
Role: an Andrews Sister and Girl on the Beach (stage show)
After graduating from drama school, Debbie worked in rep for some years, travelling around the country, performing at theatres in Malvern, Worcester, Belfast, Northampton and Chesterfield. She has appeared in musicals, such as *Chu Chin Chow*, playing the slave girl, and as Jane in *Salad Days*.

BLACK HORSE, THE
A pub in Walmington that Wilson and Pike visit while searching for Frazer, who misses a parade in 'The Miser's Hoard'.

BLACK MARKET
If you had the cash and the right contacts, food and items that were scarce could usually be obtained. The black market was rife as the effects of rationing started taking their toll, and spivs like Joe Walker appeared all over the place, ready to make money at other people's expense. In *Dad's Army*, everyone uses Walker for obtaining black market goods, although no one wants openly to admit it. He supplies Frazer with a bottle of whisky each week, and regularly secures items for the others, including Mainwaring, who orders whisky, razor blades and cheddar cheese amongst other things, while Wilson's order includes milk stout. He's seen as such an important person around town that when he receives his call-up papers, Mainwaring and Wilson visit the War Office to try and get his enlistment postponed.

Walker is well known in Walmington and supplies many people, not just members of the platoon. He's also been known to supply Miss Fortescue at the Marigold Tea Rooms and the Peabody Rooms, whenever a function is taking place.

BLACKOUT
Established under the Emergency Powers (Defence) Act in 1939, the blackout was trialed by the Home Office on London streets in August that year. As the realities of blackout drew nearer, councils around the country began painting white bands around obstacles, along major streets and kerbs, while traffic lights were adapted to reduce the amount of light emitted.

The introduction of the blackout had a dramatic effect on the British landscape, with whole cities being plunged into darkness; many historians believe its impact on the public was far greater than most other aspects of wartime life. Every evening people had to black out their windows with the aid of heavy curtains, blackout card, or other means, and industry was expected to do the same, at a great cost to many companies.

The introduction of the blackout also led to a rise in accidents, with the number of road accidents doubling during September 1939. Walking the streets also became a hazard, with many incidents being reported as a result of the darkness. People were eventually allowed to use hand torches, so long as their brightness was dimmed, and cars were fitted with masked headlights.

The blackout began 30 minutes after sunset and lasted until 30 minutes before sunrise, but eventually a small amount of light was allowed in shop windows, signs and street lights, making everywhere a little safer. Any source of light still had to be extinguished whenever an air raid siren sounded.

In September 1944, with the end of hostilities in sight, the blackout was replaced by a dim-out.

BLACKWELL, MR
A non-speaking character who works at the town hall. He arrives with Frazer in his hearse during the final scenes of 'Is There Honey Still For Tea?', with news that the aerodrome is going to be slightly repositioned, meaning Godfrey and his two sisters won't have to leave their home after all.

BLANCH, DENNIS (1947–)
Born: Barnet
Role: 2nd Lieutenant (S5, episode 6: 'If the Cap Fits…') (TV)
While Dennis attended drama school in the evenings, he worked in the London markets, driving lorries around the city. When he completed his training he worked the rep scene, including

spells at Exeter and Newcastle, before making his TV debut in *The Insider*, a play for ATV. He's also appeared in several episodes of *Heartbeat*, and spent four years (1978–1982) in the Granada series, *Strangers*.

Recently, Dennis has appeared in *The Bill*, *The Full Monty*, playing a managing director, the BBC series *The Broker's Man*, as a police sergeant and *Lost for Words*, a play for Yorkshire TV.

BLEWITT, HORACE
By the time we hear about Sidney's brother, Horace, he's already dead. In 'No Spring for Frazer' he's buried in a coffin Frazer thinks holds a butterfly spring he's lost from the Lewis gun. Horace had lived with his brother at 21 Marigold Avenue, and worked as a meter reader for the Gas Light and Coke Company.

BLEWITT, SIDNEY
Played by Harold Bennett (TV and radio)
Address: 21 Marigold Avenue, Walmington-on-Sea
One of Walmington's many old age pensioners, Mr Blewitt is regularly seen around town. He's been married over 50 years, and was celebrating his golden wedding when Mainwaring and his men came visiting at 2.30 in the morning, demanding to examine a chicken he'd specially ordered for his anniversary celebration.

For years, Sidney ran a photographic concession on the West Promenade, selling snaps to tourists for two bob a time, but since retiring he has become something of a handy man: as well as being the Vicar's gardener, he turns his hand to sign writing, uses his woodwork skills to repair old picture frames and keeps chickens in the back garden of his tudor-style home in Walmington's peaceful Marigold Avenue.

Sidney doesn't suffer fools gladly and is quick to put people in their place, like the time he told Hodges about the funny face people made behind his back.

Note: Also known as Norman and Mr Bluett during the life of the show.

BLIGHT, RON
Film sound recordist on four episodes of the fifth series (TV): episode 2 'Keep Young and Beautiful', episode 3 'A Soldier's Farewell', episode 5 'The Desperate Drive of Corporal Jones' and episode 7 'The King was in his Counting House'

BLODWEN, MISS
Played by Sally Douglas (TV)
Frazer's guest at the platoon dance in 'War Dance' was Miss Blodwen, an attractive land girl who happens to be his niece.

BLONDE, THE
Played by Gilda Perry (TV)
When Mainwaring and Wilson spend an evening in the underground station at London's Trafalgar Square after visiting the Brigadier in 'The

Loneliness of the Long-Distance Walker', Mainwaring ends up sleeping next to a pretty blonde called Judy.

BOB

Played by Ronnie Brody (TV); Michael Middleton (radio, although character called 'Driver's Mate')

The engine fireman in 'The Royal Train' who, along with Henry the driver, has to stop the train at the station because of a faulty part.

BOND, DEREK (1919–)

Born: Glasgow

Role: Minister (S5, episode 2: 'Keep Young and Beautiful') (TV)

Derek Bond started his professional career in 1937 in two early TV plays: *Gallows Glorious* and *RUR*. He then played a small part at London's Garrick Theatre in *As Husbands Go* before joining Colchester Rep in 1938 as the juvenile lead.

At the outbreak of war Derek joined the Grenadier Guards. He was wounded in Tunisia in 1942 and awarded the Military Cross. Once he'd recovered from his wounds he became a staff captain at the Royal Military College for a year before rejoining the Grenadiers in Italy where he was taken prisoner.

While he was recovering from the wounds sustained in Tunisia, Derek had been film tested and put under contract by Ealing Studios. Within eight weeks of returning from the prison camp, Ealing sent him to Germany to play a prisoner of war in *The Captive Heart*, with Michael Redgrave and Basil Radford. Next, he played the title role in *Nicholas Nickleby* and the film offers kept coming. He co-starred with Googie Withers in *The Loves of Joanna Godden*, appeared in *Uncle Silas* with Jean Simmons, and Phyllis Calvert in *Broken Journey*. His extensive film career has included over 40 pictures, such as *The Weaker Sex*, *Tony Draws a Horse*, *Stormy Crossing*, *Wonderful Life* and *Press for Time*.

He has also worked on TV, and co-presented the successful *Picture Parade* for over two years. He joined the original team on the *Tonight* programme, making 40 film reports in the show's first year. Other TV credits include the first *Callan* series, playing Hunter.

In the 1980s he starred in the West End for over six years before taking a break and writing his first book, which was published in 1991. He has since been tempted back to the theatre, playing Colonel Julyan in a tour of *Rebecca*, amongst other projects.

BOOKS

Over the years many books have been published about *Dad's Army*, or the actors who appeared in the show. A comprehensive list follows:

Dad's Army (a novel based on the film) by John Burke, Hodder Paperbacks, 1971 (ISBN: 0340150270).

Dad's Army – the official souvenir of the popular television series. A Peter Way Magazine Special, 1972.

Dad's Army by Jimmy Perry and David Croft. As well as several small actor and character profiles, the book contains five scripts: 'Asleep in the Deep', 'The Deadly Attachment', 'The Godiva Affair', 'Everybody's Trucking' and 'Keep Young and Beautiful'. First published in hardback by Elm Tree Books in 1975, it was put into paperback the following year by Sphere Books (ISBN: 0722104065).

Dad's Army Annual. Six editions of the annual were published by World Distributors, Manchester between 1973 and 1978.

Dad's Army – The Defence of a Front Line English Village by Paul Ableman, edited by A Wilson MA. The book was published by BBC Books in 1989 and contains novelisations based on four of Perry and Croft's scripts: 'The Battle of Godfrey's Cottage', 'Getting the Bird', 'Mum's Army' and 'My British Buddy' (ISBN: 0563208503).

Dad's Army – The Making of a Television Legend by Bill Pertwee was originally published in 1989 by David and Charles (ISBN: 0715394894). It was published in paperback before being revised and republished by Pavilion Books in 1997.

Dad's Army Song Book was produced by Wise Publications and distributed by Music Sales Ltd in 1995.

Dad's Army – A Guide to Television, Radio and Stage by David Hamilton, Alan and Alys Hayes was published by Homefront Publications in 1996 and originally sold through the appreciation society. It was revised and extended under the title *Dad's Army Handbook* in 1998 and published by DAAS Publications. An extended second edition followed in 1999.

Dad's Army – A Celebration by Richard Webber was published in hardback by Virgin Books in 1997 (ISBN: 1852276940). It was issued in paperback in 1999 (ISBN: 0753503077).

Dad's Army – The Lost Episodes by Jimmy Perry and David Croft was published by Virgin Books in 1998. It contains the six scripts of the second series, five of which no longer exist in the BBC archives (ISBN: 1852277572).

OTHER TITLES THAT HAVE A DAD'S ARMY LINK

A Jobbing Actor by John Le Mesurier. This autobiography was published in hardback by Elm Tree Books in 1984. A paperback version was released in 1985 (ISBN: 0722160321).

Permission to Speak, an autobiography by Clive Dunn was published in hardback by Century in 1986 (ISBN: 0712612165).

Arthur Lowe – A Life, a biography by his son, Stephen Lowe, was first published by Nick Hern Books in 1996 (ISBN: 1854592793). Virgin Books released a paperback the following year.

A Funny Way To Make A Living, an autobiography by Bill Pertwee, was published in hardback by Sunburst Books in 1996 (ISBN: 1857782682).

Lady Don't Fall Backwards by Joan Le Mesurier was first published in hardback by Sidgwick and Jackson in 1988. A paperback was released by Pan Books the following year (ISBN: 0330309942).

Who Do You Think YOU ARE KIDDING! by Colin Bean was published in paperback by the Minerva Press in 1998 (ISBN: 0754104990).

A *Dad's Army* colouring and dot-to-dot book was published by World Distributors in 1971 (ISBN: 723532893).

A *Dad's Army Activity Book* was issued by World Books of Manchester in 1973.

Piccolo Dad's Army Comic Strips was published by Pan Books in 1973.

The magazine *Look In* published a series of *Dad's Army* cartoon strips between 1970 and 1980.

BOOTS, BOOTS, BOOTS

Recorded: Friday 31/7/70

Original transmission: Friday 9/10/70, 8.00–8.30pm

Original viewing figures: 13.2 million

Repeated: 13/6/71, 10/3/85, 31/10/92, 5/11/92 (Wales), 29/6/96, 16/7/00

CAST

Arthur Lowe . . . . .Captain Mainwaring
John Le Mesurier . . . . .Sergeant Wilson
Clive Dunn . . . . .Lance Corporal Jones
John Laurie . . . . .Private Frazer
James Beck . . . . .Private Walker
Arnold Ridley . . . . .Private Godfrey
Ian Lavender . . . . .Private Pike
Bill Pertwee . . . . .ARP Warden
Janet Davies . . . . .Mrs Pike
Erik Chitty . . . . .Mr Sedgewick
Platoon: Colin Bean, Hugh Hastings, Vic Taylor, Leslie Noyes, Freddie Wiles, Frank Godfrey, Desmond Cullum-Jones, Freddie White, George Hancock, Ken Wade
Stuntman: Johnny Scripps

PRODUCTION TEAM

Script: Jimmy Perry and David Croft
Producer/Director: David Croft
Production Assistant: Harold Snoad and Donald Clive
Film Cameraman: Stewart Farnell
Film Sound: Les Collins
Film Editor: Bill Harris
Lighting: Howard King
Studio Sound: John Holmes
Design: Paul Joel
Assistant Floor Manager: David Taylor
Vision Mixer: Dave Hanks
Costume Supervisor: Barbara Kronig
Make-Up Supervisor: Cynthia Goodwin

Mainwaring decides to introduce the three F's to his platoon: fast feet, functional feet and fit feet. He checks everyone's feet and feels there's a lot of work needed to get them up to scratch, so he starts a fitness campaign with a series of arduous route marches. After a seven-mile walk Main-

'Boots, Boots, Boots'

To put a halt to Mainwaring's exercise campaign, a mischievous plan is hatched.

'Boots, Boots, Boots'

waring decides to inspect the platoon's feet, but before doing so takes Wilson into the office and says he won't show him up by asking him to show his feet in front of the platoon – he'll check them in the office instead because they can't have one rule for some, another for others.

With all the platoon's feet lined up along wooden benches, Walker paints smiling faces on Pikey and Frazer's feet, but Mainwaring isn't amused. To harden everyone's feet he organises more exercise, including a football match in bare feet (not much fun with a leather ball), racing – or tip-toeing – across the pebbled beach and marching in the sea on Walmington beach, where Mainwaring falls down a hole. It's all getting too much for Pikey who has nightmares of Mainwaring's marches.

The men are getting concerned about their Captain's plans for a 20-mile route march. Pikey has an idea which he shares with Wilson: if they exchanged a smaller pair of boots for Mainwaring's, they'd hurt his feet and he wouldn't be able to go on the march, but unbeknown to Pikey and Wilson, the rest of the platoon come up with the same idea.

As the boots cost 36 shillings a pair, Frazer's concerned about the expense, but he goes with Walker, Jones and Godfrey to a shop to buy a pair. Godfrey acts as a decoy, claiming he's not very well, and while the shopkeeper is out the back getting a glass of water, they swap the boots.

Unaware that their colleagues have already exchanged the boots, Wilson and Pike visit the shop to buy a pair of brown boots, the same sort as Captain Mainwaring's. When Wilson pretends to feel faint, the shopkeeper asks whether a glass of water will do, and while he goes off to fetch a drink, Pikey swaps the boots.

Mainwaring arrives wearing the smaller boots and it looks like their plan will work, but they hadn't bargained on the shopkeeper returning a pair of boots Mainwaring had had repaired.

BOTANICAL GARDENS
The gardens are situated north of Walmington's town centre and are referred to in 'Operation Kilt'.

BOURNE, ROGER
Role: Member of the platoon's back row in 28 episodes (S3, episodes 8, 9, 11 & 12; S6, episodes 1–5; S7; S8, episodes 1, 2, 4– 6; 'My Brother and I'; 'The Love of Three Oranges'; S9) (TV)
Roger, who served in the Royal Artillery with Jimmy Perry in India, was part of the double-act Bourne and Barbara. He did a lot of walk-ons and appeared in small parts in films and on television, including playing a picnicker in 'The Great Race', an episode of *Whatever Happened To The Likely Lads?*. Roger retired in 1980 but shortly after suffered a nervous breakdown. Ill health affected him until his death in early 1997.

BOWNESS, FELIX
Born: Harwell
Roles: Driver (S7, episode 1: 'Everybody's Trucking'), Special Constable (S8, episode 1: 'Ring Dem Bells'), Van Driver (S9, episode 5: 'Number Engaged') (TV)
Felix has been in the entertainment business over four decades performing in variety shows around the country. A veteran warm-up man, winning a talent contest in Reading led to him turning semi-pro. Whilst working in cabaret, he was spotted by a BBC producer and given a small part in radio.

With great tenacity, Felix – an amateur boxing champion in his late teens – kept plugging away, eventually making his TV debut as a stand-up comic before moving into comedy roles in shows like *Porridge*, playing Gay Gordon.

Felix, best known for his role as jockey Fred Quilley in *Hi-De-Hi!*, has worked frequently for Perry and/or Croft: he was a customer in *Are You Being Served?*, a grocer in *You Rang, M'Lord?* and he also appeared in *Hugh and I*. He played a relief guard in the series, *Oh, Doctor Beeching!*, as well as warming up the audiences prior to recordings.

BOXER
An eight-ton steam roller used during the TV episode, 'Everybody's Trucking'. It can now be seen at the Bressingham Steam Museum. (See 'Vehicles'.)

'Museum Piece'

BOYER, CHARLES

Played by Robert Gillespie (TV)

Boyer appears alongside Greta Garbo (played by Joan Savage) in the movie, *Marie Walewska*, which the Walmington Home Guard watch at the pictures one evening in 'A Soldier's Farewell'.

BOYLE, MR

Played by Arthur Brough (TV)

The aged chief clerk at the Eastgate branch of Swallow Bank. Seen in 'A Wilson (Manager)?', Wilson asks his chief clerk to arrange a staff meeting as it's his first day in the manager's hot seat. Mr Boyle must be close to retirement and one wonders whether Arthur Wilson would have been looking for younger blood if his excursion into management hadn't been cut short.

BOYS, THE

Played by Colin Daniels and Carson Green (TV)

The two boys who have been swimming in the local reservoir and are told off by Mainwaring in 'The Lion has 'Phones'.

BOY SCOUT, THE

Played by Michael Osborne (TV)

The bespectacled boy scout appears in the episode 'Museum Piece'. When Pike arranges to borrow a cart from the scouts, their leader insists

on coming along to make sure it's looked after. He ends up being the one who informs Mainwaring that the Chinese Rocket Gun, which has been requisitioned by the Home Guard, is ready for firing.

BRACEWELL, ADAM

Played by John Ringham (TV)

Adam Bracewell, who was 40 and 'something in the city' when the series started, doesn't do his chances of an extended stay in the LDV any good when he turns up for the first parade dressed in a dinner suit and asking how long they'll be required because he's taking his wife to dinner.

In fact, Bracewell was dropped after the first episode: writers Jimmy Perry and David Croft intended to make him a principal character, but when it came to recording the first episode, realised they had too many regular parts, and Bracewell was the unlucky one who got the chop. The writers also felt Bracewell was too similar to Godfrey.

Although he wasn't seen, Mr Bracewell was referred to in the second episode, 'Museum Piece'. When talking about the platoon's dearth of fighting equipment with Wilson, Mainwaring mentions Bracewell's number three iron as a possible weapon.

BRAIN VERSUS BRAWN

Recorded: Friday 17/11/72

Original transmission: Friday 8/12/72, 8.30–9.00pm

Original viewing figures: 18.6 million

Repeated: 1/9/73, 19/12/91, 11/11/95, 8/2/96 (Wales), 14/6/97, 30/3/00

CAST

Arthur Lowe	Captain Mainwaring
John Le Mesurier	Sergeant Wilson
Clive Dunn	Lance Corporal Jones
John Laurie	Private Frazer
James Beck	Private Walker
Arnold Ridley	Private Godfrey
Ian Lavender	Private Pike
Bill Pertwee	ARP Warden
Robert Raglan	Colonel
Edward Sinclair	Verger
Anthony Roye	Mr Fairbrother
Maggie Don	Waitress
Geoffrey Hughes	Bridge Corporal
David Rose	Dump Corporal

Platoon: Colin Bean, Leslie Noyes, Hugh Hastings, George Hancock

Girl at Bar: Leonnie Jessel

Guests at Dinner: Desmond Cullum-Jones, Michael Moore, Freddie Wiles, Colin Bean, Ned Hood, Rex Diamond, Bob Blaine, Arthur Parry, Harry Davies, William Curran, Tony West, Sid Cosson

PRODUCTION TEAM

Script: Jimmy Perry and David Croft

Producer/Director: David Croft

Production Assistant: Gordon Pert

Film Cameraman: James Balfour

Film Sound: Les Collins

Film Editor: Bill Harris

Lighting: Howard King

Studio Sound: John Delany

Design: Paul Joel

Assistant Floor Manager: Peter Fitton

Vision Mixer: Dave Hanks

Costume Supervisor: Susan Wheal

Make-Up Supervisor: Anna Chesterman

Visual Effects: Tony Harding

Mainwaring has asked Wilson along to the Rotarian dinner as his guest. He tells his chief clerk that some of Walmington's most influential people are attending and tries desperately to introduce him to the chairman of the town's Rotary club, who turns out to be an old school friend of Wilson's, much to Mainwaring's chagrin.

Jones is there representing not only the butchers of Walmington but also the Athletic Association, instead of Mr Cutforth, who had to attend the Darby and Joan Club. Walker is also there because he supplied the sherry and rabbit for the chicken croquettes! The Colonel bumps into Jones, Walker and Mainwaring and lets slip that there's a scheme on Saturday, which they haven't been invited to, to form a Home Guard commando unit out of the younger, fitter men – a

PLAYING BRACEWELL

'There are different sections in showbiz. No one section is better than the other. I am a classically trained actor, a jobbing character man, trying to make a living to feed my four offspring and pay the mortgage. I don't feel that category makes me superior – or inferior – to the other activities in my trade.

'I am now an old man with 52 years of professional work under my belt. Throughout my career I always accepted work in – for want of a better description – light entertainment on TV. My hope was to meet and work with people I had idolised and respected when I was young. So when my agent told me that I had an offer to play a rather stupid, middle-aged man who was "something in the city" for a new comedy series called *Dad's Army*, I was chuffed. I was told that Arthur Lowe (an exceptional talent), John Le Mesurier (I'd worked with him in films and admired his subtle skill greatly) and John Laurie (a great classical actor in the 1930s) were already in the cast, and of course I accepted.

'Then I discovered my character, Bracewell, was to be a regular, running through the series. This raised some doubts in me. We hadn't even begun yet, but if the series was to prove successful I could find myself typecast and I'd always managed to avoid that so far.

'As I said earlier, I'm a jobbing actor. At that time my face was reasonably well known by the public but nobody knew my name – that's still true – nor could they remember what they had seen me in. Consequently casting directors never had a problem suggesting me for a wide variety of parts. I could play Bully Bottom in *A Midsummer Night's Dream*, appear in a BBC classic serial, support Frankie Howerd or Dick Emery or go off to work in my first love, the theatre. Never a star, it seemed to me I'd got the best of all worlds. I wasn't sure, then, that I wanted to be identified with just one part.

'I was saved by the bell. On the first day's rehearsal for the opening episode of *Dad's Army*, David Croft took me to one side, clearly not happy. He said that they (him and Jimmy Perry) had decided there were too many regular parts and one of them would have to go – and that was me. David is a gen-uinely decent man and he handled what could have been an unpleasant situation courteously and kindly. Typically, he found a way of using me on four subsequent occasions during the series playing a captain in the army as compensation for having to ditch me; there was no obligation for him to do that. On one level I was disappointed but on another there was a sense of relief.

'In some ways I think it was a mistake to get rid of my character, whether I was to play him or not, because the part was very interesting. He was a foolish man though very comfortably off. His sense of priorities was confused. For example, Mainwaring had asked everyone to come to the next parade armed with a weapon of some sort. My man arrived in black tie and dinner jacket, plus a golf club – his idea of a weapon – and he told Mainwaring he couldn't stay long because he had a dinner engagement. There are great possibilities there for development. Only James Beck was around the same age. All the rest, except Ian Lavender, were old men. It could have been a valuable balance. However, given the immense success of the series my views have been proved wrong and irrelevant.

'Thirty-two years have passed since that first episode and it is hard to recall details. What I do remember very well, though, is that the cast gelled themselves into a team very quickly. Even at that very early stage it was possible to see that this was probably going to be a success. They had a first rate cast but the really vital point was the script written by Jimmy Perry and David Croft.

'You can't play Hamlet without Shakespeare's words. Nor can you have an outstanding comedy series without an outstanding script and that's what they came up with throughout. If I have regrets about what happened to my part it is in that area. There still isn't enough really good writing about.

'I still regard it a privilege to have been cast in *Dad's Army*, and with great pride I manage to slip into conversations the fact that I, too, was in the very first episode of one of the greatest series the BBC has ever produced.'

JOHN RINGHAM

striking force operating behind enemy lines. Mainwaring says he thinks it's a farce, but Walker and Jones class it as an insult to the older members and accept the Colonel's subsequent invitation to take part and show that veterans still have a role to play.

Their task is to place a bomb inside the Officer Commanding's office inside a petrol dump, which is highly secured. The platoon discuss ideas about how they can infiltrate the camp to place their bomb. They decide to dress up as firemen and by using Walker's old fire engine – he bought it from the fire station for £10 – they can drive to the dump and not be stopped. Their secret agent, the Verger – who replaced Mrs Pike when she couldn't decide what to wear – will set a fire going just outside the fuel dump. But the plan falls apart when the Verger's fire is quickly extinguished by one of the soldiers, and the men are diverted to a real fire by Hodges, when a stick of incendiaries sets a house alight.

The Colonel arrives on the scene and compliments Mainwaring, before telling him the training major was shocked to receive the bomb through the post, especially after the Home Guard commandos were caught. The bomb had been posted yesterday, on Wilson's advice, giving him the upper hand once again!

BRAN
A tracker dog that Walker brings along to help find enemy parachutes in 'Man Hunt'.

BRANDED
Recorded: Friday 14/11/69

Original transmission: Thursday 20/11/69, 7.30–8.00pm

Original viewing figures: 11.1 million

Repeated: 13/6/70, 19/11/82, 3/10/92, 11/2/93, 22/6/96, 11/7/00

CAST
Arthur Lowe . . . . .Captain Mainwaring
John Le Mesurier . . . . .Sergeant Wilson
Clive Dunn . . . . .Lance Corporal Jones
John Laurie . . . . .Private Frazer
James Beck . . . . .Private Walker
Arnold Ridley . . . . .Private Godfrey
Ian Lavender . . . . .Private Pike
Bill Pertwee . . . . .Chief Warden
Nan Braunton . . . . .Miss Godfrey
Stuart Sherwin . . . . .Bill (2nd ARP Warden)
Roger Avon . . . . .Doctor
Platoon: Hugh Hastings, Desmond Cullum-Jones, Vic Taylor, George Hancock, Freddie Wiles, Martin Dunn, Freddie White, Leslie Noyes, Jimmy Mac, Roger Bourne

PRODUCTION TEAM
Script: Jimmy Perry and David Croft
Producer: David Croft
Production Assistant: Steve Turner
Director: Harold Snoad
Lighting: Howard King

Studio Sound: Michael McCarthy
Design: Richard Hunt
Assistant Floor Manager: Bill Harman
Vision Mixer: Dave Hanks
Costume Supervisor: Michael Burdle
Make-Up Supervisor: Cecile Hay-Arthur

Mainwaring calls Wilson into the church hall office because Godfrey has sent him his written resignation, giving two weeks' notice. While Wilson summons Godfrey to explain himself, Mainwaring checks the duties rota and decides that due to his tea-making responsibilities, he's too valuable to lose.

Godfrey tells Mainwaring the reason he wants to leave the Home Guard is partly due to a little mouse he found in his larder: being unable to kill it, he realised he certainly wouldn't be able to kill a German. When Mainwaring enquires how it affected him during the First World War, Godfrey admits being a conscientious objector. Shocked and disgusted, Mainwaring orders Godfrey home and informs the troops of the situation.

Later, while on patrol, Jones' section stop off at a hut for a cup of tea Pikey has made. When Godfrey arrives with some of his upside-down cakes, everyone cold-shoulders him.

The platoon attend a civil defence exercise organised by Hodges which teaches the men how to rescue an unconscious person from a smoke-filled room. When Mainwaring collapses inside, it's Godfrey who saves his life. Later, while Godfrey recovers in his bedroom from the ordeal, the platoon visit. Mainwaring thanks him for saving his life, and when he notices a picture on the wall of Godfrey wearing his Military Medal, he realises he judged him too quickly. They apologise and appoint Godfrey as the platoon's medical orderly.

BRANDON, RONNIE
Role: Mr Drury (S3, episode 13: 'No Spring for Frazer') (TV)
When Frazer wanted to speak to him about the coffin he'd supplied, Mr Drury, the Walmington undertaker, brushed past, too busy to stop.

BRAUNTON, NAN
Role: Cissy Godfrey (S2, episode 2; S3, episodes 8, 9 & 11) (TV); ('The Battle of Godfrey's Cottage' and 'Branded') (radio)
Nan Braunton, real name Minnie Bevans, died in 1978. During her career she appeared in films, such as 1955's It's A Great Day, and various television shows, including The Grove Family as Miss Jones, BBC's 1960 production Yorky as Miss Sedgebeer, Heidi, a Sunday Night Theatre production titled Figure of Fun, Detective in 1964, playing Florence Gill and the ITV series of 1969, Strange Report, playing a character called Miss Blake. She also appeared in a 1958 episode of the sci-fi series, Quatermass and the Pit, playing Miss Dobson.

BRENNAN, MICHAEL (1912–1982)
Born: London
Roles: Sergeant Major ('Fallen Idol') and Tom and George Pearson ('Absent Friends') (radio)
Michael Brennan, who was once John Gielgud's stage manager, was frequently cast as a tough villain, particularly in films. Although usually seen in small roles, he became a familiar face in British post-war movies, appearing in Captain Boycott, Morning Departure, No Trace, Tom Brown's Schooldays, Emergency Call, 13 East Street, Up in the World, The 39 Steps, Dunkirk and many more. He was also a regular on TV and in the theatre.

BRESSINGHAM STEAM MUSEUM
Based at Bressingham, near Diss in Norfolk, the steam museum is now the home for three of the vehicles used in Dad's Army: the fire engine, the traction engine and the threshing machine (used in 'All is Safely Gathered In'). Jonathan Wheeler is the collections manager at the museum. Bressingham Steam Museum, Bressingham, Diss, Norfolk IP22 2AB. Tel: 01379 687386.

BREUSTER, MR
Not seen or heard in the sitcom, Mr Breuster's death is reported to Frazer by Doctor McCeavedy in 'The Miser's Hoard'. As Mr Breuster was a resident of Walmington, Frazer spots a business opportunity and intends contacting the relatives as soon as possible.

BRIGADIER, THE
Played by Patrick Waddington (TV); Jack Watson (radio)
The official watched Jones successfully complete, or so he thought, the assault course in 'The Showing Up of Corporal Jones'. He's seen again in 'The Loneliness of the Long-Distance Walker'. He calls the church hall office and ends up speaking to Walker. The Brigadier had visited Mainwaring at the bank that afternoon and was given a glass of whisky; he liked it so much he wants Walker to supply six bottles every month. When Walker points out he can't because he's joining up, the Brigadier promises to do something about it, but never does.

BRIGADIER, THE
Played by Jeffrey Segal (TV)
The Brigadier in 'The Making of Private Pike' organises a big exercise involving two brigades of infantry, a battery of 25 pounders, air support and several tanks.

BRIGADIER, THE (WAR OFFICE)
Played by Anthony Sharp (TV)
When Walker received his call-up papers in 'The Loneliness of the Long-Distance Walker', Mainwaring and Wilson travel to London to see the Brigadier at the War Office in the hope that he'll prevent Walker joining up.

BRITISH RESTAURANT
These self-service cafeterias were run by local authorities and named British Restaurants at the suggestion of Winston Churchill. They sprang up during the Blitz to help feed families who lost their homes through the bombing. Providing cheap, basic, yet wholesome meals, the restaurants became popular and expansion plans were soon drawn up; but although over two thousand had opened their doors by September 1943, the total fell well short of the government's original targets.

The Walmington-on-Sea branch of the British Restaurant is seen in the episode, 'The Two and a Half Feathers', when Mainwaring and Wilson have a portion of toad in the hole for lunch. Its

'The Two and a Half Feathers'

rather bleak look isn't helped by the brown and cream walls. The tables are adorned by white tablecloths, and its self-service style means queues are not uncommon, particularly during the lunch period. Portions are far from generous but the food is cheap and cheerful, even if it is dished out by the mouthy Edna, who manages the restaurant. One of the regular items on the menu, which is scribbled on a blackboard, is snoek fishcakes, mentioned by Mainwaring in 'The Honourable Man'.

BRODY, RONNIE (1918–1991)
Born: Bristol
Roles: Bob (S6, episode 3: 'The Royal Train'), Mr Swann (S8, episode 5: 'High Finance'), GPO Man (S9, episode 5: 'Number Engaged') (TV)
Son of music hall artistes Bourne and Lester, Ronnie joined the merchant navy at 15 before serving with the RAF in North Africa during the Second World War.

After demob he spent several years in variety and rep but by the 1950s his career was dominated by both the big and small screen. Over the years he became one of the most instantly recognisable comedy character actors in the business.

During his career he worked with many top comedians in shows such as *Dave Allen at Large, The Dick Emery Show, Rising Damp, Bless This House, Home James, The Lenny Henry Show* and *The 19th Hole*. He was seen in films such as *Help!, A Funny Thing Happened on the Way to the Forum, Superman III, Carry On Don't Lose Your Head* as the Little Man and *Carry On Loving* as Henry. Although he concentrated on comedy, he appeared occasionally in TV drama.

BROOKS, MAJOR

Not seen, but referred to by the cashiers (Doreen and Betty) at the Plaza Cinema, Walmington. He visits the cinema every week and is well-liked by the two girls.

BROUGH, ARTHUR (1905–1978)

Born: Petersfield
Role: Mr Boyle (S4, episode 11: 'A Wilson (Manager)?') (TV)

In his early life, Arthur's great love was running and acting in repertory companies. With their wedding money as financial backing, Arthur and his wife opened the East Pavilion, Folkestone, in 1929.

He went on to open successful companies at Leeds, Bradford and Lincoln before the war thwarted any more plans. After demob from the navy, he opened two more reps before branching out into TV and films.

During his career he worked on several films including *The Green Man* with Alastair Sim, but it is TV for which most people will remember him. He appeared in many bit parts in shows such as *Upstairs, Downstairs* and *The Persuaders*. But for millions of viewers he will always be the churlish Mr Grainger from five years of *Are You Being Served?*. He'd been written in for another series of the sitcom when he died in 1978, six weeks after his wife's death.

BROWN, KEN

The BBC graphic designer who redesigned the opening credits when *Dad's Army* was first recorded in colour.

After graduating from art school in Birmingham, Ken moved to London and joined an advertising agency. He spent ten years at the BBC, designing graphics for countless shows, including *Review*, an arts show, *Call My Bluff* and *The Wednesday Play*. He left the Beeb in 1974 to set up his own production company, directing commercials.

BROWN, MR

(See 'Volunteer, The'.)

BROWNE, JENNIFER

Born: London
Role: WAAF Sergeant (S3, episode 8: 'The Day the Balloon Went Up') (TV)

Jennifer, whose mother was a musician, trained at RADA. She quickly found work upon graduating, working in rep and provincial theatres. During the 1960s she was busy on stage and TV, including appearances in *The Charlie Drake Show, Hugh and I* and *Sunday Night Theatre*, but upon marrying a RAF pilot she moved to Singapore for two years. Jennifer's appearance as the WAAF Sergeant in 1969 marked the resumption of her acting career after returning from Singapore. She raised three children but found it hard to relaunch her career, so took a long break. However, four years ago she returned to acting, since when she has worked mainly in theatre, including several tours.

BRUSH WITH THE LAW, A

Recorded: Sunday 26/11/72

(The *Christmas Night with the Stars* insert was recorded the same evening)

Original transmission: Friday 15/12/72, 8.30–9.00pm

Original viewing figures: 15.4 million

Repeated: 26/2/91, 18/11/95, 15/2/96 (Wales)

CAST

Arthur Lowe	Captain Mainwaring
John Le Mesurier	Sergeant Wilson
Clive Dunn	Lance Corporal Jones
John Laurie	Private Frazer
James Beck	Private Walker
Arnold Ridley	Private Godfrey
Ian Lavender	Private Pike
Bill Pertwee	ARP Warden
Geoffrey Lumsden	Captain Square
Frank Williams	Vicar
Edward Sinclair	Verger
Stuart Sherwin	Reg Adamson (Junior Warden)
Jeffrey Gardiner	Mr Wintergreen
Marjorie Wilde	Lady Magistrate
Chris Gannon	Mr Bone, the Clerk of the Court
Toby Perkins	Usher

Platoon: Colin Bean, Hugh Cecil, Leslie Noyes, George Hancock, Evan Ross, Desmond Cullum-Jones, Hugh Hastings, Freddie Wiles, Michael Moore, Freddie White

Extras in Court: Philip Becker, Simon Jusel, Richard Attherton, Eileen Matthews, Pat Symonds

PRODUCTION TEAM

Script: Jimmy Perry and David Croft
Producer/Director: David Croft
Production Assistant: Gordon Pert
Lighting: Howard King
Studio Sound: John Delany
Design: Paul Joel
Assistant Floor Manager: Peter Fitton
Vision Mixer: Dave Hanks
Costume Supervisor: Susan Wheal
Make-Up Supervisor: Anna Chesterman

Reg, one of Hodges' ARP wardens, reports seeing a light burning in the church hall office. Hodges can't believe his luck, it's his golden opportunity: he's finally got Mainwaring.

Meanwhile, Mainwaring and Wilson inspect the platoon's rifles, after Captain Square, from the Eastgate platoon, had taken it upon himself to inspect one of the weapons recently and remarked that he thought there were birds' nests inside the barrels. Hodges arrives at the church hall and, with the aid of a policeman, serves a summons on Mainwaring – the Warden is determined to see him in court; even when the Verger advises Hodges against legal action, it's to no avail, he's set his mind on nailing Mainwaring.

'A Brush with the Law'

'The Face on the Poster'

Boys (in Church Choir): Tony Carpenter, Thomas McCade and Freddy Shakespeare

Note: In the original script, Captain Pringle was called Captain Marsh

PRODUCTION TEAM

Script: Jimmy Perry and David Croft
Producer/Director: David Croft
Production Assistant: Harold Snoad
Film Cameraman: James Balfour
Film Editor: Bob Rymer
Lighting: Howard King
Studio Sound: Michael McCarthy
Design: Paul Joel
Assistant Floor Manager: Bill Harman
Vision Mixer: Dave Hanks
Costume Supervisor: Odette Barrow
Make-Up Supervisor: Cecile Hay-Arthur
Special Effects: Peter Day

On the day of the court case, the men arrive to support their Captain, but he's so confident that he's decided to conduct his own defence, calling the men as witnesses. The Verger arrives and is desperate to inform the court of the truth but Hodges prevents him. To make matters worse for Mainwaring, Captain Square, his arch enemy, is presiding over the court as magistrate.

As proceedings unfold, Mainwaring's prospects look bleak. But things start to buck up when Walker takes to the witness box. He claims seeing the light come on after Mainwaring had turned it off; he'd just been delivering a couple of illegal bottles of black market whisky – it turns out the customer was Captain Square – but while he deliberately ponders over the name, Square realises his game. Just as he's about to drop the case in order to save his own face, the Verger owns up: he's the culprit; he's writing his memoirs and used the office to pen his thoughts.

BUCKMASTER, FRUITY

Not seen in the sitcom, Fruity is a friend of Wilson's who told him the Eastgate platoon was captured after just an hour at a weekend exercise. The Walmington Home Guard attend the same exercise in 'Gorilla Warfare' and are determined to do better than their rivals just along the coast.

Note: In the original script, the character was called Tubby Glossip.

BUFFET ATTENDANT

Played by Deirdre Costello (TV)

The pink-uniformed blonde attendant serves Mrs Gray at the railway station in 'Mum's Army', while she awaits her London-bound train.

BUGDEN, MR

Played by Peter Butterworth (TV)

The unorganised printer owns a business in Walmington and is given the job of printing Mainwaring's recruitment posters in 'The Face on the Poster'. Unfortunately for Jones, whose face was to appear on the poster, a mix-up results in the butcher's mug being posted on billboards around the town as a wanted criminal.

BULLET IS NOT FOR FIRING, THE

Recorded: Sunday 22/6/69

Original transmission: Thursday 2/10/69, 7.30–8.00pm

Original viewing figures: 11.8 million

Repeated: 25/4/70, 22/8/92, 15/6/96, 14/6/99

CAST

Arthur Lowe . . . . Captain Mainwaring
John Le Mesurier . . . . Sergeant Wilson
Clive Dunn . . . . Lance Corporal Jones
John Laurie . . . . Private Frazer
James Beck . . . . Private Walker
Arnold Ridley . . . . Private Godfrey
Ian Lavender . . . . Private Pike
Janet Davies . . . . Mrs Pike
Frank Williams . . . . Vicar
Tim Barrett . . . . Captain Pringle
Michael Knowles . . . . Captain Cutts
Edward Sinclair . . . . Verger
Harold Bennett . . . . Mr Blewitt
May Warden . . . . Mrs Dowding
The Choir: Fred Tomlinson, Kate Forge, Eilidh McNab, Andrew Daye and Arthur Lewis
Platoon: Colin Bean, Frank Godfrey, Hugh Cecil, Desmond Cullum-Jones, Richard Kitteridge, Vic Taylor, Michael Moore, George Hancock, Freddie Wiles, Leslie Noyes

The platoon return to the church hall after being out on patrol all night, while Wilson and Mainwaring – who were enjoying forty winks back at the church hall office, not that they'd admit it – prepare a cup of tea. Mainwaring asks his men to hand over the ammunition, and is startled when Jones admits that they haven't got any left. They engaged enemy aircraft in rapid fire, shooting at a low-flying Heinkel. Mainwaring says it's serious as they only had five rounds each; if Jerry were to arrive tonight they would be forced to stay at home.

When Mainwaring says he must report it to HQ, Wilson questions the decision, and Walker even offers to supply some 'under the counter' ammunition, at a bob a round, from his contact at the Irish battalion based up at Galshead. Mainwaring won't hear of it, but Wilson thinks it would get them out of a jam.

Before the inquiry begins the ammunition arrives from Area HQ, just as the two officers' arrival is announced by Godfrey. But Mainwaring continues with proceedings, while Wilson records the evidence.

The inquiry is interrupted by people entering the hall to attend a meeting the Vicar is holding in the office, which annoys Mainwaring. Walker is the first witness called and proceeds to explain that they were swanning around the water works, when this low-flying Heinkel flew over, and they started firing. The inquiry is interrupted again by the Vicar's singing practice. When a clap of thunder is followed by bucketing rain, the whole platoon – who'd been waiting outside – rush into the hall and it's decided they should demonstrate what happened!

BUNNY BABES DANCING DISPLAY

Before the war Mrs Pike knitted furry headwear with big ears for a dancing display team mentioned in 'The Showing Up of Corporal Jones'.

BURBURY, JULIA (1942–)

Born: London

Role: Miss Ironside (S4, episode 9: 'Mum's Army') (TV)

Julia became interested in acting while studying at Durham University, and upon graduating turned professional and began working the repertory theatres. Shortly after, she moved to Australia and started doing regular TV work, during which time she was nominated for a best actress award in 1969.

She spent two and a half years down under before returning to the UK and resuming her acting career, mainly in theatre. Julia still acts, writes and narrates audio guides on various subjects, including stately homes. She is currently busy writing a musical from her West Country home.

BURDLE, MICHAEL

Costume designer on seven episodes (TV): S3, episodes 8, 9, 10, 11, 12, 13 & 14

Born in Weymouth, Michael left school and took a general art course in Poole, before studying theatre design for three years at Wimbledon. He graduated in 1967 and worked for a small theatre company in London before joining the BBC as a trainee costume designer later that year.

After a six-month training course, he was promoted to assistant designer and worked on numerous shows, including *Dr Finlay's Casebook*, *Nicholas Nickleby* and *Treasure Island*. Upon becoming a fully fledged costume designer, he began specialising in period productions, working on several adaptations of Charles Dickens' novels and Shakespeare plays. Michael was working on a series of Somerset Maugham stories when he was assigned to *Dad's Army*. Other credits include *The Edwardians* and *Doctor Who*.

Michael took voluntary redundancy and left the BBC in 1991. For a while he worked freelance before retiring to Italy, where he'd owned a house since the 1970s.

BURLINGTON, MICHAEL

Roles: Wig Maker ('Keep Young and Beautiful'), Signaller ('A Question of Reference') (radio)

On the big screen, the late Michael Burlington was seen in Paramount's 1984 picture, *Top Secret*, while a year later he was seen in the TV production, *A Night of the Campaign*.

BURSTALL, HENRY

Played by Freddie Earlle (TV); Fraser Kerr (radio, although called 'The Train Driver')

The train driver in 'The Royal Train' who phones George Marshall at the railworks and complains about a broken part that causes his train to break down. He then falls asleep after taking four sleeping pills having mistaken them for saccharin tablets.

BURT

Played by Alan Travell (TV)

In 'Command Decision' Burt, the soldier helps deliver rifles to Mainwaring at the church hall.

BUTLER, BLAKE (1924–1981)

Born: Barrow-in-Furness

Role: Mr West (S4, episode 11: 'A Wilson (Manager)?') (TV)

Blake trained at RADA before appearing at the Mermaid Theatre in the opening production of *Lock Up Your Daughters*. He spent many years in theatre, including some time in Australia for the Elizabethan Theatre Trust, alongside Margaret Rutherford, where he received rave reviews for his Polonius in *Hamlet*.

Blake, who used to act under the name David Butler, found that his career took off on his return from down under. He was soon busy on stage and TV, playing character parts, including a porter in *Emergency – Ward 10*, Eric in *Paul Temple*, parts in *Rob Roy*, *Martin Chuzzlewit* and *Elizabeth R*. Later he appeared in *Last of the Summer Wine* and as a van driver in 'Just My Bill', an episode of *The Good Life*. His last appearance on TV was in *Worzel Gummidge*, playing a boat owner.

He died a year later of a heart attack.

BUTLER, DAVID (1936–1996)

Born: Bristol

Role: Farmhand (S7, episode 6: 'Turkey Dinner') (TV)

After leaving school, David worked for Butlins. He started as a redcoat but progressed to become the camp's longest-serving comic, clocking up 20 years with the company. In between seasons with the holiday giant, David – primarily a stand-up comedian – worked in revues, clubs and pantos around the country, as well as appearing in walk-on roles in several films.

Although he did little television work, he appeared in the first series of Granada TV's, *The Comedians*, after which he worked for over five months at the London Palladium. Some of his other TV work included appearances on *The Good Old Days* and the *Wheeltappers' and Shunters' Social Club*.

Later in his career, David was a regular entertainer on cruise ships, mainly sailing the Mediterranean. He was taken ill while appearing on a ship and was diagnosed with cancer. He died on Christmas Day 1996.

BUTLER, THE

Played by Charles Hill (TV)

Seen in 'Command Decision' and 'Wake-Up Walmington', Perkins, the snooty butler from the big hall, annoys Mainwaring considerably in the latter episode when he interrupts the platoon's rifle practice. He tells Mainwaring that his Lordship wants them to cease firing because he's taking his afternoon rest and points out that as they're not 'real soldiers' they can't use the range.

BUTTERWORTH, PETER (1919–1979)

Born: Bramhall

Role: Mr Bugden (S8, episode 6: 'The Face on the Poster') (TV)

One of the famous faces from the *Carry On* films, Peter Butterworth spent most of the war years as a prisoner of war. While serving with the Fleet Air Arm his plane was shot down and he was taken to a POW camp, where he was persuaded by Talbot Rothwell, who went on to write many of the *Carry On* movies, to take part in the concerts being staged in the camp.

When the war ended, Peter returned to England and continued with acting, appearing in summer shows, revues and repertory theatre, before branching out into television, initially in children's programmes. As his career developed, he started being offered more than just comedy roles, and was seen in shows like *Emergency – Ward 10*, a 1964 episode of *Danger Man*, in which he played a character called Umbrella and *Public Eye*.

As well as small-screen success, Peter was kept busy on the stage and from the late 1940s onwards, in films too, including *Murder at the Windmill*, *Night and the City*, *Blow Your Own Trumpet*, *Murder She Said*, *A Home of Your Own* and *The Day the Earth Caught Fire*.

Peter died of a heart attack.

'The Face on the Poster'

CADBURY, CAPTAIN

Played by Jonathan Cecil (TV); John Barron (radio)
The eccentric Captain Cadbury runs the dog training school in 'Things That Go Bump in the Night'. The school, which is owned by the War Office, trains tracker dogs to sniff out enemy parachutists, and Cadbury deals with all the admin, mainly because he's scared of dogs.

CALEDONIAN SOCIETY

This society in Walmington-on-Sea is mentioned in 'My British Buddy'. Since Jock McLean was kicked out for refusing to pay the increased subscriptions of five shillings, James Frazer has been the only member and the president.

CAMERAMEN (FILM)

James Balfour, Stewart A Farnell, Len Newson and Peter Chapman were the film cameramen who worked on the TV version of *Dad's Army* during its nine-year run. Their job entailed filming all the location shots for a particular series, which were later fed into the overall recording at Television Centre, when the studio scenes were completed.

CAPTAIN'S CAR, THE

Recorded: Sunday 17/11/74

Original transmission: Friday 13/12/74, 7.45–8.15pm

Original viewing figures: 14.4 million

Repeated: 12/6/75, 7/5/91, 26/11/94, 2/2/95 (Wales), 26/7/97

CAST

Arthur Lowe . . . . .Captain Mainwaring
John Le Mesurier . . . . .Sergeant Wilson
Clive Dunn . . . . .Lance Corporal Jones
John Laurie . . . . .Private Frazer
Arnold Ridley . . . . .Private Godfrey
Ian Lavender . . . . .Private Pike
Bill Pertwee . . . . .Chief Warden Hodges
Talfryn Thomas . . . . .Private Cheeseman
Frank Williams . . . . .Vicar
Edward Sinclair . . . . .Verger
Robert Raglan . . . . .Colonel
Eric Longworth . . . . .Town Clerk
Fred McNaughton . . . . .Mayor
Mavis Pugh . . . . .Lady Maltby
John Hart Dyke . . . . .French General
Donald Morley . . . . .Glossip
Platoon: Colin Bean, George Hancock, Michael Moore, Freddie White, Freddie Wiles, Roger Bourne, Evan Ross, Leslie Noyes, Desmond Cullum-Jones, Hugh Cecil

PRODUCTION TEAM

Script: Jimmy Perry and David Croft
Producer/Director: David Croft
Production Assistant: Bob Spiers
Film Cameraman: Len Newson
Film Sound: John Gatland
Film Editor: Bill Harris
Lighting: Howard King
Studio Sound: Michael McCarthy
Design: Bryan Ellis
Assistant Floor Managers: Anne Ogden and Sue Bennett Urwin
Vision Mixer: Dave Hanks
Costume Supervisor: Susan Wheal
Make-Up Supervisor: Sylvia Thornton

A French general is visiting Walmington and the Home Guard have to form a guard of honour, which doesn't please Captain Mainwaring; he doesn't like the French much, what with all that sloppy kissing.

At the church hall, Wilson and Mainwaring are visited by Lady Maltby. Mainwaring tells Wilson she probably wants to deal with an officer so Wilson can leave after the initial welcome, so he's annoyed when he discovers Lady Maltby knows Wilson and they greet each other enthusiastically. Lady Maltby wants to donate her Rolls for the war effort and has decided to give it to the Home Guard; Mainwaring is very grateful and eyes it up as a potential staff car.

Later, the Colonel arrives and explains

LIFE AS A CAMERAMAN

'The film cameraman's role is much the same for a light entertainment programme such as *Dad's Army* as it is for any other drama. It is the cameraman's job to interpret the director's wishes and get them onto film. To this end he has a knowledge of film types and filters, both for correction (such as balancing light colours) and for effect (low contrast, diffusion, graduated filters for skies, etc).

'An extensive knowledge of light sources and their uses is vital. The cameraman needs to be able to produce the required lighting effect quickly and artistically, enabling the director to concentrate on working with the actors.

'When I filmed *Dad's Army* I used to do my own camera work and so relied on my chief electrician (aka the Gaffer) to carry out my lighting plots whilst I worked out the shots with the director and the grips (the chaps responsible for tracking the camera on its dolly or crane, or for mounting it in strange places like the roof of Mr Jones' van). The lighting plot must produce the correct feel for the scene whilst leaving a spot for the microphone boom to get at the actors without throwing shadows into the frame.

'Continuity of lighting is important. If the actors are seen to be entering a cottage in strong sun then the interior must be lit to reproduce that sunny interior, although the cottage interiors may not be shot for several weeks after the location filming is completed.

'The filming for *Dad's Army* took place around Thetford making extensive use of the army facilities and ranges. It was insert filming which means that most of the interiors were recorded on video tape in the London studios by a separate crew. Nowadays there is very little insert shooting as most programmes are produced complete in themselves either on video, like *Casualty* and *The Bill*, or all on film such as *Silent Witness* and *Dangerfield*.'

PETER CHAPMAN

another reason the platoon are providing the guard of honour is because Wilson speaks French and the final speech has to be in French.

While Pike and Wilson are alone in the office, Lady Maltby's chauffeur, Mr Glossip, phones to say the newly acquired staff car has run out of petrol on the way to the garage, where it's to be painted in camouflage. Pike and Wilson go off to help. Later, Jones heads off in his van to help tow the Rolls to the paint shop, but there's a mix-up and the Mayor's Rolls ends up being camouflaged, too.

When Mainwaring inspects his newly camouflaged staff car outside the church hall, Jones and Frazer turn up in the other Rolls. It's all confusion, but to rectify the problem Frazer tries repainting it black, ready for the French General. But Frazer can't get any quick-drying paint, as the General and Hodges soon find out.

CARAVEL FILMS

Based in Slough, Caravel Films were responsible for filming the sitcom's opening credits on two separate occasions, both times in colour. Caravel worked extensively for the BBC, carrying out rostrum camera work.

John Astley, one of four people in the company's rostrum camera team, was responsible for filming the animation sequence designed by Colin Whitaker. Nowadays, John works as a project manager in marine salvage, using photography and video to complete underwater surveys on shipwrecks.

CARDINAL PUFF

An initiation ceremony referred to in 'Fallen Idol' which involves heavy drinking. Captain Mainwaring becomes interested and gets sloshed in the process.

CARELESS TALK COSTS LIVES

This campaign was launched in February 1940 by the Ministry of Information, which had become increasingly concerned about the risk to national security from war gossip. Millions of posters were distributed throughout Britain warning people against the dangers of gossiping. Adopting the slogan, 'Careless Talk Costs Lives', the posters carried various designs, some depicting Hitler eavesdropping from telephone boxes and overhearing unsuspecting women on the Tube. The Ministry's film department made several films focusing on the subject, including *The Next of Kin*, which Mainwaring arranged for his men to watch at an Eastgate cinema in 'The Battle of Godfrey's Cottage'.

The 'Careless Talk Costs Lives' campaign was also mentioned outside The Six Bells pub in 'Wake Up Walmington' and by Mrs Gray in 'Mum's Army'. In 'Operation Kilt' we learn that Mainwaring is taking the matter very seriously by hanging 'Careless Talk Costs Lives' posters in the bank, even though head office don't approve.

CARETAKER, THE
Played by Edward Sinclair (TV)

Edward Sinclair's first appearance was in series one as a caretaker in 'The Showing Up of Corporal Jones'. The character, originally named Mr Harman, became the Verger in later episodes, responsible for St Aldhelm's church hall.

CARLTON, TIMOTHY (1939–)
Born: Reading
Role: Lieutenant Hope Bruce (S3, episode 3: 'The Lion has 'Phones') (TV)

Timothy entered the industry in 1961 and has had a busy career ever since, particularly on TV, where his many appearances include early shows like *World of Wooster* in 1961, *Public Eye*, *Charlie's Aunt*, *Family at War*, *Fraud Squad*, *The Liver Birds*, *The Lotus Eaters* in 1973, *The Onedin Line*, *Callan*, *Crown Court* and *The Brothers*. In 1976 he was seen in *Coronation Street*, and other credits include *Ripping Yarns*, *Bergerac*, *The Fall and Rise of Reginald Perrin*, *Don't Wait Up*, *Minder* and *Executive Stress*. On the big screen he's appeared in several films, such as *A Touch of Class*, *That Lucky Touch* and *High Road to China*.

CARR, ANDREW
Role: Operations Officer (S3, episode 8: 'The Day the Balloon Went Up') (TV)

Andrew Carr, who died in 1992, established himself as a writer during the later years of his life, penning many productions for the BBC. He attended the Webber Douglas Drama School and once his career took off he regularly appeared on TV, in shows such as *Dixon of Dock Green*, *Softly, Softly*, *War and Peace*, *The Woman in White*, *Doctor Who* and *The Bill*. His film appearances include *The Perfect Spy* and *The Curse of the Pink Panther*.

CARTER PATTERSON

In 'Sons of the Sea', Mainwaring complains that from his office window at the bank his line of fire is being blocked by Carter Patterson's horse and van. Carter Patterson was a haulage and removals firm. It's heard of again in 'The Captain's Car', when Pike collects a bucketful of manure, after the horse has gone down the High Street, and brings it to the church hall office to give to Mainwaring for his roses.

CASSON, MRS
Played by Olive Mercer (TV)

A customer in Jones' shop during the episode, 'The Armoured Might of Lance Corporal Jones'.

CATCHPHRASES

The catchphrase is a useful device frequently exploited by comedians or sitcom writers. These familiar phrases formed part of a character's make-up and became an intrinsic source of humour. Many of Britain's top comedy shows have contained characters whose lines are peppered with regularly spouted phrases,

and members of Walmington's Home Guard were no exception. Humour sprang not from the actual line of dialogue, but the blend of character, situation and the level of expectancy aroused in the audience.

Jones was frequently heard asking Mainwaring for 'Permission to speak, sir!', and was also quick to point out that as far as the enemy is concerned, 'They don't like it up 'em!'. Most of the other characters had their favourite phrases, too. Wilson would often annoy Mainwaring with his, 'Do you think that's wise, sir?', while Frazer's answer to finding himself in a tight spot was to cry: 'We're doomed!'. Godfrey was always asking to be excused, and even Mainwaring wasn't spared the use of a few catchphrases, notably 'You stupid boy!' and 'There's a war on you know'. And one can't forget that irritant, Mr 'Put that light out!' Hodges, with his 'You ruddy hooligans'.

CATER, JOHN
Born: London
Role: Private Clarke (S4, episode 8: 'The Two and a Half Feathers') (TV)

Trained at RADA, John joined Dundee Rep shortly after graduation. His first speaking role on TV was during the 1950s BBC series, *The Appleyards*. John has had a busy career on TV, including the part of batman Doublett in ATV's *Virgin of the Secret Service* in 1968, Starr in *The Duchess of Duke Street*, George Watts in *The Other 'Arf* and roles in *Up Pompeii!*, *Bergerac* and *Shelley*. John has also appeared in over 30 films, including *The Black Tulip* and *The Mill on the Floss*.

His more recent TV credits include *The Silent Witness* and *Where the Heart Is*. He was also seen as Einstein in a recent commercial.

CECIL, HUGH (1913–)
Born: London
Role: Member of the platoon's back row in 50 episodes (S1; S2; S3, episodes 1– 4, 6, 7; S4, episodes 5, 9– 13; S5, episodes 1– 9, 11–13; S7; S8, episodes 1, 2, 4, 5, 6; 'My Brother and I', 'The Love of Three Oranges'; S9, episode 1) (TV)

After finishing his education in London, Hugh worked as an office junior at an import and export company before moving into the woollen trade, employed as a buyer at the Wool Exchange, bidding on the wool arriving at the docks. When war broke out, Hugh was called up into the navy and trained as a signalman, working on minesweepers out of Lowestoft.

He was demobbed in 1946 by which time he'd reached the rank of lieutenant. With his future to consider, Hugh decided to try his luck as a professional magician and Punch and Judy man; he'd been performing magic and Punch and Judy shows since the age of 11, and joined the Magic Circle at 18. In the early years he made sufficient money to spur him on to further his career. He also drifted into acting, appearing in sketches during summer seasons, beginning at Newcastle-upon-Tyne. Although he was booked primarily for his Punch and Judy show, he was involved in sketches with the concert party.

When Hugh obtained an agent he started being offered small parts and walk-ons, and was frequently cast as old lags in prison scenes. However, he made his television debut as an ambulance man in *Z Cars*. He has since gone on to work with many of the industry's top names, appearing with Jimmy Tarbuck and on *The Two Ronnies*. He has performed his Punch and Judy show in Tommy Steele's film, *Half a Sixpence* and *The Bill*, and appeared in a Spice Girls' video. One of his latest appearances was in the BBC production, *Real Woman*, playing a bride's grandfather.

Although there is less demand for magic and Punch and Judy acts nowadays, Hugh is still working as an actor.

CECIL, JONATHAN

Born: London
Roles: Captain Cadbury (S6, episode 6: 'Things That Go Bump in the Night') (TV); Mr Norris ('A Man of Action') (radio)

Jonathan played loopy Captain Cadbury who talked to his dogs as if they were a platoon. He became involved in acting at Oxford. After a university performance at Stratford he was told he had a future in the profession, so upon graduating he joined LAMDA.

Rep work followed before Jonathan moved into TV. Early screen credits include snooty Jeremy Crichton-Jones in two series of *Romany Jones*, *The Ben Travers Farces*, *The Goodies* and *The Dick Emery Show*. As well as an extensive TV career, Jonathan has made over 20 film appearances, including *Rising Damp*, *The Yellow Rolls Royce*, *Up the Front* and *Alice Through the Looking Glass*.

Jonathan's busy career has graced all areas of the profession, and he remains busy today.

CHAFFER, DEREK

Role: Member of the platoon's back row in one episode (S3, episode 1: 'The Armoured Might of Lance Corporal Jones') (TV)

CHAIRWOMAN, THE

Played by Diana King (TV); Judith Furse (radio)
This character, who's also a JP, chairs the all-important Military Service Hardship Committee, which listens to Walker's case against being called up.

CHAMBERMAID, THE

Played by Penny Irving (TV)
The attractive chambermaid at The Red Lion in Walmington, who Captain Mainwaring's brother, Barry, takes a shine to.

CHANNON, DENNIS

In charge of studio lighting for one episode (TV): 'A Stripe for Frazer'

CHAPMAN, PETER

Film cameraman on eight episodes (TV): S8, episodes 1, 3, 4 & 6; S9, episodes 1, 2, 3 & 5
London-born Peter Chapman joined the BBC straight from school in 1956. He began his career with the Corporation as a general trainee, working as an office boy for the *Radio Times* and a junior photographic printer before becoming a trainee assistant cameraman. It took three years before he was promoted to assistant cameraman, and a further two to become a fully fledged cameraman, working on shows like *Man Alive* and *Dixon of Dock Green*.

During his 39-year career with the BBC, he worked on numerous shows, including *Doctor Who*, *All Creatures Great and Small* and *Last of the Summer Wine*. His last production before leaving in 1995 was to film Ian McShane's series, *Madson*. Among the shows he's worked on since turning freelance are *Grange Hill*, *The Bill*, *Casualty* and *The Last Salute*.

CHARLIE'S CAFÉ

Only ever mentioned in 'The Miser's Hoard', and never seen, this Walmington café is visited by Pike and Wilson while searching for Frazer who misses parade one evening. Having stopped at every pub in the town during their search, Wilson becomes drunk and stops off at Charlie's Café for a black coffee in an attempt to sober up before returning to the church hall and facing the wrath of Mainwaring.

CHATER, GEOFFREY (1921–)

Born: Barnet
Role: Colonel Pierce (S5, episode 12: 'Round and Round Went the Great Big Wheel') (TV)
Geoffrey joined the army as a teenager and served in the Far East during the Second World War. He was demobbed as a captain, and decided to pursue an acting career as an ASM at the Theatre Royal, Windsor, in 1946.

Several years of rep work followed, including a period at Hereford where he met David Croft. His extensive TV career has seen him appear in numerous programmes, including 'Project Zero', an episode of *The Champions*, *Callan*, *Special Branch*, *General Hospital*, *Father Brown*, *Hadleigh*, *Penmarric*, *Brideshead Revisited*, *Tales of the Unexpected*, *Devenish*, *Shelley*, *Nanny*, *Bergerac*, *Pie in the Sky*, *The House of Eliott* and *The Detectives*.

His film credits include *Dr Jekyll and Mr Hyde*, *The Day the Earth Caught Fire*, *Position of Trust*, *Endless Night*, *Barry Lyndon*, *Gandhi* and *Anything More Would Be Greedy*.

CHEESEMAN, CHARLIE

Played by Jimmy Perry (TV); Jack Watson (radio)
Top of the bill at Walmington's Hippodrome Theatre when the platoon go along in 'Shooting Pains' is Charlie Cheeseman, the Cheerful Chump.

CHEESEMAN, MR

Played by Talfryn Thomas (TV)
A photo-journalist who works for *The Eastbourne Gazette*, this pushy Welshman is first seen at The Red Lion in 'My British Buddy'. In this episode he informs Mainwaring that he's writing a series of articles about the Home Guard to be entitled 'Doughboy meets the Tommy', and that he particularly wants to capture the Americans' arrival. Cheeseman, who also writes a gossip column for the paper titled, 'Whispers from Walmington' is later assigned to the Walmington platoon in order to gain a deeper understanding of how the Home Guard ticks, or doesn't as the case may be!

Although Mr Cheeseman is married, we never see his wife, but we do learn that she makes lovely gravy, even if she burns everything else to a cinder.

'A Man of Action'

CHEESEWRIGHT, MR
Played by Richard Jacques (TV)

Mr Cheesewright, who manages the Plaza Cinema in Walmington, appears in 'The Lion has 'Phones'.

CHERRY TREE COTTAGE

The idyllic home of Charles Godfrey and his two sisters, Dolly and Cissy, Cherry Tree Cottage is set just outside the town of Walmington. The location is peaceful and green, surrounded by woodland. At the end of a country lane, edged by trees and hedges, a little white picket gate marks the entrance to the path which takes the visitor up through the garden, where rose bushes grow, including one that was planted by Godfrey's father over 50 years ago. As Wilson says: 'It really does look like a picture on a chocolate box.' Whenever he sees the place and admires its beauty, it reminds him just what the country is fighting for.

Inside, the thatched cottage has olde worlde lattice windows and chintz curtains. Victorian knick-knacks are everywhere, and in the corner of the sitting room is Percy, their foul-mouthed parrot. The family are quite self-sufficient, using water drawn from their own well, and eating home-made bread, cakes and raspberry jam and drinking home-made parsnip wine.

At the bottom of the secluded country garden is a revolving summer house, where the Godfreys have idled away many a summer afternoon, listening to the birds chirping. It really makes for a picturesque setting, but nothing lasts forever and for a while it looked as if the cottage was going to be demolished to make way for a new aerodrome, until Frazer, of all people, arranged for the aerodrome to be sited elsewhere. It turns out it's built just 200 yards away and although the property remains intact, the Godfreys' hearing won't be for much longer with the noise of the planes.

CHESNEAU, BILL
Film sound recordist on four episodes (TV): S8, episodes 1, 3, 4, 6

Before entering the television industry, Bill spent eight years working as a lab assistant in a physics research laboratory for a company making wires and electrical circuits. He was always interested in film-making however, and when he tired of his lab job, he applied for a job at BBC Radio. He was successful and joined as a trainee technical operator, working at Bush House on the World Service broadcasts.

After two years he transferred to TV, initially as a trainee assistant film recordist for nine months. His early assignments included *Z Cars* and numerous shows for the newly launched BBC2. Within two years of moving to TV he was promoted to film recordist, and he went on to work on numerous shows, such as *Panorama*, *Nationwide*, 13 episodes of *Bergerac*, five episodes of

Lovejoy, *Miss Marple* and *The Great Orchestras*, a series filmed around the world.

In 1992, Bill was made redundant and he turned freelance. He has since worked on several productions for Iambic Productions, two years on *Crimewatch* and a recent documentary celebrating the James Bond movies.

CHITTY, ERIK (1907–1977)
Born: Dover

Roles: Mr Sedgewick (S4, episode 3: 'Boots, Boots, Boots'), Mr Clerk (S7, episode 3: 'Gorilla Warfare') (TV); Mr Sedgewick, Mr Parsons ('Time On My Hands') (radio)

After leaving Dover College, Erik studied Law in the 1920s at Cambridge, where he co-founded and became the first treasurer of the university's acting society, before going on to RADA. Upon graduating he followed his dream and trod the boards for years in reps around the country, interrupted only by the war, during which he served as a sergeant in Egypt and Italy with the Eighth Army.

Often cast as testy old men, Erik was spotted in TV from as early as 1938 in *The White Chateau*. He made over 200 small-screen appearances, including 1946's production of *Alice*, an eerie adaptation of *Markheim*, *Hassan*, *Doomwatch*, *Fall of Eagles*, *War and Peace*, *Loyalties* and *The Goodies*. He's probably best known as Mr Smith, the English teacher, in *Please, Sir!*.

Before he died in 1977, Erik had also notched up over 40 film credits, including *Chance of a Lifetime*, *Raising a Riot*, *Casino Royale*, *Anne of the Thousand Days*, *Great Expectations*, *The Railway Children* and *A Bridge Too Far*, and had run his own repertory company at Frinton.

CHOIR, THE
Played by Fred Tomlinson, Kate Forge, Eilidh McNab, Andrew Daye and Arthur Lewis (TV); John Whitehall (radio)

Members of the church choir appear in 'The Bullet is Not for Firing' and interrupt the court of inquiry by entering the church hall to attend singing practice in the Vicar's office.

CHRISTMAS NIGHT WITH THE STARS
For over 35 years, the BBC staged their annual *Christmas Night with the Stars* extravaganza on Christmas night. Between 1958 and 1994, a variety of comedy stars appeared in short sketch versions of their popular hits. The first offering in 1958 featured *The Charlie Chester Show*, Tony Hancock, *Charlie Drake In…* , *The Ted Ray Show* and *Whack-O!*. Perry and Croft's *Dad's Army* appeared in the 1968, '69, '70 and '72 shows.

1968
The sketch was untitled

Recorded: Sunday 27/10/68

Original Transmission: Wednesday 25/12/68

CAST

Arthur Lowe . . . . .Captain Mainwaring
John Le Mesurier . . . . .Sergeant Wilson
Clive Dunn . . . . .Lance Corporal Jones
John Laurie . . . . .Private Frazer
James Beck . . . . .Private Walker
Arnold Ridley . . . . .Private Godfrey
Ian Lavender . . . . .Private Pike
Edward Sinclair . . . . .Verger
Platoon: Richard Jacques, Frank Godfrey, Alec Coleman, Hugh Cecil, Jimmy Mac, Desmond Cullum-Jones, Vic Taylor, David Seaforth, Richard Kitteridge

PRODUCTION TEAM
Script: Jimmy Perry and David Croft
Producer/Director: David Croft
Production Assistant: Harold Snoad
Assistant Floor Manager: Tony George
Designer: Paul Joel
Studio Lighting: John Dixon
Studio Sound: Buster Cole
Vision Mixer: Bruce Milliard
Costume Supervisor: Marjorie Lewis
Make-Up Supervisor: Sheila Cassidy

It's Christmas day and Mainwaring can't drop his sense of duty for even one day. He orders his men to parade and Wilson, being more relaxed about the whole affair, says they can wear civvies, but Mainwaring doesn't like his sergeant's sudden burst of decision-making.

The men arrive all dressed as Father Christmas, with various reasons why. Mainwaring views this as proof that you cannot be seen to let discipline drop for one moment.

GHQ has come up with an idea of using telegraph poles as a means of exercise and Mainwaring runs through the instructions with his men and, as usual, forgets the age of some of them, especially when he shouts 'jump' to the aged Godfrey and expects him to sit cross-legged on the floor. Eventually Mainwaring has to show them how it's done but he's saved by the bell as the Major phones through to the office with his seasonal greetings.

Mainwaring returns to the hall and delivers a speech which shows how proud he is of the platoon and how confident he is regarding the outcome of the war. In return, the men show their respect and affection for him as they wish each other a merry Christmas.

1969
RESISTING THE AGGRESSOR DOWN THE AGES

Recorded: Friday 21/11/69

Original transmission: Thursday 25/12/69

CAST

Arthur Lowe . . . . .Captain Mainwaring
John Le Mesurier . . . . .Sergeant Wilson
Clive Dunn . . . . .Lance Corporal Jones
John Laurie . . . . .Private Frazer
Jimmy Beck . . . . .Private Walker
Arnold Ridley . . . . .Private Godfrey
Ian Lavender . . . . .Private Pike
Bill Pertwee . . . . .ARP Warden
Robert Aldous . . . . .German pilot
David Hannigan . . . . .ARP Warden (non-speaking)

PRODUCTION TEAM

Script: Jimmy Perry and David Croft
Producer/Director: David Croft
Production Assistant: Harold Snoad
Assistant Floor Manager: Bill Harman
Designer: Ray London

Studio Lighting: Howard King
Studio Sound: John Holmes
Vision Mixer: Dave Hanks
Costume Supervisor: Rita Reekie
Make-Up Supervisor: Cecile Hay-Arthur

As part of the pageant in aid of 'War Weapons Week', the men of the Walmington-on-Sea platoon are rehearsing their contribution, entitled 'Resisting the Aggressor Down the Ages'. Everyone's dressed up, including Wilson as Napoleon, Jones as the Spirit of Agriculture and Walker the Spirit of Commerce. Meanwhile, the miscast Private Godfrey – once he's been excused – is dressed as Julius Caesar, but has trouble speaking his lines with sufficient aggression.

At the end of the rehearsal, the air raid sirens sound, while Hodges and one of his junior wardens bring a captured German pilot into the church hall. He puts up a struggle until Jones shows him the cold steel.

'Resisting the Aggressor Down the Ages'

1970
THE CORNISH FLORAL DANCE

Recorded: Friday 4/12/70

(This insert was recorded on the same evening as 'Uninvited Guests')

Original transmission: Friday 25/12/70

CAST

Arthur Lowe . . . . .Captain Mainwaring
John Le Mesurier . . . . .Sergeant Wilson
Clive Dunn . . . . .Lance Corporal Jones
John Laurie . . . . .Private Frazer
Jimmy Beck . . . . .Private Walker
Arnold Ridley . . . . .Private Godfrey
Ian Lavender . . . . .Private Pike
Bill Pertwee . . . . .ARP Warden
Platoon: Colin Bean, George Hancock, Hugh Hastings
Choir: Fred Tomlinson plus four male singers and four female singers

PRODUCTION TEAM
Script: Jimmy Perry and David Croft
Producer/Director: David Croft
Production Assistant: Phil Bishop
Assistant Floor Manager: Roger Singleton-Turner
Designer: Paul Joel
Studio Lighting: George Summers
Studio Sound: Mike McCarthy
Vision Mixer: Clive Doig
Costume Supervisor: George Ward
Make-Up Supervisor: Cynthia Goodwin

Mainwaring is arranging a choir rehearsal and argues with Hodges over who should conduct. On the flip of a coin Mainwaring wins – much to Hodges' distress.

Mainwaring later discovers that conducting is not such a good job after all when some of the piano keys won't work – although Walker doesn't help by hiding a half-bottle of whisky inside the instrument – and the men can't get the song right.

As usual Jones volunteers, and ends up as the soloist, but in contrast to his parading he just can't stop coming in too soon.

1972
BROADCAST TO THE EMPIRE

Recorded: Sunday 26/11/72

(This insert was recorded on the same evening as 'A Brush with the Law')

Original transmission: Monday 25/12/72

CAST

Arthur Lowe . . . . .Captain Mainwaring
John Le Mesurier . . . . .Sergeant Wilson
Clive Dunn . . . . .Lance Corporal Jones
John Laurie . . . . .Private Frazer
Jimmy Beck . . . . .Private Walker
Arnold Ridley . . . . .Private Godfrey
Ian Lavender . . . . .Private Pike
Bill Pertwee . . . . .ARP Warden
Peter Greene . . . . .BBC Engineer
Michael Knowles . . . . .Mr Willerby Troughton-Maxwell, BBC Producer

PRODUCTION TEAM

Script: Jimmy Perry and David Croft
Producer/Director: David Croft
Production Assistant: Gordon Pert
Assistant Floor Manager: Peter Fitton
Designer: Paul Joel
Studio Lighting: Howard King
Studio Sound: John Delany
Vision Mixer: Dave Hanks
Costume Supervisor: Susan Wheal
Make-Up Supervisor: Anna Chesterman

The members of the Walmington Home Guard are proud to be taking part in the lunchtime Christmas day programme, *To Absent Friends*, just before the King's speech. In preparation, the BBC producer asks for a voice test, and commends Wilson on his wonderful radio voice,

'Broadcast to the Empire'

something which irks Mainwaring, particularly when he's told to speak more clearly because he doesn't sound like an officer.

With Jones and Pike providing sea and seagull sound effects, everyone rehearses their contribution again. As they await the standby light for this memorable occasion, Hodges marches in, just as the producer advises Mainwaring and his men that a broadcast from Hong Kong overran and their moment of fame had to be chopped.

CHURCH BELLS

June 1940 saw the introduction of an order prohibiting the ringing of church bells, except to inform people of an airborne invasion, and then only the military or police were authorised to ring the bells. The ban was relaxed on Easter day 1943, when the cabinet decided bells could be rung on Sundays and special occasions. However, many of the parish churches remained silent because the bells hadn't been used for three years and their ringers were still serving in the armed forces.

The ringing ban is most noticeable in Walmington during the *Dad's Army* movie when Bert King arrives at the vicarage to take away all but one of the church bells for use in weapon-making. Wanting to hear their sound ringing out

over Walmington just one last time, the Vicar pulls the ropes, springing the whole of the town into an invasion alert.

CHURCH FABRIC FUND

When the Vicar hears that Frazer is amassing hundreds of sovereigns in 'The Miser's Hoard', he decides to tap him for a contribution to his church fund.

CITY GENT, THE
Played by Bob Hornery (TV)

In 'The Royal Train' the city gentleman is sitting in a railway carriage when Mainwaring peers in hoping to spot King George VI, whose train is expected through Walmington station that morning.

CLARK, MR
Played by Cy Town (TV)

Clark is the mess steward at the training camp where Mainwaring and his men are put to the test during a weekend exercise in 'We Know Our Onions'.

CLARK, SERGEANT

In 'The Bullet is Not for Firing' Mainwaring has a telephone conversation with the sergeant,

who's based at GHQ, and reports the lack of ammunition after his men fired all their bullets at a Heinkel while on patrol. The sergeant is not actually seen.

CLARKE, GEORGE
Played by John Cater (TV); Michael Bates (radio)

George Clarke was an unwelcome visitor to Walmington-on-Sea, casting inaccurate slurs on Jones' military past. George, nicknamed Nobby, has been living in Walmington for just a few weeks when he meets up with Frazer in The Anchor pub. He retired from the Warwickshire Regiment, in which Jack Jones served, ten years ago. In 1898 he fought in Sudan under Kitchener, along with Jones.

He arrives in the town and joins the Home Guard with the sole intention of tarnishing Jones' character by claiming he's a coward who left him in the desert to die. His claims are untrue, but before Mainwaring has a chance to put him in his place, he leaves town.

CLAY ON ROAD

In 'Everybody's Trucking', the area around Walmington has been chosen for a divisional scheme, and Mainwaring's men are tasked with signposting the area so the three battalions of regular troops involved in the exercise know where to go. The axis of advance is down the Clayton Road.

CLEGG, JOHN (1934–)

Born: Murree (Punjab), Pakistan

Role: Wireless Operator (S5, episode 12: 'Round and Round Went the Great Big Wheel') (TV)

John was just 18 months old when he moved to England, and grew up wanting to be an actor. After being educated at The Pilgrims' School, Winchester, and Canford School, he started his national service in the ranks of the Wiltshires, before being commissioned into The Royal Hampshires, his father's old regiment.

Upon returning to civvy street he joined RADA. After graduating he worked in various reps up and down the country, including Coventry and Liverpool. Later theatre credits include taking over the Brian Rix part in *One For the Pot*, Ray Cooney's first play at the Whitehall Theatre and subsequently on a long national tour. He has toured with many productions, such as *Twelfth Night* playing Andrew Aguecheek, *Nightcap*, *Run For Your Wife*, *Circumstantial Evidence*, *Spiders Web*, *Charley's Aunt*, *The Rivals*, *Cowardy Custard*, Major Flack in *Privates On Parade*, Gonzalo in *The Tempest*, *The Wizard of Oz* and some 17 pantomimes.

Although he's appeared numerous times on TV, he's best known as Gunner Graham in *It Ain't Half Hot, Mum*, a role he played for seven years. Other small-screen credits include early appearances in *Dixon of Dock Green*, *Doctor Finlay*, *Compact*, *Father Dear Father*, *Bless This House*, several Harry Worth and Reg Varney shows, *My Good Woman*, and the fast-talking encyclopedia salesman – a real *tour de force* – in Jimmy Perry's *Lollipop*. Further TV parts include: Froth in Shakespeare's *Measure For Measure*, *The Tommy Cooper Show*, *Are You Being Served?*, *Three Up Two Down*, *The Good Guys*, *Demob*, *Doctor At the Top*, Mr Franklyn in *You Rang M'Lord?*, Clifford Howes in *Crossroads*, vicars in *Keep it in the Family* and *Spooner's Patch*, and a calligraphist in *Mr Bean*. He's also appeared in several films.

John's background of the Raj, and a love for the works of Rudyard Kipling, inspired him to compile *In The Eye of the Sun*, a one-man show of Kipling's Indian writings, which won glowing praise from the critics, and a Fringe First Award at the Edinburgh Festival, before transferring to the Gate Theatre, London, and then touring theatres and venues in the UK and in France. Extracts from the show were later featured in a BBC *Omnibus* programme. He has also toured another Kipling show, *Brushes of Comets' Hair – Kipling and England*, which was honoured by a special performance at Batemans, Kipling's Sussex country house.

John classes his most important credit being the meeting of Mavis Pugh, who later became his wife, at Watford's Palace Theatre.

CLERK, MR

Played by Erik Chitty (TV)

Mr Clerk works for the RSPCA and can be seen in 'Gorilla Warfare', arriving with Hodges in an Austin 7. He's brought along a syringe to inject the gorilla, but when Pike suggests shooting it instead, Lieutenant Wood, who is in the gorilla disguise, is quick to reveal his true identity.

CLERK OF THE COURT, THE

Played by Chris Gannon (TV); Norman Ettlinger (radio)

Mr Bone is working in the local magistrates' court when Mainwaring's case is heard in 'A Brush with the Law'.

'A Brush with the Law'

CLIFFTOP HOTEL, THE

(Film only)

A hotel at the bottom of Walmington High Street. Only exterior shots are seen in the film.

CLIPPIE, THE

Played by Joy Allen (TV); Pat Coombs (radio)

In 'A Soldier's Farewell' the platoon go to the pictures to see Greta Garbo and Charles Boyer in *Marie Walewska*. As they return on the bus, the clippie collects the fares.

CLIVE, DONALD

Production assistant on six episodes of the fourth series (TV): 'The Big Parade', 'Don't Forget the Diver', 'Boots, Boots, Boots', 'Sgt – Save My Boy!', 'Don't Fence Me In' and 'Absent Friends'

COLE, JAMES

BBC sound supervisor on series one and two (TV) James' nickname while working on the programme was Buster.

COLE, MRS

Played by Rose Hill (TV)

When the wardens share the church hall office with Captain Mainwaring in 'Uninvited Guests', the ageing Mrs Cole is allocated the job of answering the phone.

COLEMAN, ALEC (1922–)

Born: London

Role: Member of the platoon's back row in 11 episodes (S1; S2, episodes 1, 2, 3, 4 & 6) (TV)

Alec left school and joined Royal Insurance, working as an office junior at the London head office before transferring to a branch near Piccadilly. When war broke out, Alec was still a member of the army cadets, and he joined the 8th City of London Battalion of the Home Guard, based in Hackney, until his call-up to the regular army in 1942.

He trained on the Isle of Wight and became a recruit lance corporal within weeks. He was posted to Lincolnshire with the Royal Warwickshire Regiment before moving to Ireland. He was eventually demobbed in 1946 as an acting-company sergeant major, based in Germany.

Alec turned to acting full-time after the war and it wasn't long before he was working on the stage. He moved into TV with a debut in *Z Cars*, a programme he appeared in three times, playing a rent collector, a dance hall manager and a butler. He was also seen in various shows, including *Compact*, *Crown Court*, *The Plane Makers*, *Wednesday Play* and *The Tommy Cooper Show*. As a sideline, he worked as a London cabby whenever he was between jobs.

One of the platoon's original members, Alec – who is an authority in military traditions and

advised original costume designer, George Ward – left the sitcom after the second series because of other work commitments.

In 1972 he moved to Manchester and worked in the ceremonial department at Manchester Town Hall while doing the occasional acting job for Granada in shows like *Country Matters* and film appearances, such as the French president in *Chariots of Fire*.

After more than 20 years in Lancashire, Alec returned to Essex in 1999 after the death of his second wife from cancer. He continues to act, appearing most recently in two episodes of *Midsomer Murders*, as a hotel porter and a man drinking outside a pub.

COLLINS, JOHN D (1942–)
Born: London
Role: Lieutenant Short, the Naval Officer (film)

Educated at Harrow, John worked as a shop assistant for a year before joining RADA after winning Ivor Novello and Robert Donat scholarships. A busy career has included a ten-year association with Spike Milligan as assistant director and actor, and running his own theatre company at Frinton-on-Sea between 1963 and 1964.

Among his TV credits are *Get Some In!*, *A Family at War*, *Some Mothers Do 'Ave 'Em*, *Only Fools and Horses*, *Yes Minister*, *Peak Practice* (playing David Cornish) and several shows produced by David Croft, such as the Q series, *Hi-De-Hi!*, Fairfax in *'Allo, 'Allo*, Jerry in *You Rang M'Lord?* and *Oh, Doctor Beeching!*.

COLLINS, LES
Sound recordist on eight episodes (TV): S4, episodes 1, 2, 3, 5, 8, 10, 13 and 'Battle of the Giants'

COLONEL, THE
Played by Anthony Sharp (TV)
When a problem with his leg prevents the Colonel umpiring at a large exercise involving two brigades of infantry in 'The Making of Private Pike', he orders Captain Mainwaring to take his place as his deputy.

COME IN, YOUR TIME IS UP
Recorded: Thursday 10/7/75
Original transmission: Friday 26/9/75, 8.00–8.30pm
Original viewing figures: 14.6 million
Repeated: 15/5/76, 11/6/91, 31/12/94, 1/3/97, 2/3/97 (Wales)

CAST
Arthur Lowe . . . . .Captain Mainwaring
John Le Mesurier . . . . .Sergeant Wilson
Clive Dunn . . . . .Lance Corporal Jones
John Laurie . . . . .Private Frazer
Arnold Ridley . . . . .Private Godfrey
Ian Lavender . . . . .Private Pike
Bill Pertwee . . . . .Chief Warden Hodges
Frank Williams . . . . .Vicar
Edward Sinclair . . . . .Verger
Harold Bennett . . . . .Mr Bluett
Colin Bean . . . . .Private Sponge
Platoon: George Hancock, Desmond Cullum-Jones, Michael Moore, Freddie Wiles, Leslie Noyes, Hugh Cecil, Freddie White, Roger Bourne, Evan Ross
Extras: John Daniels, Brian Smith, Allan Brennan, Terry Kelly, Anthony Brown, Spencer Bradley, Paul Preston, John Clark, Andrew Bysouth, Paul Walker, Timothy Ball, Rae Parish

PRODUCTION TEAM
Script: Jimmy Perry and David Croft
Producer/Director: David Croft
Production Assistant: Jo Austin
Film Cameraman: Peter Chapman
Film Sound: Bill Chesneau
Film Editor: John Stothart
Lighting: Howard King
Studio Sound: Alan Machin
Design: Robert Berk
Assistant Floor Manager: Anne Ogden
Vision Mixer: Dave Hanks
Costume Designer: Mary Husband
Make-Up Artist: Sylvia Thornton

The platoon is supplied with two-man bivouac tents and a weekend camp is organised in order to try them out. Before going on camp they practise erecting the tents in the Vicar's garden, and discuss eating hedgehogs and lighting camp fires.

Mainwaring's men set up camp next to a small lake and while Godfrey and Frazer prepare rabbit stew, the rest of the platoon undertake a rigorous exercise routine. But things are halted when Hodges' lorry appears, giving a lift to Mr Yeatman and his Sea Scouts, and the Vicar, who are camping at the same site. When Hodges discovers his van has run out of petrol, he ends up having to sleep in the vehicle.

During the night Frazer spots a German plane on fire, but he fails to notice that the crew has bailed out and landed in the lake. Next morning, the Germans are spotted drifting in an inflatable craft, but when they refuse to come to the shore, Mainwaring, Wilson, Pike, Jones and Hodges – acting as an interpreter because he speaks the language – sail out on a raft to capture them. Hodges falls in the water and when the raft starts sinking they are forced to return to shore. Jones volunteers to swim underwater to puncture the inflatable, but fails in his attempt. Eventually Pikey punctures the inflatable with a bow and arrow.

'Come In, Your Time is Up'

COMMAND DECISION

Recorded: Monday 29/4/68 (made in black and white)

Original transmission: Wednesday 14/8/68,
8.20–8.50pm

Original viewing figures: 8.6 million

Repeated: 31/1/69, 28/7/98, 11/8/98, 17/5/99

CAST

Arthur Lowe . . . . .Captain Mainwaring
John Le Mesurier . . . . .Sergeant Wilson
Clive Dunn . . . . .Lance Corporal Jones
John Laurie . . . . .Private Frazer
James Beck . . . . .Private Walker
Arnold Ridley . . . . .Private Godfrey
Ian Lavender . . . . .Private Pike
Caroline Dowdeswell . . . . .Janet King
Geoffrey Lumsden . . . . .Colonel Square
Charles Hill . . . . .Butler
Gordon Peters . . . . .Soldier
Platoon: Hugh Hastings, Richard Jacques, Colin Bean,
Chris Franks, David Seaforth, Alec Coleman, Hugh Cecil,
Vic Taylor, Jimmy Mac, Peter Whitaker
Soldier (Burt): Alan Travell

PRODUCTION TEAM

Script: Jimmy Perry and David Croft
Producer/Director: David Croft
Production Assistant: Harold Snoad
Lighting: George Summers
Studio Sound: James Cole
Design: Alan Hunter-Craig and Paul Joel
Assistant Floor Manager: Evan King
Vision Mixer: Bob Hallman
Costume Supervisor: George Ward
Make-Up Supervisor: Sandra Exelby
(Animals by Winships Circus)

'Command Decision'

Morale is low in the platoon due to the dearth of weapons, so Mainwaring promises he'll get them their rifles by the end of the week. Colonel Square, a World War One veteran, makes his first appearance in the sitcom when he turns up at the bank, trying to throw his weight around by offering his rifles so long as he takes over command of the platoon. Mainwaring has a tricky dilemma: should he keep his promise and deliver the rifles or retain command of the platoon? When GHQ still can't promise any rifles, Mainwaring sees no alternative but to march the men to Marsham Hall to hand over command. But things don't turn out as planned: it's clear from his performance that Square still feels cavalry is the way to fight; the trouble is his animals, being ex-circus horses, can only perform tricks, and his rifles are relics. When Mainwaring realises this he marches the men back to the church hall and is saved by a late delivery of rifles.

CONNIE

Not seen in the sitcom, Connie is mentioned by Wilson in 'A Man of Action'. When he meets Fire Officer Dale in the church hall office, Wilson comments on how she wears 'awfully well'.

'Command Decision'

CONNOR, PATRICK (1926–)

Born: Margate

Role: Shamus (S4, episode 6:'Absent Friends') (TV)

After completing his national service, Patrick returned to his job as a studio manager at the BBC. He'd always been interested in acting, and had worked for the Tavistock Theatre and the Beeb's own internal theatre group, The Ariel Players. Eventually he decided to try his luck at acting professionally and joined Oldham Rep for five months.

His TV career started in the days of live broadcasting, and he went on to appear in many shows, such as *Dixon of Dock Green*, *The Army Game*, *Z Cars*, *The Persuaders*, *Danger Man* playing a receptionist in the episode, 'The Ubiquitous Mr Lovegrove', *The Professionals*, *Special Branch*, *The Love Boat* and *The Bill*.

After spending more than four decades in the entertainment business Patrick, who worked for Jimmy Perry in rep at Watford, has semi-retired from the profession.

CONSCIENTIOUS OBJECTOR

A conscientious objector refuses to take part in military action for reasons of conscience. During the Second World War 5000 men and 2000 women registered as conscientious objectors. Decisions regarding their exemption from military action varied from region to region, but the majority were exempted, allowing them to work in hospitals, the emergency services or on the land instead. People who refused to help the war effort in any way were prosecuted and usually found themselves imprisoned.

CONWAY, COUNCILLOR

Mainwaring tells Hodges in 'The Big Parade' that he'll be speaking to Councillor Conway the following Monday at the Rotary luncheon. He promises to discuss Hodges' decision to put the Home Guard at the back of the parade celebrating the start of the Spitfire Fund Week. The councillor is not seen in the sitcom.

COOMBS, PAT (1926–)

Born: London

Roles: Mrs Hall (film); Clippie and Marie ('A Soldier's Farewell') (radio)

After training at LAMDA Pat began working on the stage before establishing herself as a familiar face on TV, chiefly playing comedy parts. Her early credits include Lana Butt in the pilot of *Beggar My Neighbour* and the three subsequent series between 1967 and 1968. She also appeared as Violet Robinson in *Lollipop Loves Mr Mole* in 1971 and the series, *Lollipop*, the following year. Other series in which she's been cast include two runs of *Don't Drink the Water!*, four series of *You're Only Young Twice*, as Mrs Carey in *In Sickness and in Health*, Gloria in *Birds of a Feather* and Marge Green in *EastEnders*.

Pat has made a handful of films, such as *Adolf Hitler – My Part in his Downfall* and *Ooh! You Are Awful*.

COOPER, JOAN (1922–1989)

Born: Chesterfield

Roles: Miss Baker (S3, episode 13:'No Spring for Frazer'), Miss Fortescue (S5, episode 13:'Time On My Hands'), Dolly (S8, episode 3:'The Love of Three Oranges' & S9, episode 6:'Never Too Old') (TV); Miss Baker and Cissy Godfrey ('Is There Honey Still For Tea?') (radio); Mrs Holdane Hart and Gert (stage show)

Joan's parents were musicians and although she learnt to play the piano, her inclinations veered towards another strand of the entertainment world: the stage. At 15 she joined a residential drama school at Stratford-upon-Avon, run by Randle Ayrton, the famous Shakespearean actor. Her professional career began at the age of 17, working for Donald Wolfit, before joining various rep companies, starting at Colchester, where she became stage manager while acting in small roles. Other reps she worked at include Farnham, Manchester and Hereford. Before taking a break from acting to raise her family, she spent six months at the Arts Theatre and played in Basil Dean's *Hassan* at the Cambridge Theatre, among other productions.

Theatre was the mainstay of her career, but she made various TV appearances, including BBC's *Rookery Nook* in 1970, Mrs Marriott in 1985's *Don't Wait Up*, *Softly, Softly* and three separate roles in *Dad's Army*, most notably as Dolly, one of Private Godfrey's sisters. She appeared in several films such as *Sweet William*, *The Bawdy Adventures of Tom Jones* and *The Ruling Class*.

Joan, who was married to Arthur Lowe, never recovered from the shock of losing her husband in 1982. She died in 1989.

COPELAND, JAMES (1919–)

Born: Helensburgh

Role: Captain Ogilvy (S2, episode 1:'Operation Kilt') (TV)

As a young boy, James Copeland, the son of a house painter, earned pocket money by helping the local milkman on his rounds, before leaving school at 14 and helping his grandfather as a shoe repairer. He hated the job and decided he wanted to become a journalist, so studied shorthand and typing at night school.

Before he could pursue his chosen career, James was sent to work at a Glasgow aircraft factory in 1938. In his spare time he tried his hand at amateur acting and writing, before joining the Air Auxiliary Transport as a flight engineer in 1943. His varied career continued after the war when he spent three years as a policeman in Dumbarton, and had a spell as a water bailiff. By this time, James knew that he wanted to make his living as an actor, so studied during the evenings at Glasgow's Citizens' Theatre.

His breakthrough came straight after an appearance in *Three Estates* at the 1951 Edinburgh Festival, and within a short time he was employed full-time back at the Citizens' Theatre.

James has worked extensively in all strands of the profession, including films, clocking up more than a dozen credits, such as the 1960 film, *Tunes of Glory*, in which he played an officer. He also appeared in *Laxdale Hall*, *Singlehanded*, *Mask of Dust*, *Rockets Galore*, *The Big Catch*, *The Big Man*, *Innocents in Paris* and *The Maggie*. On TV he's been seen in many shows, such as *King's Ransom*, *Dr Finlay's Casebook* and *Take the High Road*, in which he played Jamie, a regular character for three years. Meanwhile, on stage he's appeared with numerous reps and touring companies all around the British Isles.

CORNIOLI, TINA

Role: Olive, a Land Girl ('All is Safely Gathered In') (TV)

CORTEZ, LEON (1898–1970)

Born: London

Role: Milkman (S1, episode 2:'Museum Piece'), Small Man (S3, episode 12:'Man Hunt') (TV)

Leon grew up in London. He served in the army during the Great War, then worked in cinema management before turning to the stage. A well-known Cockney comedian and variety actor, his voice was a familiar one on radio for over three decades with his Cockney Coster Band and his own series *Happy Half-Hour*. He is also remembered for his Shakespearean comedy monologues.

On TV, he popped up in *Beggar My Neighbour*, *The Saint*, *Dixon of Dock Green* and *The Max Bygraves Show*. He continued to work on the stage throughout his life and toured in the comedy, *Doctor at Sea*, Roy Plomley's *Devil's Highway*, and during 1969 was the detective in *The Case of the Frightened Lady*. Film appearances included *You Can't Help Singing* with Judy Garland, *Live Now Pay Later* and *Striptease Murder*.

Leon, who was also a regular pantomime performer, was due to begin rehearsals for two TV plays when he died in 1970, aged 72.

COSTELLO, DEIRDRE

Born: Elland

Role: Buffet Attendant (S4, episode 9:'Mum's Army') (TV)

After graduating in English from London University, Deirdre taught at a grammar school for a while before turning to acting. Offers of TV work soon followed. She has appeared in various programmes from early appearances in *Z Cars* and *Dixon of Dock Green* to *The Professionals*, *The Sweeney* and semi-regular roles in *Grange Hill*, playing a mother, three years as Joan, the betting shop manageress in *Big Deal*, and *London's Burning*. More recently, Deirdre has appeared in films like *The Full Monty*, *Elephant Man*, Ken Russell's *Valentino* and *Jack the Ripper*, starring Michael Caine. On TV, her more recent credits include *Coronation Street*, *City Central* and *The Cops*, while on radio she's just played Mrs Patterson in Radio 4's *King Street Junior*.

COSTUMES

When the series began in 1968, most costumes were hired from Berman's, a London costumiers. George Ward, the sitcom's first costume designer, found men's civilian costumes dating from the war years difficult to find, whereas military outfits were easier to trace.

COWLING, BRENDA

Born: London

Role: Mrs Prentice (S5, episode 8: 'All is Safely Gathered In') (TV)

As a child, Brenda Cowling wanted to be a film star but after leaving school she trained as a shorthand typist. Eventually she changed direction and joined RADA (she was in the same class as Warren Mitchell and Jimmy Perry). She appeared as a drama student in Hitchcock's *Stage Fright* while still at RADA.

Plenty of rep work followed before Brenda made her TV debut. Early appearances include several series of an afternoon keep-fit show and *The Forsyte Saga*. Her career has focused mainly on TV but she has also worked on stage. Brenda was cast in several films, such as *The Railway Children*, *International Velvet*, *Carry On Girls*, *Carry On Behind* and made brief appearances in two Bond movies.

Post-*Dad's Army*, Brenda worked for David Croft and Jimmy Perry in *It Ain't Half Hot, Mum* as a WVS lady, and as a maid in the final instalment of *Hi-De-Hi!*. She's played many nurses, including the sister in an episode of *Fawlty Towers* and a matron in *Only When I Laugh*. Brenda was cast as Jane in three series of *Potter*, two of which starred Arthur Lowe.

Recent years have been dominated by four series of *You Rang, M'Lord?* in which she played Mrs Lipton. She was also seen recently in *The Detectives*, *Casualty* and *The Legacy of Reginald Perrin*, as CJ's housekeeper, Mrs Wren.

CRISP, CAPTAIN

(See 'Marine Officer, The'.)

CROFT, DAVID

Born in Poole, Dorset, into a theatrical family, David finished his education at Rugby School. During the Second World War he rose to the rank of Major and served in the Royal Artillery and Dorset Regiment in North Africa, India and Singapore; for a time, he was also on Montgomery's staff at the War Office.

After the war, he returned to the theatre playing in rep at Hereford and Wolverhampton and appeared in various musicals in the West End. The 1950s saw David begin turning his attention to writing: in 1952 he collaborated with Ian Carmichael and Ted Kavenagh on a new TV

David Croft (right) felt Arthur Lowe (left) played Mainwaring perfectly.

series, and began a successful partnership with Cyril Ornadel writing the music and lyrics for the Ciceley Courtnedge musical, *Starmaker*. He went on to write several shows for the London Palladium, and pantomimes for Howard and Wyndhams, and Derek Salberg.

In 1954 he joined Rediffusion as head of the light entertainment script department, before turning to producing and directing. His early work in this capacity included many summer shows at resorts around the country, such as Weymouth, Great Yarmouth, Clacton and Scarborough, and his own musical, *The Pied Piper*, at Worthing.

In 1959 he helped set up Tyne Tees Television, and was responsible for over 300 TV shows, producing as many as five a week at one stage. He later joined the BBC where he produced and directed countless hit shows, including *The Benny Hill Show*, *The Dick Emery Show*, *Hugh and I*, *Beggar My Neighbour*, *Steptoe and Son*, *'Till Death Us Do Part*, *Tales of the Lazy Acre* and *Up Pompeii!*.

As a comedy writer he's written many Palladium pantomimes featuring stars like Norman Wisdom, Charlie Drake, Bruce Forsyth, Harry Secombe, Cliff Richard, Arthur Askey and Engelbert Humperdinck. He has also become one of the country's top sitcom writers, thanks to a string of classic shows. With Jimmy Perry he co-wrote shows including *Dad's Army*, *It Ain't Half Hot, Mum* and *Hi-De-Hi!*, while with Jeremy Lloyd he created *Are You Being Served?*, *'Allo, 'Allo* and *Grace and Favour*.

David's standing in the profession has seen

him produce and direct TV shows in Australia and America, and in recognition of his services to television, he was awarded the OBE in 1978. Four years later, he was awarded the Desmond Davies Award for his outstanding contribution to the industry, and in 1992 received the Judges Award from the Royal Television Society. In 1999 David, who is married to Ann (a former agent) and has seven children, was the proud recipient of the Eric Morecambe Award for lifetime achievement, presented by Comic Heritage.

Nowadays, he divides his time between homes in London, Norfolk and Portugal.

CROWN FILM UNIT

Harold Forster and Queenie Beal are employees of the Crown Film Unit in 'Ring Dem Bells', in which the Walmington Home Guard play Nazis in a training film. During the Second World War, the Ministry of Information's Crown Film Unit produced plenty of films, many of which were short-length documentaries.

CROXTON, MR

Not seen in the sitcom, Mr Croxton is mentioned in 'My Brother and I' and lives in Eastbourne. Frazer misses a parade because he's off to see Croxton, who's a client of his. Mainwaring also knows Mr Croxton and classes him a 'chatterbox'.

CULLUM-JONES, DESMOND (1924–)

Born: Washington, USA

Role: Member of the platoon in 63 episodes (S2; S3, episodes 2–6, 8, 9, 11, 12, 14; S4, episodes 1, 3, 6, 9–13; S5; S6; S7; S8; 'My Brother and I'; S9) (TV); (Film)

Although he was born in America, Desmond

moved to Broadstairs, Kent, at the age of three. After leaving school, he joined the navy and during the Second World War sailed on the Russian convoys and spent time in Ceylon, Algeria and Malta, before being invalided out with lung problems.

After a series of jobs, none of which lasted very long, including two weeks administering teachers' salaries at the Ministry of Education and sales assistant at a greengrocers before getting the sack, Desmond became a self-employed demonstrator of small companies' products, travelling around the country. He stayed in the business for several years until he became a travelling salesman for a soft drinks company in 1949.

His last job before turning to acting and photographic modelling was as a West End rep for Skol lager. When he received a driving ban he lost his job and took up photographic modelling whilst he looked for alternative employment. He quickly became busy and was regularly photographed for magazines and knitting patterns. So profitable was the work, he decided to open the London Charm School for Men, teaching modelling.

Soon he decided to diversify and began getting walk-on work for TV, working with stars like Shirley Bassey and Arthur Askey. He appeared several times in *Dixon of Dock Green*, including roles as a market trader and shopkeeper but continued working in adverts, including a job in Jersey promoting the Ford Cortina.

Other TV credits include: *Maigret*, playing a nightporter, two episodes of *Father, Dear Father*, several appearances in *Z Cars*, *Softly, Softly*, *The Desperate People*, *Compact*, *Wuthering Heights*, as a servant, a probation officer in *The Newcomers*, *Doctor Who* in 1966, a police sergeant in *Public Eye*, *Adam Adamant Lives!*, *Shoestring*, a magistrate in the TV adaptation of Catherine Cookson's *The Rag Nymph*, a ticket collector in *Thomas and Sarah*, *The Valiant Years*, Prince Regent in *Vanity Fair*, and *The Singing Detective*. He's also appeared in several movies, such as *Impact*, playing a prison warder, *Curse of the Werewolf*, a Scottish Dean in *Bolero*, *The Bargee*, *Quilp*, *Foreign Affairs*, *The Steal* and worked in Hollywood for three months.

On stage he's appeared as Doolittle in *Pygmalion* and the Major General in *Halfway Up A Tree*.

Desmond no longer actively seeks work and is enjoying retirement in Bournemouth.

CUNDELL, PAMELA

Born: Croydon
Roles: Marcia Fox ('The Armoured Might of Lance Corporal Jones', 'The Big Parade', 'Mum's Army', 'Getting the Bird', 'My British Buddy', 'The Honourable Man' 'Everybody's Trucking' 'The Godiva Affair' 'Turkey Dinner', 'The Love of Three Oranges',

'The Making of Private Pike' and 'Never Too Old'), Lady in the Queue (S3, episode 3: 'The Lion has 'Phones') (TV); Mrs Fox and British Restaurant Lady (stage show at Billingham and The Shaftesbury); Daisy (stage show at The Shaftesbury)

Both Pamela's parents were in the entertainment business and she never wanted to do anything else. Her training at the Guildhall School of Music and Drama was followed by steady work in rep and summer tours, as a stand-up comic.

She made her TV debut in *Yes, It's the Cathode-Ray Tube Show!* in 1957 with Peter Sellers and Michael Bentine, and worked on *Jim's Inn* during the same period.

Pamela's been fortunate enough to work with all the great comics, including Benny Hill, Harry Worth, Bill Fraser and Frankie Howerd. In recent years, she's played Vi Box in three series of BBC's *Big Deal* and Mrs Monk, the housekeeper, in *The Choir*, and she remains busy, particularly on stage. She has appeared in panto at the Palace Theatre, Watford, for three years: *Cinderella* in 1996, *Jack and the Beanstalk* and most recently *Robinson Crusoe*, all written by Roy Hudd. In 1977, she played Mrs Orlock in *Plunder* at the Savoy Theatre, and earlier this year finished a film, *Paradise Grove*.

Theatre credits include: *High Spirits*, understudying Cicely Courtnedge, *Wham Bam Thank You Mam*, *Lil Ole King Cole*, with Charlie Drake at the Palladium, *The Rose and the Ring*, *Beer Glorious Beer*, *Climb the Greased Pole*, *Magic Carpet*, *Corsican Brothers*.

TV credits include: Fat Alice in *Bootsie and Snudge*, *No Hiding Place*, Maggie in several episodes of *The Newcomers*, *Beggar My Neighbour* as Madame Gladys, *Calas*, *Show of the Week*, *The Benny Hill Show*, 'These Men Are Dangerous' in the *Thirty-Minute Theatre* series, *My Husband and I*, *The Barry Humphries Show*, *The Doctors*, *Z Cars*, *Doctor in the House*, *Gentle to Norah*, *The Root of all Evil*, *Never Say Die*, *Clochemerle*, *Pardon My Genie*, *The Frankie Howerd Show*, *Oh, Father*, *Thirty Minutes Worth*, *Beryl's Lot*, *Clayhanger*, *The Growing Pains of PC Penrose*, *Are You Being Served?*, *On the Buses* and the BAFTA award-winning production, *The Borrowers*.

Film credits include: *Half A Sixpence*, *Mrs Brown You've Got A Lovely Daughter*, *The Waiters*, *Love Thy Neighbour*.

CUTFORTH, JIM

Not seen in 'Brain versus Brawn', Jim is mentioned by Jones, who represents the Walmington Athletic Society at the Rotarian dinner in his absence. Jim had to attend the Darby and Joan Club instead.

Note: In the original script the character was called Mr Cutter.

CUTTS, CAPTAIN

Played by Michael Knowles (TV and radio)
A captain based at the War Office, he's around when Mainwaring and Wilson travel to London to see the Brigadier about getting Walker's call-up postponed in 'The Loneliness of the Long-Distance Walker'. He appears again in 'The Bullet is Not for Firing', by which time he has transferred to Area Command, and is sent down to Walmington to attend the court of inquiry Mainwaring has requested.

D

DAD'S ARMY APPRECIATION SOCIETY (DAAS)

The society, formed back in 1993, boasts over 1000 members. With Bill Pertwee and Frank Williams as its president and vice-president respectively, it's co-ordinated by the commander-in-chief, 78-year-old retired civil servant Jack Wheeler, who watches at least three episodes of the sitcom every evening. The society's adjutants are Tony Pritchard, Paul Carpenter and Nick Randall. Members receive a quarterly newsletter, the content of which is agreed by the society's editorial team, comprising of Jack, Paul Carpenter and Tony Pritchard.

Members range from age 8 to 80 and span the globe, some living in America and Australia. There is also a branch in New Zealand, co-ordinated by platoon commander, Dave Homewood. His adjùtants are Robert Cant and Martin Smith. Like its British cousin, the New Zealand branch produces a quarterly magazine.

Jack Wheeler says: 'I think it's the gentle comedy that makes *Dad's Army* so successful, and for older members the chance to reminisce about an important period of history. It's a realistic study of life in the Home Guard; in fact, some members say their experiences were even worse than those seen in the sitcom!'

The society continues to grow and for fans of Perry and Croft's classic slice of wartime life, it provides a wonderful source of information and opportunity. Trips to many of the Norfolk locations used for filming, merchandise for sale and detailed information on the sitcom are just some of the aspects offered to members.

If you would like to join the Society, or require further information, write (enclosing a sae) to Jack Wheeler, DAAS, 8 Sinodun Road, Wallingford, Oxon OX10 8AA.

DAD'S ARMY MUSEUM

In May 2000, a museum dedicated to the memory of *Dad's Army* opened at the Bressingham Steam Museum in Norfolk. Visitors can experience what it must have been like as a resident in the fictional town of Walmington, thanks to sets based on the original designs. The church hall forms the centrepiece of the display. Up to a third of the total floor space at the steam museum has been set aside for *Dad's Army*, with shop fronts and the bank exterior, a fire engine, steam roller and traction engine used in the series on display. There is also a large collection of memorabilia. For more information, call the museum on 01379 687382.

DAICOP

(Dad's Army Appreciation Society Information and Continuity Project)

Set up by two members of the Dad's Army Appreciation Society (Gordon Brodie and Christopher Leather), DAICOP is a database of information relating to the sitcom. Collated from hours of research, watching and listening to both the TV and radio versions of the programme, Gordon and Christopher have created a myriad of computer files, each dedicated to a particular aspect of *Dad's Army*, such as the vehicles used in the show, character profiles and the church hall, in which Mainwaring and his men spent so many hours. The project is ongoing, and at the time of writing 57 computer files have been established. Copies of these files are available to members of the Society.

DALBY, AMY (1888–1969)

Role: Dolly Godfrey (S2, episode 2: 'The Battle of Godfrey's Cottage') (TV)

Amy Dalby was a character actress who built up a long list of credits playing mainly cameo roles in numerous films, stage productions and TV shows. Among her big-screen appearances were roles in *Quiet Wedding* (1941) and nine other films that decade, such as *The Night Has Eyes*, playing Miss Miggs, *Millions Like Us*, *The Gentle Sex*, *Waterloo Road*, *The Wicked Lady* and *My Sister and I*. She popped up in many more pictures, *The Spy with a Cold Nose* (as Miss Marchbanks) and *Smashing Time* among them.

DALE, FIRE OFFICER

Played by Arnold Peters (TV)

In 'A Man of Action', Dale is involved in discussions regarding what can be done when a mine causes havoc in Walmington. He seems a little short of ideas.

DANIELS, COLIN

Role: Boy (S2, episode 1: 'Operation Kilt', S3, episode 3: 'The Lion has 'Phones') (TV)

DARBY AND JOAN CLUB, THE

Walmington's Darby and Joan Club is mentioned by Jones in 'Brain versus Brawn'. He attends the Rotary dinner instead of Mr Cutforth who is attending the Club. Darby and Joan Clubs were originally set up by the WRVS, and it is believed the names Darby and Joan originate from an 18th-century ballad written by Henry Woodfall.

DAVENPORT, DAVID (1921–1995)

Born: Berkhamsted

Role: Military Police Sgt (S1, episode 4: 'Enemy Within the Gates') (TV)

Educated at Berkhamsted School and Stowe College, David was 12 when given ballet lessons by his mother's friend, dancer Anton Dolin. After a year at college, he left to join London's Cone Ripman Ballet School full-time.

By 1938 he was dancing with the Lydia Kyasht Russian Ballet, and four years later the Royal Ballet. During a glittering dancing career he appeared with Margot Fonteyn and Robert Helpmann in various performances including *Miracle in the Gorbals*.

Four years (1942–1946) as a wireless operator in the RAF interrupted his dancing career, which he then resumed until concentrating on the musical stage in the early 1950s. Soon his talent had spread to films and TV.

Film credits include: *Carry On Cleo* (as Bilius), *Carry On Henry* (as Major Domo), *King's Rhapsody* and *You Only Live Twice*. On TV he's perhaps best known as Malcolm Ryder, Noele Gordon's husband, in *Crossroads*, but he appeared in many other shows including *All Creatures Great and Small*.

David's final West End appearance was in *The Secret Diary of Adrian Mole* in 1986, before bad health prevented him working again.

DAVIES, JANET (1930–1986)

Born: Wakefield

Role: Mrs Mavis Pike (30 episodes: S1, episodes 1, 2, 5

& 6; S2, episodes 1, 2, 4 & 6; S3, episodes 1, 3, 4, 5, 9 & 12; S4, episodes 1, 3, 4, 6, 9 & 11; S6, episodes 2 & 5; S7, episodes 3 & 6; S8, episodes 2 & 5; 'The Love of Three Oranges'; S9, episodes 2, 3 & 6 (TV) and stage show

Janet's father, a solicitor, died in his early thirties, and as a result she was sent to boarding school. She started training as a solicitor but left and qualified as a shorthand typist instead. She worked as a secretary at the BBC for two years, assigned to programmes including *Dick Barton* and *Special Agent* before eventually moving into rep in 1948.

She worked at various reps in Leatherhead, Watford, Shrewsbury, Bedford and Northamp-

Mrs Pike, played by Janet Davies, mollycoddled her son.

ton while early TV work included several episodes of *Dixon of Dock Green* and *Z Cars*. She also made a few films.

When she wasn't acting, Janet exploited her typing and shorthand training by working with various theatrical agencies. A true jobbing actress she kept busy throughout her career, but will always be remembered as Mrs Pike. She died of cancer in 1986, aged 56.

Theatre credits include: *The Love Match*, *Saturday Night at the Crown* and *Three Months Gone*, playing Ivy Hanker.

TV credits include: playing a librarian in *The Last of the Summer Wine*, Roz Hatch in *The Professionals*, *General Hospital*, *All Right*, *Two's Company*, *That's My Boy*, *Diamonds are a Man's Best Friend*, *Castle Haven*, *The Dick Emery Show*, *The Fall and Rise of Reginald Perrin*, *All Creatures*

Great and Small, Mrs Watkins in 1983's *The Citadel*, a mini-series of *Pride and Prejudice* in 1979, *Are You Being Served?*, *Sadie, It's Cold Outside*, *General Hospital*, 'Breath' a *Play for Today*, *Marked Personal*, *Vienna 1900* and *Casanova 74*.

Film credits include: *This House of Brede*, *Something in Disguise*, *The Hiding Place*, 1971's *Under Milk Wood* with Richard Burton and *Shot in the Dark*.

DAVIES, RICHARD
Born: Dowlais, Glamorgan
Role: Volunteer ('The Armoured Might of Lance Corporal Jones') (radio)

Richard, who's best known for playing Mr Price, a teacher, in *Please, Sir!* has led a busy career ever since joining the Oxford Pilgrim Players as a student and touring the country performing religious dramas.

Whilst serving in the Forces he was a member of the Army Topical Theatre and Stars in Battledress; he continued acting upon demob at the end of the Second World War by appearing in the West End production, *Little Lambs Eat Ivy* and *Carrington VC*.

In addition to plenty of radio work, including the 1972 series, *The Motorway Men*, which also starred Jimmy Beck, Richard appeared in various television shows, such as *Robert's Robots* for Thames in 1973, *Oh No! It's Selwyn Froggitt* in 1976, LWT's *Bottle Boys*, *Whoops Apocalypse!*, playing the Chancellor of the Exchequer, *The Citadel*, *The Max Boyce Show*, *To Serve Them All My Days*, *Angels*, *Fawlty Towers*, *Yes, Minister*,

Don't Wait Up, *Brookside*, *Coronation Street* and *EastEnders*.

His film credits include *The Night My Number Came Up*, *Zulu*, *Under Milk Wood*, *Sky West and Crooked* and *Oh, What a Lovely War!*.

DAWKINS, PAUL
Role: Nazi General (film)

On TV Paul appeared as the Reverend Graham in the 1978 mini-series of *Wuthering Heights*, a tramp in 'Stopover', a 1979 episode of *The Professionals*, Sam Pearson in a 1961 instalment of *The Avengers*, titled 'Death on the Slipway' and the 1966 series, *Pardon the Expression*. Other film credits include *Far from the Madding Crowd* in 1967, *Hot Millions* a year later, *Lock Up Your Daughters* in 1969, the foreman of the jury in *My Lover My Son*, Tim Mackay in *The Plane Makers*, Hogben in Granada's 1966 series, *The Man in Room 17*, *Nearest and Dearest*, *The Onedin Line* and *O Lucky Man!*.

DAWSON, GLADYS (1898–1970)
Born: London
Role: Mrs Witt (S2, episode 6: 'Under Fire') (TV)

Gladys always wanted to be an actress and made her stage debut at Drury Lane, when she was carried on as a baby. She turned professional as soon as she left school, and spent most of her career in theatre. During the Great War she helped entertain the troops, before forming a double-act with her husband and touring the provinces and London theatres. She later toured as a double-act with George Formby.

She got into TV from the beginning, and went on to appear in numerous productions, such as *Up The Junction*, *Cathy Come Home* and *Crossroads* playing an old woman in prison, which turned out to be one of her last jobs. She also made a few films, including *Chitty Chitty Bang Bang* and *Oliver!*.

DAY, PETER
Visual effects designer on 20 episodes: S3, episodes 1, 4, 5, 6, 7; S4, episodes 8, 9, 11, 12, 13; S5, episodes 1, 2, 3, 4, 5, 6, 7, 12; S6, episode 4; S8, episode 4

Born in Richmond, Peter trained in theatre design at Wimbledon Art School, before joining the Doyly Carte Opera Company making costumes and millinery. He also worked in architectural model-making, and for Pearl and Dean, making filmlets, before spending two years at the Arts Theatre. During the two-year period he was employed as a scenic artist he was offered a few walk-on parts. In 1958 he joined the BBC as a design assistant in the Visual Effects Department.

Initially Peter worked on school programmes before moving into mainstream TV. His skills were called upon for numerous shows, including *Doctor Who*, *Tomorrow's World*, *It's a Square World*, *The Goodies* and *Some Mothers Do 'Ave 'Em*. The last programme he worked on examined the life of Shackleton, the explorer, and resulted in a month in Greenland. Peter retired from the Beeb in 1985.

DAY, PRIVATE

Played by Peter Honri (TV)

In 'The Godiva Affair', Private Day plays a concertina while the platoon practise their morris dancing, in preparation for the weekend procession to help raise money for the town's Spitfire Fund.

DAY THE BALLOON WENT UP, THE

Recorded: Thursday 23/10/69

Original transmission: Thursday 30/10/69, 7.30–8.00pm

Original viewing figures: 12.5 million

Repeated: 23/5/70, 5/9/71, 5/11/82, 19/9/92, 30/12/95, 30/10/99

CAST

Arthur Lowe	Captain Mainwaring
John Le Mesurier	Sergeant Wilson
Clive Dunn	Lance Corporal Jones
John Laurie	Private Frazer
James Beck	Private Walker
Arnold Ridley	Private Godfrey
Ian Lavender	Private Pike
Bill Pertwee	ARP Warden
Frank Williams	Vicar
Edward Sinclair	Verger
Nan Braunton	Miss Godfrey
Jennifer Browne	WAAF Sgt
Andrew Carr	Operations Room Officer
Thérèse McMurray	Girl in the Haystack
Kenneth Watson	RAF Officer
Vicki Lane	Girl on the Tandem
Harold Bennett	Mr Blewitt
Jack Haig	Gardener

Platoon: Hugh Hastings, Desmond Cullum-Jones, Vic Taylor, Freddie Wiles, George Hancock, Martin Dunn, Leslie Noyes, Roger Bourne, Freddie White, Jimmy Mac Extras: Brian Nolan (RAF officer), Christine Cole (WAAF Private), Jean Fadgrove (WAAF Corporal), Iona MaCrae (WAAF Sgt), Sandy Stein (Wing Commander) Stuntman: Johnny Scripps

PRODUCTION TEAM

Script: Jimmy Perry and David Croft
Producer/Director: David Croft
Production Assistant: Harold Snoad
Film Cameraman: James Balfour
Film Editor: Bob Rymer
Lighting: Howard King
Studio Sound: Mike McCarthy
Design: Ray London
Assistant Floor Manager: Bill Harman
Vision Mixer: Dave Hanks
Costume Supervisor: Michael Burdle
Make-Up Supervisor: Cecile Hay-Arthur

When Godfrey turns up wearing a slipper and Walker has a bag of sugar and sultanas stuffed in his blouse pockets, Mainwaring tells the platoon they're getting very slovenly in their appearance. To make matters worse, the CO came through the town recently and didn't receive a single salute, and Jones had his hands in his pockets – the reason being he had forgotten his braces. So they practise saluting.

The Vicar complains about obscene words scribbled in wax crayon on the back of the spare harmonium which is kept in the church tower, and while Mainwaring's men climb the tower to see if their writing matches that on the harmonium, they spot the Verger hanging on the cable of a stray barrage balloon. The Home Guard rescue the Verger and then phone the RAF to report the balloon. The RAF promise to arrive as soon as they can, but it's down to the platoon to take charge in the meantime. They guide the balloon out into Pinner Fields but before they can secure it, Mainwaring is hoisted up by the balloon. As the platoon give chase in Jones's van, Hodges uses a tricycle and a tandem to try and keep up.

The stray balloon sends alarm bells ringing at RAF headquarters; classing it as an unidentified object they scramble some planes to investigate. The men try their utmost to rescue Mainwaring, finally pulling him to safety at a railway bridge, seconds before a train arrives. But there is more trouble in store when an RAF officer arrives.

DAYE, ANDREW

(See 'Tomlinson, Fred'.)

DEADLY ATTACHMENT, THE

Recorded: Friday 22/6/73

Original transmission: Wednesday 31/10/73, 6.50–7.20pm

Original viewing figures: 12.9 million

Repeated: 25/4/74, 24/6/78, 21/11/89, 23/8/90 (N Ireland), 2/10/93, 3/10/93 (Wales), 25/4/95, 28/6/97

CAST

Arthur Lowe	Captain Mainwaring
John Le Mesurier	Sergeant Wilson
Clive Dunn	Lance Corporal Jones
John Laurie	Private Frazer
James Beck	Private Walker
Arnold Ridley	Private Godfrey
Ian Lavender	Private Pike
Philip Madoc	U-Boat Captain
Bill Pertwee	Chief Warden Hodges
Edward Sinclair	Verger
Robert Raglan	Colonel
Colin Bean	Private Sponge

Platoon: Desmond Cullum-Jones, George Hancock, Evan Ross, Leslie Noyes, William Gossling, Freddie White, Freddie Wiles, Roger Bourne, Michael Moore Policeman: Ray Emmins Nazi Sailors: Les Conrad, Reg Turner, Clive Roger, Danny Lions, Alan Thomas, Emmett Hennessy, Barry Summerford

PRODUCTION TEAM

Script: Jimmy Perry and David Croft
Producer/Director: David Croft
Production Assistant: Gordon Pert
Film Cameraman: James Balfour
Film Sound: John Gatland
Film Editor: Bob Rymer
Lighting: Howard King
Studio Sound: Michael McCarthy
Design: Paul Joel
Assistant Floor Managers: Peter Fitton and Steven Morris
Vision Mixer: Dave Hanks
Costume Supervisor: Susan Wheal
Make-Up Supervisor: Ann Ailes

The phone rings during parade, and while Pike goes off to answer, Mainwaring asks Wilson whether he's primed their stock of Mills bombs and is annoyed to discover that he hasn't. Wilson's excuse is that it's very dangerous, but that doesn't cut any ice with Mainwaring.

The Colonel from GHQ is on the line: a fishing boat has just picked up a U-boat captain and seven crew members. They're down at the harbour, and Mainwaring is asked to escort them to the church hall and guard them until the armed escort can pick them up later; a responsibility Mainwaring gladly accepts.

'The Deadly Attachment'

While Mainwaring goes off with the rest of the men to pick up the Germans, Wilson and Pike are asked to stay behind and arm the grenades, but Wilson still thinks this is dangerous and primes them with dummy detonators. Frazer sets up the Lewis gun and Pike gets the Tommy gun to help guard the insolent, cigarette-puffing German captain and his men.

The Colonel phones and tells Mainwaring he'll have to look after them all night, as the armed escort won't be there until morning. The Colonel suggests buying them fish and chips, because they'll need to be fed. When Walker takes everyone's order, the German captain demands plaice and no soggy chips!

When Hodges and the Verger arrive on the

'The Deadly Attachment' has become one of the most popular episodes.

scene the Nazi captain feigns violent stomach pains and they rush to his aid against Mainwaring's advice. Within moments, the captain is holding a gun against Hodges' throat, and moves into the office. The Germans demand to be taken back to the fishing boat so they can escape to France or they'll blow Hodges' head off. Mainwaring is given until dawn to make up his mind.

Mainwaring reluctantly agrees to their terms, hoping that someone will raise the alarm *en route* to the harbour, or that the navy will blow them out of the water. To ensure no one makes any false moves, the German captain puts a grenade down Jones' trousers and says that he won't hesitate pulling the string connected to the pin, if necessary. As they are marching to the harbour the Colonel comes up the road and asks where everyone's going, before pulling a string he notices protruding from Jones' jerkin. Thinking the grenade will explode, everyone dives to the ground except Wilson, who quickly regains control of the prisoners.

'The Deadly Attachment'

DELANY, JOHN
Studio sound recordist on seven episodes (TV): S5, episodes 7–13

After leaving school at 16, John had various jobs before joining the BBC in 1960 as a technical studio trainee. Initially he worked in an office, then moved on to a photographic company, before qualifying as a lab technician after a five-year part-time evening class and working for the Coal Board. But John had always been interested in the entertainment world, and helped out behind the scenes at local amateur companies for many years.

In his early television career, he specialised in dramas, working on *Maigret* and *The Sunday Play*. He was promoted to sound supervisor in 1968 and started working on comedy, including the original series of *Monty Python's Flying Circus*. Post-*Dad's Army* credits include *The Good Life*, *The Morecambe and Wise Show*, *The Two Ronnies*, *Dave Allen*, *Parkinson*, *Russell Harty*, *Wogan* and *Grandstand*.

Since retiring from the BBC in 1992, John has tutored in television sound at the National Film School.

DENTON, ROY (1901–1989)
Born: Hull

Role: Mr Bennett (S3, episode 7: 'Big Guns') (TV)

Although his mother wanted him to become a jeweller, Roy left school and worked as a barman at Hull's Grand Theatre. Realising he wanted to make a career out of the entertainment world, he eventually succeeded in becoming a light comedian in end-of-pier shows and reviews around the country, including Tenby, where he met his wife.

Later in his career he developed an interest in theatre management, and after a spell managing a cinema he took charge of the Theatre Royals in Lincoln, Southampton and Bournemouth. During the 1970s he managed hotels for the same company, before leaving the industry behind and opening his own café in Putney, London. Sadly, his business went bust and to help earn some money, his son – a theatrical agent – secured him small-part work on TV, including appearances in *Doctor Who*, *The Likely Lads*, *Farewell to Arms*, *The Secret Agent* and *The Railway Children*. He also appeared in the occasional film, such as *The Darwin Adventure* in 1971, as well as many commercials, often for foreign TV.

Roy worked solidly until his death from a stroke.

DENYER, JAY (1913–1996)
Born: London

Role: Inspector Blake (S7, episode 2: 'A Man of Action') (TV)

Jay trained as a dental mechanic upon leaving school at the age of 14. He worked in the industry for 12 years before leaving to pursue his dream of becoming a singer. After attending singing classes, his first professional engagement was in *Me and My Girl* at the Victoria Palace in 1939, before embarking on the production's first tour.

During the war, Jay worked at an engineering factory in Coventry, but when the plant was bombed, he was transferred to a site in Derbyshire. By the end of the war, Jay had joined ENSA, and for a year (1945–1946) toured the Far East.

Returning to civvy street, he appeared in numerous variety shows and revues, as well as many commercials. He continued working in the theatre and spent over three years on the London stage in *The Sound of Music*, and an equally long stint in *Annie*, the final show he worked in.

Jay appeared in TV shows as far back as the 1950s, with productions such as BBC's *Parovia* in 1956 and *The Gentle Flame* three years later, playing a shopkeeper. Other shows he worked on include *Scotland Yard* in 1960, a year on the *Five O'Clock Club* and Thames' *Six Days of Justice* in 1975, as Henry Paulton. He also appeared in several films, including *The Intimate Stranger* in 1956.

DESMOND, PRIVATE
Played by Desmond Cullum-Jones (TV)

Private Desmond was a regular member of the Home Guard, playing a more significant role in the episode, 'Sons of the Sea'. When Mainwaring secures the services of *The Naughty Jane*, a rowing boat, he sets up river patrols for his platoon. Desmond is involved in the trial run when Mainwaring and some of his men get lost at sea. We also hear Mainwaring ask Private Desmond to help Jones in 'Things That Go Bump in the Night'.

DESPERATE DRIVE OF CORPORAL JONES, THE
Recorded: Friday 16/6/72

Original transmission: Friday 3/11/72, 8.30–9.00pm

Original viewing figures: 15.8 million

Repeated: 28/7/73, 16/4/91, 28/10/95, 1/2/96 (Wales), 15/3/97

CAST
Arthur Lowe . . . . .Captain Mainwaring
John Le Mesurier . . . . .Sergeant Wilson
Clive Dunn . . . . .Lance Corporal Jones
John Laurie . . . . .Private Frazer
James Beck . . . . .Private Walker
Arnold Ridley . . . . .Private Godfrey
Ian Lavender . . . . .Private Pike
Bill Pertwee . . . . .ARP Warden
Frank Williams . . . . .Vicar
Edward Sinclair . . . . .Verger
Robert Raglan . . . . .Colonel
Larry Martyn . . . . .Signals Private
James Taylor . . . . .Artillery Officer
Platoon: Colin Bean, Hugh Hastings, Evan Ross, George Hancock, Freddie Wiles, Leslie Noyes, Michael Moore, Hugh Cecil, Freddie White, Desmond Cullum-Jones
Stuntmen: Billy Hughes and Leslie Conrad

PRODUCTION TEAM
Script: Jimmy Perry and David Croft
Producer/Director: David Croft
Production Assistant: Gordon Pert
Film Cameraman: Stewart A. Farnell
Film Sound: Ron Blight
Film Editor: Bill Harris
Lighting: Howard King
Sound: Michael McCarthy
Design: Paul Joel
Assistant Floor Manager: Peter Fitton
Vision Mixer: Dave Hanks
Costume Supervisor: Susan Wheal
Make-Up Supervisor: Cynthia Goodwin
Visual Effects: Peter Day

The platoon is involved in a divisional scheme at the weekend, where they'll be facing a battery of 25 pounders. Their job is to occupy a deserted barn and deny it to the enemy. Area Command call to give the grid reference for the barn, but as Mainwaring is talking to the men he asks Jones to record the reference. When his pencil breaks while recording the details, Jones rushes off to get a replacement only for Godfrey to pick up the receiver and jot down the reference points in the wrong order.

En route to the barn, Jones' van breaks down and they end up marching to their position; Jones stays with the van and is tasked with notifying HQ when the platoon is ready, an event they'll mark by sending smoke signals.

Upon reaching the barn, smoke signals are sent with the help of a fire and Mainwaring's specially tailored greatcoat, which burns in the process. Spotting the smoke, Jones notifies HQ, but what no one realises is that Mainwaring and his men are waiting at the target for the 25 pounders! When Jones and Godfrey realise their mistake they know the only way they can reach Mainwaring before the firing begins is to drive, even though Godfrey has never been behind a wheel before. Luckily, Walker and the Colonel have parked their cars nearby, so Jones drives the Colonel's car and tows Godfrey, who's driving Walker's car. Experiencing trouble on the way, it's a desperate race against time.

DEVLIN, J G (1907–1991)
Born: Belfast

Role: Regan (S4, episode 6: 'Absent Friends') (TV)

J G Devlin was out of work when he was invited to join a local amateur dramatics society. He enjoyed the experience so much that he knew he wanted to be an actor. He began his distinguished career in 1932, and worked in all mediums from the stage, including a spell with Peter Hall at the National Theatre, to TV roles in shows like *Z Cars*, *The Champions*, *The Sweeney*, *Steptoe and Son*, *Taggart* and *Bread*, playing

J G Devlin (2nd from right) is arrested by Mainwaring's men in 'Absent Friends'.

Father Dooley. He also made over 20 films, including *Attempt to Kill*, 1961's *The Frightened City* and *The Reckoning*.

Early on in his career he was heard in various radio plays, and during the war helped organise amateur theatricals for factory and foundry workers. After the war he was part of several touring companies, including the Ulster Group Theatre in the 1950s. He worked extensively on the stage throughout his career.

DIAMOND, ARNOLD (1915–1992)
Born: London
Role: Major-General Anstruther Stephenson ('My Brother and I') (TV)
Arnold started his working life as a librarian, acting as an amateur during the evenings.

During the war he was wounded and taken to an Italian hospital for POWs. Whilst there he wrote and directed plays for fellow prisoners. After demob he decided to try it professionally, studying at RADA, before working in various reps around the country, such as Bolton and Southwold. He later worked with the Royal Shakespeare Company in Stratford.

Many years in rep followed before his TV career began to dominate. He appeared in *The Borgias*, *Randall & Hopkirk (Deceased)* as a poker player, *Citizen Smith* and *Master Spy*. His final appearance in a series was *In Sickness and in Health*. Among his 60 plus films are classics such as *The Italian Job*, *The Constant Husband*, *Carry On Sergeant* (as the 5th Specialist treating Kenneth Connor), *Zeppelin* and the 1961 picture, *The Frightened City*, appearing as Moffat.

Although most of his roles were small, his services were in demand in every aspect of the entertainment business, including theatre and radio, particularly playing suave official types. Arnold died in 1992 after being hit by a car. He was 77.

DIG FOR VICTORY
This campaign, launched in October 1939, urged townsfolk to turn their gardens over to growing vegetables. Royal parks set the example by replacing geraniums with cabbages, while railway embankments and bombsites were also cultivated. The number of allotments in use increased substantially as the campaign caught on.

DIGBY
An employee of the Walmington branch of Swallow Bank, Digby never featured in any of the episodes but the character, whom Mainwaring referred to as an 'old fool', was mentioned in the original script of 'Battle School'. This scene was eventually cut before the episode was recorded.

DOCTOR, THE
Played by Roger Avon (TV); Norman Ettlinger (radio)
In the episode, 'Branded', the doctor treats Godfrey at his home after an ordeal that involved saving Mainwaring from a smoke-filled hut during a civil defence exercise.

DOCTOR, THE
Played by Tim Barrett (TV)
This doctor runs the two-day blood-donoring session at Walmington church hall during the episode, 'When You've Got to Go'.

DOG AND PARTRIDGE, THE
In 'My Brother and I', this Walmington pub is mentioned by Pikey in an article he pens for a writing competition about the Home Guard.

DOIG, CLIVE
Vision mixer on five episodes (TV): S1, episodes 1, 5 & 6; S4, episode 9 & 12; production assistant on two episodes (TV): S2, episode 5 & 6
Clive, who joined the BBC in 1958, had worked with David Croft on several of his shows, including the popular sitcom *Hugh and I*, before joining the production team for *Dad's Army*.

After completing his education he travelled Europe before joining the Beeb's technical operations team. Once he had undergone training at the BBC's engineering college he joined the camera crews. When a vision mixer was taken ill, Clive stepped in and from then on he continued vision mixing for seven years before turning his attention to directing. Among his many credits in this capacity is *Vision On*, which he directed and produced.

Clive left the BBC in 1981 and formed his own production company, Brechin Productions Ltd.

DON, MAGGIE
Role: Waitress (S5, episode 10: 'Brain versus Brawn') (TV)
Other TV credits include playing Louise Perrott in Granada's 1968 production, *The War of Darkie Pilbeam*, Liz in the BBC show, *Spice Island*, *Farewell* in 1976, and *Hazlitt in Love* for Thames a year later.

DON'T FENCE ME IN
Recorded: Friday 10/7/70
Original transmission: Friday 23/10/70, 8.00–8.30pm
Original viewing figures: 16.4 million
Repeated: 27/6/71, 7/11/92, 12/11/92 (Wales), 24/5/94, 10/5/97, 7/5/01

CAST
Arthur Lowe	Captain Mainwaring
John Le Mesurier	Sergeant Wilson
Clive Dunn	Lance Corporal Jones
John Laurie	Private Frazer
James Beck	Private Walker
Arnold Ridley	Private Godfrey
Ian Lavender	Private Pike
Edward Evans	General Monteverdi
John Ringham	Captain Bailey
Larry Martyn	Italian POW

Platoon: Colin Bean, Desmond Cullum-Jones, George Hancock, Hugh Cecil, Hugh Hastings, Freddie Wiles, Vic Taylor, Leslie Noyes, Frank Godfrey, Ken Wade
MPs: Derek Shaffer, Anthony Powell
Italian POWs: Jeremy Higgins, Lee Warren, Peter Morre, Trevor Lawrence, Mario Zoppellini, Ronnie Laughlan, M N Eddy, Roy Kanaris, Tony Cordell, Steve Cornell, Ian Selman, Paul Holroy, Robert Marshall, Antonio Di Maggio, Clive Rogers, Andrew Andreas, Steve Peters

PRODUCTION TEAM
Script: Jimmy Perry and David Croft
Producer: David Croft
Production Assistant: Donald Clive

Director: Harold Snoad
Film Cameraman: Stewart Farnell
Film Sound: Les Collins
Film Editor: Bill Harris
Lighting: Howard King
Studio Sound: John Holmes
Design: Paul Joel
Assistant Floor Manager: David Taylor
Vision Mixer: Dave Hanks
Costume Supervisor: Barbara Kronig
Make-Up Supervisor: Cynthia Goodwin

The Colonel calls Mainwaring to tell him his men will be taken off active duty for the next two weekends to relieve the regular guards at an Italian POW camp, holding 60 men. When Mainwaring and his men arrive at the camp there's no one in sight: the guards have already left and the prisoners are taking a siesta!

Walker knows the Italian general and is overheard telling him he'll get all the prisoners out via the escape tunnel. Although Walker is in fact helping the Italians to get to his shed where they help him to repair radios, Mainwaring suspects he's a fifth columnist.

That evening Walker is caught loading the men into Jones' van, and has some explaining to do. Meanwhile, Mainwaring gets stuck in the tunnel and Captain Bailey arrives wanting to count the POWs, so a little skulduggery is called for during this evening of mayhem.

DON'T FORGET THE DIVER

Recorded: Friday 24/7/70
Original transmission: Friday 2/10/70, 8.00–8.30pm
Original viewing figures: 12.3 million
Repeated: 6/6/71, 3/3/85, 12/5/85 (N Ireland), 24/10/92, 29/10/92 (Wales), 10/2/96, 14/3/96 (Wales), 19/11/00

CAST

Arthur Lowe . . . . .Captain Mainwaring
John Le Mesurier . . . . .Sergeant Wilson
Clive Dunn . . . . .Lance Corporal Jones
John Laurie . . . . .Private Frazer
James Beck . . . . .Private Walker
Arnold Ridley . . . . .Private Godfrey
Ian Lavender . . . . .Private Pike
Bill Pertwee . . . . .ARP Warden
Edward Sinclair . . . . .Verger
Frank Williams . . . . .Vicar
Geoffrey Lumsden . . . . . . .Captain Square
Robert Raglan . . . . .HG Sergeant
Colin Bean . . . . .Private Sponge
Don Estelle . . . . .2nd ARP Warden
Verne Morgan . . . . .Landlord
Platoon: Desmond Cullum-Jones, Freddie Wiles, Hugh Hastings, Vic Taylor, Leslie Noyes, Frank Godfrey, Freddie White, Ken Wade.
Extras: Eileen Matthews (Woman in Pub); Leonard Kingston, Thomas Liard, Geoffrey Brighty, Francis Batfoni, Bill Lodge, Charles Faynor, Paul Blomley (Soldiers)
Stuntman: Johnny Scripps

PRODUCTION TEAM

Script: Jimmy Perry and David Croft
Producer: David Croft
Production Assistant: Donald Clive
Director: Harold Snoad
Film Cameraman: Stewart Farnell
Film Sound: Les Collins
Film Editor: Bill Harris
Lighting: Howard King
Studio Sound: Michael McCarthy
Design: Paul Joel
Assistant Floor Manager: David Taylor
Vision Mixer: Dave Hillier
Costume Supervisor: Barbara Kronig
Make-Up Supervisor: Cynthia Goodwin
Visual Effects: John Friedlander and Ron Oates

There's a big exercise on Sunday and all Home Guard units are involved. With Captain Square and the Eastgate platoon occupying a windmill, Mainwaring's men have to lay high explosives in the windmill without being caught. While the platoon discuss their plans, the Verger creeps around listening out for any snippets of information he can pass on to Captain Square because he's tired of the way Mainwaring's men treat him.

The plan is that Frazer, who'll be dressed in a diving suit, will push an artificial log up river. A message will be relayed and a diversion will attract Square's attention, at which time, Jones, who'll be inside the log, will advance towards the windmill, climb the ladder and throw the bomb inside the mill window.

They practise their routine. On the day of the exercise the Verger is keeping a look out from a nearby graveyard. The plan proceeds well but Jones can't open the flap in the log and falls into the river. But he sorts himself out while Walker and Godfrey launch the second diversion to make Square believe the men are disguised as sheep. Jones reaches the windmill, climbs the ladder on the side of the mill, and throws the explosive inside before getting tangled on one of the sails. But Square is a bad loser and refuses to surrender.

DON'T PANIC!
THE DAD'S ARMY STORY

Transmitted: BBC1, Sunday 28/5/00, 6.40–7.30pm
To coincide with the 60th anniversary of the Home Guard's formation, this was the first documentary dedicated solely to Dad's Army. It was produced by BBC Manchester.

DOREEN

Played by Gilda Perry (TV)

The 28-year-old Doreen is a busy woman: not only does she work as a cashier at the Plaza Cinema in Walmington ('The Lion has 'Phones'), but she also helps out at lunchtimes in the British Restaurant ('The Two and a Half Feathers').

DOREEN

Played by Bernice Adams (TV)

An ATS girl, Doreen has a phone conversation with a Scottish sergeant in 'Number Engaged'. They fix a date to visit the Regal Cinema.

DORIS

Played by Janet Mahoney (TV)

Doris, a tall blonde, works as a barmaid at The Six Bells pub, a quiet place in the country, or it was until the Walmington Home Guard arrive dressed as German soldiers in 'Ring Dem Bells'. While Mainwaring was phoning GHQ, the platoon became hot hanging around in the van, so nipped over to the pub for a swift drink.

DORIS AND DORA

Played by Vicki and Cathy Graham (The Graham Twins) (TV)

Twin sisters, Doris and Dora are invited to the platoon dance by Walker in 'War Dance'.

DORNING, ROBERT (1913–1989)

Born: St Helens
Role: Bank Inspector (S3, episode 5: 'Something Nasty in the Vault') (TV)

Robert trained as a ballet dancer before turning to musical comedy prior to the war. Following demob from the RAF, he resumed his career in musical comedies and moved into acting.

He worked for three years with Arthur Lowe in Granada's Pardon the Expression playing Walter Hunt, having previously appeared with him in Coronation Street. He also spent four years in Bootsie and Snudge (1960–1964), with Clive Dunn, and appeared in countless other comedies and dramas, including Bergerac.

Robert made over 25 films including 1940's They Came By Night, The Secret Man, No Safety Ahead, Company of Fools, Dreamhouse, Man Accused, The Black Windmill and Carry On Emmanuelle playing the Prime Minister.

DOUBLEDAY, MAJOR

A non-speaking character, the Major attends the sherry party thrown by the Home Guard officers in 'My Brother and I'.

DOUGLAS, SALLY (1942–c 1992)

Role: Blodwen (S3, episode 9: 'War Dance') (TV)

At the age of 15, Sally Douglas decided that her ambition was to become an actress, so she contacted an agent, who told her she was too young and to try again in two years. Upon leaving school she worked as a secretary in an iron foundry before approaching the agent again when she was 17. Although he tried dissuading her from joining the profession, she remained intent on making a living from acting.

Sally achieved her goal and went on to appear in several films and various TV shows, such as Weekend with Lulu, playing a can-can girl. Her other small-screen credits include an appearance as a stripper in an episode of *Doctor in the House*, Susie in a 1970 episode of *On the Buses* and a rent-a-girl in *Up Pompeii!*. On the big screen, she popped up in five *Carry On* movies, playing an Amazon Guard in *Spying*, Antony's dusky maiden in *Cleo*, Kitkata in *Cowboy*, a girl in *Screaming*, a harem girl in *Follow That Camel* and a girl at Dirty Dick's in *Jack*. She was also seen in the 1968 picture, *Witchfinder General* and the strangely titled, *Can Heironymus Merkin Ever Forget Mercy Humppe and Find True Happiness?* a year later.

DOWDESWELL, CAROLINE (1945–)

Born: Oldham

Role: Janet King (S1: episodes 1, 2, 3, 4, 6). (TV) She appeared in the fifth episode, but the scene was cut. Caroline, whose grandparents were actors, knew from an early age it was the life for her. At the age of 12 she attended theatre school for four years and joined her first company, Bromley Rep, aged 17, moving to York a year later.

After appearing in *Dad's Army*, Caroline made a good living out of acting for a further ten years until retiring from the profession in 1978 due to ill health. She'd worked mainly on TV, presenting the Sunday evening religious programme *Friends and Neighbours*, appearing as Thora Hird's daughter, Vera Parker, in two series of *Ours is a Nice House*, as Anna in *Casanova*, in *Softly, Softly, Redcap*, as Miss Parton in *Murder Must Advertise* and six months in *Crossroads* as Ann Taylor, David Hunter's secretary and love interest. She was also seen in numerous sitcoms, including *Man About the House*, as Richard O'Sullivan's girlfriend, as Sandra in *On the Buses* and in *Billy Liar*.

Caroline is now a partner in a publishing company, often travelling the world on business. The company publishes a course on how to wheel and deal in the futures and commodities market, plus books and newsletters.

Designer Paul Joel's photo shows the Swallow Bank set.

MY MEMORIES OF *DAD'S ARMY*

'I remember being rather underwhelmed when I initially read for the part of Janet King. David Croft told me that he didn't want any women in the series at all, but that Michael Mills, then the head of comedy at the BBC, said he couldn't possibly do a comedy series without sex. I don't remember being remotely sexy in a 1940s wig, and David Croft was proved right; in fact *Dad's Army* has been possibly the most successful comedy series ever with the only mention remotely of sex being Mrs Pike and Sergeant Wilson!

'I also remember being taken aback at the read-through on the first day, because upon reading the cast list I had imagined John Le Mesurier and Arthur Lowe in the opposite roles – so had most of the others there.

'It was enjoyable working with the rest of the cast. I was at York Rep in 1963 as ASM and juvenile aged 18. Jimmy Beck came up to play in *The Merchant of Venice* and was considered by one and all to be the finest Shylock they had seen. I was on the prompt book and remember sobbing my heart out during rehearsals as he gave a truly poignant performance. He was certainly underrated as an actor following *Dad's Army* and it was a tremendous shock to everyone when he died so prematurely.

'I was about 22 during the first series of *Dad's Army* but extremely naïve. I gravitated towards dear old Arnold Ridley as I already knew him via my agent, but was somewhat taken aback as the old boy used to tell the most risqué of jokes! I was rather shocked – it was as if the Pope swore. He and John Laurie had a sort of rivalry going between them as to who should be the most venerated. Arnold was only a couple of years older than John, but all the make-up girls used to rush around with cups of tea and chairs for him, whereas poor old John was left to fend for himself. He used to get very disgruntled and mutter away about being neglected.

'Meanwhile, John Le Mesurier somehow or other adopted the role of Grand Seigneur. I could never find a make-up girl to powder me down as they were all fussing over either Arnold or John. John always had about three of them at a time: one doing his hair, one giving him a manicure and another running errands or getting him a sandwich. He was always so languid and would call everyone 'dear lady' in a world-wearied drawl whilst they fell over themselves to fetch and carry for him. As Arthur Lowe didn't feature highly on their list of priorities I later on developed the idea that the make-up department and crew were subconsciously reacting to the social class of the characters that we all played.

'I was invited to dinner once at Arthur Lowe's house. I was somewhat intimidated by him although he had been a great favourite of mine as Leonard Swindley in *Coronation Street*. Somehow I always thought of him as a cloth-capped northerner, so I was gobsmacked to find that he lived in an elegant mews house in Knightsbridge, and after dinner he entertained us by playing on the spinet! He was an extremely intelligent and articulate man, but very modest and retiring. He used to disappear straight after rehearsals – I can't remember him ever going to the bar with the rest of us. I liked his wife, Joan, too, and she occasionally did a line here and there on the series.'

CAROLINE DOWDESWELL

DOWDING, MRS

Played by May Warden (TV)

An old woman who enters the church hall in 'The Bullet is Not for Firing', interrupting the court of inquiry in the process. The original script for 'The Day the Balloon Went Up' had the character appearing again, this time trying her best to help hold the stray barrage balloon, but the role in the actual recording was taken by Miss Godfrey.

Note: A different and much younger Mrs Dowding is seen in the episode, 'War Dance', attending the platoon dance with her husband.

DOWNSEND WOODS

In 'Man Hunt' a suspicious-looking man asks Hodges, who's preoccupied trying to recover a parachute from a tree, the way to Downsend Woods, a few miles from Walmington. The man is suspected of being a German, but turns out to be an Austrian ornithologist.

DRAKE, VERNON (1897–1987)

Born: Gateshead

Role: Member of the platoon's back row in seven episodes ('The Love of Three Oranges'; S9) (TV)

Vernon, who represented the Royal Flying Corp

at singing during the Great War, was a well-known music hall and variety performer. For 25 years he was part of the successful double-act, Connor and Drake, playing the straight man, as well as appearing in many successful musical comedies. Although he didn't appear on TV a great deal, he worked at Covent Garden for 20 years, appearing in small acting roles. He died at the age of 90.

DRIVER, THE

Played by Felix Bowness (TV)

He drives the coach which is used by the OAPs to take them out on their annual party in 'Everybody's Trucking'. The Vicar and Verger are also in the coach when it stops to try and help pull Jones' and Hodges' vans out of the mud; but the coach gets stuck, too.

DRIVER'S MATE, THE

The driver's mate is heard in the radio version of 'The Royal Train'. (See 'Bob'.)

DRURY, MR

Played by Ronnie Brandon (TV)

Mr Drury owns a funeral director's in Walmington, and appears in 'No Spring for Frazer'. He deals with the funeral arrangements for Horace Blewitt.

DUNN, CLIVE (1920–)

Born: London

Role: Lance Corporal Jones (all TV episodes and *Christmas Night with the Stars* inserts; the film, the stage show and all radio episodes)

Clive's parents were in the entertainment business and his grandfather was a music hall comedian in the 1890s, so it came as no surprise when he entered the profession at the age of 16. However, he made his acting debut even before leaving school, appearing in the Will Hay films, *Boys Will Be Boys* and *Good Morning Boys*.

Clive made his professional stage debut during Christmas 1936 in a production of *Where the Rainbow Ends*, playing a dancing frog and a flying dragon at the Holborn Empire. The following years were spent in a national tour of *Peter Pan*, working with a touring revue and in rep at Abergavenny before war was declared. He volunteered to serve his country and was called up in 1940. Initially serving with the 52 Heavy Training Regiment, he was later transferred to the 4th Queen's Own Hussars.

He fought in the Greek campaign before being captured. After spells in three POW camps he was transported via cattle trucks to Austria, where he spent four years in Nazi labour camps. When locked in a room for periods of time, he starting drawing portraits to entertain his fellow inmates, and so his passion for drawing began. Although he gave up art after the war when his acting career took over, he has resumed his interest in drawing, painting and sculpting in recent years.

In 1945, after marching across Austria for four weeks, he was finally released from the camp thanks to American soldiers. Two years later, he was demobbed and returned to the stage, spending many years working in theatres and music halls, including the famous Players Theatre in London. Although he'd made his debut on television back in 1947 with Frank Muir at Alexandra Palace, it wasn't until the early 1960s that he became a household name playing Old Johnson in *Bootsie and Snudge*. When the offer to play Jones in *Dad's Army* came along, Clive was appearing in *The World of Beachcomber* with Spike Milligan.

Other small screen successes have included numerous roles in *It's A Square World*, and numerous children's shows, including playing the old caretaker in *Children's Caravan* and his own series, *My Old Man*. He played Charlie Quick in the 1970s children's show *Grandad*, a programme he devised. He also recorded the theme song which reached number one in November 1970, and stayed in the charts for 27 weeks.

Clive, who was awarded the OBE in 1975, has had a successful career on stage and screen. Among the myriad of highlights are appearances in Royal Command Performances, time with the National Opera Company where he played Frosch in *Die Fledermaus*, and nine months at the Palladium, with second billing to the legendary Tommy Cooper.

Nowadays Clive, who's married to actress Priscilla Morgan, divides his time between homes in London and Portugal.

TV credits include: *New Faces, Treasure Island, After Hours, Beachcomber*.

Theatre credits include: *Where the Rainbow Ends, Everybody Cheer, Don't Shoot, We're English, The Bed Sitting Room, The Chiltern Hundreds, An Italian Straw Hat*.

Films include: *You Must Be Joking, Just Like a Woman, Thirty is a Dangerous Age, The Fiendish Plot of Dr Fu Manchu, She'll Have to Go*.

Radio credits include: *Hancock*.

DUNN, LINDSEY

Role: Small Boy (S6, episode 7: 'The Recruit') (TV)

The small boy, Hamish, takes the mickey out of the Home Guard and the wardens. He turns out to be Hodges' nephew. Lindsey was a child actor who has now left the profession.

DUNN, MARTIN

Role: Member of the platoon's back row in five episodes (S3, episodes 8, 9, 11, 12; S4, episode 2) (TV)

DUNSTAN, JOHN

Film editor on four episodes (TV): S9, episodes 1, 2, 3 & 5

After leaving school John, from Newcastle upon Tyne, dreamt of working in entertainment, but as his dreams were yet unfocused he chose to train as a solicitor. He qualified in 1966 but was by then confirmed in his belief that this was not the life for him, and had already made applications to the BBC and Tyne-Tees Television.

He moved to the capital and, concentrating on the film side of the profession, attempted to join the BBC's editing training course only to be told that he lacked professional experience. After writing to a myriad of film companies he was finally given a chance by the Overseas Film and Television Centre in London. During his two-year stay he was occasionally able to assist an editor working on BBC programmes, including *The Frost Report*, *Monty Python's Flying Circus* and *Marty*.

When the 'overseas' side of the work collapsed, John was made redundant but managed to join the BBC in 1969 as a holiday relief assistant film editor. After spending nearly two years working on a current affairs programme, he was, in 1971, appointed to a permanent post and then in 1976 promoted to film editor having already begun specialising in comedy.

By the time he left the Beeb in 1995, he'd worked on countless top shows, including *The Dick Emery Show*, *Porridge*, *The Two Ronnies*, *Happy Ever After*, *The Good Life*, *Rings On Their Fingers*, *To the Manor Born*, *Rosie*, *Sorry!*, *Yes, Minister*, *Bread*, *One Foot in the Grave*, *Only Fools and Horses*, *'Allo! 'Allo!* and *Waiting for God*. Since turning freelance, he's continued to work on hit series such as *Next of Kin*, *Roger, Roger* and *Bob Martin*.

DUTCH OVEN, THE

A bakery/coffee shop in Walmington, The Dutch Oven is never seen but is mentioned by Pike in 'Mum's Army'. He tells the rest of the platoon that Mr Mainwaring and Mrs Gray meet there. They used to patronise Ann's Pantry but kept seeing too many familiar faces.

DYMCHURCH

The Kent coastal town got a mention in 'Wake-Up Walmington'. During a phone conversation with Mainwaring, the Colonel mentions that he inspected the Dymchurch Home Guard recently and there were so many absentees it reminded him of 'walking down a fish queue'.

DYMWHICH

A town near Walmington-on-Sea. Never visited in the life of the sitcom, but referred to on occasions, for example in 'Round and Round Went the Great Big Wheel'. It has its own Home Guard platoon, led by Captain Graham.

In many ways, Captain Mainwaring was an inspiration to his men – a true fighter.

EARLLE, FREDDIE

Born: Glasgow

Roles: Henry (S6, episode 3: 'The Royal Train'), Italian Sergeant (S7, episode 8: 'When You've Got to Go') (TV)

Freddie was only five when he made his first radio broadcast with his school's percussion band. He always wanted to act and worked in various amateur companies before joining the army at the start of the Second World War. Between 1943 and 1945 he toured India in a concert party, providing good experience for his later appearances in *It Ain't Half Hot, Mum*. After demob, he set up double-acts initially with a friend and later with his first wife.

After his agent persuaded him to have a nose job to reduce its size, he made his first TV appearance wearing a false one while impersonating Jimmy Durante, renowned for his large nose!

Other TV credits include: *Cool for Cats* during the 1950s, two years of Granada's *People and Places*, children's show *Play Time*, numerous appearances in *The Bill* and various commercials. He also worked on one series of *Room Service*, written by Jimmy Perry in the late 1970s, and two of *It's a Square World*, with Clive Dunn.

EAST LITTLETON

The Home Guard unit at East Littleton is mentioned briefly by Frazer in 'A Stripe for Frazer', when he announces they're playing them at the weekend and he's looking for a referee. It's not clear which sport they intend to play.

EASTBOURNE GAZETTE

The regional newspaper employs Mr Cheeseman as a photo-journalist, who first appears in 'My British Buddy'. Although Walmington has its own local rag (as mentioned in the radio version of 'Sons of the Sea') the *Eastbourne Gazette* is read in the area. It ran a series of articles focusing on Mainwaring's platoon.

EASTGATE

The town of Eastgate is ten miles along the coast from Walmington. Its Home Guard unit is controlled by Captain Square, ably assisted by Sergeant Parkins, who we see in 'Battle of the Giants!'.

EASTGATE HOSPITAL

The hospital is not seen during the series, but in 'The Desperate Drive of Corporal Jones', Walker refers to it because he's made three scooters and is giving them to the kiddies there.

EASTGATE MORRIS DANCERS

The dancers give a display to help mark the climax of Walmington's 'Wings for Victory' campaign in 'Knights of Madness'.

ECCLES, MR AND MRS

Guests at the platoon dance in the episode 'War Dance'.

EDEN, ANTHONY (1897–1977)

A former Conservative prime minister (1955–1957), he was the secretary for war and then foreign secretary during the Second World War. His speech, during which he announced the LDV's formation, was heard on the radio at Mainwaring's office in the bank during the first TV episode, 'The Man and the Hour', and at Elliott's Radio Store in the film.

EDNA

Played by Queenie Watts (TV); Avril Angers (radio)

The loud-mouthed manageress of the British Restaurant in Walmington is seen in 'The Two and a Half Feathers'.

EDWARDS, PERCY (1908–1996)

Born: Ipswich

Role: Percy the Parrot 'The Battle of Godfrey's Cottage' (radio)

From the age of 12 Percy was entertaining friends and family with his wildlife impressions. He was first heard on the radio in the 1930 series *Vaudeville*, and went on to make hundreds of broadcasts until retiring from the business in 1989. He became well known for his creations: Gregory the chicken in *Ray's A Laugh* and Psyche the dog in *A Life of Bliss*.

Percy's voice was also in demand for films and television, including productions like *Orca – Killer Whale* and *The Belstone Fox*. He was awarded an MBE in 1993.

EGAN, E C

Played by Freddie Trueman (TV); Anthony Smee (radio)

Ernie Egan, a professional cricketer, turns out for the wardens in a match against the Home Guard in 'The Test'. Hodges keeps his inclusion secret and is confident he'll rip Mainwaring's team apart. But his plans are soon disrupted when Egan pulls a muscle bowling his first ball and has to retire hurt.

Note: In the radio version, 'The Test', the character is called G C Egan.

ELGOOD, PRIVATE

Not seen or heard in the sitcom, Elgood is a member of the Walmington Home Guard. In 'When You've Got to Go' Wilson classes him as ineligible to donate blood and whispers the reason to Mainwaring, fuelling speculation that he's got some embarrassing condition.

ELLIOTT'S RADIO STORE

(Film only)

Elliott's is the store Mainwaring, Wilson and Pike visit to hear Eden's speech on the radio. It is situated in Walmington High Street.

ELLIS, BRYAN

BBC designer on series 7

Born in Wallasey, Merseyside, Bryan left school and worked in architectural design before joining the BBC as an assistant designer in 1967. During his national service he worked in a drawing office for the Royal Engineers, helping design, amongst other things, bridges. Upon returning to civvy street he worked for an architect in Chester for two years, before briefly working in exhibition design prior to joining the Beeb.

Within a couple of years he was promoted to designer and went on to work on shows such as *It Ain't Half Hot, Mum*, *Some Mothers Do 'Ave 'Em*, *The Dick Emery Show*, *The Dave Allen Show* and *Hold the Back Page*.

Bryan took voluntary redundancy from the BBC in 1992 and worked freelance for a while, including working on *Absolutely Fabulous* (he'd worked on the first series while still at the Beeb). He's now retired from the business.

ELSBURY, GORDON
Production assistant on series 9
Gordon, who died in 1994, worked as assistant stage manager at Glasgow's Citizens' Theatre in the late 1960s before joining BBC Scotland and working on *Dr Finlay's Casebook*. He transferred to Television Centre in London and continued working in drama until he became David Croft's production assistant on *Dad's Army*. Later on in his career he returned to the drama department.

For a time, Gordon ran his own rollerdisco alongside his BBC job, after spotting the potential for such a business while holidaying in the States.

EMMETT, E V H (1902–1971)
The voice behind the Gaumont-British and Universal News which kept the nation informed of worldwide events via newsreels, particularly during the war years. Emmett went on to become an associate producer at Ealing Studios after the war, making documentaries. Each episode in the first series of *Dad's Army* began by combining original newsreel clippings and Perry and Croft's own version, with Emmett as the announcer.

ENEMY WITHIN THE GATES, THE
Recorded: Monday 6/5/68 (made in black and white)
Original transmission: Wednesday 28/8/68/, 8.20–8.50pm
Original viewing figures: 8.1 million
Repeated: 7/2/69, 4/8/98, 11/8/98 (Wales), 24/5/99

CAST
Arthur Lowe . . . . .Captain Mainwaring
John Le Mesurier . . . . .Sergeant Wilson
Clive Dunn . . . . .Lance Corporal Jones
John Laurie . . . . .Private Frazer
James Beck . . . . .Private Walker
Arnold Ridley . . . . .Private Godfrey
Ian Lavender . . . . .Private Pike
Caroline Dowdeswell . . . . .Janet King
Carl Jaffé . . . . .Captain Winogrodzki
Denys Peek and
Nigel Rideout . . . . .German Pilots
Bill Pertwee . . . . .ARP Warden
David Davenport . . . . .Military Police Sergeant
Platoon: Colin Bean, Hugh Hastings, Richard Jacques, Alec Coleman, Hugh Cecil, Vic Taylor, Jimmy Mac, Peter Whitaker
Other Military Police: Michael Ely, Joe Santo, Dennis Balcombe

PRODUCTION TEAM
Script: Jimmy Perry and David Croft
Producer/Director: David Croft
Production Assistant: Harold Snoad

Lighting: George Summers
Studio Sound: James Cole
Design: Alan Hunter-Craig and Paul Joel
Assistant Floor Manager: Evan King
Vision Mixer: Bob Hallman
Costume Supervisor: George Ward
Make-Up Supervisor: Sandra Exelby

The Walmington Home Guard is gradually being supplied with kit. So far they have five rifles, rounds of ammunition for each rifle, four hot water bottles and a cap each. Mainwaring gives a lecture on German agents and the various disguises they'll use. When a foreign-speaking

'The Enemy Within the Gates'

captain strolls in to the church hall and asks for information about the weapons they have, Mainwaring seems only too happy to help. But when Wilson points out he could be a German, Mainwaring puts him under arrest and tries to find out if he really is German with the aid of a a pronunciation test and a general knowledge test.

The captain is found to be from the Polish Free Forces attached to GHQ. He informs the platoon that GHQ are concerned that British pilots could be shot by mistake if the Home Guard shoot lone pilots who bail out of their planes. Therefore a bounty of £10 will be paid for every pilot captured alive. Walker can't believe his luck, particularly as he's on patrol with Jones and Pike that evening. Pound signs ring up in his eyes.

That night two German airmen bail out of their plane, and are caught and taken to the church hall. Godfrey foolishly allows the Germans to go and wash their hands. They run away, but the Polish captain saves the day by recapturing the prisoners, and says he'll claim the reward instead.

When the MP arrives, he assumes there are three prisoners. Walker doesn't put him straight

and the Polish captain is arrested as well. Walker therefore receives £30 bounty which can be claimed from brigade HQ. As there's an extra £10 in the kitty, Mainwaring calls for a celebratory platoon dinner and Walker suggests roast swan on the menu.

Note: Nigel Rideout was paid an extra £10 for writing the German dialogue in the script.

ENGINEER OFFICER, THE
Played by Michael Knowles (TV)
Arrives on the beach in 'Sgt – Save My Boy!' to help rescue Pike who's caught in barbed wire and in danger of being cut off by the tide.

ENGLISH, ARTHUR (1919–1995)
Born: Aldershot
Role: Policeman (S4, episode 6: 'Absent Friends') (TV)
Arthur began his career by entertaining fellow soldiers during the Second World War. He turned professional after demob, having worked as a waiter and shop assistant before the war, and as a navvy and painter and decorator afterwards.

Beginning his career as a light comedian, he toured music halls for years, after initial success at the Windmill Theatre. He became well known for his spiv character Tosh, and Prince of the Wideboys, wearing a white trilby, outrageously shoulder-padded suit, pencil moustache and kipper tie.

A radio favourite in the early 1950s – he became resident comedian on *Variety Bandbox* in 1951 – Arthur realised his variety days were numbered and moved towards TV and straight theatre roles during the 1960s. After several lean years, he began a busy small-screen career which included *How's Your Father?* playing Ted Cropper, the stablehand in the 1970s children's series *Follyfoot*, Doolittle in a production of *Pygmalion*,

Never Say Die, a traffic warden in *Bless this House*, *Dixon of Dock Green* and Alf Garnett's mate in *In Sickness and in Health*.

He appeared in a handful of mainly low-budget films, including *The Hi-Jackers* as a lorry driver, *Echo of Diana* as a bookmaker, *Percy, Love Thy Neighbour* and *For the Love of Ada*. Arthur died at the age of 75.

ENSA

The Entertainments National Service Association (ENSA) was formed before the Second World War to come into operation at the start of hostilities, providing entertainment of all sorts for the troops at home and abroad. It was directed by Basil Dean and was based at Drury Lane Theatre, London. The Association worked alongside the NAAFI (Navy, Army and Air Force Institute), which was responsible for the finances. It provided all types of entertainment, not only in the camps and factories of Britain, but on all the war fronts as well.

ESPLANADE HOTEL, THE

Mentioned in 'Never Too Old', the hotel at Eastgate is where Jones decided to spend his honeymoon after marrying Mrs Fox, but when the platoon are placed on standby, his plans are scuppered.

ESTELLE, DON

Born: Manchester
Roles: Man from Pickfords (S3, episode 7: 'Big Guns'), 2nd ARP Warden (S4, episode 2: 'Don't Forget the Diver'), Gerald (S4, episodes 10: 'The Test' & 12: 'Uninvited Guests') (TV)

Don, who sang from childhood, worked as an amateur singer at night in clubs during the 1950s, while working for a soft furnishing company during the day. After writing to Granada TV, he was given work as an extra in *Coronation Street* and several television plays.

Don will always be grateful to Arthur Lowe for helping lift his career from being a stand-up singer working the club circuit and occasional extra, to speaking parts on television. While appearing as a walk-on in *Coronation Street*, Don, on Arthur's advice, wrote to David Croft enquiring about a part in *Dad's Army*, and shortly after got a job.

Initially appearing as a removal man delivering a naval gun, he returned three times, establishing a semi-character called Gerald, who reported to Hodges. Don is best known for playing Lofty in *It Ain't Half Hot, Mum*, and singing the subsequent spin-off record, 'Whispering Grass' with Windsor Davies, which topped the charts in 1975.

Nowadays, he still sings around the world and runs his own music publishing company.

ETTLINGER, NORMAN

Roles: Sergeant ('Don't Forget the Diver'), Doctor ('Branded'), Clerk to the Court ('A Brush with the Law') and Pritchard ('Fallen Idol') (radio)

As well as working on radio, Norman appeared on stage, television and film. He was seen in the 1961 picture, *The Mask*, *Nobody Waved Goodbye*, four years later, and various shows on the small screen, including *I, Claudius*, playing a senator, as Percy Hoskins in *Rumpole of the Bailey* and in the 1978 mini-series, *Love for Lydia*. Norman died in 1979.

EVANS, EDWARD (1915–)

Born: London
Role: Mr Reed (S2, episode 3: 'The Loneliness of the Long-Distance Walker'), Mr Rees (S3, episode 7: 'Big Guns'), General Monteverdi (S4, episode 5: 'Don't Fence Me In') (TV)

Both Edward's parents were actors but he didn't follow in their footsteps immediately. After working in advertising and training as a pub cellarman, he secured some work in the late 1920s as a stuntman in films; this led to small parts and crowd work.

During the war, Edward, who speaks fluent Italian, served in Italy. He later utilised his language skills playing several Italian characters, such as General Monteverdi. After the war his big screen career began in earnest. He's since made over 30 films, among them *The Small Voice*, *The Man Upstairs* and *Till Death Us Do Part* (he also appeared in the TV series).

On TV he spent eight months of 1965 in *Coronation Street* as Lionel Petty, who bought the corner shop from Florrie Lindley. He was also seen in many episodes of *Compact*. His TV highlight was playing Bob Grove between 1954 and 1957 in BBC's first soap, *The Grove Family*. Edward has now retired from acting.

EVERYBODY'S TRUCKING

Recorded: Sunday 27/10/74

Original transmission: Friday 15/11/74, 7.45–8.15pm

Original viewing figures: 14.1 million

Repeated: 15/5/75, 14/5/91, 19/11/94, 16/2/95 (Wales), 30/11/97

CAST

Arthur Lowe	Captain Mainwaring
John Le Mesurier	Sergeant Wilson
Clive Dunn	Lance Corporal Jones
John Laurie	Private Frazer
Arnold Ridley	Private Godfrey
Ian Lavender	Private Pike
Bill Pertwee	Chief Warden Hodges
Frank Williams	Vicar
Edward Sinclair	Verger
Pamela Cundell	Mrs Fox
Harold Bennett	Mr Bluett
Olive Mercer	Mrs Yeatman
Felix Bowness	Driver
Colin Bean	Private Sponge

Platoon: Desmond Cullum-Jones, George Hancock, Evan Ross, Leslie Noyes, Freddie White, Freddie Wiles, Hugh Cecil, Roger Bourne, Michael Moore

Auntie Elsie: Nellie Griffiths

PRODUCTION TEAM

Script: Jimmy Perry and David Croft
Producer/Director: David Croft
Production Assistant: Bob Spiers
Film Cameraman: Len Newson
Film Sound: John Gatland
Film Editor: Bill Harris
Lighting: Howard King
Studio Sound: Michael McCarthy
Design: Bryan Ellis
Assistant Floor Managers: Anne Ogden and Sue Bennett-Urwin
Vision Mixer: Dave Hanks
Costume Supervisor: Susan Wheal
Make-Up Supervisor: Sylvia Thornton
Visual Effects: Jim Ward

Three battalions of regular troops are to move into the area of Walmington and Eastgate as part of the divisional scheme. The platoon are tasked with sign-posting the area; as sign posts have been removed, the men are asked to come up with some secret signs which will help the troops to travel safely.

One wrong sign and the whole scheme could be wrecked, a great responsibility for the warriors from Walmington and they head off cross-country to install the signs. The last signpost is erected but on their way back they can't get past an old traction engine, steam roller and caravan. A note from the driver says he's gone to collect some coal. Mainwaring decides to drive around the vehicles, against Wilson's better judgement, and gets stuck. They can't get the van out of the mud, so when Hodges drives along he's dragged in to help. But it's no good, before long Hodges' van is stuck, too.

When the Vicar and Verger come along with a coachload of OAPs on their annual party, they try to help but the coach gets stuck as well. With the convoy due down the road shortly, things are getting desperate. In the end it's down to Godfrey's Auntie Elsie to save the day by diverting the convoy.

EXELBY, SANDRA

Make-up supervisor on six episodes (TV): S1

After leaving school in Doncaster, where she grew up, Sandra moved to London to train in beauty therapy and hairdressing at the Jean Reid School of Beauty. Upon completion of her six-month course, she joined a beauty salon in Soho. Soon realising it wasn't the career for her, she applied to the BBC and joined the Corporation's training school in 1963 before working as an assistant make-up artist for two years.

During the ten years she spent at the Beeb she worked on countless shows, including *Doctor Who*. She left in 1972 to work freelance, initially for other TV companies, before moving into

MEMORIES OF BEING AN EXTRA

Thetford resident Tim Ball was lucky enough to be chosen to appear in an episode of *Dad's Army*. In 'Come In, Your Time is Up', originally transmitted in September 1975, Tim played the sea scout who's persuaded to play his bugle outside Mainwaring's tent. It was a memorable occasion for Tim.

'It all started with the bi-annual Thetford Scouts and Guides Gang Show. It was November 1974 and in the audience was a researcher from the BBC looking for some 'talent'. Three months later someone from the BBC contacted Ray Parish, leader of the 2nd Thetford, and told him he wanted to meet and tell us some 'exciting' news. I remember the evening well: it was troop night and we were told we'd been selected to be extras in a forthcoming episode of *Dad's Army*. We were to film in June and spend a Friday and Saturday filming. We were told what we'd be doing, and then the man from the BBC had a quiet word with Ray and said he wanted someone who could play a bugle to join the filming on the Wednesday as well. I was honoured to be asked and from that moment it seemed as if June would never come.

'When it did, our troop met up with all the stars at The Bell Hotel for an evening meal on the Monday. Afterwards a couple of them toddled off next-door to The Anchor, while the rest adjourned to the bar in The Bell, by which point it was time for the members of my troop to set off with Mary Husband, the costume designer, to have our short back and sides complete with brylcreem in the make-up caravan outside.

'Wednesday, the day of filming, finally arrived and it was a scorcher – so hot. My parents dropped me at The Bell, where Ray Parish and I sat chatting with Arthur Lowe and Ian Lavender, when all of a sudden there was great applause and cheering, for down the corridor came Clive Dunn grasping a copy of *The Daily Mirror* which bore the headlines: "Clive Dunn, OBE". We joined the cast for breakfast before setting off on the 15-minute coach journey to West Tofts, where the filming took place.

'After watching the cast film the keep-fit and rabbit stew scenes, it was my turn. We pretended to have a tent full of scouts when the "Come on boys, into the trees" bit was said by Frank Williams, but in fact it was only me in there. That only took about one hour to film. After lunch, Mary Husband made me up and explained what was going to happen – she really became a mum to us all. As the time for filming the bugle scene drew nearer, Bill Pertwee joked that if I got it right first time he would let me keep the sixpence! But then I got my first shock: when the guy from the Beeb came to our scout hut he had said he wanted the bugler to play reveille, which I practised until all the neighbours moved out! Now they wanted it to sound different, a bit more "painful".

'We practised for about one hour and then it was for real. It was planned for all the small tents to be full but it was so hot only Arthur was in his. I was very nervous but when the time came for shooting the butterflies went and it took just two takes. First time, one of my lips was too dry and the bugle just squeaked; after the hilarity ceased we did it again and all went well. Everybody clapped and we broke for tea. The remainder of the day was spent rehearsing for the next day's filming.

'On the Saturday it was time to film the pirate scenes, which took many takes as some of us got the giggles, along with the crew! I was amazed how long it took to film considering how short each part lasted in the actual episode. We finished at 5pm and went home buzzing after the day's events.

'As for my wages, I consider I did very well with £50 in my pocket, plus the sixpence Bill Pertwee let me keep. At the time I was 14, I'm now 38, but I still remember it as if it was yesterday. At school, I had to stand in front of everyone and tell them of my escapades. It was a great time.'

TIM BALL

films, including *Bugsy Malone*, *Highlander* and *Back to Secret Garden*. But she still occasionally works for TV, with recent projects including *Crazy Like A Fox* and *Around the World in 80 Days* with Eric Idle.

Sandra is also chairwoman for the National Association of Screen Make-up Artists and Hairdressers.

EXTRAS

Most of the extras used in *Dad's Army* were professionals, making a living out of walk-on parts. But when it came to scenes on location in Norfolk that required crowds or large groups of people, particularly for background shots, local residents were often given the chance to appear. Keith Eldred, who has run Thetford's drama society since 1969, became the contact point for the various production assistants, whose job it was to arrange for the necessary extras. Whenever people were required for background scenes, or non-speaking parts, Keith was contacted. He never had any problems recruiting the people, and always had too many volunteers. At first, they weren't paid, but eventually fees in the region of £7.50 plus fittings were paid per episode. Keith appeared himself as a fielder in 'The Test' and as an official observer in 'Round and Round Went the Great Big Wheel'.

Occasionally scenes required the services of local bands or specialists in a particular field to add authenticity; the Newmarket Town Band appeared in 'The Honourable Man', and received a payment of £100; in 'If the Cap Fits…', Pipe Major Donald Macleod received an appearance fee of £57, while £17.25 had to be paid for the use of the music.

SHOWING THE RUSHES

Brian Fisher, who lives in Thetford, worked at the town's cinema, and found himself entertaining the cast and crew of *Dad's Army* one evening.

'From 1956 until its closure in 1984, I was a relief projectionist at our local cinema, the Palace, which was actually used in the episode, "A Soldier's Farewell". On one occasion my stint in the projection box coincided with a period of location shooting. In those days it was all filmed on 35mm film stock, whereas nowadays it's on videotape. The day's footage was sent to laboratories in London for processing and returned the same day, without soundtrack, by Red Star rail service. I was asked to stay behind after the regular cinema programme to show the rushes to the cast and crew (about 25 people) who came up to the cinema to view them.

'I remember the train didn't reach Thetford until around 10pm and as there was half an hour to spare I offered to put on a reel of cartoons which was in our particular programme that week to keep them amused. This was much appreciated. When the reel of processed film arrived I spooled it up and ran it through for them, although it was only about 15 minutes' worth of location shots. For this extra hour I was paid the princely sum of £5 by the BBC, which I remember was pretty good because at that time my weekly wage was only about £20!'

BRIAN FISHER

FACE ON THE POSTER, THE

Recorded: Thursday 17/7/75

Original transmission: Friday 10/10/75, 8.00–8.30pm

Original viewing figures: 15.5 million

Repeated: 5/6/76, 18/6/91, 29/3/97

CAST

Arthur Lowe . . . . .Captain Mainwaring
John Le Mesurier . . . . .Sergeant Wilson
Clive Dunn . . . . .Lance Corporal Jones
John Laurie . . . . .Private Frazer
Arnold Ridley . . . . .Private Godfrey
Ian Lavender . . . . .Private Pike
Bill Pertwee . . . . .Chief Warden Hodges
Frank Williams . . . . .Vicar
Edward Sinclair . . . . .Verger
Peter Butterworth . . . . .Mr Bugden
Harold Bennett . . . . .Mr Bluett
Gabor Vernon . . . . .Polish Officer
Colin Bean . . . . .Private Sponge
Bill Tasker . . . . .Fred
Michael Bevis . . . . .Police Sergeant
Platoon: Desmond Cullum-Jones, Michael Moore,
George Hancock, Leslie Noyes, Hugh Cecil, Freddie
Wiles, Freddie White, Roger Bourne, Evan Ross

PRODUCTION TEAM

Script: Jimmy Perry and David Croft
Producer/Director: David Croft
Production Assistant: Jo Austin
Film Cameraman: Peter Chapman
Film Sound: Bill Chesneau
Film Editor: John Stothart
Studio Lighting: Howard King
Studio Sound: Alan Machin
Design: Robert Berk
Assistant Floor Manager: Anne Ogden
Vision Mixer: Dave Hanks
Costume Designer: Mary Husband
Make-Up Supervisor: Sylvia Thornton

There are changes in the air: Mainwaring thinks he'll become a major, as he has plans to make the platoon into a company. This would leave Wilson in line for promotion; not that Mainwaring has rated his sergeant highly in the report he has to complete on him – he points out there is room for improvement.

'The Face on the Poster'

Mainwaring has decided to begin a recruitment campaign in order to treble the platoon's size. A poster has been designed similar to Kitchener's: 'Your Country Needs You!', but as everyone wants to be the face of the campaign, a secret ballot is organised, which Jones wins.

Frazer knows a photographer, or so he says, so he arranges for Mr Bluett to come to the church hall to take Jones' photo, even if the set-up is a little antiquated.

Mr Bugden the printer is overloaded with work and not very organised. Wilson comes in with the poster design, not knowing that a police sergeant has been in before him wanting an escaped POW poster.

When the proof of the poster is delivered to Mainwaring, they realise the wrong head is on the poster. Jones's face is plastered all over the area as an escaped POW. While Jones is on his way to Mrs Prosser he sees the poster, so does a Polish Soldier who arrests him. Before long Jones is being interrogated by the Polish military and sent to the compound. Mr Bluett informs Mainwaring and the men that he saw Jones being driven off by Polish soldiers. The platoon visit Jones at the POW camp and before long they're being questioned by the Polish officer and end up in the camp themselves.

FACILITIES

The success of any show involving location shooting is determined by a number of factors, not least the helpfulness of local residents and services. During the years spent shooting scenes in the Norfolk countryside, many services were called upon to help in various ways. On 12 October 1972, the Norfolk County Council Fire Service Committee supplied water for the special effects involved in filming the burning house scene in 'Brain versus Brawn', for which they were paid £99.

Two days earlier the cast had completed a filming sequence at Bridge No 327 on the railway line between Forncett and Tivetshall, and British Railways (Eastern Region) at Norwich received a fee of £15.

Back in series one the Richmond Theatre was used to record the Charlie Cheeseman scenes in 'Shooting Pains', for which a facilities fee of £30 was paid, while £25 was paid to the military at Preston Barracks, Lewes Road, Brighton, the site used for filming indoor shots in 'We Know Our Onions' when a strike prevented the scenes being recorded in the studio.

FAIRBROTHER, TONY
Played by Anthony Roye (TV); Stuart Sherwin (radio)
Mr Fairbrother, who's seen in 'Brain versus Brawn', is Chairman of the Walmington Rotary Club as well as being managing director of Pre-

'The Face on the Poster'

cision Extrusions. Although Mainwaring sets out to introduce him to Wilson, his guest at the Rotarian dinner, it turns out Fairbrother and Wilson are old school buddies, having shared a study together in Meadowbridge.

FAIRMAN, BLAIN
Born: Canada
Role: US Sergeant (S6, episode 2: 'My British Buddy') (TV)
When Blain came to England in his early twenties to further his acting career, he was already an established performer in his native country. Since settling this side of the pond, he has worked on the stage, television and film, including the 1966 picture, *The Trap*, with Oliver Reed and Rita Tushingham. His other TV work includes playing the television presenter Sheridan Honeydew in *The Fall and Rise of Reginald Perrin*. He has also written and produced for the BBC and completed numerous voice overs.

Blain is now a partner in a London conference and production company.

FAITH, ROSEMARY
Born: Belfast
Roles: Ivy Samways (S4, episode 9: 'Mum's Army'), Barmaid ('Battle of the Giants'), Waitress (S7, episode 4: 'The Godiva Affair') (TV)
Diminutive Rosemary Faith first worked for David Croft in BBC's *Beggar My Neighbour* in 1967 as a hairdresser's assistant, and was subsequently offered the part of Deidre Garvey (the daughter of June Whitfield's character) in the following two series. Rosemary's involvement with *Dad's Army* began with Ivy Samways in 'Mum's Army', but when the character reappeared in 'My British Buddy', a stage engagement

in *Gypsy* meant that she was unavailable and the part went to Ian Lavender's then-wife, Suzanne Kerchiss.

Before attending drama school at the Webber Douglas Academy aged 17, Rosemary's first professional job was as a student acting-ASM in Bangor, County Down, for a summer season, followed by an Arts' Council tour of *The Reluctant Debutante*. The same year she also starred in an award-winning short amateur film screened at the National Film Theatre; but her first work was in amateur dramatics.

In the audience at the Press Show on her graduation from drama school were David Croft and his wife, whom she'd met whilst working as ASM in Coventry. Eight months later, while she was working in panto at Swansea, David offered her the part in *Beggar My Neighbour*.

Besides working in rep at Coventry and Swansea, during her early career Rosemary did several seasons at Worthing and Folkestone, toured around the country in shows such as *Lady Frederick*, *Under Milk Wood* and *One For*

the Pot and toured with Clive Dunn in *The Chiltern Hundreds*. She made her West End debut as Lucy Rabbit in *Toad of Toad Hall* after which she went on to play a multitude of animals, including Algy Pug in *The Rupert Show* at the Victoria Palace, and also Baby Bear and a Hip Hen in *Once Upon A Time* at the Duke of York. Her last West End appearance was at the Prince of Wales theatre in *Seven Brides for Seven Brothers*.

On radio she had a spell in *The Dales*, while on TV she appeared in the drama series *People Like Us*, *Oppenheimer*, the last 12 episodes of *Please, Sir!* and popped up in *The Goodies*. In the late-1980s she returned to Northern Ireland to nurse her mother, and upon resuming her career in 1988 soon decided to give up acting. Nowadays Rosemary works in theatre administration in Worthing.

FALLEN IDOL
Recorded: Friday 11/12/70
Original transmission: Friday 18/12/70, 8.00–8.30pm
Original viewing figures: 13.1 million
Repeated: 29/8/71, 17/3/85, 26/2/00

CAST
Arthur Lowe . . . . .Captain Mainwaring
John Le Mesurier . . . . .Sergeant Wilson
Clive Dunn . . . . .Lance Corporal Jones
John Laurie . . . . .Private Frazer
James Beck . . . . .Private Walker
Arnold Ridley . . . . .Private Godfrey
Ian Lavender . . . . .Private Pike
Geoffrey Lumsden . . . . .Captain Square
Rex Garner . . . . .Captain Ashley-Jones
Michael Knowles . . . . .Captain Reed
Anthony Sagar . . . . .Sergeant Major
Tom Mennard . . . . .Mess Orderly
Robert Raglan . . . . .Captain Pritchard
Platoon: Colin Bean, Desmond Cullum-Jones, Hugh Hastings, Vic Taylor, Freddie Wiles, George Hancock, Leslie Noyes, Freddie White, Hugh Cecil, Frank Godfrey
Girl in Canteen: Anita Archdale

PRODUCTION TEAM
Script: Jimmy Perry and David Croft
Producer/Director: David Croft
Production Assistant: Phil Bishop
Film Cameraman: Stewart Farnell
Film Sound Recordist: Les Collins
Film Editor: Bob Rymer
Studio Lighting: George Summers
Studio Sound: Michael McCarthy
Design: Paul Joel
Assistant Floor Manager: Roger Singleton-Turner
Vision Mixer: Dave Hanks
Costume Supervisor: George Ward
Make-Up Supervisor: Cynthia Goodwin

Mainwaring and his men are on a weekend course at the School of Explosives. When Pike brings in Wilson's bedding from the lorry, Main-

'Fallen Idol'

'Fallen Idol'

waring reminds him it's a democratic platoon: they eat together, sleep together and do everything together. Later when Captain Square tells Mainwaring it's not right for him to sleep with the men because officers should distance themselves, Mainwaring doesn't practise what he preaches and divides the tent, separating himself and Wilson from the rest of the men. Such action doesn't go down too well and Frazer thinks he's got ideas above his station.

Each member of the platoon is allowed two pints of beer free and Mainwaring intends joining his men, but when Captain Square says he should be drinking in the officers' mess, Mainwaring agrees with him, and again annoys the men, who are no longer in a drinking mood.

By the end of the evening, Mainwaring is drunk and staggers back to the sleeping quarters. He oversleeps in the morning and endures a terrible hangover while joining the men for a lecture on sticky bombs, conducted by a nervous Captain Reed – the explosions do nothing for Mainwaring's head!

When a grenade lands inside Jones' van by accident, just as he's driving away, Mainwaring spots a chance to restore his credibility among his men and sets off in pursuit. He clambers on the back of the van, orders Jones to stop, and jumps out. The driverless van careers into an electricity sub-station but, worried that the van will explode and put the county out of action, Mainwaring charges back to the van and throws the grenade away. What he didn't anticipate is that a stray dog, who loves bringing things back, is standing nearby.

FANY

While travelling to Walmington-on-Sea by train in the episode 'The Bullet is Not for Firing', Captain Pringle tells his colleague, Captain Cutts, that he hopes Mainwaring's court of inquiry is over quickly because he wants to return to London for a date. He's taking a FANY to a five-shilling utility dinner at The Ritz. The acronym stands for the First Aid Nursing Yeomanry.

FARMER, THE

Played by Verne Morgan (TV)
In 'Gorilla Warfare' the farmer allows Mainwaring and his men to sleep in his barn while they attend a weekend's exercise. His wife cooks the whole platoon eggs and bacon, which goes down well.

FARMHAND, THE

Played by David Butler (TV)
The farmhand works for Mr Boggis at the North Berrington Turkey Farm, looking after the 210 turkeys and carrying out odd jobs around the place. Mainwaring doesn't get much out of him while visiting the farm during 'Turkey Dinner', in the hope of finding out whether the farm's lost a turkey.

FARNELL, STEWART A

Film cameraman on 12 episodes (TV): S4, episodes 1, 2, 3, 5, 8, 10 & 13; S5, episodes 2, 3, 5 & 7

FARTHING, TIMOTHY

Played by Frank Williams (all mediums)
The bespectacled Timothy Farthing, whose weakness is alcohol, is vicar at St Aldhelm's, Walmington-on-Sea. A keen campanologist, until the outbreak of war puts paid to his hobby, he was also editor of *The Ring-A-Ding Monthly*,

until the magazine's closure. Now the only highlight of his year is the annual boy scouts' pantomime.

Before joining the sleepy parish of Walmington, the Vicar's background had involved missionary work, including a spell visiting the Umbarla-Umbarla. Ineffectual and rather huffy at times, he's regularly in dispute with Captain Mainwaring over life-threatening issues such as whose turn it is to use the church hall.

Although he never fought during the war, he fancies donning khaki and doing his bit for the nation, so he joins the Walmington Home Guard for a short time; but when Mainwaring – recovering in hospital from an operation – finds out, his time defending the home shores comes to an abrupt end.

FEATHERS, THE

(Film only)
A pub in Walmington's High Street, The Feathers is only seen from the outside in the film.

FENEMORE, HILDA

Born: London
Role: Queenie Beal (S9, episode 7: 'Ring Dem Bells') (TV)
Hilda, who appeared as the costume designer measuring up the platoon members for a training film, is a veteran character actress of film, TV and stage. For four years she played Jack Warner's affable neighbour who frequently brought him meals in *Dixon of Dock Green*. Among many other TV credits are appearances in *Are You Being Served?*, *Goodnight Sweetheart*, *Crown Court*, *Duchess of Duke Street*, *Minder*, *Brookside* and *French and Saunders*.

Hilda always wanted to become an actress and when she acted as an amateur in a play directed by the late Bill Owen everybody thought she was a professional, so she decided to make it her career.

In over four decades in the profession, Hilda – who's still acting – has appeared in 90 films, including *Room in the House*, *The Tommy Steele Story*, *Clash by Night* and two *Carry On*s: as Rhoda Bray in *Nurse* and as an agitated woman in *Constable*.

FENNELL, DAVID

Role: Platoon member (film)
David made an appearance as a member of the Walmington Home Guard platoon in the movie.

FIERCE LADY, THE

Played by Olive Mercer (TV)
In 'Man Hunt', it was thought this character had bought a pair of knickers from Walker's market stall. As they were made from parachute material and Mainwaring wants to find out whether it was a German or British parachute, he visits her home with Wilson and Walker asking to see her knickers!

FIFTH COLUMNISTS

During the war there were concerns that large numbers of German spies and British Nazi sympathisers, referred to as fifth columnists, were listening in on people's conversations. The government therefore encouraged people to inform the authorities if they came across anyone making defeatist comments, a campaign that became unpopular and was eventually stopped, but not before many thousands of German and Italian citizens residing in Britain had been arrested as suspects.

FIGHTING TIGERS, THE

This was the title Jimmy Perry gave his first TV script, which was eventually to become *Dad's Army*. While working as a young actor with the legendary Joan Littlewood, he penned a script about the adventures of a Home Guard unit. Eventually he completed it and was able to convince BBC producer, David Croft, to read it. (See 'History'.)

FILM

During the 1970s, transferring a hit sitcom to the big screen seemed the done thing. Many British shows were converted, but very few lived up to expectations, struggling to capture the atmosphere of their small-screen cousins. Storylines confined to 30 minutes screen time each week packed a punch, but extending them for the big screen wasn't so easy, with many becoming pallid versions of the original concept. *Dad's Army*, though, was an exception: the film was warmly received and still enjoys regular outings on TV.

When Jimmy Perry and David Croft developed the idea for a big-screen version of their sitcom, they secured the help of Norman Cohen, who went on to direct the film. Cohen hawked the synopsis around the industry's moguls, and after a few rejections struck gold with Columbia Pictures, who snapped it up.

Although budgets allocated to sitcom adaptations are notoriously small, more money was available than David Croft received for the TV series. The extra funds afforded the director the chance to populate the streets of Walmington-on-Sea a little, thanks to the hiring of extras to occupy the sleepy seaside town, which in reality was the pretty Buckinghamshire town of Chalfont St Giles, situated miles from the nearest beach.

But one person unhappy with the finished product was David Croft. 'It was written to someone else's specification; there were modifications to what we originally wrote and I don't think it was well done,' he says. 'There was a lack of reaction shots, for one thing. We were very much a reaction show: if someone said a funny line, you'd cut to a close-up of the other person, to see their reaction. That's where a lot of the *Dad's Army* comedy came from, particularly

The Dad's Army film

Arthur Lowe and John Le Mesurier. Those sort of shots were lacking terribly.'

Like most films, the script went through an editing process, with scenes being cut or altered. One particular scene, early on in the film, which Jimmy Perry and David Croft fought hard to retain involved Major General Fullard leaving Martin's Bank after being prevented from cashing a cheque by Mr Mainwaring. Director Norman Cohen wanted to end the scene at the bank counter, thereby not letting the audience see the General come out of the bank and climb into a military staff car; the writers felt strongly the scene should remain. Cohen finally agreed, but not before Jimmy Perry had written to him in November 1970. He said: 'Both David and I are absolutely horrified to hear that the scene of the General coming out of the bank and getting into the car has been cut.' Jimmy explained that as far as they were concerned, the scene was 'the keystone of the whole film – if this is cut what is the purpose of putting in the scene with the General in the bank in the first place? It is nearly three quarters of an hour before we see the General again and by that time no one will remember him from the scene in the bank.' Jimmy

explained that one of the main reasons for seeing the General come out of the bank and get in the car was to establish in the minds of the audience that it was a general Mainwaring had upset, not a civilian. Perry pointed out that as far as constructing comedy in *Dad's Army* was concerned, one of the golden rules they always followed was to 'Let the audience into the joke – tell them what is going to happen – and then let them see how Mainwaring and Co tackle it.' He closed by pointing out that this had worked on television and didn't see why 'the film should suddenly depart from this rule.'

The big-screen version of *Dad's Army* was premiered in March, 1971, with the BBFC classification 'U'. It has since been shown several times on British TV. BBC transmissions: 5/5/79, 28/7/81, 5/3/83, 25/8/86, 14/5/88, 27/12/89, 31/7/93, 10/8/96, 12/7/98.

THE CAST

Captain Mainwaring	Arthur Lowe
Sgt Wilson	John Le Mesurier
L/Cpl Jones	Clive Dunn
Private Frazer	John Laurie
Private Walker	James Beck
Private Godfrey	Arnold Ridley
Private Pike	Ian Lavender
Mrs Pike	Liz Fraser
Major General Fullard	Bernard Archard
RSM (Mr Dawkins)	Derek Newark
Hodges	Bill Pertwee
Vicar	Frank Williams
Verger	Edward Sinclair
Police Sergeant	Anthony Sagar
Mrs Hall	Pat Coombs
Peppery Old Gent	Roger Maxwell
Nazi General	Paul Dawkins
Nazi Orderly	Sam Kydd
Staff Captain	Michael Knowles
Bert King	Fred Griffiths
Mayor	John Baskcomb
German Radio Operator	George Roubicek
Nazi Photographer	Scott Fredericks
Nazi Pilot	Ingo Mogendorf
Nazi Co-Pilot	Franz Van Norde
Radio Shop Assistant	John Henderson
Girl in Bank	Harriet Rhys
AA Man	Dervis Ward
Inspector Hardcastle	Robert Raglan
Naval Officer	John D Collins
Marine Officer	Alan Haines

Platoon: Desmond Cullum-Jones, Colin Bean,
Frank Godfrey, Freddie White, David Fennell,
George Hancock, Freddie Wiles, Leslie Noyes,
Hugh Hastings, Bernard Severn

TECHNICAL CREDITS

Producer . . . . .John R Sloan
Director . . . . .Norman Cohen
Screenplay . . . . .Jimmy Perry and David Croft
Director of Photography . .Terry Maher
Art Director . . . . .Terry Knight
Music composed and conducted by Wilfred Burns
'Who Do You Think You Are Kidding, Mr Hitler' Sung by
Bud Flanagan
Words by . . . . .Jimmy Perry
Music by . . . . .Jimmy Perry and Derek
Taverner
Production Manager . . . . .Leonard C Rudkin
Film Editor . . . . .Willy Kemplen
Assistant Director . . . . . . .Douglas Hermes
Camera Operator . . . . . . .Gerry Anstiss
Sound Recordists . . . . . . .Ken Ritchie and Bob Jones
Sound Editor . . . . .Dino Di Campo
Wardrobe Supervisor . . . .Bridget Sellers
Casting . . . . .Harvey Woods
Location Manager . . . . . . .Bob Simmonds
Continuity . . . . .Zelda Barron
Make-Up . . . . .Jim Evans
Hairdressing . . . . .Mervyn Medalie
Set Dresser . . . . .Dimity Collins

Filmed on location and at Shepperton Studios,
England. (See shooting schedule)
Length: 8523 ft
Certificate: 'U'
Running Time: 95 minutes

The following was completed by Perry and Croft
for the film company.

SYNOPSIS

Britain, 1940. As the Nazis mass their hordes in
France for the final assault across the Channel,
the British Government realises the situation
demands drastic measures: it inaugurates the
Local Defence Volunteers, an army of senior citizens and youths still wet behind the ears who
train without manuals, march without uniforms, drill without weapons and generally
muddle through, stoically enduring the jibes of
the population.

Dad's Army is about the LDV – later the Home
Guard – in Walmington-on-Sea where the call is
heard, the challenge accepted. Crisis throws up
leaders from unexpected quarters – the Walmington Home Guard find themselves commanded by plump, balding Captain Mainwaring,
the local bank manager. Ably supported by his
office No 2, Sgt Wilson, and the High Street
butcher, Lance Corporal Jones, Mainwaring
begins to mould his squad of patriotic anarchists
into some semblance of a fighting force.

All the Dad's Army heroes are there: Frazer the

Scottish undertaker, Pike the soppy sloppy clerk,
Godfrey the white-haired wonder who can't venture too far from the Gents – and Walker the
spiv with his pockets full of illicit petrol coupons
and anything and everything in short supply.

But the incidents are all new and the big,
cinema screen gives Dad's Army a new dimension.

BELOW The Walmington platoon were prepared
to fight to the death in the Dad's Army movie.

NEWSPAPER REVIEWS OF THE FILM

The movie critics writing for the national
press had mixed views about the success of
the show on the big screen.

'It seems a bit slow and stiff
in the limbs; it's probably hard
to galvanise the senior citizens
whose own bumbling pace sets the
scene for easy and affectionate
laughter.'
Alexander Walker, Evening Standard, 17/3/71

'Not very substantial, but it's
warm-hearted, It's for small boys
to take Dad to.'
Richard Barkley, Sunday Express, 21/3/71

'The familiar characters of the
successful TV series march over
well-trodden ground and never
plant a boot in new territory. The
main incident with the chaps
capturing German airmen in the
local church is not all that
entertaining.'
Daily Express, 15/3/71

'The film is too episodic.'
Dick Richards, Daily Mirror, 15/3/71

'Played in the best traditions of
national farce... uproariously funny.'
The Times

The original shooting schedule
(issued 5 August 1970)

Monday 10 August
SET: (external) country road and field
LOCATION: Chobham Common
CHARACTERS/VEHICLES: The Squad, Jones' van

Tuesday 11 August
SET: (external) country roads
LOCATION: Chobham Common
CHARACTERS/VEHICLES: The Squad, AA man, AA motorcycle
combination, van with gas bag

Wednesday 12 August
SET: (external) High Street, Walmington
LOCATION: Chalfont St Giles
CHARACTERS/VEHICLES: The Squad, Hodges, Spinster Lady,
Miss King, 1940 vehicles

Thursday 13 August
SET: (external) High Street, Walmington
LOCATION: Chalfont St Giles
CHARACTERS/VEHICLES: The Squad, Hodges, Mrs Hall,
General Fullard, Staff Captain, Driver of staff car, army
convoy

Friday 14 August
SET: (external) High Street, Walmington
LOCATION: Chalfont St Giles
CHARACTERS/VEHICLES: The Squad, Vicar and Verger

Saturday 15 August
SET: (external) road on hill (oil slick)
LOCATION: Chobham Common
CHARACTERS/VEHICLES: The Squad, General Fullard, Staff
Captain, stunt driver, staff car

Monday 17 August
SET: (external) grass slope / water / army fixing pontoon bridge
LOCATION: Chobham/Littleton Lake / Cliveden boathouse
CHARACTERS/VEHICLES: The Squad, stuntman

Tuesday 18 August
SET: (external) Mount Street – road block / horse rehearsal
on river
LOCATION: Charlton Road, Shepperton and Cliveden
boathouse
CHARACTERS/VEHICLES: The Squad, Hodges, Bert King, open
lorry (bells)

Wednesday 19 August
SET: (external) road block / weekend camp
LOCATION: Charlton Road, Shepperton / the lot at
Shepperton Studios
CHARACTERS/VEHICLES: The Squad, Staff Captain, General
Fullard, RSM, staff car, army lorries

Thursday 20 August
SET: (external) weekend camp
LOCATION: the lot at Shepperton Studios
CHARACTERS/VEHICLES: The Squad, Staff Captain, General
Fullard, RSM, horse, army vehicles

Facing a dearth of real weapons, the Walmington platoon
were never short of alternatives.

Friday 21 August
SET: (external) weekend camp
LOCATION: the lot at Shepperton Studios
CHARACTERS/VEHICLES: Staff Captain, RSM, army vehicles

Saturday 22 August
SET: (external) weekend camp / (internal) inside tent
LOCATION: the lot at Shepperton Studios

Monday 24 August
SET: (external) brow of hill / river / pontoon bridge
LOCATION: Cliveden
CHARACTERS/VEHICLES: The Squad, General Fullard, Marine
Sergeant plus three marines, horse

Tuesday 25 August
SET: (external) brow of hill / river / pontoon bridge
LOCATION: Cliveden
CHARACTERS/VEHICLES: The Squad, General Fullard, horse

Wednesday 26 August
SET: (external) bridge / riverbank
LOCATION: Cookham
CHARACTERS/VEHICLES: The Squad, General Fullard, horse

Thursday 27 August

SET: (external) shallow water / horse ridge / bridge

LOCATION: Cliveden

CHARACTERS/VEHICLES: The Squad, canoes, horse

Friday 28 August

SET: (external) shallow water / horse ridge / bridge

LOCATION: Cliveden

CHARACTERS/VEHICLES: The Squad, canoes, horse

Saturday 29 August

SET: (external) vicarage / (internal) bell tower and loft / (internal) church yard

LOCATION: lot at Shepperton Studios and Littleton Church

CHARACTERS/VEHICLES: Vicar and Bert King

Tuesday 1 September

SET: (external) hedge / war memorial / museum / stage / farm building

LOCATION: lot at Shepperton Studios

CHARACTERS/VEHICLES: The Squad, museum guide

Wednesday 2 September

SET: (external) French coast

LOCATION: Seaford

CHARACTERS/VEHICLES: Nazi General, Schultz (Orderly), Nazi staff officers, German staff car

Thursday 3 September

SET: (external) English coast

LOCATION: Seaford

CHARACTERS/VEHICLES: The Squad

Friday 4 September

SET: (external) English coast

LOCATION: Seaford

CHARACTERS/VEHICLES: The Squad

Saturday 5 September

SET: (external) church hall

LOCATION: Littleton Church

CHARACTERS/VEHICLES: The Squad, Hodges, Verger, dust cart

Monday 7 September

SET: (internal) bank and manager's office

LOCATION: studio

CHARACTERS: Mainwaring, Wilson, Pike, General Fullard, Miss King

Tuesday 8 September

SET: (internal) bank and manager's office / police station and cell

LOCATION: studio

CHARACTERS: Mainwaring, Wilson, Pike, General Fullard, Miss King, Jones, Frazer, Godfrey, rest of squad, police sergeant

Wednesday 9 September

SET: (internal) police station and cell, undertakers, kitchen

LOCATION: studio

CHARACTERS: Mainwaring Wilson, Pike, General Fullard, Miss King, Jones, Frazer, Godfrey, rest of squad, police sergeant, Walker, Mrs Pike

Thursday 10 September

SET: (internal) radio store / butcher's shop / (external) woods / farm / window

LOCATION: studio

CHARACTERS: Mainwaring, Wilson, Jones, Walker, Frazer, Godfrey, Pike, Mrs Hall

THE FILM THAT NEVER HAPPENED

Although Jimmy Perry and David Croft weren't entirely happy with the way the big-screen adaptation panned out, they did consider writing a second movie. A treatment, titled, 'Dad's Army and the Secret U-boat Base', was completed by the writers, but the project never progressed to the stage where a full script was commissioned. Jimmy Perry takes up the story.

'Laurence Olivier loved the show so much, he had indicated he was interested in playing the lead, which was the part of a villain. The story was that British ships were being sunk in the Irish Sea, and in North Wales there was an inlet where a German U-boat used to go under the rocks and into a base that was sited there, manned by Germans. There was a country house above and all the sailors masqueraded as the staff, with the Nazi leader acting as the lord of the manor.

'The War Office knew there was a secret U-boat base somewhere along that coast.

They didn't want to rouse people's suspicions, so instead of sending the regular army, they decided to send a bunch of idiots, and that turned out to be the Walmington-on-Sea Home Guard, who went along to take part in manoeuvres.

'That was as far as we got with the plot, except that the denouement would be that they got the platoon on the submarine and intended taking them back to Germany to use as propaganda and show they thought the Home Guard were idiots. But the platoon overcame the crew but they didn't know how to drive the U-boat, and that's how it ended.

'We never finished the plot and would have probably completed several treatments, but it didn't go any further because David and I were very busy; we also didn't think the first film had succeeded, so we dropped the whole idea.'

JIMMY PERRY

Friday 11 September

SET: (internal) crypt / choir changing room / recce place / (external) field / churchyard

LOCATION: studio

CHARACTERS: The Squad, Nazi pilot and two crew

Saturday 12 September

SET: (internal) German operations room

LOCATION: Syon House

CHARACTERS: Nazi General, Schultz (Orderly), Nazi staff officers, orderlies

Monday 14 September

SET: (internal) church hall and vicar's office

LOCATION: studio

CHARACTERS: The Squad, Hodges, Mrs Pike, peppery gent

Tuesday 15 September

SET: (internal) church hall and vicar's office

LOCATION: studio

CHARACTERS: The Squad, Hodges, Mrs Pike, peppery gent

Wednesday 16 September

SET: (internal) church hall and vicar's office

LOCATION: studio

CHARACTERS: The Squad, Hodges, Mrs Pike, peppery gent

Thursday 17 September

SET: (external) church

CHARACTERS: The Squad, General Fullard, Vicar

Friday 18 September

SET: (internal) church hall and Vicar's office

LOCATION: studio

CHARACTERS: The Squad, Mrs Pike, Hodges, peppery gent

Monday 21 September

SET: (internal) church hall

LOCATION: studio

CHARACTERS: Mainwaring, Wilson, Jones, Walker, Frazer, Godfrey, Pike, Vicar, Nazi pilot and two crew

Tuesday 22 September

SET: (internal) church hall

LOCATION: studio

CHARACTERS: Mainwaring, Wilson, Jones, Walker, Frazer, Godfrey, Pike, Vicar, Nazi pilot and two crew

Wednesday 23 September

SET: (external) church wall, gas company entrance, street by church

CHARACTERS: The Squad, Hodges, General Fullard, Vicar, Verger, Nazi pilot and two crew

Thursday 24 September

SET: (internal) bath and Jones' van

CHARACTERS: Jones, Walker, Frazer, Godfrey, Pike, rest of Squad

Friday 25 September

pick-ups and inserts (all the Squad were required)

FIREMAN, THE
Played by Gordon Peters (TV)
Probably the most famous scene to be cut from the sitcom involved Gordon Peters in the first episode, 'The Man and the Hour', in which he played a chief fire officer. It was intended that Peters' character would become an integral part of the sitcom, providing another pain in Mainwaring's neck, especially as the fire service would need to share the church hall with the wardens and the Home Guard. However, when the opening episode was seriously overrunning, the fireman's scene was cut. (See 'Cut Scenes'.)

'When You've Got to Go'

FISH AND CHIP RESTAURANT, THE
The restaurant in Walmington where members of the platoon throw a farewell supper for young Pikey, who they think is joining the RAF. However, he's been turned down because it's discovered he has a rare blood group and is too high a risk for the Air Force. But, not wanting to miss out on his fish and chip supper, Pike decides not to tell anyone until the end of the evening.

FISH FRYER, THE
Played by Frankie Holmes (TV)
This character owns the fish and chip shop in Walmington where Pike has his so-called farewell supper in 'When You've Got to Go', even though he's known for days that he won't be joining up. The money-grabbing fish fryer isn't one for customer service. Although the platoon ensure the day's takings are healthy, especially as Pikey tucks into more than one portion, the fish fryer is keen to move the men on as soon as possible.

FIZZER
Military slang for being placed on a charge, which Frazer is very keen on in 'A Stripe for Frazer'.

FLANAGAN, BUD (1896–1968)
Bud Flanagan (real name Robert Winthrop) sang the theme song 'Who Do You Think You Are Kidding, Mr Hitler?'. He was a comedian who, for many years, teamed up with Chesney Allen to form part of the Crazy Gang. He wrote and sang, penning many well known songs such as 'Underneath the Arches'.

FLETCHER, MRS
Not seen in the programme, but the Verger mentions her in 'A Man of Action'. She's a regular member of the Vicar's congregation and is in hospital having her fifth child. The Vicar is probably keen for her to get back to church because his average congregation consists of ten people.

FOREST, JOHN
Role: Lieutenant Hope-Bruce ('Sorry, Wrong Number') (radio)

FORGE, KATE
Born: Liverpool
Role: Member of the Choir (S3, episode 4: 'The Bullet is Not for Firing') (TV)
Kate left school, got married at 19, raised a family and emigrated to Canada before becoming a professional singer. She studied at the Faculty of Music in Toronto, where she gained qualifications in music, before joining the Canadian National Opera Company.

Soon after returning to England in 1962 she joined the George Mitchell Singers and sang at the London Palladium, and also at Drury Lane in *My Fair Lady* before going out on tour. For the next 16 years she worked for several companies including The Fred Tomlinson Singers, singing and dancing on stage and television, as well as providing backing vocals on records, including the Beatles' *A Hard Day's Night*. Among the TV shows she worked on are *The Two Ronnies*, *The Harry Secombe Show*, *Pickwick* and *Harry Worth*.

Kate hasn't sung professionally since 1978. Nowadays she sings regularly with the London Symphony Chorus at various venues, including the Barbican, the Festival Hall and the Albert Hall. (See 'Tomlinson, Fred'.)

FORKUS, MR AND MRS
Guests at the platoon's dance in the TV episode, 'War Dance'.

FORSTER, HAROLD
Played by John Bardon (TV)
Working as a production assistant for the Crown Film Unit, Harold travels down to Walmington in 'Ring Dem Bells' to make a training film.

FORTESCUE, MISS
Played by Joan Cooper (TV)
The aged proprietor of the popular Marigold Tea Rooms in Walmington is seen in 'Time On My Hands'.

FOSTER, MRS
Referred to, but not seen, in the episode, 'Command Decision'. Mrs Foster is a friend of Jones, who helps him count the ration book coupons in return for a little meat for her cat.

FOUNTAIN BREWERY, THE
A local brewery run by Mr Fountain. Not seen or heard in the sitcom, but originally mentioned in the script of 'Shooting Pains', before the reference was cut. See 'Shooting Pains' in 'Cut Scenes'.

FOX, MARCIA
Played by Pamela Cundell (TV and stage); Mollie Sugden (radio)
Mrs Fox, who has a brother in the army, is slightly eccentric and always dresses outlandishly. Her married life remains something of a mystery, and one could question whether she might be a bigamist by marrying Jones in 'Never Too Old'! In 'The Armoured Might of Lance Corporal Jones' she tells Jones that the reason she hasn't used many of the coupons in her ration book is because she's been away with her husband, but in 'Mum's Army' she tells Mainwaring she's a widow. We can only presume her husband died in between, allowing her the chance legally to tie the knot with Jones.

Marcia is adored by Jack Jones, who sees her face everywhere he looks, even on the gas works!

FRANK

Not seen in the series, Frank chats with Hodges on the phone in 'A Brush With the Law'. A local bookmaker, Hodges places a ten bob each way bet with him on Farmer's Boy in the 3.15 at Lincoln.

FRANKLIN, JIM

Production assistant on two episodes (TV): S3, episodes 2 & 3: 'Battle School' and 'The Lion has 'Phones'

FRANKS, CHRIS

Role: Member of the platoon's back row in five episodes (S1, episodes 1, 2, 3, 5 & 6) (TV)

FRASER, LIZ (1935–)

Born: London

Role: Mavis Pike (film)

Liz studied at the London School of Dramatic Art before beginning a successful career, particularly in films where she's built up over 20 credits, mainly in comedy pictures such as *I'm All Right, Jack* with Ian Carmichael and Peter Sellers, *The Smallest Show on Earth*, *The Night We Dropped a Clanger*, *Two Way Stretch*, *The Bulldog Breed* and several *Carry Ons*: *Regardless*, *Cruising*, *Cabby* and *Behind*.

On TV, one of her first jobs was in the 1955 serial, *Sixpenny Corner*, but she's also played, among other parts, the matron in *Whack-O!*, Delilah in *Minder*, Edith in 1993's *Demob* and been seen in *The Bill*, *Robin's Nest* and two series of *Fairly Secret Army*.

FRAZER, PRIVATE JAMES

Played by John Laurie (TV, film and radio); Hamish Roughead (stage)

Address: 91, The High Street, Walmington-on-Sea

James 'We're doomed!' Frazer runs a funeral director's in Walmington at a property rented from Miss Twelvetrees for a tenner a month. He's helped in his duties by his young assistant, Heathcliff.

During the First World War he was a chief petty officer in the Royal Navy's catering branch, serving at the Battle of Jutland. The last ship he served on was *HMS Defiant*. He kept the rank until busted for hitting another officer with a boat hook while drunk. One benefit of his naval days was that he became a crack shot picking off mines at sea, a skill that proves useful more than once in the Home Guard.

From the outset the acerbic Frazer, who's a keen knitter, reveals his impudent streak by remarking that Mainwaring's invasion committee reminds him of the Boys' Brigade. With a peremptory manner, he took over the running of the platoon in 'If the Cap Fits…', but his command was short-lived. Not the most popular platoon member, Mainwaring wouldn't trust him an inch because his eyes are too close together, 'denoting a mean streak'.

Before moving to Walmington, Frazer grew up on the Isle of Barra and earned a living fishing the Hebridean seas and making coffins, before travelling to the other side of the world and diving for pearls in the South Seas, with his friend, Wally Stewart.

Although he's always been a bachelor, James Frazer nearly married a long-legged Scottish lass called Jessie. One day she failed to return from a cliff-top walk and it was thought she'd fallen off the edge, until a letter arrived from Singapore, where she'd travelled without informing him. She wanted to return home and marry Frazer but needed the £40 fare: as expected, Frazer didn't post the cash. Frazer still has an eye for the girls though, especially those with 'big, firm thighs'.

As far as hobbies are concerned, the peppery Scotsman enjoys nothing more than counting

his gold sovereigns, sitting down with his favourite whisky or tending his allotment where he grows his own vegetables, including runner beans and tomatoes. He's also known to dabble in hypnosis and tread the boards occasionally, referring to his performance in the drama society's production of *The Lighthouse Keeper* in the episode, 'Menace from the Deep'. A member of the Chamber of Commerce, and president of Walmington-on-Sea's Caledonian Society, which can't be much fun bearing in mind he's been the sole member since Jock McLean was thrown out for refusing to pay increased subscriptions, Frazer isn't one of life's instantly likeable characters. A great cynic, he spreads gloom wherever he goes. With his wild, staring eyes he's forever deriding Mainwaring's plans.

However, his absent mindedness finds him calling his new wife Mildred on his wedding day, a mistake made by Mainwaring, too. However, she was also known as Muriel during the show's run, so she must have got used to answering to several names. By the end of the series, Mrs Fox tells us that she has no male relatives, so we can only assume that her brother, mentioned earlier in the run, had died, too.

She's frequently seen around Walmington and lives above a hat shop in the High Street. The Edwardian property is busily furnished with chintzy covers, dolls and 1930s knick-knacks, and boasts a chromium-plated lamp with a chromium-plated table to match. Always wearing a smile, Mrs Fox is an ebullient member of the community who attracts the interest of several men, including the town clerk, Mr Gordon.

FOX, THE

A pub in Walmington which Wilson and Pike visit while searching for Frazer, who missed a parade in 'The Miser's Hoard'. It's also where the Colonel buys Mainwaring a drink after the selection parade in 'Keep Young and Beautiful', to celebrate not losing any of his platoon to the ARP wardens.

FOX AND PHEASANT, THE

A pub in Walmington which Wilson and Pike visit while searching for Frazer in 'The Miser's Hoard'.

Note: In the original 'The Man and the Hour' script, Frazer was a bearded ex-commander, and not a chief petty officer. This description altered prior to the actual episode being recorded.

FRED
Played by Bill Tasker (TV)

Appears in 'The Face On the Poster'. He's an old chap who works for Mr Bugden, the local printer in Walmington, and eats jam sandwiches while working the printing machines.

FREDA
(See 'Telephone Operator, The'.)

FREDERICKS, SCOTT (1943–)
Born: Cork
Role: Nazi Photographer (film)

Scott entered the industry in the mid-1960s and worked initially in the theatre before film and TV parts came his way. On the big screen he has been seen in *The Rise and Rise of Michael Rimmer*, *Blind Terror* (1971), as Mark in the 1976 production *Deadly Females* and in *The Big Red One*. On TV he played Carnell in a 1978 episode of *Blakes 7*, appeared in several episodes of *Doctor Who*, and also worked on *Z Cars*, *Barlow*, *The Man Outside*, *Triangle* and *The Enigma Files*. In 1980, he wrote and performed *Yeats Remembers* at Dublin's Gate Theatre and America's university circuit.

FRENCH GENERAL, THE
Played by John Hart Dyke (TV)

Visits Walmington-on-Sea in 'The Captain's Car' and becomes a victim of Frazer's slow-drying paint.

FRENCHY
Played by Michael Stainton (TV)

Appears in 'Wake-Up Walmington' as a merchant seaman drinking at The Six Bells. He heads back to his ship with his colleagues, including Bert, only to meet up with Mainwaring and his men, who think they're fifth columnists.

FRIEDLANDER, JOHN
Visual effects designer on one episode (TV): S4, episode 2: 'Don't Forget the Diver'

After graduating from art college in Hornsey, John served in the army. Upon demob, he freelanced as a sculptor for several months, before joining an exhibition and display studio for seven years. When he married, the need for a steadier income saw him join the BBC in 1960, initially as a visual effects design assistant.

During an 18-year career with the Beeb he worked on numerous programmes, including *It's A Square World*, *Monty Python's Flying Circus*, *The Mayor of Casterbridge* and *I, Claudius*. John left the BBC in 1978 and worked freelance for film and TV companies. He has since retired.

FULLARD, MAJOR GENERAL
Played by Bernard Archard (film)

The general is disgusted when Mainwaring refuses to cash his cheque, so when he comes up against him again at a big Home Guard exercise he's running, he is determined to make life as difficult as possible for the bank manager.

FURSE, JUDITH (1912–1974)
Role: Chairwoman ('The Loneliness of the Long-Distance Walker') (radio)

Judith was a supporting actress who first appeared on stage at the age of 12. She worked in theatre, television and in films, with over 50 credits to her name, including three *Carry On*s: a teacher in *Regardless*, Battleaxe in *Cabby* and Dr Crow, her biggest role, in *Spying*. Other films she appeared in include *Goodbye Mr Chips!*, *A Canterbury Tale*, *Quiet Weekend*, *Helter Skelter*, *The Browning Version*, *A Day to Remember*, *Doctor at Large*, *In the Doghouse*, *The Iron Maiden* and *Man in the Wilderness*.

FUZZY WUZZIES
Constantly referred to as such by Jones, the Fuzzy Wuzzies were Sudanese soldiers fighting in a war in which Jones was involved. The indigenous army was beaten by an Anglo-Egyptian army under the command of General Kitchener (1896–1898).

GALSHEAD

An Irish battalion is based at Galshead, near Walmington. When the platoon use up their ammunition in 'The Bullet is Not for Firing', Walker tells Mainwaring he could obtain some 'under the counter' ammo for a bob a round from the Irish battalion, but Mainwaring's not interested.

GANNON, CHRIS

Role: Clerk of the Court (S5, episode 11: 'A Brush with the Law') (TV)

Chris Gannon's other appearances on the small screen include playing a salesman in an episode of *Randall & Hopkirk (Deceased)*, a drunk in *Doctor in the House* during 1969, a patient in the 1981 version of *The Day of the Triffids*, Horace Murphy in the 1979 series *Room Service*, and appearances in *Thirty-Minute Theatre*, *The Onedin Line* as an Irish immigrant, *The Fenn Street Gang* as Luigi, *Poldark*, *Six Days of Justice* and *Rumpole of the Bailey*. He also appeared in a handful of films, such as 1979's *Yesterday's Hero* and 1976's *Office Party* as Mr Palmer. He died in 1983.

GARBO, GRETA

Played by Joan Savage (TV); Pat Coombs (radio)

In 'A Soldier's Farewell' the Walmington-on-Sea Home Guard go to the pictures, where they see Joan Savage play Greta Garbo alongside Robert Gillespie's portrayal of Charles Boyer in the movie *Marie Walewska*.

GARDENER, THE

Played by Jack Haig (TV)

While the gardener is tending his garden in 'The Day the Balloon Went Up', Mainwaring flies by on the end of the barrage balloon cable, swiping a much-treasured bush in the process.

GARDENIA GARDENS

Mentioned in 'Put That Light Out!', this road in Walmington is where a new air raid warden lives. Pike reckons the warden resembles Hitler. It's one of the Walmington streets never seen in the series.

GARDINER, JEFFREY

Born: Richmond

Role: Mr Wintergreen (S5, episode 11: 'A Brush with the Law') (TV)

Jeffrey served with the army during the war, but once demobbed he joined drama school. Several years in rep followed, including a spell at Oldham, before he branched out and began appearing on TV, making his debut as a television interviewer in an episode of *The Larkins* in 1959. Jeffrey has been seen on stage and TV in numerous roles, *The Canterbury Tales* being a favourite. Other credits include: *Sherlock Holmes*, *Hugh and I* – his first job for David Croft, *My Wife Next Door*, *Terry and June* and *You Rang M'Lord?*.

GARNER, REX (1921–)

Born: Wolverhampton

Role: Captain Ashley-Jones (S4, episode 13: 'Fallen Idol') (TV)

Rex left school at 15 with ambitions of becoming a draughtsman. He joined an architectural metalwork company in Wolverhampton and learnt his trade. When the Second World War broke out Rex volunteered for the army and joined the local Worcester Infantry, but after seven weeks he had left the Forces. A shortage of aircraft meant Rex's skills as a draughtsman were needed, and he was sent to work at a factory in Wednesbury as a jig and tool designer, which was classed as a reserved occupation.

When he wasn't working he served with the local Home Guard, and also found time to run an amateur dramatics society in Wolverhampton. He enjoyed himself so much that he decided to make it his new career as soon as the war finished.

Rex's first step towards achieving his goal was moving to London and joining a small rep company based in Henley-on-Thames. He learnt the trade in reps around the country, including Ipswich and Birmingham.

Although he never established a strong film career, appearing in just a few pictures such as *The Plank*, *Murder at 3am* and *The Birds of Paradise*, Rex has built up a healthy list of television

credits, dating back to 1957 and the Associated Rediffusion series, *Shadow Squad*, in which he played the private eye, Vic Steele. He was also seen in shows like *My Wife and I* playing David Finley, *The Whole World Over*, *Lollipop Loves Mr Mole* and more recently *Rhodes*, playing Sir Henry Loch in BBC's expensive 1996 miniseries.

In 1968, Rex moved to South Africa. Initially he returned to appear in the occasional production, such as *Dad's Army*, but decided to make it his permanent home in 1974. As well as acting, he worked as an artistic director at a theatre in Johannesburg, where he has since had a theatre named after him. After 30 years in the country, circumstances saw him return in 1999 to England, where he hopes to return to television acting.

GARSTANG, MRS

Not seen in the sitcom, but she attends the special dinner at the church hall in the episode, 'Turkey Dinner'. Mrs Garstang doesn't like turkey so asks Mrs Fox, who in turn asks Mr Jones, whether there is anything else. Mr Jones replies abruptly that she shouldn't come to a turkey dinner if she doesn't like the meat.

GARTLAND, ROGER

Born: London

Role: Bert ('Ten Seconds From Now') (radio)

After studying English at Cambridge University, Roger joined a repertory company in Lincoln as acting ASM. From there he joined Prospect Productions, a touring theatre company, and within a year of leaving university he was making his West End debut in a 1967 production of *The Cherry Orchard*.

Ten years in rep followed before Roger spent six months with the BBC Drama Rep, which led to the role of Bert in the episode 'Ten Seconds From Now'. Although he has done little television or film work during the course of his career, Roger has worked extensively on the stage, including seven years at the National Theatre. He also spent several years helping to run his own theatrical company.

All we see of the Gas Light and Coke Company are the entrance gates.

GAS LIGHT AND COKE COMPANY

The nearest we come to seeing the premises of this Walmington business is during the episode 'The Recruit', when the Vicar and Verger stand guard outside the company's gates. Miss Ironside, who Frazer helps recruit in 'Mum's Army', works there.

GAS MASKS

Also known as the civilian respirator, 38 million gas masks were issued to the public shortly after the 1938 Munich crisis showed the threat of war was real. To help people use their masks and survive air raids, instructions were issued on posters and even on cigarette cards, while children were given special lessons at school. However, a substantial percentage of the population constantly forgot, or didn't bother, to carry their masks with them at all times, and in 1940 the Government instructed air raid wardens to instigate monthly inspections of masks, with the person having to pay for a replacement or its repair, if the mask's condition required such action.

GATLAND, JOHN

Film sound recordist on nine episodes (TV): S6, episode 1, 3, 4, 5, 6; S7, episodes 1, 3, 5 & 6

John left school and applied to do national service in the RAF but was failed on medical grounds. He set out to find a job and joined Barclays Bank in 1952. In need of a change, he left three years later to become a trainee technical operator on BBC radio. After two years he was given a permanent contract as a technical operator, a job he kept until 1959, when he switched to TV. Expansion of the Beeb's film department led to several vacancies, and he became an assistant sound recordist.

In the years following he worked on numerous shows as sound recordist, including two years on *Z Cars*, two series of *Maigret*, and *Last of the Summer Wine*. John took early retirement from the BBC in 1992.

GERALD

Played by Don Estelle (TV)

An ARP warden who works for Hodges and is seen in 'Don't Forget the Diver', 'The Test' and 'Uninvited Guests'.

GERMAN PILOT, THE

Played by Robert Aldous (TV)

The pilot appears in the final scenes of 'Man Hunt'. After parachuting out of his plane he gives himself up when he sees Mainwaring.

GERMAN PILOT, THE

Played by Christopher Sandford (TV); Fraser Kerr (radio)

In 'Time On My Hands' the German pilot gets caught on the town hall clock after bailing out of his plane. Anyone would be frightened hanging precariously from such a height, but his high-pitched wailing was most irritating!

GERMAN PILOTS, THE

Played by Denys Peek and Nigel Rideout (TV); David Sinclair (radio)

In 'The Enemy Within the Gates', Jones, Walker and Pike are out on patrol when they capture the two pilots. In return, the platoon members receive a £20 bounty from GHQ. The airmen escape from the church hall, but are recaptured.

GERMAN RADIO OPERATOR, THE

Played by George Roubicek (film)

The radio operator has the unfortunate task of telling the Nazi General the news that the reconnaissance plane has crashed over England.

GETTING THE BIRD

Recorded: Friday 19/5/72

Original transmission: Friday 27/10/72, 8.30–9.00pm

Original viewing figures: 17.5 million

Repeated: 21/7/73, 5/4/85, 22/1/91, 13/11/93, 21/11/93 (Wales), 5/10/96, 7/12/96 (Wales), 3/5/97 (Scotland), 21/2/99

CAST

Arthur Lowe . . . . .Captain Mainwaring
John Le Mesurier . . . . .Sergeant Wilson
Clive Dunn . . . . .Lance Corporal Jones
John Laurie . . . . .Private Frazer
James Beck . . . . .Private Walker
Arnold Ridley . . . . .Private Godfrey
Ian Lavender . . . . .Private Pike
Bill Pertwee . . . . .ARP Warden
Frank Williams . . . . .Vicar
Edward Sinclair . . . . .Verger
Pamela Cundell . . . . .Mrs Fox
Alvar Lidell . . . . .Newsreader
Olive Mercer . . . . .Mrs Yeatman
Serretta Wilson . . . . .Wren
Platoon: Colin Bean, Desmond Cullum-Jones, Vic Taylor, Freddie White, Hugh Cecil, George Hancock, Leslie Noyes, Freddie Wiles, Hugh Hastings, Michael Moore
Doris (works in Jones' shop): Leila Forde
Congregation in Church: Ernest Blythe, Rose Edwards, Philip Beckar, Ernest Jennings, Kathleen Hurd, Mary Masters, Betsy White

PRODUCTION TEAM

Script: Jimmy Perry and David Croft
Producer/Director: David Croft
Production Assistant: Gordon Pert
Studio Lighting: Howard King
Studio Sound: Michael McCarthy
Design: Paul Joel
Assistant Floor Manager: Peter Fitton
Vision Mixer: Dave Hanks
Costume Supervisor: Susan Wheal
Make-Up Supervisor: Cynthia Goodwin
Visual Effects: Peter Day

Frazer spreads rumours in the butchers, telling Jones that Wilson hasn't been seen all day in the bank and he believes there are problems with Mrs Pike. Walker brings in a rabbit, but says he can't get any more even though Jones is desperate for meat. Spotting a picture of Trafalgar Square on a calendar hanging in the shop, Walker has an idea.

Everyone is talking about Wilson before parade begins: Godfrey admits seeing him leaving Alexander Park with his arm around a girl. Rumours are rife that he's quarrelled with Mrs Pike and has another woman.

The evening parade starts without Wilson, and it's not long before Walker arrives and assures Jones that all his troubles are over: he's got the off-ration meat (several dozen pigeons) and they're being stored alive in the boiler room next to Mainwaring's office.

'Getting the Bird'

Mainwaring tells the men that on Sunday there's a voluntary church parade, and that they're all expected to attend. He then finds a drunken Wilson asleep behind the stage curtain and orders him into the office for a talk. When Wilson keeps seeing a pigeon over Mainwaring's shoulder, his captain thinks he's gone loopy and orders him to pull himself together. But it's not long before Mainwaring's office is alive with pigeons, and Walker and Jones are ordered to sort everything out.

During that evening's patrol, while Mainwaring and his men watch the German bombers flying overhead, they turn on the radio for the news and discover pigeons are missing from Trafalgar Square. Jones doesn't want to be involved with stolen goods and tells Walker to clear the birds from his shop.

On Sunday, everyone arrives at the church for the service, including Wilson, for whom the day has been a trial. Just before he enters, Frazer sees a beautiful blonde kiss Wilson goodbye. It turns out she's Wilson daughter and on leave from the navy. Her mother left Wilson when she was young and he hasn't seen much of his daughter since.

The service turns out to be very memorable because the mystery of where Walker put the pigeons is soon answered. When Jones plays the organ, feathers and pigeons fly everywhere!

GHQ DRIVER, THE

Played by David Sinclair (radio)

The GHQ driver appears in the radio episode 'Command Decision' while delivering 500 LDV armbands and five rifles to the Walmington platoon. In the TV episode, the character was called 'The Soldier'.

'Getting the Bird'

GIBBONS, VIOLET

Played by Jenny Thomas (TV); Wendy Richard (radio)

Frank Pike's first real love, or so he thinks, is Violet Gibbons whom he invites to the platoon 'do' in 'War Dance' to announce their engagement. The gum-chewing, blonde-haired Violet will do irreparable damage to Pike's banking career claims Mainwaring, and Wilson is given the task of telling him. But he fails dismally and when Pikey announces his engagement, Mavis Pike faints. However, she needn't have worried, the engagement is short-lived.

Violet, a local ATS girl, is on leave when Pike asks her to the dance. Her mother used to clean for Mainwaring twice a week, while Violet's working life prior to joining up included stints at Woolworths and a fish and chip shop. Walker fancied her for a while, but when she started working in the chippie, he quickly went off her: whenever she got hot the fish and chip odour became unbearable.

GILCHRIST, DAVID

Role: Serviceman ('Mum's Army') (TV)

The serviceman asks for Mainwaring's chair in the station café.

GILLESPIE, ROBERT (1933–)

Born: Lille, France

Role: Charles Boyer (S5, episode 3: 'A Soldier's Farewell') (TV)

Gillespie being asked to play actor Charles Boyer in a scene from the 1937 movie, *Marie Walewska*, in which the Frenchman was cast as Napoleon, was a consequence of David Croft not being allowed to use a clip from the actual picture.

Robert was cast in his first sitcom by David Croft, playing a Moroccan policeman in *Hugh and I Spy*, a role that led to him playing numerous policemen.

He spent his early years in Nantes, until his parents moved to Manchester. He eventually began performing as a semi-professional at the city's Library Theatre, before joining RADA. After graduating he worked at the Old Vic until he was offered the role of Matthew in the TV production of *Jesus of Nazareth*.

Although Robert is normally cast in comedy roles, such as the gas man in *Rising Damp*, five series of *Keep It in the Family*, *The Fall and Rise* of *Reginald Perrin*, *Robin's Nest*, *Butterflies*, *George and Mildred* and *Whatever Happened To The Likely Lads?*, he's appeared in numerous dramas, including *Maigret*, *Crane*, *New Scotland Yard*, *The Sweeney*, *Van Der Valk*, *The Professionals* and *Secret Army*.

Robert, who also writes and directs, has made a handful of films, and has appeared regularly on stage, including two years with the RSC.

GILL'S THE TAILORS

A shop in Walmington that makes Mainwaring's new hat in time for the ceremonial church parade in 'Battle of the Giants!'. Although we never see the shop, or the owner, we know a delivery boy is employed by the firm because he drops the hat round to the church hall.

GILPIN, JEAN

Born: London
Role: Sylvia (S9, episode 2: 'The Making of Private Pike') (TV)

Jean's father worked for the United Nations and, although she was born in England, she left with her family before the age of one and spent most of her early years in other parts of the world, including Cuba, China, Thailand and the USA. She returned to England aged ten, while her parents moved to Africa. She attended schools in the UK, France and Switzerland before studying drama and English at Bristol University in the late 1960s. After graduating she started her acting career and for the next ten years concentrated on building a life in England, before deciding to move back to the States.

Upon completing her degree she was offered a place at a London drama school with the following year's intake. In the meantime, she looked for work and it wasn't long before she found it at the Nottingham Playhouse, her first professional job. After a short time at drama school – she never completed the course – Jean started being offered rep and TV work, making her debut in *The Duchess of Malfi* in 1972, by which time she'd already made her first film appearance, playing a ground stewardess in *To Catch A Spy*. Other credits on the big screen include Miss Field in *The World is Full of Married Men* (1979), the musical *The Bawdy Adventures of Tom Jones*, *The Tip-off* and the 1999 short *That Marino Thing*. Her TV work includes playing Margaret Eddington in *Quincy*, Staff Nurse Harper in *Angels* and roles in *Skeletons* and *Survivors*.

While developing her career this side of the pond, Jean started writing letters to producers and directors in search of work, one of which was answered by David Croft, whom she read for and who later offered her the part in 'The Making of Private Pike'. She worked for David again shortly after in his less popular sitcom, *Come Back Mrs Noah*, and appeared in an episode of *The Professionals* ('The First Night') as Debra in the same year (1977).

After finding it hard to steer her career in the direction she wanted, Jean returned to America in 1979. She has since established a successful career in voice work, and although she hasn't appeared on TV for some time, she's still seen on the stage and in the occasional film. Jean lives in California.

GIRL AT THE WINDOW, THE
Played by Thérèse McMurray (TV)

Appears in the newsreel-style footage of 'The Showing Up of Corporal Jones' as a woman watering her flowers – she doesn't speak. Also seen in 'Shooting Pains'.

GIRL IN THE BANK, THE
(See 'King, Janet'.)

GIRL IN THE HAYSTACK, THE
Played by Thérèse McMurray (TV)

While Mainwaring is being carried along by the barrage balloon in 'The Day the Balloon Went Up', he crashes through a haystack, revealing the girl in the process.

GIRL ON THE TANDEM, THE
Played by Vicki Lane (TV)

When trying to keep up with a stray barrage balloon in 'The Day the Balloon Went Up', Hodges commandeers a tandem. When the man gets off, Hodges climbs on and pedals off with the girl.

GLEESON, TIM
Designer on three episodes (TV): S9, episode 1: 'Wake-Up Walmington'; episode 3: 'Knights of Madness' and episode 4: 'The Miser's Hoard'

Tim studied at the Chelsea College of Art and joined the BBC as a holiday relief design assistant in 1958. Initially he worked on drama productions such as The *Murders in the Rue Morgue*,

The Borderers, *Softly*, *Softly* and *Dixon of Dock Green*, but occasional sitcoms started coming his way. During his time with the Beeb he's worked on many top shows, including *The Likely Lads*, *Yes, Minister*, *Open All Hours*, *Porridge*, *Last of the Summer Wine* and *Keeping Up Appearances*. Tim left the BBC in 1991 and worked freelance for a while. He's now retired.

GLOSSIP, MR
Played by Donald Morley (TV)

Glossip is Lady Maltby's chauffeur. When she donates her Rolls Royce to the Walmington Home Guard in 'The Captain's Car', Glossip takes the vehicle to the paint shop where it will be painted in camouflage, but he runs out of petrol *en route*.

GODALSTON

Not far from Walmington, Godalston is where the RAF holding station is situated. It's here that Walker hires a band in 'War Dance'.

GODFREY, PRIVATE CHARLES
Played by Arnold Ridley (all mediums)
Address: Cherry Tree Cottage, Walmington-on-Sea

Godfrey – who possesses a kind, welcoming face – leads a quiet life at Cherry Tree Cottage with his two geriatric sisters. Every morning Godfrey, who's a bachelor, gets up at 7.30am and makes tea for his sisters. Life at their country home is peaceful and, perhaps, a little lonely. Once Godfrey admitted to having had his phone cut off for two weeks – due to non-payment – before realising, because hardly anyone ever called. His isolation is compounded by his inability to drive, meaning excursions from the cottage are few and far between, and usually through necessity rather than pleasure. Anyone contemplating visiting the Godfreys should avoid Wednesdays,

particularly in winter, because it's the day they don't light a fire due to a coal shortage. As a result, the house becomes so cold Cissy Godfrey keeps warm by staying in bed all day with a hot-water bottle.

Their idyll looked in danger of being shattered when they discovered plans were afoot to build a new runway and demolish their cottage. At the eleventh hour, just as the furniture was being loaded into the removal van, their house is reprieved, thanks to Frazer, of all people.

Godfrey deserves to lead a peaceful life, especially after clocking up 35 years' service in the Civil Service Stores, some of which were spent in the sports department. He could have moved on to a better job in accounts but declined the offer because it was based on the fifth floor and he hates heights.

A mild-mannered man – except for the time he smashed a chair over an American soldier's head at The Red Lion during a brawl between Mainwaring's men and an advance party of Yanks – Godfrey is one of life's gentlemen; but when he first appeared back in 'The Man and the Hour', he was rather more confrontational. On the day Walmington's LDV are formed, and everyone returns to the church hall to present their makeshift weapons, Godfrey brings a rifle that belongs to his friend. When Mainwaring announces he wants the gun, Godfrey refuses to let him have it.

Godfrey mellows as life in Walmington moves on, and his amiable manner is occasionally derided by the more vociferous members of the platoon, particularly Frazer, who once claimed that he was as 'soft as a cream puff'. But his loyalty and dedication are commendable: when the platoon are guilty of being AWOL in 'Absent Friends', he's the only one to return to the church hall instead of playing darts with the wardens, even though Frazer calls him a blackleg.

He's a gentle and frail man who hates loud noises because they bring on headaches, which is why he dislikes Guy Fawkes' Night. He suffers from a weak bladder and continuously wants to be 'excused'; he also has a touch of gout and rheumatism in his shoulder, brought on by his sister, Dolly, forcing him to eat breakfast by the window. His eyesight is failing, too, but he won't wear glasses because he claims they make him look old.

Although Godfrey was a conscientious objector during the Great War, he volunteered to join the Medical Corps and at the Battle of the Somme went out into no man's land under heavy fire saving several lives. As a result, he was later appointed the platoon's medical orderly. He was decorated for his bravery by being awarded the Military Medal: a picture of him wearing the medal hangs above his bed.

His hobbies include beekeeping. He regards bees as very friendly, which explains why he doesn't worry about his beekeeping veil having plenty of large holes. But he doesn't like dogs and feels he brings out the worst in them. His sister Dolly once owned a Pekingese, but it kept jumping up at him and he had no option but to order it to leave.

When time permits, Charles is also a keen bowls player, a sport which has made him late for meetings with Mr Mainwaring on more than one occasion. He used to play cricket when he was younger, regularly turning out for the Gentlemen's Outfitting Team in the Civil Service Stores for the annual match against the Tobacco and Cigarette Department. While a working man, he also performed in The Gay Gondoliers, the company's troupe who did a few shows for charity.

GODFREY, CISSY

Played by Nan Braunton and Kathleen Sainsbury (TV); Nan Braunton and Joan Cooper (radio)
Address: Cherry Tree Cottage, Walmington-on-Sea
Little is known about Cissy Godfrey from the five appearances she made in the TV series, other than that she's Godfrey's sister, lives at Cherry Tree Cottage, and during the winter stays in bed all day on Wednesdays to save fuel. She's a mild-mannered, polite old lady, who relishes a bit of company at the cottage, like the time Mainwaring, Pike and Wilson come visiting in 'Is There Honey Still For Tea?'.

GODFREY, DOLLY

Played by Joan Cooper and Amy Dalby (TV)
Address: Cherry Tree Cottage, Walmington-on-Sea
Charles' sister, Dolly, who's three years younger than him, is famous around Walmington for making delicious upside-down cakes, although she's not entirely happy with the standard because food shortages mean she can't include certain ingredients. Nevertheless, the cakes are always popular among the men of the Home Guard whenever Charles brings them with him on patrol. She also makes parsnip wine, although she won't have any other form of alcohol in the cottage. Dolly appears in four episodes.

GODFREY, FRANK

Role: Member of the platoon's back row in 23 episodes (S2; S3, episodes 1–7; S4, episodes 1–3, 5, 6, 9–13) (TV); (Film)
Frank was an old pro who had been a performer all his life before moving into theatre management, including a spell at the Palace Theatre, Watford.

GODFREY (SENIOR), MR

Not seen in the episode, but we learn a little about Charles Godfrey's father in 'The Battle of Godfrey's Cottage', when we hear that he died five years previously, aged 92, after spending the last year of his life confined to bed. To help provide a little company, and to make their father's final days more bearable, Charles and his sisters, Dolly and Cissy, bought him a parrot called Percy. But when Mr Godfrey (Senior) dies, he causes something of a scandal in the area by leaving his money not to his children, but to a young girl in Walmington.

GODIVA AFFAIR, THE

Recorded: Sunday 3/11/74
Original transmission: Friday 6/12/74, 7.45–8.15pm
Original viewing figures: 13.8 million
Repeated: 5/6/75, 30/4/91, 9/12/95, 2/8/97

CAST

Arthur Lowe . . . . .Captain Mainwaring
John Le Mesurier . . . . .Sergeant Wilson
Clive Dunn . . . . .Lance Corporal Jones
John Laurie . . . . .Private Frazer
Arnold Ridley . . . . .Private Godfrey
Ian Lavender . . . . .Private Pike
Bill Pertwee . . . . .Chief Warden Hodges
Talfryn Thomas . . . . .Private Cheeseman
Frank Williams . . . . .Vicar
Edward Sinclair . . . . .Verger
Janet Davies . . . . .Mrs Pike
Pamela Cundell . . . . .Mrs Fox
Eric Longworth . . . . .Town Clerk
Peter Honri . . . . .Private Day
Rosemary Faith . . . . .Waitress
Colin Bean . . . . .Private Sponge
George Hancock . . . . .Private Hancock
Platoon: Michael Moore, Desmond Cullum-Jones, Freddie White, Freddie Wiles, Evan Ross, Leslie Noyes, Roger Bourne, Hugh Cecil
Young Girls: Penny Lambirth, Yasmin Lascelles, Elaina Grand, Belinda Lee

PRODUCTION TEAM

Script: Jimmy Perry and David Croft
Producer/Director: David Croft
Production Assistant: Bob Spiers
Studio Lighting: Howard King
Studio Sound: Michael McCarthy
Design: Bryan Ellis
Assistant Floor Manager: Anne Ogden and Sue Bennett-Urwin
Vision Mixer: Dave Hanks
Costume Supervisor: Susan Wheal
Make-Up Supervisor: Sylvia Thornton

The town of Walmington is only £2,000 off its target to buy a Spitfire and during the week the citizens will be doing their best to raise the money, climaxing in a procession on Saturday afternoon, when the platoon will be morris dancing.

After they practise their routine in the church hall, Mainwaring notices Jones isn't himself and has a private chat with him in the office. He explains his arrangement with Mrs Fox, but that recently her attention has been elsewhere: she has eyes for Mr Gordon, the town clerk; it's upsetting Jones so much, he asks Mainwaring to speak to her.

'The Godiva Affair'

'The Godiva Affair'

After leaving school, David studied at Cambridge University (where he performed with the university's acting group, The Footlights) and qualified as a teacher. He taught at a grammar school in Leeds for two years before deciding to try his luck as an actor.

Within months of leaving his teaching job, David was performing in *Romeo and Juliet* at the Salisbury Playhouse. He worked with the city's rep company for two years before moving on to companies at Worcester, Liverpool, Derby and Stoke, and returning to Salisbury in 1970.

The following year he joined the BBC Drama Repertory Company and over the next two years established his name on the radio. David made his TV debut in 1969 with a leading role in the Thames' detective series, *The Mind of Mr J G Reeder*. Since then he's appeared in numerous shows, including *Bergerac*, *The Bill*, *London's Burning*, *Doctor Who* and *A Touch of Frost*, playing the pathologist. He's also been busy on the stage and writing. He started with a one-man show, *The Castaway*, and has gone on to write various plays, such as an adaptation of *The Wind in the Willows*, which enjoyed two successful years (1986–1987) in the West End. He's currently writing a visitors' guide for St Paul's Cathedral.

As well as acting and writing, for the last ten years David has directed a radio course for students.

GOODWIN, CYNTHIA
Make-up supervisor on the fourth and fifth series (TV)

GORDON, CLAUDE
Played by Eric Longworth (TV)
Claude, who takes over the role of town clerk in Walmington-on-Sea from Mr Rees, is inclined to panic. In 'A Man of Action', he's in a terrible state when he arrives at the church hall office to hear a mine has cut off the town's gas and water supplies, brought down the phone lines and badly damaged the railway track.

Mainwaring calls Mrs Fox but rumours soon spread among the platoon, thanks to Frazer who overheard the captain talking to her on the phone, arranging to meet at the Marigold Tea Rooms the following morning. Everyone plans to be there, even Cheeseman, who writes a gossip column for the *Eastbourne Gazette* called 'Whispers from Walmington'.

Mainwaring is worried about meeting Mrs Fox, because she's so brash and loud, but when he tries, with difficulty, to broach the matter of Jones' feelings with her, she gets the wrong idea, thinks Mainwaring fancies her too, and suggests Jones has Mondays and Saturdays, Mainwaring Tuesdays and Fridays, while Mr Gordon can have Wednesdays.

At parade the next evening, Jones thanks Mainwaring, but the men then find out they can't get in the hall because Hodges, the Vicar,

(Above) One of Hodges' better jobs was helping to select the right girl for Lady Godiva.

Mr Gordon and the Verger are auditioning a bunch of women, including Mrs Fox, for the part of Lady Godiva in the procession. Mr Gordon decides Mrs Fox is the ideal person for the role. But when her wig and fleshings (tights) are stolen, it's Elizabeth Mainwaring, much to her husband's horror, who steps into the breach.

GOODERSON, DAVID (1941–)
Born: Lahore
Role: Mr Murphy ('Under Fire') (radio)
David moved to England with his mother in 1945, aged four. His father, who was in the Indian Civil Service, joined them a year later.

Mr Gordon isn't universally liked; Jack Jones can't stand him while Wilson describes him as a 'bald-headed old duffer'.

GORILLA WARFARE

Recorded: Sunday 27/10/74

Original transmission: Friday 29/11/74, 7.45–8.15pm

Original viewing figures: 14.4 million

Repeated: 29/5/75, 12/6/76, 5/12/89, 6/9/90 (N Ireland), 9/10/93, 12/4/97

CAST

Arthur Lowe	Captain Mainwaring
John Le Mesurier	Sergeant Wilson
Clive Dunn	Lance Corporal Jones
John Laurie	Private Frazer
Arnold Ridley	Private Godfrey
Ian Lavender	Private Pike
Bill Pertwee	Chief Warden Hodges
Talfryn Thomas	Private Cheeseman
Edward Sinclair	Verger
Robert Raglan	Colonel
Robin Parkinson	Lieutenant Wood
Erik Chitty	Mr Clerk
Rachel Thomas	The Mother Superior
Michael Sharvell-Martin	Lieutenant
Verne Morgan	Farmer
Joy Allen	Lady with the Pram

Platoon: Colin Bean, George Hancock, Desmond Cullum-Jones, Michael Moore, Freddie White, Freddie Wiles, Evan Ross, Leslie Noyes, Roger Bourne, Hugh Cecil

Nun (non-speaking): Belinda Lee

PRODUCTION TEAM

Script: Jimmy Perry and David Croft
Producer/Director: David Croft
Production Assistant: Bob Spiers
Film Cameraman: Len Newson
Film Sound Recordist: John Gatland
Film Editor: Bill Harris
Studio Lighting: Howard King
Studio Sound: Michael McCarthy
Design: Bryan Ellis
Assistant Floor Manager: Anne Ogden and Sue Bennett-Urwin
Vision Mixer: Dave Hanks
Costume Supervisor: Susan Wheal
Make-Up Supervisor: Sylvia Thornton
Visual Effects: Jim Ward

The platoon are off on a weekend exercise which explains why Pike has his scarf, Wilson a suitcase and pyjamas, and Godfrey an eiderdown. They are supposed to be commandos who've been dropped behind enemy lines; they have to rendezvous with a secret agent – who's Mainwaring, of course – and take him to a secret place. GHQ will try stopping them by using counter agents.

The Verger and Hodges are annoyed when they hear Mainwaring's men laughing about Eastgate's effort, so they set out to get the platoon spotted. Mainwaring suspects everyone of being a counter agent, including a woman with a pram, two nuns with a broken-down car and a very suspicious man who races out from the woods saying he runs an experimental laboratory for the war office and a gorilla has escaped.

Mainwaring and his men survive the day and spend the night in a farmer's barn, but there's someone else in the barn: Lieutenant Wood, disguised as a gorilla. The gorilla reports back to GHQ that Mainwaring is the important secret agent. With only half an hour to deliver Mainwaring to GHQ, time is against them, but after Mainwaring commandeers Hodges' motorbike and sidecar and ends up riding pillion with a gorilla, with Jones in the sidecar, they reach their destination in the nick of time. On their arrival, the important secret agent is looking the worse for wear thanks to a misplaced needle!

GORT, GENERAL

Gort's name is mentioned by Wilson and Mainwaring in 'Museum Piece' after reading the newspaper headlines. General Lord Gort VC, was appointed commander-in-chief of the British Expeditionary Force (BEF) during the Second World War.

GOSSLING, WILLIAM (1912–1981)

Role: Member of the platoon's back row in seven episodes (S5, episode 12; S6, episodes 1–5 & 7) (TV)

After working in an engineer's office for most of his career William was made redundant in his fifties. Unsure what to do with his life, his actress wife persuaded him to take up walk-on work. Thanks to fellow platoon member George Hancock, William joined *Dad's Army*.

He secured work in various shows, including *The Tommy Cooper Show* and many productions of Shakespeare and also did film work. William was in demand until illness stopped him working and he died at the age of 69.

GPO MAN, THE

Played by Ronnie Brody (TV)

In 'Number Engaged', the GPO man arrives to sort out the unexploded bomb caught in the phone wires. After quickly assessing the situation he decides it's more than he can handle, which doesn't go down well with Mainwaring.

GRAHAM, CAPTAIN

Not seen in the series, Captain Graham is mentioned in 'Round and Round Went the Great Big Wheel' as the leader of the Dymwhich Home Guard, who are tasked with patrolling the aerodrome perimeter while the secret demonstration takes place.

GRAHAM TWINS, THE

Roles: Doris and Dora ('War Dance') (TV)

Vicki and Cathy Graham played the twins who were invited to the platoon dance in 'War Dance'. Other TV work included appearances in *The Saint*. They are no longer in the profession.

GRAINGE, RONNIE

Roles: Several including the Newspaper Boy and Dave, the songwriter (stage show)

Ronnie's career has included London productions like *Charlie Girl* and *Treasure Island*, pantomimes (working at the Palladium) and cabaret. He has also toured extensively, including engagements in Canada and South Africa.

GRANT HILL

Located between Walmington-on-Sea and Eastgate, Grant Hill is mentioned in 'The Making of Private Pike' by an exhausted Frank Pike, who spent an hour pushing a car up it after running out of petrol. What made the whole affair more embarrassing for Frank was that he'd taken a girl to the pictures and they were on their way home.

GRAY, FIONA

Played by Carmen Silvera (TV and radio)

Address: 31 Wilton Gardens, Walmington-on-Sea

Mrs Fiona Gray moves to Walmington with her mother from their London home near Regent's Park to escape the bombing. However, her life in the seaside town is far from active and the highlights of her days are having morning coffee in Ann's Pantry and watching the dahlias grow!

Her stay at Wilton Gardens, not far from Mainwaring's home, is short-lived. She decides to return to the capital when it is obvious a longer stay could, perhaps, lead to an affair with Mainwaring, who becomes besotted with her, seeing in this courteous, confident lady everything his wife isn't.

GREEN, CARSON (1955–)

Born: Hillingdon

Role: Boy (S3, episode 3: 'The Lion has 'Phones') (TV)

Carson, whose father worked in the film industry, was interested in following him into the business, and at the age of five appeared in two commercials advertising jam for the Co-op and beans for an American company. Although he didn't attend a full-time acting school, he trained in singing and acting during the evenings, and acquired an agent. Small parts in *Half a Sixpence* and *Chitty Chitty Bang Bang* followed, further commercials, including one for Kit Kat, and the occasional walk-on part on television, in shows such as *Boy Meets Girls*.

His first role with lines was that in *Dad's Army*, after which he spent three months with the Royal Shakespeare Company, initially at Stratford before touring in *The Merry Wives of Windsor*. Other stage worked followed (*As You Like It* and *Julius Caesar*) but he left acting at 17 to work as a runner for a commercial film company. He later got married and left the business. He's now a partner in a company that restores old cars.

GREEN, GERARD
Role: Colonel Masters ('The Captain's Car') (radio)

GREEN, MR
An unseen official from Swallow Bank's head office, who's mentioned in 'Operation Kilt'. His impending visit is the reason, or so Wilson claims, why Mainwaring leaves the bank early via the back door, so he can catch up on some Home Guard paperwork at the church hall. Mr Green is cross to miss Mainwaring again, especially as it's the third time that week. He's also unhappy at the wartime posters splashed across the walls of the bank, believing it promotes the wrong image.

GREENE, PETER
Born: London
Role: Sound Engineer (1972 *Christmas Night with the Stars* insert, 'Broadcast to the Empire') (TV)
Peter, whose mother was a professional actress, worked as a student ASM at Watford Rep for writer Jimmy Perry before joining drama school. After graduating, he toured, worked in rep and made commercials before making his TV debut in *Whack-O!*. A role as a vicar in *Doctor on the Go* during the 1970s was followed by many one-off comedy appearances, notably in *Some Mothers Do 'Ave 'Em*, *Are You Being Served?* and *It Ain't Half Hot, Mum*. He's also made cameo appearances in several comedy films.

Today, Peter works for an independent research company, but still does corporate work and directs local shows.

GREGG, MR
Not seen in the series, Mr Gregg, who owns a farm just outside Walmington, is persuaded to lend a tractor and truck full of hay to Wilson for the exercise in 'Operation Kilt'. Mr Gregg banks with the Swallow, and Mainwaring had recently refused him an overdraft, but when Wilson tells him that Mainwaring has supposedly changed his mind, the farmer soon agrees to lend the equipment.

GREGORY, DRILL SERGEANT
Played by Anthony Sagar (TV); Jack Watson (radio)
The Drill Sergeant is from the Guards and arrives at Walmington on a Friday evening to help kick any sloppiness out of the Walmington Home Guard with one hour of drill. Seen in the episode 'Room at the Bottom', he barks his commands and is not a character you would want to upset.

GRIFFITHS, FRED (1912–1994)
Born: Ludlow
Role: Bert King (film)
Fred made a living out of character parts, appearing in hundreds of film and television productions during his career. A former London fireman, he moved into acting by accident and was a regular face in British movies, especially during the 1950s when he was often cast in small parts.

His film credits included playing a barman in *Steptoe and Son*, a taxi driver in *Carry On Loving*, *Carry On Regardless*, *Perfect Friday*, *Billion Dollar Brain*, *There Was a Crooked Man* and *John and Julie* in 1955. He was also seen in *To Sir, with Love*; *Light Up the Sky*; *I Believe in You*; *I'm All Right, Jack*; *Carry On Nurse*; *Dunkirk* and a host of other movies.

GUTTERIDGE, MARTIN
BBC visual effects designer on four episodes (TV): S9: 'Wake-Up Walmington', 'The Making of Private Pike', 'Knights of Madness' and 'Number Engaged'
London-born Martin Gutteridge started his career in special effects at the age of 16 working for a company called Trading Post. He remained with the company, apart from a two-year spell completing national service, until 1961, when he left to work on the model unit of *HMS Defiant* as a special effects assistant. After this he went on to work on other films including *Lawrence of Arabia*.

In 1971 he returned to England after working on location and, with a group of colleagues, founded Effects Associates, the company of which he's now managing director. The BBC employed his company for over six years, and as well as working on the final series of *Dad's Army* he worked on other shows including *The Onedin Line*.

HACKNEY, PEARL

Born: Burton

Role: Mavis Pike in 14 episodes (radio)

Pearl, who spent nearly five decades in show-business, trained as a ballet dancer from the age of five. After leaving school she moved to London and became principal dancer at The Windmill Theatre for four years. During the late 1930s acting began dominating her career, and she worked chiefly in rep and radio. Her numerous TV appearances include *Coronation Street*, *Hi-De-Hi!*, *Meet the Wife*, *The Liver Birds*, *All Creatures Great and Small* and *Terry and June*. She made several films, including *There's a Girl in My Soup*, *Cool it Carol*, *Tiffany Jones*, *Stand Up Virgin Soldiers*, *The Ploughman's Lunch*, *The Hound of the Baskervilles*, *Yanks* and *Laughterhouse*. Pearl retired from acting in 1994.

HAIG, JACK (1913–1989)

Born: London

Roles: Gardener (S3, episode 8: 'The Day the Balloon Went Up'), Landlord (S8, episode 1: 'Ring Dem Bells') (TV); Lance Corporal Jones (part of the stage show's run)

Jack, whose parents had their own double-act, began his professional career as a comedian in revues, touring shows and pantos up and down the country.

He started his small-screen career in the late 1950s, playing Wacky Jacky, the popular children's character for Tyne Tees Television, a role he used later on *Crackerjack*. Among his many roles on TV is that of Archie Gibbs, the gardener in *Crossroads*. In his later work, Jack is probably best remembered as Monsieur Leclerc in five series of *'Allo, 'Allo*, but he appeared in countless shows, including *Keep It In the Family*. His film work was limited to small roles in pictures like *Oliver!*, *Superman* and *The Adventures of a Taxi Driver*.

Jack died of cancer in 1989.

HAINES, ALAN

Roles: Major Smith (S3, episode 2: 'Battle School') (TV); Marine Officer (film)

Among his many TV, film and stage appearances are roles in the 1972 series, *Van Der Valk*, playing

Hodges' nephew, Hamish, was just as annoying as his uncle.

Brigadier Mertens, and Constable Marlowe in the 1964 film, *The Eyes of Annie Jones*.

HALL, MRS

Played by Pat Coombs (film)

A customer in Jones' shop whose husband always insists on a bit of brisket.

HALLMAN, BOB

Vision mixer on one episode (TV): 'Under Fire'

HAMILTON, GRAHAM

Roles: Several in the stage show, particularly at Billingham and The Shaftesbury, including Private Meadows and Raymond

Graham's career has covered all areas of the entertainment business. He has appeared in West End plays, such as *Jeeves* and *The Mousetrap*, been on tours and worked in rep, with a spell at Harrogate, and a period with the Royal Shakespeare Company. He has also worked on TV, and was seen in *Last of the Summer Wine*.

HAMISH

Played by Lindsey Dunn (TV); Elizabeth Morgan (radio)

The mouthy little boy in 'The Recruit', Hamish is cheeky to the Verger and Vicar while they're on patrol during their brief service with the Home Guard. He is an annoying troublemaker around the streets of Walmington, where he frequently runs into Jones' shop shouting: 'Sainsbury's' and wanders into Swallow Bank bellowing: 'National Provincial'. It turns out he's Mr Hodges' nephew.

Note: In the original script the character was called Wilfred not Hamish.

HAMPTON, MIRANDA (1937–)

Born: Sutton Coldfield

Role: Sexy Lady (S3, episode 12: 'Man Hunt') (TV)

After studying at an Arts Education school in Hertfordshire, Miranda started her career as a dancer, specialising in classical dancing. After ten years as a dancer, she started being offered television work and appeared in shows such as *Doctor Who*, *Sherlock Holmes*, *The Benny Hill Show* and a 1972 episode of *Van der Valk*, playing a bar manageress. She also worked on stage, including a period with the Welsh Theatre Company, and made a few film appearances, like a scullery maid in 1968's *Chitty Chitty Bang Bang*.

Miranda started finding the world of acting too stressful and gave up the profession in the mid-1970s to concentrate on teaching. After a year's college course she is now a choreographer and teacher of dance, focusing on jazz and contemporary. Currently she teaches one day a week at Hampstead and regularly runs courses at Holborn.

HANCOCK, GEORGE (1906–1992)

Born: Newcastle-under-Lyme
Role: Member of the platoon's back row in 60 episodes (S3, episodes 1–4, 6–9, 11, 12; S4, episodes 1, 3, 5, 6, 9–13; 'Battle of the Giants'; S5; S6; S7; S8; 'My Brother and I'; 'The Love of Three Oranges'; S9) (TV); (Film)

Before he appeared in *Dad's Army*, George had been an opera singer, but he began his working life as a blacksmith in the coal mines until he was 17.

Interested in making singing his career, he won a scholarship at 18 to the Royal College of Music. After graduating, he launched his professional singing life by joining the Old Vic, and he later became the youngest baritone to appear at Glyndebourne. He toured South Africa, Australia and New Zealand as the leading baritone in a popular musical, returning just before war was declared.

After working at Covent Garden, George won a three-year recording contract with Columbia and made many records, before travelling to the Middle East, Asia and East Africa with an army entertainment unit during the war years.

He maintained his singing career for many years after the Second World War, clocking up over 400 radio broadcasts. Eventually he started doing TV work and adverts, including a long run in an Oxo commercial. Among his small screen credits are two episodes of *Steptoe and Son*, *The Beggars Opera*, *Z Cars* and *The Goodies*.

HANCOCK, PRIVATE

Played by George Hancock (TV)

A regular in Walmington's platoon who's mentioned by Mainwaring in 'The Deadly Attachment' when he's asked, along with Sponge, to fetch a step ladder. He is also credited in 'The Godiva Affair'.

HANKS, DAVE

Vision mixer on 56 episodes (TV): S2, episodes 1, 2 & 5; S3; S4, episodes 3, 4, 5, 6, 7, 8, 10, 11 & 13; 'Battle of the Giants'; S5; S6; S7, episodes 1, 3, 4, 5 & 6; S8, episodes 1, 3, 4 & 6

Dave joined the technical operations department of the BBC in 1959, straight from school, as a trainee cameraman. In 1962, he became a vision mixer, working on an afternoon women's programme and shows such as *Playbox* and *Last Man Out*, a wartime adventure story for children's TV.

Other than a secondment to the appointments department, Dave remained in vision mixing until he retired early through ill health in 1990. By this time he'd been promoted to senior vision mixer, and had undertaken training of new employees.

Since retiring, Dave has run adult education classes in video recording at local colleges in Surrey, and the City and Guilds' media production course for the county's Adult Education Service.

HAPPIDROME

This comedy show was popular during the Second World War and was one of Pikey's favourite programmes. In a scene that was eventually cut from 'The Two and a Half Feathers', he's listening to it in the sitting room before Wilson, who's got a lot on his mind, switches the wireless off. Some of the characters were Enoch (played by Robbie Vincent), Mr Lovejoy (Harry Korris) and Ramsbottom (Cecil Frederick).

HARBORD, GRAHAM (1958–)

Role: Little Arthur (S2, episode 4: 'Sergeant Wilson's Little Secret') (TV)

Graham, who was ten when the episode was recorded, was attending the Barbara Speake Stage School in London when he played the evacuee taken in by Mrs Pike. He joined the school at the age of nine, and remained there until he completed his education. His day was split between school work in the morning and auditions, modelling and extra work during the afternoon.

His first job in films was as a workhouse boy in *Oliver Twist*, while other credits include: *Chitty Chitty Bang Bang*, *Stig of the Dump* for TV and the original version of the musical *Joseph and the Amazing Technicolor Dreamcoat*. He was also seen as a young Tony Curtis in the opening credits of *The Persuaders*.

Upon leaving stage school, Graham took up photography; he got a job and started a City and Guilds course, but after two years gave up the profession. He moved into car sales, and now runs his own company, concentrating on leasing vehicles and contract hire in southeast England.

HARDCASTLE, INSPECTOR

Played by Robert Raglan (film)

The inspector arrives at the church during the closing scenes of the film, but while he considers, along with all the other officials, what to do about the German airmen holding hostages in the church hall, the enterprising Captain Main-

waring has already risked his life to resolve the incident.

HARDCASTLE, PRIVATE

Not seen in the sitcom, Private Hardcastle is a member of the Walmington Home Guard. Jones calls his name in 'Absent Friends'.

HARDING, TONY

Visual effects designer on two episodes (TV): S5, episode 10: 'Brain versus Brawn' and episode 13: 'Time On My Hands'

Amersham-born Tony Harding spent three years at art school before joining the art department at Guild Television Services in London, helping make commercials. After two years he moved to Century 21, a company which made puppet shows such as *Thunderbirds* and *Captain Scarlet*. By the time he left in 1968, Tony had transferred to the visual effects department. He worked freelance for a while, joining the BBC in 1970. He worked in the visual effects department for 28 years, and his credits include *Monty Python*, *The Goodies*, *Doctor Who* and *Some Mothers Do 'Ave 'Em*. Since 1998 he has returned to freelance work.

MEMORIES OF VISUAL EFFECTS

'I helped Peter Day with the episode "Round and Round Went the Great Big Wheel" and was given the job of driving the huge wheel. Inside the two big wheels was a drum which dangled and never rotated. I sat inside and operated two handles which controlled each wheel separately. I wound it like two crank handles, and if I wanted to turn a corner I wound one harder than the other. It was hard work! I didn't have any time to practise, partly because it turned up with part of the gearing not completed. For the first few shots we had to pull it on a long wire and had to shoot without seeing the wire.'

TONY HARDING

HARRIS, BILL

Film editor on 15 episodes (TV): S4, episodes 2, 3, 4 & 5; S5, episodes 3, 5, 10, 12 & 13; S6, episodes 5 & 6; S7, episodes 1, 3, 5 & 6

HARRIS ORPHANS' HOLIDAY HOME HUT

Situated on the beach at Walmington, the hut is deserted when Mainwaring and his men use it as a patrol hut in 'Sgt – Save My Boy!'. Frazer and Godfrey remember what it was like before the children were evacuated to somewhere safer

'Sgt – Save My Boy!'

after Dunkirk. Frazer recalls it was usually full with three dozen screaming kids, wearing blue aprons and straw hats. Godfrey and his sisters had three over for tea once, and he discovered they were skilled sandcastle makers.

The wooden chalet-styled hut was built to provide changing accommodation and shelter for the orphans and their escorts, and evidence of their occupation still remains in the form of buckets, spades, swimming rings and sandcastle flags.

HARRISON, JAN
Make-up designer on one episode (TV): 'Something Nasty in the Vault'

HART DYKE, JOHN (1929–)
Born: Hampton Wick
Role: French General (S7, episode 5: 'The Captain's Car') (TV)
John, who'd worked for Jimmy Perry at Watford Rep and Arnold Ridley in a production of *Ghost Train*, began training as a chartered surveyor after his national service. Halfway through his studies he met someone connected with a rep company in Perth, Scotland, and gave up surveying and joined the company for three months as an unpaid student, before becoming ASM.

He made his TV debut in an episode of a BBC children's programme, quickly followed by an appearance in *Z Cars* as a furniture removal man. John has never been a regular on TV and most of his work since *Dad's Army* has been in the theatre. However, his TV credits include *The Professionals*, *Bergerac*, *Doctor Finlay*, a judge in *EastEnders* and *All Creatures Great and Small*, playing a local squire.

Recently he's played a butler in an episode of *Poirot*, toured the Middle and Far East in the famous *Derek Nimmo Tours*, spent a few weeks in Israel appearing in *Run For Your Wife*, and worked on a cruiser in *Funny Money*, travelling from Bombay to Athens.

HASTINGS, HUGH (1917–)
Born: Sydney, Australia
Role: Member of the platoon's back row in 34 episodes: S1; S3, episodes 8, 11, 12; S4, episodes 1–10, 12, 13; 'Battle of the Giants'; S5, episodes 1–11 & 13 (TV); (Film)
Educated in Australia, Hugh came to England aged 19, determined to become an actor. He was lucky enough to be offered extra work, before joining a trio that had a cabaret act in 1938.

From there he played piano at a nightclub until joining Dundee Rep. His career was interrupted by a five-year spell in the navy during the war, but he returned to the profession after demob and was soon making his West End debut.

Hugh, an accomplished pianist, is also a playwright. He wrote the hugely successful *Seagulls Over Sorrento*, a play that since opening in 1950 has been produced around the world. Four years later he returned to Australia for five years, but upon his return found it difficult to resume his career for a while. Eventually offers of work came his way. Hugh was a regular in the platoon until 1972, when he left to join the Young Vic Company, staying eight years, during which time he toured Mexico, USA and Australia.

Although he hasn't made many films, he was seen in a small part in the 1950 picture, *The Gift Horse*, for which he also received a screenplay credit. In the late 1980s he played piano in a floating restaurant moored on the Thames. Nowadays he writes novels, and has recently completed his second, as well as several plays.

HAWTHORNE, NIGEL (1929–)
Born: Coventry
Role: Angry Man (S3, episode 1: 'The Armoured Might of Lance Corporal Jones') (TV)
Before the runaway hits of *Yes, Minister* and *Yes, Prime Minister*, Nigel played a cameo role in *Dad's Army*, but he'd been working in the medium since the mid-1950s. Among his long list of television credits are appearances in *Marie Curie*, *Holocaust*, *Edward and Mrs Simpson*, *Destiny*, *The Knowledge*, *Barchester Chronicles*, *Jenny's War* and *The Miser*. His many films include *Young Winston*, *Sweeney 2*, *Memoirs of a Survivor*, *Gandhi*, *Relatively Speaking*, *The Madness of King George*, *Richard III* and *Twelfth Night*. He has also worked extensively in the theatre.

HAY-ARTHUR, CECILE
Make-up supervisor on the third series (TV)
It's believed Cecile now lives in America.

HAYDON, DICK
Born: Exeter
Role: Raymond (S3, episode 1: 'The Armoured Might of Lance Corporal Jones') (TV)
Dick – in his early 20s when he appeared – was the first actor to be seen playing Raymond, Jones' young shop assistant. He was frequently referred to but hardly ever seen.

He joined the merchant navy at 16 for three years. But after visiting a London theatre in the early 1960s, he knew he wanted to become an actor and left the navy to join drama school. His first TV job came a year later in the drama *Compact*. Subsequent years saw him busy in shows such as *United!* and *Z Cars*. By the 1970s he worked more in theatre with various West End productions.

Dick's youthful looks meant he became typecast in young roles for some time, even when he'd reached his 30s. He last worked on stage four years ago, and has been concentrating on scriptwriting ever since from his homes in England and France.

HEADPUHF

The codename given to the High Explosive Attack Device Propelled by Ultra High Frequency, a top secret new weapon. The giant wheel, which is controlled by radio, contains two thousand pounds of high explosives and will knock out an enemy pillbox within a range of three miles. It receives its trial run at a deserted aerodrome near Walmington, with Mainwaring's men in charge of all the dirty jobs in the episode, 'Round and Round Went the Great Big Wheel'.

HEATHCLIFF

Never seen or heard in the sitcom, Heathcliff is a boy who works for Frazer. He's mentioned in 'Is There Honey Still For Tea?'.

HEINKEL

A warplane used by the Germans during World War Two. It was designed by German aircraft designer Ernst Heinkel, who became the biggest producer of military aircraft during the war. In the episode, 'The Bullet is Not for Firing', it's a Heinkel the platoon fire at whilst on patrol, using up their meagre supply of ammunition in the process.

HENDERSON, JOHN

Role: Radio Shop Assistant (film)

HENNESSY, EMMETT

Roles: Member of the platoon's back row in two episodes: (S4, episode 6 and 'Battle of the Giants'), Nazi Sailor ('The Deadly Attachment') (TV)

HENRY, THE MILKMAN

Played by Leon Cortez (TV)

Henry appeared in the episode, 'Museum Piece'. With his horse, Flash, and the milk cart, he helps Mainwaring collect the armoury from the Peabody Museum of Historical Army Weapons. When their various attempts at entering the museum fail and they return to the church hall to review their strategy, a cart is borrowed from the scouts for their return visit.

HIGGINS, CHARLIE

Not seen but mentioned by Jones in 'A Man of Action', while talking to Pike outside the park one night on patrol. Christmas 1900 found Jones in South Africa fighting in the Boer War, and he was the recipient, just like all the other soldiers, of a tin box containing a slab of chocolate, a gift from Queen Victoria. Jones didn't touch his chocolate for 25 years and it meant so much to him, he never let it out of his sight. That is until he had to go into hospital and gave it to Charlie

Higgins, a friend, to look after. While Jones was in hospital, Higgins ate the chocolate and filled the tin with sand.

HIGH FINANCE

Recorded: Friday 30/5/75

Original transmission: Friday 3/10/75, 8.00–8.30pm

Original viewing figures: 14.3 million

Repeated: 22/5/76, 21/5/91, 17/12/94, 23/2/95 (Wales), 22/3/97

CAST

Arthur Lowe . . . . .Captain Mainwaring
John Le Mesurier . . . . .Sergeant Wilson
Clive Dunn . . . . .Lance Corporal Jones
John Laurie . . . . .Private Frazer
Arnold Ridley . . . . .Private Godfrey
Ian Lavender . . . . .Private Pike
Bill Pertwee . . . . .Chief Warden Hodges
Frank Williams . . . . .Vicar
Edward Sinclair . . . . .Verger
Janet Davies . . . . .Mrs Pike
Ronnie Brody . . . . .Mr Swann
Colin Bean . . . . .Private Sponge
Natalie Kent . . . . .Miss Twelvetrees
Platoon: George Hancock, Michael Moore, Desmond Cullum-Jones, Freddie White, Evan Ross, Leslie Noyes, Roger Bourne, Freddie Wiles, Hugh Cecil

PRODUCTION TEAM

Script: Jimmy Perry and David Croft
Producer/Director: David Croft
Production Assistant: Jo Austin
Studio Lighting: Howard King
Studio Sound: Alan Machin
Design: Robert Berk
Assistant Floor Manager: Anne Ogden
Vision Mixer: Angela Beveridge
Costume Designer: Mary Husband
Make-Up Artist: Sylvia Thornton

Jones visits the bank and deposits his takings; he presents a cheque for three pounds, two and six – his weekly staff wages – but it's rejected due to insufficient funds. For the last few months he's had a £50 overdraft and it's not reducing. He can't pay it back, has no security, so until the £50 overdraft is repaid, Mainwaring can't honour Jones' cheque. Jones is facing bankruptcy unless he sorts out his affairs. Wilson and Mainwaring feel sorry for him; after the bank closes, Mainwaring, Wilson and Pike head to the butcher's shop to help Jones check his books. Mainwaring can't believe Jones' slapdash methods and, with invoices all over the place, it's no wonder his finances are in a mess. There's no alternative but for Mainwaring to take the books home to complete an audit. When he's completed the work £50 is still unaccounted for.

Suddenly Mr Swann, who runs the grocer's, enters the church hall to speak confidentially to Mr Mainwaring, but is brushed away.

Jones worries that if he has to give up his busi-

ness, he'll let the orphanage down, where he supplies meat, even though they haven't paid his bills, totalling £50, for three months. The story of what happened to the missing money has just begun.

With the Vicar a trustee of the local orphanage, he's dragged out of bed to explain why Jones hasn't been paid. He blames it all on Miss Twelvetrees, who hasn't paid the Vicar for five months. Miss Twelvetrees is interviewed and explains she owns a small shop in the High Street and the £10 per month rent she receives is donated to the orphanage, but she hasn't received the rent for five months. She has asked for the money several times but the man is so poor, yet so kind. You wouldn't think she meant Frazer, who rents the shop.

Mainwaring can't believe the web of intrigue unfolding before him and intends sorting everything out. He calls a meeting which is attended by members of the platoon, Hodges, the Vicar, Verger and Miss Twelvetrees. Frazer lent £50 to Godfrey who'd lent it to Wilson. Mainwaring blames Hodges for the trouble and calls upon Mrs Pike who explains Hodges is her landlord. A year ago he gave notice that he'd be increasing the rent from £1 a week to £2, which she couldn't afford. He said she could owe it to him, but last week took her to The Red Lion for a drink and told her she owed £50 back rent but he'd forget about it if she was 'nice' to him! The confusion is resolved and the money returns to its rightful owner.

Before the meeting is brought to an end, Mr Swann shows his face again and announces, in front of everyone, that Mrs Mainwaring hasn't paid the grocery bill for six months and she owes £49 17s 6d.

HILL, CHARLES

Born: Ulverston, Lake District
Roles: Butler at Marsham Hall (S1, episode 3: 'Command Decision'; S9, episode 1: 'Wake-Up Walmington'), Sergeant ('Battle of the Giants') (TV)
Before attending RADA for a six-month retraining course, upon demobilisation from the navy after the war, Charles Hill worked in insurance by day and did amateur acting in the evening. He became a member of local acting companies and won a silver cup at Skipton Drama Festival for the best individual performance.

He made his TV debut in the Bisto adverts, but gradually built up his career, appearing in shows such as *And Mother Makes Three*, *The Dick Emery Show* and *The Invisible Man*. He was also cast in several films, most notably *The Millionairess*, with Peter Sellers and Sophia Loren. He died of cancer in 1981.

HILL, ROSE (1914–)

Born: London
Role: Mrs Cole (S4, episode 12: 'Uninvited Guests') (TV)
Rose, who's been in the business six decades, began her career as an opera singer, after win-

ning a scholarship to train at the Guildhall School of Music and Drama. She made her debut at Glyndebourne before joining the Sadler's Wells Opera Company. Eventually she turned to acting, and appeared on stage and TV, including *Dixon of Dock Green*, Fay Bridge in the 1968 series, *Thingumybob*, *Take a Sapphire*, *Waterloo Sunset*, Mrs Temple in *The Bill* and *A Touch of Frost*. Although she's appeared in many shows, she's probably best known for playing Fanny, the bedridden old lady in *'Allo, 'Allo*.

Rose has also appeared in a few films, including *Wildcats of St Trinian's*, *Footsteps*, *For the Love of Ada* and *Heavens Above!*.

HIPPODROME THEATRE

The platoon visit the theatre in Walmington during the episode 'Shooting Pains', to cheer themselves up after a poor display on the rifle range, and watch a show with Charlie Cheeseman top of the bill. The theatre is a regular haunt of Walker's, as he visits every Saturday on the look out for orders, and it's here that he spots Laura La Plaz, a crack shot, who, with a little persuasion, helps out Mainwaring's platoon during a shooting competition.

HISTORY

Back in 1968, when colour TV was still in its infancy and man hadn't set foot on the moon, a sitcom, shot in black and white, emerged in rather inauspicious circumstances. Titled *Dad's Army*, its producer and co-writer David Croft had the foresight to judiciously withhold from his boss some rather unflattering results obtained from an audience survey conducted just after the recording of the first episode, 'The Man and the Hour'. The negative views concerned David. 'It was a terrible reaction,' he admits. 'I think the most positive comment was: "I quite like it", while most people said things like: "Don't the authors know the war's over?"' His decision to suppress the results probably saved the show's life. 'If people had got to hear about it I don't think there would have been a second series.'

Critics too weren't bowled over by the escapades of the largely aged part-time soldiers from Walmington-on-Sea when the series was first aired. Opinions were mixed regarding the programme's future, but views quickly changed as the show began attracting a loyal and large audience.

Few, if any, programmes continue to earn their rightful place in the audience-hungry transmission schedules of prime time television so long after they received their small-screen baptism. While many sitcoms from a bygone age collect dust on the shelves of the archives at Television Centre, *Dad's Army* remains as fresh and accessible today as when it was first shown, and continues to be welcomely repeated on BBC1, attracting new and younger audiences all the while.

When Jimmy Perry began penning his thoughts for a new sitcom, while travelling by train to the East London suburb of Stratford, where he was working for Joan Littlewood's theatre company, little did he know he was creating, arguably, his nation's finest example of television comedy. At this point in his life, Jimmy's only experience in the medium of TV was as an actor; his writing output consisted of pantomimes and comedy sketches, but he'd always dreamed of writing for the small screen. 'I kept telling myself that I must write for TV because I could create a good part for myself – that was the main reason for writing *Dad's Army*,' laughs Jimmy.

On his daily train ride to Stratford East, he pondered over the idea. He was convinced of one thing: the success of *Bilko* and *The Army Game* proved that a good service comedy series never failed. 'It was important I wrote about something I'd experienced and understood; then I thought about the Home Guard, after all, I'd served in it at Barnes and Watford during the Second World War. It seemed a wonderful subject for comedy – and one that hadn't been tackled before.'

But it was 1967, over 20 years since the Second World War had finished, and no one mentioned the Home Guard anymore. Jimmy acknowledged ruefully that everyone had forgotten about the Home Guard's role during the war, including the librarian at his local public library. 'I went along to see what books they had on the subject and was astonished when the librarian asked: "The Home Guard, what's that then?"'

Next stop on his research trail was the Imperial War Museum. After returning home with pamphlets describing how to make Molotov cocktails, the memories came flooding back. 'I was a 16-year-old boy in the Home Guard, and it was an exciting time. I was convinced this was a subject that could be explored through comedy.'

Jimmy set to work. He sketched out a brief synopsis, gave some thought to the principal characters and settled down to write the first script. 'For a while I puzzled over how to construct the first episode – there was so much to consider,' he says. He gained much-needed inspiration from the Will Hay movie, *Oh! Mr Porter*, which was being screened one Sunday afternoon. 'One of the movie's strengths was the wonderful balance of characters: a pompous man, a boy and an old man. The combination made for perfect comedy.' This was a key influence when writing his first script, which he titled, 'The Fighting Tigers', especially with the drawing of characters like Mainwaring, Pike and Godfrey.

Switch on any episode of *Dad's Army* and one laughs at the almost crazy antics Captain Mainwaring and his ill-equipped, ill-trained platoon get up to; but all the time Jimmy Perry and David Croft were drawing on their own wartime experiences when scripting the memorable scenes. Although comedy itself demands exaggeration and exploitation of situations, the storylines of Perry and Croft's wartime sitcom were founded in realism, which is one of the show's greatest attractions. For those old enough to understand and have experienced the war years *Dad's Army* provided a nostalgia trip to a time when the country was united against a common foe, pulling together in a desperate fight to retain dignity and independence. And anyone too young to have experienced the period was able to see, perhaps for the first time, what life must have really been like during wartime in dear old Blighty.

The dearth of weapons at the beginning of the series, the makeshift alternatives comprising of golf clubs, old shotguns and other oddities were all reflections of what life was like for Jimmy in the real Home Guard. 'One section of the first episode considers how to tackle a tank with a burning blanket – I remember having lectures about that,' he says.

When the first script was completed, he was chuffed with the result. But he put it aside for several weeks and got on with work at Joan Littlewood's Theatre Workshop. During the summer of 1967, while the theatre was taking a two-month break, Jimmy's then-agent, who also happened to be David Croft's wife, rang offering him a small part in *Beggar My Neighbour*, which

'The Love of Three Oranges'

David was directing for the BBC. Playing Reg Varney's uncouth brother, Reg, led to an opportunity Jimmy wasn't going to miss. 'We were rehearsing at a boys' club on a hot summer's day. I saw David fiddling about with his white sports car and grasped the opportunity to tell him about my script. He was non-committal but agreed to read it.'

The following Monday saw Jimmy and David back in the studio preparing to record the episode of *Beggar My Neighbour*. As the hours ticked by, Jimmy – who was expecting some feedback from David regarding his script – began fearing the worst, until David approached him enthused by the idea. Once a second script had been written, titled 'The Sharpshooters', which later formed the basis for the episode 'Shooting Pains', David Croft showed the idea to Michael Mills, then BBC's head of light entertainment. Mills shared Croft's avidity but wasn't convinced about the title 'The Fighting Tigers'; it was his masterstroke that saw the programme renamed *Dad's Army*. On the proviso that David worked with Jimmy on the scripts, taking into account his experience as a TV writer, Michael Mills was keen to proceed, although he made a few suggestions for improving the script.

Mills didn't care for some of the names Jimmy had employed, and Private Duck was renamed Private Frazer, while Joe Fish became Joe Walker. Jim Jones was turned into Jack Jones, and the original setting of Brightsea-on-Sea became Walmington-on-Sea. Michael Mills' scribbled notes on the original scripts also reveal he felt

one or two of the characters could be from another part of the country, perhaps Scotland. When it came to finding them a position in the society, Mills suggested making one of the platoon members an ex-colonel or admiral, another could be the ex-colonel's gardener, and Pike could be a poacher or local bad boy – which would have been an interesting departure for the young, thumb-sucking Pikey!

After sitting down and discussing Mills' suggestions, Jimmy and David set to work. From the beginning their writing styles complemented one another's. Upon roughing out detailed plots for two episodes, discussing the odd joke or piece of dialogue, the writers went their separate ways to write an episode alone. In all the years they scripted *Dad's Army*, neither Jimmy nor David ever felt the need to swap scripts and read each other's work. 'It was extraordinary how our writing styles were so similar,' says David. 'Whenever I watch an episode now, I can't tell who wrote it.'

Within six weeks of the day Jimmy passed 'The Fighting Tigers' script to David, the BBC hierarchy had given the green light for six episodes to be made, but not before some concerns had been voiced. 'Nearly everyone involved was enthusiastic,' says Jimmy, 'and any opposition came from people worried about whether we were sending up the efforts of the Home Guard.' The programme's format, and in particular the closing credits, was battled over for some time before it was cleared for transmission. 'The original closing credits, for which I fought very hard, showed vignettes of the artists against a background of authentic war scenes,' explains David Croft.

Enormous phalanxes of marching troops contrasted the might of the German army with its tanks and guns against what Michael Mills described as the 'pathetic, comic, but valorous nature of the Home Guard'.

'We also had shots of refugees in the opening credits but Paul Fox, BBC1's controller at the time, was against it,' says David. 'I fought hard to keep the credits the way they were and remember attending a meeting with Paul, Bill Cotton and Tom Sloan. Paul, realising how strongly I felt about the matter, finally agreed to the format I wanted. But having fought for so long, Tom Sloan suddenly decided that if Paul wasn't happy the credits should be changed.'

Sir Paul Fox believes the credits were not apposite for the type of programme being made. 'The shots I was unhappy about showed refugees and Nazi troops, and to me had absolutely nothing to do with the subject of the series, that was my concern.'

'Paul was also very worried about whether the show was taking the mickey out of Britain's Finest Hour,' David explains. 'For a while Dad's Army was on the verge of not going ahead. Then someone suggested having a prologue before the credits on the first episode showing the cast in the present day supporting the "I'm Backing Britain" campaign. So that's what happened but it meant the first episode appeared to start three times: first you had the prologue, then the familiar swastika and union jack credits and also the

newsreel-style clippings before the show finally started. It was like a dog's dinner in my view, but that was the compromise that got the show on the air.'

David Croft didn't let the matter rest there, and when a second series was commissioned he tried, once again, to use authentic filming sequences within the closing credits, referring to an earlier survey the Audience Research Department had conducted for him, in which the majority of people asked had stated the closing captions containing factual background material were not offensive. Sadly, David lost the fight again. In a memo dated 1 November 1968, Michael Mills informed David that the controller of BBC1 and the head of light entertainment had felt the first series had been 'a success as it was, so why change it?'. David, who had already started

making the second series using his preferred style of closing credits, was told to remake them with the revised captions used previously.

With six episodes finally commissioned, David and Jimmy set about refining the main characters. One of the first to receive their attention was Frazer. 'We wanted a Scotsman in the programme,' says Jimmy. 'In those days, every English southern town seemed to have a Scot who was always treated with great reverence by the English, although they were inclined to be a bit disdainful of the English people around them.' From this generalisation, the character of Frazer was born.

Next came the spiv, who Jimmy had originally planned to be a 45-year-old bookmaker. 'Everybody did a spiv, it was a common wartime char-

acter. Forty years ago, spivs traded out of suitcases all along London's Oxford Street, and whenever things were scarce, like during the war, you could guarantee there would be a spiv around.'

As for Jones, the ageing war veteran, Jimmy Perry delved into his Home Guard memories. With him then was an old soldier who'd seen action at the Battle of Omdurman in 1898. 'He was a lance corporal, probably in his late 60s, and kept telling me about his war experiences with Kitchener against the Fuzzy Wuzzies. When it came to writing the series, I dug all these memories up and created Jones. As for the catchphrase "They don't like it up 'em!", that came from a sergeant who taught bayonet drill at Colchester barracks when I was called up in the regular army in 1944.

'Private Godfrey, meanwhile, dated from an era long gone when shop assistants politely asked whether you were being attended to, or if they could help,' says Jimmy. 'They loved their work and took great pride in serving customers. We needed a gentle character and Godfrey evolved.'

A vicar was required to be in charge of a church hall constantly argued over by Mainwaring and Hodges concerning its usage. The Verger, so brilliantly portrayed by Edward Sinclair, started out as a caretaker and didn't don clerical attire until the sixteenth episode, 'The Bullet is Not for Firing'.

The baby of the platoon, Frank Pike, who was originally described as a 17-year-old office boy, was constantly mollycoddled by his mother, and was based on Jimmy's experiences as a boy, while the character of Hodges explored an area of society that interests Jimmy. 'I've always been obsessed with people who never had a hope in hell of doing anything more than shuffling along in life, suddenly getting power. The warden has the power to fine people for showing a light. In Dad's Army we wanted someone to upset the pompous, middle-class Mainwaring, and Hodges was certainly an irritant. In my experience, air raid wardens were often people from minor positions who exploited the power given to them by their duties. Hodges was certainly jumped up, something Mainwaring blamed on the fact that he was only a greengrocer – which incidentally generated lots of mail from real life greengrocers!'

Once the characters had been agreed, Jimmy Perry and David Croft turned their minds to casting, a crucial component in any successful show. Jimmy had already given the matter some thought, recording his views on the original script of 'The Fighting Tigers'. It's hard to imagine anyone other than Messrs Lowe, Le Mesurier, Laurie et al playing the roles, but Jimmy initially saw Arthur Lowe playing Sergeant Wilson and Robert Dorning, who later appeared as a bank inspector in the episode 'Something Nasty in the Vault', as Captain Mainwaring, a character whose name originated from Perry's interest in names that sound different from the way they're spelt. Jack Haig, meanwhile, would play two characters: Jack Jones the butcher (although Jimmy had originally considered making him an iron-monger) and his twin brother, George.

Most of the cast were undefined at this early stage, but Jimmy wanted comedy actor Arthur English to play Joe Walker, even though he'd hoped to play the part himself. 'I wrote Walker for myself, but Michael Mills and David didn't think it was a good idea. Sadly, I was in no position to argue.'

Jimmy was disappointed not to be acting in the series he had created, but in hindsight believes it was probably for the best, a view echoed by David Croft. 'I realised Jimmy was disappointed not to be playing the spiv, but I feel authors are needed in the production box to see how things are going, and that's difficult if they're also acting.'

As he possessed little power in those days, Jimmy's grateful to David Croft for allowing him the chance of becoming involved in discussions regarding casting. 'I claim credit for Arthur Lowe,' he states. 'I kept telling David he should be in the show but the BBC weren't convinced, particularly Michael Mills. I remember him saying: "Arthur Lowe? We don't know him at the BBC, he doesn't work for us."' Lowe was a big success as Mr Swindley in *Coronation Street*, but that was a Granada production. He was an actor whose reputation had been established primarily in commercial TV, which didn't appeal to the Beeb.

The part was first offered to actor Thorley Walters, and when he declined Jon Pertwee was considered. Pertwee, who had seen the original script and showed an interest in playing Captain Mainwaring, and Jack Haig, who was considered for the part of Jack Jones, were pursued by the BBC. A memo from Michael Mills dated 13 November 1967 instructed the department responsible for booking artists to negotiate a fee with both Pertwee and Haig, although neither was able to proceed.

Much to Jimmy's delight, Arthur Lowe was finally invited to meet Michael Mills, David and Jimmy at the BBC. 'One of the things I remember most about the meeting was Arthur putting his foot in it,' smiles Jimmy. 'We were sitting in the restaurant at Broadcasting House when Arthur said to David: "I'm not too fond of situation comedy, you know, I don't like the audience. One series I can't stand is that dreadful *Hugh and I*." David replied: "I produced it!" I couldn't believe how quickly Arthur changed his tack.'

After lengthy discussions, the part was finally offered to Arthur Lowe, and he swiftly stamped his inimitable style on the character of Mainwaring, proving he was perfect for the part. But initially David Croft was unconvinced. 'We were taking a risk,' he admits. 'I knew him as Mr Swindley and he was very good, but the character was quite different from Mainwaring. I needn't have worried, though, because he slotted in to the role perfectly. The electricity between him and Wilson was wonderful.'

One of the challenges David faced when working with Arthur was getting him to learn his lines. 'He wouldn't take his script home and occasionally some of the other actors would call me at home insisting I get Arthur to learn the lines. So I started sending two copies of the script to him with a note saying: "Here's one that

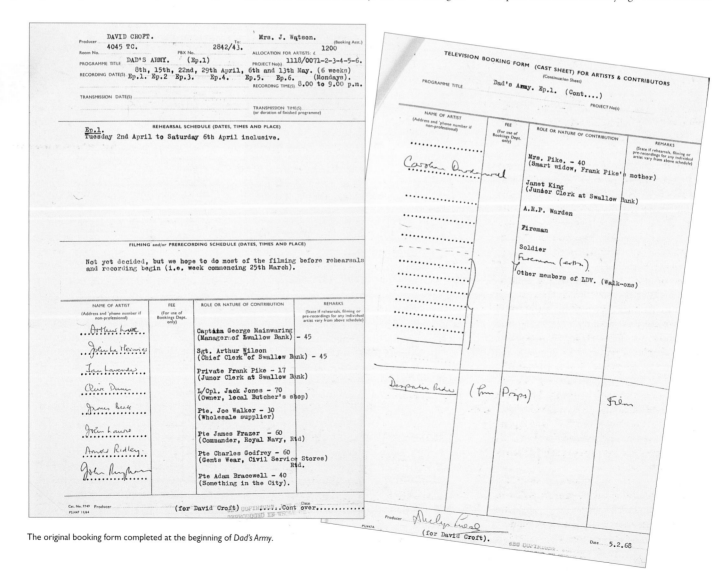

The original booking form completed at the beginning of *Dad's Army*.

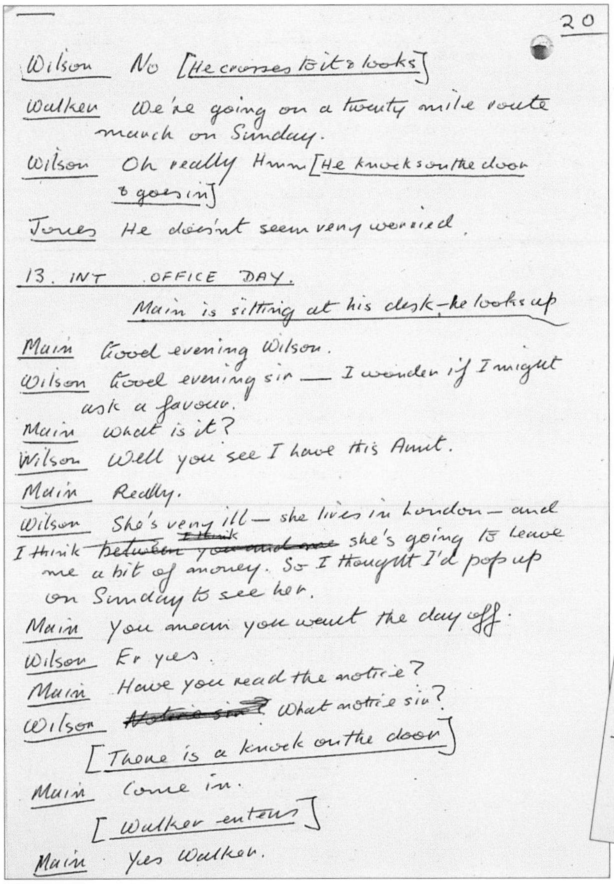

Page 20 (handwritten script):

20

Wilson   No [He crosses to it & looks]

Walker   We're going on a twenty mile route march on Sunday.

Wilson   Oh really Hmm [He knocks on the door & goes in]

Jones   He doesn't seem very worried.

13. INT   OFFICE   DAY.

Main is sitting at his desk — he looks up

Main   Good evening Wilson.

Wilson   Good evening sir — I wonder if I might ask a favour.

Main   What is it?

Wilson   Well you see I have this Aunt.

Main   Really.

Wilson   She's very ill — she lives in London — and I think ~~between you and me~~ she's going to leave me a bit of money. So I thought I'd pop up on Sunday to see her.

Main   You mean you want the day off.

Wilson   Er yes.

Main   Have you read the notice?

Wilson   ~~Notice sir~~ What notice sir?

[There is a knock on the door]

Main   Come in.

[Walker enters]

Main   Yes Walker.

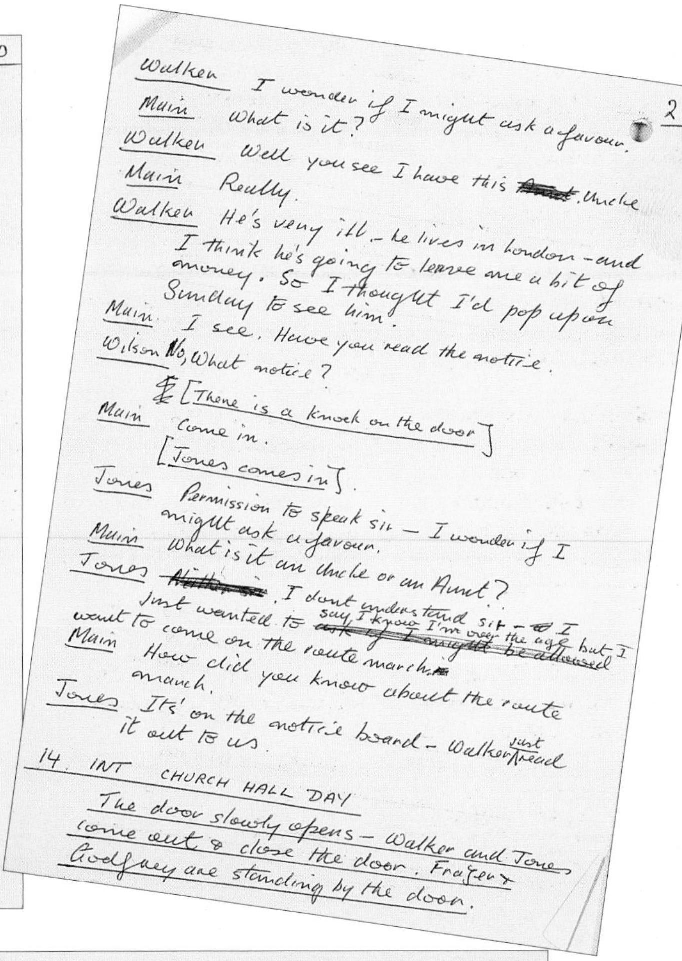

Page 21 (handwritten script):

21

Walker   I wonder if I might ask a favour.

Main   What is it?

Walker   Well you see I have this ~~Aunt~~ uncle

Main   Really.

Walker   He's very ill — he lives in London — and I think he's going to leave me a bit of money. So I thought I'd pop up on Sunday to see him.

Main   I see. Have you read the notice.

Wilson   No, What notice?

[There is a knock on the door]

Main   Come in.

[Jones comes in]

Jones   Permission to speak sir — I wonder if I might ask a favour.

Main   What is it an uncle or an Aunt?

Jones   ~~Neither~~. I don't understand sir — I just wanted to ~~say I know I'm over the age but I might be allowed~~ come on the route march.

Main   How did you know about the route march.

Jones   It's on the notice board — Walker just read it out to us.

14   INT   CHURCH HALL   DAY

The door slowly opens — Walker and Jones come out & close the door. Frazer & Godfrey are standing by the door.

Body text (printed):

you can read in the rehearsal room, and another to put under your pillow in the hope that something filters through during the night!" He wasn't amused,' laughs David.

One of the qualities of *Dad's Army* is its timeless humour making for good clean family viewing, something which must have pleased Arthur who didn't appreciate material that was in the slightest bit suggestive or risqué. Jimmy recalls an incident in his favourite episode 'The Deadly Attachment', when Arthur refused to have a bomb put down his trousers.

'In the original script Mainwaring had the bomb in his trousers, down which Frazer had to put his arm. Arthur never read his scripts until the last minute, and while we were on location having breakfast at The Bell Hotel, Thetford, he started rustling his script. He said: "James, could you spare a minute, please." I went over and he mumbled: "I'm not having this, I'm not having a bomb down my trousers." I reminded him that we were filming in an hour and enquired why he hadn't read the script before now. He replied that was his concern and restated that he wasn't having a bomb down his trousers, and certainly not John Laurie's arm!'

David Croft arrived and Jimmy broke the news. They had anticipated Arthur's reaction to the scene and prepared a contingency plan. After feigning surprise they reverted to plan number two, and when the episode was transmitted, it

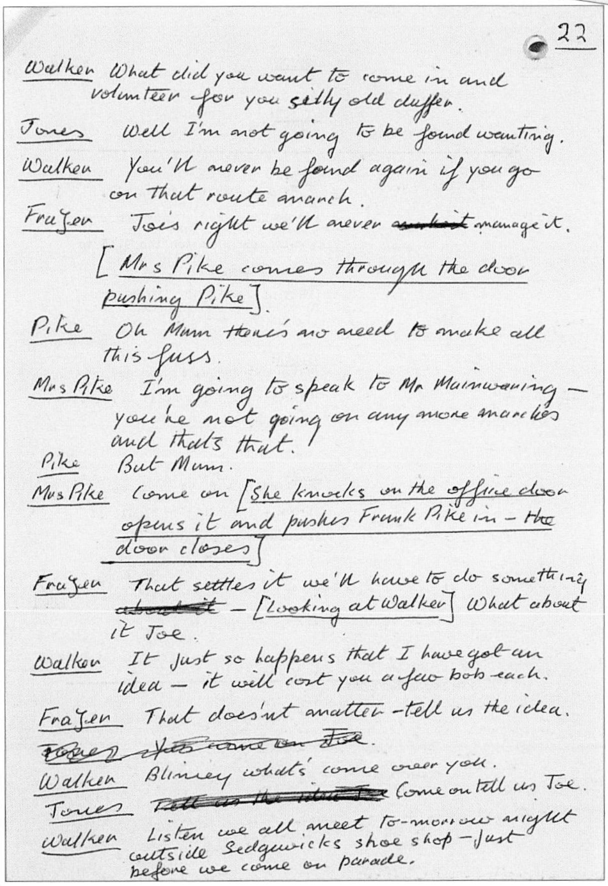

Page 22 (handwritten script):

22

Walker   What did you want to come in and volunteer for you silly old duffer.

Jones   Well I'm not going to be found wanting.

Walker   You'll never be found again if you go on that route march.

Frazer   Joe's right we'll never ~~do it~~ manage it.

[Mrs Pike comes through the door pushing Pike]

Pike   Oh Mum there's no need to make all this fuss.

Mrs Pike   I'm going to speak to Mr Mainwaring — you're not going on any more marches and that's that.

Pike   But Mum

Mrs Pike   Come on [She knocks on the office door opens it and pushes Frank Pike in — the door closes]

Frazer   That settles it we'll have to do something ~~about it~~ — [Looking at Walker] What about it Joe.

Walker   It just so happens that I have got an idea — it will cost you a few bob each.

Frazer   That doesn't matter — tell us the idea.

~~Jones   Yes come on Joe~~

Walker   Blimey what's come over you.

Jones   ~~Tell us the idea Joe~~ Come on tell us Joe.

Walker   Listen we all meet to-morrow night outside Sedgewicks shoe shop — just before we come on parade.

A script begins to take shape.

was Corporal Jones who ended up having the bomb in his trousers.

The rest of the casting was down to David Croft and Michael Mills, who were responsible for bringing John Laurie's name into the frame. Perry explains: 'Michael said: "I've got you John Laurie." To me, John Laurie was a legend. A great Shakespearean actor and one of the finest supporting actors I knew. But then came the embarrassment: his character was described simply as "A Scotsman"! Not exactly inspiring for an actor of his standing.' Initially there were plans to make Frazer a fisherman, but Jimmy and David felt there was insufficient depth in the characterisation and chose the job of undertaker.

Arnold Ridley was selected to play the incontinent Private Godfrey because he'd worked for David Croft on *Hugh and I*. 'He was terribly

funny and a lovely actor. And I was keen on Jimmy Beck for Walker, while Ian Lavender, who was one of my wife's clients, had just played a marvellous part in *Flowers at My Feet*. He was obviously a good actor and as young as we could go for Pikey.'

When it came to casting Jack Jones, the butcher, David Croft agreed with Jimmy that Jack Haig, who subsequently made a handful of appearances in the series, was the ideal candidate for the job. 'The trouble was he'd just been offered 26 programmes of *Whacky Jacky*, a character he more or less created himself for children, and that's the part he accepted,' David recalls. 'So we offered the part to Clive Dunn, who'd played a lovely old man in *Bootsie and Snudge*.

'Michael Mills suggested John Le Mesurier and he was cast as Sergeant Wilson. John was an

extraordinary performer because he never seemed totally with it. But he was a very clever man, always word-perfect and at rehearsals 15 minutes before everyone else.'

David Croft knew that Bill Pertwee possessed a tremendous sense of humour and was also a great enthusiast, so he was an ideal choice as a member of the cast. 'He's a bubbly character and one of his functions was to make the others happy, and he achieved that. He's a lovely man and one of the few actors who never rang me up asking whether there's anything for them in the next show – he knew I'd use him when I could.

'I've cast Frank Williams in clerical roles several times before and he's a marvellous actor, while I've used Edward Sinclair as a short-sighted funeral director before, and he was terribly funny as the Verger. His partnership with the Vicar was wonderful.'

Other storylines considered for use in *Dad's Army*.

As far as the setting was concerned, clearly the series had to be based in a coastal town in southern England, the region closest to the Nazi threat a few miles across the English Channel. Jimmy thought up the name Brightsea-on-Sea, but this was changed to Walmington-on-Sea before the first episode got under way. 'I pictured a small seaside town along the coast from Folkestone, an area of the world I know well,' says Jimmy.

When it came to filming out on location, the military grounds near the Norfolk town of Thetford were chosen as the ideal spot. It wasn't just the cast that enjoyed spending time out on location because it became a family affair with wives usually accompanying their husbands to Norfolk. An essential part of the set each season were the chairs designated to each of the principal actors, who were the only people allowed to use them, something Kay Beck was reminded of by her husband, Jimmy. 'When I first went on location with him he took me on one side and said: "We have these special chairs and not even you're allowed to sit on them. If you'd accidentally sat on it there's no way I could've told you to move, so I thought I'd better warn you." He was being so gentle because he thought I wouldn't understand this!' she laughs. 'Jimmy was later given his chair, and I still have it.'

Location shooting usually involved a fortnight in Norfolk, although everything could have been wrapped up in about ten days. Ian Lavender once asked producer David Croft why. 'He replied: "You haven't seen each other for nine months, so the nights sitting around talking after dinner are very important because you get rid of all your stories. Then when we get to the rehearsal room, we just work."'

The happy, family-like atmosphere surrounding the production was shattered by the death of Jimmy Beck, one of the public's favourite characters. Casting a shadow over the production, it was a distressing time for all. 'But we had to get the show out and ended up rewriting scenes on the spot,' says David Croft. Walker's absence in the episode 'The Recruit', made directly after his death, was explained via a note left on the church hall floor. Thankfully, there was never any intention to engage another actor to replace Jimmy Beck; the part was dropped and for the seventh season a new character, Mr Cheeseman, played by Welsh actor Talfryn Thomas, was introduced. But the move wasn't successful and by the eighth series, he'd gone.

'We made a mistake: it was wrong introducing such a strong character to a series that had been running several years. Cheeseman was an irritating character. It wasn't Talfryn's fault, it was just how the character had been created.'

The Jimmy Perry, David Croft partnership was ideally suited to the development of a programme like *Dad's Army*. Perry brought an incredible enthusiasm and first-hand knowledge of the Home Guard to the partnership, whereas Croft's professional background in TV meant he knew what sort of jokes and visual effects would work on the small screen.

Writing 30-minute episodes for a bunch of actors eager for their fair share of lines, particularly as their characters developed, threw up constant challenges for Jimmy Perry and David Croft. Actor Ian Lavender often found weeks where there wasn't much to do, but he didn't mind. 'We all knew that eventually we'd get a bite of the cherry. For one episode I found I might only have four lines but the next focused entirely around my character – that's the way it worked. All the characters had a share of the lines eventually. We accepted that because there's no way everyone could have hundreds of lines each episode.'

And so came the first day of location filming, a memorable occasion for Jimmy Perry. The *Dad's Army* team were blessed with brilliant weather throughout the years of location shooting, but that day back in April 1968 was a cruel exception – it was snowing! 'We were trying to get the first shot in the can and waited and waited,' he says. 'David owned a Rolls Royce in those days and had parked it in a field. It was full up: Arthur, John Le Mesurier and several others were sitting in it. It was 11am by the time we were ready to shoot and David asked me to get everyone together. Because this was my first TV series, I was very enthusiastic and my one bugbear was that many of the cast didn't seem to share my enormous, mad, eccentric enthusiasm.

'The windows of the Rolls were steamed up as I pulled open one of the doors. Everyone was sitting there looking bellicose, and I was given the most terrible glares. I told them we were ready to film in ten minutes, and Arthur replied: "We'll come when we're ready." I went back to David and told him they were on the way before adding: "We've got a miserable lot of old sods here." But overall, we didn't have much trouble on the set. Some would mutter and get a bit sullen, but nothing to worry about.'

Over the years everyone got to know each other well. One of the things Jimmy Perry remembers about Arthur Lowe was his insatiable appetite. 'He loved his grub,' says Jimmy. 'He'd have a full English breakfast, wade through bacon and sausage sandwiches at the 11 o'clock break, followed by a full lunch. For afternoon tea it would be Mr Kipling cakes and cucumber sandwiches. And back at the hotel, he enjoyed browsing through the pile of menus to select his evening meal. One day we had a young floor manager working with us, and Arthur asked whether I'd told him about the Mr Kipling cakes. I hadn't, so Arthur insisted I did because he didn't want any misunderstandings, it had to be Mr Kipling's cakes. We always ended up with a wide selection of Mr Kipling cakes on location!'

As the years passed, Jimmy Perry and David Croft were delighted with how the series developed and are flattered people still ask about *Dad's Army*, even though they've written other TV shows. Although the show ran for nine years there were times when the cast were unsure whether a new series was to be written. The programme reached an important juncture in its life at the close of 1975, when the stage show gave Jimmy and David a welcome break from script writing. It was the ideal opportunity to step back and consider the programme's future – a decision influenced by David Attenborough, who was then controller of BBC1. It was Attenborough who persuaded the writers to continue. 'He took us to lunch and simply said we couldn't let the show go. He's a very persuasive man so we carried on,' David recalls.

The question always being asked is why *Dad's Army* has retained its appeal while other shows from the genre have drifted into obscurity. When you examine the success of this golden sitcom, it doesn't take long to realise its ingredients were propitious for a successful sitcom. Jimmy Perry believes this success is partly because he wrote about a subject he knew, and that the series reflected Britain at its best. David Croft, meanwhile, says: 'I don't think the basis of comedy changes, and it was universal family entertainment. Jimmy and I were both well-versed in pantomime and summer show comedy, and an enormous amount of the show was based on that style of humour.'

In fact, whatever aspect of this perennial favourite you consider, it's clear that *Dad's Army* is perfect family viewing in every respect. The show is predominantly a character-driven, not a gag-driven series and, therefore, the characters with all their idiosyncrasies and foibles remain just as funny as when they made their first appearances all those years ago.

One trademark was the show's supply of gentle humour, and the occasional excursion into pathos, varying the mood and tone. While a string of episodes would contain pure farce, the next might be a gentle character exploration of more serious themes. A good example is the episode 'Branded', where Godfrey is cold-shouldered for admitting being a conscientious objector during the Great War. When the episode was first transmitted, many viewers wrote congratulating Jimmy and David on their treatment of such a delicate issue. Whenever a serious or straight scene was required, the writers could deliver the goods, as Ian Lavender points out. 'The scene might only last two minutes, and may not contain a serious social slant, but when required they could write such scenes beautifully.'

Another well-crafted example is 'Mum's Army', an episode full of pathos. Making a guest appearance was Carmen Silvera, who later played Edith Artois in *'Allo, 'Allo*. 'I'd worked for David in *Hugh and I* and *Beggar My Neighbour*, so when he rang saying he'd written a special episode of *Dad's Army* and wanted me to play Mrs Gray, I was absolutely thrilled,' she says. But when the episode, which saw Mainwaring being tempted into a brief encounter by the attractiveness of Mrs Gray, was transmitted it met with negative reaction from certain quarters of the Press, as Carmen explains: 'They didn't think it was funny enough and questioned its serious nature. But David didn't mind and still classes it as one of his favourites. What's interesting is that critics have grown to love the episode.'

Reflecting on the success of the series, there are only two things David Croft would have done differently. 'First, I would have employed more extras because the streets of Walmington-on-Sea were always deserted. The trouble is they're expensive: you've got to find them, dress them, feed them and pay them and it was money we didn't have. And second, I would have used more incidental music. That's expensive as well,' he says. 'One had to economise so on *Dad's Army* we used archival music and it worked well.'

The curtain finally came down on the series in 1977 with the transmission of the episode, 'Never Too Old'. Although Jimmy and David knew it was time to stop, the final recording was still an emotional event. Susan Belbin, now a BBC producer, was assistant floor manager that evening. 'It was so moving I had to leave the studio because I was crying so much,' she says. 'As well as realising that this was the end of a wonderfully successful series, Jimmy and David's writing made me think about the war and the grit of the people who were the real Dad's Army. It was an emotional time!'

We're now into the 21st century and the *Dad's Army* phenomenon lives on. Episodes, many of which have been repeated endlessly, still grace our screens and pull in large audiences, proving that Perry and Croft have certainly created a small-screen legend. But whenever we watch an episode today, chances are it's received a touch of polishing from Charles Garland, whose job it is to ensure each instalment's visual and audio quality is in tiptop condition. Garland describes his duties as those that producer David Croft would have done at the time of the original recording, if the technology had existed. Although some people question whether giving the episodes a makeover in this way is detrimental to their origins, it's clearly an essential job if fans of the show want to continue watching their favourite sitcom on mainstream TV in years to come. Garland's objectives are to enhance the picture and sound quality, which cannot be seen as anything but constructive.

Whenever the Beeb are planning to rerun a few episodes, freelance producer Charles Garland, who looks after a large amount of BBC's comedy archive and acts as series editor on reruns of *Dad's Army*, visits the editing suites

BUDGET FOR 'THE MAN AND THE HOUR'

Excluding the writers' and actors' fees, the first episode of *Dad's Army*, 'The Man and the Hour' cost £3175 to make. The cost breakdown is as follows:

Signature tune:
  recording fee for Bud Flanagan = £105
  musicians = £252
  conductor = £30

Design = £1255
Costume = £300
Make-up = £35
Film sequences = £1009
Recordings (Film/VTR) = £80
Film hire = £90
Filming facilities:
  Stanford = £15
  Anchor Hotel, Thetford, Norfolk = £4

at Television Centre, London, and obtains copies of the episodes. He works through each tape frame by frame, and with the aid of computer equipment he's able to remove scratches and blemishes from the tape. Once he's happy with the picture quality, the programme is then moved into sound dub, enabling him to enhance the quality where necessary, or bring the sound forward if it is muffled or distant. Charles Garland works on each episode for approximately three days before he's in a position to show Perry and Croft the end result, ensuring they're happy with the quality before transmission.

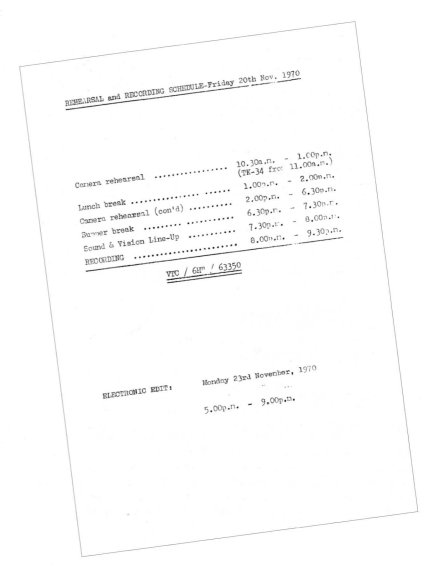

REHEARSAL and RECORDING SCHEDULE-Friday 20th Nov. 1970

Camera rehearsal .... 10.30a.m. - 1.00p.m.
                                    (TK-34 from 11.00a.m.)
Lunch break .... 1.00p.m. - 2.00p.m.
Camera rehearsal (con'd) .... 2.00p.m. - 6.30p.m.
Supper break .... 6.30p.m. - 7.30p.m.
Sound & Vision Line-Up .... 7.30p.m. - 8.00p.m.
RECORDING .... 8.00p.m. - 9.30p.m.

VTC / 6HT / 63350

ELECTRONIC EDIT: Monday 23rd November, 1970

                    5.00p.m. - 9.00p.m.

HODGES, WILLIAM
Played by Bill Pertwee (all mediums)

Mainwaring's adversary, Hodges, who's not the bravest of men, is always screaming 'Put that light out!' around the streets of Walmington in his capacity as air raid warden, later to be promoted to chief warden. He also has the use of the church hall on Wednesday evenings for his ARP meetings, which often leads to arguments with Mainwaring.

He's an unpopular person around town, especially with members of the Home Guard; even Godfrey doesn't like the man, classing him as the 'most vulgar and commonest man he's ever encountered'. Donning the familiar white helmet, Hodges has let the newly found power of being chief warden go to his head. On a personal crusade to challenge Mainwaring's inflated

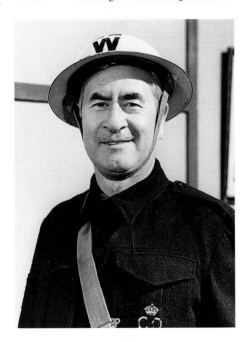

status in the town, Hodges will do anything to get one over on the portly bank manager.

By day, he runs a greengrocer's shop in the High Street. He employs an assistant, Mabel, to help run the shop.

When he's not working, Hodges – who served in the army during the last campaign, spending part of his time as a guard at a prison camp where he learnt to speak German – is a keen sportsman and happens to be the best bowler in the town's cricket eleven.

HOLLAND, JEFFREY (1946–)
Born: Walsall
Role: Soldier (S9, episode 1: 'Wake-Up Walmington') (TV)

Jeffrey didn't contemplate acting as a career until joining an amateur company at the age of 15. Unsure what to do with his life, he worked at a wine merchants straight from school, before working in the office of a cardboard box

manufacturer. It was then he decided to become an actor.

After more than four years in theatre at Coventry, small TV parts came his way. His first speaking role was a young husband in *Dixon of Dock Green*, but he also played a market stall trader in ten episodes of *Crossroads* in the mid-1970s before *Dad's Army*.

Jeffrey, who classes *Dad's Army* as his favourite programme, was offered the part of the truck-driving soldier after appearing in the stage show. Post *Dad's Army* his career blossomed and the 1980s saw him spend seven years playing Spike Dixon in *Hi-De-Hi!* and appear with Russ Abbot on his *Madhouse* shows. Other TV credits include playing James Twelvetrees in *You Rang, M'Lord?*, *Are You Being Served?* and Cecil Parkin in *Oh, Doctor Beeching!*.

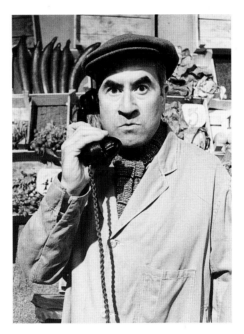

HOLLAND, MAJOR-GENERAL SIR CHARLES

Works at the War Office and is in charge of Operation Catherine Wheel in 'Round and Round Went the Great Big Wheel', although the everyday co-ordination is delegated to Colonel Pierce.

HOLMES, FRANKIE (1922–)
Born: Ilkeston
Role: Fish Fryer (S8, episode 2: 'When You've Got to Go') (TV)

Frankie left school at 14 and worked as an errand boy for a chain of grocery shops. In his spare time he developed his interest in magic by performing locally. Until his call-up at the age of 20, Frankie joined a concert party who entertained at RAF stations and army barracks in the area. During the war he served with the RAF in North Africa and Italy, where he met Alfred Marks. When he was off duty Frankie occasion-

ally performed his magic act, and he impressed Marks so much he suggested he turned professional upon demob.

Back on civvy street, Frankie followed Marks' advice and worked at Nottingham's Empire Theatre for a week, before returning home to take over the running of his mother's grocery shop, while continuing his magic shows during the evenings. Gradually his career in the entertainment world took off and in 1951 he did his first summer season. Frankie did summer shows for the next 31 years, and it was during one show that David Croft contacted him with a view to offering him a part in *Dad's Army*. Work commitments prevented this happening but he later turned up as the owner of the fish and chip shop. Other television work has included *Hugh and I*, playing a husband for Pat Coombs' character, *Crackerjack*, *Hey Presto It's Rolf* and six years in Southern TV's *Little Big Time* as the crazy Professor Frantic.

Frankie also spent nine years as resident entertainer on a cruise ship sailing out of Miami around Caribbean Islands, worked in South Africa, played Dame in panto and recently appeared on *The Big Breakfast* and *Ready, Steady, Cook*. He still works, concentrating mainly on his magic show and stints in the old time music halls around the country.

HOLMES, JOHN
Sound supervisor on four episodes (TV): S3, episode 12: 'Man Hunt' and S4, episode 1: 'The Big Parade', episode 2: 'Don't Forget the Diver', episode 3: 'Boots, Boots, Boots' and episode 5: 'Don't Fence Me In'

Mitcham-born John Holmes spent eight years in the RAF, flying in Shackletons, before joining the BBC in 1958. Early shows he worked on include *Dixon of Dock Green* and *The Charlie Drake Show*. He was promoted to sound supervisor in 1964. During the 1970s he worked on a lot of drama, sport and political programmes before returning to sitcoms with *Terry and June*, *Porridge* and *Steptoe and Son*.

After 30 years' service, John accepted redundancy from the BBC in 1985, by which time he was working in a managerial role. He is now retired and mends clocks as a hobby.

HOLT, JONATHAN
Role: 2nd Soldier (S3, episode 14: 'Sons of the Sea') (TV)

Jonathan's TV career has included roles in Yorkshire's *Play for Love* in 1978, ATV's 1974 production, *Antony and Cleopatra*, playing Dercetas, a reporter in Granada's 1968 series, *Spindoe*, and ATV's 1967 series, *Trapped*.

HOME GUARD

One of the frustrations for the men who did their bit for Britain by joining the Home Guard was that they were frequently ridiculed, becoming the butt of jokes. This was explored beautifully in the episode, 'Wake Up Walmington'. Perkins, the butler from the big hall, interrupts Mainwaring and his men while they practise at the firing range. He tells them they can't use the range because his lordship is trying to take an afternoon nap. When a fuming Mainwaring complains, the butler retorts by reminding him that the range is only for 'real' soldiers. Later, Mainwaring agrees to see a deputation back at the church hall, and Jones brings a disgruntled platoon into the office, with Frazer admitting that around town they're known by the nickname, the geriatric fusiliers.

Originally called Local Defence Volunteers, Mainwaring finds out in the episode, 'Command Decision' that they've been renamed the Home Guard, and during 'The Showing Up of Corporal Jones', discovers that his platoon, the first to be set up in the area, is responsible for patrolling the stretch of coastline between the Jolly Roger Pier and Stones' Amusement Arcade.

It's not until they become fully armed in the episode, 'Shooting Pains', that the men feel like real soldiers, and no longer have to put up with being called 'the broomstick army'. But their duties are quite intense, especially after a long day at work. When Mainwaring suggests the platoon start undertaking river patrols in 'Sons of the Sea', Wilson reminds him that they're on patrol five nights a week, they guard the railway bridge, gas works, telephone exchange and carry out mobile patrols in Jones' van.

In reality, the Home Guard played an important part during the war years. At its peak, recruitment had reached nearly two million men, whose duties included guarding and patrolling key areas, as well as manning searchlights and anti-aircraft guns. With the increasing threat of invasion causing concern amongst government officials, the Home Guard was formed during May 1940. When Eden appealed for men aged between 17 and 65, who were outside the scope for call-up, to do their bit for Britain, a quarter of a million had volunteered within 24 hours. At first, broomsticks, shotguns and the like were used as makeshift weapons until rifles were procured from America, while uniforms consisted of a single armband. In sparsely populated areas several Home Guard mounted patrols were established. A member of such a unit would be issued with a pair of cord pantaloons and a pair of puttees instead of battledress trousers.

Although the Home Guard were often mocked, they gradually gained the respect of the general public as the years passed.

HOME GUARD (HG) SERGEANT

Played by Robert Raglan (TV); Norman Ettlinger (radio)

A sergeant from the Eastgate platoon who's drinking in the pub with Captain Square when Mainwaring enters in 'Don't Forget the Diver'.

JIMMY PERRY'S DAYS IN THE HOME GUARD

Facing the frightening Nazi war machine just across the channel, a 16-year-old Jimmy Perry, like millions of others in Britain, was ready to fight for his life. As he pedalled his bike to join the Watford Home Guard, he knew he was prepared to die for his country, if necessary.

He spent four years as a member of the real Dad's Army, an experience he'll never forget. 'I couldn't wait to get my hands on a rifle,' says Jimmy. 'My mother didn't like it very much, especially as we had to bring our rifle home. But young boys like me weren't allowed any ammunition. What is interesting is that back then over two million people had rifles, pistols and machine guns at home, and there were never any hold-ups or bank robberies.'

After working all day in a munitions factory, Jimmy spent several evenings a week attending lectures, or guarding various sites around Watford. 'We had lectures on subjects like aircraft recognition, which used to drive me mad because it was so boring, and I remember one on how to make petrol bombs. We also used to strip down and reassemble Lewis guns; there were two teams, and everyone was blindfolded. When the whistle went we'd strip it down as quickly as possible, then put it back together again. There were cheers for each side; it was like The Generation Game only we were dead serious.'

The platoon also received regular training in the dangers of gas warfare. 'We went to a regular army depot, and the worst part was how to deal with mustard gas. A drop would be put on your hand, you'd leave it five seconds, wipe it off and then apply anti-gas ointment. It was eerie because you knew that if you left it on it could burn right through your hand! I was excited, just like Pikey. I couldn't wait for the Germans to come. It was a terrible time for the nation but, just like many other youngsters, it didn't affect me as much.'

Once a week, Jimmy spent the night out on patrol, looking for saboteurs or fifth columnists. 'After the novelty wore off, the duties became tedious. We'd patrol power stations and railway sidings, in case someone tried blowing them up, which was very unlikely.

'I remember one night I stopped someone to check their identity card. He gave me his card, and I casually looked at it. Suddenly the man said: "No, no, son, you're doing it all wrong. You're supposed to examine it carefully, I'll show you how to do it." So there I was being shown how to examine an identity card!

'We were always trying to amuse each other by mucking about. One night we were on duty in a very old house, and I pretended to be a ghost. It was only harmless amusement and it was important to let off steam once in a while.'

Accidents are inevitable when millions of people possess weapons, but Jimmy can only recall one incident. 'I remember one idiot stood up during grenade training. Everyone else was lying down and safe, but he was badly wounded in the shoulder by flying shrapnel. Luckily, he was standing some distance from the explosion, else it could have been fatal.'

When it came to writing Dad's Army, Jimmy relied upon his memories of Home Guard life. Obviously scenes were exaggerated, but storylines were often based on the sort of incidents he encountered. 'More than anything, the attitude was accurate. But don't forget most of the actors had experienced the war, so were able to inject a sense of realism into the show.'

As well as relying on personal memories, Jimmy Perry and David Croft did plenty of research, spending hours ploughing through the Daily Mirror from the period. 'We'd go to the newspaper office and look through hundreds of yellowing papers – it was marvellous.'

Musing over the reasons for Dad's Army's timeless appeal, Jimmy believes its truthfulness is a major factor. 'And it's funny, of course,' he adds. The dearth of weapons in Mainwaring's platoon in the early episodes, the makeshift alternatives comprising of golf clubs, old shotguns and other oddities, were all reflections of what life was like for Jimmy in the real Home Guard.

Whenever he watches an episode of the sitcom now, Jimmy's thoughts drift back to the years he spent in the Home Guard, some of the most important of his life. 'This may sound a bit hammy, but I was very proud to be alive during a period that is, in my view, the greatest time in the British people's history: a time when the whole nation stood shoulder to shoulder.

'Everything was black and white, no one had any doubts – we were simply fighting for our lives. We lived within an almost authoritarian society, when black marketeers were imprisoned and looters during air raids could be shot on sight, but it was a great time to be alive.'

HONOURABLE MAN, THE

Recorded: Sunday 8/7/73

Original transmission: Wednesday 28/11/73,
6.50–7.20pm

Original viewing figures: 12.1 million

Repeated: 23/5/74, 2/4/91, 2/12/95, 11/4/96 (Wales)

CAST

Arthur Lowe . . . . .Captain Mainwaring
John Le Mesurier . . . . .Sergeant Wilson
Clive Dunn . . . . .Lance Corporal Jones
John Laurie . . . . .Private Frazer
James Beck . . . . .Private Walker
Arnold Ridley . . . . .Private Godfrey
Ian Lavender . . . . .Private Pike
Bill Pertwee . . . . .Chief Warden Hodges
Frank Williams . . . . .Vicar
Edward Sinclair . . . . .Verger
Eric Longworth . . . . .Town Clerk
Janet Davies . . . . .Mrs Pike
Gabor Vernon . . . . .Russian
Hana-Maria Pravda . . . . . . .Interpreter
Robert Raglan . . . . .Colonel
Pamela Cundell . . . . .Mrs Fox
Fred McNaughton . . . . .Mayor
Platoon: Colin Bean, Desmond Cullum-Jones, Michael
Moore, George Hancock, Evan Ross, Leslie Noyes,
William Gossling, Freddie White, Freddie Wiles, Roger
Bourne
Other Extras: Leila Ford and Eileen Matthews
Band: The Newmarket Town Band

PRODUCTION TEAM

Script: Jimmy Perry and David Croft
Producer/Director: David Croft
Production Assistant: Gordon Pert
Film Cameraman: James Balfour
Film Sound Recordist: John Gatland
Film Editor: Bill Harris
Studio Lighting: Howard King
Studio Sound: Michael McCarthy
Design: Paul Joel
Assistant Floor Manager: Peter Fitton
Vision Mixer: Dave Hanks
Costume Supervisor: Susan Wheal
Make-Up Supervisor: Ann Ailes

A meeting is called by the town clerk to nominate someone to co-ordinate the visit of the Russian worker, a hero of the Soviet Union, whose team has made 5,723 tanks. Hodges, the Vicar, the Verger, Walker, Jones, Wilson, Mrs Fox, Frazer, Pike – who's there as a messenger – Godfrey and Mrs Yeatman are among those attending. They discuss what form the welcome should take: Frazer offers a £10 voucher towards funeral costs; Mrs Fox, representing the WVS, says they should all smile a lot and Wilson suggests giving him the freedom of the town. Mainwaring likes Wilson's idea and they agree a wooden key can be presented at the welcoming, during which the Home Guard and ARP wardens will parade.

At the bank a letter arrives from Wilson's solicitors addressed to the Honourable Arthur Wilson. Mainwaring can't believe his eyes and discovers from Wilson that a childless uncle has died which means he's now entitled to call himself 'The Honourable'. Mainwaring is amazed again when Wilson's reason for arriving back late from lunch is that the golf club has invited him to join. Mainwaring's been trying for years. One thing he's sure about: it won't make any difference to their relationship, so he asks Wilson to pull his socks up.

During parade, the town clerk arrives for a quiet word with Mainwaring; he hopes Mainwaring doesn't take this amiss, but as there is only one 'Honourable' person in the town, he thinks Wilson should present the key to the Russian. Mainwaring won't hear of it, and

becomes even more annoyed when the Vicar wants Wilson to be co-opted onto the parochial church council and agree the crest for his own private pew.

Wilson is getting fed up with all the fuss but Mainwaring feels he's revelling in it. He'll present the key and Wilson must learn to ride the motorbike the platoon has been given and no one wants to ride. Forced to go for an hour's spin, Wilson rides around out of control, eventually falling off, just as the Russian visitor comes along in a staff car.

At the ceremony, Mainwaring presents the key, only for the Russian to announce he represents the workers and that the people on the stand, including Mainwaring and the Mayor, are bourgeois middle class and that they should honour their workers. He gets a dishevelled

MEMORIES OF THE HOME GUARD

As well as being a member of Mainwaring's platoon, Alec Coleman had served in the real Home Guard.

'The day Anthony Eden made his broadcast for volunteers (Local Defence Volunteers) I was just about 18 and employed as a junior in an insurance office. Immediately after work I rushed home to Hackney, collected some of my cadet and ex-school pals, and we all dashed off to Hackney Police Station to register our names.

'Within a short while we had a base in the TA barracks, where we carried out our drills and lectures. We were issued LDV armbands, which we wore when attending bombing incidents during the early days of the Blitz. Later we had patches bearing the words "Home Guard" which my mother stitched over the "LDV".

'As the organisation built we were issued denim battle dress, caps, boots, belts, anklets and rifles with ten rounds of ammunition. We were fast becoming the fighting force Captain Mainwaring wanted. Eventually we were given serge battle dress, sleeve titles "Home Guard" and, in our case, formation ID: 8 Col (8th Battn County of London).

'Our duties varied from assisting rescues at bomb sites, cordoning off streets in the case of unexploded bombs, first aid, fire prevention/fighting, providing guards at HQ, power stations, civic buildings and being on standby during the Blitz nights.

'We were taken to army rifle ranges for firing practice. On Hackney Marshes we fired mortars, were taught how to make Molotov cocktails (petrol-filled bottles) and how to throw grenades. Sundays were usually spent at

Chigwell, Essex, carrying out fieldcraft attack and defence. We learnt battle drill as well as ceremonial drill. All this training proved useful at the time of my call-up, and when on active service in an infantry battalion.

'Some years after the war, the agent Hugh Cecil, Peter Whitaker, Vic Taylor, Jimmy Mac and I shared, called me into his office to say David Croft and Jimmy Perry had written a series about the Home Guard, and was I interested? I was interested very much, especially when he asked me to attend a wardrobe fitting at Berman's. I was to meet George Ward, the wardrobe supervisor. My agent also said that it would help the agency if I shared my expertise with George. This I was most happy to do; I was in my element dealing with uniforms and dress. David Croft also requested advice on drills, weapon handling, etc.

'Commencing the new series, the first call was at Thetford, Norfolk, where most of the location shooting was carried out. Some of us felt we had been called up again, what with having uniforms and arms issued, and dashing about in battle dress!

'Later in the studios, recording with an audience, Dad's Army proved a winner. Even today's viewers enjoy the antics of the platoon. It was great entertainment value, possibly more so than the present day soaps. I feel everyone involved in the production had a wonderful working relationship, whether it was outside rehearsals, location, or in the studio. The audience loved it, we enjoyed it, no one was temperamental which proved how good it all was.'

ALEC COLEMAN

Wilson out of the car and introduces him as a true worker, who should have the key.

HONRI, PETER (1929–)
Born: Pimlico
Role: Private Day (S7, episode 4: 'The Godiva Affair') (TV)

Both Peter's parents worked in the entertainment industry: his mother was an actress, his father a film technician at Ealing Studios. But Peter didn't follow in their footsteps initially, although he'd studied dancing and piano playing, and made his stage debut as a five-year-old dancing policeman!

Peter was employed as a cub reporter on the *Surrey Herald* before giving up journalism to study part-time at LAMDA. His first London appearance was in 1948 playing a concertina – which he later did in *Dad's Army* – at a music hall, and he went on to establish a successful career, initially in variety. By 1955, he was working as a comic feed in revues and pantos, and by the sixties was also seen in musicals, including 16 in the West End.

Peter, who's also a writer, appeared on stage in *Beyond the Fringe* and *Our Man Crichton* with Kenneth More, as well as various TV productions, including *Upstairs, Downstairs* and, more recently, an episode of *Hippies*.

HOOPER, LINDSAY
Role: Member of the platoon's back row in one episode ('The Battle of the Giants') (TV)

HOPE, PRIVATE
Not seen in the sitcom, Private Hope is a member of the Walmington Home Guard and is announced by Jones in 'Absent Friends'.

HOPE-BRUCE, LIEUTENANT
Played by Timothy Carlton (TV); John Forest (radio)
A member of the Coldstream Guards, Hope-Bruce is a touch arrogant and dismissive towards the Home Guard in 'The Lion has 'Phones', when he arrives at the reservoir where Mainwaring and his men have been guarding an enemy plane that has crashed.

HORNERY, BOB
Role: City Gent (S6, episode 3: 'The Royal Train') (TV)

Bob appeared in an episode of *Sapphire and Steel*, *The Miscallef Programme* playing Jack Adams and the Rev Chasuble in the 1992 production of *The Importance of Being Earnest*. His film roles have included a BBC cameraman in the 1982 film, *Britannia Hospital*, a waterseller in the 1985 picture, *Mad Max Beyond Thunderdome* and a meteorologist in 1987's *Ground Zero*.

HORSE AND GROOM, THE
This pub in Walmington is where Walker meets the two girls, Doris and Dora, whom he's invited

to the platoon celebration in 'War Dance'. It's also frequented by Jones' section while on patrol one cold night, in 'Turkey Dinner'. The men enjoyed a rum before moving on to The King's Head.

HORSE AND HOUNDS, THE
A pub in Walmington that Wilson and Pike visit while searching for Frazer, who misses a parade in 'The Miser's Hoard'.

Frazer was a first-class rumour monger, always indulging in tittle-tattle.

HORSFALL, SQUADRON-LEADER
Played by Michael Knowles (radio)
A character in the radio episode, 'The Day the Balloon Went Up', Horsfall works in the operations room at Biggin Hill when the stray barrage balloon is on the scene. In the television version this character is known as the Operations Room Officer.

HOSKINS, MRS
Mrs Hoskins, a resident of Walmington, is referred to but not seen in the first episode, 'The Man and the Hour'. While gazing out of the office window at the bank, Mainwaring and Wilson spot her enter the phone box in the High Street. While Wilson explains she's calling her sister in Thetford, so it'll be just a three-minute call, Mainwaring wishes she'd hurry up because she's blocking his line of fire, since he's set up a gun just in case Germans begin storming the town.

HOUSEWIFE, THE
Played by Elizabeth Morgan (radio)
The housewife is heard in the radio episode 'The Great White Hunter'.

HUBBARD, KEVIN
Born: Leicester
Roles: Member of the Home Front Company and a Dervish (stage show)

Kevin trained at the Arts Theatre in Ipswich before working as an actor/ASM at Hornchurch and touring Northern clubs singing and dancing as part of the Jayne Mansfield Show. He's also appeared in theatre and numerous summer seasons around the country.

HUCKIN, PAUL (1955–)
Born: Barnes
Role: Messenger Boy ('Battle of the Giants') (TV)

When a family friend, who ran a vehicle hire business used by television and film companies, was asked whether he knew any children who would be interested in doing crowd scenes, Paul was given his chance to act. For eight months he appeared in several productions, including playing a schoolboy in *Please, Sir!*, a slave in *Doctor Who*, a schoolboy in *Young Winston* and another schoolboy in a Nimble advert.

When his O-levels came along, Paul gave up acting to concentrate on his school work. Upon finishing his education he joined the family printing business, but is now a self-employed builder.

HUGHES, GEOFFREY (1944–)
Born: Liverpool
Role: Bridge Corporal (S5, episode 10: 'Brain versus Brawn') (TV)

Geoffrey began acting at Newcastle University

and gained some early stage experience at a rep company in Stoke-on-Trent. Although he's best known for his roles as Eddie Yeats in *Coronation Street* and Onslow in *Keeping Up Appearances*, he's had a busy career. His many TV credits include *The Likely Lads*, *Shadows of Fear*, Harper the gardener in *Randall & Hopkirk (Deceased)*, *Don't Drink the Water*, *Doctor Who*, *Spender*, playing Kenny Coates, Tim Watkins in *Boon* and Ray in *The Upper Hand*. Among his film credits are appearances in *Carry On At Your Convenience*, *'Till Death Us Do Part* and providing the voice of Paul McCartney in *Yellow Submarine*.

HUGHES, NEVILLE (1945–)

Born: St Clears, Wales
Role: Soldier (S1, episode 1: 'The Man and the Hour') (TV)

Neville Hughes, who earnt £35 playing the soldier in 'The Man and the Hour', caught the acting bug at school but followed in his father's footsteps by studying medicine initially. A year into his studies he reconsidered his future and decided he wanted to be an actor.

He joined RADA in 1965, after spending 18 months working for a television production company in London. Upon graduating he worked in various rep companies, including the Theatre Royal, Windsor, and the Sybil Thorndike Theatre in Leatherhead. He made his television debut in *Dad's Army* and went on to appear as the Rev Peter Hope in *Crossroads* for four years, an episode of *The Avengers*, *Department S*, *The Protectors*, *Emergency – Ward 10*, ATV's 1974 production, *Father Brown*, and BBC's series, *Rebecca in 1979*. He also appeared in the 1973 movie, *Soft Beds, Hard Battles* with Peter Sellers, and plenty of commercials.

In 1974, Neville was offered an assignment with car manufacturer BMW, and a year later he decided to give up acting and join the company full-time. Within three years he was the company's top salesman and later worked as their national training manager. Nowadays Neville works as an industrial psychologist.

HUGHES, TONY (1928–)

Born: Bristol
Role: Mr Billings (S5, episode 9: 'When Did You Last See Your Money?')

While Tony's father played professional football for Bristol City, his mother was a professional actress, so it was no surprise when Tony eventually followed in her footsteps. After leaving school, he worked for a tobacco company until completing his national service.

When he returned to civvy street he decided to pursue an acting career. Initially he worked in rep, but by the 1960s he was appearing on TV, beginning with a presenter's job on a children's maths show. Has also made over 100 commercials, including a contract with Italian TV for a Lenor advert, and a handful of films. Now semi-retired, the last two years have been taken up recovering from replacement knee joint surgery.

HUNT, RICHARD

BBC designer on three episodes (TV): S3, episode 9: 'War Dance', episode 11: 'Branded' and episode 13: 'No Spring for Frazer'

HUNTER-CRAIG, ALAN

Designer on six episodes (TV): S1

Alan finished his education at Dulwich College in 1954 and spent two years in the army completing national service. When he re-joined civvy street he enrolled on a foundation course at Bromley College of Art. Quickly realising he didn't want to study fine art, he transferred to Beckenham School of Art and earned a degree in graphic design.

After graduating he struggled to get a job but finally struck lucky and joined a design company. When the BBC advertised for trainee production designers and art directors for BBC2, Alan applied and was offered a position in 1963. He eventually progressed to the position of production designer, clocking up 18 years' service. Alan worked for David Croft on several programmes before joining him on *Dad's Army*. Other shows he worked on include: *Z Cars*, *Softly, Softly*, *Sykes*, *The Dick Emery Show* and *The Likely Lads*.

In 1969 Alan left the BBC to go freelance and started at LWT, where he worked on *On the Buses* and *The Train Now Standing* in 1972. He also did work for ATV in Birmingham, HTV in Bristol, Thames TV and independent production companies. He now concentrates mainly on architectural work, designing houses, extensions, loft conversions, etc.

HUSBAND, MARY

Costume designer on 14 episodes (TV): S8; S9; 'My Brother and I' and 'The Love of Three Oranges'; and the stage show

Mary is a distinguished costume designer who has worked on a myriad of top television and stage shows. Educated at the Queens School, Chester, and the Liverpool College of Art, from where she gained a National Diploma in Design, Mary was the first costume designer for BBC Wales at the age of 23, before moving to Television Centre in London.

Specialising in comedy, she has worked on shows like *Hi-De-Hi!*, *Open All Hours*, *Sorry!*, *Porridge*, *Are You Being Served?*, *Clarence*, *It Ain't Half Hot, Mum*, *You Rang, M'Lord?*, *Nice Day at the Office* and *Oh, Doctor Beeching!*. She also designed costumes for *The Two Ronnies*, *The Stanley Baxter Show* and dramas including *Middlemarch*, *Coming Up for Air*, *Lord Raingo*, *Joy* and Channel 4's *The War That Still Goes On*.

As far as her stage credits are concerned, she's worked on shows such as *The Two Ronnies* at the London Palladium, *It Ain't Half Hot, Mum* and *Bedful of Foreigners* at London's Victoria Palace.

After a successful career with the BBC, which saw her promoted to senior costume designer, she left and continues to work freelance.

HUTTON, LEN

Visual effects designer on the TV special: 'Battle of the Giants'

Len started his career as a film projectionist at the Rex Cinema in Hanworth, but after completing his national service joined Farey Aviation in Hayes, later moving to a model-making company in Middlesex. He joined the BBC in 1964 as a design assistant, was promoted to designer in 1973 and went on to work on shows including *It Ain't Half Hot, Mum*, *Up Pompeii!* and *The Goodies*. He died of a heart attack in 1987 after having spent 23 years in the Visual Effects Department.

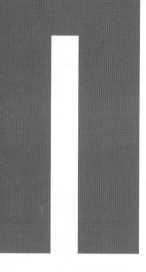

IF THE CAP FITS...

(The working title for this episode was 'Turnabout')

Recorded: Friday 30/6/72

Original transmission: Friday 10/11/72, 8.30–9.00pm

Original viewing figures: 15.5 million

Repeated: 4/8/73, 12/2/91, 4/11/95, 7/6/97

CAST

Arthur Lowe . . . . .Captain Mainwaring
John Le Mesurier . . . . .Sergeant Wilson
Clive Dunn . . . . .Lance Corporal Jones
John Laurie . . . . .Private Frazer
James Beck . . . . .Private Walker
Arnold Ridley . . . . .Private Godfrey
Ian Lavender . . . . .Private Pike
Bill Pertwee . . . . .ARP Warden
Campbell Singer . . . . .Major General Menzies
Robert Raglan . . . . .Colonel
Edward Sinclair . . . . .Verger
Alex McAvoy . . . . .Sergeant
Dennis Blanch . . . . .Second Lieutenant
Platoon: Colin Bean, Desmond Cullum-Jones, Evan Ross, Michael Moore, Freddie White, Leslie Noyes, George Hancock, Hugh Hastings, Hugh Cecil, Freddie Wiles
Piper: Pipe Major Donald MacLeod
Extra: James Haswell (Barman)

PRODUCTION TEAM

Script: Jimmy Perry and David Croft
Producer/Director: David Croft
Production Assistant: Gordon Pert
Studio Lighting: Howard King
Studio Sound: Michael McCarthy
Design: Paul Joel
Assistant Floor Manager: Peter Fitton
Vision Mixer: Dave Hanks
Costume Supervisor: Susan Wheal
Make-Up Supervisor: Cynthia Goodwin
Visual Effects: Peter Day

While Mainwaring prepares a lecture on identifying the enemy, the men are getting restless, especially Frazer who hates wasting a beautiful summer's day cooped up in the church hall. He begins stirring up trouble by getting the platoon singing 'Why are we waiting?'. Eventually, the lecture starts with Jones controlling the projector, a monocle-wearing Wilson reading notes, and

'If the Cap Fits...'

Mainwaring explaining the slides, warning everyone that a Nazi's eyes are mean, shifty and set too close together; he also tells them to watch out for dopey expressions, and seems more interested in describing their general demeanour than identifying uniforms.

Later, Frazer storms into Mainwaring's office and berates him for wasting their time with useless 'blether', recalling occasions on 6 November 1940, when he wasted three hours explaining why Germans don't play cricket; 28 January 1941, when he lectured them on how Hitler bites the carpet when he's in a rage and then had the temerity to follow it up with a two-hour session planning how they could send him a poisoned hearth rug!

Mainwaring is fed up with Frazer's grousing; he's been a thorn in his side since the platoon was formed. He refers to his trusty old Home Guard manual and invites anyone in the platoon to take over command for a couple of days if they're unhappy with how he's running things. Not expecting anyone to volunteer, he's shocked when Frazer demands his pips.

'If the Cap Fits...'

Frazer takes charge and starts throwing his weight around. He busts Wilson, demoting him to the rank of private, and ruffles a few more feathers by telling Jones he's a woolly-minded old ditherer, causing him to resign to the ranks. Jones goes off to cry on Mainwaring's shoulder and tells him he's not serving under such a rude man. In their place, Pike is promoted to corporal and Walker becomes sergeant.

Later, Major General Menzies, who's just taken over at Area Command, enters the church hall and introduces himself to Frazer. Mistaking the Scotsman for Mainwaring, he explains that he's visiting all the Home Guard units. Noticing Frazer is Scottish, too, he invites him to his planned Highland get-together at the officers' mess at HQ.

Everything returns to normal in the platoon, with Mainwaring back at the helm. The invitation to the Highland do arrives; Frazer tries telling Mainwaring it involves playing the bagpipes, but Mainwaring tells him to stop interrupting. Just when it looks like the captain will make a fool of himself, he surprises everybody.

Note: In the closing scenes of the transmitted episode we discover that Mainwaring learnt how to play the bagpipes while honeymooning in Invergeike, but the original script saw him spending a whole winter there as a relief bank manager.

I'M BACKING BRITAIN

The first episode of *Dad's Army* kicks off with a white-haired George Mainwaring addressing a party formed to launch Walmington-on-Sea's 'I'm Backing Britain' campaign. The nationwide movement was the brainchild of five Surbiton typists (Carol Fry, Joan Southwell, Brenda Mumford, Valerie White and Christine French) in January 1968.

With the country gripped in a battle against rising inflation and economic gloom, the five women, all employed by Colt Heating and Ventilation Ltd, sparked a mini-revolution in workplace attitudes when they suggested everyone at the company work an extra half-hour for free. Their idea was conceived as a way of helping the stumbling economy, and 'I'm Backing Britain' fever, albeit short-lived, spread like wildfire. The company was inundated with phone calls and letters supporting the women's stance, and extra telephone lines were installed to cope with the deluge.

As interest picked up, a telegram was sent to the Prime Minister (Harold Wilson) asking him to suggest ways that would encourage others to follow suit. Colt Heating and Ventilation received a telegram from Prince Philip, congratulating them on their idea. Colt launched the 'I'm Backing Britain' campaign by writing to 40,000 employers urging them to join the scheme, and planned issuing Union Jack lapel badges to firms taking part, after a Lincolnshire company offered to print 100,000 badges for nothing.

Governmental interest saw a junior minister for economic affairs conducting a fact-finding trip and printing a poster promoting the slogan. Mr O'Hea, Colt's chairman, told a journalist at the *Surrey Comet*, 'The response has been absolutely overwhelming. It has taken us completely by surprise. It is very encouraging for the good of the country.'

The five typists decided to act upon receiving a memo from the company's marketing director, who stated that everyone in Britain working an extra half-day for free would quickly solve the nation's balance of payments problem. The girls sent a memo back suggesting Colt lead the way.

The wave of enthusiasm spread to other firms, with the owner of two hairdressing salons in Kingston slashing prices by five per cent. Express Dairy announced they would suspend price increases, Independent Food Services, which represented more than 5,000 independent retailers, froze increases on many products for six months, while other companies, with the backing of their staff, adopted the idea of working extra time for free.

The *Surrey Comet* of Wednesday 10 January 1968 reported that the on-going running of the 'I'm Backing Britain' campaign had been passed over to the Industrial Society, a decision announced by Edmund Dell, Under-Secretary of the Department of Economic Affairs, when he visited the Colt offices. By then, the campaign had attracted worldwide interest, with the typists being interviewed by TV reporters from Germany to Japan.

Inevitably, not everyone agreed with this principle of working for free, dismissing claims that it would help the country's economy. It was suggested that the only people benefiting from such employee generosity were the employers who'd be getting something for nothing. Sceptics felt such a stance would have no bearing on the nation's overall economic status.

INTERPRETER, THE
Played by Hana-Maria Pravda (TV)
The interpreter is employed to help translate when the Russian hero visits Walmington-on-Sea in 'The Honourable Man'.

INVASION
In the event of an invasion, Walmington-on-Sea's Home Guard had a clear strategy, which was explained in 'The Battle of Godfrey's Cottage'. As soon as the church bells were sounded to warn the town's residents that an invasion was on the cards, the unit would proceed to the Novelty Rock Emporium, which would act as a command post. From there, the platoon would divide into two sections, to be led by Mainwaring and Wilson. The first section would move to the crossroads, a mile away, that lead into the town, where they would establish a second command post at Godfrey's cottage. Patrols would be sent out from each of the command posts, and communication between them would be via runners. Luckily for everyone, including the residents of Walmington, the platoon's defence skills were never put to the test.

INVASION COMMITTEE
The Walmington-on-Sea invasion committee is established in the opening episode, 'The Man and the Hour'. Upon hearing Anthony Eden's speech on the radio, announcing the formation of a new force called the Local Defence Volunteers, Mainwaring identifies a golden opportunity to show his leadership flair, which some might question, and form an invasion committee.

Mainwaring has his critics, but at least he shows the backbone and get-up-and-go qualities required to shake the residents of sleepy Walmington-on-Sea into action. Appointing himself as the commander of the committee, Wilson as second in command – again – and Pike as information officer, the first steps towards the formation of his future platoon were taken. Pike nips on his bike and tours the town announcing LDV volunteers should report to the church hall at six that night. During a rather chaotic evening, that includes the arrival of Mainwaring's biggest irritant, in the shape of ARP Warden Hodges, the self-appointed commander enlists volunteers into the LDV.

IRONSIDE, MISS
Played by Julia Burbury (TV)
When the women of Walmington want to join the platoon to help the war effort in 'Mum's Army', Mainwaring supports their wish, initially, because he feels they can relieve his men of certain duties, allowing them more time to 'grapple with the enemy'. Frazer knows Miss Ironside, who works for the Gas Light and Coke Company, and brings her along to the parade. She is constantly described by Frazer as having 'big, strong thighs' and a 'fine, firm body'.

IRVING, PENNY (1955–)
Born: Hitchin
Role: Chambermaid (Christmas Special, 'My Brother and I') (TV)
Former model, Penny Irving regularly popped up on the screen, most notably as Miss Bakewell, Young Mr Grace's longest serving secretary in *Are You Being Served?*. Other appearances include playing Mary in several episodes of *Hi-De-Hi!*, and Pam in the first episode of *The Professionals*. On the big screen, she was seen in *Carry On Dick*, playing one of the Birds of Paradise, Chiquita in *Percy's Progress*, Sandy in the film version of *The Likely Lads*, in *Vampira* with David Niven, and as a serving wench in *The Bawdy Adventures of Tom Jones*. Penny has now left the profession.

ISAACS, SAM

Not seen or heard in the sitcom, Sam Isaacs owns a pawnbrokers' shop in Walmington. He's mentioned in a scene that was cut before the final recording of 'The Big Parade'.

ISTED, RON

Vision mixer on one episode (TV): 'A Man of Action'

IS THERE HONEY STILL FOR TEA?

Recorded: Thursday 26/6/75

Original transmission: Friday 19/9/75, 8.00–8.30pm

Original viewing figures: 12.8 million

Repeated: 8/5/76, 4/6/91, 3/12/94, 9/2/95 (Wales), 26/4/97

CAST

Arthur Lowe . . . . Captain Mainwaring
John Le Mesurier . . . . Sergeant Wilson
Clive Dunn . . . . Lance Corporal Jones
John Laurie . . . . Private Frazer
Arnold Ridley . . . . Private Godfrey
Ian Lavender . . . . Private Pike
Bill Pertwee . . . . Chief Warden Hodges
Gordon Peters . . . . Man with the Door
Robert Raglan . . . . Colonel
Campbell Singer . . . . Sir Charles Renfrew
                              McAllister
Joan Cooper . . . . Dolly
Kathleen Sainsbury . . . . Cissy
Platoon: Colin Bean, Desmond Cullum-Jones, Evan Ross, George Hancock
Walk-on: Jimmy Mac

PRODUCTION TEAM

Script: Jimmy Perry and David Croft
Producer/Director: David Croft
Production Assistant: Jo Austin
Film Cameraman: Peter Chapman
Film Sound Recordist: Bill Chesneau
Film Editor: John Stothart
Studio Lighting: Howard King
Studio Sound: Michael McCarthy
Design: Robert Berk
Assistant Floor Manager: Anne Ogden
Vision Mixer: Dave Hanks
Costume Designer: Mary Husband
Make-Up Artist: Sylvia Thornton

The Colonel arrives to inform Mainwaring and Wilson of bad news concerning Godfrey: his house, Cherry Tree Cottage, has to be demolished to make way for a new aerodrome; the Colonel thinks it's best that one of the platoon tell him. At Godfrey's age the shock could easily kill him, as Frazer points out when they discuss how to break the news. Neither Frazer nor Jones, who are called to an emergency meeting by Mainwaring, offer to do the job, so Mainwaring decides to visit the cottage with Wilson and Pike the following afternoon. But things don't go to plan and they spend the entire time stuffing themselves with upside-

'Is There Honey Still for Tea?'

down cakes, and leave the cottage without broaching the subject.

In the end it's down to Jones to break the news to Godfrey, but after going round the houses for ages, he finds out that Godfrey knows already. Jones suggests Godfrey stays with him while his sisters live with friends. But Frazer saves the day when he phones London in the middle of the night and speaks to Sir Charles Renfrew McAllister, the minister in charge of the aerodrome project, and asks him to move the aerodrome. When he refuses, Frazer blackmails the minister by threatening to disclose his shady past; the decision is altered and the aerodrome is moved 200 yards away, leaving the cottage standing.

IT STICKS OUT HALF A MILE

This radio series was written by Harold Snoad and Michael Knowles for BBC Radio 2. Although 13 episodes were transmitted on the radio, a further two were written but never recorded, as Snoad's and Knowles' contracts with the BBC stipulated 15 scripts had to be written. None of the episodes were titled.

At the end of the original run of *Dad's Army* on TV, Harold Snoad felt it a pity that such good characters should go to waste. He suggested to Michael Knowles that they team up and develop a vehicle, something Jimmy Perry and David Croft were agreeable to. Snoad and Knowles, who'd already successfully adapted the TV scripts for radio, sat down and dreamt up the idea for *It Sticks Out Half a Mile*.

It was Harold's decision to focus on just a few of the *Dad's Army* characters for the spin-off; he felt that retaining the small-screen cast in its entirety would be like trying to reinvent the wartime sitcom.

When Harold and Michael floated the idea of working together again to the appropriate members of the *Dad's Army* cast, it met with a favourable response. The basis of the idea focused on Mainwaring and Wilson meeting up, unexpectedly, after the war, with one significant difference: a reversal of roles finds Wilson as the bank manager and Mainwaring in need of a loan. The writers can't remember how they formed the idea of basing the series around the purchase of a pier; initially the basic storyline of Mainwaring returning to the country to find Wilson as a bank manager appealed to them, from which they had to decide for what purpose he would need a loan. From this premise, the series grew.

The programme was based in the fictional seaside resort of Frambourne. Thinking it would be too pat for Mainwaring to return to Walmington and find Wilson running the bank he'd controlled, they created another little town further along the coast. Moving away from the Walmington setting meant the show was removed from the basis of *Dad's Army*, and they wouldn't have to worry about listeners questioning the whereabouts of the excluded characters.

It was originally intended that Mainwaring and Wilson would be the only characters taken from *Dad's Army*. Harold discussed the idea with Arthur Lowe, and left him a script to read. The

'IT STICKS OUT HALF A MILE' BY HAROLD SNOAD

FIRST PILOT – NEVER TRANSMITTED BECAUSE OF ARTHUR LOWE'S DEATH

Since the end of the war and the Home Guard days – a couple of years earlier – Wilson has moved down the coast and become manager at the Frambourne branch of the bank. The episode starts with Miss Perkins, his middle-aged secretary – who obviously has a crush on him – telling Wilson that one of the people who had an appointment to see him has dropped out but she has replaced him with someone else – a Mr Mainwaring. Wilson double-takes on the mention of that name but, from the description Miss Perkins gives him, he realises that it must be the same one. Mainwaring is equally amazed to hear that the person he will be seeing is called Wilson – and horrified to discover that it's not only the same man but that he's the manager!

We learn that Mainwaring moved to Switzerland after the war where he was employed as a supervisor in a firm making cuckoo clocks ('Any cuckoo that didn't spring out was thrown out'). They have just moved back to this country because the air in Switzerland didn't suit Elizabeth's chest and they have settled in Frambourne. He tells Wilson that he was horrified to discover that Frambourne council have plans to demolish the pier and he wants to buy it – although we realise that he is very embarrassed finding himself having to ask his old chief clerk for a loan in order to do so.

Wilson reluctantly agrees to his request and the next scene finds the two of them walking down the length of the pier (having had trouble with the locked gates) with Mainwaring enthusiastically mapping out his plans. They get to the section which was removed during the war and, although Wilson advises against it, Mainwaring decides to use the rope bridge to cross over the gap. Unfortunately the rope is rotten and it breaks, sending Mainwaring into the sea. He is thrown a rope by Wilson and a council workman and has to leave the pier wearing the latter's spare boiler suit.

The final section is based around a meeting at the town hall a couple of days later between members of the committee who are very pleased that some 'idiot' wants to buy the pier and actually has the necessary five thousand pounds. Mainwaring and Wilson are shown in. At first Mainwaring's nose is put out because everyone knows Wilson who, in turn, knows all of them – on Christian-name terms – but nobody knows Mainwaring. He outlines his plans for the pier (they point out that the theatre is quite small – he says he'll have to book Arthur Askey. Does anyone know where the fortune teller is now – yes she works for the council, in Forward Planning, etc) and it is agreed that he can buy the pier. Because they are keen to get if off their hands they have already had the agreement drawn up and it is signed there and then.

The episode finishes with the town clerk suggesting that it might be a nice idea to have a drink to celebrate the deal. The glasses are poured and the town clerk proposes a toast: 'To the new owner of Frambourne Pier' at which point (because of the loan) Wilson adds – much to Mainwaring's chagrin – 'Swallow Bank'!

SECOND PILOT

Hodges has arranged to meet Frank (Pike) in a pub and the episode starts with the former arriving back at the table with Frank's glass of orange. During the course of the conversation we discover that Hodges is thinking of getting out of the greengrocery business he still has in Walmington and has his eyes set on a new venture – namely buying Frambourne Pier which is closed and due for demolition unless someone buys it. When Pike asks why Hodges wanted to meet up with him he says it was because he was looking for a partner for this new project. Pike is rather surprised but, as he is not at all happy with his job in the ironmongery department at Woolies, he isn't uninterested.

In reality it becomes obvious to the listener that the only reason Hodges wants Pike as a partner is to further his chances of getting a loan from Wilson who is now manager at the Frambourne branch of Swallow Bank. In the pub scene we established that Wilson left Walmington and came to Frambourne and, coincidentally, Mavis also felt the need for a change! She and Pike, therefore, also moved to Frambourne. In fact nothing has changed between Wilson and Mavis.

Pike goes to the bank to see Wilson (who isn't expecting him as his secretary has only put Pike in at the last moment when someone else dropped out) and tells him that he wants to withdraw his money (which amounts to very little – to be precise two pounds, seventeen and six) from his post office account and open a bank account. He then goes on to ask 'Uncle Arthur' for a loan – to buy the pier. It is obvious that he has been put up to this by Hodges. Wilson refuses to give him a loan – even after Frank becomes quite angry – until Pike casually mentions a girl who works at Woolworths who has told him that her mother had a bit of a fling with Wilson who, when he first arrived at Walmington, was looking for somewhere to stay and moved into their house for a few weeks. Pike says Uncle Arthur wouldn't like his mother (Mavis) to know about that, would he? Pike gets his loan!

Pike asks Wilson to join him and Hodges at the meeting at the town hall to give their attempt to purchase the pier more clout – him being such a respected person in Frambourne. Wilson doesn't really want to get involved – until Pike mentions the lady friend again, at which point he succumbs. Wilson then asks Pike who his partner is and is horrified to learn that it's Bert Hodges.

The three of them attend the meeting with Hodges and Pike passing Wilson off as their 'financial advisor'. Plans for the future of the pier are discussed along roughly the same lines as in the original version but, in this instance, of course, with the added bonus of being able to use Pike's ignorance or mis-quotation of facts (for instance, the pier being built by Ignoramus Burke instead of Eugenius Birch).

The episode finishes in the same way as the original pilot but this time with Hodges and Pike protesting at Wilson's comment.

Some of the *Dad's Army* characters lived on in Snoad and Knowles' radio series.

following day, Lowe called to say he liked the idea, but it should be on TV instead of radio. Harold asked the BBC, but they weren't interested in taking it for the small screen, so a pilot was written for BBC radio. It was recorded in 1982, but before it could be broadcast Arthur Lowe died. At his memorial service, Arthur's widow, Joan Cooper, told Harold and Michael how much Arthur had loved the idea, and that she wanted them to continue with the project. So with Joan's blessing, they set about altering the plot by introducing Hodges, and Pike, who team up to buy the pier. As Hodges had always been a rather aggressive character, the writers consciously toned down his quarrelsome streak.

When it came to the writing process, Snoad and Knowles would meet to agree the storylines, then go their separate ways, write an episode each and reconvene to discuss the scripts. Other than for the two pilots, which were written together, this is the working practice Snoad and Knowles adopted throughout the life of *It Sticks Out Half A Mile*, the same as they had used when they adapted *Dad's Army* for radio.

The series, as far as radio was concerned, came

to an end upon the death of John Le Mesurier. But still believing the idea would make a suitable subject for the small screen, Harold Snoad tried again. He shot a pilot, with location filming including scenes on an actual pier. *Walking the Planks* was transmitted on 2 August 1985, and was watched by 11 million people.

But the BBC still didn't want to commission a series, so Snoad and Knowles were forced to look elsewhere. They took the idea to Yorkshire TV, who decided to give the show a try. Transmission of the series, *High and Dry*, started on 7 January 1987, but Harold (who used the pseudonym, Alan Sherwood, for the series) and Michael were not happy with the results, especially as no location filming took place, resulting in the pier being a set built in a large studio. With no horizon, seagulls or wind, the atmosphere was very unrealistic and artificial, which the writers felt led to the sitcom's demise after just seven episodes.

IT STICKS OUT HALF A MILE
(Broadcast on BBC Radio 2)

Producers: Jonathan James Moore (1st pilot);
Martin Fisher (2nd pilot and series)

First Pilot
Recorded: 19/7/81
Never transmitted
CAST
Arthur Lowe (George Mainwaring)
John Le Mesurier (Arthur Wilson)
Josephine Tewson (Miss Baines)
Dougie Brown (Stephen Rawlings)
Timothy Weston (Guthrie)
Anthony Sharp (Charles Hunter)
Sidney Bronty (Percy Short)
Hayden Wood (the Man)

Second Pilot
Recorded: Saturday 11/9/82
First broadcast: Sunday 13/11/83, 1.30–2pm
CAST
John Le Mesurier (Arthur Wilson)
Ian Lavender (Frank Pike)
Bill Pertwee (Bert Hodges)
Vivienne Martin (Miss Perkins)
Robin Parkinson (Mr Hunter)
Edward Burnham (Mr Short)
Gordon Peters (Mr Rawlings)
Spencer Banks (council employee)

SERIES ONE
Episode 2
Recorded: Saturday 19/2/83
First broadcast: Sunday 20/11/83, 1.30–2pm
CAST
John Le Mesurier (Arthur Wilson)
Ian Lavender (Frank Pike)
Bill Pertwee (Bert Hodges)
Vivienne Martin (Miss Perkins)
Glynn Edwards (Fred Guthrie)
Michael Bilton (Mr Johnson)

Episode 3
Recorded: Wednesday 23/2/83
First broadcast: Sunday 27/11/83, 1.30–2pm
CAST
John Le Mesurier (Arthur Wilson)
Ian Lavender (Frank Pike)
Bill Pertwee (Bert Hodges)
Vivienne Martin (Miss Perkins)
Glynn Edwards (Fred Guthrie)
Barry Gosney (Mr Watkins, the electrician)
James Bryce (the bank cashier and the librarian)
Stuart Sherwin (electricity showroom assistant)

Episode 4
Recorded: Wednesday 23/2/83
First broadcast: Sunday 4/12/83, 1.30–2pm
CAST
John Le Mesurier (Arthur Wilson)
Ian Lavender (Frank Pike), Bill Pertwee
(Bert Hodges), Vivienne Martin (Miss Perkins)

Episode 5

Recorded: Saturday 19/2/83
First broadcast: Sunday 11/12/83, 1.30–2pm
CAST
John Le Mesurier (Arthur Wilson)
Ian Lavender (Frank Pike)
Bill Pertwee (Bert Hodges)
Vivienne Martin (Miss Perkins)
Carol Hawkins (Avril)
Janet Davies (Mrs Pike)
Gordon Salkild (telephone engineer)

Episode 6

Recorded: Saturday 26/2/83
First broadcast: Sunday 18/12/83, 1.30–2pm
CAST
John Le Mesurier (Arthur Wilson)
Ian Lavender (Frank Pike)
Bill Pertwee (Bert Hodges)
Vivienne Martin (Miss Perkins)
Glynn Edwards (Fred Guthrie)
Michael Knowles (Ernest Woolcot)
Hilda Braid (Olive Briggs)

Episode 7

Recorded: Saturday 5/3/83
First broadcast: Sunday 1/1/84, 1.30–2pm
CAST
John Le Mesurier (Arthur Wilson)
Ian Lavender (Frank Pike)
Bill Pertwee (Bert Hodges)
Glynn Edwards (Fred Guthrie)
Michael Knowles (Ernest Woolcot)
Hilda Braid (Olive Briggs)
Michael Bilton (the elderly man)
Madi Hedd (the woman)
Jill Lidstone (the young lady)

Episode 8

Recorded: Tuesday 8/3/83
First broadcast: Sunday 8/1/84, 1.30–2pm
CAST
John Le Mesurier (Arthur Wilson)
Ian Lavender (Frank Pike)
Bill Pertwee (Bert Hodges)
Vivienne Martin (Miss Perkins)
Paul Russell (Derek)

Episode 9

Recorded: Saturday 5/3/83
First broadcast: Sunday 15/1/84, 1.30–2pm
CAST
John Le Mesurier (Arthur Wilson)
Ian Lavender (Frank Pike)
Bill Pertwee (Bert Hodges)
Janet Davies (Mrs Pike)
Vivienne Martin (Miss Perkins)
Michael Knowles (Ernest Woolcot)
Hilda Braid (Olive Briggs)
Gordon Clyde (Willoughby Smallpiece)
Miranda Forbes (the waitress)

Episode 10

Recorded: Saturday 26/2/83
First broadcast: Tuesday 21/8/84, 10.30–11pm
CAST
John Le Mesurier (Arthur Wilson)
Ian Lavender (Frank Pike)
Bill Pertwee (Bert Hodges)
Vivienne Martin (Miss Perkins)
Glynn Edwards (Fred Guthrie)
Stella Tanner (Myrte Spivy)
Gordon Clyde (Mr Fisher)
Carole Harrison (the builders' receptionist)
Katherine Parr (the Irish nun)

Episode 11

Recorded: Tuesday 8/3/83
First broadcast: Tuesday 4/9/84, 10.30–11pm
CAST
John Le Mesurier (Arthur Wilson)
Ian Lavender (Frank Pike)
Bill Pertwee (Bert Hodges)
Vivienne Martin (Miss Perkins)
Reginald Marsh (Sir Wensley Smithers)
Gordon Clyde (civil servants 1 and 5)
Job Glover (civil servants 2 and 4)
Michael Bilton (Mr Thornedyke and civil servant 3)

Episode 12

Recorded: Tuesday 15/3/83
First broadcast: Tuesday 18/9/84, 10.30–11pm
CAST
John Le Mesurier (Arthur Wilson)
Ian Lavender (Frank Pike)
Bill Pertwee (Bert Hodges)
Vivienne Martin (Miss Perkins)
Christopher Biggins (Dudley Watkins)
Robin Parkinson (Mr Hunter)

Episode 13

Recorded: Tuesday 15/3/83,
First broadcast: Tuesday 9/10/84, 10.30–11pm
CAST
John Le Mesurier (Arthur Wilson)
Ian Lavender (Frank Pike)
Bill Pertwee (Bert Hodges)
Vivienne Martin (Miss Perkins)
Glynn Edwards (Fred Guthrie)
Betty Marsden (Madame Zara)

NOTE: Only four recordings are retained in the BBC archives: the first pilot, featuring Arthur Lowe, (master tape No SLN29/289G753); the second pilot (master tape No SLN37/289T783); the second episode of series one (master tape No SLN08/288M519) and episode five from series one (archive No 80735)

Walking the Planks

One episode, lasting 30 minutes, was transmitted by BBC1: Friday 2/8/85, 8.30pm
CAST
Michael Elphick (Ron Archer)
Richard Wilson (Richard Talbot)
Vivienne Martin (Miss Baxter)
Gary Raynsford (Trevor Archer)

High and Dry

Seven episodes, each lasting 30 minutes, were transmitted by Yorkshire TV: between 7/1/87 and 18/2/87, on Wednesdays, 8.30pm
CAST
Bernard Cribbins (Ron Archer)
Richard Wilson (Richard Talbot)
Vivienne Martin (Miss Baxter)
Angus Barnett (Trevor Archer)
Arthur English (Fred Whattle)
Diana Coupland (Mrs Briggs)

ITALIAN POW

Played by Larry Martyn (TV); Sion Probert (radio)
In 'Don't Fence Me In', Mainwaring finally attracts this Italian POW's attention and gets him to open the prison camp gates.

ITALIAN SERGEANT

Played by Freddie Earlle (TV)
This Italian sergeant is one of the POWs who Jones herds up to help Mainwaring win the blood-donoring competition in 'When You've Got to Go'.

IVY CRESCENT

A street in Walmington featured in 'Absent Friends', where an IRA suspect is found at number 27.

JACKSON, MR

Not seen or heard in the sitcom, Mr Jackson talks to Mr Mainwaring on the phone during the episode, 'Knights of Madness'. While Mainwaring's working at the bank, he has a conversation with Jackson about building a dragon for the grand finale of the town's 'Wings for Victory' week. His estimate is too expensive and Mainwaring decides to look elsewhere. Although we never know for sure, we can only assume that Mr Jackson works as a carpenter in the town.

JACQUES, RICHARD (1931–2000)

Born: Liverpool

Roles: Member of the platoon's back row in 17 episodes (S1; S2; S3, episodes 1, 2, 3 & 7; S5, episode 12), Mr Cheesewright (S3, episode 3: 'The Lion has 'Phones') (TV)

When war broke out, Richard's family moved to Southport, where he enjoyed a happy childhood. After finishing his education at Wycliffe College, he trained at Bradford's Northern Theatre School, making his acting debut at the age of 16 as Ronnie in *The Winslow Boy* at the old Halifax Grand Theatre. Two years later he started his national service, which was mostly spent in Singapore, where he played leading roles for the Arts Theatre of Singapore, completed over 100 broadcasts for Radio Malaya – as actor and announcer – and made many broadcasts for Radio Singapore, as a disc jockey.

Returning to civvy street, Richard resumed his acting career and spent several years in various reps, including York, Lincoln, Ipswich, Folkestone and Ashford. He then moved to London, and whilst working at Palmers Green, met Jimmy Perry. Richard was one of the original members of the back row, and stayed into the third season, bowing out in 'Big Guns'. He left the sitcom to accept a five-year contract at The Arts Theatre as leading actor and director, prior to co-founding The English Theatre of Sweden (based in Stockholm) and directing all the theatre's productions during the next five years.

When Richard returned to England he became a teacher, director and lecturer at several drama schools, including The Drama Studio, The Italia Conti Academy of Theatre Arts and The Acad-emy. Richard also directed the stage version of Perry and Croft's *It Ain't Half Hot, Mum*.

Having worked in America for a while, where one of the plays he'd written for children was presented, with Richard co-directing and playing a leading role, he decided to concentrate on playwriting. He emigrated to Toronto, Canada, in 1991 and began directing cabaret productions in the city, and two major productions at The Red Barn Theatre. He completed two full-length plays for the adult market, and a book on training actors and directors. He returned to England most years to teach and direct. He died of cancer.

JAFFÉ, CARL (1909–1974)

Born: Germany

Role: Captain Winogrodzki (S1, episode 4: 'The Enemy Within the Gates') (TV and radio)

Jaffé arrived in England in 1936 as a refugee. Although by then he was well known on the continent for acting, he was unknown here and unable to speak a word of English. He set about learning the language, secured an agent and was sent to J B Priestley, who offered him a part in his play, *People at Sea*. There he was spotted by Raymond Massey who recruited him for his West End show, *Idiot's Delight*, in 1937.

As his film career blossomed he was frequently cast as officials and aristocrats. His movie credits include playing Meyer in the 1947 movie *The Blind Goddess*, a German general in *Appointment in London*, *The Saint in London*, *Two Thousand Women*, *Counterblast*, *Ivanhoe*, *Timeslip*, *Rockets Galore*, *Man on a String*, *Battle Beneath the Earth* and his last picture, *Fiddler on the Roof*, playing Isaac.

JAMES, LINDA

Born: Ilford

Role: Betty (S3, episode 3: 'The Lion has 'Phones' and S4, episode 8: 'The Two and a Half Feathers') (TV)

On the proviso that she qualified as a teacher, Linda's parents allowed her to enrol on a drama course at The Royal Academy of Music. Three years later, she graduated as a speech and drama teacher.

She worked in rep before making her TV debut in 1969's comedy, *The Gnomes of Dulwich*, written by Jimmy Perry. The series about garden gnomes meant her appearance as one of the humans was restricted to shots of her feet! Other TV credits include *Keeping Up Appearances*, *Waiting for God*, *Only Fools and Horses*, *Don't Wait Up*, *Last of the Summer Wine*, *Some Mothers Do 'Ave 'Em*, *Doctors at the Top*, *The Liver Birds* and *The Dick Emery Show*.

In a career spanning 15 years, she was seen mainly in comedy parts. Nowadays Linda – who's married to actor Michael Knowles – is a dialect coach for film and TV, and teaches at two drama schools.

JESSIE

Mentioned by Frazer in 'Never Too Old' Jessie was a long-legged Scottish lass who Frazer dated prior to his days in Walmington. When she didn't return from a cliff-top walk one day, it was feared she'd fallen off the cliff. It turned out she had left the country for Singapore, but after getting fed up with life there, she wrote to Frazer explaining she wanted to return and marry him, but needed £40 for the ticket. It didn't take long for Frazer to decide he wasn't made of money.

JETHRO

A friend of Frazer's, mentioned by the Scotsman in the TV episode, 'Uninvited Guests'. They spent time together in the South Seas some fifty years before; when Jethro took a ruby from an idol, a witch doctor placed a curse on him. It couldn't have worked because he died at the age of 86. Not seen in the sitcom.

JOEL, PAUL (1942–)

Designer on 52 episodes: S1; S2, episodes 1, 3, 4, 5, 6; S3, episodes 1–7; S4: 'Battle of the Giants'; S5; S6

Born in 1942, Paul left school in 1960 and studied architecture in London, working for several architects, including Eric Lyons, before going on to work in interior design. He joined the BBC in 1965 as a design assistant and was promoted to designer in 1968. His career in the BBC spanned almost 30 years, designing all types of productions, including *Blue Peter*, *Q5* with Spike Milligan, *Monty Python's Flying Circus*, the pilot of *It*

MY MEMORIES OF *DAD'S ARMY*

'I was a war baby. The nearest I came to the action was being left to sleep in the garden one afternoon just before a bomber jettisoned its remaining load into a nearby street, which sent a piece of shrapnel hurtling into the side of my pram, grazing my buttocks. I don't appear to have any scars, but the thirst for knowledge of this extraordinary period lives on and it was with painstaking care that I researched the *Dad's Army* series. To me it was a slice of history, made funny by the characters and personalities involved – a comedy drama rather than a sitcom – so my sets were designed to reflect the reality of the period as well as the comic situation.

'*Dad's Army* was a production I looked forward to designing – always stimulating and usually a challenge. Jimmy and David's scripts were full of genuine humour and, sensibly, never demanded more sets than the series budget could afford. Sometimes they would ask me at an early stage in writing the script how much could be built to accommodate a specific situation. They realised that there was only a finite amount of space in front of the studio audience to plan the sets and all of the comedy would need to be seen to get the best natural reaction from that audience. It was comforting to know that, on occasions, the sets themselves provided Jimmy and David with a spontaneous gag or two, such as Mainwaring being unwittingly trapped in the corner of the Vicar's office behind the two doors which opened against each other.

'One notable challenge was "Asleep in the Deep", where the platoon were marooned in the basement of a bombed local waterworks with water rising around them. I designed the whole set to be suspended in a large, purpose-built water tank to a depth of four feet, so as not to exceed the studio floor weight loading (the script did not require the platoon to fall into the video editing rooms below!), and instead of the water rising at one point in the proceedings, the set and props were lowered in by three feet and Peter Day, the visual effects designer, donned a wetsuit and snorkel to pilot Bill Pertwee around in a small bathtub from beneath the water, whilst the rest of the cast bravely acted being in the deep.

'Quite often the situation demanded a full-studio set piece, as in "Sgt – Save My Boy!", for which I designed a beach, together with the Harris Orphans' Holiday Home Hut (interior and exterior), and a starlit sky over Walmington-on-Sea in the background. The beach was supposed to be mined and the platoon had to creep gingerly forward on their stomachs, prodding the sand with bayonets to find the mines. The majority of the beach was fine sawdust, but BBC Studio Planning waived their usually stringent regulations and I was allowed to build a six-inch deep trench across the studio and fill it with sand so that close-ups of the action looked real. However, I was not allowed to use real barbed wire for the sea defences as Pike had to become entangled in it! The illusion seemed to work well on camera except for the stars. They were actually pealights pinned to a black gauze and one minute before the studio recording they collapsed into a congealed heap! That wouldn't happen now, with today's sophisticated technology.

'Jones' van was the most delightful "big prop". I found the old Ford with the help of a specialist vehicle supplier. It was a bit of a wreck, but mechanics made it work well enough for its filming sequences near Thetford. My job was to design the signwriting, so I chose a florid, late-Victorian style to go with Jones' butcher's shop. Later, portholes were cut in the sides and roof for the platoon's rapid response rifle drill, and a large gas bag strapped to the roof as an alternative source of fuel. This, of course, was punctured by the rifles' bayonets – great fun!

'By far the most difficult episode to design and build was 'Time On My Hands', where an enemy parachutist dangles from the town clock projecting from the clocktower, and Corporal Jones takes a ride on the mechanical figures moving in and out of the tower. This was to have been recorded in the largest studio with a day to prepare the scaffolding to support the large and complicated set, and arrange the intricate special effects. Just before recording the studio planning department changed it to a night set-up in a middle-sized studio – a serious compromise! It was necessary for me to supervise "hands on" throughout the night and the following rehearsal/recording day to make up the lost 12 hours, and adjust the set to the smaller studio space. However, with literally seconds to go before the final rehearsal, everything was in place and working well, and the platoon coped gamefully with the mayhem – as always.'

PAUL JOEL

Ain't Half Hot, Mum, Colditz, David Copperfield, When the Boat Comes In, The Duchess of Duke Street, Tomorrow's World, Marie Curie, Not the Nine O'Clock News, The Tempest, Sense and Sensibility, Frost in May, Beau Geste, Strangers and Brothers, The Prisoner of Zenda, Double Image, Dancin' Thru the Dark, Adam Bede, A Breed of Horses and many more. He has been nominated for various design awards during his career.

Paul left the BBC in 1994 and occasionally works freelance. Now living in a studio in Cornwall with his artist wife, Judy, much of his time these days is devoted to organising and designing art exhibitions. Ian Lavender opened one of Judy's solo art exhibitions, for which Judy presented him with her own painting of *Dad's Army*.

JOHNSON, KAY
Producer's assistant on 34 episodes (TV): S3, episodes 8, 9, 10, 11, 12, 13 & 14; S4; 'Battle of the Giants'; S5

JOHNSON, MR
Mr Johnson is not seen in the series, but in 'Sons of the Sea' we're informed of his death, at which point his Swallow Bank account is overdrawn by £33 12s 6d. He has no relatives and his only possessions are the clothes he stood up in and a 15-foot rowing boat called *The Naughty Jane*, which he used for taking visitors on trips around the lighthouse. Because of the overdraft, Mainwaring gains control of his boat.

JOHNSON, MRS
Not seen in the sitcom, Mrs Johnson is mentioned by Jones in 'High Finance'. She deals with all the accounts and finances at his butcher's shop. She's a keen knitter and her handiwork can often be found inside the little cashier's booth.

JOHNSON, WENDY
Role: Mrs Binns (S5, episode 9: 'When Did You Last See Your Money?') (TV)

JOLLY ROGER ICE CREAM PARLOUR
Frequently mentioned by Mainwaring and his men, the ice cream parlour was seen in the episode, 'Put That Light Out!', when it's chosen as the rendezvous point for Jones' section before they cross the causeway. The parlour is situated at the end of a jetty on Walmington's sea front, and doubles up as a warden's post.

JONES, ANNA
Make-up artist on seven episodes (TV): S5, episodes 8, 9, 10, 11, 12 & 13; S6, episode 2
Ann trained as a primary teacher at Bedford College upon leaving school, and during the mid-1950s worked for four years at a school in Romford. She realised her future lay outside teaching and as soon as she'd saved enough money, gave up the profession and booked a place at a private school in London, studying beauty therapy, under Gertrude Hartley (Vivien Leigh's mother).

After completing the six-month course she sent speculative letters to numerous TV companies. The only station to reply was the BBC, and she was taken on as a trainee make-up artist in 1959. Three months in the corporation's own training school was followed by 14 years' service, before leaving in 1973. Among the shows she worked on are *Dixon of Dock Green*, *Marriage Lines*, *It Ain't Half Hot, Mum*, and *That Was The Week That Was*.

A period of freelance work followed before she moved to Granada Television as a senior make-up artist and designer. During this time she won a BAFTA award for her work as make-up designer on *The Jewel in the Crown*.

She then moved to LWT as head of make-up, where she remained until recently. She has largely retired from the business, although she still considers offers of freelance work.

Note: Anna's surname was Chesterman during her time on the show.

JONES, BRONWEN

Not seen in the sitcom, but mentioned by Private Cheeseman in 'Turkey Dinner', Bronwen is a big, fat Welsh girl who used to wash glasses on a Saturday night at a pub. He says she spent half her life in a haystack and became known as 'the welcome in the valley'.

JONES' BUTCHER'S SHOP

A well-established shop situated in Walmington's High Street, it is surprising it has remained in business so long considering Jones' slapdash accounting methods, which are highlighted by Mr Mainwaring in 'High Finance'. The interior is always spotlessly clean and highly decorative, with black and white tiles on the floor, and patterned examples covering the walls. Serving behind the counter in his straw hat and striped apron, there is no doubting the fact that Jack Jones takes pride in his work, ever since he took over from his father, also a butcher by trade, who couldn't afford proper sawdust so had to make do with secondhand stuff.

During the course of the sitcom we get to see, or hear, about some of the staff Jones employs, including Bailey, who's missing from parade in 'Museum Piece' because he's counting coupons back at the butcher's shop. Mrs Foster also helps out with coupon-counting, although it's unclear whether she's a paid employee or simply a volunteer, because in 'Command Decision' we learn that she helps him in return for a few scraps for her cat. As Jones' feelings towards Mrs Fox strengthen, she starts helping count the coupons on the last Wednesday of the month, after which she makes him a nice cuppa.

Miss Doris Mortimer, who earns 30 shillings a week, is the cashier, while Raymond assists Jones by serving customers and collecting a wage packet of 22s 6d for his efforts. Mrs Johnson,

This butcher's in London was the inspiration behind many of Paul Joel's designs when he created the interior of Jones' shop.

meanwhile, also uses the little cashier's booth because she's responsible for keeping the accounts up to date.

When customers keep on Jones' good side they can expect quality service, but if anyone upsets him he gives them gristle, and enjoys thinking about them while he sits at home tucking into his Sunday lunch. Another way of getting his revenge is to add them to his sausage blacklist.

Just like everything else, the war is taking its toll on Jones' shop, stripping it of much of the produce and delicacies he's used to serving, with sausages and brawn becoming unlikely favourites instead.

JONES, ELSIE

Although she's never seen, Elsie is referred to in 'Museum Piece'. While Mainwaring's men try getting into the Peabody Museum of Historical Army Weapons, Jones' father, George, who's employed as the caretaker while the museum is closed for the duration, asks his son how Elsie is. It's not clear what relation she is to either of them, but we do learn that she has troublesome legs. George is far from complimentary when he says she has such fat legs she resembles an elephant.

JONES, GEORGE
Played by Eric Woodburn (TV and radio)
George Jones, who's a long-standing customer of the Swallow Bank, is Jack's father. At 88, he still works as caretaker at the Peabody Museum of Historical Army Weapons. A cantankerous old man, who's been married three times, George does everything in his power to prevent Mainwaring and his men entering the museum in the episode 'Museum Piece'. However, he finally lets his predilection for alcohol get the better of him, and while sipping some of Frazer's whisky, the platoon enter the building.

JONES, LANCE CORPORAL JACK
Played by Clive Dunn (all mediums)
Works address: 42, The High Street, Walmington-on-Sea, although we later learn in 'A Brush With the Law', that he lives and works at 19, The High Street
A butcher by trade, 70-year-old Jack 'They don't like it up 'em!' Jones, who keeps his feet in condition by bathing them in tea, has an impeccable

military record, with 29 years' service in the regular army under his belt. Although it's ages since he joined up, he'll never forget that day. After having his hair shaved off, being washed all over with carbolic soap, given a large basin of cold, fatty soup and a prickly blanket, he cried himself to sleep.

He signed on as a drummer boy in 1884, and later saw service with the Warwickshire Regiment in Sudan, fighting the Fuzzy Wuzzies. He was invalided out of the army in 1915, when sight problems set in. During his time in khaki he spent 14 years as a lance corporal, a rank he's allowed to retain in the Home Guard, something Mainwaring and Wilson were happy to honour, even though slipping them both a little steak didn't harm his chances!

As a boy, Jones used to rise at 5am and help the local milkman on his round. For tuppence a week, and a bruised toe or two thrown in, Jones would hold the milkman's horse while he took the bottles to the houses.

Always a second or two behind the rest of the men during drill, Jones is one for the ladies, particularly Mrs Fox, whom he finally weds in the last episode after fancying her for 17 years. But before this joyous occasion, rumours circulate about his so-called relationship with the timid Mrs Prosser. Jones flatly denies anything but a friendly relationship, and is fully aware of what people think. When Mainwaring starts reading a letter from Hodges in 'The Test', Jones butts in and states that if the note is about him and Mrs Prosser being found down the air raid shelter, everything can be explained: she came over a bit faint and he had no alternative but to take her down to rest.

Even though Jones is as keen as mustard, his health and age are beginning to take their toll: at one point his ability to cope with the rigours of Home Guard duties are questioned and put to the test by Major Regan, and if it hadn't been for the help of his loyal comrades, he could have been pensioned off for good. Despite his inability to keep up during drill, his knack of distracting all around him, his inclination to panic in tricky situations, drift off into the 'realms of fantasy' with some hare-brained scheme or idea and recurrent attacks of malaria, something he's suffered for 40 years, Jones is one of the more valuable members of the platoon. He is a lionheart, always faithful to the cause, and is a vital cog in Walmington's defence machine, despite his shortcomings.

In his spare time, Jack Jones, who is secretary of the local Darby and Joan Club, is occasionally seen playing the organ at St Aldhelm's Church, but only when 'Onward Christian Soldiers' is chosen by the Vicar, because it's the only tune he can play. His desire to take up the instrument was driven by passion: some time ago he fell in love with a woman from Leamington Spa, although he admits she had an 'acid face'; it was her flat knees that caught his eye, something she gained from praying too much. The liaison ended in heartache when he rushed round to see her one day, only to find she'd moved to Bournemouth. He also played first cornet in the town band before the war.

When it comes to entertaining, there's only one woman he wants to spend time with, other than long-time friend Mrs Prosser, and that's

Mrs Fox. He starts dating her and, prior to their marriage, spends Saturday evenings at her place. After enjoying a couple of pork chops, they sit down and listen to *In Town Tonight* on the radio.

JONES, MRS

We discover very little about Jack Jones' mother. She never appears and is only mentioned once, during the episode 'Turkey Dinner', when Jones states she's gone to Angmering, in West Sussex.

JONES, PEGGY ANN

Born: Peterborough
Roles: Member of the Home Front Company (stage show), Britannia (stage show at Billingham)
For several years Peggy was principal mezzo-soprano with the D'Oyly Carte Company, touring Canada and America. She has also worked on TV and films, including Gene Wilder's satire, *The Adventure of Sherlock Holmes' Smarter Brother*.

JUDY

Played by April Walker (TV)
Judy is a land girl who works on Mrs Prentice's farm. In 'All is Safely Gathered In', she spends more time chatting with Walker than helping thresh the wheat.

JUTLAND, BATTLE OF

It is often mentioned how Frazer was serving with the Royal Navy during the Battle of Jutland. This major naval engagement during the Great War took place off the Jutland Peninsula in northern Europe in 1916.

KEANE, MRS

Heard in the radio episode, 'Under Fire'. (See 'Keen, Mrs'.)

KEEN, MRS

Played by Queenie Watts (TV); Avril Angers (radio, although character called Mrs Keane)

A middle-aged blonde who lives in the same block of flats as Mr Murphy in 'Under Fire'. Murphy and Mrs Keen don't see eye to eye over anything, and he remarks that she entertains sailors and the Canadian Air Force!

KEEP YOUNG AND BEAUTIFUL

Recorded: Friday 9/6/72

Original transmission: Friday 13/10/72, 8.30–9.00pm

Original viewing figures: 16 million

Repeated: 7/7/73, 26/9/89, 24/1/90 (N Ireland), 6/8/93, 10/1/97, 21/2/99

CAST

Arthur Lowe . . . . .Captain Mainwaring
John Le Mesurier . . . . .Sergeant Wilson
Clive Dunn . . . . .Lance Corporal Jones
John Laurie . . . . .Private Frazer
James Beck . . . . .Private Walker
Arnold Ridley . . . . .Private Godfrey
Ian Lavender . . . . .Private Pike
Bill Pertwee . . . . .ARP Warden
Derek Bond . . . . .Minister
Robert Raglan . . . . .Colonel
James Ottaway . . . . .1st Member of Parliament
Charles Morgan . . . . .2nd Member of Parliament
Platoon: Colin Bean, Desmond Cullum-Jones, Evan Ross, George Hancock, Hugh Hastings, Leslie Noyes, Hugh Cecil, Freddie White, Freddie Wiles, Michael Moore

PRODUCTION TEAM

Script: Jimmy Perry and David Croft
Producer/Director: David Croft
Production Assistant: Gordon Pert
Film Cameraman: Stewart A Farnell
Film Sound Recordist: Ron Blight
Film Editor: Bob Rymer
Studio Lighting: Howard King
Studio Sound: Michael McCarthy
Design: Paul Joel
Floor Assistant: Richard Cox

'Keep Young and Beautiful'

Vision Mixer: Dave Hanks
Costume Supervisor: Susan Wheal
Make-Up Supervisor: Cynthia Goodwin
Visual Effects: Peter Day

It's decided by Parliament that the ARP and Home Guard should exchange personnel: the younger, fitter men joining the Home Guard while the older warhorses transfer to the ARP. Such talk enrages Mainwaring and his platoon, who are determined to stay put. What makes matters worse is that a recent exercise proved that most of Mainwaring's men aren't up to scratch.

In an attempt to look young, Mainwaring decides a toupee – even an ill-fitting one – will knock years off his appearance; meanwhile, Wilson decides on a corset, or as he says, a 'gentleman's abdominal support'. Soon everyone is determined to stay put, including Hodges who hates the thought of transferring to the Home Guard, so much so that he pays Walker £1 for something that will turn his hair white – ceiling white! Godfrey and Jones turn to Frazer's skills of beautifying the dead in order to shed the years because being the oldest, they think they'll be transferred first.

The area commander is due to inspect the platoon to decide who'll transfer, but all the hard work pays off when no one is selected. Mainwaring denies having anything to do with the charades the men have been involved in, until the Colonel praises him for using his initiative.

KENT, NATALIE

Role: Miss Twelvetrees (S8, episode 5: 'High Finance') (TV)

Natalie appeared in various TV shows, including *The Sweeney*, playing Doris in the episode, 'The Jackpot'. She was also seen in *Z Cars*, *Angels* as Mrs Faulkner, *New Scotland Yard* as Mrs Walton, *Scoop* playing Sister Watts, *Swallows and Amazons*, and various productions from the 1950s, like *No Shepherds Watched* and *Huntingtower*.

KENWAY, NAN

Role: Mrs Prentice ('All is Safely Gathered In') (radio)

KERCHISS, SUZANNE

Born: London

Role: Ivy Samways (S6, episode 2: 'My British Buddy') (TV)

Suzanne, who was engaged to Ian Lavender when she appeared in the series, originally trained as a ballet dancer. She attended the Royal Ballet School (1956–1962), and upon graduating joined the original cast of *Pickwick*, understudying for Dilys Watling, in London, Manchester and on tour; the same year (1963) saw her dancing at the Royal Command Performance.

For the next ten years she remained busy, particularly in the theatre, working at The Piccadilly Theatre, The Globe, The Comedy Theatre and various venues around the country, including a production of *The Clandestine Marriage* at Canterbury in 1967, where she met Ian. She worked on radio and TV occasionally, including the series *Topol*.

Suzanne gave up the business in 1975 upon the birth of her second child, and divorced Ian in 1976. Although she retains her Equity card, she qualified as a RGN nurse in 1986 and worked full-time for 15 years. She has now scaled down her nursing career to pursue a BA Hons history degree at Birkbeck College, London University.

Pikey got annoyed when Ivy Samways (left) was chatted up by the Americans in 'My British Buddy'.

KERR, FRASER

Roles: Major General Menzies (nine episodes), Sergeant MacKenzie ('If the Cap Fits...'), Captain Swan and Inspector ('A Man of Action'), Mr West ('A Wilson (Manager)?'), Russian Visitor ('The Honourable Man'), Policeman ('The Great White Hunter'), Colonel Winters ('The Deadly Attachment'), Train Driver ('The Royal Train'), German Pilot ('Time On My Hands'), Sir Charles McAllister ('Is There Honey Still For Tea?') (radio)

KING, BERT

Played by Fred Griffiths (film)

The stocky, cockney-speaking Bert is responsible for taking the Vicar's bells away in aid of the war effort, as well as driving his lorry all over the vicarage lawn.

KING, DIANA (1919–1986)

Born: London

Role: Chairwoman (S2, episode 3: 'The Loneliness of the Long-Distance Walker') (TV)

Diana, whose career was spent mainly in the theatre, always wanted to be an actress and attended the Fay Compton School of Dramatic Art. During the war years she performed in various reps, including Peterborough and Buxton, and continued developing her stage career after the war. She also became busy on TV, appearing in several sitcoms, such as *Marriage Lines* playing Prunella Scales' mother, Captain Peacock's wife in *Are You Being Served?* and *You're Only Young Twice*.

She made sporadic film appearances, beginning with *Spellbound* in 1941 and also including *The Man in Grey*, *My Teenage Daughter*, *The Man Who Wouldn't Talk*, *A Farewell to Arms* with Rock Hudson and *They Came from Beyond Space*.

Diana died of cancer at the age of 67.

KING, HOWARD

Lighting supervisor on six series (TV): S3, S5–S9, 'Battle of the Giants', 'My Brother and I' and 'The Love of Three Oranges'

KING, JANET

Played by Caroline Dowdeswell (TV); Harriet Rhys (film); Elizabeth Morgan (radio)

Janet King, a junior clerk at the Walmington-on-Sea branch of Swallow Bank, appeared in five out of six episodes in the opening series, and would have appeared in 'The Showing Up Of Corporal Jones' had it not been for the editor's knife. Viewers never got to know anything about her background, but she seemed an efficient bank employee, providing a bit of glamour around an otherwise sombre-looking workplace.

In the film, the mild-mannered clerk was described on the closing credits as the 'Girl in Bank', and was told off in the picture's early scenes for wearing lipstick which the stuffy Mr Mainwaring regards as too bright for the Swallow Bank's image.

KING WAS IN HIS COUNTING HOUSE, THE

Recorded: Friday 23/6/72

Original transmission: Friday 17/11/72, 8.30–9.00pm

Original viewing figures: 16 million

Repeated: 11/8/73, 31/10/89, 2/8/90 (N Ireland), 13/8/93, 25/9/94 (Scotland), 7/2/97

CAST

Arthur Lowe . . . . .Captain Mainwaring
John Le Mesurier . . . . .Sergeant Wilson
Clive Dunn . . . . .Lance Corporal Jones
John Laurie . . . . .Private Frazer
James Beck . . . . .Private Walker
Arnold Ridley . . . . .Private Godfrey
Ian Lavender . . . . .Private Pike
Bill Pertwee . . . . .ARP Warden
Frank Williams . . . . .Vicar
Edward Sinclair . . . . .Verger
Wendy Richard . . . . .Shirley

'The Loneliness of the Long-Distance Walker'

Colin Bean . . . . .Private Sponge
Platoon: Desmond Cullum-Jones, Michael Moore,
George Hancock, Leslie Noyes, Hugh Hastings, Evan
Ross, Hugh Cecil, Freddie Wiles, Freddie White
Wardens: Clifford Hensley and Harry Davies
Stuntman: Tom Atkins

PRODUCTION TEAM
Script: Jimmy Perry and David Croft
Producer/Director: David Croft
Production Assistant: Gordon Pert
Film Cameraman: Stewart A Farnell
Film Sound Recordist: Ron Blight
Film Editor: Bob Rymer
Studio Lighting: Howard King
Studio Sound: Michael McCarthy
Design: Paul Joel
Assistant Floor Manager: Peter Fitton
Vision Mixer: Dave Hanks
Costume Supervisor: Susan Wheal
Make-Up Supervisor: Cynthia Goodwin
Visual Effects: Peter Day

Mainwaring has arranged a party at his house because he feels it's time to meet with everyone on equal terms. He's provided sandwiches and beer for his guests, although Mrs Mainwaring is concerned they'll get drunk and smash the place up. Things aren't running very well and the atmosphere is tense. Mainwaring announces his wife, who's upstairs, will come down soon and then they can start the refreshments. Walker surprises everyone and turns up with an uninvited guest, Shirley, a real dolly bird, and, as Walker remarks, 'It's like an undertakers' convention'. While Mainwaring is out of the room, Pikey breaks an ornament containing artificial snow and water, so Walker fills it up with water from the goldfish bowl. When Mainwaring re-enters the room and becomes conscious of the silence, he shows off his curios, but is surprised when no snow falls!

Mrs Mainwaring is slow in coming down and when she's finally on her way, the air raid siren sends her racing to the shelter. Three bombs drop, one on the bank. It puts paid to the party – which everyone is relieved about – because the men have to guard the money in the damaged bank. All the money, totalling £96,478 11s 4d, is taken to the church hall for safe keeping.

While Jones' section count the currency, the rest of the platoon form a guard around them. Pike, meanwhile, phones the manager of the Eastgate branch, who agrees to keep the money in his vault if they bring it over the following day. Wilson is sent to order a couple of taxis: one for the money, the other for the armed guard, but the garage was bombed and all the vehicles are out of order. Walker comes to the rescue and secures a vehicle for transporting the money, even if it is a horse and cart.

Mainwaring – who tells Wilson he knows how to handle horses – drives the cart while the men

follow on their bikes. When the money blows out of the basket it's being carried in, Pike gives chase but can't catch up. Instead, he fires his gun to grab Mainwaring's attention, frightening the horse in the process, which gallops off with Mainwaring desperately trying to keep control.

KING'S HEAD, THE
A pub in Walmington, mentioned in 'Turkey Dinner', where Jones takes his section while on patrol one cold night. The men enjoy a couple of pints before moving on to The Goat and Compasses.

apprenticeship in motor mechanics before giving it up to attend the London Academy of Modelling. He joined Equity in 1967, and combined a modelling career with walk-on parts on TV, with his first job being a soldier in a BBC play.

After leaving *Dad's Army* he was involved mainly in photographic work until quitting the profession and taking a complete change in direction by purchasing a petrol station in 1986. He subsequently ran a business selling go-kart parts and drove a minicab during the evening. Nowadays he works for the local council in Bromley.

KITCHENER, GENERAL (1850–1916)
Constantly mentioned by Jones, who served under him during the Sudanese campaign in the 1880s, Kitchener was born in County Kerry. He joined the Royal Engineers in 1871 and, from 1892, became the Commander-in-Chief of the Egyptian army, winning back the Sudan for Egypt. His military successes followed him to South Africa, where he brought the Second Boer War to an end. In 1914 he had been appointed Secretary of War, but two years later was drowned off the Orkneys, when his ship, *HMS Hampshire*, was mined.

KITTERIDGE, RICHARD (1944–)
Born: St Neots
Role: Member of the platoon's back row in 11 episodes (S2; S3, episodes 1–4, 6, 7) (TV)
Richard, who was in his twenties when he appeared in the back row, was scheduled to become a regular until other work prevented him doing so. Upon leaving school he started an

The platoon frequented many of the pubs around the area of Walmington.

KNIGHTS OF MADNESS
Recorded: Friday 22/7/77
Original transmission: Sunday 16/10/77, 8.10–8.40pm
Original viewing figures: 19 million
Repeated: 25/9/78, 14/8/79, 20/9/91

CAST
Arthur Lowe . . . . .Captain Mainwaring
John Le Mesurier . . . . .Sergeant Wilson
Clive Dunn . . . . .Lance Corporal Jones
John Laurie . . . . .Private Frazer
Arnold Ridley . . . . .Private Godfrey
Ian Lavender . . . . .Private Pike
Bill Pertwee . . . . .Chief Warden Hodges
Frank Williams . . . . .Vicar
Edward Sinclair . . . . .Verger
Janet Davies . . . . .Mrs Pike
Colin Bean . . . . .Private Sponge
Olive Mercer . . . . .Mrs Yeatman

Eric Longworth . . . . .Town Clerk
Fred McNaughton . . . . .Mayor
Platoon: Desmond Cullum-Jones, George Hancock, Freddie White, Freddie Wiles, Michael Moore, Jimmy Mac, Roger Bourne, Vernon Drake, Evan Ross
Note: The Thetford ATC 1109 Squadron appeared as the Sea Cadet band.
Doubles for Arthur Lowe: Derek Ware and William Sully
Double for Bill Pertwee: Jimmy Lodge

PRODUCTION TEAM
Script: Jimmy Perry and David Croft
Producer/Director: David Croft
Production Assistant: Gordon Elsbury
Film Cameraman: Peter Chapman
Film Sound Recordist: Graham Bedwell
Film Editor: John Dunstan
Studio Lighting: Howard King
Studio Sound: Laurie Taylor
Design: Tim Gleeson
Assistant Floor Manager: Susan Belbin
Vision Mixer: Angela Beveridge
Costume Designer: Mary Husband
Make-Up Artist: Sylvia Thornton
Visual Effects: Martin Gutteridge

At a committee meeting the town clerk mentions that the grand march past on Saturday afternoon will mark the climax of 'Wings for Victory' week. First in the procession will be the Sea Scouts' Drum and Bugle Band, then a keep-fit display by the ladies netball team (led by Mrs Yeatman), then some morris dancing by the Eastgate Morris Dancers.

There are arguments between Mainwaring and Hodges as to whether the Home Guard or the wardens will be chosen to do the grand finale, so it's decided the privilege will be shared between them, fuelling the personal rivalry.

As the finale coincides with St George's Day, Mainwaring thinks the Home Guard should re-enact the fight between George and the dragon. The trouble is the wardens have the same idea, so it's a race to see who can outdo the other.

KNOWLES, MICHAEL
Born: Spondon, Derbyshire
Roles: Captain Cutts (S2, episode 3 & S3, episode 4), Engineer Officer (S4, episode 4), Captain Reed (S4, episode 13), Captain Stewart (S5, episode 12), BBC Producer (Christmas Night with the Stars 1972) (TV); Captain Bailey ('A Stripe for Frazer' and 'A Wilson (Manager)?'), Captain and Mr Rees ('The Loneliness of the Long-Distance Walker'), Captain Pringle ('The Bullet is Not for Firing'), Mr Wintergreen ('A Brush with the Law'), Squadron Leader ('The Day the Balloon Went Up'), Captain Stewart ('Round and Round Went the Great Big Wheel') (radio)
Michael had considered studying medicine before turning his attention to acting. Graduating from RADA, he worked at reps in Richmond, Bromley and Watford.

Thanks to his time at the Palace Theatre, Watford, Michael was recruited to the cast of Dad's Army to play various silly-ass captains. This began a 20-year career in TV, with notable appearances as Captain Ashwood in It Ain't Half Hot, Mum, Fanshaw in BBC's 1978 sitcom, Come Back, Mrs Noah, The Dick Emery Show, Brush Strokes and the Honourable Sir Teddy Meldrum in Perry and Croft's You Rang, M'Lord?. In collaboration with Harold Snoad, he was responsible for adapting 67 Dad's Army episodes for radio.

Michael – who's married to Linda James – is still a regular face on TV, particularly in sitcoms. Together with Harold Snoad, he's written for radio, theatre and TV. They began writing material for Bill Pertwee's cabaret show, before moving on to TV and radio, including two episodes of Thames Television's Bless This House, with Sid James, although their scripts were never recorded.

KRONIG, BARBARA
Costume designer on six episodes: S4, episodes 1–6
Barbara attended art college in London for three years, during which time she studied all aspects of costume design, including the history of costume. After graduating, she spent two years working for a company specialising in period dress, before setting up her own business making period costume for TV and film. In 1965 she joined the BBC as a designer, and her early credits include Comedy Playhouse, Butterflies and shows with Harry Secombe and Roy Hudd. Although she did her fair share of light entertainment shows, she worked mainly on period productions and dramas, including the last recording of Z Cars, The Mayfly and the Frog, Lord Peter Wimsey, The Brothers, The Lost Boys and I, Claudius.

By the time Barbara left the BBC in the 1980s she had moved into management. For a while post-Beeb she ran a company with a partner, helping promote TV and film productions as well as working on them. She now works as a freelance costume designer.

KYBER ROAD
During a raid on the area, Kyber Road in Walmington is patrolled by the air raid wardens in 'Uninvited Guests'.

KYDD, SAM (1915–1982)
Born: Belfast
Roles: Yokel (S9, episode 1: 'Wake-Up Walmington') (TV); Nazi Orderly (film)
Sam Kydd, who moved to England as a child, always wanted to work in the entertainment business, and by the time war broke out in 1939, he'd already started acting with an appearance in the film, They Came by Night. He became a prisoner of war in 1940, and while interned in a Polish POW camp, he got involved in running and acting in the theatrical productions staged to entertain fellow prisoners.

He resumed his acting career upon his return to England after the war, and soon became a regular face playing small parts in a myriad of post-war British movies, including The Captive Heart, Scott of the Antarctic, Portrait from Life, Passport to Pimlico, The Small Back Room, No Trace, Seven Days to Noon, Doctor in Distress and Smokescreen.

On TV, he's probably best known for appearing in Crane, although he popped up in lots of other shows, including Shadow Squad, The Pickwick Papers and Here's Harry.

Sam died from a respiratory ailment.

LA PLAZ, LAURA
Played by Barbara Windsor (TV)
Crack shot Laura La Plaz is entertaining at the Hippodrome Theatre, Walmington, when Mainwaring and his men are in the audience. Supposedly straight from South America, Laura is an expert shot when she fires over her shoulder or through her legs. With a shooting competition looming, Walker asks her to shoot for the platoon, but what he doesn't realise is that she can only hit the target when shooting in this unconventional manner.

LADIES IN THE QUEUE
Played by Pamela Cundell, Bernadette Milnes and Olive Mercer (TV)
While Mainwaring teaches his platoon how to use the telephone box in 'The Lion has 'Phones' a queue forms. In it are three ladies who Walker exploits by convincing them that phone calls are going to be rationed.

LADY MAGISTRATE, THE
Played by Marjorie Wilde (TV)
This monocle-wearing magistrate sits alongside Captain Square to hear the case brought against Captain Mainwaring in 'A Brush With the Law'.

LADY WITH THE PRAM, THE
Played by Joy Allen (TV)
While quietly pushing her baby along in a pram in 'Gorilla Warfare', this lady is startled when Mainwaring and his men surround and search the pram, worried that she's really a counter agent out to ruin their chances of succeeding in a weekend exercise.

LADY WITH THE UMBRELLA, THE
Played by Adele Strong (TV)
In 'Ring Dem Bells' this old lady starts poking Mainwaring with her umbrella while accusing him of being a quisling.

LANDLORD, THE
Played by Verne Morgan (TV)
The landlord of The Red Lion in Walmington, where the platoon set up a darts match to wel-

come the Americans to the town is the same landlord at the pubs where members of the Walmington and Eastgate platoons drink in 'Don't Forget the Diver', and where the darts match between the Home Guard and the wardens take place in 'Absent Friends'. It's unclear whether the same pub is visited on all three occasions or if the landlord swapped pubs on a regular basis.

LANDLORD, THE

For the landlord in 'Ring Dem Bells', see 'Palethorpe, Mr'.

LANE, VICKI (1941–)

Born: Abingdon

Role: Girl on the Tandem (S3, episode 8: 'The Day the Balloon Went Up') (TV)

Vicki played the girl who's riding peacefully along on a tandem with her boyfriend when it's commandeered by Hodges. He orders the man off the back, and sets off in pursuit of Mainwaring who's drifting along on the end of the stray barrage balloon.

Vicki left school at 15 and went straight into panto at Bournemouth, playing a tiller girl, before joining a touring company for two years, working summer months around English coastal resorts and winters in Scotland.

Most of Vicki's acting career was spent in variety, but in the 1970s she started being offered the occasional small part on TV, including a role in *Softly, Softly*. In 1978, she started travelling with her husband, the comedian Ken Goodwin, and gradually retired from the business. She now divides her time between England and Spain, where she bought a home in 1978.

LANKESHEER, ROBERT (1914–1993)

Born: South Wales

Role: Medical Officer (S2, episode 3: 'The Loneliness of the Long-Distance Walker') (TV)

While working for local government in the land registry department before the Second World War, Robert qualified as a lawyer via evening classes. The war years prevented him following a legal career and by the time he was demobbed with the rank of Major, he had decided his future lay in acting.

He spent many years in reps around the country before starting in films and television, where his credits included *The Professionals*, playing a vicar in 1978, a 1970 production of *David Copperfield* as Mr Sharp, an MP in *Young Winston* and an episode of *Fawlty Towers*.

LARGE MAN, THE

Played by Robert Moore (TV)

An angry husband in 'Man Hunt', this man complains to Hodges when Mainwaring, Wilson and Walker come calling on his wife asking to see her knickers.

LAURIE, JOHN (1897–1980)

Born: Dumfries

Role: Private James Frazer (all TV episodes and *Christmas Night with the Stars* inserts, the film and 64 episodes of the radio series)

John experienced a tough upbringing. His father – who was a foreman of a mill before opening his own gentlemen's outfitters – died when he was only three. John won a scholarship to the

Dumfries Academy, before taking up an apprenticeship in a local architect's office. Starting as an articled clerk, he earnt £5 a year and stayed with the firm until he received his call-up.

During the Great War he served with the Honourable Artillery Company and fought at the Somme. Invalided out due to bronchial problems, he finished his war service in London. When he was demobbed he needed a job quickly. Deciding he couldn't afford to return to his apprenticeship in the architect's office, he turned his mind to acting. Upon joining a local dramatic society he soon discovered he possessed a talent for the stage and that people enjoyed listening to him.

While attending a two-week summer school at Stratford-upon-Avon run by Elsie Fogerty, he was persuaded to take up acting professionally. His early theatrical career was heavily focused on Shakespeare and he established a reputation as an adept classical actor.

John served in the Home Guard during the Second World War, by which time he'd become leading man at Stratford, playing the likes of Hamlet, Macbeth, Othello and Richard III. His film career had also taken off with appearances in over a dozen films at that point.

The cessation of hostilities in 1945 marked a significant juncture in John's professional life. He resumed his big-screen career with ease but

his stage career never returned to the heights it had reached during the 1930s. During a career spanning six decades, John made nearly 100 films. With his pronounced facial features, bushy brows and wild-eyed expressions, he was often cast as irascible eccentrics. Although the financial rewards were greater than those he could possibly earn on the stage, he wasn't impressed with many of the pictures he appeared in.

Very much a homebird, John was a private man who enjoyed nothing more than relaxing with a good book or completing *The Times* crossword. A septuagenarian by the time *Dad's Army* started in 1968, John had reached the twilight of his career. Despite his initial reservations, he was grateful for the work at this late age, regarding it to be the best pension an old man could have.

John died of emphysema in 1980. A week before his death he had spent three days in Glasgow recording a play for Scottish television.

TV credits include: *Rosmersholm, Julius Caesar, Henry V, Jackanory, The Avengers, Man of the World, The Alcoa Hour, Strange Report, The Teckman Biography, The Three Hostages, Duty Bound, Shadow Squad, Murder Bag, Wednesday Magazine.*

Theatre credits include: *The Merry Wives of Windsor, King John, The Winter's Tale, Much Ado About Nothing, Macbeth, Hamlet, King Henry V, Richard III, The Improper Duchess, Napoleon, Twelfth Night, Crime on the Hill, A Midsummer Night's Dream, The Rivals, The Duchess of Malfi, Hedda Gabler, Othello, Heartbreak House, The Cherry Orchard, The Hero of a Hundred Fights.*

Film credits include: *Juno and the Paycock, The 39 Steps, The Tudor Rose, The Edge of the World, Q Planes, Ships With Wings, The Life and Death of Colonel Blimp, The Way Ahead, Fanny By Gaslight, I Know Where I'm Going, Mine Own Executioner, Madeleine, Treasure Island, Trio, Laughter in Paradise, The Fake, The Black Knight, Hobson's Choice, Rockets Galore, The Prisoner of Zenda, Kidnapped, The Reptile, One of Our Dinosaurs is Missing.*

LAVENDER, IAN (1946–)

Born: Birmingham

Role: Private Frank Pike (all TV episodes and *Christmas Night with the Stars* inserts; the film, the stage show and 59 episodes of the radio series)

The son of a policeman, Ian considered becoming a detective, but quickly dropped the idea upon realising he would have to train as a policeman first. Although he doesn't know why he chose the acting profession, it was the only job he considered after giving up any thoughts of being a detective.

After finishing his schooling at Bourneville Technical College in 1965, Ian headed for drama school at Bristol's Old Vic. He graduated in 1967 and a season playing juvenile leads followed at the Marlowe Theatre, Canterbury.

In 1968, he made his TV debut in an ATV play, *Flowers At My Feet*. During the same year, Ian was interviewed for the role of Pike in *Dad's Army*. After filming a commercial for *Woman's Own* – for which he had to spread marmalade on corn flakes – he phoned his agent to discover he'd got the part of Pike. At the time, Ian didn't think of the role as his big TV break, seeing it from a financial viewpoint, being the offer of several weeks of television work.

Between series of *Dad's Army*, Ian remained busy, appearing in TV shows like *Z Cars*, *Smokescreen* (a BBC *Wednesday Play*) and *The Canterbury Tales*. He also made his West End debut as Teddy Widgett in the musical *Ann Veronica*, enjoyed a successful run in the Mermaid Theatre production of *The Apple Cart*, and toured in numerous other shows.

Since playing Pike, Ian has been heard on the radio and seen in various small-screen comedies, including *Yes, Minister*, *Rising Damp* and *Goodnight Sweetheart*. He is also busy on the stage, and is regularly involved in writing and directing pantomimes.

TV credits include: *Casualty*, *Peak Practice*, *Call My Bluff*, *Harry Hill Show*, *Who's Cooking Dinner?*, *Funny You Ask*, *Keeping Up Appearances*, *Westbeach*, *Come Back Mrs Noah*, *Cluedo*, *The Glums*, *The Hello Goodbye Man*, *Have I Got You … Where You Want Me?*.

Theatre credits include: *Noel and Gertie*, *Who's Afraid of Virginia Woolf?*, *The Ghost Train*, *Out of Order*, *And Then There Were None*, *Plaintiff in a Pretty Hat*, *Run For Your Wife*, *Not Now Darling*, *The Mating Game*, *School Days*, *She Stoops to Conquer*, *Twelfth Night*, *Two and Two Make Sex*, *Why Not Stay For Breakfast?*, *Outside Edge*, *My Fat Friend*, *One for the Road*, *Risky Kisses*, *Buster Keaton*, *Noises Off*, *Cash on Delivery*.

Film credits include: *Carry On Behind*.

Radio credits include: *A Murder is Announced*, *The Sexton's Tales*, *He's a Wonderful Wife*, *It Sticks Out Half a Mile*.

LE MESURIER, JOHN (1912–1983)
Born: Bedford
Role: Sergeant Arthur Wilson (all TV episodes and *Christmas Night with the Stars* inserts; the film, the stage show and all radio episodes)

John turned his back on a law career – both his father and grandfather had been lawyers – in preference for acting, but he never regretted the decision.

John attended Sherborne School, Dorset, before embarking on a life in law. He had read the subject for three years and been articled to a firm of solicitors in Bury St Edmunds, but he had always nurtured a desire to try his hand at acting, and when he was 20, his parents finally gave their blessing. A career spanning five decades began with a six-month course at the Fay Compton Studio of Dramatic Art.

Interrupted only by a spell in the army, where

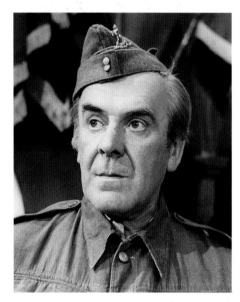

he finished his service as a captain on the north-west Indian frontier, John was busy throughout his career, initially with repertory and touring companies. His work incorporated all mediums of the acting profession, but it was film work he enjoyed most, and he made his first appearances in 1948's *Escape from Broadmoor* and *Death in the Hand*.

John became so busy on the film and television arena that he appeared rarely on stage as his career progressed. Among his numerous TV credits is a part in Dennis Potter's play *Traitor*, which won him a BAFTA for Best Actor in 1971, even though it took Joan, his wife, three weeks to persuade him to accept the part. Other appearances included: Colonel Maynard in *George and the Dragon*, Lord Bleasham in *A Class By Himself*, guest roles in *Hancock's Half Hour*, *Brideshead Revisited*, *Thriller*, *Marry the Girls*, *The Goodies* and *Worzel Gummidge*. His was also the voice behind various Homepride flour commercials and Bod, the children's character.

Equally adept playing serious roles as well as comedy, he clocked up more than 150 film credits during his long career, with classics such as *Private's Progress*, *I'm All Right, Jack*, *The Bulldog Breed* and *The Battle of the River Plate*. John became one of those familiar character faces popping up in seemingly every postwar British movie made.

John died in 1983, aged 71, having been ill for some time. While rehearsing a play – *The Miser* – in Perth, Australia, he experienced difficulties learning his lines; he blamed the intense heat until he collapsed and was rushed to hospital suffering from liver failure, which was later blamed on the cumulative effect of alcohol consumption. For a year, John followed a strict alcohol-free diet and consequently lost a lot of weight, which explains his unusually gaunt appearance in the final series of *Dad's Army*. Although he stuck to the diet, he felt increasingly miserable. Finally, he decided he'd had enough and returned to the occasional drink. Almost immediately he resembled the old John Le Mesurier, and enjoyed another five years of life before a series of liver haemorrhages saw him bedridden in hospital. He never recovered.

TV credits include: *Adam Adamant Lives!*, *George and the Dragon*, *Flint*, *A Married Man*, *The Bachelors*, *Doctor At Large*, *The Dick Emery Show*, *Hi-De-Hi!*, *The Morecambe and Wise Show*.

Radio credits include: *It Sticks Out Half a Mile*, *Hancock*, *Brothers in Law*.

Theatre credits include: *Hamlet*, *Dangerous Corner*, *Twelfth Night*, *Draw the Fires*, *The Three Sisters*, *Peace In Our Time*, *French Without Tears*, *Gaslight*, *Journey's End*, *The Winslow Boy*, *The Browning Version*, *An Inspector Calls*.

Film credits include: *Escape from Broadmoor*, *Death In the Hand*, *Never Take No For an Answer*, *Beautiful Stranger*, *Dangerous Cargo*, *The Baby and the Battleship*, *Brothers in Law*, *Happy is the Bride*, *I Was Monty's Double*, *Blood of the Vampire*, *Gideon's Day*, *Operation Amsterdam*, *School for Scoundrels*, *The Rebel*, *The Pure Hell of St Trinian's*, *Very Important Person*, *The Pink Panther*, *The Early Bird*, *The Sandwich Man*, *The Italian Job*, *Jabberwocky*, *The Shillingbury Blowers*, *The Fiendish Plot of Doctor Fu Manchu*.

LE WHITE, JACK
Role: Porter (S4, episode 9: 'Mum's Army') (TV)

Jack, who died in 1999, led a busy film and television career. On the small screen he appeared in shows like *No Hiding Place* as a newspaperman, a judge in *The Prisoner*, *The Jazz Age*, *Paul Temple*, *The Adventures of Black Beauty*, *Doctor Who*, *Colditz* playing a café owner, a newsagent in *Public Eye*, an old man in *The Howerd Confessions* and *Upstairs, Downstairs*. He also had a semi-regular role in *The Liver Birds*, as Grandad. His film credits include 1958's *Further Up the Creek*, *Danny the Dragon* and the 1983 picture, *Bloodbath at the House of Death*.

LEE ENFIELD RIFLE

The Lee Enfield rifle was mentioned by Lance Corporal Jones during the episode 'A Brush With the Law'. The bolt-action weapon was used extensively by the British Empire and the Commonwealth upon its introduction in 1895. During its lifetime of over 60 years it underwent several upgrades, and was still being used in the Korean War during the 1950s.

LEESON, JOHN (1943–)

Born: Leicester

Role: 1st Soldier (S3, episode 14:'Sons of the Sea') (TV)

All John's relatives had been clergymen, but he'd always wanted to act, ever since joining drama groups at school. He spent time in amateur dramatics in Leicester before training at RADA, from where he graduated in 1964. Rep work followed, including spells at Colchester, Newcastle and Nottingham, before he started being offered TV parts.

After *Dad's Army*, he spent several years working as an announcer on the Forces network in Germany, before returning to this country and appearing in various shows, including *Rings On Their Fingers* and *My Wife Next Door*. John also supplied the voice for K9 in *Doctor Who* and played the original Bungo Bear in the children's show *Rainbow*. Nowadays he mainly works in the theatre and corporate videos, and has been a freelance announcer at Channel 4 for over ten years.

Recently, John appeared in the Channel 4 film *Longtitude*, playing a BBC radio producer. He is also a member of the Association of Wine Educators, and teaches at seminars.

LEONARD, MRS

Played by Elizabeth Morgan (radio)

In the radio episode 'The Armoured Might of Lance Corporal Jones', Mrs Leonard is a customer in Jones' shop who gives him a tin of tobacco.

LESLIE, PRIVATE

Played by Leslie Noyes (film)

One of the platoon regulars, Private Leslie is the soldier who, whilst hanging precariously from the bridge, manages to grab Major General Fullard from his horse as he floats down the river.

LEWIS, ARTHUR

(See 'Tomlinson, Fred'.)

LEWIS GUN

The Lewis gun was designed in 1911. Mainwaring has a Mark One in his office at the bank, from where he can keep his eye on the High Street.

LEWIS, MARJORIE

Costume supervisor on six episodes (TV): S2

The Lieutenant (left) tried his best to fool Mainwaring and his men in 'Gorilla Warfare'.

LIDELL, ALVAR

Born: Wimbledon

Role: Newsreader (S5, episode 4:'Getting the Bird') (TV and film)

Alvar, whose parents were Swedish, started acting at Oxford. He began his professional career as a singer, but when a producer wanted someone who spoke Swedish, he was given the opportunity to work in radio. Although he did little TV work, he appeared in various films and was a BBC newsreader for a while during the 1950s.

He retired from the profession in 1969, and died of cancer in 1981, after being ill for two years.

LIEUTENANT, THE

Played by Michael Sharvell-Martin (TV)

In 'Gorilla Warfare' Mainwaring and his men attend a weekend exercise. While trying their best to avoid counter agents, they meet a white-jacketed man who comes running from the woods. He explains he works for the War Office at an experimental laboratory, training animals for secret war work, and that a gorilla has got loose. Mainwaring isn't prepared to listen, which is just as well because the man is out to deceive the Walmington Home Guard.

LIGHTHOUSE KEEPER, THE

Played by Gordon Peters (TV); Stuart Sherwin (radio)

Seen in 'Put That Light Out!', he's in charge of the lighthouse situated just off the coast from Walmington. He used to live there until the salt started getting into his lungs.

LINEHAN, BARRY

Born: Ireland

Role:Van Driver (S9, episode 1:'Wake-Up Walmington') (TV)

Barry entered the entertainment industry in England in 1961 and was seen in various productions, particularly on television, including *The Tomorrow People*, *The Andromeda Breakthrough*, *Canterbury Tales*, *Ivanhoe*, *Witches Daughter*, *Armchair Theatre* and *To Play the King*.

His film credits include 1962's *Death Trap*, playing Detective Sergeant Rigby, *The Devil-Ship Pirates* in 1964 and the gatekeeper in 1974's *Dark Places*.

Barry died in 1996.

LION HAS 'PHONES, THE

(The working title for this episode was 'Sorry, Wrong Number')

Recorded: Sunday 8/6/69

Original transmission:Thursday 25/9/69, 7.30–8.00pm

Original viewing figures: 11.3 million

Repeated: 2/5/70, 29/10/82, 15/8/92, 6/1/96, 11/1/96 (Wales), 31/5/97

CAST

Arthur Lowe	Captain Mainwaring
John Le Mesurier	Sergeant Wilson
Clive Dunn	Lance Corporal Jones
John Laurie	Private Frazer
James Beck	Private Walker

Arnold Ridley . . . . .Private Godfrey
Ian Lavender . . . . .Private Pike
Janet Davies . . . . .Mrs Pike
Bill Pertwee . . . . .ARP Warden
Avril Angers . . . . .Telephone Operator
Timothy Carlton . . . . .Lieutenant Hope Bruce
Stanley McGeagh . . . . .Sergeant Waller
Pamela Cundell,
Olive Mercer and
Bernadette Milnes . . . . .Ladies in the Queue
Gilda Perry . . . . .Doreen
Linda James . . . . .Betty
Richard Jacques . . . . .Mr Cheesewright
                    and Member of Platoon
Colin Daniels
and Carson Green . . . . .Boys
Platoon: Colin Bean, Frank Godfrey, Hugh Cecil, Vic
Taylor, Desmond Cullum-Jones, Richard Kitteridge,
Michael Moore, George Hancock, Freddie Wiles
Boy outside Phone Box: John Watters

PRODUCTION TEAM
Script: Jimmy Perry and David Croft
Producer: David Croft
Production Assistant: Jim Franklin
Director: Harold Snoad
Film Cameraman: James Balfour
Film Editor: Bob Rymer
Studio Lighting: Howard King
Studio Sound: Michael McCarthy
Design: Paul Joel
Assistant Floor Manager: Bill Harman
Vision Mixer: Dave Hanks
Costume Supervisor: Odette Barrow
Make-Up Supervisor: Jan Harrison
Special Effects: Peter Day

Mainwaring is giving a lecture on communications. He believes that in the event of an invasion the prime spots the enemy will try capturing in Walmington are the gasometer, railway bridge, telephone exchange and reservoir. Such places are vital to the town, so two men will be posted at each of the points and in the event of an invasion, they will call Mainwaring at the church hall. They discuss various forms of communication just in case the local phone boxes are out of order, including heliograph and sign language.

When he discovers Godfrey and Pike don't know how to use a public phone, a demonstration at the call box outside the reservoir gates is called for. One at a time the men use the phone with Mainwaring. When it's Pike's turn he practises by calling the church hall, and is shocked when his mother, who just happened to be there, answers the phone. She ends up rowing with Mainwaring and Wilson because she doesn't like Frank using public phones because they're unhealthy.

When the queue begins building up outside the box, Walker seeks an opportunity to earn some extra cash by convincing some ladies that there will soon be rationing of phone calls.

Later, while out on patrol, Frazer and Walker see a plane crash in the local reservoir; Walker calls Mainwaring, who joins up with Frazer soon after. They try to persuade the Germans to surrender but to no avail. Meanwhile, Jones calls GHQ but misdials and ends up speaking to the Plaza Cinema. Total confusion leaves Jones thinking a British aircraft has crashed with Googie Withers and Eric Portman inside, but he calls the emergency services asking for help as it is an enemy aircraft.

Eventually Lieutenant Hope Bruce of the Coldstream Guards turns up; they've surrounded the reservoir and his pompous attitude sees him belittle Mainwaring by telling him it's a job for the regular army. But Hope Bruce had underestimated the endeavour of the Home Guard because Walker arrives back on the scene. After contacting the official who looks after the reservoir, the sluice gates are opened and in two hours the plane will sink, so the aircrew will have to swim for their lives.

LITTLE ARTHUR
Played by Graham Harbord (TV)
Little Arthur is the evacuee who Mrs Pike looks after in 'Sgt Wilson's Little Secret'. She doesn't tell Arthur Wilson of her plans, and a misunderstanding leads him to think that Mavis is expecting his child!

LITTLEBOURNE-ON-SEA
The Home Guard unit from Littlebourne-on-Sea attend a course at the School of Explosives at the same time as Mainwaring's men in 'Fallen Idol'. The coastal town is never visited during the series.

LIVINGS, MR
Never seen in the series, Mr Livings has a telephone conversation with Mainwaring in 'The Honourable Man'. As bank manager, Mainwaring refuses to cash his £32 cheque because his bank account only holds a meagre £1 4d at the time.

LOCAL DEFENCE VOLUNTEERS (LDV)
In July 1940, the Local Defence Volunteers became known as the Home Guard on the insistence of Winston Churchill. By this time over a million men had joined the LDV to help defend the country against Hitler. Within 24 hours of Anthony Eden broadcasting his appeal in May of that year, over 250,000 men had rushed to their local police station to put themselves forward. Although there was a lack of arms and uniforms for some time, it didn't prevent the volunteers from undertaking their primary duties of keeping watch for German parachutists.

LOCATIONS
Although the fictitious town of Walmington-on-Sea was situated on the south coast of England, virtually all location shooting took place in Norfolk. There were specific reasons for this. Filming for the first series started in April and producer David Croft wanted somewhere with plenty of evergreen because the scripts were set in summertime; he also wanted to film undisturbed and the big battle area at Stanford, near Thetford, was ideal.

There were rumours that Norfolk was picked because David lived nearby, but that was incorrect. David did eventually buy a house just across the county border in Suffolk, but only after filming had begun.

The man responsible for finding suitable locations when the television series started was Harold Snoad, then a production assistant on the show, and here he answers a few questions about this often difficult and time-consuming task.

When it came to selecting locations for the TV series, what requisites did you have?

'I realised that the location work was going to involve an awful lot of filming on roads and open areas so it was necessary to take into account that this was a "period" piece and we couldn't have "modern" vehicles or members of the public in the background. It's also necessary to be able to accommodate the artists and members of the unit not far from the location because every hour of the day spent travelling is an hour less filming.'

How did you find the area in Norfolk?

'I hit upon the idea of using a private military area and although I investigated two or three of these sites I decided to opt for the Stanford Practical Training area in Norfolk because it offered plenty of opportunities: roads, fields, woods, bridges, a river and different types of properties – some damaged having been used for military purposes, farms, a church, etc. Having based the majority of the filming in a specific area it is then necessary, for logistical reasons, to keep all

ABOVE   Arnold Ridley has time to sign a few autographs.

BELOW   Another scene in rehearsal in Norfolk.

OUT ON LOCATION

The first two series saw little location work for the cast, but in 'Operation Kilt', one of the episodes from the second series that no longer exists in the BBC archives, a farmstead was required to represent Manor Farm, which the Highland Regiment use as their headquarters during an exercise involving the Walmington Home Guard. When Wilson suggests infiltrating their base, a pantomime cow is used as disguise, with Walker and Frazer inside, although a professional double-act, The Lynton Boys, were employed for the job.

Hatches Farm in Great Kingshill, Buckinghamshire, was chosen for the location shooting back in 1968, and it is an occasion that owner David Davies, who still lives there, remembers well.

'One day I received a called from the regional office of the NFU (National Farmers' Union). I was told the BBC were looking for a farm that could be used for location work, and mine had been suggested. I was already a fan of *Dad's Army* so didn't have any hesitation about agreeing to let the crew film at the farm.

'Part of the filming involved the Lynton Boys dressing up as a pantomime cow and sitting in amongst a herd of cows, but of course no one knew, including me, how the animals would react to this strange object amongst them. When they caught sight of the panto cow, they stared for a moment before scattering in all directions. Then they turned round and charged back. For a moment, we were worried they were going to charge the pantomime cow, but they all stopped within a ten-yard radius and formed a circle around the actors, looking at the panto cow in amazement.

'Another scene saw my Angus bull running across the field. It was supposed to be chasing the pantomime cow but in fact we had put down a pile of food, and the bull was running to get something to eat.

'They filmed some other scenes at the farm and we received the princely sum of £25, which was a lot of money in those days. I enjoyed watching the episode when it was first shown, and it's nice to think we helped in the making of an episode of *Dad's Army*.'

DAVID DAVIES

ABOVE The cast dry their feet on Winterton beach.

RIGHT David Croft looks on
as preparations are made for the next scene.

the rest in or around a 20 mile or so radius, and I
was able to do this using Thetford and surrounding areas.

'I usually looked at four or five possible sites
for any particular scene and then made a decision. More often than not David Croft didn't see
my chosen location until the actual day of filming but we had worked together well on other
shows before this and he trusted me and was
always happy with my choice.'

With the exception of the first two series, where
little location shooting took place, most of the
episodes involved filming in the Norfolk countryside. Such scenes added realism to the show,
and fans of the sitcom have become interested to
find out the true identity of the buildings, roads,
rivers, railway lines and other locations used
during the making of *Dad's Army*. Over the last
three years, Tony Pritchard, one of the adjutants
of the Dad's Army Appreciation Society, has
dedicated almost 30 days to a personal crusade
to discover the whereabouts of all the locations
used during the sitcom's run. Family holidays

Episode	Actual Name	Place		O S Map No	Grid Reference	Place/Setting in Episode	Status
69	A 500-year-old cottage	East Wretham	Thetford	144		Cherry Tree Cottage	
26	Acle New Road	Nr Gorleston				Railway Line	Not confirmed
47,57,58,63,65,67,63	All Saint's Church	Honington	Suffolk	144	913 746	St Aldhelm's Church	
5	Assault Training Course	Stanford Training (MOD)	Nr Thetford			Training Course	Not found
28	Bardwell		Suffolk	144	945 738	Marching with rifles behind wall	
58	Bardwell Green	Bardwell	Suffolk	144	944 737	Village Green	
26	Beccles		Norfolk			River	Not confirmed
61,75,79	Blackrabbit Warren	Stanford Training (MOD)	Nr Thetford	144	915 935	Unnamed Road and Camp	
27	Brandon Station	Brandon	Nr Thetford	144	784 873	Unnamed	
57	Brighton Barracks	Brighton				Initiative Training Centre	
22	Britannia Pier	Lowestoft	Suffolk			Walmington Pier	
34	British Ind Sands Ltd	Leziate	King's Lynn	132	675 195	Desert	
36,29	Buckenham Tofts	Stanford Training (MOD)	Nr Thetford	144	835 945	Walmington Cricket Pitch	Destroyed 1982
3	Buckenham Tofts	Stanford Training (MOD)	Nr Thetford	144	853 945	Marsham Hall	
40	Buckenham Tofts Bailey Bridge	Stanford Training (MOD)	Nr Thetford	144	836 953	Iron Road Bridge	
15	Bury Sugar Beet Works	Bury St Edmunds	Suffolk	155	859 657	Walmington Reservoir	
66	Caston Hall, Caston	Attleborough	Norfolk	144	974 975	North Berrington Farm	
20,63	Croxton Heath	Stanford Training (MOD)	Nr Thetford	144	878 917	Pinner Fields	
28	Drinkstone Mill	Nr Woolpit	Suffolk	155	964 622	Mill	
39	Electric Sub Station	Honington to Euston Rd	Suffolk			Sub Station	Destroyed ?
40	Elveden Hall Water Tower	Elveden	Nr Thetford	144	823 795	Unnamed Tower	
3	Ferngate Farm	Weeting	Norfolk	144	775 881	Unnamed Road	
24,16,47,63	Frog Hill	Stanford Training (MOD)	Nr Thetford	144	873 911	Unnamed	
45	Furze Heath	Stanford Training (MOD)	Nr Thetford	144	825 955	Unnamed Road	
72	Gorse Industrial Est	Barnham	Thetford	144	875 793	Prisoner War Camp	
59	Grange Farm	Sapiston	Suffolk	144	918 943	Tracker Dog Training School	
39	Grenade Training Area	Stanford Training (MOD)	Nr Thetford			Sticky Bomb Training	Not confirmed
7	Hatches Farm	Great Kingshill	High Wycombe			Manor Farm	
42,45,50	High Lodge	Brandon	Thetford	144	813 855	Unnamed	
75	Ixworth House	Ixworth	Suffolk	144	928 711	Flour Mill	
25	Langford Church	Stanford Training (MOD)	Nr Thetford	144	837 965	St Matthew's Church	
75	Lynford Hall	Nr Mundford	Thetford	144	821 943	The Big Hall	
54	Mill Lane	Thetford	Norfolk	144	871 825	Walmington Road	
13,24,27,53	Nether Row	Thetford	Norfolk	144	872 828	Percy Street	
2,15	Newtown	Thetford	Norfolk	144	866 828	Unnamed Street	
72	Old Bury Road	Thetford	Norfolk	144	868 829	Free Polish Club	
2	Oxburgh Hall	Oxborough	Norfolk	143	743 014	Peabody Museum	
43,27	Palace Cinema	Thetford	Norfolk	144	873 830	Inside	
47,57,58,65,67	Primary School	Honington	Suffolk	144	913 746	St Aldhelm's Hall	
9	Regent's Park Barracks	Albany Street	London			Army Camp Scenes	
6	Richmond Theatre					Hippodrome Theatre	
50	Santon Downham	Nr Brandon	Nr Thetford	144	817 878	Unnamed Village and Bridge	
58,67	Sapiston		Suffolk	144	918 748	Wilson falls off motorbike, Pike gives salute from van	
77	Sapiston Church	Sapiston	Suffolk	144	921 743	Walmington Green and Church	
67	Sapiston Church	Sapiston	Suffolk	144	921 743	Walmington Church	
2	St Mary's The Less (1567)	Old Bury Road	Thetford	144	865 828	Church	
70	Stanford Lake	West Tofts (MOD)	Nr Thetford	144	842 950	Unnamed Lake	
59	The Black Bourn River	Sapiston	Suffolk	144	927 744	River Crossing	
53,65	The Guildhall		Thetford	144	870 832	Town Hall	
67,75	The Six Bells	Bardwell	Nr Thetford	144	946 737	The Six Bells	
31	Thrope Camp	Stanford Training (MOD)	Nr Thetford	144	901 901	Italian POW camp	
52	Wacton Village		Norfolk	134	181 914	Unnamed Village	
48	Walnut Tree Farm	Wilney Green Fersfield	Norfolk	144	067 817	Mrs Prentice's Farm	
50	Walnut Tree Farm	Wilney Green Fersfield	Norfolk	144	067 817	House on fire	
52	Wash Lane Railway Bridge	Wacton	Norfolk	144	168 917	Unnamed	
52	Watton Airfield	Watton (MOD)	Norfolk	144	943 995	Disused Airfield	
14	Wendling Rail Station	Wendling	Dereham	132	932 130	Unnamed Station	
15	West Tofts Church	Stanford Training (MOD)	Nr Thetford	144	836 929	Walmington Church	
40	West Tofts Cross Roads	Stanford Training (MOD)	Nr Thetford	144	837 944	Unnamed Crossroads	
67	West Tofts Field, by Church	Stanford Training (MOD)	Nr Thetford	144	837 930	Field, hoisted on to a horse, also all marquee shots	
24	West Tofts T-junction	Stanford Training (MOD)	Nr Thetford	144	837 943	Warden removing parachute	
56	Weybourne Station	Weybourne	Norfolk	133	118 419	Walmington Station	
29	Winterton Beach	Winterton	Norfolk	134	505 185	Walmington Beach	
24	Unknown					Farm Buildings	Not found
43	Unknown					Farm Buildings	Not found
3	Unknown		Thetford			Block of Flats	Not found
43	Unknown	Stanford Training (MOD)	Thetford			Waterloo Battlefield	Not found

Platoon members (left to right) George Hancock,
Hugh Cecil and Vic Taylor relax while on location.

have centred in and around Thetford, from
where Tony, together with his wife and family,
have scoured the region on the hunt for the sites
where scenes may have taken place.

The rewards of his hard work were plentiful,
with virtually all the places used during the
series identified. A few locations have been
added from other sources, but the lion's share of
the list on page 124 is down to Tony's research.

LOCKE, PRIVATE
Not seen, but referred to by Wilson in 'The
Showing Up of Corporal Jones', Private Locke is
a member of the platoon and owns a shop in
Walmington.

LOMAX, MICHAEL
Role: 2nd ARP Warden (S4, episode 6: 'Absent Friends')
(TV)

LONDON, RAY
BBC designer on four episodes (TV): S3, episode 8:
'The Day the Balloon Went Up', episode 10: 'Menace
from the Deep', episode 12: 'Man Hunt' and episode
14: 'Sons of the Sea'

LONELINESS OF THE LONG-DISTANCE WALKER, THE
Recorded: Sunday 27/10/68 (made in black and white)
Original transmission: Saturday 15/3/69, 7.00–7.30pm
(This episode was originally planned for
transmission on 20 January)
Original viewing figures: 11.3 million
(The *Christmas Night with the Stars* insert, which was
transmitted Wednesday, 25/12/68, was recorded the
same evening)
This episode has never been repeated

CAST
Arthur Lowe . . . . .Captain Mainwaring
John Le Mesurier . . . . .Sergeant Wilson
Clive Dunn . . . . .Lance Corporal Jones
John Laurie . . . . .Private Frazer
James Beck . . . . .Private Walker
Arnold Ridley . . . . .Private Godfrey
Ian Lavender . . . . .Private Pike
Anthony Sharp . . . . .Brigadier (War Office)
Diana King . . . . .Chairwoman
Patrick Waddington . . . . . .Brigadier
Edward Evans . . . . .Mr Reed
Michael Knowles . . . . .Captain Cutts
Gilda Perry . . . . .Blonde
Larry Martyn . . . . .Soldier
Robert Lankesheer . . . . . . .Medical Officer
Colin Bean . . . . .Private Sponge
Platoon: Richard Jacques, Frank Godfrey, Alec Coleman,
Hugh Cecil, Jimmy Mac, Desmond Cullum-Jones, Vic
Taylor, David Seaforth, Richard Kitteridge

PRODUCTION TEAM
Script: Jimmy Perry and David Croft
Producer/Director: David Croft
Production Assistant: Harold Snoad
Studio Lighting: John Dixon
Studio Sound: James Cole
Design: Paul Joel
Assistant Floor Manager: Tony George
Vision Mixer: Bruce Milliard
Costume Supervisor: Marjorie Lewis
Make-Up Supervisor: Sheila Cassidy

Walker arrives late on parade with news that he's
been called up for his medical in ten days' time,
even though he'd listed his occupation as a
banana salesman and wholesale supplier of illuminated signs in the hope that it would be

classed as a reserved occupation and release him
from the need to join up.

For Mainwaring and the rest of the platoon,
who rely on Walker for their black market goods,
it's tragic news and something needs to be done.
Mainwaring plans on telling the War Office he's
important, valuable and needed by the people of
Walmington.

Wilson and Mainwaring visit the Brigadier at
the War Office to discuss their case and confusion leads to Mainwaring and Wilson falsely
believing the Brigadier will help. The following
day Wilson attends a meeting of the Military Service Hardship Committee, designed for address-

'The Loneliness of the Long-Distance Walker'

demobbed in 1946. His first professional job was at Oldham Rep, where he stayed 11 years. Eric moved behind the scenes and became theatre manager between 1951 and 1957, and then took the same position at Guildford until 1963. Returning to acting, Christmas Day 1963 saw him in Granada's 90-minute epic *Mr Pickwick*, with Arthur Lowe playing lead. This was his second TV appearance, the first being in *Shadow Squad* in the late 1950s. Usually cast as businessmen and retired colonels, other small-screen credits include *Z Cars* and *No Hiding Place*.

Eric believes his appearance in a 1972 episode of TV's *Lollipop*, written by Jimmy Perry, led to the offer of work in *Dad's Army* later that year. He understudied Arthur Lowe in the *Dad's Army* stage show but didn't tour with the production due to work commitments, after making his only leading role in a documentary drama for Yorkshire Television in 1974, *Who Killed Julia Wallace?*, playing William, the husband.

He has made a handful of minor film appearances, including a scene with Ursula Andress in 1970's *Perfect Friday*, *No Sex Please, We're British* and *Tom Jones*. Other TV parts include two appearances in *Coronation Street*, one playing a policeman alongside Jimmy Beck.

ing cases where people with one-man businesses will be ruined if they're called up. Mainwaring suggests the committee hear Walker's case, and he helps by giving Walker moral support at the hearing, where his appeal is considered.

At the end of the meeting, it's decided that Walker must present his books, which will be difficult because he doesn't keep any. Frazer, Jones and the rest of the platoon try another course of action to help him fail the medical: jumping off a ladder in the hope it makes him flat-footed. But nothing works and Walker is passed A1.

Walker swaps his spiv suits for khaki as he arrives at the infantry training barracks. But it's not long before Walker's pacing the streets of Walmington again thanks to corned beef fritters that led to blotches and his face swelling up.

LONGWORTH, ERIC (1918–)

Born: Shaw
Roles: Claude Gordon (S5, episode 13), Town Clerk (S6, episode 5; S7, episodes 2, 4, 5; S8, episodes 2; 'The Love of Three Oranges'; S9, episode 5) (TV)
When his father died Eric was only 17 and his ambitions to become an actor were sidetracked while he helped support the family. He worked as a salesman at a printing company in Shaw, but maintained an interest in acting by joining the Crompton Stage Society, a local amateur company, playing character parts until his call-up in 1939.

In 1943–1944, while serving with the army in Bombay, he got involved with the dramatic society and pursued an acting career once

RANDOM THOUGHTS FROM A RETIRED CIVIL SERVANT

'Little did I think in 1972, when I first appeared as Claude Gordon, town clerk of Walmington-on-Sea, that it was going to put a morsel of jam on my bread in old age, or that an appreciation society would be holding conventions up and down the country 20-odd years later.

'One thing I did realise was the fact that *Dad's Army* appealed to young and old alike and this was brought home to me one sunny Sunday in 1975. The stage version had just opened at the Shaftesbury Theatre and all the Longworths had attended the first night, with the exception of my seven- and eight-year-old granddaughters, who'd been promised a visit to a Saturday matinee. This was fixed for the Saturday following that sunny Sunday when, with Mum and Dad, they had come over to Guildford for the day. There was I up a very large Bramley apple tree picking apples, assisted by my youngest granddaughter, Amanda, down below. There had been no mention of *Dad's Army* since their arrival when

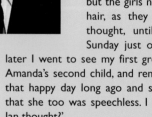

suddenly, out of the blue, Amanda said: "Grandpa, can I meet Pike?" I nearly fell out of the tree – she was only seven!

'Come the following Saturday I conducted the two girls round every dressing-room, after the matinee and eventually arrived at Ian's door. I knocked, "Come in!" he called. I flung open the door and ushered the two girls in and then realised that Ian was sitting there stark naked, or so it appeared at first glance until a closer inspection revealed that he was wearing the briefest of briefs I had, up to that moment, ever seen. I was speechless, but the girls never turned a hair, as they say, or so I thought, until one sunny Sunday just over 24 years later I went to see my first great grandson, Amanda's second child, and reminded her of that happy day long ago and she confessed that she too was speechless. I wonder what Ian thought?'

ERIC LONGWORTH

There have been no recent long-running TV roles or theatre parts (his last appearance on TV was in the 1989 BBC production *Oedipus the King*) but Eric, who spent more than five decades in showbiz, is kept busy with commercials. Last year, he travelled to Amsterdam to film an advert for Dutch Rail, and has recently filmed in Stockholm and Oslo. His last commercial for British TV was in 1998, for Macdonald's.

LORD HAW-HAW

In the opening scene of 'The Showing Up of Corporal Jones', Mainwaring enters the church hall office to find Wilson listening to Lord Haw-Haw on the Vicar's radio. He promptly tells him to switch it off; Wilson says he just switched it on and that was how the set was tuned. Whether this was true, or Wilson was trying to pass the buck, is unclear.

Wilson was listening to the voice of Lord Haw-Haw, alias William Joyce, a broadcaster who sent propaganda messages from Hamburg during the war. The news blackout by censors resulted in the public being susceptible to rumour, and Joyce's broadcasts became popular in Britain, with an estimated one million people tuning in. The regular broadcasts concentrated on issues that would touch a nerve, such as food prices, censors and the progress being made by the British armed forces.

Joyce was captured in May 1945 and was tried at the Old Bailey for high treason. Found guilty, he was hanged in Wandsworth jail in January, 1946, at the age of 39.

LOVE OF THREE ORANGES, THE

Recorded: Friday 10/12/76

Original transmission: Sunday 26/12/76, 7.25–7.55pm

Original viewing figures: 13.7 million

Repeated: 25/12/90, 26/2/00

CAST

Arthur Lowe . . . . .Captain Mainwaring
John Le Mesurier . . . . .Sergeant Wilson
Clive Dunn . . . . .Lance Corporal Jones
John Laurie . . . . .Private Frazer
Arnold Ridley . . . . .Private Godfrey
Ian Lavender . . . . .Private Pike
Bill Pertwee . . . . .Chief Warden Hodges
Frank Williams . . . . .Vicar
Edward Sinclair . . . . .Verger
Pamela Cundell . . . . .Mrs Fox
Janet Davies . . . . .Mrs Pike
Olive Mercer . . . . .Mrs Yeatman
Joan Cooper . . . . .Dolly
Eric Longworth . . . . .Mr Gordon (Town Clerk)
Colin Bean . . . . .Private Sponge
Platoon: Freddie Wiles, Hugh Cecil, Roger Bourne, Michael Moore, Evan Ross, George Hancock, Freddie White, Jimmy Mac, Vernon Drake
Little Girl: Jayne Toffman
Other Extras: 12 ladies and 3 men in bazaar scene

'The Love of Three Oranges'

PRODUCTION TEAM

Script: Jimmy Perry and David Croft
Producer/Director: David Croft
Production Assistant: Jo Austin
Studio Lighting: Howard King
Studio Sound: Michael McCarthy
Design: Barry Newbery
Assistant Floor Manager: Susan Belbin
Vision Mixer: Angela Beveridge
Costume Designer: Mary Husband
Make-Up Artist: Sylvia Thornton
Visual Effects: Peter Pegrum

The parish council decide to organise a church bazaar, to raise money for comforts for the troops. Mainwaring forms a committee to organise the event. Mrs Yeatman agrees to run the tombola, Godfrey will provide chutney, wine and honey, Jones will donate a monster brawn, Mrs Fox will tell fortunes at sixpence a time, Mrs Mainwaring is providing lampshades that she makes to occupy her time in the shelter and Hodges is donating three oranges, which causes plenty of excitement.

Mrs Mainwaring's table is bare and Mr Mainwaring is relieved because, as he admits to Wilson, her shades are rather bizarre and could have led to ribald remarks. But an incident involving the bath is the reason for her absence. He decided to paint it but Elizabeth took a bath before it was dry and the paint

'The Love of Three Oranges'

went all over her. There was hell to pay and she shut herself in the bedroom; however if he could secure one of Hodges' oranges, because Elizabeth is partial to oranges, it might help smooth things over.

When he comes out of the office with Wilson, the lampshades have turned up, thanks to Pike who collected them *en route* to the church hall. The town clerk officially opens the bazaar. Everyone tries Godfrey's wine but no one buys it, and Jones's brawn is run over by a dispatch rider on a motorbike. When it comes to auctioning the oranges, Mainwaring is determined to get one for his wife. But when Hodges hears he's going to bid, he does his utmost to prevent him winning. When there is just one orange left to auction, Pike tries helping his captain by bidding, but ends up bidding against Mainwaring and the price rockets.

Mainwaring outbids everyone and secures the orange at an extortionate price, but he shows his gratitude to his men for a hard day's work by sharing his orange with them. What Hodges forgot to tell Mainwaring was that the oranges are bitter and for making marmalade.

LOWE, ARTHUR (1915–1982)
Born: Hayfield
Role: Captain George Mainwaring (all TV episodes and *Christmas Night with the Stars* inserts; the film, the stage show and all radio episodes)

Arthur – the only son of a railwayman – worked as a stagehand at the Manchester Palace of Varieties during his teenage years. He enjoyed his brush with the acting world, but never considered it a serious career option, partly because his parents expected him to pursue a managerial career. But Arthur wasn't so keen and instead decided to join the merchant navy.

Sadly, poor eyesight thwarted his ambitions and he worked at an aeroplane factory before joining the army on the eve of the Second World War. Whilst serving abroad in the Middle East, Arthur began taking part in shows put on for the troops. He enjoyed the experience so much that he set about making a career out of acting upon returning to civvy street, at the age of 30. By the time Arthur made his professional stage debut at a Manchester rep in 1946, he was already balding, making him well-suited to character parts.

After years of slogging away in the provinces and reps around the country, including Hereford, Bromley, Richmond and Croydon, he made his West End debut in the 1950 production, *Larger than Life*, at the Duke of York's. By this time he'd already made a handful of films, including *London Belongs to Me*, *Flood Tide*, both in 1948, and *Kind Hearts and Coronets*, *Stop Press Girl*, *Until Tomorrow* and *The Intruder*, a year later. His portly appearance and bumbling disposition were regularly requested and in a career covering over 30 years, he was seen in hundreds of plays, such as *Kelly's Eye*, *Inadmissible Evidence*, *The Soldier's Fortune*, *The Tempest* and *Bingo*. During the 1950s he appeared in several musicals, including *Call Me Madam* and *The Pajama Game*. He also appeared in more than 50 films, such as *The Green Man*, *This Sporting Life*, *Go To Blazes*, *The White Bus* and *O Lucky Man*, for which he received the SFTA Award for Best Supporting Performance.

Arthur also conquered the transition into small-screen acting, beginning in 1951 with *I Made News: Big Band* and *To Live in Peace*. Besides *Dad's Army*, two roles he'll be remembered for are draper Leonard Swindley in *Coronation Street*, and the cantankerous Redvers Potter in BBC's sitcom, *Potter*. After the success of the *Coronation Street* role, Arthur was given his own series, *Pardon the Expression*, in 1965. Other television credits include playing Mr Micawber in *David Copperfield*, Dr Maxwell in *Doctor at Large* and an Irish priest, Father Duddleswell, in the comedy series, *Bless Me Father*.

Although Arthur, who was married to actress Joan Cooper, was seen in a great many TV shows, his true love was film work. He remained busy throughout his career, and reached the level where he could pick and choose his work. Though it was his roles in *Coronation Street* and *Dad's Army* that made him a household name, he built up a long and distinguished career as a character actor, covering all areas of the entertainment business.

Arthur died in 1982 after suffering a stroke in the dressing room at Birmingham's Alexandra Theatre, where he was performing in *Home at Seven*.

TV credits include: *Turn Out the Lights*, *Microbes and Men*, *Philby*, *A J Wentworth B A*.

Theatre credits include: *Bedtime Story*, *Hassan*, *Pal Joey*, *A Dead Secret*, *The Ring of Truth*, *Home and Beauty*, *Ann Veronica*, *Caught Napping*, *Home at Seven*.

Film credits include: *The Ruling Class*, *Stormy Crossing*, *The Rise and Rise of Michael Rimmer*, *Theatre of Blood*, *The Bawdy Adventures of Tom Jones*, *The Lady Vanishes*, *Britannia Hospital*.

LUCAS, EVE
Producer's assistant on four episodes (TV): S1, episode 1; S2, episodes 1, 2 & 3

LUMSDEN, GEOFFREY (1915–1984)
Born: London
Role: Colonel Square (S1, episode 3), Corporal-Colonel Square (S2, episodes 5 & 6), Captain Square (S4, episodes 2 & 13; 'Battle of the Giants!'; S5, episode 11; S9, episode 1) (TV); same character in seven episodes of the radio series

Geoffrey's character was the guffawing old war veteran who took charge of the Home Guard's Eastgate platoon. There was intense rivalry and constant tension between Square and Mainwaring, partly because Square always pronounced his rival's name wrongly.

By the time Geoffrey left school both his parents had died, so he stayed with his uncle. Against his wishes he worked at a colliery training as an engineer. Whilst there, he helped to organise several concerts. Realising that his future lay in the entertainment world, he left the mines and won a scholarship which enabled him to train at RADA.

His busy rep career was interrupted when the war began. But after serving with the army in Burma he returned to rep at Dundee. Geoffrey, who was also a playwright, moved into TV and worked on various shows, including *Sykes*, *Edward and Mrs Simpson* playing Geoffrey Dawson, *Bergerac*, *The Saint* and *The Mind of Mr J G Reeder*. He also appeared in a few films, such as *The Horror of Frankenstein*, *The Night Caller*, *Dateline Diamond* and the 1968 movie *Hostile Witness*, with Ray Milland. Geoffrey died in 1984, aged 69.

MABEL

Not seen in the sitcom, Mabel is Hodges' assistant at his greengrocery business. The only reference to the character is when we hear Hodges calling to her in 'Keep Young and Beautiful'.

MAC, JIMMY (1903–1984)

Born: Glasgow

Role: Member of the platoon's back row in 22 episodes (S1; S2; S3, episodes 8, 11, 12; 'The Love of Three Oranges'; S9) (TV)

Jimmy started his career in a Glasgow circus, aged 12. He worked as a boy entertainer in Blackpool before later managing his own summer shows and pantomimes. A famous panto performer, he appeared at the Theatre Royal, Bath, for 31 years. He was also seen in numerous TV shows, including *The Two Ronnies* and *Are You Being Served?*, the occasional film, such as *Oliver!* and was often in demand for photographic work.

MACDONALD, KENNETH (1950–)

Born: Manchester

Role: Army Sergeant (S9, episode 5: 'Number Engaged') (TV)

Kenneth – whose father was a professional wrestler – had already become a well-known face on TV by the time he appeared in *Dad's Army*: for seven years he was Gunner Nobby Clark in *It Ain't Half Hot, Mum*.

He turned to acting straight from school, with his first job at Leatherhead. After years of rep and theatre he made his TV debut as a villain in *Z Cars*. He worked in many TV shows, most recently for 13 years as Mike the landlord in *Only Fools and Horses*. He is still busy in the theatre and on TV.

MACEY, PRIVATE

Not seen in sitcom, Macey is a member of the Walmington Home Guard. Jones calls his name in 'Absent Friends'.

MACHIN, ALAN

Studio sound supervisor on seven episodes (TV): S8 and 'My Brother and I'

Bradford-born Alan Machin left school after

completing his A-levels and joined the BBC in 1963, working at London's Television Centre. Upon completing his probationary period as a trainee technical operator, he moved into the sound department, initially as a floor operator. He was promoted to sound supervisor in 1973, whilst still only 25. Most of his career has been spent working on classic comedy shows like *The Liver Birds*, *Whatever Happened To The Likely Lads?*, *It Ain't Half Hot, Mum*, *'Allo, 'Allo*, *Only Fools and Horses*, *Bread* and *Yes, Minister*.

In the 1990s, Alan got more involved in drama, but has recently been working on shows such as *They Think It's All Over*, *Crimewatch*, *Watchdog*, *Blue Peter* and *Chambers*. Alan still works for the BBC.

MACKAY, FULTON (1922–1987)

Born: Paisley

Roles: Captain Ramsey (S6, episode 4: 'We Know Our Onions'), Dr McCeavedy (S9, episode 4: 'The Miser's Hoard') (TV)

Best known for playing Chief Warden Mackay in *Porridge*, Fulton Mackay was a familiar face on TV and stage. He grew up in Clydebank and trained as a quantity surveyor upon leaving school, before volunteering for the RAF in 1941. A perforated ear drum prevented him joining the Force, and he spent the war years serving with the Black Watch.

Returning to civvy street, Fulton decided he wanted to become an actor, and after training at RADA he spent nine seasons at Glasgow's Citizens' Theatre, until 1958. Later, he worked in Edinburgh and various rep theatres, before moving on to the Arts Theatre Club in London and spells with the Royal Shakespeare Company and the Old Vic.

His TV career included many Scottish productions, such as *Three Tales of Orkney*, *The Master of Ballantrae* and *Clay*, as well as roles in shows like *Special Branch* as Chief Superintendent Inman, *The Foundation*, *Some Mothers Do 'Ave 'Em*, *Going Straight* and the captain in *Fraggle Rock*.

Fulton also appeared in more than 20 films, including 1952's *I'm a Stranger*, *The Brave Don't Cry*, *Mystery Submarine*, *Britannia Hospital* and *Gumshoe*.

MACLEOD, NORMAN
Roles: Several in the stage show, including Private Maple at Billingham and The Shaftesbury; also Clive Dunn's stand-in

A founder member and lead singer of the Maple Leaf Four vocal team, Norman toured variety venues around the country. For several years he wrote *Smokey Mountain Jamboree* for BBC radio, as well as appearing on stage. One of his performances saw him work alongside Ginger Rogers in *Mame* at London's Drury Lane.

MADOC, PHILIP
Born: Merthyr Tydfil
Roles: U-boat Captain (S6, episode 1:'The Deadly Attachment') (TV); Captain Muller (radio)

For someone who only appeared in one episode, it's unbelievable how many people recall vividly Philip's role as the U-boat Captain.

After working as an interpreter in German, he entered the industry in the 1960s, studying at RADA. He worked for a while in rep before moving into TV, one of his first TV appearances being in the 1956 production *The Count of Monte Cristo*. Other TV work includes: Detective Chief Supt Tate in *Target*, Fison in *A Very British Coup*, *The Avengers* and *Doctor Who*. He also appeared in 'Get Me Out Of Here!', an episode of *The Champions*, playing Angel Martes; as Rawlins in a *Randall & Hopkirk (Deceased)* episode, titled 'Never Trust a Ghost' in 1968 and an episode of *Man in a Suitcase*.

Philip also made over 30 films including *The Quiller Memorandum*, *Daleks: Invasion Earth 2150AD* and *Operation Daybreak*, while recent years have been dominated by theatre. His own TV detective series, *A Mind to Kill*, in which he plays the lead, has been sold all over the world.

MAGINOT LINE, THE
A line of fortifications built between 1929 and 1938 to protect the eastern borders of France, the Maginot Line was named after the French minister of war, who authorised their construction. The invading Germans never put the fortifications to the test during the Second World War, deciding to outflank them instead. Built mainly underground, the forts were linked by tunnels and were shielded by tank traps and gunposts.

MAHONEY, JANET
Role: Doris, the Barmaid (S8, episode 1:'Ring Dem Bells') (TV)

Janet's other work in the profession includes appearances in two comedy films of 1970: *Carry On Loving* playing Gay, and *Doctor in Trouble* as Ms Dailey.

MAINWARING, BARRY
Played by Arthur Lowe (TV)

This red-faced, garishly dressed, drunken character turns out to be Captain Mainwaring's brother. Certainly the black sheep of the family, Barry hasn't a good word for his brother, and used to call him 'po-face'. He's a salesman in jokes and carnival novelties, who hasn't spoken to George for some 15 years. His unexpected

visit to Walmington in 'My Brother and I' is motivated by his wish to collect a gold watch which belonged to their father.

In his younger days, Barry was a good sportsman, and George feels he let his talents go to waste.

MAINWARING, EDMUND
Never seen in the sitcom because he died in 1922, Captain Mainwaring's father left very little of substance because he had a weakness for the bottle. We learn a lot about Mr Mainwaring Snr, who kept horses, in 'The King was in his Counting House', while Captain Mainwaring entertains at home. He claims that his father had a flourishing tailoring business situated on the Parade at Eastbourne and was a member of the Master Tailors' Guild.

Mainwaring is proud of his father, but whether the summary of his life is strictly true is questionable, especially when Jones, who's known Eastbourne 50 years, states his business wasn't on the Parade, it was a pokey little draper's shop up a side street called East Street, with workmen's trousers hanging up outside. Jones feels justified in spilling the beans because his brother bought a pair of trousers there and before long the gusset fell out. Jones' comments are backed up later when George's drunken brother, Barry, arrives in Walmington.

MAINWARING, ELIZABETH
Address: 23 Lime Crescent, Walmington-on-Sea
Wife of Mr Mainwaring, the nearest we come to seeing the mysterious recluse, Elizabeth, who makes bizarre lampshades and has two sisters, is when her huge bulbous-shaped body looms towards Mr Mainwaring while they sleep in bunkbeds in the Anderson shelter.

Her refusal to attend various social functions arranged by the Home Guard, and her obvious anti-social nature, make her husband the butt of jokes among his platoon. Few people have seen Mrs Mainwaring and those who have are far from complimentary. While Wilson says she's 'a bit odd', Pikey claims she's 'always cross', but there is no doubting she's a highly strung woman, who tosses and turns at night upon hearing the slightest noise.

Elizabeth has many foibles, such as being sensitive to smells. When Captain Mainwaring attends Pikey's special supper, he admits she'll have a fit if she smells fish and chips on him, so he decides to take a long walk in the fresh air before going home. Her aversion to smells saw George banished from the sitting room for three days after smoking a cigarette.

Elizabeth, who's a vegetarian, finds change difficult to accept, and still hasn't adjusted to the introduction of 'talkies' at the cinema, claiming they encourage headaches. She's also terrified by the war and doesn't feel safe unless she sleeps in the air raid shelter all night, forcing George to join her: she's even been known to shut herself away in the cupboard beneath the stairs, such is her nervous disposition.

The Mainwarings have no children, but Elizabeth is very fond of her cat, Empress, who's almost certainly her only friend. She regards the men of the Walmington Home Guard as ruffians. When George arranges a get-together at his house, which Walker compares to an 'undertak-

DAVID CROFT ON MRS MAINWARING

'Never seeing Mrs Mainwaring became a good gimmick and any appearance by her would have been a letdown. We never set out to keep her a mystery, it's just something that happened.'

ers' convention', Elizabeth is concerned they will all get drunk and smash the place up.

Although her marriage to George has lasted some while, it's hard to believe they're still together, especially as from day one George never felt at ease with Elizabeth's parents, believing they were always looking down their noses at him. Her family is well connected, with her father being the suffragan Bishop of Clagthorpe. But for all her parents' concerns, George believes he's introduced Elizabeth to all the little treats she's been deprived of by her sheltered upbringing, including tomato sauce!

Mrs Mainwaring in 'The Sharpshooters'

EVENING. THE LOUNGE IN GEORGE MAINWARING'S HOUSE
(George is seated at the table with his wife, Elizabeth. She is a thin, shivery lady about 40. They are having supper. All around the walls are pictures of generals and battle scenes. On the mantelpiece are various model cannons and machine guns. Everything on the table has a military motive. The pepper and salt shakers are two heavy machine gun bullets. The mustard pot is a figure of General Gordon in heroic posture. They are both eating in silence.)

GEORGE Pass the Vickers Gun Bullet Mark I, please, Elizabeth. (**She hands him the salt. He shakes it on his food. At each shake it gives a little squeak.**)

ELIZABETH May I have the pepper? (**He glares at her.**) I mean the Vickers Gun Bullet Mark II, please, dear. (**This also squeaks when she shakes it.**) Oh, and General Gordon, please. (**He hands her the mustard pot.**) You're very quiet tonight, dear. Is something wrong?

GEORGE I don't know how to tell you, Elizabeth.

ELIZABETH Oh come on, George, it can't be as bad as that.

GEORGE Oh yes it is. I made myself a laughing stock in front of the men today. I fired my revolver on the range.

ELIZABETH What happened?

GEORGE I ended up in the arms of Major Smythe-Smith.

ELIZABETH Oh really, dear? Well never mind. I'll get the sweet. (**She starts to rise.**)

GEORGE No, thank you.

ELIZABETH But it's Foreign Legion pudding, dear. Your favourite.

GEORGE I'm in no mood for all that gritty sago, tonight.

ELIZABETH (**Getting up and going to sideboard.**) How about a nice piece of cheese then? (**Puts the cheese dish on the table. It is shaped like a little fort.**) I got the whole ration for the week for the both of us. (**She lifts up the lid. There is a small piece of cheese about two inches square on the dish.**) You have my share as well, George. Must keep up the spirits of our fighting men, you know. (**George takes piece of cheese and starts to nibble it.**)

ELIZABETH (**Looking very coy**) Now, how about a nice war game, dear?

GEORGE Well as long as you're feeling in the mood, Elizabeth.

ELIZABETH You know I'm always in the mood for that, George.

GEORGE Very well then.

ELIZABETH (**Gently taking him by the hand.**) Come along then, dear.
(**They cross to a table. On it are rows of model soldiers drawn up facing each other.**)

ELIZABETH I know dear. Just for a treat I'll let you be the Duke of Wellington and I'll be Napoleon. (**She hands him a model of the Duke of Wellington and starts to shake the dice.**)

THE REAL MRS MAINWARING

Prior to Jimmy Perry's original script, 'The Fighting Tigers', being commissioned, he wrote a second script to prove his idea for a sitcom about the Home Guard extended beyond one episode. In that script, entitled 'The Sharpshooters', Mrs Mainwaring makes an appearance. The script was later turned into 'Shooting Pains', the final episode in the first series, and the scene involving Elizabeth was dropped; conse-

quently, Mrs Mainwaring was never to appear in the sitcom. If the scene had been retained, it's clear she wouldn't have been seen as an old dragon, or attracted such irreverence. Jimmy's script refers to a thin 40-year-old woman, who plays war games to keep her husband happy, holds his hand, looks coy, gives him her tiny ration of cheese each week, and calls him 'dear' – not the aggressive, miserable character we got to know.

MAINWARING, 'FRUITY'
George Mainwaring's uncle commanded an army unit on the North West Frontier of India. He experienced a tough time and ended up a nervous wreck. He's not seen in the sitcom, but Mainwaring mentions him in 'Operation Kilt'.

MAINWARING, GEORGE
Played by Arthur Lowe (all mediums)
Address: 23 Lime Crescent, Walmington-on-Sea
George takes his role in society very seriously. His dedication to duty and hard work are perhaps the main reasons he's become a pillar of society in the community. Banker, soldier, magistrate, alderman and secretary of the Rotary Club, Mainwaring is certainly a

respected figure around town, although not always the most popular. With an air of pomposity he manages the Walmington-on-Sea branch of Swallow Bank, and captains the local Home Guard platoon. Although no one could justifiably knock his achievements in life (even if he does struggle to understand the 24-hour clock) Mainwaring still has an enormous chip on his shoulder when it comes to social standing. He blames his grammar school education in Eastbourne for his lack of progression up the Swallow Bank career ladder. When Wilson assumes the title 'The Honourable', Mainwaring believes that if he'd possessed a title, he'd be on the Bank's board of directors, not managing some 'tin-pot branch'. Furthermore, his attempts to join the local golf club would never have been thwarted.

Mainwaring, who despises red tape, has been manager at Walmington for over ten years. Starting as an office boy, he moved steadily through the ranks, from clerk to assistant chief clerk (which involved a spell at the Guildford branch just after the Great War), to assistant manager and finally manager after 25 years.

To some people, George Mainwaring would appear a power freak, never content unless he's organising and controlling. Any obsession with managing the lives of others is not simply a reflection of his leadership skills, which are often questioned, but stems back, perhaps, to his lonely childhood when there was little chance to make decisions on behalf of others, or practise the skills of teamwork. George's schooldays were very lonely: he was always a forlorn figure in the playground, possessing few friends. Even at home, life consisted of little more than the obligatory cold bath each day and reading books.

Mainwaring is certainly a man of habit – he gets annoyed with Miss King at the bank if she doesn't bring him his morning coffee promptly at 10.30 – and also an impractical idealist, seeing his mainly aged platoon as a real fighting force, able to withstand and defeat anything the Nazis may throw at them.

His military record involves serving as a commissioned officer in the army of occupation in France, during 1919. Although he missed the Great War, he qualifies his position by explaining he was one of the those tasked with clearing up the mess. His absence from the battlefields of Europe meant he returned to civvy street without any medals, a fact that often leads to bouts of insecurity and is embarrassing in the company of his highly decorated platoon members.

What he lacks in medals, he makes up for in resolve and drive. In the very first episode, Mainwaring talks of Britain's 'bulldog tenacity' and, despite his shortcomings, it's a quality he possesses in bundles; he'd do anything to have a crack at the enemy. He's a brave man, always ready to risk his own well-being for the sake of others, with no better example than in 'The

Royal Train', when he clambers over the carriage roof to retrieve the brake wheel. He may be pompous and exasperating, but his valorous Churchillian attitudes are admirable: he has an inner strength, an unwillingness to surrender and is a braveheart, which he proves by standing up to the German airmen in the closing scenes of the movie.

The highlight of his day is parading each evening with the Home Guard. The war has afforded him plenty of opportunities to prove to everyone, including himself, that not having medals doesn't mean he's an unworthy leader. He likes his role so much that he admits to getting excited upon finishing his tea, and feels a warm glow when he slips on his uniform and walks down to the church hall for another Home Guard parade. Age may have prevented him grabbing his piece of the action this time, but he pursues his duties in the Home Guard with the utmost efficiency.

George is married to Elizabeth and claims he has an 'almost' blissful marriage, though dealings with his wife suggest differently. Undoubtedly henpecked, he often gets his ear chewed off by his beloved when she calls him at the church hall, much to the merriment of Wilson. Any resistance to her demands is met with an abrupt drop of the receiver.

Wartime restrictions and an equally restrictive wife mean life for George revolves around Walmington, with one of his last ventures beyond the town being a 1936 holiday to Bognor Regis. His working and personal life have been in a rut for some time, and any love that existed between George and Elizabeth is long gone, which explains the occasion he let his attentions be drawn elsewhere. In Mrs Gray, who moved to Walmington from London to avoid the bombing, he found, if only for a brief moment, a woman with everything he could ever want from a wife.

When he gets the chance to relax, George likes

working in his garden, although one of the town's senior citizens, Sidney Blewitt, classes it as being in a 'terrible state'. Mainwaring has got a penchant for dahlias but isn't allowed to grow them because his wife says they attract earwigs. He also enjoys the occasional blast on the bagpipes ever since learning to play while honeymooning at Invergeike, Scotland.

MAJOLIER, SUSAN (1949–)
Born: Gayton Thorpe
Role: Nurse (S6, episode 7: 'The Recruit') (TV)
Susan worked as a dancer before switching to acting. From the age of 11 she was educated as a boarder at a ballet school in East Grinstead; she fulfilled a lifetime's ambition when she became a professional dancer and appeared in top shows including *The Black and White Minstrel Show*.

After a while she veered towards acting, and upon graduating from a two-year course at Bristol's Old Vic drama school in 1968, she went into commercial theatre, starting off with a Ray Cooney summer season in Jersey. Small parts on TV started coming her way and she balanced a career encompassing theatre, commercials and TV. She continued working on stage – including a spell in South Africa – and filming commercials (Marmite, Galaxy, etc) until she decided to raise a family, at which point she gave up theatre work.

Although she's not actively seeking work, spending as much time as possible with her children, she has in recent years taken work on the box, including appearances in *Peak Practice* and *The Bill*, where she has a semi-regular role as Marion, the Chief Superintendent's secretary.

MAKE-UP
The make-up designers took care of the actors' appearances, including hair styles. A number of people worked on make-up for the programme, including Cynthia Goodwin, Anna Chesterman, Sylvia Thornton and Cecile Hay-Arthur.

MAKING OF PRIVATE PIKE, THE
Recorded: Friday 1/7/77
Original transmission: Sunday 9/10/77, 8.10–8.40pm
Original viewing figures: 10.3 million
Repeated: 18/9/78, 7/8/79, 2/7/91, 28/9/96, 25/3/00

CAST
Arthur Lowe	Captain Mainwaring
John Le Mesurier	Sergeant Wilson
Clive Dunn	Lance Corporal Jones
John Laurie	Private Frazer
Arnold Ridley	Private Godfrey
Ian Lavender	Private Pike
Bill Pertwee	Chief Warden Hodges
Frank Williams	Vicar
Edward Sinclair	Verger
Jean Gilpin	Sylvia
Anthony Sharp	Colonel

MEMORIES OF A MAKE-UP ARTIST

In charge of make-up for the first series on TV was Sandra Exelby, who shares her memories of those days back in 1968.

'As a make-up designer at BBC TV, we were allocated productions as they came up and we became free, but I was the lucky one who got *Dad's Army*. I read the scripts and discussed with David Croft any ideas he had about the main characters, but he left the final details to me and the actors.

'As the original six shows were to be shot in black and white, not much hair colouring had to be done and, after a phone call to Arthur Lowe we decided on a neat hair cut to keep his character uncluttered.

'Clive Dunn, however, was a different matter. Clive was still a young man when he started playing Corporal Jones, so this meant a grey wig, eyebrows and, of course, the famous moustache. We went along to the wig makers and sorted out the wig, then along to the BBC's postiche department and talked about a moustache. Clive wanted something with waxed ends and after some discussion the idea of a very small moustache with waxed ends seemed to fit the bill.

'John Le Mesurier was no problem, neither was Ian Lavender as Pike, but Private Walker needed something. Jimmy Beck and I talked about the character and felt he should look like a "wide boy" or "spiv" and the pencil moustache just finished off his characterisation. Janet Davies, who played Mrs Pike, had her own long hair which we dressed in a 1940s hairstyle with just a little make-up.

'We had the location filming to do first so we went off to Thetford to film on the army shooting range, which could be quite dangerous so we had to be careful not to stray away from the unit.

'Arthur Lowe and I became great friends, and even after I left the BBC we used to phone each other frequently, right up to his death.

'After completing the six shows in the studios, we all knew how great the show was going to be, just by the way the "behind the camera crew" laughed during rehearsals. I'm still thrilled that I was lucky enough to have lent a hand in creating those famous characters so well-loved all over the world.'

SANDRA EXELBY

Jeffrey Segal . . . . .Brigadier
Pamela Cundell . . . . .Mrs Fox
Janet Davies . . . . .Mrs Pike
Melita Manger . . . . .Nora
Platoon: Michael Moore, Freddie White, Freddie Wiles, Evan Ross, Desmond Cullum-Jones, Vernon Drake, Jimmy Mac, George Hancock, Roger Bourne

PRODUCTION TEAM
Script: Jimmy Perry and David Croft
Producer: David Croft
Production Assistant: Gordon Elsbury
Director: Bob Spiers
Film Cameraman: Peter Chapman
Film Sound Recordist: Graham Bedwell
Film Editor: John Dunstan
Studio Lighting: Howard King
Studio Sound: Laurie Taylor
Design: Geoff Powell
Assistant Floor Manager: Susan Belbin
Vision Mixer: Angela Beveridge
Costume Designer: Mary Husband
Make-Up Artist: Sylvia Thornton
Visual Effects: Martin Gutteridge

Mainwaring has to be umpire at a local exercise, but there's a welcome compensation: a staff car, even if Hodges describes it as so small it reminds him of a roller skate.

Pike, meanwhile, meets Hodges' niece, Sylvia, at the local milkbar and ends up agreeing to take her to the pictures at Eastgate. The trouble is he's got to get out of going with Wilson. Once that's achieved, Sylvia tries persuading Pikey into taking Mainwaring's new staff car; not wanting to seem a 'soppy boy', he gives in to Sylvia's demands and they head off in the vehicle.

Sylvia is a happy-go-lucky kind of girl who's looking for a bit of fun while she's on leave from the ATS. Unfortunately she's chosen the wrong partner in Pike whom she ends up calling retarded. To top it all, the car runs out of petrol on the way home and Pike pushes it nine miles. By the time they arrive back at the church hall, Mainwaring has to rush off to umpire. Wilson, meanwhile, attempts to have a man-to-man chat with Pike.

MALTBY, LADY ANGELA
Played by Mavis Pugh (TV); Betty Marsden (radio)
With petrol shortages hitting hard, Lady Maltby, who arrives at the church hall smartly dressed in Conservative blue, donates her Rolls Royce to the Home Guard to help towards the war effort. Mainwaring eyes it up as a potential staff car. She turns out to be an old friend of Wilson's, and she also knows Jones because he's been supplying meat to the household since 1933 when Lord Maltby, who was in the greengrocery business, fell out with Sainsbury's. Her son, Nigel, is serving in the Forces. She appears in the episode, 'The Captain's Car'.

MEMORIES OF PLAYING SYLVIA

'At the time I was offered the part of Sylvia I couldn't drive, and of course the episode involves the character driving Pikey to the pictures at Eastgate. At the end of my interview with David Croft, he said: "You're too intelligent for this role and you don't drive, but if I don't find anybody more suitable I'll cast you." I went away thinking that was the end of that, but then I got a call from my agent saying I'd better learn how to drive quickly because he was offering me the role.

'I immediately took some lessons but didn't have time to take my test before we went off to film some of my scenes on location; private land was used for the driving scenes, which meant it didn't matter that I hadn't passed my test. Ian Lavender was extremely apprehensive about being driven by me and I was equally nervous about driving!

'The car was old-fashioned and you pressed a button for the ignition, not a key; when it came to the studio shots I couldn't get the car to start, so someone in the production crew told me not to worry, they'd pull the car off the set, to make it look like the two characters (Sylvia and Pikey) were driving off, and then put engine noises over the filming afterwards. Not being a driver, I thought: "Oh, that means I don't have to do anything." To my horror, I found we were being pulled right into the camera, and afterwards people said: "You should have been steering." The poor cameraman was horrified when we were pulled straight towards him – but the audience loved it!

'It was a wonderful experience doing *Dad's Army* because it was not the kind of role that I tended to get at that point in my career. I was usually offered more offbeat characters, so I was grateful to David for his willingness to take a chance and offer me something different. It was enormous fun working with those lovely men, and was the first time I'd gone to the BBC to rehearse and no one wore jeans.

'It was one of my more memorable jobs because of the wonderful characters I worked with. They were mostly experienced, distinguished character actors, and it was a rare opportunity to work with such people at the end of a special and successful series.'

JEAN GILPIN

MAN AND THE HOUR, THE

Recorded: Monday 15/4/68 (made in black and white)

Original transmission: Wednesday 31/7/68, 8.20–8.50pm

(This episode was originally planned for transmission on Monday 5 June)

Original viewing figures: 7.2 million

Repeated: 17/1/69, 8/10/82, 14/7/98, 22/3/99

CAST

Arthur Lowe . . . . .Captain Mainwaring
John Le Mesurier . . . . .Sergeant Wilson
Clive Dunn . . . . .Lance Corporal Jones
John Laurie . . . . .Private Frazer
James Beck . . . . .Private Walker
Arnold Ridley . . . . .Private Godfrey
Ian Lavender . . . . .Private Pike
Janet Davies . . . . .Mrs Pike
Caroline Dowdeswell . . . . .Janet King
John Ringham . . . . .Bracewell
Bill Pertwee . . . . .ARP Warden
Neville Hughes . . . . .Soldier
Gordon Peters . . . . .Chief Fire Officer (scene was cut prior to recording)
Platoon: Colin Bean, Richard Jacques, Hugh Hastings, Chris Franks, David Seaforth, Alec Coleman, Hugh Cecil, Vic Taylor, Jimmy Mac, Peter Whitaker
Other Extras: Jack Yeomans, Bill Straiton, Brian Nolan (played firemen during rehearsals, but scene was cut prior to recording)
Despatch Rider: Jack Wright

PRODUCTION TEAM

Script: Jimmy Perry and David Croft
Producer/Director: David Croft
Production Assistant: Harold Snoad
Studio Lighting: George Summers
Studio Sound: James Cole
Design: Alan Hunter-Craig and Paul Joel
Assistant Floor Manager: Evan King
Vision Mixer: Clive Doig
Costume Supervisor: George Ward
Make-Up Supervisor: Sandra Exelby

The prologue shows Mainwaring being introduced as the guest of honour at Walmington-on-Sea's 'I'm Backing Britain' campaign. Mainwaring talks about 1940 when everyone backed Britain against Hitler.

At the bank it's Tuesday 14 May 1940, Mainwaring's office is being prepared for Hitler's arrival; Mainwaring is putting the sandbags up at the windows ready for his machine gun so he can guard the High Street.

A letter arrives from GHQ informing Mainwaring that a force of local volunteers is to be set up, called the LDV (Local Defence Volunteers) in view of the grave danger of enemy paratroopers parachuting into the Home Counties. Their responsibilities involve guarding strategic points in the area. Anthony Eden announces the formation of the new force on the radio.

Seizing this opportunity to show his leadership qualities, although some would consider these dubious, Mainwaring says the first thing they must do is set up an Invasion Committee. He appoints himself as the Commander, Wilson as 2nd in Command and Pike as the Information Officer. Mainwaring sends Pike off on his bike to tell the town that LDV volunteers must report to the church hall that evening, but not before ending up with a sooty mouth after showing Pike how to use the megaphone, a converted coal scuttle.

Later, Mainwaring and Wilson start enrolling the men until they're rudely interrupted by Hodges who comes in shouting at Mainwaring to clear the hall, as an ARP lecture is taking place

'Is There Honey Still For Tea?'

in five minutes' time. He has requisitioned the hall for civil defence purposes. To speed up the enrolment everyone squashes into the office and all that can be seen of the self-appointed captain is a bald pate.

An hour later they return for an inspection of their weapons. When Godfrey refuses to give Mainwaring the rifle that belongs to his friend, they decide to share it and set up a rota. Bracewell is dressed for dinner: it's his wife's birthday and they're dining out. Mainwaring's impressed with the turnout and a demonstration on how to blow up an enemy tank is organised. But then Mrs Pike comes to collect Frank, as it's his bedtime.

MAN FROM PICKFORDS, THE

Played by Don Estelle (TV); Michael Middleton (radio)
This character delivers the naval gun to the Home Guard in 'Big Guns'.

MAN ON THE STATION, THE

Played by Ralph Ball (TV)
In 'Sons of the Sea' the city gent is waiting on the railway platform at Eastbourne when Mainwaring and his men, who think they're on the continent, open the door of the railway wagon and in schoolboy French ask the name of the station.

MAN WITH THE DOOR, THE

Played by Gordon Peters (TV)
When the Walmington branch of Swallow Bank is bombed, it takes three months before Mr Mainwaring's new office door arrives in 'Is There Honey Still For Tea?'. 'The Man with the Door' fixes it for Mainwaring who isn't happy with the quality because it's made of paper.

MAN HUNT

Recorded: Friday 21/11/69

Original transmission: Thursday 27/11/69, 7.30–8.00pm

Original viewing figures: 11.8 million

(The *Christmas Night with the Stars* insert, titled 'Resisting the Aggressor Down the Ages', transmitted Thursday 25/12/69, was recorded the same evening)

Repeated: 20/6/70, 26/11/82, 10/10/92, 15/10/92 (Wales), 8/6/96

CAST

Arthur Lowe . . . . .Captain Mainwaring
John Le Mesurier . . . . .Sergeant Wilson
Clive Dunn . . . . .Lance Corporal Jones
John Laurie . . . . .Private Frazer
James Beck . . . . .Private Walker
Arnold Ridley . . . . .Private Godfrey
Ian Lavender . . . . .Private Pike

Bill Pertwee . . . . .Chief Warden
Janet Davies . . . . .Mrs Pike
Patrick Tull . . . . .Suspect
Robert Moore . . . . .Large Man
Leon Cortez . . . . .Small Man
Olive Mercer . . . . .Fierce Lady
Miranda Hampton . . . . .Sexy Lady
Robert Aldous . . . . .German pilot
Bran . . . . .as himself
Platoon: Leslie Noyes, Jimmy Mac, Hugh Hastings, Roger Bourne, Desmond Cullum-Jones, Vic Taylor, George Hancock, Freddie Wiles, Martin Dunn, Freddie White

PRODUCTION TEAM
Script: Jimmy Perry and David Croft
Producer/Director: David Croft
Production Assistant: Harold Snoad
Studio Lighting: Howard King
Studio Sound: John Holmes
Design: Ray London
Assistant Floor Manager: Bill Harman
Vision Mixer: Dave Hanks
Costume Supervisor: Michael Burdle
Make-Up Supervisor: Cecile Hay-Arthur

The war has been raging 18 months and a memo from GHQ claims empty parachutes are being dropped to cause confusion; the trouble is, as Jones points out on parade, how do they tell the difference between German and British parachutes? Mainwaring clears up any uncertainty by stating that British ones are white, and the German ones dirty, off-white.

After the platoon are dismissed and head to the pub, Walker tells Mainwaring and Wilson he found a parachute in the woods a while ago and used it to make eight-dozen pairs of women's knickers. But he can't say whether it was a British or German parachute. As all the knickers were sold on Walker's market stall there is no alternative but to try and track them down. When the bank closes the following day, Walker, Wilson and Mainwaring have the unenviable task of visiting the homes of likely purchasers to look at their knickers! They don't have any luck, until a young woman invites Wilson in to look – they turn out to be blue. All the people they've called on complain to Hodges who asks Mainwaring what he's doing.

To help in the search, Walker brings a tracker dog on parade the following evening. They decide to test the dog out, with Jones pretending to be a Nazi parachutist. They let the dog smell the scent and it starts hounding out Jones but as the men are charging after the dog on the church hall staircase, a visiting Mrs Pike gets knocked over and reveals her white undies, which answers Mainwaring's question: it was a British parachute!

Hodges, meanwhile, discovers a parachute stuck in a tree and is so pre-occupied he doesn't think anything of the man asking for directions to Downsend Woods. When the platoon travel by in Jones' van they get out and the dog quickly picks up the scent from the parachute. Hodges tells Mainwaring that a man with a German voice asked for directions to the woods, and they give chase.

They eventually catch up with the man who turns out to be a Viennese ornithologist who'd read in the papers that the Golden Oriel – a rare bird – was spotted in the wood. Before the day is out a frustrated German airman arrives on the scene desperate to give himself up.

MAN OF ACTION, A
Recorded: Tuesday 7/5/74
Original transmission: Friday 22/11/74, 7.45–8.15pm
Original viewing figures: 16.4 million
Repeated: 22/5/75, 16/4/82, 28/11/89, 30/8/90 (N Ireland), 20/11/93, 17/12/93 (Wales), 24/8/96

CAST
Arthur Lowe . . . . .Captain Mainwaring
John Le Mesurier . . . . .Sergeant Wilson
Clive Dunn . . . . .Lance Corporal Jones
John Laurie . . . . .Private Frazer
Arnold Ridley . . . . .Private Godfrey
Ian Lavender . . . . .Private Pike
Bill Pertwee . . . . .Chief Warden Hodges
Talfryn Thomas . . . . .Mr Cheeseman
Frank Williams . . . . .Vicar
Edward Sinclair . . . . .Verger
Eric Longworth . . . . .Town Clerk
Harold Bennett . . . . .Mr Bluett
Arnold Peters . . . . .Fire Officer Dale
Jay Denyer . . . . .Inspector Baker
Robert Mill . . . . .Captain Swan
Colin Bean . . . . .Private Sponge

Platoon: George Hancock, Michael Moore, Desmond Cullum-Jones, Freddie White, Evan Ross, Leslie Noyes, Roger Bourne, Hugh Cecil

PRODUCTION TEAM
Script: Jimmy Perry and David Croft
Producer/Director: David Croft
Production Assistant: Bob Spiers
Studio Lighting: Howard King
Studio Sound: Michael McCarthy
Design: Bryan Ellis
Assistant Floor Manager: Anne Ogden
Vision Mixer: Ron Isted
Costume Supervisor: Susan Wheal
Make-Up Supervisor: Sylvia Thornton

While Jones and Pike patrol outside the park one evening, they reminisce about when, as a young boy, Pike used to push his head through the park gates. He gives Jones a demonstration and gets his head stuck between the bars.

Meanwhile, back at the church hall, Wilson doesn't think Mainwaring's decision to let the *Eastbourne Gazette* write a series of articles about the platoon is a good idea. Mainwaring says he didn't want to offend the press: when the editor of the paper phoned, he didn't see any reason to object, even if it does involve a reporter joining the ranks of the platoon.

Mr Cheeseman arrives and announces the first article will be called 'Captain Mainwaring – Man Of Action'. Mainwaring wants to impress upon the reporter that the platoon is an efficient fighting force, so when Jones phones to report Pike's head is stuck, he shields the purpose of the call from Cheeseman before heading off to investigate.

'A Man of Action'

'A Man of Action'

While the platoon try freeing Pike, the air raid sirens sound. With more important matters to deal with the problem has to be solved as quickly as possible. Mainwaring also wants to keep the matter quiet, and the platoon ends up lifting the gate off its hinges and taking it back to the church hall. Back at base, Cheeseman is confused as to why Pike has his head stuck in the railings, and even more so when Mainwaring says it's a secret.

Freeing Pike takes second place when an emergency occurs: a land mine has been dropped on the railway line just outside town. There are no casualties but over 100 yards of track are destroyed and the town's gas and water supplies are cut off. To add to the confusion the telephone lines are down as well. Mainwaring halts the panic and decides to take charge, declaring martial law, much to everyone's anger.

Wilson, Jones and Frazer are ordered to get on their bikes and shout orders through the town, including the shooting of looters and imprisonment of rumour-mongers. Power goes to Mainwaring's head, but his bubble is burst when Captain Swan arrives from GHQ to take charge.

MANGER, MELITA

Born: Neath

Role: Waitress (S4, episode 9: 'Mum's Army'), Nora (S9, episode 2: 'The Making of Private Pike') (TV)

Playing the waitress in 'Mum's Army' was Melita's first part on TV. During rehearsals she was so nervous she shook the tray she was carrying and spilt the tea. When it came to recording, Melita, who was in her 20s, noticed the tea cups hadn't been filled quite so high.

Melita always wanted to be a dancer and after leaving school she studied at Brighton School of Music and Drama. Pantos, summer seasons and her first professional play (a production of Arnold Ridley's *The Ghost Train*) came her way. Small TV parts also began arriving, including roles in *Are You Being Served?*, *Doctor on the Go* and *The Basil Brush Show*.

Throughout the 1970s, Melita was also busy in commercials. After getting married she took a break from acting to raise a family. Today, she helps run the family business in Wales but still acts when asked: her last appearance was as a Welsh woman in *Waiting for God*.

MANOR FARM

This farm situated three miles from Walmington is utilised by the Highland Regiment during the exercise in 'Operation Kilt'. It acts as the Regiment's headquarters.

MANSON, PAMELA (1929–1988)

Born: London

Role: NAAFI Girl (S6, episode 4: 'We Know Our Onions') (TV)

Pamela entered the industry in 1952 and after years of theatre work began what was to become a busy TV career, with appearances in *The Good Life*, *Are You Being Served?*, *Jackanory*, *The Professionals*, *Charles and Diana* and many other shows. Though Pamela was a versatile actress, working with the likes of Tony Hancock and Peter Sellers, she spent most of her career in comedy.

Before turning to acting, Pamela had worked as a secretary on the *News Chronicle*. She was also employed as a public relations officer in the fashion industry and managing theatrical artists for a time. Pamela was only 59 when she died.

MARIE
Played by Pat Coombs (radio)
Pat Coombs played Marie Antoinette in a film showing at the cinema during the radio episode, 'A Soldier's Farewell'.

MARIGOLD TEA ROOMS
Situated in Walmington-on-Sea's High Street, the tea rooms are where Mainwaring and Wilson frequently go for their morning break, indulging in a cup of coffee and some rich tea biscuits, unless it's Tuesday, when they opt for rock cakes, fighting over the one with the most fruit.

Before the war, afternoon customers could sip their tea or enjoy one of the tea rooms' delicious buns, which were filled with cream on the premises, while listening to Miss Rowlands and her friends entertain with a little light music, a musical treat that was well-received by older patrons. But those days have gone and now, in the event of an invasion, the tea rooms would double-up as the Home Guard's advanced headquarters because the property is near the Novelty Rock Emporium and Stones' Amusement Arcade, the stretch of coastline patrolled by Mainwaring and his men.

Owned by Miss Fortescue, the Marigold Tea Rooms is a cosy, quaint little place where residents of Walmington can idle away an hour or so, and, if they're lucky, they might be able to secure the bay window seats and watch the world go by in the High Street outside. With its oak-beamed ceiling, little round tables decorated in lace tablecloths, Mainwaring describes the tea rooms as a typical English setting, and whenever he's there it's difficult to imagine there is a war on.

The Marigold Tea Rooms are seen in 'Time On My Hands' and 'The Godiva Affair'.

MARINE OFFICER, THE
Played by Alan Haines (film)
Captain Crisp, the marine officer, arrives at the church during the closing scenes of the film, but while he considers, along with all the other officials, what to do about the German airmen who are holding hostages in the church hall, the enterprising Captain Mainwaring has already risked his life to bring the incident to an end.

MARKS & SPENCER
The town of Walmington has a branch of this nationwide store, and in 'The Bullet is Not for Firing' it's shot at by a low-flying Heinkel.

MARQUIS OF GRANBY, THE
A pub in Walmington that Wilson and Pike visit while searching for Frazer, who missed parade in 'The Miser's Hoard'.

MARSDEN, BETTY
Role: Lady Maltby ('The Captain's Car') (radio)
Betty died in 1998.

MARSHALL, GEORGE
George is not seen in the series, but his name crops up in 'The Royal Train'. He's a railway employee who works in the steam maintenance department. Henry, the driver, phones him to complain about the square boss on the steam brake wheel, a part that has gone wrong and caused him to stop his train at the station.

MARTIN'S BANK LIMITED
It was originally intended that Mainwaring would be the bank manager of Martin's Bank, but when the series was commissioned a bank existed with the same name, so Swallow Bank was chosen instead, although Mr Mainwaring gets a little confused and is heard saying he's the manager of Martin's Bank whilst enjoying a coffee at the Marigold Tea Rooms in 'Time On My Hands'. By the time the film was released in 1971, the bank no longer existed and Swallow Bank was dropped in favour of Martin's.

The real Martin's bank was in business until 1969 when it merged with Barclays by private act of Parliament.

MARTINI-HENRY
A type of rifle, the Martini-Henry is mentioned by Jones in 'A Brush With the Law'.

MARTYN, LARRY (1934–1994)
Born: London
Roles: Soldier (S2, episode 3: 'The Loneliness of the Long-Distance Walker'), 2nd Sailor (S3, episode 10: 'Menace from the Deep'), Italian POW (S4, episode 5: 'Don't Fence Me In'), Signals Private (S5, episode 5: 'The Desperate Drive of Corporal Jones') (TV); Joe Walker (32 radio shows)
Larry entered the industry in the 1950s, working in variety as a singer and comedian until the age of 22. His early small-screen career was dominated by drama until the 1970s, when he was employed more and more in light entertainment. His TV appearances included *Rising Damp, Spring and Autumn, The Dick Emery Show, Up Pompeii!, Mike Yarwood in Persons, Never Mind the Twain* and *The Bill*. He also made several films, such as *Up the Junction, The Great St Trinian's Train Robbery, Carry On at Your Convenience* and *Carry On Behind*, playing an electrician.

Larry served with the parachute regiment during the war and continued the activity as a hobby.

MAXWELL, MR
Played by Michael Bilton (TV); Timothy Bateson (radio)
The solicitor in 'Sons of the Sea' who visits Mr Mainwaring at the bank to inform him that Mr Johnson, who banked with the Swallow, has died.

MAXWELL, ROGER (1900–1971)
Role: Peppery Old Gent (film)
The late Roger Maxwell appeared in many television shows and films, including 1951's *Mr Drake's Duck* as Colonel Maitland, *Treasure Hunt* and *Glad Tidings*, both in 1952, *Colonel March Investigates* as Major Rodman a year later, Colonel Smythe in 1953's *Deadly Nightshade*, General Holt in *John Wesley*, the Major in *No Smoking* in 1955 and a party chairman in 1970's *The Rise and Rise of Michael Rimmer*.

MAYOR, THE
Played by Fred McNaughton (TV)
Alderman Bickerstaff, the mayor of Walmington, appears at all the necessary functions, including standing on ceremony as King George VI passes through the station in 'The Royal Train'.

MAYOR, THE
Played by John Baskcomb (film)
The mayor of Walmington-on-Sea was one of the unfortunate residents taken hostage by German airmen in the closing scenes of the movie.

McALLISTER, SIR CHARLES RENFREW
Played by Campbell Singer (TV); Fraser Kerr (radio)
Sir Charles is the government minister responsible for overseeing the building of the new aerodrome in 'Is There Honey Still For Tea?'. When its construction means Godfrey's cottage will have to be demolished, Frazer takes up the case. While McAllister's father owned a fish and chip shop on the Isle of Barra, Sir Charles was expelled from his school on Barra for cheating, got Maisie McIntosh into trouble and got the sack from a draper's shop for being caught with his fingers in the till. When Frazer threatens to sell this information to a certain society magazine, Sir Charles agrees to relocate the aerodrome so that Godfrey's cottage is just outside the perimeter.

McAVOY, ALEX (1928–)
Born: Glasgow
Role: Sergeant (S5, episode 6: 'If the Cap Fits…'), Sergeant (S6, episode 4: 'We Know Our Onions') (TV)
Alex was a boy soprano and sang on the radio in 1944, aged 16. When he left school he wanted to become a commercial artist so trained at evening classes at Glasgow School of Art, while working during the day, first in the inspections department at a gun factory, then as a display artist for various organisations, including department stores.

Before joining the RAF for national service in 1946, Alex had begun working behind the scenes at a local theatre. Shortly after leaving the forces he studied full-time at Glasgow's drama academy. Four years of variety and broadcasting for the BBC followed combined with various rep work. In 1962 he left for France to study mime and movement with the world-renowned Lecoq.

Alex was often cast as youngsters and during his early TV career played Sunny Jim (an 18 year old, even though he was 39) in BBC's *Vital Spark* in 1967.

He's made a few film appearances, most notably as the teacher in Pink Floyd's *The Wall*. He remains busy today, mainly in the theatre (he was the original Jacob in *Joseph and the Amazing Technicolor Dreamcoat*). Alex also teaches mime and movement at a drama college in Edinburgh.

McCARTHY, MICHAEL

Studio sound recordist on 61 episodes (TV): S3–S8; 'The Love of Three Oranges' and 'Battle of the Giants'

In 1961, Wimbledon-born Michael McCarthy left school and immediately joined the BBC, employed as a trainee in the sound department. He gained experience assisting on top shows like *Steptoe and Son* and Michael Bentine's *It's A Square World*, helping with the music and sound effects. In 1967, he was promoted to sound supervisor, and was responsible for the sound department's contribution to shows including *Harry Worth*, *Oh Brother!*, *The Morecambe and Wise Show* and *The Two Ronnies*. More recently he's worked on *The Generation Game*, *Big Break* and the *National Lottery*. Michael still works for the BBC.

McCEAVEDY, DOCTOR

Played by Fulton MacKay (TV)

McCeavedy is the doctor in 'The Miser's Hoard' who comes round to tell Frazer that Mr Breuster has died, only to knock over his tin containing hundreds of gold sovereigns. Believing Frazer needs to take better care of his money, the doctor pops in to see Mr Mainwaring at the bank and suggests he offers some financial advice.

McCULLY, GENERAL

General McCully is not seen but is mentioned by Jones in the episode, 'All is Safely Gathered In'. Jones remembers him for saying: 'Let's take it in turns'.

McCULLY, MR

Not seen or heard in the sitcom, Mr McCully attends the dinner in the episode, 'Turkey Dinner' and asks Pikey whether there are seconds.

McGARRY, PARNELL

Role: Elizabeth (S4, episode 8: 'The Two and a Half Feathers') (TV)

The late Parnell McGarry didn't appear in the sitcom, but she provided the voice of the mysterious Mrs Mainwaring who was sleeping in a bunk bed above her husband, George. Other credits include two films from 1973: *The Love Ban*, playing a nun, and *Bedazzled* as Gluttony.

McGEAGH, STANLEY

Role: Sergeant Waller (S3, episode 3: 'The Lion has 'Phones') (TV)

Stanley, who now lives in Australia, appeared regularly on the screen during the 1960s and '70s. On television he played the hero in 'An Author in Search of Two Characters', an episode of *Jason King*, a police sergeant in a 1969 episode of *Doctor in the House*, and several appearances in *Doctor Who*. His film credits include playing a prison guard in *Gandhi* (1982), a reporter in *Carry On Emmannuelle*, a short-sighted man in *Carry On Behind* and Hiller in the 1975 picture, *The Land That Time Forgot*.

McGUGAN, STUART

Born: Stirling

Role: Scottish Sergeant (S9, episode 5: 'Number Engaged') (TV)

After leaving school, Stuart worked as a journalist for six years before turning to acting. His last job as a newspaper man was a sub editor with *The Daily Mail*. While attending drama school in Glasgow, he worked as a freelance journalist, but as soon as he graduated he spent time in rep, beginning at Canterbury in 1967, with Ian Lavender; he later moved on to Stratford, Newcastle, Leeds and spent a period in America.

His career has been busy, and on TV he appeared as Gunner Mackintosh in *It Ain't Half Hot, Mum* and spent nine years presenting *Play School*. Other TV appearances include the chief inspector in *The Chief*, *Tutti Frutti* and *Hamish Macbeth*.

McGUIRE, ARTHUR (1926–1987)

Role: Member of the platoon's back row in two episodes (S2, episode 4: 'Sgt Wilson's Little Secret', S3, episode 9: 'War Dance') (TV)

While serving 20 years with the Royal Navy, Arthur McGuire accepted the chance to appear as an extra in a handful of films, including *A Matter of Life and Death*, for which he was paid £3 a day, and *The Baby and the Battleship*. When he joined civvy street he turned to walk-on work and was regularly employed in shows such as *The Saint* and *The Persuaders*. He also did commercials. Arthur died of a heart attack at the age of 61.

McINTOSH, MAISIE

Not seen or heard in the sitcom, Maisie is mentioned by Frazer in 'Is There Honey Still For Tea?'. Sir Charles Renfrew McAllister got her pregnant on the Isle of Barra, and Frazer uses this, together with other sordid details about the minister's past, to persuade him to shift the proposed site for the aerodrome, saving Godfrey's cottage in the process.

McMURRAY, THÉRÈSE

Born: Herne Bay

Role: Girl at the Window (S1, episodes 5: 'The Showing Up of Corporal Jones' and 6: 'Shooting Pains), Girl in the Haystack (S3, episode 8: 'The Day the Balloon Went Up') (TV)

Thérèse, who made her acting debut in *Snow White* while at St Mary's Convent, Whitstable, believes it was a foregone conclusion that she would become an actress. Previous generations had had successful stage careers, including her aunt, who was the world famous contortionist, Cochran's Eve.

Thérèse grew up in Whitstable and was attending Saturday drama classes at Italia Conti Stage School when Lord Grade, her godfather, offered to pay the fees for five years' full-time tuition. She quickly established herself as a leading child actress and appeared in many stage and TV productions. At 18 she was cast as Nurse Parkin in *Emergency – Ward 10* for two years. In 1968, she kept the nurse's uniform for an appearance in *Hugh and I Spy*, produced by David Croft, which led to the first of her appearances in *Dad's Army*. Other TV credits include two series of *The Dick Emery Show*, *Second Time Around*, *Are You Being Served?* and *The Brighton Belles*.

Married to actor Donald Hewlett, Thérèse retired from acting in 1981 to bring up her family. She now runs a production company, writing and producing corporate videos.

McNAB, EILIDH

(See 'Tomlinson, Fred'.)

McNAUGHTON, FRED (1903–1981)

Born: London

Role: Mayor (S6, episode 3: 'The Royal Train', episode 5: 'The Honourable Man', S6, episode 5: 'The Captain's Car', S9, episode 5: 'The Knights of Madness') (TV)

A direct relative of music-hall star Marie Lloyd, Fred was the fourth generation of a theatrical family. He was training as a lawyer when his father died in 1920. Having to support his family, he began a 60-year career by joining Archie Pitt's Lido Follies as juvenile lead.

Straight man and scriptwriter for top variety double acts with first Raymond Bennett, then Stan Stanford, Fred was a radio star in the 1930s and '40s. From 1946, he was lead comedian in provincial pantos and tours of Whitehall farces.

In the mid-1950s series like *Emergency – Ward 10*, *Dixon of Dock Green*, *Z Cars*, *Softly, Softly*, *The Plane Makers* and *Crossroads* brought him to TV, and later to films. He was stage director at the London Palladium and understudied Frankie Howerd and Max Bygraves there for more than ten years.

Over six feet tall, Fred was often cast in uniform on stage, including appearances in *Journey's End*, *Seagulls Over Sorrento*, *Worm's Eye View*, and in films such as *Charge of the Light Brigade*. His wide range of dialects gave him contracts at the Gate Theatre, Dublin, and countless voice-overs. A back injury, sustained when wearing full armour, slowed him down after 1978. He died in 1981 after a short illness.

MEADOWBRIDGE

The minor public school attended by Wilson, which housed 300 boys.

MEADOWS, MISS

Played by Jean St Clair (TV); Diana Bishop (radio)

A bespectacled, grey-haired customer in Jones' shop, Miss Meadows appears in 'The Armoured Might of Lance Corporal Jones'.

MEADOWS, PRIVATE

A platoon member who, along with Private Woods, was ordered by Mainwaring to prevent anyone entering the church hall while the rest of the men practised their dance for the procession to be held to help raise money for the Spitfire fund in 'The Godiva Affair'.

MEDALS

In 'The Showing Up of Corporal Jones', Jack Jones explains the medals he has collected during his time in the army. He proudly displays six general service medals, a medal for the Egyptian Campaign 1884–1885 and the Caliph's Star, the Khedive's Star and the Queen's Sudan Medal. All the platoon members except Walker and Pike – who let no one forget that he'd earnt some badges from the scouts – wore their medals when the occasion dictated, something that annoyed and embarrassed Mainwaring because he didn't have any.

MEDICAL OFFICER

Played by Robert Lankesheer (TV)

The doctor appears in the penultimate scene of 'The Loneliness of the Long-Distance Walker' when Walker has been taken ill after eating corned beef fritters. He examines Walker, who lies groaning in his bunk with a swollen and blotchy face.

MEMBER OF PARLIAMENT, 1ST

Played by James Ottaway (TV)

This Member of Parliament appears in 'Keep Young and Beautiful' and debates the idea of transferring men between the Home Guard and ARP.

MEMBER OF PARLIAMENT, 2ND

Played by Charles Morgan (TV)

The other Member of Parliament involved in discussions to transfer the fit, young members of the ARP in to the Home Guard, with their places being taken by the older, less able members of the Home Guard.

MEMORABILIA

Successful television shows can be turned into profit-making commodities for companies who specialise in spin-off merchandise, such as jig-saws, model vehicles, annuals, cigarette cards, mugs and painting books. In today's aggressive climate it seems no small-screen success is left untouched, but even back in the seventies shows like *Dad's Army* were just as marketable. Over the years, many items of memorabilia have been manufactured, as Jack Wheeler of the DAAS found out when he compiled a list:

Dad's Army Sweet Cigarette Cards

A set of 25 cards depicting scenes from the 1971 feature film was produced by Primrose Confectionery Co Ltd.

Dad's Army Jigsaws

Between 1974 and 1978, it is understood that ten jigsaws were manufactured by Whitman Publishing (UK) Ltd. Each puzzle had a colour picture, a scene from the TV series. The photos included: Jones' van parked in a field, the platoon donning firemen's uniforms sitting on a Dennis Fire Engine, the platoon in camouflage, the platoon lined up in the church hall, a steam traction engine with the platoon members, three platoon members on horseback, the platoon lined up outside a railway station, the platoon in a field with a threshing machine and the platoon on the steps of the town hall.

Dad's Army Board Games

Ovaltine produced a board game (On Patrol with *Dad's Army*) in 1971, which people could obtain by collecting six tokens. Another board game was launched in 1974 by Denys Fisher, under the Strawberry Fayre label.

Dad's Army Bubble Bath

In the early 1970s, Lever Brothers sold bubble bath inside *Dad's Army* characters.

Dad's Army Mug

In 1977, a pottery in the Devon town of Newton Abbot produced a mug for a promotion by the company manufacturing Daddies sauce. Three labels had to be collected in order to obtain a mug which was personalised by having your own photo fired onto it. The mug depicted the sitcom's main characters plus your own photo as part of the platoon.

Dad's Army Model Vehicles

Model manufacturer Lledo have manufactured several *Dad's Army* sets, which have normally been sold through the BBC or *Radio Times*. The first set was issued in 1991 under the banner, 'BBC *Dad's Army* Comedy Classics' and contained Jones' van, a BBC outside broadcast van, a fire engine and two other vehicles. Jones' van provided the only link with the TV series. A second set, titled 'Radio Times' *Dad's Army* Series' was sold in 1995. The set included Jones' van, Hodges' van, a Walmington taxi, a Walmington newspaper delivery van and a LDV truck. A Walmington single-decker bus was later added, although like some of the other items, such a vehicle had never been seen in the television show. Hodges' van and Jones' van had been part of a 1993 set of vehicles promoted through the *Radio Times*, which also included items depicting other classic shows. A *Hi-De-Hi!* bus, an army truck for *It Ain't Half Hot, Mum*, a delivery van for *Are You Being Served?* and a horse and cart for *Steptoe and Son* completed the set.

Dad's Army First Day Cover

Issued to celebrate the 30th anniversary of the sitcom, one thousand editions were produced by Benhams and signed by Jimmy Perry, David Croft, Bill Pertwee, Ian Lavender, Frank Williams, Clive Dunn and Pamela Cundell. The cover was stamped in Thetford on 31 July 1998, 30 years after the first episode was transmitted.

Dad's Army Miniature Figures

A company called SDD produced 50 sets of miniature *Dad's Army* figures before they were forced to stop production due to copyright difficulties.

MENACE FROM THE DEEP

Recorded: Friday 7/11/69

Original transmission: Thursday 13/11/69, 7.30–8.00pm

Original viewing figures: 13.3 million

Repeated: 6/6/70, 12/11/82, 5/9/89, 3/1/90 (N Ireland), 29/1/91, 9/1/93, 14/1/93 (Wales), 12/7/96

CAST

Arthur Lowe . . . . .Captain Mainwaring
John Le Mesurier . . . . .Sergeant Wilson
Clive Dunn . . . . .Lance Corporal Jones
John Laurie . . . . .Private Frazer
James Beck . . . . .Private Walker
Arnold Ridley . . . . .Private Godfrey
Ian Lavender . . . . .Private Pike
Bill Pertwee . . . . .ARP Warden
Stuart Sherwin . . . . .2nd ARP Warden
Bill Treacher . . . . .1st Sailor
Larry Martyn . . . . .2nd Sailor

No other members of the platoon appeared in this episode

PRODUCTION TEAM

Script: Jimmy Perry and David Croft
Producer/Director: David Croft
Production Assistants: Harold Snoad and Steve Turner
Film Cameraman: James Balfour
Film Editor: Bob Rymer
Studio Lighting: Howard King
Studio Sound: Michael McCarthy
Design: Ray London
Assistant Floor Manager: Bill Harman
Vision Mixer: Dave Hanks
Costume Supervisor: Michael Burdle
Make-Up Supervisor: Cecile Hay-Arthur

The home guard are given the job of guarding the pier at Walmington and manning the machine-gun post for the next four nights whilst the navy regulars have a break from duties. Mainwaring is in his element and has meticulously, and laboriously, planned the strategies.

When Mainwaring tells Pike to fetch the

food from the boat, he returns empty-handed. A little sheepish, he explains that although he tied the boat to a small cable, it's been washed away in the strong tide, pulling the telephone line with it, so they're cut off as well. The only way left to communicate is by Morse code, but when the light they use is spotted by Hodges, he uses a children's paddle boat to reach the pier. The boat sinks before he gets there, leaving him no alternative but to swim the rest of the way.

As the hours pass, the men become increasingly hungry, so everyone is excited when Pike spots a machine full of chocolate. After Frazer – the only one who has some pennies – loses a small fortune trying to win some chocolate, Walker gives the machine a quick slap and wins the jackpot in terms of chocolate bars. The trouble is they're all artificial except for Frazer's bar.

As morning breaks, Jones spots a mine drifting perilously close to the pier, and therefore wakes Mainwaring. They try to fend it off the girders but struggle until Hodges arrives on the scene. He falls while still wearing his helmet and being a magnetic mine, it follows him. Eventually Hodges clambers back on the pier, lobs an object at the mine which blows it up, and saves the day.

MENNARD, TOM (1918–1989)
Born: Leeds
Role: Mess Orderly (S4, episode 13: 'Fallen Idol') (TV)

Tom left school and became an apprentice in the family undertaker's business until he was called up into the army during the Second World War. Once demobbed he became a taxi driver for a company in Hove, before working as a bus driver in and around Brighton.

In his spare time he helped his local church put on stage shows and, upon being noticed in one of the productions, was offered the chance to work at the Windmill Theatre as a stand-up comic. During his career he worked in all strands of the profession, including films like *The Flesh and Blood Show*, *The Four Dimensions of Greta* and *Tiffany Jones*. His TV career included appearances in *The Good Old Days*, the children's show *Rainbow* back in 1981, and Granada's *Foxy Lady* a year later. In 1985, he joined the cast of *Coronation Street*, playing Sam Tindall – who fell in love with Phyllis Pearce – for four years. He was also seen in shows such as *All Creatures Great and Small* playing Mr Scargill, Cyril in *Open All Hours*, Challis in *Bergerac*, a mayor in *Sorry!* and a police sergeant in *Brothers McGregor*. He was also regularly heard on the radio and had his own show, *Local Tales*, for a while.

Tom – who owned a guest house in the Cornish town of Newquay, which his sister ran – died in 1989 after a battle against cancer.

MENZIES, MAJOR GENERAL
Played by Campbell Singer (TV); Fraser Kerr (radio)
A Scottish officer who takes over at Area Command in 'If the Cap Fits…', Menzies visits all the Home Guard units to introduce himself. When he enters the church hall at Walmington, he mistakes Frazer for Mainwaring. Noticing he's Scottish, Menzies invites Frazer along to his planned Highland get-together at the officers' mess at HQ.

MERCER, OLIVE (1906–1983)
Born: London
Roles: Mrs Casson (S3, episode 1: 'The Armoured Might of Lance Corporal Jones'), Lady in Queue (S3, episode 3: 'The Lion has 'Phones'), Mrs Yeatman (S3, episode 9: 'War Dance', S5, episode 4: 'Getting the Bird', S7, episode 1: 'Everybody's Trucking', S7, episode 6: 'Turkey Dinner', 'The Love of Three Oranges', S9, episode 3: 'The Knights of Madness'), Fierce Lady (S3, episode 12: 'Man Hunt') (TV)
After graduating from RADA, Olive worked briefly with her father before joining a rep. But in 1931 she left to marry and raise a family. While her children were growing up, she produced shows for various companies as well as local children's shows in Ruislip. She also helped set up a drama school, Mime and the Spoken Word, in the town (the most famous pupil being Russell Grant).

Olive didn't concentrate on acting again until in her 50s, joining various reps including Watford with Jimmy Perry. It wasn't until she was 60 that she moved into TV, clocking up a myriad of small parts, including roles in *The Forsyte Saga*, *Emergency – Ward 10*, the cleaner in *Please, Sir!*, *Doctor in the House*, *On the Buses*, an aunt in *The Likely Lads* and *Monty Python*. Olive regularly appeared in *Crossroads*, as one of her final jobs. She worked mainly in TV – often in stern parts – but was also frequently hired for newspaper and magazine adverts.

She contracted shingles at 70 and her health never fully recovered. She died of a heart attack.

MESS ORDERLY, THE
Played by Tom Mennard (TV)
The mess orderly is in charge of catering at the School of Explosives in 'Fallen Idol'.

MESS STEWARD, THE
(See 'Clark, Mr'.)

METHODIST CHURCH
Referred to by Mainwaring in 'The Man and the Hour', the church stands across the road from the Swallow Bank in Walmington-on-Sea. Always believing the residents of the town are unaware of just how real the threat of Nazi invasion is, Mainwaring suggests that hordes of German paratroopers, dressed as nuns, could drop out of the sky and set up their HQ at the church and no one would be any the wiser.

MIDDLETON, MICHAEL
Roles: American sergeant ('My British Buddy'), Man from Pickfords ('Big Guns'), Sergeant Baxter ('We Know Our Onions'), Driver's Mate ('The Royal Train') (radio)

MIKE
In 'The Royal Train' the Walmington Home Guard are gathered in the railway station waiting room, awaiting the King, who'll be passing through the station. Frazer makes a cup of tea, only to find there is no milk or sugar. Before Walker comes to the rescue, he asks: 'Couldn't Mike let you have any?' It's not clear who Mike is and it's the last we hear of him.

MILFORD, ANN
Producer's assistant on three episodes: S2, episodes 4, 5 & 6

MILITARY POLICE SERGEANT
Played by David Davenport (TV)
In 'The Enemy Within the Gates' the police sergeant arrives at the church hall to collect the German pilots whom Jones, Walker and Pike capture while out on patrol.

MILITARY SERVICE HARDSHIP COMMITTEE
In 'The Loneliness of the Long-Distance Walker', Joe Walker's case for call-up deferment is heard by this local committee, chaired by a justice of the peace, who's described as a 'tight-lipped efficient-looking lady'. Making up the three-piece panel are a 'stroppy' Welsh trade unionist and Sergeant Wilson, whose responsibilities involve considering whether Walker should be forced to join up. As far as his mates back in the platoon, including Mainwaring, are concerned, he shouldn't because if Walker leaves the town, their supply route for black market goods will be cut.

The committee's purpose is to address cases where people with one-man businesses will be ruined if they're called up.

MILKMAN, THE
The milkman is seen in 'Museum Piece'. (See 'Henry, the milkman'.)

MILL, ROBERT
Born: London
Roles: Captain Swan (S7, episode 2: 'Man of Action'), Army Captain (S9, episode 5: 'Number Engaged') (TV)
After finishing national service, Robert began reading Classics at Oxford but left before gaining a degree. He moved between jobs for two years before joining RADA.

He became an ASM at Margate, before spending time at reps in Cambridge, Coventry and 18 months at Northampton starting in 1963. His great love is the theatre (he appeared in Tom

Conti's 1991 production *Otherwise Engaged* at Windsor) but he's worked on TV in *Enemy of the State* in the 1960s, a version of Oscar Wilde's *The Canterville Ghost* with Bruce Forsyth, a vicar in *In Sickness and In Health, Are You Being Served?* and *The First Churchills*. He has also made a few films. Robert hasn't worked on TV or stage for over a year, but he's still a busy member of the Equity Council.

MILLS BOMB

Mills bombs are first mentioned in 'Command Decision' when Walker, always on the lookout for situations to exploit, tells Mainwaring he can supply Mills bombs at £1 each. In this instance, the captain isn't interested.

The bomb resembled a hand-grenade and was serrated on the outside to produce shrapnel on explosion. It was designed by engineer Sir William Mills (1856–1932).

MILNES, BERNADETTE

Role: Lady in the Queue (S3, episode 3: 'The Lion has 'Phones') (TV)
Other TV shows Bernadette has appeared in include a 1953 episode of *The Quatermass Experiment* playing an usherette and *The Sweeney* as a character called Maureen Whittle. She's also appeared in a few films, such as *Gutter Girls* in 1964 and *The Elephant Man* in 1980.

MINISTER, THE

Played by Derek Bond (TV)
This minister in the House of Commons debates the swapping of personnel from the Home Guard and ARP in the episode, 'Keep Young and Beautiful'. The plan is to ensure the Home Guard is full of young, fit men, while the old guard transfer to ARP duties.

MINISTER, THE

Played by Jeffrey Segal (TV)
This bespectacled minister visits the aerodrome to see the Operation Catherine Wheel demonstration in 'Round and Round Went the Great Big Wheel'.

MISER'S HOARD, THE

Recorded: Friday 24/6/77
Original transmission: Sunday 23/10/77, 8.10–8.40pm
Original viewing figures: 11.1 million
Repeated: 2/10/78, 21/8/79, 25/6/91, 3/8/96

CAST

Arthur Lowe . . . . .Captain Mainwaring
John Le Mesurier . . . . .Sergeant Wilson
Clive Dunn . . . . .Lance Corporal Jones
John Laurie . . . . .Private Frazer
Arnold Ridley . . . . .Private Godfrey
Ian Lavender . . . . .Private Pike
Fulton Mackay . . . . .Doctor McCeavedy
Bill Pertwee . . . . .Chief Warden Hodges
Frank Williams . . . . .Vicar

Edward Sinclair . . . . .Verger
Colin Bean . . . . .Private Sponge
Platoon: Freddie Wiles, Freddie White, Evan Ross, George Hancock, Michael Moore, Desmond Cullum-Jones, Roger Bourne, Jimmy Mac, Vernon Drake

PRODUCTION TEAM

Script: Jimmy Perry and David Croft
Producer: David Croft
Production Assistant: Gordon Elsbury
Director: Bob Spiers
Studio Lighting: Howard King
Studio Sound: Laurie Taylor
Design: Tim Gleeson
Assistant Floor Manager: Susan Belbin
Vision Mixer: Angela Beveridge
Costume Designer: Mary Husband
Make-Up Artist: Sylvia Thornton

Frazer's business is booming, with profits for the week hitting over £18. He has got over £3,000 savings, with any profits from his business being used to buy gold sovereigns.

Doctor McCeavedy visits to inform him Mr

'The Miser's Hoard'

Breuster has died, but before leaving he knocks Frazer's gold sovereigns all over the place. Worried for Frazer's mind if the gold were to be stolen, the doctor visits Mainwaring and suggests he offers some financial advice. Mainwaring has the idea of selling him an annuity, but assures Wilson that it has nothing to do with earning himself commission.

A check on Frazer's bank statement reveals

just £15 in his account, so Mainwaring, who decides to be tactful, will raise the matter during that evening's parade. He talks to the platoon about savings and finance, but when he refers to gold and their citizens' duty to sell it towards the war effort, Frazer realises his game and warns him he won't get his hands on the gold.

Frazer phones to tell Mainwaring he's putting his fortune where no one will ever find it. Mainwaring believes Frazer would bury his gold, but he's not sure where. Some of the men decide to shadow him and when he takes a cash-box to the churchyard everyone thinks that's where he's buried his gold. But on digging up the tin box, Mainwaring is in for a big surprise: it contains nothing but a brick!

MITCHELL, NORMAN (1919–2001)

Born: Sheffield
Role: Captain Rogers (S3, episode 5: 'Something Nasty in the Vault') (TV)
Veteran actor and scriptwriter Norman Mitchell built a career out of small parts in film, TV and theatre. After studying medicine at Sheffield University for three years, he changed direction and began acting at a local rep. Other than a six-year spell in the Royal Army Medical Corps during World War Two, he led a busy career, and since his screen debut in the 1950s, clocked up over 2000 TV credits, including *Crossroads, All Creatures Great and Small, Are You Being Served?, Yes, Minister, Beryl's Lot, One by One, You Rang*

M'Lord?, Whatever Happened To The Likely Lads? and *Worzel Gummidge*. He also appeared in over 100 films, such as *Barry Lyndon, Revenge of the Pink Panther, A Night to Remember, Invasion, Oliver!, Mess Mates, Carry On Spying, Carry On Cabby, Carry On Cleo, Carry On Screaming, Legend of the Werewolf, Goodbye Mr Chips* and *The Price of Silence.*

His numerous stage appearances included Anthony Quayle's production of *The Clandestine Marriage* in the West End, *A View from the Bridge, The Visit* and *Shadow of Heroes*. He was also a member of the RSC for three years, touring Australia. Norman was recently seen in the film, *The Lighthouse*, playing Brownlow, the lighthouse keeper.

MOGENDORF, INGO

Born: Germany

Role: Nazi Pilot (film)

Ingo, who now lives in Spain, has worked on the small and big screen. On television he was seen as a German businessman in *Auf Wiedersehen, Pet*, a CID man in *The Brief*, Naujocks in *Spy – Frontiers of War*, Ludwig in *By the Sword Divided, Unity* and *The Train*. His film credits include *The Dirty Dozen – The Next Mission, A View to a Kill, Jenny's War, Up the Front, Murphy's War* and *Darling Lili.*

MONTEVERDI, GENERAL

Played by Edward Evans (TV); Cyril Shaps (radio)

Franco Monteverdi is the Italian general in the POW camp in 'Don't Fence Me In'. Mainwaring's men guard the camp for two weekends while the regular troops take some leave. He's overly friendly towards Walker, whom he knows, because on the quiet, Walker has been using some of the prisoners to assemble radio parts in one of his sheds.

MOORE, MICHAEL (1909–1979)

Born: Woolwich

Role: Member of the platoon's back row in 45 episodes: S3, episodes 1–4, 6,7; 'Battle of the Giants'; S5; S6, episodes 1–5, 7; S7; S8, episodes 1, 2, 4–6; 'My Brother and I'; 'The Love of Three Oranges'; S9 (TV)

Michael finished his education at Berkshire's Wellington College and trained as a medical student before turning to journalism. He spent eight years in Fleet Street working for the *Daily Express, Sporting Life* and *The Daily Telegraph* during the 1930s. Always interested in the entertainment world, Michael became a popular impressionist and comedian before the war, making his debut in cabaret in 1936.

He spent five years in the RAF where he was able to continue his entertaining, spending over ten months in the popular RAF Gang Show.

After the war he became a professional entertainer, best known as a radio star in *Ignorance is Bliss*. He also worked in the theatre and was offered small parts on television, including *The Benny Hill Show, The Carol Gibbons Show* and *Variety Bandbox.*

MOORE, ROBERT

Role: Large Man (S3, episode 12: 'Man Hunt') (TV)

As well as a number of television appearances Robert was seen in a handful of films, including playing the First Coroner's Officer in 1947's *Green Fingers*, a police inspector in 1952's *The Ghost Ship, Forces Sweetheart, The Gift Horse, Tiger by the Tail* in 1955, *The Ladykillers* during the same year, Dr Macfarlane in 1962's *Jigsaw* and the father in 1963's *Hide and Seek.*

MOORE, WILLIAM (1917–2000)

Born: Birmingham

Role: Station Master (S6, episode 3: 'The Royal Train') (TV)

William turned to acting after qualifying as an engineering draughtsman. Always interested in amateur dramatics, he began working in the crowd scenes at Birmingham Rep, and liked the experience so much that he decided to make acting his future.

William, who was married to actress Mollie Sugden, has worked extensively on TV and the stage. His credits include: *Z Cars, Softly, Softly, Dombey and Son, The Dick Emery Show, The Cedar Tree, The Fenn Street Gang* and *My Husband and I*. On the small screen he was probably best known as Ronnie Corbett's father in *Sorry!*, and Sergeant Turpin in *Coronation Street*, a role he played for two years.

On stage he appeared in many productions, such as *Great Expectations* and *When We Are Married*. He also taught at Bristol's Old Vic Theatre School.

MORGAN, CHARLES (1909–1994)

Born: Tredegar

Role: 2nd Member of Parliament (S5, episode 2: 'Keep Young and Beautiful') (TV)

A friend of Le Mesurier, who he'd worked with in rep at Croydon during the 1930s, and Lowe, who he knew from the TV series *All Aboard*, in 1958, Charles Morgan worked down the mines before moving to London and joining a repertory company.

Before serving in the RAF during the war, he worked as a film extra and at numerous rep companies around the country. Upon demob, he joined Worthing Rep and stayed eight years, and became the leading man, before moving on to the Savoy Theatre in 1954.

His TV career started shortly after and he went on to appear in numerous comedy shows

Trouble brews when it's announced the king will be passing through Walmington station.

and sitcoms, including *Never the Twain*, *Bless This House*, *Man About the House*, as well as dramas such as *Doomwatch*. He remained busy until a heart attack forced him to reduce his workload. He died aged 85.

MORGAN, ELIZABETH
Born: Llanelli
Roles: Mrs Leonard ('The Armoured Might of Lance Corporal Jones'), Janet King ('Something Nasty in the Vault'), Nurse ('The Recruit'), Housewife ('The Great White Hunter') (radio)

Elizabeth studied English at a London teacher-training college, but gave up the profession to attend the Royal Academy of Music, where she trained in speech and drama. Not long after graduating she was offered a comedy slot on a regular afternoon show for TV Wales and the West, the forerunner of the independent television company, HTV.

Later she became busy doing voice-overs and appearing in various theatres around the country, including Bath. She also worked for the National Theatre and toured American universities with her one-woman shows.

Other TV work includes a spell in *Crossroads* as Rachel Fisher (she also helped write the show for three months), *The Dick Emery Show*, *The Two of Us* and *To Have and To Hold*.

She has also spent many years working for the BBC's Repertory Company on the radio, provided the voices for the famous Angels in *Thunderbirds* and written 25 plays for Radio 4. Nowadays she continues to do voice-overs and writes. After seeing many articles and a book about living in France published, she is now working on her first novel.

MORGAN, VERNE (1900–1984)
Born: Sidcup
Roles: Landlord (S4, episode 2: 'Don't Forget the Diver', S4, episode 6: 'Absent Friends', S6, episode 2: 'My British Buddy'), Farmer (S7, episode 3: 'Gorilla Warfare') (TV)

Verne always wanted to act and upon leaving school got involved in variety shows and concert parties. Primarily a comedian, he had a double-act with his wife, Betty Moore, for many years. He was also a regular in panto before the war during which he joined ENSA. *En route* to the Middle East his ship was torpedoed and he was lucky to survive.

After the war, Verne resumed his acting career and appeared in the West End as well as the occasional film. In 1953 he popped up in *The Limping Man* as Stone, a taxi driver, and during the 1970s in two Hammer productions: *That's Your Funeral*, as a pensioner, and a records clerk in *Man at the Top*.

In addition to *Dad's Army* he had small parts in various shows including *The Best of Benny Hill* (1974), a waiter in an episode of *The Professionals* and a butler in *Shoulder to Shoulder*, a

BBC series about the suffragettes. Verne was also a writer, penning magazine articles, numerous plays and pantomimes for local companies. He died at the age of 84.

MORLEY, DONALD
Born: Richmond-upon-Thames
Role: Glossip (S7, episode 5: 'The Captain's Car') (TV)

Donald enjoyed a full career. On TV he appeared in *Coronation Street* as Walter Fletcher, *Compact*, *The Gold Robbers*, *Freewheelers*, *Emmerdale Farm*, *The Spy Killer*, *Duchess of Duke Street* as a barrister, *Crown Court*, *Going Straight*, *The Sweeney*, *No Place Like Home*, *All Creatures Great and Small* as a bank manager, *Bless This House*, *Van Der Valk*, *Are You Being Served?*, *Open All Hours*, *Bergerac*, *The Brittas Empire* and *Grace and Favour*. He was also seen as Sloane in 'Project Zero', an episode of *The Champions*, and Inspector Clayton in 'Never Trust a Ghost', an episode of *Randall & Hopkirk (Deceased)*.

His film appearances include *Mix Me A Person*, *Catch Us If You Can*, *Blowing Hot and Cold* and *Out of Sight*.

MORTIMER, DORIS (MISS)
Doris works for Jones as cashier in his butcher's shop. Never seen, or heard in the series, she is referred to in 'The Armoured Might of Lance Corporal Jones', and 'Getting the Bird' when Jones tells her how much to charge for Mrs Yeatman's ration. She earns 30 shillings a week.

MORTIMER STREET
While keeping guard on the roof of the church tower, Frazer and Godfrey spot a light flashing from a house on the corner of Mortimer Street. Many of the houses in this street in Walmington are three-storey Victorian terraced houses that have been converted into flats.

MOTHER SUPERIOR, THE
Played by Rachel Thomas (TV)
When her car breaks down in 'Gorilla Warfare' and the mother superior asks Mainwaring and his men for help, they totally ignore her just in case she's a counter agent, out to ruin their plans of succeeding in the weekend exercise.

MRS NOLAN'S
Mentioned in 'Under Fire', this little drapery in Walmington High Street is where Mainwaring and Wilson buy long johns for the cold evenings when they're on guard.

MULLER, CAPTAIN
(See 'U-Boat Captain'.)

MULLEY, JACK
Jack owned and hired out Hodges' greengrocer's lorry for the TV series.

MUM'S ARMY
Recorded: Friday 13/11/70
Original transmission: Friday 20/11/70, 8.00–8.30pm
Original viewing figures: 16.4 million
Repeated: 25/7/71, 3/10/89, 7/2/90 (N Ireland), 12/12/92, 17/12/92 (Wales), 23/11/97

CAST
Arthur Lowe . . . . .Captain Mainwaring
John Le Mesurier . . . . .Sergeant Wilson
Clive Dunn . . . . .Lance Corporal Jones
John Laurie . . . . .Private Frazer
James Beck . . . . .Private Walker
Arnold Ridley . . . . .Private Godfrey
Ian Lavender . . . . .Private Pike
Carmen Silvera . . . . .Mrs Gray
Wendy Richard . . . . .Edith Parish
Janet Davies . . . . .Mrs Pike
Pamela Cundell . . . . .Mrs Fox
Julia Burbury . . . . .Miss Ironside
Rosemary Faith . . . . .Ivy Samways
Melita Manger . . . . .Waitress
Deirdre Costello . . . . .Buffet Attendant
David Gilchrist . . . . .Serviceman
Eleanor Smale . . . . .Mrs Prosser
Jack Le White . . . . .Porter
Platoon: Colin Bean, Hugh Hastings, Vic Taylor, Hugh Cecil, Desmond Cullum-Jones, Leslie Noyes, Freddie Wiles, George Hancock, Frank Godfrey, Freddie White
Servicemen: Eric Stark, Les Conrad, David Melbourne, Peter Wilson
Service Girls: Hillary Martin, Ann Downs, Carol Brett
Customers: Clifford Hemsley, Maria Cope

PRODUCTION TEAM
Script: Jimmy Perry and David Croft
Producer/Director: David Croft
Production Assistant: Phil Bishop
Studio Lighting: George Summers
Studio Sound: Michael McCarthy
Design: Paul Joel
Assistant Floor Manager: Roger Singleton-Turner
Vision Mixer: Clive Doig
Costume Supervisor: George Ward
Make-Up Supervisor: Cynthia Goodwin
Visual Effects: Peter Day

The town's womenfolk want to join the platoon to help with the war effort. Mainwaring thinks it's a good idea because taking on some of the responsibilities currently shouldered by his men will allow more time to prepare for grappling with the enemy.

The following evening the women are interviewed by Mainwaring and Wilson. Applicants include Mrs Fox, Ivy Samways, invited along by Pike, and Edith Parish, Walker's girlfriend. Before the evening is out Mrs Gray turns up unexpectedly, and Mainwaring is smitten with her from the start; he's taken with her attitude and is keen to sign her up.

The evening after that Mainwaring teaches the women the rudiments of footdrill and is forever praising Mrs Gray's contribution. Knowing Fiona Gray often frequents Ann's Pantry, Mainwaring decides to visit the following day and is pleased when he meets her. Remembering her comment that he looks so much better without his glasses, he tries removing them, even though he can't see a thing.

Later on parade, Frazer stirs it up by suggesting Mainwaring is making a fool of himself over Mrs Gray. Edith Parish reports they've been to the cinema three times, and Pike says they have coffee together each morning.

Meanwhile, Mainwaring decides to disband the women's section, except for a few special helpers, but when he discovers Mrs Gray is missing from parade and Ivy Samways saw her heading for the station with two heavy suitcases, he dashes off in pursuit. He meets up with her at the station buffet and opens his heart, imploring her to stay. But with tongues starting to wag, and Mainwaring's reputation with the bank to consider, Fiona thinks it's best she leaves, although she promises to write.

MURPHY, SIGMUND

Played by Ernst Ulman (TV); David Gooderson (radio)

A short, plump continental man with a thick accent, Sigmund has lived in a flat in Mortimer Street for 25 years. In 'Under Fire' he's accused of being a quisling when Frazer and Godfrey spot a light shining from his room. The fact that he cooks with garlic and walks out of the cinema when the national anthem starts adds to the suspicions held by Mainwaring and his men when they go along to investigate the incident. It transpires that he was born in Salzburg but is a naturalised Englishman. His real name is Sigmund Von Schickenhausen, which he changed because of the war. He owns a dachshund called Fritz, who is a nuisance because he often roams into Mrs Keen's flat and chews her slippers. It turns out that Mr 'Siggy' Murphy isn't a spy, and used to be married to Hodges' Auntie Ethel.

MUSEUM CARETAKER

(See 'Jones, George'.)

MUSEUM PIECE

Recorded: Monday 22/4/68 (made in black and white)

Original transmission: Wednesday 7/8/68, 7.00–7.30pm

(This episode was originally planned for transmission on Wednesday 12 June)

Original viewing figures: 6.8 million

Repeated: 24/1/69, 31/12/88 (C4), 21/7/98, 4/8/98, 10/5/99, 29/7/99

CAST

Arthur Lowe . . . . .Captain Mainwaring
John Le Mesurier . . . . .Sergeant Wilson
Clive Dunn . . . . .Lance Corporal Jones

John Laurie . . . . .Private Frazer
James Beck . . . . .Private Walker
Arnold Ridley . . . . .Private Godfrey
Ian Lavender . . . . .Private Pike
Janet Davies . . . . .Mrs Pike
Caroline Dowdeswell . . . . .Janet King
Leon Cortez . . . . .Henry, the milkman
Eric Woodburn . . . . .George Jones,
the Museum Caretaker
Michael Osborne . . . . .Boy Scout
Platoon: Colin Bean, Hugh Hastings, Richard Jacques, Chris Franks, David Seaforth, Alec Coleman, Hugh Cecil, Vic Taylor, Jimmy Mac, Peter Whitaker

PRODUCTION TEAM

Script: Jimmy Perry and David Croft
Producer/Director: David Croft
Production Assistant: Harold Snoad
Studio Lighting: George Summers
Studio Sound: James Cole
Design: Alan Hunter-Craig and Paul Joel
Assistant Floor Manager: Evan King
Vision Mixer: Bob Hallman
Costume Supervisor: George Ward
Make-Up Supervisor: Sandra Exelby

Mainwaring tells Wilson he's concerned the platoon doesn't possess the unthinking obedience required to make an efficient fighting unit. There is further bad news when he finds out it will be a further six weeks before the uniforms and rifles arrive, and to top it all, the Peabody Museum of Historical Army Weapons closes its bank account for the duration because the cura-

tor has joined the navy. Mainwaring suddenly realises they might be able to use the situation to their advantage because the museum may contain equipment that could be put to good use by the Home Guard. As a result, Operation Gun Grab begins, with Mainwaring requisitioning anything he finds useful for his cause. The trouble is that they have to get past the caretaker, who happens to be Jones' 88-year-old father, who's rather cantankerous.

They try a scaling ladder and using a battering ram but to no avail, and with cold water being poured over them, they call it a day. They change tack and try cunning, with Frazer playing a key role, especially as it involves whisky. His job is to tempt Jones Snr out of the museum, while the others nip in and take what equipment they want. They achieve their goal and sneak into the museum but there seems to be little of use until Walker spots a 1901 Chinese Rocket Gun. Back at the church hall Mainwaring is happy with the men's initiative but thinks the gun is too antiquated. When it fires rockets everywhere, he's not so sure.

MUSIC

When it came to using incidental music in the series, David Croft turned to archival recordings instead of commissioning his own compositions. Relying on music from the period undoubtedly complemented the sitcom's feel of authenticity. When an audience survey was conducted by the BBC after the showing of 'The Showing Up of Corporal Jones', back in 1968, it was clear viewers felt the same. The author of the report stated: 'Attention to detail and the inclusion of excerpts from wartime songs … added greatly to the atmosphere of authenticity.'

As well as adding a touch of authenticity, there was another motivation behind Croft's decision to use archival music: money. 'You didn't get much value for money in those days,' David admits. 'I forget the actual conditions, but you could only do something like one programme at a time in a three-hour session, then things were improved and you could record the music for three episodes at a time, but it was still very expensive. So we turned to archival music which turned out to be a terrific asset, making a nostalgic impact on the listener.'

EPISODE-BY-EPISODE GUIDE TO INCIDENTAL MUSIC

Series One
THE MAN AND THE HOUR

RECORDS DUBBED ONTO FILM

'In Torment' composed by Trevor Duncan. Performed by the New Concert Orchestra.

'In the News' composed by Peter Yorke. Performed by the Band of the Royal Netherlands Navy.

'Pig Iron' composed by A Rayner. Performed by the Westway Studio Orchestra.

'Coronet March' composed by Ivor Slaney. Performed by the New Concert Orchestra.

ON TAPE, TRANSFERRED FROM DISCS

'There'll Always be an England' composed by Ross Parker and Hugh Charles. Performed by the Jack Payne Orchestra. Vocals by Robert Ashley.

'There's a Boy Coming Home on Leave' composed by Jimmy Kennedy. Performed by Ambrose and his Orchestra. Vocals by Jack Cooper.

'Wish Me Luck' composed by Harry Parr-Davies. Lyrics by Phil Park. Performed by Gracie Fields with Orchestra.

MUSEUM PIECE

RECORDS DUBBED ONTO FILM

'Three Cheers (March)' composed by Hugo de Groot. Performed by The Celebrity Orchestra.

ON TAPE, TRANSFERRED FROM DISCS

'Seventeen Candles' composed by Strauss, Dale and Miller. Performed by Ambrose and his Orchestra. Vocals by Jack Cooper.

'Let the People Sing' composed by Gay, Eyton and Grand. Performed by Geraldo and his Orchestra. Vocals by Evelyn Laye.

'In the Mood' composed by Garland and Razaf. Performed by Joe Loss and his Band.

'Till the Lights of London Shine Again' composed by Connor and Pola. Performed by Lew Stone and his Band. Vocals by Sam Browne.

COMMAND DECISION

ON TAPE, TRANSFERRED FROM DISCS

'You've Done Something to My Heart' composed by Noel Gay. Lyrics by Ian Grant. Performed by Geraldo and his Orchestra. Vocals by Evelyn Laye.

'If Ever a Heart was in the Right Place' composed by Harry Woods. Performed by Geraldo and his Orchestra. Vocals by Al Bowlly.

'Blue Skies are Round the Corner' composed by Ross Parker and Hugh Charles. Performed by Jack Hylton and his Orchestra.

'It's a Hap, Hap, Happy Day' composed by Al Neiburg, Sammy Timberg and Winston Sharples. Performed by Arthur Askey with Orchestra.

'Goodnight Children Everywhere' composed by Gabby Rogers and Harry Phillips. Performed by Phyllis Robins with Orchestra.

ENEMY WITHIN THE GATES

RECORDS DUBBED ON FILM

'Jack Boot' composed by Peter Franklyn. Performed by Celebrity Symphony Orchestra.

'Crystal Palace March' composed by Hugo de Groot. Performed by Celebrity Symphony Orchestra.

RECORDS DUBBED ON TAPE

'You Never Miss the Old Faces' composed by Hughes and Wallace. Performed by Geraldo and the Savoy Hotel Orchestra. Vocals by Cyril Grantham.

THE SHOWING UP OF CORPORAL JONES

RECORDS DUBBED ON FILM

'Three Cheers March' composed by Hugo de Groot. Performed by The Celebrity Orchestra.

RECORDS DUBBED ON TAPE

'If Ever a Heart was in the Right Place' composed by Harry Woods. Performed by Geraldo and his Orchestra. Vocals by Al Bowlly.

'There'll Always be an England' composed by Parker and Charles. Performed by Jack Payne and his Band. Vocals by Robert Ashley.

'I'm Singing a Song for the Old Folks' composed by Box, Cox and Roberts. Performed by Jack Hylton and his Orchestra.

'Wishing' composed by Boulanger and Kennedy. Performed by Vera Lynn with Fela Sowande at the organ.

'Good Morning' composed by Freed and Herb Brown. Performed by Arthur Askey with Orchestra.

SHOOTING PAINS

RECORDS DUBBED ON FILM

'New Realm March' composed by Ivor Slaney. Performed by Amsterdam Select Orchestra.

'Coronet March' composed by Ivor Slaney. Performed by The Celebrity Orchestra.

'We're Off to See the Wizard' composed by Leigh, Harline and Ned Washington. Performed by Victor Young and his Orchestra. Vocals by The Ken Sarby Singers.

RECORDS DUBBED ON TAPE

'An Apple for the Teacher' composed by Monaco and Burke. Performed by Ambrose and his Orchestra. Vocals by Evelyn Dall.

'I Shall be Waiting' composed by Ross Parker, Hughie Charles and Joe Irwin. Performed by Issy Bonn with Orchestra.

'There'll Always be an England' composed by Parker and Charles. Performed by Joe Loss and his Orchestra. Vocals by Monte Ray.

Series Two
OPERATION KILT

RECORDS DUBBED ON TAPE

'Hi Diddle De Dee' taken from the Disney cartoon, Pinocchio. Composed by Ned Washington. Performed by Jay Wilbur and Orchestra.

'Tiggerty Boo' composed by Hal Halifax. Performed by Joe Loss and his Orchestra.

'Run, Rabbit, Run' composed by Gay and Butler. Performed by Ambrose and his Orchestra. Vocals by Jack Cooper.

'A Nightingale Sang in Berkeley Square' composed by Maschwitz, Sherwin and Strachey. Vocals by Vera Lynn.

THE BATTLE OF GODFREY'S COTTAGE

RECORDS DUBBED ON TAPE

'There'll Always be an England' composed by Parker and Charles. Performed by Joe Loss and his Orchestra.

'If I Only had Wings' composed by Sid Colin and Ronnie Aldrich. Performed by Harry Roy and his Band.

'In an 18th Century Drawing Room' composed by Raymond Scott. Performed by Ambrose and his Orchestra.

During the episode, it was planned that Clive Dunn would sing 'The White Cliffs of Dover' (composed by Burton and Kent). It is unclear whether this scene was ever recorded.

THE LONELINESS OF THE LONG-DISTANCE WALKER

RECORDS DUBBED ON TAPE

'Fools Rush In' composed by Johnny Mercer and Rube Bloom. Performed by Ambrose and his Orchestra.

'Fools Rush In' composed by Johnny Mercer and Rube Bloom. Performed by Carroll Gibbons and his Orchestra.

'I'm Stepping Out With a Memory Tonight' composed by Allie Wrubel and Herb Magidson. Performed by Harry Roy and his Band.

'I've Got My Eyes On You' composed by Cole Porter. Performed by Ambrose and his Orchestra. Vocals by Jack Cooper.

'I'm Nobody's Baby' composed by Milton Ager, Benny Davis and Leslie Santly. Performed by Nat Gonella and his New Georgians.

'There'll Always be an England' composed by Charles and Parker. Performed by Jack Payne and his Orchestra. Vocals by Robert Ashley.

'It's a Lovely Day Tomorrow' composed by Irving Berlin. Performed by Jack Hylton and his Orchestra.

'Tiggerty Boo' composed by Hal Halifax. Performed by Joe Loss and his Orchestra.

SGT WILSON'S LITTLE SECRET

RECORDS DUBBED ON TAPE

'Tiggerty Boo' composed by Hal Halifax. Performed by Joe Loss and his Orchestra.

'I've Got No Strings' composed by Leigh Harline and Ned Washington. Vocals by Pat Kirkwood.

'Whose Baby are You?' composed by Anne Caldwell and Jerome Kern. Vocals by Louise Leight and Will String.

'If I Should Fall in Love Again' composed by Jack Popplewell. Performed by Ambrose and his Orchestra.

'Only Forever' composed by Johnny Burke and James Monaco. Performed by Joe Loss and his Orchestra.

A STRIPE FOR FRAZER

RECORDS DUBBED ON TAPE

'Faithful Forever' composed by Robin and Rainger. Performed by Jack Hylton and his Orchestra.

'A Tisket, A Tasket' composed by Fitzgerald and Feldman. Performed by Joe Loss and his Orchestra.

UNDER FIRE

RECORDS DUBBED ON FILM

'New Realm March' composed by Ivor Slaney. Performed by The Amsterdam Select Orchestra.

'Coronet March' composed by Ivor Slaney. Performed by The Celebrity Orchestra.

'We're Off to See the Wizard' composed by Leigh Harline and Ned Washington. Performed by Victor Young and his Orchestra. Vocals by The Ken Darby Singers.

'Fools Rush In' composed by Johnny Mercer and Rube Bloom.

'The Army, the Navy and the Airforce' composed by Herman Darewski.

Series Three
THE ARMOURED MIGHT OF LANCE CORPORAL JONES

RECORDS DUBBED ONTO TAPE

'It's a Hap-Hap-Happy Day' composed by Freed and Herb Brown. Performed by Arthur Askey with Orchestra.

'I Came, I Saw, I Conga'd' composed by Frank Weldon, Al Neiburg and Sammy Timberg. Performed by Nat Gonella and his Georgians. Vocals by Stella Moya.

'Hey Little Hen' composed by Butler and Gay. Performed by Donald Peers with Jay Wilbur and his Orchestra.

LIVE FROM THE STUDIO

'I Dreamt I Dwelt in Marble Halls' composed by Balfe. Vocals by Clive Dunn and James Beck.

'Heil Hitler, Ra-Ra-Ra, Ya-Ya-Ya' composed by M Crick. Vocals by Clive Dunn and James Beck.

'Sometimes I Feel Like a Motherless Child'. Vocals by Clive Dunn.

BATTLE SCHOOL

RECORDED ON FILM

'Who Do You Think You Are Kidding, Mr Hitler?' composed by Jimmy Perry and Derek Taverner. Whistled by the cast.

'We'll Meet Again' composed by Parker and Charles. Vocals by Arthur Lowe, John Le Mesurier, Clive Dunn, John Laurie, James Beck, Arnold Ridley, Ian Lavender and Colin Bean.

RECORDED ON TAPE

'Chattanooga Choo Choo' composed by Gordon and Warren. Performed by Glenn Miller and his Orchestra.

'The Girl Who Loves a Soldier' composed by Gay and Butler. Performed by Billy Cotton and his Band, with Vocal.

'Little Drummer Boy' composed by Noel and Pelosi. Performed by Lew Stone and his Band. Vocals by Al Bowlly.

'The King is Still in London' composed by Hunter and Charles. Performed by Billy Cotton and his Band. With vocals.

'Fools Rush In' composed by Mercer and Bloom. Performed by Carroll Gibbons and his Orchestra. Vocals by Anne Lenner.

THE LION HAS 'PHONES

RECORDS DUBBED ON TAPE

'Carry On' composed by Hamilton. Performed by Ambrose and his Orchestra.

'Tiggerty Boo' composed by Hal Halifax. Performed by Joe Loss and his Orchestra.

'A Nightingale Sang in Berkeley Square' composed by Maschwitz, Sherwin and Strachey. Performed by Joe Loss and his Orchestra.

'Flying Squadron' (Band 1, Side B) composed by Jack Shaindlin.

SOMETHING NASTY IN THE VAULT

LIVE IN STUDIO

'Jubilate Deo' performed by Fred Tomlinson and four singers (Kate Forge, Eilidh McNab, Andrew Daye and Arthur Lewis).

'Nunc Dimittis' performed by Fred Tomlinson and four singers (see above).

ROOM AT THE BOTTOM

RECORDS DUBBED ON TAPE

'This is Worth Fighting For' composed by De Lang and Stept. Performed by Hutch.

'You Don't Have to Tell Me, I Know' composed by Noel and Pelosi. Performed by Harry Roy and his Band. Vocals by Jean Farrar.

'Amapola' composed by Lacalle and Gamse. Performed by The Royal Air Force Dance Orchestra.

'I Yi Yi Yi Yi Like You Very Much' composed by Gordon and Warren. Performed by Harry Roy and his Band. Vocals by Harry Roy.

'The London I Love' composed by Purcell and Posford. Performed by Joe Loss and his Orchestra.

'When They Sound the Last All-Clear' composed by Charles and Elton. Performed by Vera Lynn accompanied by Mantovani and his Orchestra.

'Who am I?' composed by Styne and Bullock. Performed by Oscar Rabin and his Orchestra.

BIG GUNS

RECORDS DUBBED ON TAPE

'You Say the Sweetest Things, Baby' composed by Harry Warren and Mack Gordon. Performed by Billy Cotton and his Band. With vocals.

THE DAY THE BALLOON WENT UP

RECORDS DUBBED ON TAPE

'Furioso No 1' composed by Tony Lowry. Performed by The Crawford Light Orchestra.

'Amy, Wonderful Amy' composed by Horatio Nicholls and Joseph Gilbert. Performed by Jack Hylton and his Orchestra.

WAR DANCE

RECORDS DUBBED ON TAPE

'Let the People Sing' composed by Noel Gay, Eyton and Grant. Performed by Jack Hylton and his Orchestra. With vocal refrain.

'It's a Lovely Day, Tomorrow' composed by Irving Berlin. Performed by Carroll Gibbons and his Band.

'Oh Johnny' composed by Rose and Olmen. Performed by Pat Kirkwood with Orchestra.

'Love in Bloom' composed by Robin and Rainger. Performed by Billy Scott-Coomber.

LIVE FROM STUDIO

'Trees', 'Deep Purple', 'Flat Foot Floogie', 'Monday Night at Eight', 'Big Hearted Arthur they call me', 'In a Monastery Garden', 'He's a Fine Old English Gentleman' all performed by Hugh Hastings, Mike Pullen and Jack Whiteford.

MENACE FROM THE DEEP

RECORDS DUBBED ON TAPE

'If I Had My Way' composed by Klein and Kendis. Performed by Ambrose and his Orchestra. Vocals by Jack Cooper.

'I Shall be Waiting' composed by Parker, Charles and Irwin. Performed by Jack Payne and his Band. Vocal chorus by Billy Scott Coomber and the Singing Grenadiers.

'Bless 'em All' composed by Stillman, Hughes and Lake. Performed by Billy Cotton and his Band. With vocal chorus.

'So Deep is the Night' composed by Chopin, Nelfi and Miller. Performed by Ambrose and his Orchestra. Vocals by Jack Cooper.

BRANDED

RECORDS DUBBED ON TAPE

'Only Forever' composed by James Monaco. Performed by Joe Loss and his Orchestra.

'I'm Nobody's Baby' composed by Milton Ager and Leslie Santly. Performed by Nat Gonella and his New Georgians.

'It's a Blue World Without You'.

'Faithful Forever' composed by Robert Wright and G Forest.

MAN HUNT

RECORDS DUBBED ON TAPE

'Watch the Birdie' composed by Don Raye and Gene De Paul. Performed by Jack Simpson's Sextette. Vocal chorus by Betty Kent.

'Walking Through Mocking Bird Lane' composed by Peters and Jones. Performed by Al Bowlly.

NO SPRING FOR FRAZER

RECORDS DUBBED ON TAPE

'Scatterbrain' composed by Burke, Keene – Bean and Masters. Performed by Jack Hylton and his Orchestra. Vocals by Sam Brown.

'That's For Me' composed by Charles and Towers. Performed by Beryl Davies.

'I Shall Always Remember You Smiling' composed by Parker and Charles. Performed by Ambrose and his Orchestra. Vocal Vera Lynn.

'Today I Feel So Happy' composed by Abrahams. Performed by Jack Hylton and his Orchestra.

SONS OF THE SEA

RECORDS DUBBED ON TAPE

'The Last Time I Saw Paris' composed by Hammerstein 2nd and Kern. Performed by Noel Coward with Orchestra.

'Little Sir Echo' composed by Smith, Fearis, Girard and Marsala. Performed by Ambrose and his Orchestra. Vocal chorus by Vera Lynn and Denny Dennis.

Series Four
THE BIG PARADE

RECORDS DUBBED ON FILM

'Teddy Bears' Picnic' composed by Kennedy and Bratton. Performed by Henry Hall and his Orchestra, with chorus.

'Teddy Bears' Picnic' composed by Kennedy and Bratton. Performed by the Belgrave Salon Orchestra.

'In the News' composed by Peter Yorke. Performed by the Band of the Royal Netherlands Navy.

RECORDS DUBBED ON TAPE

'Tomorrow's World Belongs to You' composed by Shelly, Karel and Mayne. Performed by Issy Bonn.

DON'T FORGET THE DIVER

RECORDS DUBBED ON TAPE

'When that Man is Dead and Gone' composed by Irving Berlin. Performed by Bebe Daniels (vocal), accompanied by Jay Wilbur and his Band.

'Fun and Games' composed by Connor and Sherwin. Performed by Harry Roy and his Band with vocal chorus.

BOOTS, BOOTS, BOOTS

RECORDS DUBBED ON TAPE

'Boots, Boots, Boots' words by Rudyard Kipling. Music by J McCall.

'I Came, I Saw, I Conga'd' composed by Weldon. Performed by Nat Gonella and his Georgians. Vocals by Stella Moya.

'If I Had a Talking Picture of You' composed by Ray Henderson and Nacio-Herb Brown. Performed by Ambrose and his Orchestra.

'You Don't Have to Tell Me' composed by Noel and Pelosi. Performed by Harry Roy and his Band. Vocals by Jean Farrar.

'Sand in My Shoes' composed by Robin and Rainger. Performed by Carroll Gibbons and the Savoy Hotel Orpheans. Vocals by Leslie Douglas.

DON'T FENCE ME IN

RECORDS DUBBED ON TAPE

'A Nightingale Sang in Berkeley Square' composed by Maschwitz and Sherwin. Performed by New Faces, with Leslie Hutchinson at the piano.

'Don't Fence Me In' composed by Cole Porter. Performed by Bing Crosby with The Andrews Sisters. With Vic Shoen and his Orchestra.

ABSENT FRIENDS

RECORD DUBBED ON TAPE

'Thanks to Love' composed by Connor and Sherwin. Performed by Harry Roy and his Band, with vocal chorus.

PUT THAT LIGHT OUT!

RECORD DUBBED ON TAPE

'When the Lights Go On Again (all over the world)' composed by Benjemen. Performed by Issy Bonn with orchestral accompaniment.

THE TWO AND A HALF FEATHERS

RECORDED ON TAPE AND DUBBED ON FILM

'Scheherazade' composed by Rimsky-Korsakov. Performed by Czech Philharmonic Orchestra, conducted by Zdenek Chalabala.

RECORD DUBBED ON TAPE

'The Old Brigade' composed by Barri and Weatherley. Performed by Peter Dawson and Orchestra.

MUM'S ARMY

RECORDS DUBBED ON TAPE

'Run, Rabbit, Run' composed by Noel Gay. Performed by Gracie Fields with the troops.

'Love in Bloom' composed by Robin and Rainger. Performed by Bing Crosby with Irving Aaronson and his Commanders.

THE TEST

RECORDS DUBBED ON TAPE

'Country Garden' composed by Percy Grainger. Performed by the Band of H M Welsh Guards, conducted by Lieutenant T S Chandler LRAM, ARCM, PSM.

'There'll Always be an England' composed by Parker and Charles. Performed by Jack Payne and his Band. Vocal chorus by Robert Ashley.

'There'll Always be an England' composed by Parker and Charles. Performed by Joe Loss and his Concert Orchestra. Featuring Monte Rey.

A WILSON (MANAGER)?

ON RECORD, PLAYED OVER FILM INSERT

Piano concerto No 1 in B flat minor op 23 (1st movement) composed by Tchaikovsky. Performed by Katchen/London Symphony Orchestra, conducted by Pierino Gamba.

RECORDS DUBBED ON TAPE

'Waltzing in the Clouds' composed by Stolz and Kahn. Performed by Deanna Durbin with Charles Previn and his Orchestra.

'I'll Never Smile Again' composed by Lowe. Performed by Tony Martin.

'Sergeant of the Line' composed by Squire.

UNINVITED GUESTS

RECORD DUBBED ON TAPE

'I've Got No Strings' composed by Ned Washington. Performed by Pat Kirkwood.

FALLEN IDOL

RECORDED ON TAPE AND DUBBED ONTO FILM

'Furioso No 1' composed by Tony Lowry. Performed by The Crawford Light Orchestra.

RECORDS DUBBED ON TAPE

'It's a Hap, Hap, Happy Day' composed by Neilburg, Sammy Timberg and Winston Sharples. Performed by Arthur Askey and Orchestra.

'Warsaw Concerto' composed by Richard Addinsell. Performed by the Melachrino Orchestra, conducted by G Melachrino. Solo pianist: William Hill-Bowen.

'Chattanooga Choo, Choo' composed by Gordon and Warren. Performed by The Andrews Sisters.

Christmas Special
BATTLE OF THE GIANTS

RECORDS DUBBED ON TAPE

'There's a Land of Begin Again' composed by Parker and Charles. Performed by Jay Wilbur and his Band with Jack Cooper (vocal chorus).

'There'll Always be an England' composed by Parker and Charles. Performed by Jack Payne and his Band with Robert Ashley (vocals).

'Country Gardens' composed by Percy Grainger. Performed by Band of H M Welsh Guards.

'Lords of the Air' arranged by North and Burnaby. Performed by Jack Hylton and Orchestra.

'The Little Boy that Santa Claus Forgot' composed by Carr, Connor and Leach. Performed by Issy Bonn with Orchestra.

'Hush, Hush, Hush, Here Comes the Bogey Man' composed by Lowton and Benson. Performed by Henry Hall and his Orchestra.

'Furioso No 1' composed by Tony Lowry. Performed by the Crawford Light Orchestra.

Series Five
ASLEEP IN THE DEEP

RECORDS DUBBED ON TAPE

'Who Are You A-Shovin Off?' composed by Arkell and Gay. Performed by Lupino Lane and Orchestra.

'Without a Word of Warning' composed by Gordon and Revel. Performed by Ambrose and his Orchestra.

'Let the People Sing' composed by Gay, Eyton and Grant. Performed by Evelyn Laye with Geraldo and Orchestra.

'Rule Brittania' performed by the King's Military Band.

KEEP YOUNG AND BEAUTIFUL

RECORDS DUBBED ON TAPE

'Keep Young and Beautiful' composed by Al Dubin and Harry Warren. Performed by Harry Roy and his Orchestra. From The Mayfair Hotel with vocal refrain.

'I'd Know You Anywhere' composed by Jimmy McHugh and Johnny Mercer. Performed by Bob Crosby and his Orchestra. Vocals by Bonnie King.

A SOLDIER'S FAREWELL

RECORDS DUBBED ON TAPE

'Changing Scenes' composed by Sidney Torch. Performed by The Queen's Light Hall Orchestra.

'1812 Overture' composed by Tchaikovsky. Performed by the London Symphony Orchestra with the Grenadier Guards.

'Romeo and Juliet Fantasy Overture' composed by Tchaikovsky. Performed by the Vienna Symphony Orchestra.

'Lords of the Air' composed by North and Burnaby. Performed by Harold Williams and Orchestra.

'Why Don't We Do This More Often' composed by Newman-Wrubel. Performed by Geraldo and Orchestra.

'You Oughta be in Pictures' composed by Heyman and Suesse. Performed by Al Bowlly.

GETTING THE BIRD

RECORDS DUBBED ON TAPE

'Sing-a-song of London' composed by Kennedy and Carr. Performed by Ambrose and his Orchestra. Vocal chorus by Sam Browne.

'In the Chapel in the Moonlight' composed by Hill. Performed by Ambrose and his Orchestra. Vocal chorus by Sam Browne.

'Smile When You Say Goodbye' composed by Harry Park-Davies. Performed by Ambrose and his Orchestra. Vocal chorus by Sam Browne.

'It Looks Like Rain in Cherry Blossom Lane' composed by Mercer and Whiting. Performed by Ambrose and his Orchestra. Vocal chorus by Sam Browne.

THE DESPERATE DRIVE OF CORPORAL JONES

'Adolf' composed by Annette Mills. Performed by

Billy Cotton and his Band, with Chorus.

'There'll Come Another Day' composed by Stranks and Pattison. Performed by Ambrose and his Orchestra, with Chorus.

'Chase-Struggle-Agitato No 7'. Performed by Scherzo Dramatique Orchestra.

IF THE CAP FITS…

RECORDS DUBBED ON TAPE

'Adolf' composed by A Mills. Performed by Ambrose and his Orchestra.

Music used (visual): improvisation performed by Pipe Major Donald MacLeod.

THE KING WAS IN HIS COUNTING HOUSE

RECORDS DUBBED ON TAPE

'Pennies from Heaven' composed by Johnston and Burke. Performed by Ambrose and his Orchestra.

'Blue Champagne' composed by Brady Watts and Ryerson. Performed by Geraldo and his Orchestra.

ALL IS SAFELY GATHERED IN

RECORDS DUBBED ON TAPE

'Hey Little Hen' composed by Butler and Gay.

'Sergeant Sally' composed by Kennedy and Evans. Performed by Bunny Boyle with Orchestra.

'Calling All Workers' composed by Eric Coates. Performed by Eric Coates and Orchestra.

WHEN DID YOU LAST SEE YOUR MONEY?

RECORDS DUBBED ON TAPE

'Money is the Root of All Evil' composed by Whitney and Kramer. Performed by Paul Fenoulehet and The Skyrockets' Dance Orchestra.

'I Want Some Money' composed by Confrey. Performed by The Gilberts with Orchestra.

'With Her Head Tucked Underneath Her Arm' composed by Weston, Lee and Weston. Performed by Billy Cotton and his Band, with Choir.

'Moonlight Becomes You' composed by Burke and Van Heusen. Performed by Carroll Gibbons and the Savoy Hotel Orpheans.

BRAIN VERSUS BRAWN

RECORDS DUBBED ON TAPE

'Furioso No 1' composed by Tony Lowry. Performed by Crawford Light Orchestra.

RECORDS TRANSFERRED TO TAPE AND RECORDED ONTO VTR

'Jolly Good Company' composed by Wallace. Performed by Jack and Claude Hulbert.

'Any Rags, Bottles and Bones' (from *Band Waggon*) Performed by Arthur Askey, Richard Murdoch and Company.

A BRUSH WITH THE LAW

RECORDS DUBBED ON TAPE

'Eleven More Months and Ten More Days' composed by Fields and Hall. Performed by Ambrose and his

Orchestra at the Mayfair Hotel.

'My Devotion' composed by Hillman and Napton. Performed by Ambrose and his Orchestra. Vocals by Ann Shelton.

ROUND AND ROUND WENT THE GREAT BIG WHEEL

RECORDS TRANSFERRED TO TAPE AND DUBBED ON VTR

'Goodbye Sally' composed by Riscoe and Borelli. Performed by Arthur Riscoe.

'Follow the White Line' composed by Burnaby and North. Performed by Arthur Riscoe.

'If I Only Had Wings'. Sung by Bebe Daniels.

'Cortege' composed by Arnold Steck. Performed by the New Era Symphonic Band, conducted by Michael John.

'Hi, Gang!' (Forces programme) – BBC programme, side 2, 20/10/40. A 15-second extract was used.

Series Six
THE DEADLY ATTACHMENT

RECORDS DUBBED ON TAPE

'Whistle While You Work' composed by Churchill and McRey. Performed by Billy Cotton and his Band.

'I've Got My Eye on You' composed by Cole Porter. Performed by Geraldo and the Savoy Hotel Orchestra.

'All Over the Place' composed by Eyton and Gay. Performed by Jay Wilbur and his Band.

MY BRITISH BUDDY

RECORDS DUBBED ON TAPE

'My British Buddy' composed by Irving Berlin. Performed by Ambrose and his Orchestra with Bob Arden (vocal).

THE ROYAL TRAIN

RECORDS DUBBED ON TAPE

'The King is Still in London' composed by Campbell and Hunter. Performed by Carroll Gibbons and the Savoy Orpheans.

THE HONOURABLE MAN

RECORDS DUBBED ON TAPE

'Russian Rose' composed by Miller and Charles. Performed by Ambrose and his Orchestra. Vocals by Ann Shelton.

'If I Had My Way' composed by Klein and Klendie. Performed by Carroll Gibbons and the Savoy Orchestra.

THINGS THAT GO BUMP IN THE NIGHT

RECORDS DUBBED ON TAPE

'Deep Purple' composed by Parish and De Rose. Performed by Jack Hylton and his Orchestra.

'They Ride By Night' composed by Charles Williams. Performed by the Queen's Hall Light Orchestra.

'Violence' composed by Robert Mersey. Performed by the Queen's Hall Light Orchestra.

'Suspicion' composed by Charles Williams. Performed by the Queen's Hall Light Orchestra.

Series Seven
EVERYBODY'S TRUCKING

RECORD DUBBED TO TAPE

Bliss Suite 'Things to Come' composed by Arthur Bliss. Performed by London Symphony Orchestra, conducted by Sir Arthur Bliss.

GORILLA WARFARE

RECORD DUBBED ON TAPE

'Tiptoe Thro' the Tulips With Me' composed by Joe Burke and Al Dubin. Performed by Arthur Lowe.

THE GODIVA AFFAIR

RECORDS DUBBED ON TAPE

'Don't Sit Under the Apple Tree' composed by Brown, Tobias and Stept. Performed by Billy Cotton and his Band.

'Cocktails For Two' composed by Johnston and Coslow. Performed by Carroll Gibbons and the Savoy Orpheans.

'Now It Can Be Told' composed by Irving Berlin. Performed by Lew Stone and his Band. Vocals by Al Bowlly.

'Jealousy' composed by Jacob Gade. Performed by Mantovani and his Orchestra.

'Yes We Have No Bananas' composed by Silver and Cohn. Performed by Brass Band.

'Entry of the Gladiators' composed by Fucik. Performed by Brass Band.

MUSIC PLAYED LIVE

Morris dance tunes composed by Cecil Sharp and Herbert Macilwaine. Performed by Peter Honri.

THE CAPTAIN'S CAR

RECORD DUBBED ON TAPE

'Pardon My English' composed by Carter and Ellis. Performed by Frances Day and the Saville Theatre Orchestra.

'The Last Time I Saw Paris' composed by Hammerstein and Kern. Performed by Ambrose and his Orchestra.

MUSIC SANG ON FILM

'The Marseillais' performed by the Thetford Church Choir.

TURKEY DINNER

RECORDS DUBBED ON TAPE

'Turkey in the Straw' composed by Maurice Baron (traditional arrangement). Performed by Harry Davidson and his Orchestra.

'There'll Always Be an England' composed by Charles and Parker. Performed by Jack Payne and his Band. Vocals by Robert Ashley.

Series Eight
RING DEM BELLS

RECORD DUBBED ON TAPE

'You Oughta Be In Pictures' composed by Heyman and Suesse. Performed by Ray Noble and his Orchestra.

WHEN YOU'VE GOT TO GO

RECORDS DUBBED ON TAPE

'If I Only Had Wings' composed by Sid Colin and Ronnie Aldrich. Performed by Geraldo and the Savoy Hotel Orchestra.

'When They Sound the Last All-clear' composed by Charles and Elton. Performed by Charles and Elton. Performed by Billy Cotton and his Band. With vocal chorus.

IS THERE HONEY STILL FOR TEA?

RECORD DUBBED ON TAPE

'Sing Everybody Sing' composed by Long. Performed by Billy Cotton and his Band. With vocal chorus.

RECORDS DUBBED ON FILM

'Follow the White Line' composed by Burnaby and North. Performed by Billy Cotton and his Band. With vocal chorus.

'Country Gardens' composed by Artock and Grainger. Performed by The Light Music Society Orchestra.

COME IN, YOUR TIME IS UP

RECORDS DUBBED TO TAPE

'Adolf' composed by Annette Mills. Performed by Billy Cotton and his Band. With vocal chorus.

HIGH FINANCE

RECORD DUBBED ON TAPE

'Follow the White Line' composed by Burnaby and North. Performed by Billy Cotton and his Band. With vocal chorus.

'Sing, Everybody, Sing' composed by Long. Performed by Billy Cotton and his Band. With vocal chorus.

THE FACE ON THE POSTER

RECORD DUBBED ON TAPE

'That Started It' composed by Will, Eyton and Gay. Performed by Billy Cotton and his Band. With vocal chorus.

Christmas Special
MY BROTHER AND I

'We Must All Stick Together' composed by Wallace and Butler. Performed by Billy Cotton and his Band. With vocal chorus.

Series Nine
WAKE-UP WALMINGTON

RECORDS DUBBED ON TAPE

'We Must All Stick Together' composed by Wallace and Butler. Performed by Billy Cotton and his Band. With vocal chorus.

'You Started Something' composed by Robin and Rainger. Performed by The Royal Air Force Dance Orchestra. Vocal chorus by J Miller.

'Moonlight Becomes You' composed by Van Heusen and Burke. Performed by Ambrose and his Orchestra. Vocal refrain by Leslie Douglas. Taken from *The Road to Morocco*.

THE MAKING OF PRIVATE PIKE

RECORDS DUBBED ON TAPE

'Carry On, On the Home Front' composed by Jimmy Perry and David Croft. Performed by Bill Pertwee, Frank Williams, Edward Sinclair, Pamela Cundell, Janet Davies, Joan Cooper and ensemble. Taken from side one of the Warner Brothers' LP *Dad's Army* (LP56186).

'Curtain Up' composed by Sidney Torch. Performed by The Melodi Light Orchestra, conducted by Ole Jensen. (Side 1, band 9 of *Crime Cameos*.)

'Chord into Chord' composed by Charles Williams. Performed by The Melodi Light Orchestra, conducted by Ole Jensen. (Side 2, band 1 of *Dramatic Story*.)

'I Live in Grosvenor Square' (film soundtrack from EMI Elstree).

KNIGHTS OF MADNESS

RECORDS DUBBED ON TAPE

'Let's Call the Whole Thing Off' composed by Gershwin. Performed by Ambrose and his Orchestra. Vocal chorus by Sam Browne and Evelyn Dall.

'Lords of the Air' composed by Burnaby and North. Performed by Jack Payne and his Band. Vocal chorus by Robert Ashley.

'Smoke Gets in Your Eyes' composed by Otto Harbach and Jerome Kern. Performed by Ambrose and his Orchestra, with vocal chorus.

RECORDS DUBBED ON FILM

'Skater's Waltz (Les Patineurs)' composed by Emile Waldteufel. Performed by The Foden Motor Works Band. From *Marching and Waltzing*.

'Marching Strings' composed by Marshall Ross. Performed by 1109 Thetford Squadron, ATC.

'Willow Tree', 'Bean Setting' and 'Shooting' (traditional) played on whistle by Jill Slee for the Morris dance sequence.

THE MISER'S HOARD

RECORDS DUBBED ON TAPE

'Pennies From Heaven' composed by Johnston and Burke. Performed by Ambrose and his Orchestra. Vocals by Sam Browne.

'And That Started It' composed by Winn, Eyton and Gay. Performed by Joe Loss and his Band.

'You Are My Sunshine' composed by Davis and Mitchell. Performed by The Andrews Sisters.

'One, Two, Button Your Shoe' composed by Johnston and Burke. Performed by Ambrose and his Orchestra. Vocals by Sam Browne.

'With Her Head Tucked Underneath Her Arm' composed by Weston, Lee and Weston. Performed by Billy Cotton and his Band.

NUMBER ENGAGED

RECORDS DUBBED TO TAPE

'Tristesse' composed by Chopin, Nelfi and Miller. Performed by Alfred Piccaver.

'Dream Lover' composed by Schertzinger. Performed by Olive Groves.

'Here We Are Again' composed by C Knight. Performed by Tommy Handley from *Let's Join in the Chorus*.

NEVER TOO OLD

RECORDS DUBBED TO TAPE

'Only Forever' composed by James Monaco. Performed by Geraldo and the Savoy Hotel Orchestra.

'In an 18th Century Drawing Room' composed by Raymond Scott. Performed by Ambrose and his Orchestra.

'There'll Always Be an England' composed by Parker and Charles. Performed by Jack Payne and his Band.

'Love is the Sweetest Thing' composed by Ray Noble. Performed by Al Bowlly.

'Wedding March' composed by Wagner. Performed by Ole Jensen.

Sketches for the annual *Christmas Night with the Stars*: 1972

BROADCAST TO THE EMPIRE

A programme of Christmas Greetings broadcast throughout the empire was played during the sketch, narrated by Howard Marshall.

MY BRITISH BUDDY

Recorded: Friday 8/6/73

Original transmission: Wednesday 7/11/73, 6.50–7.20pm

Original viewing figures: 12.5 million

Repeated: 2/5/74, 12/3/91, 25/9/93, 24/10/93 (Wales), 21/2/97

CAST

Arthur Lowe	Captain Mainwaring
John Le Mesurier	Sergeant Wilson
Clive Dunn	Lance Corporal Jones
John Laurie	Private Frazer
James Beck	Private Walker
Arnold Ridley	Private Godfrey
Ian Lavender	Private Pike
Bill Pertwee	Chief Warden Hodges

'My British Buddy'

'My British Buddy'

Alan Tilvern . . . . .US Colonel
Frank Williams . . . . .Vicar
Edward Sinclair . . . . .Verger
Janet Davies . . . . .Mrs Pike
Wendy Richard . . . . .Shirley
Pamela Cundell . . . . .Mrs Fox
Verne Morgan . . . . .Landlord
Talfryn Thomas . . . . .Mr Cheeseman
Suzanne Kerchiss . . . . .Ivy Samways
Robert Raglan . . . . .Colonel
Blain Fairman . . . . .US Sergeant
Platoon: Colin Bean, George Hancock, Michael Moore,
Desmond Cullum-Jones, Evan Ross, Freddie White,
Freddie Wiles, Roger Bourne, Leslie Noyes,
William Gossling
US Soldiers: Steve Kelly, Hugh Elton, Michael Stevens,
Douglas Rowe, Clinton Morris, John Cannon,
Danny Lyons

PRODUCTION TEAM
Script: Jimmy Perry and David Croft
Producer/Director: David Croft
Production Assistant: Gordon Pert
Studio Lighting: Howard King
Studio Sound: Michael McCarthy
Design: Paul Joel
Assistant Floor Managers: Peter Fitton and Tony
Newman
Vision Mixer: Dave Hanks
Costume Supervisor: Susan Wheal
Make-Up Supervisor: Anna Chesterman

Mainwaring informs the platoon that the Americans have joined the battle against Hitler, and a small advance party will be arriving in Walmington-on-Sea at the weekend; it's up to them to make the Yanks feel welcome. Jones suggests inviting them to a darts match at The Red Lion, a typical evening in a traditional English pub – the women folk can come, too.

While the platoon and Mrs Pike, Mrs Fox, Shirley and Pike's girlfriend, Ivy, wait for the Americans at the pub, Mr Cheeseman turns up with his camera. He's writing a series of articles for the *Eastbourne Gazette*, and tells Mainwaring he wants to take a photo.

As the Americans arrive, the flashgun goes off just as Mainwaring gives his welcome speech. When he tells them to relax and make themselves at home, they rush off and sit with the womenfolk. The Americans are having a ball with the ladies, much to the platoon's disgust. Tension starts to rise when Mainwaring buys the Colonel a pint and he spits it out because it's warm, and when he can't get a scotch on the rocks, he insults their hospitality. Mainwaring sticks up for the British, but when Hodges insults the Americans, a punch is thrown, which accidentally catches Mainwaring, just as Cheeseman clicks his camera. A perfect picture for the local paper.

GHQ orders Mainwaring, who's sporting a black eye, to make a public apology because they're concerned the Nazi propaganda machine will have a field day. It seems Mainwaring's men aren't entirely innocent: when Mainwaring asks them about the night it materialises they played an active part in the fight.

But it looks like Mainwaring will be saved the embarrassment of having to apologise when the American Colonel arrives at the church hall office offering the olive branch, admitting he didn't realise what the British had endured since the war began. The *Gazette* photographer is ready with his flash. The Americans hand out chocolate bars but when Jones realises Mrs Fox has befriended the Colonel he insults the American, who, in turn, swings out, once again catching Mainwaring in the process. Another scoop for the *Eastbourne Gazette*!

MY BROTHER AND I

Recorded: Friday 23 and Saturday 24/5/75
Original transmission: Friday 26/12/75, 6.05–6.45pm
Original viewing figures: 13.6 million
Repeated: 29/5/76, 31/12/80, 25/12/89, 20/8/93,
11/3/00

CAST
Arthur Lowe . . . . .Captain Mainwaring
John Le Mesurier . . . . .Sergeant Wilson
Clive Dunn . . . . .Lance Corporal Jones
John Laurie . . . . .Private Frazer
Arnold Ridley . . . . .Private Godfrey
Ian Lavender . . . . .Private Pike
Bill Pertwee . . . . .Chief Warden Hodges
Frank Williams . . . . .Vicar
Edward Sinclair . . . . .Verger
Penny Irving . . . . .Chambermaid
Arnold Diamond . . . . .The Major-General
Colin Bean . . . . .Private Sponge
Platoon: Desmond Cullum-Jones, George Hancock,
Michael Moore, Freddie White, Evan Ross, Leslie Noyes,
Roger Bourne, Freddie Wiles, Hugh Cecil

PRODUCTION TEAM
Script: Jimmy Perry and David Croft
Producer/Director: David Croft
Production Assistant: Jo Austin
Studio Lighting: Howard King
Studio Sound: Alan Machin
Design: Robert Berk
Assistant Floor Manager: Anne Ogden
Vision Mixer: Angela Beveridge
Costume Designer: Mary Husband
Make-Up Artist: Sylvia Thornton

The Home Guard officers of the district are throwing a sherry party for various local civic dignitaries and officers of surrounding units, and Mainwaring has volunteered to play host with Jones' section acting as stewards.

Frazer, meanwhile, is missing the night's parade because he's been away on business in Eastbourne, interviewing a client. On his way home, he sits in the same railway compartment as a red-faced, garishly dressed man who has a striking resemblance to Captain Mainwaring. He's a salesman in jokes and carnival novelties, and when he announces himself as Barry Mainwaring, Frazer's ears prick up. He asks whether his father was a master tailor in Eastbourne and he laughs, stating that he owned a little draper's shop in East Street with workers' clothes hanging up outside. Frazer discovers the man is Mainwaring's brother and that they have a strained relationship. Barry tells Frazer he's on his way to see George to reclaim a gold watch. Barry says that he looked after his father until his death, but that George had taken the watch.

Frazer agrees to tell Mainwaring he met his drunk brother on the train, and he also delights in telling the rest of the platoon about his meeting. Captain Mainwaring will be pleased to see

'My Brother and I'

Barry out of Walmington as soon as possible, but he agrees to meet him at The Red Lion. George tells his brother that he won't give him the watch, so Barry threatens to come round to the sherry party and embarrass him. George then agrees to give Barry the watch so long as he leaves Walmington.

At the sherry party, a drunken Barry Mainwaring turns up, and when the other guests arrive the men usher him into the side office. Mainwaring, when he finds out, asks Jones, Frazer and Pike to get Barry out of the office and as far away from the party as possible. Barry is too big to push through the window so they plan to get him out in a cupboard. Wilson retrieves the watch for Mainwaring, but George takes pity on Barry and asks Wilson to give it back to him and see him off on the train.

NAAFI GIRL, THE
Played by Pamela Manson (TV)

In 'We Know Our Onions', the NAAFI girl takes tea to Mainwaring and his men during the weekend efficiency test, only to find herself being attacked by the Home Guard.

NAUGHTY JANE, THE
This 15-foot rowing boat is owned by Mr Johnson, who used to run pleasure trips, taking people round the lighthouse before the war. When he dies his bank account is overdrawn by £33 12s 6d, so the boat becomes the property of the Swallow Bank. Instead of selling it to offset the overdraft, Mainwaring plans using it for river patrols. It's moored just a few miles up river from Walmington, and some members of the platoon try it out. But the idea falls flat when they find themselves drifting out to sea, lost in fog. The boat features in the episode 'Sons of the Sea'.

NAVAL OFFICER, THE
Played by John D Collins (film)

Lieutenant Short arrives at the church during the closing scenes of the film. He considers, along with all the other officials, what to do about the German airmen who are holding hostages in the church hall, but the enterprising Captain Mainwaring has already risked his life to bring the incident to a close.

NAZI CO-PILOT, THE
Played by Franz Van Norde (film)

This character co-pilots the German reconnaissance plane which is brought down near Walmington-on-Sea while on an important mission.

NAZI GENERAL, THE
Played by Paul Dawkins (film)

The Nazi General prepares his invasion plans throughout the film.

NAZI ORDERLY, THE
Played by Sam Kydd (film)

Assigned to the Nazi General, the orderly's duties include driving the officer around the French coastline.

NAZI PHOTOGRAPHER, THE
Played by Scott Fredericks (film)

The photographer is a member of the crew whose plane is shot down over England. Together with his two colleagues, he ends up holding hostages in the church hall until lionheart George Mainwaring comes to Walmington-on-Sea's rescue.

NAZI PILOT, THE
Played by Ingo Mogendorf (film)

This character pilots the German aircraft that is shot down over Walmington-on-Sea.

NEVER TOO OLD
Recorded: Friday 29/7/77

Original transmission: Sunday 13/11/77, 8.10–8.45pm

Original viewing figures: 12.5 million

Repeated: 16/10/78, 4/9/79, 1/12/91, 8/5/95, 28/5/00

CAST
Arthur Lowe . . . . .Captain Mainwaring
John Le Mesurier . . . . .Sergeant Wilson
Clive Dunn . . . . .Lance Corporal Jones
John Laurie . . . . .Private Frazer
Arnold Ridley . . . . .Private Godfrey
Ian Lavender . . . . .Private Pike
Bill Pertwee . . . . .Chief Warden Hodges
Frank Williams . . . . .Vicar
Edward Sinclair . . . . .Verger
Pamela Cundell . . . . .Mrs Fox
Janet Davies . . . . .Mrs Pike
Colin Bean . . . . .Private Sponge
Joan Cooper . . . . .Dolly
Robert Raglan . . . . .Colonel
Platoon: Roger Bourne, Desmond Cullum-Jones, Freddie White, Michael Moore, Freddie Wiles, George Hancock, Evan Ross, Jimmy Mac, Vernon Drake

PRODUCTION TEAM
Script: Jimmy Perry and David Croft
Producer/Director: David Croft
Production Assistant: Gordon Elsbury
Studio Lighting: Howard King
Studio Sound: Laurie Taylor
Design: Geoff Powell
Assistant Floor Manager: Susan Belbin
Vision Mixer: Angela Beveridge

Costume Designer: Mary Husband
Make-Up Artist: Sylvia Thornton

Life's wonderful for Lance Corporal Jones, but Mainwaring's worried that he's becoming woolly-headed. The glint in Jones's eye is explained however when he asks Mainwaring for permission to marry Mrs Fox. Jones is besotted by her and sees her face wherever he goes.

Mrs Fox is calling at 8pm with her answer and Jones is on tenterhooks. She agrees to wed, but later calls Mainwaring and asks him to pop round and see her in the strictest confidence. She wants a few minutes alone with him before Mrs Pike, Mr Wilson, Jones and Frank arrive. Mainwaring feels uneasy at Mrs Fox's home, what with underwear all over the place – and then she admits to always having had a soft spot for him. But he needn't have worried because Mrs Fox only wanted to ask whether he'd give her away.

With the wedding over, the reception takes place in the church hall, but the Colonel calls and asks Mainwaring to put his men on 30-minute standby.

In his speech Mainwaring hopes that Jones and Mrs Fox will be as happy as he's been with Elizabeth, even though, as expected, she can't be there because she's away staying with her sister. As the cake is cut, Sponge tells Mainwaring the Colonel wants to speak to him again. Barges are moving around the North Sea coast, the weather is right, so no chances can be taken and all Home Guard units are put onto immediate standby.

The action across the channel means Jones spends his wedding night on duty with Pike instead of with his newly-wed at Eastgate's Esplanade Hotel. While they're on patrol at the end of the pier, Mainwaring, Wilson, Godfrey and Frazer come along with a bottle of champagne to toast Jones. But Hodges spoils the occasion by arriving and insulting them by claiming the Germans could walk all over them. They take no notice and toast the Home Guard.

NEWARK, DEREK (1933–1998)
Role: Regimental Sergeant Major (film)

Derek entered the industry in 1961 and built up

a busy career in both TV and film. On the small screen his early appearances include playing Inspector Wright in an episode of *Out of this World* in 1962, Za in *Doctor Who* a year later, a mess sergeant in *Redcap*, Baggio in *The Baron*, Maurice in *Man in a Suitcase*, as well as roles in *The Saint*, *Callan*, *The Champions*, *The Avengers*, *Department S*, *Jason King*, *Juliet Bravo*, *Dempsey and Makepeace*, *Some Mothers Do 'Ave 'Em* and *Rising Damp* as the loud-mouthed wrestler, Spooner. On the big screen he was seen as Detective Wilson in *The Little Ones*, and numerous other films including *Front Page Story*, *The Blue Max*, *Fragment of Fear*, *The Offence* and *Bellman and True*, in 1987.

NEWBERY, BARRY
Designer on one episode (TV): 'The Love of Three Oranges'

Born in Stockwell, Barry earned a scholarship to an engineering school and worked in the industry until he left to undertake national service in the RAF, working as a motor fitter. After returning to civilian life he changed direction and studied fine art for five years. He subsequently worked as a draughtsman designing jewellery and in exhibition design before joining the BBC as a design assistant in 1957.

He was promoted to designer in 1963 and went on to work on shows including a six-part children's programme, *Last Man Out*, *The Count of Monte Cristo*, *Z Cars*, *Softly, Softly*, *Doctor Who*, *When the Boat Comes In*, *The Citadel*, *Lost Boys*, *Paul Temple*, *The Critic* and *Prince Regent*, for which he received a BAFTA nomination.

Barry, who mainly worked in drama, retired early from the BBC in 1983.

NEWMAN, SID
Not seen in the sitcom, Sid is referred to in 'The Loneliness of the Long-Distance Walker'. He sells secondhand car accessories, and his office can be reached via a green door in Slope Alley, just off the High Street in Walmington. He rents out two garages to Joe Walker.

NEWSON, LEN
BBC film cameraman on four episodes (TV): S7, episode 1: 'Everybody's Trucking', episode 3: 'Gorilla Warfare', episode 5: 'The Captain's Car' and episode 6: 'Turkey Dinner'

NEWSPAPERS
Dad's Army met with a mixed reception from the critics when it was first broadcast in 1968. However audiences loved it and by the second series, the TV critics across the British Isles had agreed that it was likely to join other shows of the genre in the pantheon of classic comedy. The following range of reviews shows just how divided members of the Press were about Perry and Croft's wartime show.

'It is nice to see a comedy like *Dad's Army*, which has enough confidence in its actors to force the pace. It is a humorous recollection of the Home Guard of 1940, but it is played in such an easy-going natural fashion that one imagines even the most hard-bitten professional anti-patriots must find it amusing.'
Stanley Reynolds, *The Guardian*, August 1968

'The trouble with this, though, is that it isn't situation or character comedy, it's only gag comedy, the easiest to write and the quickest wearing on the ear.'
Peter Black, *The Daily Mail*, August 1968

'I must admit to being agreeably surprised by the first episode of *Dad's Army*. It was lively, inventive, full of amusing characters and, above all, funny. With the last not too common quality, any defects are immediately forgiven.'
Maurice Tasnier, *Western Daily Press*, 1 August 1968

'*Dad's Army* is a nice little thing.'
N Banks-Smith, *The Sun*, 1 August 1968

'I cannot say I cracked a rib, split my sides, or even raised a belly-laugh – but some instinct is still telling me that the BBC is about to come up with a classic comedy series… The script mercifully avoided all the tempting cliché traps… Give it a week or two and I'll tell you whether this is really comedy's finest half-hour. All I say now is that the possibilities are tremendous.'
Ron Boyle, *Daily Express*, 1 August 1968

'It seemed to me to blend sentiment and humour rather uneasily as if afraid of making too much fun of a hallowed wartime institution… The one solid pleasure last night was watching the performance of Arthur Lowe as the organizing hero.'
Michael Billington, *The Times*, 1 August 1968

'I'm fairly hopeful that this may prove an interesting series, though in the opening instalment the balance between humour and nostalgia seemed to be held uneasily.'
Maureen Wiggins, *Sunday Times*, 4 August 1968

'Jimmy Perry's and David Croft's inaugural script was pretty feeble, with an over reliance on strained little jokes, but again this may be only a scene-setting problem.'
The Sunday Telegraph, 4 August 1968

'After two episodes it looks as though *Dad's Army* is a real winner. It's situation comedy of the very best sort, because it's drawn from a rich fund of experience and not from the artificial hatchery of a script conference.'
Peter Tinniswood, *The Western Mail*, 10 August 1968

'Humour must be dead in those who cannot get a few laughs out of *Dad's Army*.'
Granville Wilkinson, *Telegraph and Argus* (Bradford), 14 August 1968

'A gentle vein of satire is admirably played off against a good honest background of slapstick which warms us to the men (perhaps unwisely) to tackle Hitler's invaders with broomsticks and relics from the armament museums.'
A G S, *Bath and Wilts Evening Chronicle*, 15 August 1968

'This is the first time I've seen the series and, though it doesn't revive any memories for me, I can only say that I'll be watching it regularly from now on. With a good cast, witty script, and the ability to make fun out of a serious business without being unkind, I'm sure *Dad's Army* will go marching into the top charts.'
Fergus Wood, *Evening Times* (Glasgow), 15 August 1968

'Arthur Lowe, the captain of *Dad's Army*, is its kingpin. And what holds it together. It's no effort to reel back to the days of Dunkirk. You could put Mr Lowe into any era. He is the man for any hour.'
Daily Mirror, 15 August 1968

'Why has *Dad's Army*… become a "must" for a vast viewing public? The answer, once more, is that this brilliant production portrays an authentic picture of the behaviour of people during the Second World War.'
The Yorkshire Post, 15 August 1968

'Well worth watching for a half-hour's respite from the day's cares.'
Stewart Lane, *Morning Star*, 24 August, 1968

'Talking of television, I'm delighted to find that I'm not alone in having a sneaking liking for the BBC's *Dad's Army* series… The treatment is affectionate and, no doubt, that's why the series has been such a success that it's to be brought back in the new year.'
West Lancashire Evening Gazette, September 1968

'As the Walmington volunteers assembled, Messrs Perry and Croft showed a real gift for satire. Two things defeated them. One was the inexcusable use of a modern studio audience: every time it reacted 1940 was lost and we were back in 1968. The other was a tendency to go for laughs at all costs, even if they punctured the atmosphere.'
Sean Day-Lewis, *The Daily Telegraph*, September 1968

NEWSREADER, THE
Played by Alvar Lidell (radio)

The man who reads the news in 'Getting the Bird', reports pigeons are mysteriously disappearing from Trafalgar Square. The culprit, of course, is Walker, who planned to sell them to Jones.

NEWSREEL
Genuine newsreel footage, followed by fictional contributions from the cast of *Dad's Army*, was used to open each of the six episodes in series one. Narrated by the respected voice of E V H Emmett, newsreels became an integral part of early cinema, particularly pre-television. Events around the world were captured in nine-minute packages, filmed by roving cameramen. The use of newsreel lost its way in the 1960s, when TV grew in importance; as the quality and frequency of news bulletins on the small screen improved, the big screen became a venue for entertainment, with the public only wanting to see the latest movies.

Producer David Croft felt using newsreel footage during the first series of *Dad's Army* gave the show an authentic feel. 'It was a way of pitching people into the atmosphere and the events of what was happening at that time. There was no television news during the war years, so the Gaumont British news was an important part of the era; each week when people went to the cinema they came across Gaumont British news.' Once the sitcom was up and running, and established in the minds of the viewers, it was felt the introductory newsreel style had served its purpose. 'We had to quickly show the audience what the series was about and using a newsreel style helped,' explains Jimmy Perry. 'When everyone knew the series well enough, we changed the format.'

The original footage was obtained from the Imperial War Museum in London at an agreed royalty charge. For example, some 'Dig for Victory' footage used in the episode 'The Showing Up of Corporal Jones' cost the BBC ten shillings a foot.

NEXT OF KIN, THE
Released in 1942 by Ealing Studios, *The Next of Kin* was a film that explored the devastating results of careless talk, leading to loss of life in a commando raid. Originally intended as an instructional film, its production qualities saw it become a commercial success. The cast included: Mervyn Johns, Nova Pilbeam, Stephen Murray, Basil Radford and Naunton Wayne.

In 'The Battle of Godfrey's Cottage', Wilson is planning to take 18 members of the Home Guard over to the cinema in Eastgate to watch the picture, but the ringing of the church bells, signifying a possible invasion, puts paid to his plan.

NIGHT OF ONE HUNDRED STARS
Members of the cast (John Le Mesurier, Bill Pertwee, Ian Lavender and Frank Williams) appeared in London Weekend Television's *Night of One Hundred Stars*, which was transmitted on ITV, on Sunday 21 December 1980. In the presence of Princess Margaret, Terry Wogan introduced a range of stars from the world of entertainment, many involved in successful shows like *Dad's Army*. A copy of the show is retained in LWT's archives and involved the cast members in a short sketch.

NO SPRING FOR FRAZER
Recorded: Friday 28/11/69

Original transmission: Thursday 4/12/69, 7.30–8.00pm

Original viewing figures: 13.6 million

Repeated: 25/7/70, 3/12/82, 19/9/89, 17/1/90 (N Ireland), 16/1/93, 24/2/96, 1/7/00

CAST
Arthur Lowe . . . . .Captain Mainwaring
John Le Mesurier . . . . .Sergeant Wilson
Clive Dunn . . . . .Lance Corporal Jones
John Laurie . . . . .Private Frazer
James Beck . . . . .Private Walker
Arnold Ridley . . . . .Private Godfrey
Ian Lavender . . . . .Private Pike
Frank Williams . . . . .Vicar
Edward Sinclair . . . . .Verger
Harold Bennett . . . . .Mr Blewitt
Joan Cooper . . . . .Miss Baker
Ronnie Brandon . . . . .Mr Drury
Extras: Jay Neil, Brian John, Roy Hatterway and Walter Turner

PRODUCTION TEAM
Script: Jimmy Perry and David Croft
Producer/Director: David Croft
Production Assistant: Harold Snoad
Film Cameraman: James Balfour
Film Editor: Bob Rymer
Studio Lighting: Howard King
Studio Sound: Michael McCarthy
Design: Richard Hunt
Assistant Floor Manager: Bill Harman
Vision Mixer: Dave Hanks
Costume Supervisor: Michael Burdle
Make-Up Supervisor: Cecile Hay-Arthur

On parade, Mainwaring inspects the platoon's armoury, only to discover Frazer has lost the butterfly spring from the Lewis gun. *En route* to the recreation hall, where the men are having a lecture, they stop off at Frazer's shop to pick up the spring. But it seems Frazer put it in a coffin for storage, which has now been passed to HE Drury's, the funeral directors, where they discover the box has already been used for Horace Blewitt. He's lying at rest at his brother's, Sidney Blewitt, so Jones and Frazer go to pay their respects. At the same time, they hope to retrieve the spring, but fail.

Later that night, the men go round to Sidney Blewitt's house. They break in to allow Frazer the chance to look in the coffin, but he finds that the coffin has been screwed down. They have to escape quickly when Sidney wakes up.

Next morning, Frazer is officiating at the funeral but still doesn't have the opportunity to retrieve the spring. Mainwaring devises a plan involving a fictitious unexploded bomb, which has the mourners running for their lives, leaving the graveyard deserted. When darkness falls, members of the platoon go to the graveyard and try opening the coffin but are disturbed by the Verger who arrives to fill in the grave. When the dirt is thrown back in his face, the Verger is petrified until he spots members of the Home Guard running away. He takes the matter up with Mainwaring and threatens to tell the Vicar. To add to his headache, Mainwaring has no option but to report the lost spring to GHQ. While he's on the phone, Frazer suddenly finds the missing item.

NORA
Played by Melita Manger (TV)

Nora works as an assistant at the milk bar in Walmington where Pike and Sylvia – Hodges' niece – get chatting in 'The Making of Private Pike'.

NORRIS, MR
Played by Jonathan Cecil (radio)

Mr Norris is a newspaper reporter in the radio episode, 'A Man of Action'. The role is played by Talfryn Thomas in the TV episode, although his character is called Mr Cheeseman.

NORTH BERRINGTON TURKEY FARM
The platoon visit the farm, which is owned by Mr Boggis, and is situated just a few miles from Walmington in the episode, 'Turkey Dinner'. Jones had accidentally shot a turkey while out on patrol, so Mainwaring and his men visit to apologise and pay for the bird. The trouble is, the owner has gone to market, and his employee, a brainless farmhand, is no help. With 210 birds at the farm, it's difficult knowing whether the turkey did, in fact, come from there, so the platoon decide to keep the bird and throw a turkey dinner for the Walmington OAPs instead.

NOVELTY ROCK EMPORIUM
A seaside confectionery kiosk, the emporium acts as the platoon's guard post while they patrol the stretch of coastline from Stones' Amusement Arcade to the Jolly Roger Pier. In the event of an invasion, the emporium would have strategic significance as far as the defence of Walmington is concerned because it would become the Home Guard's command post, or as Mainwaring describes it, 'our nerve centre'. This choice was made by GHQ in the episode, 'The Battle of Godfrey's Cottage'.

NOYES, LESLIE

Role: Member of the platoon's back row in 49 episodes: S3, episodes 4, 6–9, 11, 12; S4, episodes 1–3, 5, 6, 9–13; 'Battle of the Giants'; S5; S6, episodes 1–5, 7; S7; S8, episodes 1, 2, 4–6; 'My Brother and I'

Leslie, originally a tap dancer, worked as a stooge for Arthur Haynes for many years. Although he worked in America for a while as a dancer, his career was dominated by variety. He died of cancer in 1976.

NUMBER ENGAGED

Recorded: Friday 15/7/77

Original transmission: Sunday 6/11/77, 8.10–8.40pm

Original viewing figures: 9.6 million

Repeated: 9/10/78, 28/8/79, 13/9/91, 16/12/95, 22/2/96 (Wales), 23/8/97

CAST

Arthur Lowe . . . . .Captain Mainwaring
John Le Mesurier . . . . .Sergeant Wilson
Clive Dunn . . . . .Lance Corporal Jones
John Laurie . . . . .Private Frazer
Arnold Ridley . . . . .Private Godfrey
Ian Lavender . . . . .Private Pike
Bill Pertwee . . . . .Chief Warden Hodges
Frank Williams . . . . .Vicar
Edward Sinclair . . . . .Verger
Ronnie Brody . . . . .GPO Man
Robert Mill . . . . .Army Captain
Kenneth MacDonald . . . . . . .Army Sergeant
Felix Bowness . . . . .Van Driver
Colin Bean . . . . .Private Sponge
Stuart McGugan . . . . .Scottish Sergeant
Bernice Adams . . . . .ATS Girl
Platoon: Desmond Cullum-Jones, Vernon Drake, Michael Moore, Freddie White, Freddie Wiles, George Hancock, Roger Bourne, Jimmy Mac, Evan Ross

Extras: (Regular Army Soldiers) Mike Harrington-Spier and Lyndon Redpath
Stuntmen: Jim Dowdall (for Ian Lavender) and Derek Ware (for Clive Dunn)

PRODUCTION TEAM

Script: Jimmy Perry and David Croft
Producer: David Croft
Production Assistant: Gordon Elsbury
Director: Bob Spiers
Film Cameraman: Peter Chapman
Film Sound Recordist: Graham Bedwell
Film Editor: John Dunstan
Studio Lighting: Howard King
Studio Sound: Laurie Taylor
Design: Geoff Powell
Assistant Floor Manager: Susan Belbin
Vision Mixer: Angela Beveridge
Costume Designer: Mary Husband
Make-Up Artist: Sylvia Thornton

A highly secret invasion warning device has been set up just along the coast from Walmington – its purpose being to detect enemy boats and landing craft early, giving as much warning as possible. All the information travels along telephone wires, which are guarded by the regular army, to GHQ. For 24 hours, Mainwaring's men have to guard the two-mile stretch within their area, a highly important job.

En route they see a sign stating the road is up and there's a diversion. A diversion will cause too much of a delay because they're late already, so Mainwaring orders the signs to be taken up and they move on.

The platoon settle down, with Frazer being put in charge of the catering. Pikey is told to look after the porridge, and it's left simmering all night. During the night there is an air-raid, but it passes without any apparent problem, or so the men think.

Next day, the Vicar, who had suggested an open-air service, arrives with Hodges. He's soon interrupted when a stray bomb is spotted caught in the telephone wires. Sponge alerts the GPO and the Home Guard await a team of experts, but when just one engineer arrives on a bike, and refuses to climb the pole, Mainwaring tries unsuccessfully to scale it, ripping Hodges' trouser leg in the process. Frazer tries catching the bomb with his fishing rod, which he'd brought to catch trout in the local stream. Next, they requisition a lorry carrying furniture and build a tower. Pikey climbs it but falls into a pile of manure when the tower collapses. Eventually a crane, which Wilson had spotted the previous day, is borrowed. Jones climbs into the crane's bucket and climbs on to the telegraph pole. He's soon in trouble and drops the bomb into the cauldron of porridge Pikey had made for breakfast. Fortunately it doesn't detonate, but there's still a shock in store for Jones.

NURSE, THE

Played by Susan Majolier (TV); Elizabeth Morgan (radio)

The nurse works in Walmington's cottage hospital where Mainwaring goes for his ingrowing toenail operation in 'The Recruit'. When Wilson and Jones visit, Wilson tries chatting her up by commenting on how tiny her waist looks in her uniform.

OATES, RON
Visual effects designer on one episode (TV): S4, episode 2: 'Don't Forget the Diver'
The late Ron Oates worked in the film industry before joining the BBC's visual effects team in 1958. He worked on numerous shows, including *The Goodies*, *It's A Square World* and *Maigret*.

OGILVY, CAPTAIN
Played by James Copeland (TV); Jack Watson (radio)
A tough, Scottish captain in the Highland Regiment, Ogilvy co-ordinates an exercise in 'Operation Kilt'. While their HQ is at nearby Manor Farm, his men will try infiltrating the town of Walmington and then take control of the church hall.

OLD FLOUR MILL, THE
Just outside Walmington-on-Sea, the Old Flour Mill is a disused building which Mainwaring and his men adopt as their HQ during Operation Wake-Up in 'Wake-Up Walmington'.

OLD MAN, THE
Played by Harold Bennett (TV); Richard Davies (radio)
This character takes part in the air raid exercise in 'The Armoured Might of Lance Corporal Jones'. He's the unfortunate patient when Mainwaring's men are acting as stretcher bearers. After various mishaps, he climbs off the stretcher and decides it's safer to walk to the hospital.

OLIVE
Played by Tina Cornioli (TV)
Olive is a land girl who works on Mrs Prentice's farm. She is seen in 'All is Safely Gathered In'.

OPENING TITLES
A graphic designer from the BBC and freelance animator, Colin Whitaker, who worked regularly for the Beeb, were assigned the task of creating the famous opening titles for *Dad's Army*. Union Jacks and swastikas battle it out over a map of northern Europe, which was nothing more than a piece of airbrushed artwork.

David Croft, who was keen to create titles that were indicative of the kind of graphics used in the period, and seen in publications like *Picture Post*, discussed his ideas with the graphic designer, whose job was to translate the producer's ideas onto a storyboard. At that stage, the project was discussed with Colin Whitaker who, after completing the necessary hand animation, filmed the original black and white titles in his converted garage at Hemel Hempstead. The titles were shot straight onto 16mm cine film, and later transferred to telecine ready for the first episode's transmission in 1968.

Over the sitcom's lifetime, the credits were filmed three times: after the initial black and white version they were reshot in colour on two separate occasions. On both occasions graphic designer Ken Brown designed a storyboard and Colin completed the hand animation, but instead of filming everything in his studio at home, he turned to John Astley at Caravel Films in Slough, who completed the camera work.

The credits were shot in single frame, with 25 frames equating to a second of screen time. The trails which followed the arrowheads across the land were airbrushed onto cell and every time they needed shortening, paint was scratched off the cell; the arrowheads (which were made from paper) were then repositioned along a semi-translucent paper template.

When the positioning was correct against the background, a glass cover held everything in place while another frame was shot. The length each arrow moved between frames was determined by a pre-arranged scale Whitaker had calculated to tie-in with the overall time allocated for the opening credits. This process continued until the credits were complete.

OPERATION CATHERINE WHEEL
This secret operation in 'Round and Round Went the Great Big Wheel' sees the trial run for a secret weapon, codenamed Headpuhf. The giant wheel contains two thousand pounds of explosive, enough to demolish an enemy pillbox within a range of three miles. Co-ordinated by Colonel Pierce, the demonstration for other senior members of the military and the minister takes place at a deserted aerodrome near Walmington. Three Home Guard platoons are employed to help. While the Eastgate mob, under Captain Square, guard the aerodrome entrances, and Captain Graham and his men from Dymwhich patrol watch the aerodrome perimeter, Mainwaring and his men are allocated all the dirty jobs, including potato-peeling and washing-up.

OPERATION DANCE
Mainwaring adopts this code name when organising the platoon dance in 'War Dance'. A dance committee is formed, comprising of Mainwaring, Wilson, Jones, Walker and Godfrey. While drink is being provided by the golf club (although Walker obtains their supplies), Godfrey organises the food. To help, Jones agrees to donate some sausages and Mainwaring says his wife will turn them into sausage rolls. Music, meanwhile, is down to Private Hastings, with Walker agreeing to hire a band from the RAF holding station at Godalston.

OPERATION GUN GRAB
Mainwaring dreams up this operation in 'Museum Piece'. When he hears a local museum, the Peabody Museum of Historical Army Weapons, has closed because the curator has joined the navy, Mainwaring wants to acquire any weaponry which might be of use to the Home Guard. The operation kicks off at 6pm, but the platoon experience great difficulties getting into the museum because of the miserable caretaker, who's 88 years old and Jones' father. After using a scaling ladder, battering ram and having cold water thrown over them, they're on the brink of calling it a day, when they decide to change tack and try cunning. Eventually the platoon manage to get in the building, but find most of the equipment unsuitable for their needs, until Walker spots a 1901 Chinese rocket gun.

OPERATION KILT
Recorded: Sunday 13/10/68 (made in black and white)
Original transmission: Saturday 1/3/69, 7.00–7.30pm
Original viewing figures: 13.9 million
This episode has never been repeated

CAST
Arthur Lowe . . . . Captain Mainwaring
John Le Mesurier . . . . Sergeant Wilson

Clive Dunn . . . . .Lance Corporal Jones
John Laurie . . . . .Private Frazer
James Beck . . . . .Private Walker
Arnold Ridley . . . . .Private Godfrey
Ian Lavender . . . . .Private Pike
Janet Davies . . . . .Mrs Pike
James Copeland . . . . .Captain Ogilvy
Colin Daniels . . . . .Small Boy

Platoon: Colin Bean, Richard Jacques, Frank Godfrey, Alec Coleman, Hugh Cecil, Jimmy Mac, Desmond Cullum-Jones, Vic Taylor, David Seaforth, Richard Kitteridge

Highland Soldiers: Alex Donald, Robin Williams, Dennis Halcombe, Barry Raymond, Bruce Wells

Pantomime Cow: The Lynton Boys

PRODUCTION TEAM
Script: Jimmy Perry and David Croft
Producer/Director: David Croft
Production Assistant: Harold Snoad
Studio Lighting: George Summers
Studio Sound: James Cole
Design: Paul Joel
Assistant Floor Manager: Tony George
Vision Mixer: Dave Hanks
Costume Supervisor: Marjorie Lewis
Make-Up Supervisor: Sheila Cassidy

Mainwaring leaves the bank early – via the back door, perhaps to escape Mr Green from head office – to catch up on Home Guard paperwork. Later, at the church hall, Jones delivers an envelope which contains instructions that in future all HG units will do 25 minutes of physical training before parade. There's just time for this before Captain Ogilvie of the Highland Regiment arrives to brief the unit about the night manoeuvres on Saturday. By the time Ogilvie arrives Mainwaring is in agony, but not wanting to admit to being unfit, he blames his lumbago.

Ogilvie tells Mainwaring the plan: his men will try infiltrating the town and take over the church hall. As Mainwaring's men outnumber the Highland Regiment three to one, he doesn't think they'll find it too difficult to win the battle, even against highly trained professional soldiers.

Desperate to discover Ogilvie's plans, the Home Guard intend creeping into Manor Farm where the regiment are based; their disguise must be something that doesn't look unfamiliar on a farm, and Walker returns later with a pantomime cow. Mainwaring doesn't think it will work, and he's right; their next scheme involves borrowing a tractor and truck full of hay from Mr Gregg's farm. Wilson is to drive the truck into Manor Farm and leave it there with Pike hidden underneath the hay – Pike's hay fever however means that Jones has to take his place.

After Jones manages to hear Ogilvie's plans, the Walmington platoon make a start setting traps along the eight paths that lead through the woods. Things don't go entirely to plan and Jones finds himself hanging upside down next to the kilt-wearing Captain Ogilvie.

OPERATIONS ROOM OFFICER
Played by Andrew Carr (TV)
The officer is in charge of the operations room when Mainwaring calls to report the stray barrage balloon in 'The Day the Balloon Went Up'. In the radio version this character is known as Squadron-Leader Horsfall.

ORCHARD, JULIAN (1930–1979)
Born: Wheatley
Roles: Mr Upton, the Town Clerk ('A Man of Action', 'The Honourable Man', 'The Godiva Affair' and 'Big Guns') (radio)
Although Julian appeared in many television shows, including *Culture for the Masses*, *Whack-O!*, *Odd Man Out* and an episode of *The Goodies*, playing the Minister for the Arts, he's best known for the busy film career he established before his untimely death at the age of 49. From *The Great Van Robbery* in 1959 to *The London Connection* in 1979, he appeared in numerous character roles, including four *Carry On* pictures: *Follow That Camel* as a doctor, *Don't Lose Your Head*, *Doctor* as Fred and *Henry*, playing Duc de Poncenay. Other movies included *Crooks Anonymous*, playing a jeweller, *Father Came Too* as a bath salesman, Tom Hobbs in *Bless this House*, a producer in *Man About the House*, *The Slipper and the Rose* and *The Revenge of the Pink Panther*.

ORPHANAGE
The local orphanage, where the Vicar is a trustee, is mentioned in 'High Finance' and is the cause of Jack Jones' financial problems. He supplies meat there, but hasn't had his bills paid for three months.

OSBORNE, MICHAEL (1956–)
Born: London
Role: Boy Scout (S1, episode 2: 'Museum Piece') (TV)
When his sister's dance tutor was involved in casting a children's film, Michael was offered the chance to appear. He obtained an agent and went on to do several crowd scenes as a child actor, before appearing in *Dad's Army*, aged 12. A year later, he appeared in the first of two series of *Country Boy*, for Southern TV.

At 15, he emigrated to Australia with his family, where he became involved in the theatre, working with various rep companies and the Queensland Theatre Company. He also started running drama classes for children.

He returned to England in 1976 to appear in a show, but it never materialised. By the late 1970s, he had diversified and was writing shows and songs as well as acting in theatre. Today he's involved in Banana Cabaret, a comedy venue in London, and runs acting classes.

OTTAWAY, JAMES (1907–1999)
Role: 1st Member of Parliament (S5, episode 2: 'Keep Young and Beautiful') (TV)
James' television career included appearances in *The Sweeney* playing Uncle Billy in a 1978 episode, *The Gentle Touch*, *Boon*, *Jeeves and Wooster*, *The Bill* as Gordon Picket, and Mr Wellington in an episode of *As Time Goes By*. He appeared in several films, such as *Passport to Shame*, back in 1958, *In the Wake of a Stranger*, *The Man Who Liked Funerals*, *The Man Who Finally Died*, *Inadmissible Evidence*, *That'll Be the Day* playing Grandad, and the 1981 picture *Absolution*.

P

PALETHORPE, MR
Played by Jack Haig (TV)
The landlord of The Six Bells pub, Mr Palethorpe is seen in 'Ring Dem Bells'. It's a country pub where very little happens, so you can imagine the excitement when Mainwaring's men turn up dressed in German uniforms.

PALMER'S STORES
A department store situated in the Walmington High Street, Palmer's Stores is mentioned by Godfrey in the 1968 *Christmas Night with the Stars* sketch. He explains that the reason he arrives dressed as Santa is because he has been helping out in the store's toy department over the Christmas holidays. He got locked in the store and when he was finally released he had no time to change as he was late for parade.

PARISH, EDITH
Played by Wendy Richard (TV and radio)
Address: 35 Berwick Road, Walmington-on-Sea
Edith was one of Walker's many girlfriends, first appearing in 'The Two and a Half Feathers', sitting in a shelter with Joe. She was seen again in 'Mum's Army', when Mainwaring decides she's unsuitable to join the platoon. The attractive Edith is an usherette at the Tivoli Cinema in the town, and lives with her father.

PARKINS, SERGEANT
Played by Charles Hill (TV)
Seen in 'Battle of the Giants!', Parkins is the sergeant of the Eastgate Home Guard, reporting directly to Captain Square.

PARKINSON, MR
Mr Parkinson is not seen, but is referred to in 'The Test'. Frazer had just attended Mr Parkinson's funeral which explains why he turns up at the cricket ground in his undertaker's outfit.

PARKINSON, MRS
Referred to in 'No Spring for Frazer', Mrs Parkinson is never seen. When Frazer arrives at H E Drury's, the funeral directors, to find out whether a recently made coffin has been used, Miss Baker, the receptionist, is talking to Mrs

'Ring Dem Bells'

Parkinson on the phone. Mrs Parkinson was enquiring whether a reservation was needed because someone had just died.

PARKINSON, ROBIN (1929–)
Born: Coventry
Role: Lieutenant Wood (S7, episode 3: 'Gorilla Warfare') (TV)
Robin left school and worked for his father (a commercial artist) before changing direction and deciding to attend drama school. He entered the business in 1958, appearing in a TV series while finishing his studies at drama school. He then started being offered regular TV and film work.

On the big screen Robin made his debut as a jeweller's assistant in the 1963 movie *Billy Liar*. Other film credits include *Twisted Nerve*, *Catch Me A Spy* and *The Family Way*. He has made numerous television appearances, including 20

episodes of the 1970s series *The Many Wives of Patrick*, an episode of *Rising Damp*, *The Dick Emery Show*, *Girls About Town*, three series of *'Allo, 'Allo* and an episode of *Outside Edge*.

PARRISH, PAT
Producer's assistant on 12 episodes: S1, episodes 2, 3, 4, 5 & 6; S3, episodes 1, 2, 3, 4, 5, 6 & 7

PARSONS, MR
Played by Erik Chitty (radio)
Mr Parsons winds the town hall clock twice a year, and ascends the clock tower with Mainwaring and his men in the radio episode 'Time On My Hands'. At the end of the episode he finds himself marooned on the clock.

PATHANS
Jones fought the Pathans while serving on the North West Frontier in India.

PAYNE, FREDDIE

Role: Member of the platoon's back row in one episode (S2, episode 5: 'A Stripe for Frazer') (TV)

PEABODY MUSEUM OF HISTORICAL ARMY WEAPONS

This museum in Walmington featured in 'Museum Piece'. Mainwaring receives notification from the curator, who has decided to join the navy, that he wants the museum's bank account closed for the duration, with all the funds being transferred to a deposit account. Mainwaring has an idea: rather than let the exhibits gather dust, he launches Operation Gun Grab to see if there are any weapons that could be used by the Home Guard. Unfortunately they have to get past the museum's caretaker, who turns out to be Jones' cantankerous 88-year-old father. When they finally manage that, their find is disappointing as most of their weapons were antiquated, originating from the Boer and Crimean Wars. This does not surprise Wilson, who earlier quipped that the chief exhibit was a full-scale replica of Boadicea's chariot.

PEABODY PARK

Pike suggests Frazer might bury his gold sovereigns in this Walmington park during the episode, 'The Miser's Hoard'.

PEABODY ROOMS

Various functions and dinners are held at this plush venue in Walmington, such as the Rotarian dinner in 'Brain versus Brawn' and regular whist drives.

PEARMAN, VIVIAN

Born: Godalming
Role: Member of the Home Front Company (stage show)
Vivian grew up in Devon and went on to study at college before going into repertory theatre. She then married, raised a family and spent three years lecturing for a computer company. However, she returned to the theatre with an appearance in a Mike and Bernie Winter's pantomime at Croydon.

PEARSON, GEORGE

Played by Michael Brennan (radio)
George is an escaped convict in the radio episode 'Absent Friends', replacing the IRA suspect in the TV version. He has a twin brother, Tom.

PEARSON, TOM

Played by Michael Brennan (radio)
Tom is George Pearson's twin brother in the radio episode 'Absent Friends'.

PEASHMARSH PLATOON

(Film only)
The Peashmarsh Home Guard platoon attend the weekend camp, where they are assigned the task of attacking the enemy (a detachment of Royal Marines) on the left flank.

PEEK, DENYS

Role: German Pilot (S1, episode 4: 'The Enemy Within the Gates')

'The Enemy Within the Gates'

Other productions Denys has appeared in include Rediffusion's 1965 series, *Object Z*, playing Robert Duncan, George in BBC's *I Measured the Skies* in 1970, and several films, like 1968's *Curse of the Crimson Altar* as Peter Manning, and *The Limbo Line* the same year.

PEMBROKE GARDENS

In 'Put That Light Out!' we learn that enemy agents have been flashing lights from 17 Pembroke Gardens.

PEPPERY OLD GENT, THE

Played by Roger Maxwell (film)
This character, whose name is General Wilkinson, enrols for the LDV when Mainwaring takes charge. He turns up with a shotgun, but when he refuses to hand it over to Mainwaring, he's classed as a troublemaker and Mainwaring is determined to get rid of him.

PERCY STREET

Mainwaring is told to report to Percy Street in Walmington for the air raid exercise in 'The Armoured Might of Lance Corporal Jones'.

PERCY THE PARROT

Appearing in 'The Battle of Godfrey's Cottage', Percy is the Godfreys' foul-mouthed parrot who lives with Charles and his sisters, Cissy and Dolly. The bird is nearly 100 years old and belonged to their father, who died aged 92, some five years ago. Mr Godfrey's children bought the parrot as company for their father who was confined to bed for the last year of his life. It's unclear where Percy picked up his bad habits!

PERKINS

See 'Butler, The'.

PERKINS, TOBY

Role: Usher (S5, episode 11: 'Brush with the Law') (TV)
Toby Perkins, who died in 1983, appeared in a handful of films, including the 1959 film, *The Night We Dropped a Clanger*, *Double Bunk*, *Take Me Over* and *Games That Lovers Play*. He also appeared in a *Jackanory Playhouse* in the 1970s.

PERRY, GILDA (1933–)

Born: London
Roles: Blonde (S2, episode 3: 'The Loneliness of the Long-Distance Walker'), Doreen (S3, episode 3: 'The Lion has 'Phones' and S4, episode 8: 'The Two and a Half Feathers') (TV)
Dancer, comedienne and choreographer, Gilda Perry worked in theatre, cabaret and television. A trained dancer, she was a member of the world famous Ballet Rambert. She was also an actor/manager at Watford's Palace Theatre between 1956 and 1964.

During her career, she was seen in numerous West End musicals and three Royal Command shows at the London Palladium, as well as appearing occasionally on TV in shows like *Are You Being Served?* playing Mr Humphries' next-door neighbour. Unwilling to join the ranks of unemployed, ageing actresses, she turned her hand to building a house in the country and designing the large garden, while she qualified as a physiotherapist.

PERRY, JIMMY (1924–)

Actor, singer, theatre director, composer and writer, Jimmy Perry was born in Barnes, southwest London. From the age of five he was taken to the theatre by his parents, and as a result of these experiences he fell in love with the entertainment world and could hardly wait to get on the stage, into the spotlight and to show off.

This became his magnificent obsession and has carried him through his entire life – which he has translated into dramatic terms: starting with the Home Guard at the age of 16 (*Dad's Army*), serving as a sergeant in The Royal Artillery in the Far East (*It Ain't Half Hot, Mum*), as a red coat at Butlins (*Hi-De-Hi!*) and listening to stories from his grandfather, who was a gentleman's gentleman (*You Rang, M'Lord?*).

While based at Oswestry during his army days, he set up a concert party, and when he was later posted to India, he established an entertainments unit. Upon being demobbed, he trained at RADA, and during the summer breaks worked as a singer and comic feed at Butlins holiday camps.

After graduating from drama school he worked with various repertory companies before taking over the lease of Watford's Palace Theatre, which he ran with his wife for eight years.

In 1968, Jimmy first met David Croft when he worked for him as an actor in the TV comedy series, *Beggar My Neighbour*. Jimmy's first impression of David was that he seemed rather cross, but they managed to work together for 30 years without hitting each other.

PERT, GORDON

Production assistant on 20 episodes (TV): S5 and S6

PERTWEE, BILL (1926–)

Born: Amersham

Role: Chief Warden William Hodges (60 TV episodes and *Christmas Night with the Stars* inserts; the film, the stage show and 33 radio episodes)

Bill has enjoyed a varied career in entertainment which began in earnest when Beryl Reid accepted some of his comedy material for a London revue. As a result, he was later invited to join the company, turning professional some months later.

Before entering the world of showbiz, Bill held down a number of jobs, including making parts for Spitfires, window-cleaning and being assistant baggage boy to the Indian cricket team in 1946.

Bill experienced a precarious early education and was unable to write even his own name accurately until he was 12. But after moving to a small private school where learning became fun, Bill's education was back on track.

When war broke out in 1939, he was evacuated to Sussex, a part of the country he's grown to love. When he finished his education at 16, he went looking for work. Until he broke into the entertainment business in 1954, some 12 years later, he experienced a chequered career encompassing numerous jobs. In the 1950s he began spending time with various acting groups, and when the offer to help his cousin, the late Jon Pertwee, on a variety tour came along, he jumped at the chance, even though it involved no actual acting.

When the tour finished, Bill found employment at a school outfitters in London. One day he received a phone call from producer Ronnie Hill that was to change his life. The producer's call led to Bill joining Beryl Reid's revue at the Watergate Theatre. For eight weeks, Bill continued working at the outfitters during the day while appearing in the revue in the evenings. But by 1955 he knew he wanted to act professionally and settled down to concentrate on his future career.

His first professional summer season saw him spending two weeks with a small acting company playing at Bognor Regis. The eight performers, who made up the company, then moved on to Gorleston on Sea, near Great Yarmouth, for the main season.

As the years passed, Bill kept busy with radio, small TV parts and plenty of variety seasons. The 1950s closed in style with an offer to join the second series of radio's popular weekly comedy show, *Beyond Our Ken*, with Kenneth Williams and Kenneth Horne among the cast. Soon after the show finished in 1964, Bill was recruited for the equally funny series, *Round the Horne*.

In 1967 he was offered a couple of lines in an episode of *Hugh and I*, a BBC sitcom produced by David Croft. Working for Croft in this one-off episode proved advantageous because a year later he was given a few lines as the air raid warden in *Dad's Army*. The character appeared again in the fourth episode, before expanding into a regular role.

His other TV appearances include *Lollipop Loves Mr Mole*, *Jackanory*, *The Dick Emery Show*, *Frost Weekly*, *Billy Liar* and *The Larry Grayson Show*.

Since the series finished Bill has continued with theatre work (he toured as Sergeant Beetroot, the Crowman's assistant in *Worzel Gummidge*), pantomimes and TV, including the role of Police Constable Wilson in Perry and Croft's *You Rang, M'Lord?*. He has also written several books, including his autobiography, *A Funny Way To Make A Living!*, which was published in 1996.

TV credits include: *Night Spot*, *Two in Clover*, *Beggar My Neighbour*, *Mike and Bernie*, *Worzel Gummidge*, *It Ain't Half Hot, Mum*, *Chance in a Million*, *Hi-De-Hi!*, *Candid Camera*.

Theatre credits include: *The Watergate Review*, *Summertime*, *Comedy Cocktail*, *Goodie Two Shoes*, *Old Time Music Hall*, *Caught Napping*, *Find The Lady*, *Run For Your Wife*, *It Runs in the Family*, *Funny Money*, *Die Fledermaus*.

Film credits include: *Carry On Loving*, *Carry On Girls*, *Psychomania*, *Love Thy Neighbour*, *Man About The House*, *Confessions of a Pop Performer*, *What's Up Nurse*, *The Seven Magnificent Deadly Sins*.

Radio credits include: *Meet the Huggets*, *The Motorway Men*.

PETERS, ARNOLD (1925–)

Born: London

Role: Fire Officer Dale (S7, episode 2: 'A Man of Action') (TV)

Arnold, who's the voice behind Jack Woolley in the long-running radio series, *The Archers*, joined a dance band as a schoolboy until being called up to the RAF during the Second World War. Returning to civvy street, he became a professional actor and entertainer, with his first job being on radio's *Children's Hour*, in a programme called *Hastings of Bengal*.

Offers of work were plentiful and he joined the BBC Drama Repertory Company in Birmingham. As well as radio and theatre work, Arnold is also a busy screen actor. His television appearances include: *Citizen Smith*, *Please, Sir!*, *The Siege of Golden Hill*, *Shoulder to Shoulder*, *United!*, *The Tomorrow People* and, in 1998, the BBC series, *Prince Among Men*.

Arnold has had a long-standing interest in English folk music and plays in a folk dance band.

PETERS, GORDON (1935–)

Born: County Durham

Roles: Soldier (S1, episode 3: 'Command Decision'), Policeman (S2, episode 5: 'A Stripe for Frazer'), Lighthouse Keeper (S4, episode 7: 'Put That Light Out!'), Man with the Door (S8, episode 3: 'Is There Honey Still For Tea?') (TV)

Gordon was also booked as the Fire Chief for episode one, sharing a scene with Mainwaring arguing over the use of the church hall, but the scene was dropped.

A chorister at Durham Cathedral for six years, Gordon worked for Standard Bank as a clerk, and emigrated to Southern Rhodesia with the job. Whilst there he rekindled his interest in acting, winning a talent contest in the process.

He returned to the UK aged 25 and kicked off his professional acting career, initially working as a stand-up comic until club work became scarce. *Dad's Army* was the first of many TV parts alongside his role as a warm-up artist, including a series of his own, *The Gordon Peters Show* and *Now Take My Wife*. Recent work includes cameos in *Keeping Up Appearances* and *One Foot in the Grave*.

Lately, Gordon has been doing old-time music hall acts around the country and cabaret work on cruises. Last Christmas he appeared in cabaret at Butlins in Minehead, and he has recently worked as many of the voices for the TV cartoon, Fred Bassett.

PETERS, MRS
Played by Queenie Watts (TV)
One of Jones' customers in 'The Armoured Might of Lance Corporal Jones', Mrs Peters buys three small lamb chops, corned beef and a couple of sausages.

PETERSEN, JUNE
Role: Woman (S2, episode 6: 'Under Fire') (TV)
June's other television work includes playing a stewardess in BBC's 1953 production, *The Teckman Biography*.

PICKERING, MRS
Not seen or heard in the show, Mrs Pickering is referred to in 'The Miser's Hoard'. Frazer writes her a letter in which he hopes she found the funeral arrangements for her late husband satisfactory. This seems unlikely bearing in mind that the hearse ran out of petrol and she had to help push the vehicle, together with her mother, to her husband's final resting place.

PIERCE, COLONEL
Played by Geoffrey Chater (TV); John Barron (radio)
Colonel Pierce is the military official who co-ordinates Operation Catherine Wheel in 'Round and Round Went the Great Big Wheel'.

PIKE, MAVIS (MRS)
Played by Janet Davies (TV and stage); Liz Fraser (film); Pearl Hackney (radio)
Described by the writers as a 'smart widow, age 40' when the series began, Mrs Pike, who's been known to go out with Hodges occasionally, was seen in the opening episode dragging Frank, her son, from the Home Guard's first parade because it's his bed time, something Mainwaring finds

intolerable, particularly as he's trying to conduct a lecture in the church hall.

Although she rents her house from Hodges, Mrs Pike banks at the Swallow and has invested in shares, so she's not short of a penny or two. She moved to Walmington from the Somerset town of Weston-super-Mare at the same time as Wilson transferred with the bank, a fact that

fuels rumours that Arthur is Frank's real father. Mavis dotes on Wilson, and each year enjoys a *tête-à-tête* supper to celebrate the anniversary of their first meeting. The fact she keeps Wilson's ration book suggests they cohabit, although it's always a topic of conversation Mavis and Arthur avoid.

PIKE, PRIVATE FRANK
Played by Ian Lavender (all mediums)
Raspberryade-loving Frank Pike is a mollycoddled teenager with a delicate disposition, who supposedly suffers from a bad chest, hence the trademark scarf that his mother insists he wears. He's a rather sickly character, whose ailments include hay fever and croup, which are made worse by his mother's incessant pampering – she won't allow him to use a public phone because it's unhygienic. Frank also suffers from vertigo, weak ankles and sinus problems, which his mother used to treat by placing a hot water bottle over his face and ice packs on his feet.

It's never confirmed whether Frank's father is actually Sergeant Wilson, but strong hints are often dropped, especially as he was allowed to call Wilson 'daddy' as a young boy.

When Wilson is promoted to manager of the Eastgate branch, Frank, who's been a clerk since leaving school, is briefly assigned the post of relief chief clerk, but his position of responsibility is

---

MEMORIES OF *DAD'S ARMY*

'I remember the phone call from David Croft's office. "Would you like to play a fire chief in a new sitcom? It's about the Home Guard; there's going to be six episodes, and you'll be in the first one." Of course I accepted. Any television is worth accepting.

'At the first day of rehearsal I met the cast: only Arthur Lowe, John Laurie and Bill Pertwee were known to me. Lasting impressions of the first two days were of David Croft saying again and again to Bill: "Louder, Bill – bully him." Bill was and is one of the quietest people I know, so for him to shout and rail at another person was not easy. The fact that he was in all the series showed that he succeeded in shouting loud enough for David!

'My scene as the fire chief was a two-hander – Arthur and me. We stood in the middle of the church hall and argued over who had the right to be there: Arthur with his soldiers, me with my firemen. All the time we were arguing, my lads were running hoses out between our legs, which gave Arthur ample opportunity to rant and rave, and go purple with exasperation.

'On the third day David took me to one side and said: "We are going to be four minutes over and the only way I can see of getting it to time is to cut your scene completely. I promise I'll book you again as soon as possible." I was very disappointed. I felt it was a reflection on me rather than a logistical problem. However, two weeks later he did phone and I was in again. Actually, I was "in" four times playing different roles.

'I would have been very, very disappointed if I had known what a success the series was going to be. At the time it was just another attempt at a sitcom. I often wonder what would have happened to my career if the Fire Chief had stayed in? It was such a funny scene it would have made an impact with the viewers.

'Several years later, David said: "We should have used that scene in another episode, it was too good to leave out." However, it was left out. Despite that I am still pursuing a career, the mortgage has been paid off years ago, and people don't shout after me: "Put that fire out!"'.

GORDON PETERS

Frank is destined to see out the war years in Walmington, after being refused entry into the RAF. Having passed his medical with flying colours, he is preparing to join the Forces, when a blood-donoring session reveals that he has a very rare blood group and is too high a risk for the Air Force.

Away from his duties at the bank and the Home Guard, Frank is an avid reader of comics, with his greatest literary challenge each week being *The Hotspur*. He's also a keen movie-goer, and is always merging fantasy with reality, comparing real-life events with something he's seen in a Jimmy Cagney movie, or some other silver-screen offering.

Although he's incredibly naïve, foolish and diffident, Frank is full of kindness and may have quite a bright future in the bank by the time he reaches his fifties!

PINNER FIELDS

Located outside Walmington, Pinner Fields is where Walker suggests taking the stray barrage balloon in 'The Day the Balloon Went Up'.

PLATOON

Mainwaring's men (No1 platoon, 'B' Company) wore the insignia of The Queen's Own Royal West Kent Regiment. Although at times members of the Walmington platoon sniped at Mainwaring and disliked his leadership style, particularly Frazer, who was frequently talking behind his captain's back, his men always came to his defence in his hour of need. This is exemplified beautifully in 'Something Nasty in the Vault'. Several members of the platoon put their lives at risk, even though Mainwaring orders them to leave the bank, when he and Wilson find themselves holding the bomb in the strongroom.

'Ring Dem Bells'

temporary because when a bomb flattens the Eastgate branch, Wilson returns to Walmington to resume his old job under Mainwaring's thumb.

Frank, who's a boy scout, also flirted with responsibility in the Home Guard, taking over as lance corporal of the Walmington platoon in 'If the Cap Fits…'; but the opportunity, again, is temporary, which is just as well because he's far too green for such responsibility; after all, would the people of Walmington want to trust their hard-earned pennies, and the defence of their town, to an overgrown boy who spends his sweet ration on hundreds and thousands and used to enjoy mashing up bananas, cream and sugar, before taking a big mouthful and squeezing it through the gaps in his teeth?

DAVID CROFT'S VIEW

'The Mavis Pike – Arthur Wilson relationship added a lovely element to the series. The fact that we never knew if they were partners, or just friends, and whether Pike was Wilson's son was a nice little mystery which was left unresolved, although in my estimation he was always Wilson's son.'

PLATOON MEMBERS

As well as the main characters there were other faces who made up the Walmington Home Guard. Only two episodes ('Menace from the Deep' and 'No Spring for Frazer') didn't require the services of the men who formed the essential back rows. When the first series was transmitted in 1968, the silent soldiers were paid six guineas for each appearance, and their services were required partly to add authenticity to the show. Many of those who stood behind the main cast in the church hall were seasoned pros who were coming to the end of their professional careers, or actors who had turned to walk-on work as a source of income after retiring from a different career.

Although a few of the faces changed during the sitcom's run, a nucleus became an inherent

NOT INCLUDING PRODUCTION TEAM OR MAIN CAST
BACK ROW (LEFT TO RIGHT): Richard Jacques, Arthur McGuire, Hugh Cecil, Frank Godfrey, Jimmy Mac, David Seaforth, Desmond Cullum-Jones, Vernon Drake, Richard Kitteridge, Colin Bean

NOT INCLUDING MAIN CAST
LEFT TO RIGHT: Roger Bourne, Colin Bean, Jimmy Mac, Freddie White, George Hancock, Desmond Cullum-Jones, Evan Ross, Michael Moore, Freddie Wiles, Vernon Drake

component of the platoon's make-up. Even though few were even given a line to say, it was still important that they knew the business. Competent performers know how not to stand out, which was vital in a show like *Dad's Army*.

LEAGUE TABLE OF BACK ROW
APPEARANCES
1. Colin Bean (76)
2. Desmond Cullum-Jones (63)
3. George Hancock (60)
4. Freddie Wiles (57)
5. Freddie White (51)
6. Hugh Cecil (50)
7. Leslie Noyes (49)
8. Michael Moore (45)
9. Vic Taylor (37)
10. Hugh Hastings and
    Evan Ross (34)
12. Roger Bourne (28)
13. Frank Godfrey (23)
14. Jimmy Mac (22)
15. Richard Jacques (17)
16. David Seaforth,
    Richard Kitteridge and
    Alec Coleman (11)
19. William Gossling and
    Vernon Drake (7)
21. Peter Whitaker,
    Martin Dunn and
    Chris Franks (5)
24. Ken Wade (3)
25. Emmett Hennessy and
    Arthur McGuire (2)
27. Freddie Payne,
    Derek Chaffer and
    Lindsay Hooper (1)

PLAZA CINEMA

Residents in the area have two choices when it comes to the cinema. They can either travel over to Eastgate or frequent Walmington's Plaza Cinema, which is run by Mr Cheesewright, with Doreen and Betty in the box office. In the episode 'The Lion has 'Phones', Jones calls the cinema by mistake. He should be phoning GHQ to report a plane crashing in the reservoir, but gets into a muddle regarding the telephone number.

PLOUGH, THE

Wilson and Pike visit The Plough while searching for Frazer, who misses a parade in 'The Miser's Hoard'.

POLICE FORCE, THE

Walmington, being a small town, has a police force that consists of Inspector Baker, who we see in 'A Man of Action', a sergeant and two constables: Dick and George. It's a pretty toothless set-up with Baker being powerless when it comes to preventing Mainwaring declaring martial law when a land mine lands on a railway line, cutting off Walmington's gas and water supplies,

BEHIND THE LINES WITH *DAD'S ARMY*

Hugh Cecil appeared in 50 episodes of the sitcom as a member of the platoon's back row. Although he never uttered a word, his presence was valuable, as was that of the other members.

'It all started as a run-of-the-mill engagement for a dozen older men or types who were unlikely to be called up to serve in the regular forces. I never did find out whether we were chosen from photographs and descriptions in the agent's book, or whether it was just a matter of luck in phoning the agent at the right moment.

'Appearing in *Dad's Army* was a good job inso-far as we were booked for two days a week for six or seven weeks. In addition there were periods of four days upwards when we were on location in Thetford where we would do all the pre-filming for the coming six or seven episodes. Several of us knew each other from previous TV shows, and we were all experienced professionals from one branch or another of showbusiness. This meant, of course, that there was always plenty to talk about – the usual thing when a bunch of pros get together!'

HUGH CECIL

LIFE IN THE BACK ROW

Desmond Cullum-Jones was the second longest-serving member of the Walmington-on-Sea platoon's back row, making 63 appearances in the sitcom. The men who stood behind the principal actors played a crucial part in building a sense of reality about the Home Guard unit. With most of them becoming regular members of the show, stability was provided. If the faces peering over the front line's shoulders were changing each week, it would detract from the fact that this was supposed to be a town's Home Guard where the personnel wouldn't be constantly changing. But I've always wondered whether Desmond, Hugh Cecil and the rest found the job frustrating, bearing in mind they never spoke. I asked Desmond this question, and more, which hopefully provides an insight into the life of the 'back row'.

What was it like being a platoon member in one of this country's greatest sitcoms?
'Initially it was just a job, but after a while a spirit of *esprit de corps* emerged and everyone was very nice to work with. The management was helpful and we weren't "put down" as extras; consequently we were helpful ourselves and interested in the show and its success, and I'm sure it shows.'

Wasn't it frustrating never being able to speak?
'Yes, but most of us, being actors in the main, realised the wisdom of this; being semi-motionless we did not detract from the front rank and "scene steal". Also, those of us who had a commercial bent realised that to speak meant being paid a lot more money and screwing up the budget!'

How was the job explained to you when you started?
'It wasn't. You just kept your eyes open and realised what was happening. If you did it well you were rebooked.'

Could anyone have done the job, or did it take particular skills?
'Possibly the "skills" were in not appearing to have any but avoiding looking like speechless numbskulls.'

Were you made welcome within the team?
'Very much so. A little of the "them and us" occurred but it was very important that the principals should be close-knit and after a while, it all fell into place as people's idiosyncrasies emerged and were allowed for.'

Who were you most friendly with on the show?
'Jimmy Beck and Ian Lavender. We sometimes played poker together, both in my house and occasionally on the film.'

Why do you think the sitcom worked?
'The attitude of the management (David Croft missed nothing). Arthur realised very quickly that the episodes featuring the squad were most popular; he even spoke to us using our names on a couple of shows which helped to make us feel part of the family.'

How much were you paid?
'It started at £3 per day and £10 per day on location. But this grew to £12 and then £15.'

Do the 'back row' platoon members earn repeat fees? If so, has it been a good earner over the years?
'Yes and yes.'

Do you have any regrets about being involved in Dad's Army?
'None whatsoever. In fact, I'm quite proud of it.'

DESMOND CULLUM-JONES

and pulling down the telephone lines. With Mainwaring threatening to imprison anyone who disobeys him, Inspector Baker is worried he won't be able to cope, especially as there are only two cells at the station.

POLICE SERGEANT, THE
Played by Michael Bevis (TV)
In 'The Face On the Poster', the sergeant leaves a poster design, warning the public of an escaped prisoner, at Mr Bugden's printing shop.

POLICE SERGEANT, THE
Played by Anthony Sagar (film)
This unfortunate policeman is on duty at Walmington Police Station when the crowd of local men, who have just heard Eden's plea on the radio, barge in wanting to join the LDV.

POLICEMAN, THE
Played by Gordon Peters (TV)
In 'A Stripe for Frazer' the policeman rushes into the church hall upon hearing Mainwaring blowing a whistle while training his men in how to cope during a gas attack.

POLICEMAN, THE
Played by Arthur English (TV); Stuart Sherwin (radio)
The policeman in 'Absent Friends' calls for the help of the Walmington Home Guard when he discovers an IRA suspect is staying in Ivy Crescent.

POLICEWOMAN, THE
Played by Avril Angers (radio)
In the radio episode 'Brain versus Brawn', the policewoman redirects the fire engine, which the Walmington Home Guard are using, to a burning house. She also asks Mainwaring to give a lift to a 'Sister of Mercy', who is actually Godfrey in disguise. In the TV version, the character is replaced by Hodges.

POLISH OFFICER, THE
Played by Gabor Vernon (TV)
In 'The Face On the Poster' this officer interrogates Jones after he's mistakenly arrested by a Polish soldier, who suspects him of being an escaped prisoner.

PORTER, THE
Played by Jack Le White (TV)
The porter works at Walmington Station and appears in 'Mum's Army'.

POSTLETHWAITE, BERT
Played by Norman Bird (radio)
In the radio episode 'Present Arms', Bert is the stage marksman. In the TV version, 'Shooting Pains', the equivalent character is Laura La Plaz.

POWELL, GEOFF
Designer on three episodes (TV): S9, 'The Making of Private Pike', 'Number Engaged' and 'Never Too Old'

Born in Birmingham, Geoff studied at art school in the city. He taught for a while before packing in his job and driving a delivery van. After talking to a friend who had joined the BBC, Geoff applied and was recruited in 1965 as a holiday relief assistant in BBC Birmingham's design department. He moved to Television Centre (London) via a post in BBC Wales, and was soon promoted to designer. Among the programmes he's worked on are *Blue Peter*, *Top of the Pops*, *Rutland Weekend Television*, *Barlow*, *The Black and White Minstrel Show*, *The Survivors* and *The Insurance Man*, for which he won a BAFTA.

Geoff took voluntary redundancy from the BBC in 1990 and has now retired from the business, dividing his time between homes in England and Italy.

PRAVDA, HANA-MARIA
Born: Prague
Role: Interpreter (S6, episode 5: 'The Honourable Man') (TV)
Hana-Maria believes she resembles a young Maggie Thatcher wearing a strange hat in her role as the fiery interpreter accompanying a Russian visitor.

She grew up in Czechoslovakia and during the Second World War was held in a German concentration camp. As soon as hostilities ended, Hana-Maria returned to the stage and resumed her acting career.

She had already established herself as an actress in Czechoslovakia (three leading film roles and experience at the country's National Theatre) when she left for Australia. She then ran her own theatre company in Melbourne for six years before being spotted by Sybil Thorndike who invited her back to London.

Shortly after arriving, Hana-Maria was cast in a TV series with child actress Mandy Miller after which many theatre roles followed. Recent stage work has included a spell at The Globe Theatre with Tom Conti, while on TV she has been seen in Agatha Christie's *Poirot* and as Mrs Emma Cohen in BBC's *The Survivors*.

Lately, she has been working on the radio. Her war diaries, written during her time in the concentration camp, have recently been broadcast.

PRENTICE, MRS
Played by Brenda Cowling (TV); Nan Kenway (radio)
Described as a 'ruddy-faced, grey-haired woman in her middle sixties' in the original script, Mrs Prentice owns a farm outside Walmington which she's struggling to maintain. In 'All is Safely Gathered In', the platoon come to her rescue at harvest time after Mr Yates of nearby Grove Farm can't thresh her wheat because he's fallen behind with his. Mrs Prentice is an old sweetheart of Godfrey's, from their days together before the Boer War. She was in service in one of the halls in the area, but eventually married a

farmer, not Godfrey. Now a widow, with her foreman in hospital with a hernia problem, one hundred acres of wheat fields is a lot to control with just three land girls to help. In the radio version of 'All is Safely Gathered In' we learn that Mrs Prentice's Christian name is Edwina.

PRINGLE, CAPTAIN
Played by Tim Barrett (TV); Michael Knowles (radio)
Captain Pringle travels down from Area Command to attend the court of inquiry Mainwaring has requested after the platoon waste all their ammunition while on patrol in 'The Bullet is Not for Firing'.

PRITCHARD, COLONEL
Played by Robert Raglan (TV and radio)
In his first two appearances, Pritchard is still a captain. Initially, he's an adjutant at Home Guard headquarters who phones Mainwaring in 'A Wilson (Manager)?' to announce Wilson's commission has come through. He's also present at the School of Explosives in 'Fallen Idol'. Later he appears as a colonel in 14 shows: 'Battle of the Giants', 'Keep Young and Beautiful', 'Desperate Drive of Corporal Jones', 'If the Cap Fits…', 'Brain versus Brawn', 'The Deadly Attachment', 'My British Buddy', 'The Honourable Man', 'Gorilla Warfare', 'The Captain's Car', 'Ring Dem Bells', 'Is There Honey Still For Tea?', 'Wake-Up Walmington' and 'Never Too Old'. He's a levelheaded, experienced man reporting to Major General Menzies; he's also Mainwaring's superior. His responsibilities include controlling all the Home Guard units in the area.

PROBERT, SION
Born: Swansea
Roles: POW and Sentry ('Don't Fence Me In') (radio)
Sion was given his first professional job at the age of 11. He belonged to Swansea Grammar School's drama club and when one of his teachers – who was also a playwright – had a play accepted by Radio 4, Sion played the part of a boy. He was offered several other jobs before he left school and attended drama school at London's Guildhall. After graduating he worked in various plays around the country, including Arnold Ridley's *The Ghost Train*. On stage he's appeared in numerous productions over the years, several with the English Shakespeare Company.

On radio he has worked with the BBC Drama Repertory Company, with Arthur Lowe on several occasions and more recently in Ostrovsky's *The Storm*, *A Kind of Justice* and *Making the Grade*. His television credits, meanwhile, include playing a holidaymaker in *Hi-De-Hi!*, *The Citadel*, *The Sweeney*, *How Green was my Valley*, *The Bill*, *Casualty* and *Next of Kin*.

Sion is still busy acting, most of his work these days being in the theatre.

THE ROLE OF THE PRODUCER'S ASSISTANT

'The Producer's Assistant is the lynchpin of the office as she/he is the one person who knows what all the others are doing. The PA has the responsibility of making sure all the bureaucratic 'bumf' so beloved of the BBC is completed, arranging editing sessions for film and VT, sending out scripts, film schedules, rehearsal time, doing the camera script, checking times, chasing the others up to find the answers to questions they try to dodge, and generally being the fount of all knowledge.

'The PA is responsible for keeping the filming script up to date with take numbers and timings (vital), continuity, script detail, and at the end of the filming day has to make out the notes for the film editor back at London watching the "rushes" and making up a rough-cut while the unit is still away.

'In the studio the PA has to call all the shots to the cameras on the floor who depend on this to know where they are in the script, check timing, make notes of re-takes, etc, to mark up an editing script for the VT.

'When the recordings are finished the PA has to complete the programme costings for the departmental manager, and complete even more paperwork to ensure that everyone gets paid and that every single detail of the programme (music, copyright, all details of film in that episode, and all timings for extra payments for artists, etc). This is kept for life (theoretically) as the "Bible" of that show in case of any future arguments.

'The PA types all the "thank you" letters and makes sure that everyone knows which programme should go out on the due date. She/he is usually the only one left in the office to do this as everyone else has gone off either on a break or to another programme.

'All the time this is going on the telephone never ever stops ringing, unless she/he throws it across the office! This screed regarding the job of a PA makes the person seem superhuman – believe me, the good ones are!'

JO AUSTIN

PRODUCER'S ASSISTANT

During the show's life, eight people occupied the important role of producer's assistant. Assisting David Croft in a range of duties, they worked busily behind the scenes aiding the smooth process of production. The duties of the producer's assistant included typing scripts, camera scripts, rehearsal schedules and ensuring the necessary records for use of incidental and background music were obtained from the BBC's sound library.

PRODUCTION ASSISTANT

The production assistant (PA), later to be called production manager, was a crucial member of the production team. Numerous people wore the production assistant's hat during the show's nine-year run. For the eighth series and two specials ('My Brother and I' and 'The Love of Three Oranges') Jo Austin, who became the first female production manager in Light Entertainment, was the incumbent.

PROSSER, MRS

Played by Eleanor Smale (TV)
A friend of Jones, the timid Mrs Prosser, who's 83, is first mentioned in 'A Stripe for Frazer', when we learn that she's a member of the WVS. She partners him to the platoon dance in 'War Dance', but although there is the occasional suggestion that, perhaps, there is more to the friendship than meets the eye, Jones is quick to point out they're just good friends. In 'Mum's Army'

Jones explains that in return for giving her cat some meat and taking her some eggs, Mrs Prosser keeps him company from time to time.

PUGH, MAVIS

Born: Kent
Role: Lady Maltby (S7, episode 5: 'The Captain's Car') (TV)
As a child, Mavis, who came from a legal family, was a keen dancer and fond of literature so her choice to study drama at Oxford's International School of Acting upon leaving the Downs College came as no surprise to her family.

She made her first stage appearance with comedian Ernest Lotinga, making audiences laugh as the child in a tour of *My Wife's Family*. Spells in rep followed, but it wasn't long before she was at The Westminster Theatre playing Beth in *Little Women*, and taking over the title role in *Junior Miss* at the Saville Theatre and on a year-long tour. After returning, she appeared with Michael Denison and Dulcie Gray at The Westminster Theatre in *We Must Kill Toni*, before touring with a farce, *Talk of the Town Hall*, in which she was seen by Jimmy Perry. He asked her to join him at The Palace Theatre, Watford, where she was soon to meet her future husband, John Clegg.

Her television credits include appearances in *Are You Being Served?*, an episode of *Fawlty Towers* playing Mrs Chase in 'The Kipper and the Corpse', *Spooner's Patch*, *PC Penrose*, Mrs Barrable in *Sorry!*, Winnie Dempster in *Hi-De-*

Hi!, *Life Without George*, *Close to Home*, *Smith and Jones*, *Boon*, *The Stanley Baxter Show*, a belligerent army official in *It Ain't Half Hot, Mum* and four years as one of her greatest successes, the vague and zany Lady Lavender Meldrum in Jimmy Perry and David Croft's, *You Rang, M'Lord?*.

Her theatre work in an extensive career has ranged from a string of bedroom farces opposite Hugh Paddick, to Mrs Alving in *Ghosts*, Norah in *A Doll's House*, Blanche DuBois in *A Streetcar Named Desire*, Sarah Kahn in *Chicken Soup With Barley* and Mme Raquin in *Therese Raquin*.

Her film appearances include Mrs Barnet in *A Class of Miss McMichael* with Glenda Jackson in 1978, *Half a Sixpence*, *The Revenge of the Pink Panther* and the mother in *Brothers and Sisters*. Mavis, who is still acting, has also directed many plays, including farces for Ray Cooney and two one-man shows. She has one, as yet, unfulfilled ambition: to make a short comedy film.

PUT THAT LIGHT OUT!

(This episode was based on an idea by Harold Snoad)
Recorded: Friday 30/10/70
Original transmission: Friday 6/11/70, 8.00–8.30pm
Original viewing figures: 13 million
Repeated: 11/7/71, 21/11/92, 26/11/92 (Wales), 6/5/01

CAST

Arthur Lowe	Captain Mainwaring
John Le Mesurier	Sergeant Wilson
Clive Dunn	Lance Corporal Jones
John Laurie	Private Frazer
James Beck	Private Walker
Arnold Ridley	Private Godfrey
Ian Lavender	Private Pike
Bill Pertwee	ARP Warden
Stuart Sherwin	Mr Alberts (2nd ARP Warden)
Gordon Peters	Lighthouse Keeper
Avril Angers	Freda, the Telephone Operator

Platoon: Colin Bean, Hugh Hastings, Vic Taylor

PRODUCTION TEAM

Script: Jimmy Perry and David Croft
Producer/Director: David Croft
Production Assistant: Phil Bishop
Studio Lighting: George Summers
Studio Sound: Michael McCarthy
Design: Paul Joel
Assistant Floor Manager: Roger Singleton-Turner
Vision Mixer: Dave Hanks
Costume Supervisor: George Ward
Make-Up Supervisor: Cynthia Goodwin

Mainwaring has got permission to set up an observation post in the lighthouse, which nowadays is only used in special cases. Jones' section is to rendezvous at the Jolly Roger Ice Cream Parlour and cross the causeway to the lighthouse. They start their duty at 8pm and their task is to

'Put That Light Out!'

keep their eyes open for any fifth columnist spies until morning.

When they realise the telephone and electric supply have been cut off, Jones tries taking control and while searching for a solution, he turns the generator on, illuminating the entire coastline, just in time for the air raid sirens. With the light spotlighting the whole of Walmington, Mainwaring, Hodges, Walker, Wilson and Mr Alberts – another warden – discuss how to extinguish the light. Walker's suggestion to put the transformer out of action is an idea Mainwaring decides to try, but he ends up fusing all the lights in the Jolly Roger Parlour but not the lighthouse because it has its own generator, as the keeper informs them when he arrives on the scene. They phone the telephone exchange to see if they'll reconnect the line to the lighthouse. Mainwaring struggles to get through to the woman at the exchange, so Walker comes to the rescue. Instructions are eventually passed to Jones who's able to shut down the generator just in time.

THE INSPIRATION BEHIND 'PUT THAT LIGHT OUT!'

'The basic idea came to me one day when it suddenly occurred to me that there could be fun gained from the use of the Warden's slogan ("Put That Light Out!") if applied to a much larger light. I spent a lot of my youth living at Eastbourne and fairly frequently saw Beachy Head lighthouse. I remember associating the two ideas and realising the possibilities.

'I put the idea of the platoon using the lighthouse – and the problem that would arise if they accidentally switched on the huge beam lighting up Walmington just as an air raid starts – to Jimmy and David who were very keen. Obviously none of us were that conversant with the basic workings and layout of a lighthouse, so I contacted the authorities at Trinity House and gained permission for Jimmy and myself to visit the one at Beachy Head. A date was duly arranged for the recce and as access can only be gained by boat I also fixed this up with a local company. I remember driving down to Eastbourne with my wife early on the agreed date and finding the boatman on the beach declaring that, unfortunately, the sea was particularly rough that day and the trip wouldn't be possible. We met Jimmy off the train and I had to break this news to him.

'We (and the designer, Paul Joel) eventually did some other research instead – without actually visiting a lighthouse – and managed to gain enough information to make it work.'

HAROLD SNOAD

RADIO

Harold Snoad and Michael Knowles adapted many of the television scripts for radio. Harold explains how the idea came about.

'I don't really know who had the idea for doing a radio version of *Dad's Army* – probably someone in radio. What I do remember is that at the time David and Jimmy were up to their eyes writing the sixth television series and couldn't cope with anything more. So when the project came up Richard Stone, who was Michael's agent for acting and mine for writing, asked if Jimmy and David would be happy if Michael and I did it.

'Jimmy and David's answer was in the affirmative because they knew that I was inventive as I had come up with ideas for the TV series and, previously, with storylines for *Up Pompeii!* starring Frankie Howerd. Jimmy also knew that Michael and I had also come up with ideas together for the Sid James series, *Bless This House*, and had written together before, including cabaret material for Bill Pertwee.

'It also helped, of course, that I had worked on the TV version of *Dad's Army* for five years and was, therefore, pretty familiar with the episodes and the characters.'

EPISODE LIST
SERIES ONE
The Man and the Hour
Museum Piece
Command Decision
The Enemy Within the Gates
The Battle of Godfrey's Cottage
The Armoured Might of Lance Corporal Jones
Sgt Wilson's Little Secret
A Stripe for Frazer
Operation Kilt
Battle School
Under Fire
Something Nasty in the Vault
The Showing Up of Corporal Jones
The Loneliness of the Long-Distance Walker
Sorry, Wrong Number (TV equivalent is 'The Lion has 'Phones')
The Bullet is Not for Firing
Room at the Bottom

Menace from the Deep
No Spring for Frazer
Sons of the Sea

Christmas Special
Present Arms (TV equivalent is the combined episodes, 'Battle of the Giants' and 'Shooting Pains')

SERIES TWO
Don't Forget the Diver
If the Cap Fits…
Put That Light Out!
Boots, Boots, Boots
Sgt – Save My Boy!
Branded
Uninvited Guests
A Brush with the Law
A Soldier's Farewell
Brain versus Brawn
War Dance
Mum's Army
Getting the Bird
Don't Fence Me In
The King was in his Counting House
When Did You Last See Your Money?
Fallen Idol
A Wilson (Manager)?
All is Safely Gathered In
The Day the Balloon Went Up

SERIES THREE
Man of Action
The Honourable Man
The Godiva Affair
Keep Young and Beautiful
Absent Friends
Round and Round Went the Great Big Wheel
The Great White Hunter (TV equivalent is 'Man Hunt')
The Deadly Attachment
Things That Go Bump in the Night
My British Buddy
Big Guns
The Big Parade
Asleep in the Deep
We Know Our Onions
The Royal Train
A Question of Reference (TV equivalent is 'Desperate Drive of Lance Corporal Jones')
High Finance
The Recruit
A Jumbo-Sized Problem (TV equivalent is 'Everybody's Trucking')
The Cricket Match (TV equivalent is 'The Test')
Time On My Hands
Turkey Dinner
The Captain's Car
The Two and a Half Feathers
Is There Honey Still For Tea?
Ten Seconds From Now (TV equivalent is 'Broadcast to the Empire')

CAST LISTS
Arthur Lowe (Captain Mainwaring), John Le Mesurier (Sergeant Wilson) and Clive Dunn (Lance Corporal Jones) featured in each of the 67 radio episodes. Therefore, only additional cast members are listed below.

SERIES ONE
'The Man and the Hour'
Recorded: Sunday 3/6/73
First transmission: Monday 28/1/74, 6.15–6.45pm (Audience: 0.9 million) and Wednesday 30/1/74, 12.27–12.57pm (Audience: 1.2 million)
ADDITIONAL CAST
Arnold Ridley (Pte Godfrey), James Beck (Pte Walker), Ian Lavender (Pte Pike), John Laurie (Pte Frazer), Timothy Bateson (Elliott / General Wilkinson / GHQ driver)

'Museum Piece'
Recorded: Thursday 7/6/73
First transmission: Monday 4/2/74, 6.15–6.45pm (Audience: 0.9 million) and Wednesday 6/2/74, 12.27–12.57pm (Audience: 1.1 million)
ADDITIONAL CAST
James Beck (Pte Walker), John Laurie (Pte Frazer), Ian Lavender (Pte Pike), Eric Woodburn (George Jones)

'Command Decision'
Recorded: Thursday 21/6/73
First transmission: Monday 11/2/74, 6.15–6.45pm (Audience: 0.6 million) and Wednesday 13/2/74, 12.27–12.57pm (Audience: 1 million)
ADDITIONAL CAST
John Laurie (Pte Frazer), James Beck (Pte Walker), Geoffrey Lumsden (Colonel Square), David Sinclair (GHQ driver)

'The Enemy Within the Gates'
Recorded: Thursday 21/6/73
First transmission: Monday 18/2/74, 6.15–6.45pm (Audience: 1 million) and Wednesday 20/2/74, 12.27–12.57pm (Audience: 1.3 million)
ADDITIONAL CAST
James Beck (Pte Walker), Arnold Ridley (Pte Godfrey), Ian Lavender (Pte Pike), Carl Jaffé (Captain Winogrodzki), David Sinclair (German airman)

'The Battle of Godfrey's Cottage'
Recorded: Friday 6/7/73
First transmission: Monday 25/2/74, 6.15–6.45pm (Audience: 1.1 million) and Wednesday 27/2/74, 12.27–12.57pm (Audience: 0.8 million)
ADDITIONAL CAST
John Laurie (Pte Frazer), Arnold Ridley (Pte Godfrey), Ian Lavender (Pte Pike), Bill Pertwee (ARP Warden), Nan Braunton (Cissy Godfrey), Percy Edwards (Percy the Parrot)

'The Armoured Might of Lance Corporal Jones'
Recorded: Friday 6/7/73
First transmission: Monday 4/3/74, 6.15–6.45pm

(Audience: 0.9 million) and Wednesday 6/3/74, 12.27–12.57pm (Audience: no figures available due to industrial dispute)

ADDITIONAL CAST
John Laurie (Pte Frazer), James Beck (Pte Walker), Bill Pertwee (ARP Warden), Pearl Hackney (Mrs Pike), Richard Davies (the Volunteer), Elizabeth Morgan (Mrs Leonard), Diana Bishop (Miss Meadows)

'Sgt Wilson's Little Secret'
Recorded: Friday 13/7/73
First transmission: Monday 11/3/74, 6.15–6.45pm (Audience: 1.3 million) and Wednesday 13/3/74, 12.27–12.57pm (Audience: 1.1 million)

ADDITIONAL CAST
James Beck (Pte Walker), Arnold Ridley (Pte Godfrey), Ian Lavender (Pte Pike), Bill Pertwee (ARP Warden), Pearl Hackney (Mrs Pike)

'A Stripe for Frazer'
Recorded: Friday 13/7/73
First transmission: Monday 18/3/74, 6.15–6.45pm (Audience: 1 million) and Wednesday 20/3/74, 12.27–12.57pm (Audience: 1 million)

ADDITIONAL CAST
John Laurie (Pte Frazer), James Beck (Pte Walker), Ian Lavender (Pte Pike), Geoffrey Lumsden (Corporal-Colonel Square), Michael Knowles (Captain Bailey)

By the time this episode was transmitted, Jimmy Beck had died. It was his last piece of *Dad's Army* work to be broadcast. Unlike the TV series, the radio series retained his character, with Graham Stark and Larry Martyn playing the part.

'Operation Kilt'
Recorded: Monday 23/7/73
First transmission: Monday 25/3/74, 6.15–6.45pm (Audience: 1.3 million) and Wednesday 27/3/74, 12.27–12.57pm (Audience: 1 million)

ADDITIONAL CAST
John Laurie (Pte Frazer), Ian Lavender (Pte Pike), Arnold Ridley (Pte Godfrey), Pearl Hackney (Mrs Pike), Jack Watson (Captain Ogilvy)

'Battle School'
Recorded: Thursday 28/6/73
First transmission: Monday 1/4/74, 6.15–6.45pm (Audience: 1 million) and Wednesday 3/4/74, 12.27–12.57pm (Audience: 0.8 million)

ADDITIONAL CAST
John Laurie (Pte Pike), Arnold Ridley (Pte Godfrey), Ian Lavender (Pte Pike), Jack Watson (Major Smith), Alan Tilvern (Captain Rodrigues)

'Under Fire'
Recorded: Friday 27/7/73
First transmission: Monday 8/4/74, 6.15–6.45pm (Audience: 0.8 million) and Wednesday 10/4/74, 12.27–12.57pm (Audience: 0.9 million)

ADDITIONAL CAST
John Laurie (Pte Frazer), Arnold Ridley (Pte

Godfrey), Pearl Hackney (Mrs Pike), Geoffrey Lumsden (Corporal-Colonel Square), Avril Angers (Mrs Keane), David Gooderson (Mr Murphy)

'Something Nasty in the Vault'
Recorded: Monday 23/7/73
First transmission: Monday 15/4/74, 6.15–6.45pm (Audience: 0.7 million) and Wednesday 17/4/74, 12.27–12.57pm (Audience: 1.2 million)

ADDITIONAL CAST
John Laurie (Pte Frazer), Ian Lavender (Pte Pike), Bill Pertwee (ARP Warden), John Barron (Mr West), Frank Thornton (Captain Rogers), Elizabeth Morgan (Janet King)

'The Showing Up of Corporal Jones'
Recorded: Friday 20/7/73
First transmission: Monday 22/4/74, 6.15–6.45pm (Audience: 1.2 million) and Wednesday 24/4/74, 12.27–12.57pm (Audience: 0.7 million)

ADDITIONAL CAST
John Laurie (Pte Frazer), Arnold Ridley (Pte Godfrey), Graham Stark (Pte Walker), Jack Watson (Major Regan)

'The Loneliness of the Long-Distance Walker'
Recorded: Friday 20/7/73
First transmission: Monday 29/4/74, 6.15–6.45pm (Audience: 0.9 million) and Wednesday 1/5/74, 12.27–12.57pm (Audience: 1 million)

ADDITIONAL CAST
John Laurie (Pte Frazer), Arnold Ridley (Pte Godfrey), Graham Stark (Pte Walker), Jack Watson (the Sergeant / the Brigadier), Judith Furse (Chairwoman), Michael Knowles (the Captain / Mr Rees)

'Sorry, Wrong Number'
(TV equivalent is 'The Lion has 'Phones')
Recorded: Friday 27/7/73
First transmission: Monday 6/5/74, 6.15–6.45pm (Audience: 1 million) and Wednesday 8/5/74, 12.27–12.57pm (Audience: 1 million)

ADDITIONAL CAST
John Laurie (Pte Frazer), Ian Lavender (Pte Pike), Graham Stark (Pte Walker), Bill Pertwee (ARP Warden), Pearl Hackney (Mrs Pike), Avril Angers (the Telephone Operator), John Forest (Lieutenant Hope-Bruce)

'The Bullet is Not for Firing'
Recorded: Thursday 26/7/73
First transmission: Monday 13/5/74, 6.15–6.45pm (Audience: 1 million) and Wednesday 15/5/74, 12.27–12.57pm (Audience: 0.9 million)

ADDITIONAL CAST
Arnold Ridley (Pte Godfrey), Graham Stark (Pte Walker), Frank Williams (the Vicar), Michael Knowles (Captain Pringle), Timothy Bateson (Captain Marsh), John Whitehall (all members of the choir)

'Room at the Bottom'
Recorded: Monday 23/7/73
First transmission: Monday 20/5/74, 6.15–6.45pm

(Audience: 0.7 million) and Wednesday 22/5/74, 12.27–12.57pm (Audience: 1.2 million). Next repeat: Sunday 3/6/84, 11.40am on Radio 4 as *Smash of the Day*.

ADDITIONAL CAST
John Laurie (Pte Frazer), Arnold Ridley (Pte Godfrey), John Ringham (Captain Turner), Jack Watson (Sergeant Gregory)

'Menace from the Deep'
Recorded: Tuesday 24/7/73
First transmission: Monday 27/5/74, 6.15–6.45pm (Audience: 0.6 million) and Wednesday 29/5/74, 12.27–12.57pm (Audience: 0.8 million)

ADDITIONAL CAST
John Laurie (Pte Frazer), Ian Lavender (Pte Pike), Bill Pertwee (ARP Warden), David Sinclair (2nd ARP Warden)

'No Spring for Frazer'
Recorded: Thursday 26/7/73
First transmission: Monday 3/6/74, 6.15–6.45pm (Audience: 1 million) and Wednesday 5/6/74, 12.27–12.57pm (Audience: 0.8 million)

ADDITIONAL CAST
John Laurie (Pte Frazer), Arnold Ridley (Pte Godfrey), Edward Sinclair (the Verger), Joan Cooper (Miss Baker), Timothy Bateson (Mr Blewitt / Captain Turner)

'Sons of the Sea'
Recorded: Wednesday 25/7/73
First transmission: Monday 10/6/74, 6.15–6.45pm (Audience: 0.9 million) and Wednesday 12/6/74, 12.27–12.57pm (Audience: 0.6 million)

ADDITIONAL CAST
Ian Lavender (Pte Pike), John Laurie (Pte Frazer), Arnold Ridley (Pte Godfrey), Timothy Bateson (Mr Maxwell and all other characters)

Christmas Special
'Present Arms' (TV equivalent is the combined episodes, 'Battle of the Giants' and 'Shooting Pains')
Recorded: Thursday 18/7/74
First transmission: Wednesday 25/12/74, 1.15–2.15pm (Audience: 0.7 million) and Thursday 26/12/74, 7.30–8.30pm (Audience: 0.7 million)

ADDITIONAL CAST
John Laurie (Pte Frazer), Ian Lavender (Pte Pike), Arnold Ridley (Pte Godfrey), Larry Martyn (Pte Walker), Bill Pertwee (Chief Warden), Pearl Hackney (Mrs Pike), Geoffrey Lumsden (Captain Square), Jack Watson (the Brigadier / Cheerful Charlie Cheeseman), Norman Bird (Bert Postlewaite)

SERIES TWO
'Don't Forget the Diver'
Recorded: Tuesday 16/7/74
First transmission: Tuesday 11/2/75, 12.27–12.57pm (Audience: 1.1 million) and Thursday 13/2/75, 6.15–6.45pm (Audience: 0.6 million). Next repeat: Sunday 14/3/82, 5pm on Radio 2 as part of *Comedy Classics*.

ADDITIONAL CAST

John Laurie (Pte Frazer), Ian Lavender (Pte Pike), Arnold Ridley (Pte Godfrey), Edward Sinclair (the Verger), Geoffrey Lumsden (Captain Square), Norman Ettlinger (the Sergeant)

'If the Cap Fits…'

Recorded: Wednesday 17/4/74

First transmission: Tuesday 18/2/75, 12.27–12.57pm (Audience: 1 million) and Thursday 20/2/75, 6.15–6.45pm (Audience: 0.8 million). Next repeat: Sunday 24/1/82, 5pm on Radio 2 as part of Comedy Classics.

ADDITIONAL CAST

John Laurie (Pte Frazer), Ian Lavender (Pte Pike), Arnold Ridley (Pte Godfrey), Edward Sinclair (the Verger), Fraser Kerr (Major General Menzies / Sergeant MacKenzie)

'Put That Light Out!'

Recorded: Tuesday 30/4/74

First transmission: Tuesday 25/2/75, 12.27–12.57pm (Audience: 0.9 million) and Thursday 27/2/75, 6.15–6.45pm (Audience: 0.8 million)

ADDITIONAL CAST

John Laurie (Pte Frazer), Ian Lavender (Pte Pike), Arnold Ridley (Pte Godfrey), Bill Pertwee (ARP Warden), Avril Angers (the Telephone Operator), Stuart Sherwin (Lighthouse Keeper)

'Boots, Boots, Boots'

Recorded: Tuesday 16/4/74

First transmission: Tuesday 4/3/75, 12.27–12.57pm (Audience: 1.1 million) and Thursday 6/3/75, 6.15–6.45pm (Audience: 0.7 million)

ADDITIONAL CAST

John Laurie (Pte Frazer), Ian Lavender (Pte Pike), Arnold Ridley (Pte Godfrey), Erik Chitty (Mr Sedgewick)

'Sgt – Save My Boy!'

Recording: Tuesday 16/4/74

First transmission: Tuesday 11/3/75, 12.27–12.57pm (Audience: 0.9 million) and Thursday 13/3/75, 6.15–6.45pm (Audience: 0.5 million). Next repeat: Sunday 13/3/83, 5pm on Radio 2 as part of Comedy Classics.

ADDITIONAL CAST

John Laurie (Pte Frazer), Ian Lavender (Pte Pike), Arnold Ridley (Pte Godfrey), Pearl Hackney (Mrs Pike)

'Branded'

Recorded: Wednesday 17/7/74

First transmission: Tuesday 18/3/75, 12.27–12.57pm (Audience: 1.1 million) and Thursday 20/3/75, 6.15–6.45pm (Audience: 0.7 million)

ADDITIONAL CAST

John Laurie (Pte Frazer), Ian Lavender (Pte Pike), Arnold Ridley (Pte Godfrey), Bill Pertwee (Chief Warden Hodges), Nan Braunton (Cissy Godfrey), Michael Segal (2nd Warden), Norman Ettlinger (the Doctor)

'Uninvited Guests'

Recorded: Thursday 18/4/74

First transmission: Tuesday 25/3/75, 12.27–12.57pm (Audience: 0.9 million) and Thursday 27/3/75, 6.15–6.45pm (Audience: 0.7 million)

ADDITIONAL CAST

John Laurie (Pte Frazer), Ian Lavender (Pte Pike), Arnold Ridley (Pte Godfrey), Bill Pertwee (ARP Warden), Frank Williams (the Vicar), Edward Sinclair (the Verger)

'A Brush with the Law'

Recorded: Wednesday 17/7/74

First transmission: Tuesday 1/4/75, 12.27–12.57pm (Audience: 1 million) and Thursday 3/4/75, 6.15–6.45pm (Audience: 1.1 million)

ADDITIONAL CAST

John Laurie (Pte Frazer), Ian Lavender (Pte Pike), Arnold Ridley (Pte Godfrey), Larry Martyn (Pte Walker), Bill Pertwee (Chief Warden Hodges), Geoffrey Lumsden (Captain Square), Edward Sinclair (the Verger), Michael Segal (2nd Warden), Michael Knowles (Mr Wintergreen), Norman Ettlinger (the Clerk of the Court)

'A Soldier's Farewell'

Recorded: Wednesday 15/5/74

First transmission: Tuesday 8/4/75, 12.27–12.57pm (Audience: 1.4 million) and Thursday 10/4/75, 6.15–6.45pm (Audience: 0.8 million). Next repeat: Sunday 28/2/82, 5pm on Radio 2 as part of Comedy Classics.

ADDITIONAL CAST

John Laurie (Pte Frazer), Ian Lavender (Pte Pike), Arnold Ridley (Pte Godfrey), Larry Martyn (Pte Walker), Bill Pertwee (ARP Warden), Pat Coombs (the Clippie / Marie)

'Brain versus Brawn'

Recorded: Tuesday 30/4/74

First transmission: Tuesday 15/4/75, 12.27–12.57pm (Audience: 0.8 million) and Thursday 17/4/75, 6.15–6.45pm (Audience: 0.7 million)

ADDITIONAL CAST

John Laurie (Pte Frazer), Ian Lavender (Pte Pike), Arnold Ridley (Pte Godfrey), Larry Martyn (Pte Walker), Avril Angers (the Waitress / the Policewoman), Robert Raglan (Colonel Pritchard), Stuart Sherwin (Mr Fairbrother / the Corporal)

'War Dance'

Recorded: Sunday 12/5/74

First transmission: Tuesday 22/4/75, 12.27–12.57pm (Audience: 1.2 million) and Thursday 24/4/75, 6.15–6.45pm (Audience: 0.7 million). Next repeat: Sunday 24/6/84, 11.40am on Radio 4 as Smash of the Day.

ADDITIONAL CAST

John Laurie (Pte Frazer), Ian Lavender (Pte Pike), Arnold Ridley (Pte Godfrey), Larry Martyn (Pte Walker), Pearl Hackney (Mrs Pike), Wendy Richard (Violet Gibbons)

'Mum's Army'

Recorded: Sunday 12/5/74

First transmission: Tuesday 29/4/75, 12.27–12.57pm (Audience: 0.7 million) and Thursday 1/5/75, 6.15–6.45pm (Audience: 0.7 million). Next repeat: Sunday 3/4/83, 5 pm on Radio 2 as part of Comedy Classics.

ADDITIONAL CAST

John Laurie (Pte Frazer), Ian Lavender (Pte Pike), Arnold Ridley (Pte Godfrey), Larry Martyn (Pte Walker), Carmen Silvera (Mrs Gray), Mollie Sugden (Mrs Fox / the Waitress), Wendy Richard (Edith Parish)

'Getting the Bird'

Recorded: Monday 15/7/74

First transmission: Tuesday 6/5/75, 12.27–12.57pm (Audience: 0.9 million) and Thursday 8/5/75, 6.15–6.45pm (Audience: 0.6 million)

ADDITIONAL CAST

John Laurie (Pte Frazer), Ian Lavender (Pte Pike), Arnold Ridley (Pte Godfrey), Larry Martyn (Pte Walker), Frank Williams (the Vicar), Diana Bishop (Sergeant Wilson's daughter)

'Don't Fence Me In'

Recorded: Thursday 16/5/74

First transmission: Tuesday 13/5/75, 12.27–12.57pm (Audience: 0.9 million) and Thursday 15/5/75, 6.15–6.45pm (Audience: 0.8 million)

ADDITIONAL CAST

John Laurie (Pte Frazer), Ian Lavender (Pte Pike), Arnold Ridley (Pte Godfrey), Larry Martyn (Pte Walker), Cyril Shaps (General Monteverdi), John Ringham (Captain Turner), Sion Probert (the POW / the Sentry)

'The King was in his Counting House'

Recorded: Wednesday 15/5/74

First transmission: Tuesday 20/5/75, 12.27–12.57pm (Audience: 1.2 million) and Thursday 22/5/75, 6.15–6.45pm (Audience: 0.8 million). Next repeat: Sunday 10/6/84, 11.40am on Radio 4 as Smash of the Day, and Friday 15/9/89, 10.30 pm on Radio 2.

ADDITIONAL CAST

John Laurie (Pte Frazer), Ian Lavender (Pte Pike), Arnold Ridley (Pte Godfrey), Larry Martyn (Pte Walker), Bill Pertwee (ARP Warden), Wendy Richard (Shirley)

'When Did You Last See Your Money?'

Recorded: Wednesday 15/5/74

First transmission: Tuesday 27/5/75, 12.27–12.57pm (Audience: 0.7 million) and Thursday 29/5/75, 6.15–6.45pm (Audience: 0.6 million). Next repeat: Sunday 27/2/83, 5pm on Radio 2 as part of Comedy Classics, and Friday 22/9/89, 10.30 pm on Radio 2.

ADDITIONAL CAST

John Laurie (Pte Frazer), Ian Lavender (Pte Pike), Arnold Ridley (Pte Godfrey), Timothy Bateson (Mr Blewitt / Mr Billings)

'Fallen Idol'
Recorded: Tuesday 16/7/74
First transmission: Tuesday 3/6/75, 12.27–12.57pm
(Audience: 0.9 million) and Thursday 5/6/75,
6.15–6.45pm (Audience: 0.8 million). Next repeat:
Sunday 7/3/82, 5pm on Radio 2 as part of *Comedy Classics*.

ADDITIONAL CAST
John Laurie (Pte Frazer), Ian Lavender (Pte Pike),
Arnold Ridley (Pte Godfrey), Geoffrey Lumsden
(Captain Square), Jack Watson (Captain Reed),
Michael Brennan (the Sergeant-Major), Norman
Ettlinger (Pritchard)

'A Wilson (Manager)?'
Recorded: Wednesday 17/4/74
First transmission: Tuesday 10/6/75, 12.27–12.57pm
(Audience: 0.9 million) and Thursday 12/6/75,
6.15–6.45pm (Audience: 0.7 million)

ADDITIONAL CAST
John Laurie (Pte Frazer), Ian Lavender (Pte Pike),
Arnold Ridley (Pte Godfrey), Edward Sinclair (the
Verger), Michael Knowles (Captain Bailey), Fraser
Kerr (Mr West)

'All is Safely Gathered In'
Recorded: Monday 15/7/74
First transmission: Tuesday 17/6/75, 12.27–12.57pm
(Audience: 0.8 million) and Thursday 19/6/75,
6.15–6.45pm (Audience: 0.7 million)

ADDITIONAL CAST
John Laurie (Pte Frazer), Ian Lavender (Pte Pike),
Arnold Ridley (Pte Godfrey), Bill Pertwee (ARP
Warden), Frank Williams (the Vicar), Nan Kenway
(Mrs Prentice)

'The Day the Balloon Went Up'
Recorded: Thursday 18/4/75
First transmission: Tuesday 24/6/75, 12.27–12.57pm
(Audience: 0.9 million) and Thursday 26/6/75,
6.15–6.45pm (Audience: 0.8 million). Next repeat:
Sunday 31/1/82, 5pm on Radio 2 as part of *Comedy Classics*.

ADDITIONAL CAST
John Laurie (Pte Frazer), Ian Lavender (Pte Pike),
Arnold Ridley (Pte Godfrey), Bill Pertwee (ARP
Warden), Frank Williams (the Vicar), Edward Sinclair
(the Verger), Michael Knowles (Squadron Leader
Horsfall)

SERIES THREE
'Man of Action'
Recorded: Monday 28/4/75
First transmission: Tuesday 16/3/76, 12.27–12.57pm
(Audience: 0.8 million) and Thursday 18/3/76,
6.15–6.45pm (Audience: 0.5 million)

ADDITIONAL CAST
John Laurie (Pte Frazer), Ian Lavender (Pte Pike),
Arnold Ridley (Pte Godfrey), Larry Martyn (Pte
Walker), Bill Pertwee (Chief Warden Hodges), Julian
Orchard (Mr Upton – the Town Clerk), Jonathan
Cecil (Mr Norris), Fraser Kerr (Captain Swan / the
Inspector)

MICHAEL KNOWLES' VIEWS ON RADIO ADAPTATIONS

'At the time we wrote the scripts there was a fashion for adapting successful TV shows for sound radio, until radio got a bit grand and announced they weren't taking any more material from television.

'Nothing as complicated as *Dad's Army* had ever been attempted; Harold and I approached the project with great enthusiasm and a confidence born of ignorance because we had never adapted anything for radio before.

'When asked about the difficulties of adapting something so very visual I always quote the example of an episode where the final shot is of a dog scampering into the sunset with a bomb in its mouth. Of course you could just have a character say: "Look at that dog with a bomb in its mouth", but that's not awfully good radio so you write another scene which delivers a similar message in a different way.

'Harold and I were often told when we started: "You can't do that, it won't work on radio. You can't send Mainwaring up with a balloon, you can't have virtually a whole episode on a boat on the river, or the entire platoon crammed into a runaway train." But with John Dyas' help, we did a lot of those things that couldn't be done and, for the most part, they worked. In fact, I think I can say, without undue modesty, that Harold and I helped push forward the boundaries of radio sitcom!'

MICHAEL KNOWLES

'The Honourable Man'
Recorded: Monday 28/4/75
First transmission: Tuesday 23/3/76, 12.27–12.57pm
(Audience: 0.7 million) and Thursday 25/3/76,
6.15–6.45pm (Audience: 0.6 million). Next repeat:
Sunday 20/3/83, 5pm on Radio 2 as part of *Comedy Classics*.

ADDITIONAL CAST
John Laurie (Pte Frazer), Ian Lavender (Pte Pike),
Arnold Ridley (Pte Godfrey), Larry Martyn (Pte
Walker), Bill Pertwee (ARP Warden), Julian Orchard
(Mr Upton – the Town Clerk), Fraser Kerr (the
Visiting Russian)

'The Godiva Affair'
Recorded: Monday 5/5/75
First transmission: Tuesday 30/3/76, 12.27–12.57pm
(Audience: 0.7 million) and Thursday 1/4/76,
6.15–6.45pm (Audience: 0.4 million). Next repeat:
Sunday 21/2/82, 5pm on Radio 2 as part of *Comedy Classics*.

ADDITIONAL CAST
John Laurie (Pte Frazer), Ian Lavender (Pte Pike),
Arnold Ridley (Pte Godfrey), Larry Martyn (Pte
Walker), Bill Pertwee (ARP Warden), Frank Williams
(the Vicar), Julian Orchard (Mr Upton), Mollie
Sugden (Mrs Fox)

'Keep Young and Beautiful'
Recorded: Monday 12/5/75
First transmission: Tuesday 6/4/76, 12.27–12.57pm
(Audience: 0.7 million) and Thursday 8/4/76,
6.15–6.45pm (Audience: 0.6 million). Next repeat:
Sunday 20/2/83, 5pm on Radio 2 as part of *Comedy Classics*.

ADDITIONAL CAST
John Laurie (Pte Frazer), Ian Lavender (Pte Pike),
Arnold Ridley (Pte Godfrey), Larry Martyn (Pte
Walker), Michael Burlington (the Wig Maker)

'Absent Friends'
Recorded: Tuesday 6/5/75
First transmission: Tuesday 13/4/76, 12.27–12.57pm
(Audience: 0.7 million) and Thursday 15/4/76,
6.15–6.45pm (Audience: 0.5 million)

ADDITIONAL CAST
John Laurie (Pte Frazer), Ian Lavender (Pte Pike),
Arnold Ridley (Pte Godfrey), Larry Martyn (Pte
Walker), Bill Pertwee (Chief Warden Hodges), Pearl
Hackney (Mrs Pike), Michael Brennan (Tom /George
Pearson), Stuart Sherwin (the Policeman)

'Round and Round Went the Great Big Wheel'
Recorded: Wednesday 7/5/75
First transmission: Tuesday 20/4/76, 12.27–12.57pm
(Audience: 0.6 million) and Thursday 22/4/76,
6.15–6.45pm (Audience: 0.7 million)

ADDITIONAL CAST
John Laurie (Pte Frazer), Ian Lavender (Pte Pike),
Arnold Ridley (Pte Godfrey), Larry Martyn (Pte
Walker), Bill Pertwee (ARP Warden), John Barron
(Colonel Pierce), Michael Knowles (Captain
Stewart)

'The Great White Hunter'
(TV equivalent is 'Man Hunt')
Recorded: Friday 30/5/75
First transmission: Tuesday 27/4/76, 12.27–12.57pm
(Audience: 0.6 million) and Thursday 29/4/76,
6.15–6.45pm (Audience: 0.4 million). Next repeat:
Saturday 1/4/95, 7 pm on Radio 2 as part of *Comedy Classics*, introduced by Ken Bruce.

ADDITIONAL CAST
John Laurie (Pte Frazer), Ian Lavender (Pte Pike),
Arnold Ridley (Pte Godfrey), Larry Martyn (Pte
Walker), Pearl Hackney (Mrs Pike), Elizabeth Morgan
(Housewife), Fraser Kerr (the Policeman)

DIFFERENCES BETWEEN THE SCREEN AND RADIO

Because the original scripts, written by Perry and Croft, were so visual, Snoad and Knowles' job of adapting them for radio was a challenge, particularly as 67 episodes were to be broadcast on the airwaves. An example of a script that couldn't simply be transferred to radio intact was 'The Day the Balloon Went Up', which includes a scene where Mainwaring is pulled up in the air by a stray barrage balloon that the platoon are trying to guide to safety. On TV it's fine to have one character on his own, but for radio where dialogue, and situations that can evoke dialogue, are crucial, someone had to be alongside Mainwaring, holding on for their life while being pulled across the sky; so Jones, who was always a glutton for punishment, was written into the radio script, providing someone Mainwaring could talk to. Other scenes couldn't be modified and were too visual for alteration, leaving the writers no alternative but to write a completely fresh scene.

Some of the more significant changes included combining the primary storylines in the TV episodes, 'Shooting Pains' and 'Battle of the Giants' to produce 'Present Arms', in which the Eastgate and Walmington platoons compete against each other to win the right to provide the Guard of Honour for the Prime Minister's impending visit.

The small-screen episode, 'Everybody's Trucking', was renamed 'A Jumbo-Sized Problem', and included several script alterations; most significantly, instead of the road being blocked by a showman's trailer, the platoon's progress is impeded by an elephant trailer. The elephant proceeds to pull Jones' van out of mud, but only succeeds in releasing the cab, leaving the trailer behind; the elephant sits on the bonnet of Hodges' vehicle, crushing it.

'Broadcast to the Empire', which started out as a ten-minute sketch for the 1972 programme, *Christmas Night with the Stars*, was retitled, 'Ten Seconds From Now', and extended to approximately 30 minutes. The radio version followed the television script but additional scenes were introduced, including Jones teaching the platoon tactics, a build up to the rehearsals and Mainwaring trying to get his wife to listen to the broadcast instead of the popular comedy series, *Happidrome*, on another station.

Other changes affected 'The Godiva Affair'. Although the storyline is similar, the beginning of the radio version finds the platoon performing the floral dance instead of morris dancing as in the TV episode.

There are also instances of scenes being borrowed from other episodes, as in the radio version of 'Battle School'. The episode opens with the platoon learning how to deal with Nazi tanks in a scene similar to that in the small-screen episode 'The Man and the Hour'. The TV version of 'Battle School', meanwhile, opens with the platoon in the train on the way to the school.

There are also examples where lines of dialogue are spoken by a different character in the radio version. In 'Room at the Bottom', while it's the Verger who runs to Mainwaring informing him the Bismarck has been sunk, it's Frazer in the radio script. And in 'Under Fire', Sigmund Murphy is married to Hodges' Aunt Ethel in the TV version, but on radio he was married to Mrs Pike's aunt.

Finally, names were occasionally altered for the radio, an example being Walmington's town clerk: Mr Rees and Mr Gordon on TV were replaced by Mr Upton on the airwaves. And some characters weren't even used on the radio, such as one of Godfrey's elderly sisters: although Cissy featured in radio episodes, Dolly was never heard of.

'The Deadly Attachment'
Recorded: Wednesday 30/4/75
First transmission: Tuesday 4/5/76, 12.27–12.57pm (Audience: 0.8 million) and Thursday 6/5/76, 6.15–6.45pm (Audience: 0.5 million). Next repeat: Saturday 8/4/95, 7pm on Radio 2 as part of *Comedy Classics*, introduced by Ken Bruce.

ADDITIONAL CAST

John Laurie (Pte Frazer), Ian Lavender (Pte Pike), Arnold Ridley (Pte Godfrey), Larry Martyn (Pte Walker), Frank Williams (the Vicar), Philip Madoc (Captain Muller), Fraser Kerr (Colonel Winters)

'Things That Go Bump in the Night'
Recorded: Wednesday 7/5/75
First transmission: Tuesday 11/5/76, 12.27–12.57pm (Audience: 0.7 million) and Thursday 13/5/76, 6.15–6.45pm (Audience: 0.7 million). Next repeat: Saturday 15/4/95, 7pm on Radio 2 as part of *Comedy Classics*, introduced by Ken Bruce.

ADDITIONAL CAST

John Laurie (Pte Frazer), Ian Lavender (Pte Pike), Arnold Ridley (Pte Godfrey), Larry Martyn (Pte Walker), John Barron (Captain Cadbury)

'My British Buddy'
Recorded: Tuesday 6/5/75
First transmission: Tuesday 18/5/76, 12.27–12.57pm (Audience: 0.7 million) and Thursday 20/5/76, 6.15–6.45pm (Audience: 0.7 million). Next repeat: Saturday 22/4/95, 7pm on Radio 2 as part of *Comedy Classics*, introduced by Ken Bruce.

ADDITIONAL CAST

John Laurie (Pte Frazer), Ian Lavender (Pte Pike), Arnold Ridley (Pte Godfrey), Larry Martyn (Pte Walker), Bill Pertwee (Chief Warden Hodges), Jack Watson (Colonel Schultz), Pearl Hackney (Mrs Pike), Mollie Sugden (Mrs Fox), Wendy Richard (Shirley), Michael Middleton (the American Sergeant)

'Big Guns'
Recorded: Monday 5/5/75
First transmission: Tuesday 25/5/76, 12.27–12.57pm (Audience: 0.8 million) and Thursday 27/5/76, 6.15–6.45pm (Audience: 0.7 million). Next repeat: Saturday 29/4/95, 7pm on Radio 2 as part of *Comedy Classics*, introduced by Ken Bruce.

ADDITIONAL CAST

John Laurie (Pte Frazer), Ian Lavender (Pte Pike), Arnold Ridley (Pte Godfrey), Larry Martyn (Pte Walker), Julian Orchard (Mr Upton – the Town Clerk), Michael Middleton (the Pickfords Man)

'The Big Parade'
Recorded: Friday 2/5/75
First transmission: Tuesday 1/6/76, 12.27–12.57pm (Audience: 0.8 million) and Thursday 3/6/76, 6.15–6.45pm (Audience: 0.3 million)

ADDITIONAL CAST

John Laurie (Pte Frazer), Ian Lavender (Pte Pike), Arnold Ridley (Pte Godfrey), Larry Martyn (Pte Walker), Bill Pertwee (Chief Warden Hodges), Edward Sinclair (the Verger), Pearl Hackney (Mrs Pike)

'Asleep in the Deep'
Recorded: Friday 9/5/75
First transmission: Tuesday 8/6/76, 12.27–12.57pm (Audience: 0.5 million) and Thursday 19/6/76, 6.15–6.45pm

ADDITIONAL CAST

John Laurie (Pte Frazer), Ian Lavender (Pte Pike), Arnold Ridley (Pte Godfrey), Larry Martyn (Pte Walker), Bill Pertwee (ARP Warden)

'We Know Our Onions'
Recorded: Thursday 8/5/75
First transmission: Tuesday 15/6/76, 12.27–12.57pm (Audience: 0.7 million) and Thursday 17/6/76, 6.15–6.45pm (Audience: 0.5 million)

ADDITIONAL CAST

John Laurie (Pte Frazer), Ian Lavender (Pte Pike), Arnold Ridley (Pte Godfrey), Larry Martyn (Pte Walker), Bill Pertwee (ARP Warden), Alan Tilvern (Captain Ramsay), Michael Middleton (Sergeant Baxter)

'The Royal Train'

Recorded: Tuesday 29/4/75

First transmission: Tuesday 22/6/76, 12.27–12.57pm
(Audience: 0.7 million) and Thursday 24/6/76,
6.15–6.45pm (Audience: 0.6 million)

ADDITIONAL CAST

John Laurie (Pte Frazer), Ian Lavender (Pte Pike),
Arnold Ridley (Pte Godfrey), Bill Pertwee (ARP
Warden), Frank Williams (the Vicar), Stuart Sherwin
(the Station Master), Fraser Kerr (the Train Driver),
Michael Middleton (the Driver's Mate)

**'A Question of Reference' (TV equivalent is
'Desperate Drive of Lance Corporal Jones')**

Recorded: Monday 12/5/75

First transmission: Tuesday 29/6/76, 12.27–12.57pm
(Audience: 0.5 million) and Thursday 1/7/76,
6.15–6.45pm (Audience: 0.6 million)

ADDITIONAL CAST

John Laurie (Pte Frazer), Ian Lavender (Pte Pike),
Arnold Ridley (Pte Godfrey), Larry Martyn (Pte
Walker), Peter Williams (the Colonel), Michael
Burlington (the Signaller)

'High Finance'

Recorded: Friday 27/6/75

First transmission: Tuesday 6/7/76, 12.27–12.57pm
(Audience: 0.7 million) and Thursday 8/7/76,
6.15–6.45pm (Audience: 0.6 million). Next repeat:
Sunday 27/3/83, 5pm on Radio 2 as part of *Comedy
Classics*.

ADDITIONAL CAST

John Laurie (Pte Frazer), Ian Lavender (Pte Pike),
Arnold Ridley (Pte Godfrey), Larry Martyn (Pte
Walker), Bill Pertwee (Chief Warden Hodges), Pearl
Hackney (Mrs Pike), Frank Williams (the Vicar)

'The Recruit'

Recorded: Thursday 1/5/75

First transmission: Tuesday 13/7/76, 12.27–12.57pm
(Audience: 0.6 million) and Thursday 15/7/76,
6.15–6.45pm (Audience: 0.7 million)

ADDITIONAL CAST

John Laurie (Pte Frazer), Ian Lavender (Pte Pike),
Arnold Ridley (Pte Godfrey), Larry Martyn (Pte
Walker), Bill Pertwee (Chief Warden Hodges), Frank
Williams (the Vicar), Edward Sinclair (the Verger),
Elizabeth Morgan (the Nurse and the Small Boy)

**'A Jumbo-Sized Problem'
(TV equivalent is 'Everybody's Trucking')**

Recorded: Wednesday 18/6/75

First transmission: Tuesday 20/7/76, 12.27–12.57pm
(Audience: 0.7 million) and Thursday 22/7/76,
6.15–6.45pm (Audience: 0.5 million). Next repeat:
Sunday 6/3/83, 5pm on Radio 2 as part of *Comedy
Classics*, and Friday 8/9/89, 10.30pm on Radio 2.

ADDITIONAL CAST

John Laurie (Pte Frazer), Ian Lavender (Pte Pike),
Arnold Ridley (Pte Godfrey), Larry Martyn (Pte
Walker), Bill Pertwee (Chief Warden Hodges)

HAROLD SNOAD ON THE RADIO SERIES

**When Jimmy Beck died, the character of
Walker was handed over to Graham Stark
and, finally, Larry Martyn. What made you
decide, unlike the TV series, to retain the
character?**

'At the time we learned that Jimmy Beck had
died, Michael and I had already adapted the
first batch of episodes and they were being
recorded. Jimmy was last heard in episode
eight of that first series. Graham Stark took
the role over at very short notice and was
heard in four episodes of the first series of 20
episodes. When we came to do the second
batch of 20, John Dyas, the producer, asked for
my suggestion for recasting Walker on a long-
term basis and I came up with Larry Martyn
whom I had worked with in TV several times.
He was subsequently heard in 32 episodes.

'We never considered leaving the character
out because we were adapting TV episodes in
which Walker had already been established as
part of the episode storyline. David and
Jimmy, of course, were writing new episodes
much further ahead of us and, therefore, in
new storylines had a free hand when it came
to involving another character.'

**Why did you decide to change some of the
episode titles?**

'I think the idea of changing some episode
titles was the decision of John Dyas. "Sorry,
Wrong Number", for example, verbally her-
alds a storyline rather better than "The Lion
has 'Phones". "A Question of Reference" –
referring to a map reference – means a bit
more than "The Desperate Drive of Corporal Jones", "The Cricket Match" isn't quite so
vague as "The Test" and "Ten Seconds from
Now" is slightly more punchy than "Broadcast to the Empire".'

**Why did you decide to adapt just some of
the episodes for radio, and how did you
select them?**

'We started off by adapting episodes establishing the platoon – obviously essential, and
then moved on leaving out episodes that we
felt were fairly "visual". At that stage our brief
was to adapt 20 episodes – we had no idea
we were going to finish up rewriting 67 of
them! When we came to do the next batch
we tried following the same lines but as the
adventures of the platoon were, by now,
inevitably more "visual", Michael and I
accepted that we would have to change the
scheme of things and include a number of the
visual – but not too visual – episodes. We also
went back and included episodes that fitted
into this brief previously omitted when we
adapted the first batch.

'There were still certain ones that just
wouldn't work – a good example being "My

Brother and I" where Arthur Lowe played
both Mainwaring and his brother – not easy
on radio! And "Gorilla Warfare" which
involved a member of the platoon not realising that a gorilla was creeping up on him!'

**Why did you alter the occasional character
name? For example, the town clerk was Mr
Upton in the radio series and Mr Gordon on
TV.**

'I think there were occasions when John Dyas
did this so he could use actors that he had
worked with before on radio. To avoid upsetting the actor used in the TV version he
changed the character name. There were
probably also occasions when he wanted to
use someone cheaper for radio than the actor
who had played a part on TV, and he felt it was
more tactful to change the character's name.'

**Why were the radio episodes transmitted in a
different order from the TV versions?**

'This relates back to the answer to your earlier question. We started off by adapting and
recording less "visual" episodes; then with the
brief to adapt a second 20 and then a further
27 we had to concentrate on some that John
Dyas had originally told us not to include in
our plans. Therefore they were recorded and
transmitted in a different order to the TV
versions. I remember there was a Christmas
episode called "Present Arms" in which we
used a combination of elements from "Everybody's Trucking" and "Battle of the Giants"
but that still didn't make it long enough so
Michael and I wrote extra material to bring it
to the right length.'

Were you happy with the radio episodes?

'Yes, we were very happy with the radio
episodes and, obviously, the listeners enjoyed
them which made the BBC happy. In view of
the continued repeats of the TV episodes
Michael and I are amazed that the radio
episodes aren't also repeated every so often.
We feel that they would make ideal listening
at around 6pm when people are in their cars
driving home from work. Still, there you go!'

**What were some of the difficulties you
encountered when adapting episodes for
radio?**

'Some episodes were a lot more difficult than
others but I honestly can't remember the
details. It was a very long time ago! I do
remember that in "The Day the Balloon Went
Up" we decided to have Jones caught up on
the balloon with Mainwaring simply because
– without being up there with Mainwaring to
see what was happening – it seemed a better
idea to be able to hear two people talking
about their problems rather than the alternative of people on the ground below just doing
a commentary.'

'The Cricket Match' (TV equivalent is 'The Test')
Recorded: Thursday 1/5/75
First transmission: Tuesday 27/7/76, 12.27–12.57pm
(Audience: 0.5 million) and Thursday 29/7/76,
6.15–6.45pm (Audience: 0.5 million)

ADDITIONAL CAST
John Laurie (Pte Frazer), Ian Lavender (Pte Pike),
Arnold Ridley (Pte Godfrey), Bill Pertwee
(Chief Warden Hodges), Frank Williams (the Vicar),
Edward Sinclair (the Verger), Anthony Smee
(G C Egan)

'Time On My Hands'
Recorded: Tuesday 29/4/75
First transmission: Tuesday 3/8/76, 12.27–12.57pm
(Audience: 0.9 million) and Thursday 5/8/76,
6.15–6.45pm (Audience: 0.8 million). Next repeat:
Friday 29/9/89, 10.30pm on Radio 2.

ADDITIONAL CAST
John Laurie (Pte Frazer), Ian Lavender (Pte Pike),
Arnold Ridley (Pte Godfrey), Larry Martyn (Pte
Walker), Bill Pertwee (Chief Warden Hodges), Frank
Williams (the Vicar), Erik Chitty (Mr Parsons), Fraser
Kerr (German Pilot)

'Turkey Dinner'
Recorded: Friday 2/5/75
First transmission: Tuesday 10/8/76, 12.27–12.57pm
(Audience: 0.7 million) and Thursday 12/8/76,
6.15–6.45pm (Audience: 0.8 million). Next repeat:
Saturday 29/12/90, 10am on Radio 4 as *Smash of the
Day*.

ADDITIONAL CAST
John Laurie (Pte Frazer), Ian Lavender (Pte Pike),
Arnold Ridley (Pte Godfrey), Larry Martyn (Pte
Walker), Bill Pertwee (Chief Warden Hodges), Frank
Williams (the Vicar), Pearl Hackney (Mrs Pike),
Harold Bennett (Mr Blewitt)

'The Captain's Car'
Recorded: Friday 9/5/75
First transmission: Tuesday 17/8/76, 12.27–12.57pm
(Audience: 0.7 million) and Thursday 19/8/76,
6.15–6.45pm (Audience: 0.6 million). Next repeat:
Sunday 7/2/82, 5pm on Radio 2 as part of *Comedy
Classics*.

ADDITIONAL CAST
John Laurie (Pte Frazer), Ian Lavender (Pte Pike),
Arnold Ridley (Pte Godfrey), Larry Martyn (Pte
Walker), Bill Pertwee (Chief Warden Hodges), Betty
Marsden (Lady Maltby), Gerard Green (Colonel)

'The Two and a Half Feathers'
Recorded: Thursday 8/5/75
First transmission: Tuesday 24/8/76, 12.27–12.57pm
(Audience: 0.9 million) and Thursday 26/8/76,
6.15–6.45pm (Audience: 0.5 million)

ADDITIONAL CAST
John Laurie (Pte Frazer), Ian Lavender (Pte Pike),
Arnold Ridley (Pte Godfrey), Larry Martyn (Pte
Walker), Bill Pertwee (Chief Warden Hodges),
Michael Bates (Pte Clarke), Avril Angers (Edna)

'Is There Honey Still For Tea?'
Recorded: Friday 11/7/75
First transmission: Tuesday 31/8/76, 12.27–12.57pm
(Audience: 0.8 million) and Thursday 2/9/76,
6.15–6.45pm (Audience: 0.7 million). Next repeat:
Sunday 17/6/84, 11.40am on Radio 4 as *Smash of the
Day.*

ADDITIONAL CAST
John Laurie (Pte Frazer), Ian Lavender (Pte Pike),
Arnold Ridley (Pte Godfrey), Joan Cooper (Cissy
Godfrey), Fraser Kerr (Sir Charles Renfrew-
McAllister / the Colonel)

**'Ten Seconds From Now' (TV equivalent is
'Broadcast to the Empire')**
Recorded: Wednesday 18/6/75
First transmission: Tuesday 7/9/76, 12.27–12.57pm
(Audience: 0.9 million) and Thursday 9/9/76,
6.15–6.45pm (Audience: 0.6 million). Next repeats:
Sunday 14/2/82, 5pm on Radio 2 as part of *Comedy
Classics*, and Friday 1/9/89, 10.30pm on Radio 2.

ADDITIONAL CAST
John Laurie (Pte Frazer), Ian Lavender (Pte Pike),
Arnold Ridley (Pte Godfrey), Larry Martyn (Pte
Walker), Frank Thornton (BBC Producer), Roger
Gartland (Bert – the BBC Engineer)

PRODUCTION CREDITS
Scripts: the original TV scripts were adapted by
Harold Snoad and Michael Knowles.
Producer: John Dyas
Each of the episodes was introduced by BBC
announcer, John Snagge, and recorded at The
Playhouse Theatre, Northumberland Avenue,
London and the Paris Studios, Lower Regent
Street, London.

TV EPISODES NOT ADAPTED FOR RADIO
Series 7: 'Gorilla Warfare'
Series 8: 'Ring Dem Bells', When You've Got to
Go', 'Come In, Your Time is Up', 'The Face on the
Poster'
Series 9: 'Wake-Up Walmington', 'The Making of
Private Pike', 'Knights of Madness', 'The Miser's
Hoard', 'Number Engaged', 'Never Too Old'
Special Christmas Episodes: 'My Brother and I',
'The Love of Three Oranges'
Sketches for *Christmas Night with the Stars*: Only
the 1972 sketch, 'Broadcast to the Empire' was
adapted for the radio in its own right. The basis
of the 1970 sketch ('The Cornish Floral Dance')
replaced the morris dancing in the radio adapta-
tion of 'The Godiva Affair'.

RADIO FUN
Radio Fun was a comic printed during the 1930s.
When Mainwaring cracks a rare joke in 'Turkey
Dinner', Private Cheeseman says he'll send it to
the comic because they pay anything from half a
crown to five bob for jokes.

RADIO SHOP ASSISTANT, THE
Played by John Henderson (film)
When Mainwaring hears that Anthony Eden will
be addressing the nation on the radio, he,
together with Arthur Wilson and Frank Pike,
rushes across to Elliott's Radio Store in the High
Street and demands to listen to one of their
models. Sadly, as far as the shop assistant's commission is concerned, Mainwaring hasn't the
slightest intention of buying anything.

RAF OFFICER, THE
Played by Kenneth Watson (TV)
The RAF officer arrives on a motorbike in the
closing scene of 'The Day the Balloon Went Up'
to congratulate Mainwaring and his men for
looking after the stray barrage balloon.

RAGLAN, ROBERT (1906–1985)
Born: Reigate
Roles: HG Sergeant ('Don't Forget the Diver'),
Captain Pritchard ('A Wilson (Manager)?' and 'Fallen
Idol') (TV); Colonel (14 episodes) (TV); Inspector
Hardcastle (film); Colonel Pritchard ('Brain versus
Brawn') (radio)
After joining a water company office straight
from school, Robert – whose brother James was
also an actor – left to attend drama school. He
worked in various reps until war broke out,
during which he served in the REME before
touring overseas with ENSA.

Frequently cast as policemen or military officials, he resumed his acting career after demob
and quickly made his film debut. Although he
never topped the billing, a busy big-screen career
boasts over 70 films, including *Brothers in Law*,
Private's Progress, *A Night to Remember*, *Jigsaw* and
Man from Tangier, playing Inspector Meredith.

After suffering two heart attacks while appearing with Robert Morley in the West End, he
retired from the stage and concentrated on TV
in shows such as *George and Mildred*, *Are You
Being Served?*, *Shelley* and *Bless this House*.
Although he never starred in any production he
was always a solid, dependable supporting actor.

RAMSEY, CAPTAIN
Played by Fulton MacKay (TV); Alan Tilvern (radio)
During the episode 'We Know Our Onions' the
Scottish Captain Ramsey runs the weekend effi-
ciency test that Mainwaring and his men attend.

RATIONING
War means privations and even before the outbreak of hostilities, plans were being drawn up
to cater for rationing. A Ministry of Food was

David Croft and Jimmy Perry mingle
with the cast of *The Rear Guard*.

established days after war was declared, headed by Lord Woolton who went on to appeal successfully to housewives in the drive to ration supplies. Ration books had already been printed for every household, but rationing was not actually introduced until a poll showed the move had the public's backing.

Some foods were rationed by weight, others by value, while some were controlled by the use of coupons, known as points. Items such as fish and offal were never rationed, just hard to get. Such conditions created a gold mine for black marketeers, like Walker, who used their contacts to obtain items which had become luxuries.

Inevitably, rationing and food shortages were frequently spotlighted in *Dad's Army*, with Jones spending Monday evenings counting ration coupons, and always trying to do the best for his customers by providing a little on the side.

RAYMOND
Played by John Ash and Dick Haydon (TV)
Raymond is Jones' young assistant at the butcher's shop. He's a capable lad who's occasionally told to hold the fort while Jones pops out on an errand or across to see Mainwaring at the bank.

REAGAN, WALLY
Not seen in the sitcom, Wally is an old school friend of Frazer's who was the lighthouse keeper on Fairloch Rock. Frazer tells Pike about him in 'Put That Light Out!'.

REAR GUARD, THE
In 1974, Jimmy Perry and David Croft wrote a prospective script with the intention of selling their successful comedy format to an American television station. The new script was based on the first episode transmitted on British TV, 'The Man and the Hour'. Retaining the *Dad's Army* title, the script was set in Tulls Point, a small fictitious coastal town in Maine, USA. The date was early spring, 1942, a few months after Pearl Harbor.

While some of the characters retained their original *Dad's Army* name, others were changed, but all boasted character traits identified in their British forebears. Heading the bank in Tulls Point was Cornelius P Bishop, who was given the grand title of president rather than manager. 'A short, fat, bald-headed, pompous man in his mid-fifties', he resembled Mainwaring in many ways. His vice-president was Arthur Wilson, also in his mid-fifties, 'an acid-faced man' and a loser. Frank Pike, meanwhile, was a 'spotty-faced high school boy of 17 who works as a teller at the bank in his spare time and during school vacations'. Other characters were Jack Jones, owner of the town's butcher's shop, and Jethro Muldoon (the Frazer-based character) the town's undertaker. Jethro was described as 'a tall thin cadaverous character with flowing white hair and wild eyes', but unlike his Scottish counterpart, he was a 'fanatical teetotaller and prohibitionist'. Charles Godfrey was a 'gentle old bachelor', Bill Hodges the Chief Air Raid Warden, who owned a diner, and Nick Azzeretti (based on Walker) was the owner of the local pool hall; instead of exploiting the black market for a living he simply had contacts who could provide the occasional luxury.

When Jimmy Perry and David Croft set out to sell the *Dad's Army* format to the States, they soon attracted interest from a production company owned by Herman Rush, and in 1976 California-based Herman Rush Associates negotiated an agreement securing the exclusive option to produce an American version of *Dad's Army*. Part of the agreement stated that the BBC would not sell the original British version to any TV companies for prime time viewing during the life of the agreement.

At this time, Rush – an independent producer who also adapted *'Till Death Us Do Part* – was hunting for British formats he could remake for the American market. He decided to have his own script written instead of using Perry and Croft's, but was impressed with their material, and arranged to spend time watching *Dad's Army* being made in the UK. He liked the show so much, he worked out the arrangement to option the rights to bring it to the States.

Rush was confident the series could be Americanised, and although the US people didn't suffer air raids, they experienced blackouts, air raid wardens and Home Guard units. The pilot was transmitted on 10 August 1976 at 10pm by ABC. The station was initially excited by the prospect, but when it was shown to focus groups prior to full transmission, the response was poor, and the show never progressed. Reflecting on the pilot's lack of success, Rush feels the problem was that not enough people remembered those days. At that time in the 1970s, he felt there was a different generation of young people watching television, and he couldn't attract enough interest from advertisers to sponsor the programme.

The Rear Guard pilot, created by Arthur Julian

CAST

Lou Jacobi . . . . .Max Raskin
Cliff Norton . . . . .Nick Rosatti
Jim Connell . . . . .Father Fitzgerald
Ronda Copland . . . . .Marsha Wilson
Dennis Kort . . . . .Bobby Henderson
John McCook . . . . .Don Crawford
Arthur Peterson . . . . .Mr Muldoon
Eddie Foy, Jr . . . . .Bert Wagner

Conrad Janis . . . . .German Captain
James McCullion . . . . .Colonel Walsh
Dave Morick . . . . .Frank Sanicola
Don Diamond . . . . .Foster
Claude Jones . . . . .Krupinsky

PRODUCTION TEAM

Executive Producer: Herman Rush
Associate Producer: Dee Baker
Written and produced by Arthur Julian
Music by Pete Rugolo
Theme lyrics by Solomon Burke and Herman Rush
Vocals by The Willow Sisters
Art Director: Edward Stephenson
Costumes: Ed Smith
Assistant to the producer: Lorraine Sevre Kenney
Casting: Marsha Kleinman and Pat Harris
Associate director: Anthony Chickey
Post Production Associate Director: Hal Collins
Unit Manager: Robert M. Furiga
Engineering Supervisor: Gerry Bobian
Studio Supervisor: Darrell Gentry
Technical Director: Jim Doll
Lighting Director: Jack Denton

"THE REAR GUARD"

Plot ideas from the British "Dad's Army" show, transcribed from a telephone conversation with Jimmy Perry.

--

"Dad's Army" was developed to be a war series with no violence whatsoever. The (ABC pilot) was the only episode in which the characters actually meet the Germans. All of the other stories deal with the conflicts and petty jealousies of a small town and the frustrations of trying to deal with the wartime situation. The threat of conflict was always there, but mainly the characters were dealing with the people in the town and facing up to the wartime restrictions--the shortages, the rations, the black market, and the various frustrations--generally the problems of small town life. The town is located on the south coast of Kent, right on the channel.

DAD'S ARMY - Story Ideas

The type of situations our local heroes -- DAD'S ARMY -- would become involved in:

1.   German U-Boat sighted off the coast of Maine runs aground and DAD'S ARMY is in charge of holding the U-Boat captain and crew until appropriate authorities arrive.

2.   Local factory that manufactures munitions for U.S. Army is having problems. DAD'S ARMY is called to patrol, and suspects sabotage.

3.   Since town is on the Atlantic coast and because of U-Boat threat, there are local blackouts. DAD'S ARMY assists in making sure blackout rules are adhered to.

4.   A stranger arrives in town and arouses the suspicions of DAD'S ARMY that he is a spy. (He turns out to be an FBI agent and his cover is inadvertantly blown by our heroes.)

5.   There is an Army base located outside of town. DAD'S ARMY, not realizing they are holding maneuvers, decides the enemy has landed and surrounds the GIs.

6.   The British home office sends a Colonel Blimp type from their home guard to America to offer instruction to their American cousins and he is assigned to our group in Maine.

7.   On Flag Day DAD'S ARMY decides to hold a parade to display their newest uniforms and equipment. Unbeknownst to them the Army base has made the same decision and the two parades collide as they round the corner of 5th and Main.

8.   DAD'S ARMY is holding special training and conflict erupts between our General and one of the Privates as to who is in command.

9.   Washington sends a retired General to visit with DAD'S ARMY to bring them up to date on the latest methods of defense. He turns out to be a greater bumbler than our heroes.

If the pilot of *The Rear Guard* had taken off, Herman Rush already had a batch of ideas for further episodes.

Senior Video: Bud Hendricks

Audio: Art Du Pont

Stage Managers: Jerry Blumenthal and James Woodworth

Production Administrator: Ron Von Schimmelmann

Production Co-ordinator: Bryant Henry

Production Supervisor: Conrad Holzgang

Based on *Dad's Army*, created by Jimmy Perry and David Croft. A BBC production.

Video taped at ABC Television Centre, Hollywood, California.

Herman Rush Associates in association with Wolper Productions.

PROLOGUE

Much has been written about those gallant soldiers of World War Two who met and defeated the enemy. But there were those who stayed behind to defend our shores. They were the men of the Civil Defence to whom this show is dedicated.

Based on the *Dad's Army* episode, 'The Deadly Attachment', the Long Island civil defence unit find themselves guarding a German U-boat crew, after local fisherman, Frank Sanicola, spots the enemy while returning from a fishing trip. A captain and five members of his crew are picked up and, with the regular army 85 miles away, the civil defence will have to guard them.

Unlike the British version where the sailors are fed on fish and chips, one of the American soldiers goes off to buy salami sandwiches and one corned beef, for the fussy U-boat captain. But he doesn't get his way and the order is placed as six salami sandwiches.

The American version is disappointing, in my view. Obviously it's difficult seeing other actors play characters based on Mainwaring, Wilson et al, even if there are blatant differences. One example is the sergeant who's much more loud-mouthed and outspoken than Wilson, boasting none of the quiet, unassuming manner we associate with and adore in Le Mesurier's performance.

The clerical influence rests with Father Fitzgerald, while the pretty, voluptuous Marsha, who works at the local aircraft plant, adds the love interest. The captain, Nick Rosatti, is just as bravehearted as Mainwaring, and can't wait to get his hands on the enemy, while Bobby Henderson is based on Pike, constantly referring to Gary Cooper and the like. Bert Wagner is a 70 year old who always wants the toilet – so you can guess who he's based on – while Mr Muldoon is custodian of the church, and just as much a troublemaker as Mr Yeatman.

Filmed entirely in the studio, the script remains close to the original episode, but doesn't quite ring true when 'Don't tell him, Pike!' is changed into 'Don't tell him, Henderson!'

See 'Selected Scripts' for Jimmy Perry and David Croft's American version of *Dad's Army* and Arthur Julian's pilot for *The Rear Guard*.

'The Recruit'

RECRUIT, THE

Recorded: Sunday 22/7/73

Original transmission: Wednesday 12/12/73, 6.50–7.20pm

Original viewing figures: 11.5 million

Repeated: 6/6/74, 8/1/94, 13/2/94 (Wales), 19/7/97

CAST

Arthur Lowe . . . . Captain Mainwaring
John Le Mesurier . . . . Sergeant Wilson
Clive Dunn . . . . Lance Corporal Jones
John Laurie . . . . Private Frazer
Arnold Ridley . . . . Private Godfrey
Ian Lavender . . . . Private Pike
Bill Pertwee . . . . Chief Warden Hodges
Frank Williams . . . . Vicar
Edward Sinclair . . . . Verger
Susan Majolier . . . . Nurse
Lindsey Dunn . . . . Hamish, the Small Boy
Platoon: Colin Bean, Desmond Cullum-Jones, George Hancock, Michael Moore, Leslie Noyes, Evan Ross, Freddie White, Freddie Wiles, William Gossling
Assistant Warden: Jimmy Mac

PRODUCTION TEAM

Script: Jimmy Perry and David Croft
Producer/Director: David Croft
Production Assistants: Gordon Pert and Bob Spiers
Studio Lighting: Howard King
Studio Sound: Michael McCarthy
Design: Paul Joel
Assistant Floor Managers: Peter Fitton and John Cox
Vision Mixer: Dave Hanks
Costume Supervisor: Susan Wheal
Make-Up Supervisor: Ann Ailes

Mainwaring is in the Walmington Cottage Hospital having two ingrowing toenails removed. While he's away, Wilson is in charge. The platoon are against Wilson's decision to recruit the Vicar and Verger to the ranks; but with hundreds of clergymen joining up, Wilson doesn't feel he can refuse their requests.

As they start their first parade, Mainwaring – who discharged himself because beds were needed for more urgent cases – arrives at the hall and can't believe his eyes when he spots the new recruits. In the office he shows his annoyance at having them in the platoon, and promises they'll be treated just like everyone else. On duty with Jones' section that evening they are given the responsibility of standing guard.

The Verger spots someone approaching, but it turns out to be a cheeky kid calling himself Adolf Hitler. Panicking, the Vicar summons Jones and his section from the guard hut, while the Verger clips the lad round the ear. Mainwaring and Wilson arrive and tell the boy off before sending him packing.

Hodges arrives at the church hall with the boy, Hamish, who turns out to be his nephew. He's angry that Mainwaring and his men could be so cowardly as to threaten a little boy, but when Hamish says the Home Guard are nearly as funny as the Wardens, Hodges chases the boy from the hall. Mainwaring reflects on an evening of aggravation and declares the Vicar and Verger should have dealt with the matter differently, causing them to resign from the platoon.

Note: 'The Recruit' was the first episode to be transmitted without Jimmy Beck appearing in

'The Recruit'

either the studio or location scenes. His absence was explained by a note on the church hall floor stating he'd gone to London. All the dialogue originally written into the script had to be reallocated among the other cast members.

See 'Selected Scripts' for the original version of 'The Recruit' script.

REDFARN, ROGER

Roger, who was born in London, made his West End debut as a director with his production of *The King and I*, and was responsible for staging the *Dad's Army* theatre show. After training at Birmingham, he did a little acting before concentrating on stage management, initially at Lincoln, then at the Welsh National Theatre and for five years at Coventry's Belgrave Theatre, during which time he was responsible for over 50 productions as associate director.

He decided to turn freelance and during an eight-year period worked around the world, with three months touring American theatres after being awarded a Winston Churchill Fellowship. He also directed a number of top shows around the country, before being appointed artistic director at Plymouth's Theatre, a job he did for ten years.

Since leaving Plymouth in 1985 he has again turned freelance, working in this country and abroad, including spells in Austria and the Middle East.

RED LION, THE

The Red Lion in Walmington's High Street happens to be Hodges' favourite haunt. When the Americans arrive in 'My British Buddy', a darts match is arranged at the pub to welcome them

to Walmington, although the evening is a dire failure.

In 'Turkey Dinner' we discover that Jones' section visited the pub while out on patrol during a cold evening. The trouble was they'd already been to a couple of pubs beforehand, and only entered The Red Lion to help sober up Godfrey, who had begun singing raucously!

As well as being a public house, rooms are offered on a bed and breakfast basis, and it's where the drunken Barry Mainwaring stays while visiting Walmington in 'My Brother and I'.

REED, CAPTAIN

Played by Michael Knowles (TV); Jack Watson (radio)

The captain has been running the School of Explosives for a year when Mainwaring and his men attend in 'Fallen Idol'. Reed is fed up with running the courses for the Home Guard because he finds everyone too enthusiastic, so much so that he's developed a nervous twitch.

REES, MR

Played by Edward Evans (TV); Michael Knowles (radio)

A stroppy Welsh trade union representative on the Military Service Hardship Committee, Mr Rees hears Walker's case for call-up deferment in 'The Loneliness of the Long-Distance Walker'. It's unclear whether this is the Mr Rees who later becomes town clerk, even though the character is played by the same actor.

REES, MR

Played by Edward Evans (TV)

Mr Rees is the town clerk in Walmington who refuses Mainwaring's request to demolish the

bandstand in 'Big Guns'. Along with other officials, he watches Mainwaring's men make fools of themselves while trying to convince Rees that their newly acquired gun would be essential in saving the town from invaders, but only if the bandstand – which is in the line of fire – is dismantled. Mr Rees, who is far more authoritarian than his successor, Mr Gordon, is unimpressed.

REGAN, MAJOR

Played by Martin Wyldeck (TV); Jack Watson (radio)

The Major was seen in two episodes: 'The Showing Up of Corporal Jones' and 'Shooting Pains'. In the first, he was appointed by GHQ to inspect training and battle drill in all Home Guard units in the area. During his time with the Walmington platoon he questions whether Jones is too old to serve in the unit; although Mainwaring declares his support for his corporal, the Major is not convinced. In order to prove he's fit enough to remain, Jones is ordered to complete an assault course within 15 minutes.

In 'Shooting Pains' the arrogant Major Regan takes charge when the Walmington and other Home Guard units take part in some shooting practice.

REGAN, PATRICK

Played by J G Devlin (TV)

Patrick appears in 'Absent Friends' as an IRA suspect who's arrested at 27 Ivy Crescent in Walmington. He denies his identity and claims it's his brother, Shamus, they're looking for. Mainwaring and three members of the platoon place him under arrest and walk him to the church hall.

REGAN, SHAMUS

Played by Patrick Connor (TV)

Shamus arrives at the church hall in 'Absent Friends' to free his brother, Patrick, who's been arrested as an IRA suspect. He gets violent but Wilson sorts him out single-handed.

REHEARSALS

Although the very first episode of *Dad's Army* was rehearsed at St Nicholas Parish Hall, Bennett Street, London W4, and some episodes were rehearsed at the London Transport Training Centre in London's Wood Lane, most rehearsals took place at St Michael's Church Hall, Commonwealth Avenue, London W12, just behind TV Centre.

REPEATS

There is no doubting *Dad's Army* is one of the most frequently repeated sitcoms of all time, proving its perennial appeal among young and old alike. BBC schedulers feel comfortable about submitting Perry and Croft's comedy masterpiece for another outing, knowing that whatever episodes they show, the programme is an almost certain crowd puller. Its plum slot in the television timetable seems to be Saturday tea time, just when viewers have closed the door after a hectic shopping trip and put their feet up with a warm cuppa before preparing the evening meal.

It's remarkable to see a programme which has passed its 32nd birthday still entertaining today, with the humour and finely drawn character studies just as accessible and fresh as when they first hit our screens. But it's not just Britain that enjoys the antics of Walmington's senior citizens – the show continues to be shown worldwide.

The programme has been bought by broadcasting companies in numerous countries, including Jamaica, USA, Singapore, Belgium, Zambia, Australia, New Zealand, Nigeria, Barbados, Bahamas, Saudi Arabia, Sweden, Bermuda, Denmark, Yugoslavia and Holland, where it was voted the most popular comedy show on Dutch television.

RESERVED OCCUPATIONS

In 1938, a Schedule of Reserved Occupations was published by the government, followed by a booklet, which was sent to every household a few months later, listing the various full- and part-time war jobs. One of its objectives was to prevent particular skilled workers enlisting to the Forces purely on impulse, especially if it meant they would be depriving the nation of a skill essential to the war effort. Later, the method used to determine which occupations were classed as reserved was amended, allowing the blanket ban on certain professions to be lifted.

In 1939, employers were allowed to request the deferment of call-up for individuals working in one of the reserved occupations, something which by 1941 had been extended to cover men in jobs not regarded as 'reserved'. To help process such requests, advisory committees were set up to consider applications. One such committee is spotlighted in 'The Loneliness of the Long-Distance Walker' when Joe Walker has to confront the Military Service Hardship Committee, which has been set up to discuss the call-up of people who run one-man businesses and believe they'll be ruined financially if they join the Forces.

RHYS, HARRIET
Role: Girl in the Bank (film)

RICHARD, WENDY (1946–)
Born: Middlesbrough
Roles: Edith Parish (S4, episode 8: 'The Two and a Half Feathers' and S4, episode 9: 'Mum's Army'), Shirley (S5, episode 7: 'The King was in his Counting House' and S6, episode 2: 'My British Buddy') (TV); Violet Gibbons ('War Dance'), Edith Parish ('Mum's Army'), Shirley ('The King was in his Counting House' and 'My British Buddy') (radio)
Wendy moved to London as a baby when her parents took over a pub in Mayfair. As a girl she harboured dreams of becoming an archaeologist, but never pursued her ambitions. Upon fin-

ishing her education, Wendy completed a course in shorthand and typing, and worked briefly as a sales assistant at Fortnum and Mason's before joining the Italia Conti Stage School.

While she was studying she earned money as a photographic model, working for magazines and retailers. Wendy made her small-screen debut in the sixties, playing a runaway teenager in *Dixon of Dock Green*, followed quickly by an appearance with Sammy Davis Jnr in ATV's *Sammy Davis Meets the Girl*. Other credits in a busy

'My British Buddy'

career include playing Miss Brahms in *Are You Being Served?* and *Grace and Favour*, Doreen the clippie in *On the Buses*, *Please, Sir!*, *The Fenn Street Gang*, a barmaid in ITV's *Not On Your Nellie*, *Up Pompeii!*, *Harpers West One* and *Danger Man*. In the late 1960s, she also spent three years as Joyce Harker in the popular BBC series *The Newcomers*. For the last 15 years she's been playing Pauline Fowler in *EastEnders*.

On the big screen, Wendy made her debut with two lines in *Doctor in Clover*, but has appeared in a handful of other movies, including *Bless this House*, *Carry On Matron*, *Carry On Girls* and *No Blade of Grass*.

RIDEOUT, NIGEL (1942–)
Born: Petts Wood
Role: German Pilot (S1, episode 4: 'The Enemy Within the Gates') (TV)
Nigel started acting as a six year old, and by the age of ten he'd sung on a recording for HMV. Upon graduating from drama school he began

working on the stage and television, with one of his early appearances being in *The Wedding Feast*, a BBC production from 1964. Other work on television has included *The Frost Report* and *The Avengers*, but it's theatre which has dominated his career as an actor.

Nigel moved into teaching and for the last 30 years has dedicated his time to running several drama schools. He also spent 15 years working in Australia and is the author of numerous books.

RIDLEY, ARNOLD (1896–1984)
Born: Bath
Role: Private Charles Godfrey (all TV episodes and *Christmas Night with the Stars* inserts; the film, the stage show and 60 episodes of the radio series)
Arnold was educated at Clarendon School, Bath, and Bristol University, where he began his acting career. For a while after graduating he was uncertain where his future lay: he'd trained as a school teacher and taught for a short spell, but quickly turned to acting, making his first professional stage appearances in *Prunella* at Bristol's Theatre Royal, in 1913.

During the First World War he served in the army, but was invalided out in 1917 after being severely wounded at the Somme. Injuries to his arm left it virtually useless, while being hit on the head with a rifle butt led to blackouts which affected him for the remainder of his life.

Arnold resumed his acting career in 1918 at Birmingham Rep. During his three years at the company he appeared in over 40 productions.

He moved on to Plymouth but his stage career was brought to an abrupt end when he was forced to give up acting because of his war injuries. With his life in turmoil, he returned to Bath and worked in his father's boot shop while contemplating a future which looked bleak. But success was soon bestowed upon Arnold. He began writing plays and, although his first attempt was unsuccessful, the second struck gold.

In 1923, Arnold penned *The Ghost Train*, which was produced two years later and eventually became a worldwide success, being adapted for both the big and small screen. The idea emerged from an unwelcome wait of several hours at a deserted West Country railway station. The atmosphere of the occasion inspired him to write a play. Over the years many productions of *The Ghost Train* have been staged, but Arnold's career as a playwright also produced more than 30 other plays, including *Easy Money* and *Beggar My Neighbour*.

In the mid-1930s, Arnold established his own film company with a partner. The first release, *Royal Eagle*, was favourably received by the critics, but the company's life was brief. During the making of their second film, the bank who had acted as financial backers went bankrupt, leaving

Arnold and his partner seriously in debt. It took nearly 20 years for Arnold to clear this debt.

When the Second World War began, Arnold worked with ENSA, and one of the plays he went on to direct was his own, *The Ghost Train*. When the war ended he resumed his acting career, and in 1940 returned to the stage as director of productions with the Malvern Company for two years. He then appeared in the West End in several productions, such as *Twelve Angry Men*. He went on to tour with shows like *Rain* and *Roar Like a Dove*.

Although he'll forever be remembered for *Dad's Army* and writing *The Ghost Train*, Arnold also made a handful of films, notably *The Interrupted Journey*, *The Man Who Knew Too Much* and 1973's *Carry On Girls*, playing the decrepit Alderman Pratt.

On the radio he spent over two decades as Doughy Hood in *The Archers*, and on TV was also seen playing the vicar in *Crossroads* and two characters in *Coronation Street*: Herbert Whittle, who tried courting Minnie Caldwell, in 1967 and John Gilbert in 1969.

Arnold had reached the age of 88 when he died in 1984.

Theatre credits include: *Marshall's Aid*, *A Funny Thing Happened on the Way to the Forum*.

Film credits include: *Mrs Pym of Scotland Yard*, *Green Grow the Rushes*, *Stolen Face*, *Wings of Mystery*, *Crooks in Cloisters*, *The Amorous Milkman*.

RING-A-DING MONTHLY, THE

The Vicar used to edit this local campanologists' magazine before its publication was stopped because of the war. The loss of income from sales has a major knock-on effect when the phone is cut off in the church hall office because the Vicar can't afford the bill. The monthly magazine is mentioned in the episode, 'The Enemy Within the Gates'.

RING DEM BELLS

Recorded: Thursday 3/7/75

Original transmission: Friday 5/9/75, 8.00–8.30pm

Original viewing figures: 11.3 million

Repeated: 24/4/76, 17/7/81, 10/8/81 (Wales), 12/12/89, 13/9/90 (N Ireland), 23/10/93, 7/11/93 (Wales), 14/9/96

CAST

Arthur Lowe . . . . Captain Mainwaring
John Le Mesurier . . . . Sergeant Wilson
Clive Dunn . . . . Lance Corporal Jones
John Laurie . . . . Private Frazer

Arnold Ridley . . . . .Private Godfrey
Ian Lavender . . . . .Private Pike
Bill Pertwee . . . . .Chief Warden Hodges
Frank Williams . . . . .Vicar
Edward Sinclair . . . . .Verger
Jack Haig . . . . .Mr Palethorpe,
　　　　　　　　　　　　　the Landlord
Robert Raglan . . . . .Colonel
Felix Bowness . . . . .Special Constable
John Bardon . . . . .Harold Forster
Hilda Fenemore . . . . .Queenie Beal
Janet Mahoney . . . . .Doris, the Barmaid
Adele Strong . . . . .Lady with the Umbrella
Platoon: Colin Bean, George Hancock, Michael Moore,
Desmond Cullum-Jones, Freddie White, Evan Ross,
Leslie Noyes, Roger Bourne, Freddie Wiles, Hugh Cecil

PRODUCTION TEAM
Script: Jimmy Perry and David Croft
Producer/Director: David Croft
Production Assistant: Jo Austin
Film Cameraman: Peter Chapman
Film Sound Recordist: Bill Chesneau
Film Editor: John Stothart
Studio Lighting: Howard King

'Ring Dem Bells'

'Ring Dem Bells'

Studio Sound: Alan Machin
Design: Robert Berk
Assistant Floor Manager: Anne Ogden
Vision Mixer: Dave Hanks
Costume Designer: Mary Husband
Make-Up Artist: Sylvia Thornton

The platoon are making their screen debut, but as Frazer points out, it's only a training film. Colonel Pritchard arrives with Mr Forster, the production assistant from the Crown Film Unit, and Mrs Beal, his costume designer. Mainwaring can't believe it when he's told his men are play-ing the Nazis, and to make matters worse they will only be used in distant shots. It's not Main-waring's day: Queenie Beal tells the production assistant he's too round and has girls' feet, while Pike and Wilson are chosen to play the officers. Mainwaring informs the Colonel he refuses to have anything to do with the film, but he's ordered to do it, although the Colonel later sym-pathises and tells him he can stand on the touch-line and watch.

To avoid them being seen while dressed as Germans, Mainwaring drives everyone around in the van. When they arrive on the set for loca-tion work, there is no one to be found. Eventu-ally the production assistant arrives to announce the filming has been postponed for a week.

Mainwaring is outraged so stops off at a phone box to give the officials at GHQ a piece of his mind, but not until he's warned the men against getting out of the van, even though it's stifling hot. Stopping next to The Six Bells pub is a fatal mistake and the men ignore their cap-tain's order and pop out for a quick drink. The landlord, Mr Palethorpe, is understandably shocked to see German uniforms. He tells his barmaid, Doris, to warn the village. Mainwaring finishes his call and is annoyed to find the men in the pub. Soon the whole village turns out and a nervous special constable questions Mainwar-ing, who rushes off in the van. While Mr Palethorpe tries calling the Home Guard in Walmington, because that is where the lorry is heading, the special constable calls the Superin-tendent at the Eastbourne police station.

Hodges doesn't believe Mr Palethorpe when he calls, but when he spots Mainwaring and the platoon dressed as Germans as they arrive back at the church yard, he thinks they're quislings. With the Vicar and Verger in tow, they rush off to sound the alarm: the church bells. Thinking the whole country will be up in arms, Mainwar-ing and the platoon attempt to stop the bells, but not before the whole of the south coast is put on red alert. The Brigadier at GHQ is furious and wants to know who was responsible.

RINGHAM, JOHN (1928–)
Born: Cheltenham
Roles: Bracewell (S1, episode 1), Captain Bailey (S2, episodes 5 & 6; S3, episode 6; S4, episode 5) (TV);

Captain Turner ('Room at the Bottom' and 'Don't Fence Me In') (radio)

When he was told Bracewell wouldn't become a regular character, John was relieved because he didn't want to be fettered by a long-running series; but he enjoyed dropping in occasionally as Captain Bailey. Primarily a classical actor, John has spent over 50 years in the profession, subsidising his theatrical career with TV and radio work.

During the war he joined a teenagers' amateur society performing 'highbrow' material which fuelled his enthusiasm for serious roles. He turned pro in 1948 and after 11 years of rep made his TV debut. During the 1960s he appeared in *The Forsyte Saga*, *The Railway Children*, *War and Peace* and *David Copperfield*.

After *Dad's Army*, John worked with Arthur Lowe on several occasions, including the sitcom *Bless Me, Father*. He also appeared as Professor Acheson in 'A Sense of History', an episode of *The Avengers*, an instalment of *The Governor* and an advert for vegetarian sausages.

John has made over 200 theatre appearances, including appearances at the National, 300 TV roles and one film, 1961's *Very Important Person*. John is still working on TV and in the theatre; he also writes plays.

ROBINSON, MRS

Mrs Robinson appears as a non-speaking ARP warden in 'Uninvited Guests'. Hodges tells her to take charge of the incident map when the ARP wardens end up sharing the church hall office with Mainwaring.

RODRIGUES, CAPTAIN

Played by Alan Tilvern (TV and radio)

In 'Battle School', Rodrigues, who fought in the Spanish Civil War, is against the arm-waving style of military discipline. He takes charge of the Walmington Home Guard's training in the intricacies of guerilla warfare.

ROGER

Mentioned in 'The Captain's Car', Roger works at Walmington's town hall. He's off work with his old trouble again, which means Sam has to clean the mace in time for the French General's visit.

ROGERS, CAPTAIN

Played by Norman Mitchell (TV); Frank Thornton (radio)

Captain Rogers works for the army's bomb disposal unit and arrives on the scene in 'Something Nasty in the Vault' to defuse the bomb Mainwaring and Wilson end up cradling. He does little to instil confidence by announcing the bomb is a 'trembler', which isn't good news.

ROGERS, CAPTAIN

Mainwaring calls Captain Rogers in 'No Spring for Frazer' to check on the availability of Lewis gun spares when Frazer loses the butterfly spring on their gun. Rogers is not seen in the episode and although it's not clear, this is probably a different character to the one played by Norman Mitchell, who was an expert in bomb disposal.

ROOM AT THE BOTTOM

Recorded: Sunday 29/6/69 (although this episode was recorded in colour it only exists in black and white in the BBC archives)

Original transmission: Thursday 16/10/69, 8.00–8.30pm

Original viewing figures: 12.4 million

Repeated: 9/5/70, 9/9/98

CAST

Arthur Lowe . . . . .Captain Mainwaring
John Le Mesurier . . . . .Sergeant Wilson
Clive Dunn . . . . .Lance Corporal Jones
John Laurie . . . . .Private Frazer
James Beck . . . . .Private Walker
Arnold Ridley . . . . .Private Godfrey
Ian Lavender . . . . .Private Pike
Anthony Sagar . . . . .Drill Sergeant Gregory
John Ringham . . . . .Captain Bailey
Edward Sinclair . . . . .Verger
Colin Bean . . . . .Private Sponge
Platoon: Frank Godfrey, Hugh Cecil, Desmond Cullum-Jones, Richard Kitteridge, Vic Taylor, Michael Moore, George Hancock, Freddie Wiles, Leslie Noyes

PRODUCTION TEAM

Script: Jimmy Perry and David Croft
Producer/Director: David Croft
Production Assistant: Harold Snoad
Film Cameraman: James Balfour
Film Editor: Bob Rymer
Studio Lighting: Howard King
Studio Sound: Michael McCarthy
Design: Paul Joel
Assistant Floor Manager: Bill Harman
Vision Mixer: Dave Hanks
Costume Supervisor: Odette Barrow
Make-Up Supervisor: Cecile Hay-Arthur
Special Effects: Peter Day

The auditors have detained Mainwaring at the bank, so Wilson is in charge at the church hall when an officer arrives with some embarrassing news for Mainwaring. He points out that there were no commissions in the LDV, and is surprised to hear that Mainwaring appointed himself captain, particularly as it's the norm to have a lieutenant in charge of a platoon.

As Mainwaring was never a captain, he must remove one of his pips. Wilson has to break the news and almost relishes the job while practising in front of the mirror. When Mainwaring arrives and finds Wilson wearing a beret he tells him to take it off as only officers can wear them. He says the days have gone when you could promote yourself to any old rank. Wilson feels it's the opportune moment to tell Mainwaring that he's been demoted to lieutenant. Just as Mainwaring is about to pass the bad news on to the men, the Verger rushes into the church yard enthusing over the sinking of the Bismarck.

When Captain Bailey visits the church office for the second time, Mainwaring is, once again, with the auditors. It appears Mainwaring hasn't any authority over the men at all and must be demoted to private. When Mainwaring hears about the decision he's shocked, especially as Wilson is placed in temporary charge.

Though deeply upset, Mainwaring decides to stay on as a private, just in time for the one-hour drill practice being conducted at the churchyard by an aggressive drill sergeant.

Wilson is in charge of the platoon at the weekend exercise, but when he leads the men into an ambush, everyone wants Mainwaring back as captain. They write to GHQ asking for him to be reinstated because his absence has left an unbridgeable void. Frazer is not so keen, and writes asking for promotion himself.

GHQ respond by issuing Mainwaring's commission. In future, Southgate, Eastgate and Walmington platoons will be made into a company with Mainwaring second-in-command.

ROSE AND CROWN, THE

This public house in Walmington is seen in 'Something Nasty in the Vault', when Mainwaring and his men, together with Mr West from Swallow Bank's head office, celebrate after successfully dealing with the unexploded bomb.

ROSE, DAVID (1932–)

Born: Hamnish, Herefordshire

Role: Dump Corporal (S5, episode 10: 'Brain versus Brawn') (TV)

After graduating from RADA, David was soon working for the Old Vic Company, one of ten actors chosen from 500 hopefuls. The company included the likes of Richard Burton, Claire Bloom and Michael Hordern.

Much of David's career has been spent in the theatre, and he's worked all over the world, including the USA, Canada, Denmark, Holland, Belgium and Austria. His West End credits include: *The Case in Question*, *Nuts* and *Arturio Ui*. He's also worked at numerous reps around the country, such as Exeter, York and Liverpool, and has appeared in the occasional film, which has taken him to the Libyan Desert and Spain, where he co-starred in a Spanish horror movie, *Rest in Pieces*.

Recent years have seen him on a nine-month national tour of *The Sound of Music*, and appearing on Meridian's children's show, *It's A Mystery*. Other TV work includes scenes in *Yes, Prime Minister*, *Howard's Way*, *Blood Money*, *Blind Justice* and *Chain*.

ROSEMARY CAFÉ, THE

Although we never see it, we hear in 'The Recruit' that Jones and Pikey went to this café in Eastgate for lunch one day. They chose brown windsor soup, whale meat cutlets, mashed potato and swede, followed by tapioca pudding and a cup of tea, all for nine pence. It may be cheap but the standard of cooking isn't high because Pike was sick and Jones didn't enjoy it.

ROSS, EVAN

Born: Cardigan

Role: Member of the platoon's back row in 34 episodes (S5, episodes 2, 5–13; S6, episodes 1–5; S7, episodes 1–6; S8; 'My Brother and I'; 'The Love of Three Oranges'; S9) (TV)

Evan, who had to change his name from Evan Thomas when he started working on TV because he was being confused with a leading Canadian actor living in Kent, has gained much acclaim as a professional singer. Encouraged by many notable musicians to make singing his career, he was awarded a scholarship at the Royal Academy of Music.

During his studies he became a successful member of the Academy's opera class and, after graduating, spent three seasons with the Glyndebourne Festival Opera as understudy and chorister at Glyndebourne, Edinburgh and Berlin. Later, he became principal baritone at the Carl Rosa Opera Company. During a successful singing career he has sung in countless venues around the British Isles, and appeared in numerous broadcasts and TV shows.

Upon moving into acting he was quickly offered extra work. He became a regular on *Crackerjack* as a policeman in comedy sketches. Nowadays he concentrates on singing.

ROUBICEK, GEORGE

Born: Vienna

Role: Radio Operator (film)

George and his family were pre-war refugees who fled Austria. He spent his childhood in Queensland, Australia, before moving in 1954 to England, where he studied at RADA. Upon graduating he worked in various repertory theatres such as Bromley, Oxford and Ipswich, before finally making his West End debut in *Tea and Sympathy*.

As well as appearing on stage, George has worked in films and television. Among his movie credits are two James Bond pictures, including *You Only Live Twice*, *The Dirty Dozen* and *Star Wars*. On the small screen his many appearances include roles in *The Avengers* and *Z Cars*. Nowadays, George concentrates mainly on writing, directing and running a dubbing studio.

ROUGHEAD, HAMISH

Role: Private Frazer (stage show)

Hamish was still at high school in Fife, Scotland, when he appeared in a production of *The Merchant of Venice*. During his career he's appeared

in theatres throughout Britain, including time at the Birmingham Rep and various West End engagements, such as Ronald Millar's *The Affair* and *The New Man* and Lionel Bart's *Oliver!*. He has also worked abroad, including a spell in Kenya.

His TV credits include: *Doctor Finlay*, *Dr Finlay's Casebook*, *The Borderers*, *Detective*, 'Just Your Luck' in the *Play for Today* series, *Witch Wood*, *The World of Tim Frazer*, *Dark Side of the Earth*. Among the films he's appeared in are *Naughty!* in 1971 and 1959's *The Bridal Path* with George Cole.

ROUND AND ROUND WENT THE GREAT BIG WHEEL

Recorded: Friday 1/12/72

Original transmission: Friday 22/12/72, 8.30–9.00pm

Original viewing figures: 13.7 million

Repeated: 11/1/74, 6/6/84, 5/3/91, 25/11/95, 23/1/96, 21/6/97

CAST

Arthur Lowe . . . . .Captain Mainwaring
John Le Mesurier . . . . .Sergeant Wilson
Clive Dunn . . . . .Lance Corporal Jones
John Laurie . . . . .Private Frazer
James Beck . . . . .Private Walker
Arnold Ridley . . . . .Private Godfrey
Ian Lavender . . . . .Private Pike
Bill Pertwee . . . . .ARP Warden
Geoffrey Chater . . . . .Colonel Pierce
Edward Underdown . . . . . . .Major General
Sir Charles Holland
Michael Knowles . . . . .Captain Stewart
Jeffrey Segal . . . . .Minister
John Clegg . . . . .Wireless Operator
Platoon: Colin Bean, Hugh Cecil, Desmond Cullum-Jones, Michael Moore, Richard Jacques, Freddie Wiles, George Hancock, Evan Ross, Freddie White, William Gossling
Extras in War Office: Colin Thomas and Fred Davies

PRODUCTION TEAM

Script: Jimmy Perry and David Croft
Producer/Director: David Croft
Production Assistant: Gordon Pert
Film Cameraman: James Balfour
Film Sound Recordist: Les Collins
Film Editor: Bill Harris
Lighting: Howard King
Sound: John Delany
Design: Paul Joel
Assistant Floor Manager: Peter Fitton
Vision Mixer: Dave Hanks
Costume Supervisor: Susan Wheal
Make-Up Supervisor: Anna Chesterman
Visual Effects: Peter Day

It's 1941 and at the War Office top officials discuss plans for a new weapon: a giant wheel containing 2000lbs of high explosives – enough to knock out an enemy pillbox within a range of three miles. It's called the High Explosive Attack Device Propelled by Ultra High Frequency, codename 'Headpuhf'. It can be homed in to the enemy target by radio – or that's the plan. Operation Catherine Wheel involves the weapon being demonstrated at a deserted aerodrome near Walmington, and the Home Guard is being used to guard the area

Colonel Pierce intends utilising all Home Guard platoons in the operation: Eastgate – under Captain Square – will guard the entrance, Dymwhich – under Captain Graham – will patrol the perimeter, and all the fatigues, digging loos and other rough work, is to be left to Mainwaring's men. Mainwaring thinks the reason Captain Stewart struggles to tell him their responsibilities when he comes to see them, is because they're assigned to special duties. Little does he know what they entail!

On Saturday they discover that the so-called

Location filming for 'Round and Round Went the Great Big Wheel'.

special duties include potato peeling and washing-up. When he can, Pike sneaks out with Walker to hear *Hi, Gang!* on his radio, which he's carried with him in the back of the van.

The demonstration takes place in front of high officials and the minister. The wheel starts rolling and sparks fly everywhere, but just when everything is going well, *Hi, Gang!* booms out over the public address system sending the wheel out of control. As it heads towards Walmington, Captain Stewart asks to return to the town and warn residents. Mainwaring and his men head off in Jones' van, but the wheel begins catching them up, turning whenever they turn. They eventually shake it off and decide to keep it under observation by stopping the van.

When Captain Stewart arrives and warns them that the wheel must be close to exploding, the only way to put it out of action is to damage its aerial. Walker admits that it's probably Pike's portable radio which caused the trouble, so Mainwaring and Hodges plan luring it back in the motorbike and sidecar with Pike carrying the radio. Finally, with the help of Jones dangling from a bridge, one of the aerials is cut off and the wheel is put out of action.

ROWLANDS, MISS

Together with some colleagues, Miss Rowlands used to entertain the Marigold Tea Rooms' pre-war clientele with a little afternoon music. The group is suggested as a possible band for the platoon do in 'War Dance' but are quickly dismissed when Walker states they're unsuitable; he further insults them by referring to one of the group as 'an old bat from the library.'

ROYAL TELEVISION GALA PERFORMANCE

The *Dad's Army* team took part in a sketch as part of the *Royal Television Gala*, recorded on 13 May 1970, and transmitted on BBC1 on Sunday 24 May. With the Queen and the Duke of Edinburgh in the audience in Shepherd's Bush, the men were seen in an 11-minute sketch, written by Jimmy Perry and David Croft. Proceeds from the evening went towards helping the British teams at the Commonwealth Games in Edinburgh.

Cast

Arthur Lowe
John Le Mesurier
Clive Dunn
John Laurie
Arnold Ridley
Jimmy Beck
Ian Lavender
Platoon: Colin Bean, Desmond Cullum-Jones, Freddie Wiles, Jimmy Mac, Michael Moore

Overview of sketch

During parade, Captain Mainwaring notices that the platoon's old boys are struggling to keep up

Mainwaring and his men seen in a short sketch for the *Royal Television Gala*.

with the younger lads during drill. He quietly informs Wilson that he'll pick his moment carefully, but doesn't see any alternative than to tell the older members that he'll have to dispense with their services.

Before the evening is out, the platoon discuss the plans for the following day's exciting task: forming the guard at Buckingham Palace. Guarding the palace during wartime is no laughing matter, Mainwaring impresses upon his men, and they discuss the various disguises the enemy might use, including dressing up as milkmen and chimney sweeps.

When Jones reminds Mainwaring that he doesn't need to worry about a thing because everyone has been practising, Wilson enquires whether now is an opportune moment to disclose the bad news, but Mainwaring decides against it. Instead, he opts to tell them diplomatically the following day, and posts Godfrey, Frazer and Jones – the victims of ageism within the ranks – at the palace's back entrance, tucked well away from where any potential action would take place.

But when two young girls, perhaps the princesses, bring cups of cocoa to the three old-timers in order to show their appreciation for what they're doing, Mainwaring might have to think again about making them stand down.

ROYAL TRAIN, THE

Recorded: Friday 29/6/73

Original transmission: Wednesday 14/11/73, 6.30–7.00pm

Original viewing figures: 13.1 million

Repeated: 9/5/74, 5/2/88, 26/3/91, 4/12/93, 23/1/94 (Wales), 8/3/97, 30/7/00

CAST

Arthur Lowe . . . . .Captain Mainwaring
John Le Mesurier . . . . .Sergeant Wilson
Clive Dunn . . . . .Lance Corporal Jones
John Laurie . . . . .Private Frazer
James Beck . . . . .Private Walker
Arnold Ridley . . . . .Private Godfrey
Ian Lavender . . . . .Private Pike
Bill Pertwee . . . . .Chief Warden Hodges
Frank Williams . . . . .Vicar
Edward Sinclair . . . . .Verger
William Moore . . . . .Station Master
Freddie Earlle . . . . .Henry (Engine Driver)
Ronnie Brody . . . . .Bob (Engine Fireman)
Fred McNaughton . . . . .Mayor
Sue Bishop . . . . .Ticket Collector
Bob Hornery . . . . .City Gent
Platoon: Colin Bean, Desmond Cullum-Jones, George Hancock, Evan Ross, Leslie Noyes, William Gossling, Freddie White, Michael Moore, Freddie Wiles, Roger Bourne

PRODUCTION TEAM

Script: Jimmy Perry and David Croft
Producer/Director: David Croft
Production Assistant: Gordon Pert
Film Cameraman: James Balfour
Film Sound Recordist: John Gatland
Film Editor: Bob Rymer
Studio Lighting: Howard King
Studio Sound: Michael McCarthy
Design: Paul Joel
Assistant Floor Manager: Peter Fitton
Vision Mixer: Dave Hanks
Costume Supervisor: Susan Wheal
Make-Up Supervisor: Ann Ailes

The platoon head to the railway station where Mainwaring opens sealed orders concerning a special parade. In 20 minutes King George VI will travel through the station and Mainwaring's men will form a guard of honour on the platform, and ensure no unauthorised people get near the train. Although the King's fleeting visit is supposedly top secret it seems everybody, including Hodges, knows about it.

They practise their guard of honour in one of the station buildings, conscious that no one must find out what they're doing, but Mainwaring realises their attempts are futile when the Vicar, Verger and Mayor hurry into the station to await the King's arrival.

A train whistle sounds and everyone scurries out onto the platform but it's a false alarm: a driver and his mate get out of the engine – the train has broken down and they need to report the problem. While they use the office phone they decide to make a cuppa, but after mistaking some sleeping pills which Mainwaring had got for his wife, for sugar, they pass out.

The train has to be cleared from the track and when the driver can't be roused from his sleep Pike, who learnt to drive a train at a schoolboys' exhibition, steps in. When it's discovered the brake wheel has been left in the office and Mainwaring and his men won't be able to stop the engine, the Mayor, Vicar, Verger and Hodges have to try and catch them. Fearing problems when they get to Snettlefold station, Mainwaring and Jones risk their lives by climbing over the carriage roof to the back of the train in the hope of getting the brake wheel from the Vicar, who's following behind.

'The Royal Train'

Mainwaring finally retrieves the wheel and the train is stopped in a siding, just as the King's train comes into view. The Home Guard just have time to line up by the side of the track, only to see the train go racing past, soaking everyone in the process!

ROYE, ANTHONY (1922–1995)

Born: North Wales

Role: Mr Fairbrother (S5, episode 10: 'Brain versus Brawn') (TV)

Anthony made his stage debut at the age of 12 with Dame Sybil Thorndike and Sir Lewis Cannon. By the 1950s, he was dividing his time between acting, directing and management, first at York and then Wimbledon. His West End appearances included *The Fourth of June*, *Windfall*, *Power of Persuasion* and *The Farm*.

Between 1963 and 1967 he travelled around south west England with his own company and later spent four years touring the east Midlands. But he was also busy on television and his many credits include *The Sword of Honour*, *The Avengers*, *Hadleigh*, *The Old Curiosity Shop*, *The Double Agent*, *Nearest and Dearest*, *The Duchess of Duke Street*, *The Onedin Line*, *The Pickwick Papers* and *The Bill*.

Anthony suffered from motor neurone disease, and ill health eventually forced his retirement from the industry. He died aged 73.

RSM

Played by Derek Newark (film)

Mr Dawkins was the regimental sergeant major at the camp hosting the Home Guard exercise.

RUSSIAN, THE

(See 'Vladislovski, Mr'.)

RYMER, BOB

Film editor on 20 episodes (TV): S3, episodes 1, 2, 3, 4, 6, 7, 8, 12, 13, 14; S4, episodes 4, 10, 13; 'Battle of the Giants'; S5, episodes 2, 7, 8; S6, episodes 1, 3, 4

Bob grew up with the film industry because his father was an accountant for the Rank Organisation, which led to Bob being taken along to trade shows. Upon leaving school in 1946, he joined the camera department at Denham Studios, and stayed until the studio's closure in the 1950s. After working for an American film company for several years, he joined the Beeb as a film editor in the mid-1960s and worked on *Panorama*.

Bob moved to light entertainment and worked on many top shows, including *The Good Life*, *Steptoe and Son* and *Fawlty Towers*. Before retiring from the Corporation in 1996, he was assigned to the education department.

SAGAR, ANTHONY (1920–1973)
Born: Burnley
Roles: Sergeant Gregory (S3, episode 6: 'Room at the Bottom'), Sergeant Major (S4, episode 13: 'Fallen Idol') (TV); Police Sergeant (film)

Anthony enjoyed a busy career. As well as working on the stage, he appeared on TV shows such as 1972's *Spyder's Web* as Parker, *Doomwatch* in 1970 as Sergeant Harris, 1963's *Swallows and Amazons* as Ernie Kidd, a 1961 episode of *The Avengers*, Stan Wallace in ATV's *The Plane Makers*, *Special Branch* and *Randall & Hopkirk (Deceased)*.

On the big screen he appeared in many films, including playing a coxswain in 1957's *Barnacle Bill*, a customs official in 1958's *Law and Disorder*, the Sergeant of the Guards in *I Was Monty's Double* the same year, an instructor's assistant in *The Bulldog Breed* and a drunk in *The Loneliness of the Long Distance Runner*. He also appeared in six *Carry Ons*, playing a stores sergeant in *Sergeant*, an ambulance man in *Nurse*, a bus conductor in *Regardless*, a cook in *Cruising*, a policeman in *Screaming* and a man in hospital in *Loving*.

SAILORS, THE 1ST AND 2ND
Played by Bill Treacher and Larry Martyn (TV)

In 'Menace from the Deep' two sailors guard the machine gun post at the end of the pier in Walmington, and are relieved by the Home Guard for four nights while they take a well-earned break.

SAINSBURY, KATHLEEN
Role: Cissy Godfrey (S8, episode 3: 'Is There Honey Still For Tea?') (TV)

Kathleen's other television credits included an appearance in Thames' 1972 series, *Ace of Wands*.

SAINT (ST) ALDHELM'S CHURCH
The church in Walmington where Timothy Farthing is the incumbent vicar, is situated on the Eastgate Road and Mortimer Road. The church was named by David Croft, bringing back memories of his days at prep school near Swanage, where every Sunday he attended the service at St Aldhelm's, a church positioned on a hill.

Since the death of the resident organist, Mrs West, the congregation – which rarely consists of more than ten people – has been singing unaccompanied. However, if the hymn 'Onward Christian Soldiers' is due to be sung, Jack Jones is often called upon, because it's the one tune he learnt to play on the organ as a result of falling in love!

The church hall is always in demand. During the evenings and weekends, the Home Guard can be found practising their drill and discussing how they intend defending the Walmington coastline if Jerry were to attack. The wardens use the hall once a week, while various functions, dances and fêtes are frequently held at the venue.

SAINT (ST) MATTHEW'S CHURCH
Set in the countryside not far from Walmington, Mr Blewitt's brother, Horace, is buried at St Matthews church in 'No Spring for Frazer'.

SALTHAVEN
When Pike is in danger of being cut off by the tide in 'Sgt – Save My Boy!', one idea of how to rescue him involves getting a boat, but the suggestion is rejected because the vessel would have to come from Salthaven, further along the coast, taking too long.

SAM
A non-speaking character in 'The Captain's Car', Sam works at Walmington's town hall and drives the Mayor around on occasions. He's given the job of cleaning the mace prior to the French General's visit.

SAMWAYS, IVY
Played by Rosemary Faith and Suzanne Kerchiss (TV)
Address: 27 Jutland Drive, Walmington-on-Sea

The 'awfully obliging' Ivy Samways works in a sweet shop in Walmington. When Mainwaring decides to recruit females to the platoon to help with the war effort in 'Mum's Army', Pike brings this ridiculously quietly spoken girl along. She appears again in 'My British Buddy', when Pike takes her to The Red Lion to meet the Americans, only to see her chatted up by the smooth-talking Yanks.

SAMWAYS, MRS
Never seen in the sitcom, Mrs Samways is mentioned by Mainwaring in 'Command Decision'. She's the guide mistress in Walmington, and possibly the mother of Ivy Samways. She has cause to complain to Captain Mainwaring about an occasion when his platoon had to use the guide hut for arms drill, during which their bayonets cut straight through the felt roof. Now when it rains she has to send half her troop home because the roof leaks. Miss Beckworth helps her run the guides.

We hear of Mrs Samways again in 'A Brush With the Law', when Reg Alberts, an air raid warden, tells Hodges that he had to warn her about showing a light in her bungalow.

SANDFORD, CHRISTOPHER (1939–)
Born: London
Role: German Pilot (S5, episode 13: 'Time On My Hands') (TV)

Christopher joined drama school immediately after completing his education. An actors' agency was attached to the school and upon graduating he went straight into rep, including a season at Bournemouth. By the time he embarked on his national service at Catterick (where he helped run the garrison theatre) in 1960, Christopher had already made his West End debut, spending over a year in the Agatha Christie play, *Unexpected Guest*.

Back in civvy street, he resumed his acting career and soon started appearing on television in shows like *Maigret*, *No Hiding Place* and *Coronation Street*, joining the cast in 1962 as Walter Potts, the singing window cleaner. His role in the soap spawned a hit record with 'Not Too Little, Not Too Much' which reached number 17 in the charts back in December 1963.

Other television shows he's appeared in include a 1971 episode of *The Persuaders* playing Onslow. He's also appeared in several films, including 1960's *A French Mistress*, 1965's *Rapture*, Sid in *Half a Sixpence* two years later, Johnny in 1969's *When Winter Comes* and Rudolph in 1970's *The Kremlin Letter*. He also did cabaret with Clive Dunn.

In the 1970s, Christopher was in such demand

for voice-over work, he gave up acting and has concentrated on this side of the business ever since. He also launched his own radio production company and his own studio business, which he continues to run.

SANGER, MRS
Mrs Sanger, an OAP, attends the nosh-up in the television episode, 'Turkey Dinner'. Mainwaring asks if she's enjoying herself, and she confirms she is.

SAVAGE, JOAN
Born: Blackpool
Role: Greta Garbo (S5, episode 3: 'A Soldier's Farewell') (TV)
Joan, who has established herself as one of Britain's top female entertainers, grew up in Blackpool. She started her professional career aged 12 when she starred in the Blackpool Tower Children's Revue followed by the Tower Circus.

Joan, who's a popular singer, has worked in all mediums. As well as many appearances on radio, she has had series of her own, including *The Pleasure of Your Company*, *The Musical World of Joan Savage* and *Joan Savage Sings*. She's busy in cabaret and revue, and regularly entertains on worldwide cruises. On TV she's been seen on *The Les Dawson Show*, *Sez Les*, *The Black and White Minstrel Show*, *The Good Old Days*, *The Arthur Haynes Show* and many more. Her career has also covered theatre: most recently she played Flora at the Arts Theatre in *No Way to Treat a Lady* (1998), two roles in *My Fair Lady* at the Sheffield Crucible (1997/98) and Lady Brockhurst in *Divorce Me Darling* at the 1997 Chichester Festival.

SCHOOL OF EXPLOSIVES, THE
Mainwaring and his men attend a course at the school in 'Fallen Idol' during which the bank manager gets drunk.

SCHULZ, COLONEL
Played by Alan Tilvern (TV); Jack Watson (radio)
The loud-mouthed American colonel in 'My British Buddy' does little for Anglo-American relations by insulting the hospitality at The Red Lion by spitting beer on the floor and claiming it's warm.

SCOTTISH SERGEANT, THE
Played by Stuart McGugan (TV)
The sergeant has a phone conversation with Doreen, an ATS girl, in 'Number Engaged', booking a date in the process.

SEAFORTH, DAVID (1948–)
Born: London
Role: Member of the platoon's backrow in 11 episodes (S1, episodes 1,2, 3, 5 & 6; S2) (TV)
After leaving school, David embarked on an electrical engineering apprenticeship before

giving it up to become an actor. He would have become a regular in the platoon but other work commitments prevented him staying beyond the second series. Graduating from *Opportunity Knocks*, he has made the occasional appearance on TV, including two parts in *Crimewatch*, but most of his time is spent on the hotel cabaret circuit, which has taken him abroad, including a recent summer season in Rhodes, and trips to Bahrain, the Falklands, Belize, Germany and Holland.

David now works under the name David André as a comedian, impressionist and compère. He also runs a magic act, and has appeared throughout the UK in theatre, cabaret and summer seasons – three with *The Black and White Minstrel Show*. He has also played the lead in pantomimes and runs a booking agency, organising themed evenings.

SEBAG, SIR STEPHEN
The bald-headed old school friend of Wilson's attends the Rotarian dinner in 'Brain versus Brawn' but isn't seen.

SECOND AIR RAID WARDEN, THE
Played by Michael Lomax (TV)
The 2nd ARP warden takes part in the darts match at the local pub in 'Absent Friends'.

SECOND LIEUTENANT
Played by Dennis Blanch (TV)
In 'If the Cap Fits…', the second lieutenant makes a silly remark in the mess at HQ where Major General Menzies and the Colonel are busy talking.

SEDDLECOMBE PLATOON
(Film only)
This Home Guard platoon attend the weekend camp, where they are assigned the task of attacking the enemy (a detachment of Royal Marines) from the rear.

SEDGEWICK, MR
Played by Erik Chitty (TV and radio)
Seen in 'Boots, Boots, Boots', Mr Sedgewick owns a shoe shop in Walmington and always supplies Mainwaring with his Home Guard boots. Being an officer, Mainwaring is entitled to brown boots while the rest of the platoon have to wear black.

SEGAL, JEFFREY (1920–)
Born: London
Roles: Minister (S5, episode 12: 'Round and Round Went the Great Big Wheel'), Brigadier (S9, episode 2: 'The Making of Private Pike') (TV)
Jeffrey, always an active amateur actor, left school intending to be a civil servant. But the war put paid to his plans, and he joined the army, serving in Italy and Germany. When a recruitment drive was launched to gather people who could help

entertain the troops, Jeffrey took advantage and joined a theatrical unit.

Jeffrey continued acting after the war and has remained busy ever since. He first worked at the Mercury Theatre, Notting Hill Gate, and at various reps including Watford and Leatherhead. He then moved into TV, initially working as a back-up news commentator and has since worked in all genres of television, including several appearances for Perry and/or Croft, in *Are You Being Served?* and *It Ain't Half Hot, Mum*. He appeared as Mr Perkins in *Rentaghost* for five years and was seen in many other shows such as *Love Hurts* (the final series), *Bergerac*, *Lytton's Diary* and *David Copperfield*.

On radio, he was one of the writers behind the much-loved soap, *The Dales*; he made his film debut aged 13, and went on to make a handful of cameo appearances. As well as acting Jeffrey continues to write.

SEGAL, MICHAEL
Role: 2nd ARP Warden ('Branded' and 'A Brush with the Law') (radio)
Michael, who died in 1996, was a busy character actor who popped up in various television shows, such as *The Railway Children*, *Great Expectations*, *The Adventures of Tom Sawyer*, *Coronation Street* as Howard Seymour, *The Prisoner* as a lab technician, *Father, Dear Father*, *The Onedin Line*, *Robin's Nest* playing Mr Smith, *The Sweeney* as a reporter and *The Persuaders*. His numerous film credits include *Payroll* in 1961, *Hide and Seek*, *The Informers*, *Murder Most Foul*, *The Dirty Dozen*, *That's Your Funeral* and *The Black Windmill*.

SERGEANT, THE
Played by Alex McAvoy (TV); Fraser Kerr (radio)
When the Walmington Home Guard attend the Highland do in 'If the Cap Fits…', the sergeant informs Mainwaring of the procedure. He also turns up at the training camp in 'We Know Our Onions', where the Walmington Home Guard attend a weekend's efficiency course.

SERGEANT, THE
In the radio episode, 'Don't Forget the Diver', the sergeant is part of the Eastgate Home Guard based in the water mill during an exercise.

SERGEANT-MAJOR, THE
Played by Anthony Sagar (TV); Michael Brennan (radio)
The sergeant-major works at the School of Explosives, where Mainwaring and his men attend a course during 'Fallen Idol'.

SERVICEMAN, THE
Played by David Gilchrist (TV)
A member of the RAF, the serviceman asks for Mainwaring's seat at the railway station buffet in 'Mum's Army'.

From: Chief Assistant (General) Scenic Design, Tel.
room no. & building: 374 Scenery Block, T.C.   Tel.Extn.: 2434/5

Subject: DAD'S ARMY : 2/7 : Week 21 : TC.8 : 'ASLEEP IN THE DEEP'
Director: David Croft
Designer: Paul Joel

To: David Croft   Date: 27th March 1972

copies to: L.E.(Org. (C) Tel.   P.A.(Servicing)
Scenic Design Manager   P.A.(F.A.)
Asst.Sc.Des.Man.   Asst.Production
Paul Joel

Studio Weight Information
(Asst. to H.S.M.(1)
(Manager (St.Ops.)
(Construction Org.
(Property Org.
(Vision Manager
(Alloca.Org.Costume
(A/Ch.Asst.(Contracts)
(E.I.C. (Elecs.) H.S. Tel.

No filming effort required for this programme.

Studio Sets   Man Hours   Materials

1. Interior Command Post - this set is
    held from no.1   (100)
    As this episode calls for a little
    more action than that of the previous
    episode we suggest an extra 50 man
    hours for any additional set
    requirements   50   £40

2. Int. First Room Pumping Station -
    with beginnings of passage outside.   175   £150
    On one of the walls of the room are
    about 20 pipes, some with stop cocks
    on. On another wall is a small grill -
    next to a manhole cover with bolts on
    the outside. This manhole is big
    enough for a man to get through. On
    a rack there are several large spanners.
    There are two doors, one of them prac.

- more -

Studio Sets (continued)   Man Hours   Materials

3. Int. Passage Pumping Station   150   £120
    This is a length of passage which has
    a large crack in the wall and broken
    rubble standing approximately 3'0"
    high. There is a door leading to a
    second room (see details of set 4).
    The passage should have a wall which
    is required to collapse, the script
    is not quite clear whether or not
    this should take place in vision or
    sound only - page 24 - however, the
    passage and the second room should be
    built in the studio within a water tank.

    Clouds of dust are required in the studio
    in vision after the wall collapses and
    as this can only be done with Fullers
    Earth Powder, we would like to alert
    the Technical Operations Manager and
    the Property Master. There is a
    certain amount of restriction as to
    its use, F.14 Design Department Manual
    refers.

4. Int. Second Room Pumping Station (Night) 200   £200
    In the corner is a two tier bunk. At the
    head of the bunk is a manhole similar
    in character to the manhole in the first
    room, with bolts all around the edge.
    Further along the wall is a rack with
    spanners, next to that is the manhole
    cover leading to the next door. There
    are no bolts on it. Next is a grill
    which is 7'0" from the ground under
    which is a tin bath. The top tier of
    the bunk is 5'0" from the ground.

    This second room plus the passage will
    need to be built in a swimming pool
    approximately 24' x 15' + 3' as the
    action is that the Platoon is trapped
    within this room with various leaking
    water pipes from joints and cracks and
    we cut back and forth from the first
    room - to the passage - to the second
    room and the water is gradually rising
    until it reaches chest level.

    Obviously this depth of water is not
    possible in the studio and therefore a
    certain amount of illusion of depth
    will be necessary.

    TOTAL   575   £510

- more -

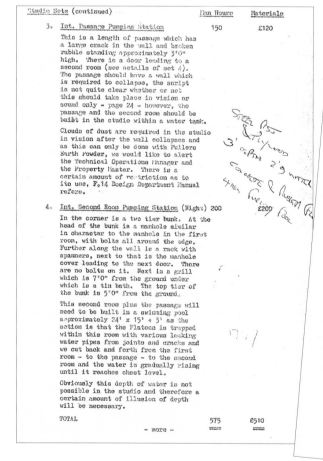

As these two sets are to stand in water it will not be permissable to use stock.

As a very rough calculation:
The weight of the tank when filled will be approx. 24 tons;
With three sources of inlet and outlet, it should fill in
150 minutes and empty in 35.
Approximately 6,750 gallons.

As this is a very important part of the programme this operation may
well need to take place three times during the day of rehearsals.

One very big snag as I see it will be that the water pumped in for
the artists to move around in will be extremely cold. A
complaint made by all artists when required to do this sort of
programme. Should any heating of this water be required, the time
factor involved may well be of an impossible nature.

I have been in contact with Asst.to H.S.M.(1) and he is forwarding
this detail to Mr.Charlwood, Clerk of Works, but seems quite confident
that in TC.8 in the non-audience area, there is no particular weight
problem.

Another problem which I foresee is that when the artists leave the
water tank they should have a dressing and drying area adjacent to
this set, with tarpaulins, and on no account be required to go near
a floor painted area with wet clothes.

During the course of the water rising we will need to see various
pipes come apart with more water bursting through and the bunk getting
lower and lower in the water and the tin bath floating with an actor
sitting in it.

Consideration will have to be given to :
(a) the construction of the tank
(b) time to erect
(c) method of transporting this in
(d) hire charge
(e) cost of specialized staff to erect and dismantle
(f) is there an insurance factor?
(g) cost of and number of filling and emptying pumps and
     noise of these
(h) number of changes of costume for artists for rehearsals
     and transmission

At first sight it does appear that this set should be filmed except
that you will find that this is quite a major part of the production.

(Frederick Knapman)

A memo from the BBC's Scenic Design Department reveals the process undertaken while making an episode such as 'Asleep in the Deep'.

SERVICEMAN'S CANTEEN APPEAL

Mentioned in 'When Did You Last See Your Money?', the appeal has collected £500 towards a new canteen in Walmington. Dick Billings is chairman and Jack Jones treasurer – perhaps not the wisest of appointments considering his appalling memory, highlighted by the incident in which he mislaid the £500 collected by local shopkeepers; he later discovers that he wrapped the notes up and gave them to Mr Billings in place of half a pound of sausages.

SETS

The original sets for *Dad's Army* were designed by Alan Hunter-Craig and Paul Joel during the first series. Research was carried out in various libraries, including the BBC's extensive reference section and the War Museum, to determine what was appropriate for the period. The BBC's stock prop department and TV and film hire companies were used for dressing the sets with everything from furniture to telephones, all of which were of the period or older. Posters, newspapers, labels, etc, were often reproduced from the originals for particular purposes.

The biggest and most used set throughout the series was the church hall, which became the platoon's headquarters. Designed by Alan and Paul, it was an amalgam of many church halls they had known as children. Final design decisions were dictated by the requirements of the script, such as the Vicar's office, which had to be positioned adjacent to the hall so that Mainwaring had immediate access to it for use as his office. Particular attention was also paid to designing the entrance to the hall. If the doorway led straight into the hall from the back of the set, problems with the artist-painted backing would be created, so the entrance led in from the side and the backing was placed behind the windows, which were divided into small panes criss-crossed with shatterproof tape.

When Paul took over the design for the second series he altered one aspect of the hall: the centre of the set at the back featured a beam supported by columns with clerestory windows over it, which had not been seen during the first series, so he reduced the height of the columns to reveal the entire architecture of the church hall and make sense of the columns. As an architect, Paul was very conscious that everything needed a sense of reality, and the sets had to be as believable as possible.

The Walmington-on-Sea branch of Swallow Bank was, again, influenced by childhood memories and research, plus visits to several older banks to determine a style suitable for the scripts. Paul Joel, who became the sitcom's longest-serving designer, drew on his own experience and that of fellow designers if it was necessary to double-check facts and plans.

When the scripts arrived, Paul's first task was to break them down into the various requirements in terms of sets, locations and props, then costing to ensure he didn't exceed the allocated budget for the series. If a lot of money was spent on an elaborate set for just one episode, like 'Time On My Hands', which was the most complicated set Paul designed for *Dad's Army*, the rest of the series had to be scaled down in expenditure.

Designing and constructing sets can be an expensive business, eating into the overall money allocation, as the following examples show. For the episode, 'The Royal Train', a locomotive cab was built by a specialist company at a cost of £962, while the design team's cost breakdown for 'My British Buddy' totalled over £2500, with over 840 man hours costing £1680, materials £538 and properties bought or hired £450.

When it came to building a set, the first step was for Paul, or one of his assistants, to produce scale drawings and sketches from which a model would be made. One set he designed was the quaint and cosy Marigold Tea Rooms, regularly frequented by Mainwaring and many of his men. Its design was influenced by various cafés Paul had visited over the years, but, amongst other things, his eventual design was also determined by the stock scenery available. Because of restricted budgets not everything could be built from new.

One set which can be attributed to a particular influence was the interior of Jones' butcher's

A breakdown of the requirements from the Scenic Design Department for an entire series.

DAD'S ARMY, NO. 4 of 7. SUB TITLE: "THE ROYAL TRAIN"
V.T.R. 29/6/73, FRIDAY, WEEK 26. STUDIO TC1.

STUDIO SETS	MAN HOURS	PROPS & MATS.
1. Side Office (Stock Set) (100)		
2. Int. Railway Waiting Room seedy type (New Set) } --	200	£ 175
3. Ante Room for Tea (New Set) This set is in composite with set 2. Very seedy. These two sets will need to match film.		
4. Cab of Railway Engine (New Set) Backed by C.S.O. or B.P.	200	£ 175
5. Roof of Railway Carriage (New Set) Backed by C.S.O. or B.P. This will be a long length of roof built up from the studio floor on sprung rostra and may be built in composite with set 4.	150	£ 180
Total Resources:	550	£ 530

FILM

L.S. of Railway Station.
Station Platform.
Various Railway Trucks.

* * * *

DAD'S ARMY, NO. 5 of 7. SUB TITLE: "THINGS THAT GO BUMP IN THE NIGHT"
V.T.R. SUNDAY 8/7/73, WEEK 28. STUDIO: TC4.

STUDIO SETS	MAN HOURS	PROPS & MATS.
1. Front Door / Porch with Hall & or Lobby & a large Staircase (New Set) } -- This is a Tudor Period House and should match to film of exterior.	200	£ 190
2. Jones Van Interior (Hired Van to match filming) against B.P. or C.S.O. N.B. This scene could be on film?	---	
3. Int. Landing Outside Bedroom (New Set)(Night) Several doors off. Panelled(Tudor Period.) This set to include Corner of Passage.	175	£ 160
4. Int. Bedroom (Night)(New Set) Practical fire, four poster bed, panelled(Tudor period.) Set 3 & 4, built in composite	150	£ 190
5. Kitchen off Hall (New Set)(Night)	150	£ 140
Total Resources:	675	£ 700

This figure should include th cost of possible P.V.C.
Tudor panelling.

.... / ....

Episode 5, continues.   - 4 -

FILM

Ext. Country Road (Night)
Jones Van required.

Int. Jones Van (Night)
Possible scene on film or in studio.

Ext. Front Door (Night)
Ext. Yard
Ext. Field
Ext. Hedge
Ext. Cuts into Field } Day
Ext. Stream
Ext. Bushes
Ext. Woods
Ext. Roads

* * * *

DAD'S ARMY, NO. 6 of 7. SUB TITLE: "THE HONOURABLE MAN"
V.T.R. 15/7/73 SUNDAY WEEK 29. STUDIO TC8.

	MAN HOURS	MATS. & PROPS
1. Int. Church Hall (Stock Set)(450)		
2. Bank (Mainwaring's) Office (New Set)	175	£200
3. Side Office (Stock Set)(100)		
Total Resources: This figure includes floor painting.	175	£200

FILMING

Outside the Church Hall
One Mid 30's Motor Cycle required.
Ext. Fields.
One Army Humber required.
Ext. Village Green
Canopy and Dias.

DAD'S ARMY, NO. 7 of 7. SUB TITLE: TBA.
V.T.R. SUNDAY 22/7/73, WEEK 30. STUDIO: TC6.

STUDIO SETS	MAN HOURS	MATS. & PROPS
1. Int. Church Hall (Stock Set)(450)	---	---
2. Int. Side Office (Stock Set)(100)	---	---
3. Int. & Ext. Command Post (New Set)	300	£ 250
4. Int. Wardens Post (New Set)	75	£ 100
5. Ward of - Cottage Hospital(New Set)	125	£ 175
Total:	500	£ 525

No filming is envisaged at this moment, although the script is still
being written.

(FREDERICK KNAPMAN)

Just one of the many sets built during the run of *Dad's Army*.

shop. Paul recalled shops that were tiled in the most elaborate way, in particular, Cope Brothers in Ealing, London. He took photos of the shop and its decorative wall tiling and used the idea in Jones' shop. Deciding to decorate it in a Victorian style, he designed various motifs which an artist painted onto the tiles, suiting Jones' florid personality to a tee.

Another source of inspiration was the lighthouse at Beachy Head, on which Paul Joel based his design of the lighthouse interior for the episode 'Put That Light Out!', including a reproduction of the huge glass lens, which threatened to illuminate the whole of Walmington-on-Sea.

SEVERN, BERNARD

Role: Member of the platoon (film)
The late Bernard Severn made an appearance as a member of the Walmington Home Guard in the movie.

SEXY LADY, THE

Played by Miranda Hampton (TV)
In 'Man Hunt', when Walker admits to having found a parachute in the woods which he had made into women's knickers, Mainwaring and Wilson go off with Walker to try and identify whether it was a German or British parachute. They knock on the doors of all the women who may have bought the knickers from Joe's market stall and ask to see their underwear. Understandably, the women are offended, except for 'the sexy lady' who doesn't mind showing her knickers to Wilson.

SGT – SAVE MY BOY!

(The working title for this episode was 'The Mine')
Recorded: Saturday 27/6/70
Original transmission: Friday 16/10/70, 8.00–8.30pm
Original viewing figures: 14.5 million
Repeated: 20/6/71, 31/12/90, 21/10/95, 18/4/96 (Wales), 17/5/97, 31/3/01

CAST

Arthur Lowe . . . . .Captain Mainwaring
John Le Mesurier . . . . .Sergeant Wilson
Clive Dunn . . . . .Lance Corporal Jones
John Laurie . . . . .Private Frazer
James Beck . . . . .Private Walker
Arnold Ridley . . . . .Private Godfrey
Ian Lavender . . . . .Private Pike
Bill Pertwee . . . . .ARP Warden
Janet Davies . . . . .Mrs Pike
Michael Knowles . . . . .Engineer Officer
Platoon: Colin Bean, Hugh Hastings, Vic Taylor

PRODUCTION TEAM

Script: Jimmy Perry and David Croft
Producer/Director: David Croft
Production Assistants: Harold Snoad and Donald Clive
Studio Lighting: Howard King
Studio Sound: Michael McCarthy
Design: Paul Joel

Assistant Floor Manager: David Taylor
Vision Mixer: Dave Hanks
Costume Supervisor: Barbara Kronig
Make-Up Supervisor: Cynthia Goodwin

Since the orphans were evacuated after Dunkirk, the Harris Orphans' Holiday Home Hut is no longer in use. The platoon is therefore using the wooden chalet, which is situated on the beach, as a patrol hut.

Mrs Pike arrives at the hut with a tin of biscuits Pike has forgotten, but is worried when she finds out that he hasn't arrived, especially as he left ten minutes before her. Frazer's on guard and hears a cry for help. It's Pike, who has got tangled up in the barbed wire which runs along the beach – to make matters worse he's in the middle of a minefield. Wilson calls the engineers but they're dealing with another emergency and won't be able to get there for three hours, which will be too late for Pikey because the tide is coming in.

Walker suggests rescuing him by boat but the idea is dismissed because it will take too long to get the boat from Salthaven. They therefore decide to negotiate a path through the minefield – a tortuous, time-consuming job.

As Mainwaring and Wilson prod their way down the beach, Godfrey appears at Pike's side. He followed the same route as Pikey from the bathing gap. As Mainwaring and the men eventually reach Pike, they suddenly notice Godfrey who enquires whether they want a cup of tea before starting back!

By the time they reach the hut, the engineering officer arrives with Hodges claiming the minefield stops 200 yards up the beach – but he's in for a shock.

SGT WILSON'S LITTLE SECRET

Recorded: Friday 4/11/68 (made in black and white)
Original transmission: Saturday 22/3/69, 7.00–7.30pm
Original viewing figures: 13.6 million
Repeated: 2/9/98, 29/8/99, 26/9/99 (Wales)

CAST

Arthur Lowe . . . . .Captain Mainwaring
John Le Mesurier . . . . .Sergeant Wilson
Clive Dunn . . . . .Lance Corporal Jones
John Laurie . . . . .Private Frazer
James Beck . . . . .Private Walker
Arnold Ridley . . . . .Private Godfrey
Ian Lavender . . . . .Private Pike
Janet Davies . . . . .Mrs Pike
Graham Harbord . . . . .Little Arthur
Platoon: Colin Bean, Richard Jacques, Frank Godfrey, Alec Coleman, Hugh Cecil, Jimmy Mac, Desmond Cullum-Jones, Arthur McGuire, David Seaforth, Richard Kitteridge

PRODUCTION TEAM

Scripts: Jimmy Perry and David Croft

Producer: David Croft
Production Assistant: Clive Doig
Director: Harold Snoad
Studio Lighting: George Summers
Studio Sound: James Cole
Design: Oliver Bayldon
Assistant Floor Manager: Tony George
Vision Mixer: Bruce Milliard
Costume Supervisor: Marjorie Lewis
Make-Up Supervisor: Sheila Cassidy

After a lecture on camouflage, the platoon find different ways of disguising themselves. Walker dresses up as a haystack, Frazer in snow camouflage, Jones disguises himself as a butcher and Godfrey wears a bee-keeping hat. Pike has a letter from his mother saying he can't dress up in a lot of damp leaves because it will set his chest off. Mainwaring isn't happy with Mrs Pike's mollycoddling, so orders Wilson to have a chat with her.

Mrs Pike meanwhile receives a letter from the WVS asking if she'll take in an evacuee. She agrees and talks to Pike about it being nice to have a little child around the house again. She asks Pike not to tell Wilson at the moment; what she doesn't know is that he's listening at the door!

Although Wilson admits to overhearing Mavis' chat with Frank, they talk at cross-purposes and Wilson remains shocked because he thinks Mavis is expecting his child.

Wilson is in a constant daze on parade so Mainwaring calls him in to the office where he confides in his captain about the baby. Mainwaring tells Wilson he must do the honourable thing and marry her. She accepts and the platoon are set to provide the Guard of Honour. Wilson and Jones – replacing Mrs Pike – practise the procession with the men, but Mrs Pike turns up to announce Little Arthur has already arrived. Fortunately for Wilson, the confusion is cleared up when he's introduced to Little Arthur, the evacuee.

SHAND, JUNE

Born: Aberdeenshire
Roles: Member of the Home Front Company, an Andrews Sisters, Girl on the Beach (stage show)
June grew up in a tiny Scottish village and won a scholarship to London's Royal College of Music, where she studied for over four years. Since graduating she has appeared in all strands of the profession, including cabaret, TV, summer seasons, rep and pantomime.

SHAPS, CYRIL (1923 –)

Born: London
Role: General Monteverdi ('Don't Fence Me In') (radio)
Upon leaving school in 1940, Cyril worked for the London County Council's ambulance service as a clerk for five years. Between 1942 and 1947

he was based with the Service Corps and Educational Corps. Before demob, Cyril, who had always wanted to be an actor, helped prepare soldiers for civvy street by teaching music and drama appreciation.

When he finally left the army he won a scholarship to RADA, and upon graduating, his first post was in rep at Guildford followed by a spell in the West End. For two years he worked on Holland's radio network, covering a range of duties including reporting, producing and announcing. He returned to England and struggled on the job front until the chance to join the BBC's own repertory company came along.

He gradually established himself on radio and television, appearing in various shows, such as *Z Cars* and *Doctor Who*. His first film role was in 1950's *Cairo Road*, but other productions he worked on include *The Silent Enemy*; *Danger Within*; *Passport to Shame*; *Never Let Go*; *Return of a Stranger*; *To Sir, With Love*; *The Odessa File*; *Operation Daybreak* and *The Spy Who Loved Me*. Cyril is still busy in the profession.

SHARP, ANTHONY (1915–1984)
Born: London
Role: Brigadier (War Office) (S2, episode 3: 'The Loneliness of the Long-Distance Walker), Colonel (S9, episode 2: 'The Making of Private Pike') (TV)
Anthony led a very busy acting career before his death at the age of 69.

A regular character player on television he was seen in numerous productions, including *To The Manor Born*, *The Young Ones* as Roland Percival, *Keep It in the Family* as Mr Baker, *George and Mildred*, *Doomwatch*, *Rising Damp* and *Counterstrike*.

His film career boasted over 30 movies, such as *Teheran*, *The Sword and the Rose*, *Left, Right and Centre*, *Invasion*, *Rebound*, *One of Our Dinosaurs is Missing*, *Never Say Never Again* as Lord Ambrose and *Crossed Swords* in 1978 as Dr Buttes.

SHARVELL-MARTIN, MICHAEL (1944–)
Born: Herne
Role: Lieutenant (S7, episode 3: 'Gorilla Warfare') (TV)
Michael always wanted to be an actor and upon completing his education joined the Bristol Old Vic drama school in 1961. He completed his two-year course and undertook a stage management course while working as an ASM with the Royal Shakespeare Company. He then worked at various reps, and was also employed as an electrician and lighting technician for a while.

While working at Cheltenham's Everyman Theatre as a production manager, Michael was offered acting jobs, and gradually he started to concentrate on this side of the business. He branched out into television in the early 1970s, making his debut as a spear carrier in *Up Pompeii!*. He went on to appear in numerous TV shows, including *Are You Being Served?*, *Terry and June*, *The Two Ronnies*, *The Benny Hill Show* and 12 years appearing in sketches with Dave Allen on his shows. Latterly, Michael appeared in seven series of *No Place Like Home* as Trevor Botting.

His film appearances include playing a Russian in *Not Now, Comrade* in 1976, a barman in *Frightmare*, a factory designer in *The Love Ban* and a policeman in *That's Your Funeral* in 1972.

Theatre takes up most of Michael's time now, and he has appeared in pantomime for the last 25 years.

SHERWIN, STUART (1927–)
Born: Stoke-on-Trent
Roles: 2nd ARP Warden (S3, episode 10: 'Menace from the Deep'), Bill, 2nd ARP Warden (S3, episode 11: 'Branded'), Mr Alberts, 2nd ARP Warden (S4, episode 7: 'Put That Light Out!'), Reg Adamson, Junior Warden (S5, episode 11: 'A Brush with the Law') (TV); Lighthouse Keeper ('Put That Light Out!'), Mr Fairbrother ('Brain versus Brawn'), Policeman ('Absent Friends'), Station Master ('The Royal Train') (radio)

Stuart's father was a pottery salesman travelling the country. When he arrived home on Fridays, the family would visit the local theatre, and that's where Stuart's interest in the stage originated. Before joining the army during the Second World War, he worked on the railways in various jobs including a booking clerk, a job he returned to briefly upon demob, before moving to an estate agents. Eventually he joined a rep company in Leeds after applying to an advert in *The Stage*.

His final spell in rep was a winter season at Bognor after which he toured in *Salad Days* in 1960. His first West End appearance was with Brian Rix at the Whitehall Theatre in *One For The Pot*. Small parts in TV came along including *Emergency – Ward 10*, *Are You Being Served?*, *The Dick Emery Show*, *Crackerjack*, *Don't Wait Up*, *The Bill*, *Little and Large* and *Keeping Up Appearances*. He has also appeared in a handful of films, such as *The Victors* and *Oh, What a Lovely War!*.

Since *Dad's Army* he's worked with Les Dawson, Terry Scott and been seen in *Keeping Up Appearances*, as a clerk of the court in *Rumpole of the Bailey* and as a hotel guest in *Fawlty Towers*. Although he recently filmed a part in *The Find*, the last few years have been dominated by long stints in theatre. He's just finished a two-year spell in *Oliver!* at the Palladium. His career has taken him around the world, including a tour of the Middle and Far East for four months visiting 14 countries as Colonel Pickering in *Pygmalion*.

Other notable theatre appearances include the stage adaptation of David Croft and Jeremy Lloyd's *Are You Being Served?* at Blackpool, the first performance of *Around The World in 80 Days* and a leading role in *Boorskale* which won the Vivian Ellis Award.

SHIRLEY
Played by Rosemary Faith (TV)
Surname unknown, Shirley is a dark-haired barmaid who works in the saloon bar frequented by members of the Eastgate and Walmington platoon after the ceremonial church parade in 'Battle of the Giants!'.

SHIRLEY
Played by Wendy Richard (radio)
Shirley is Walker's girlfriend and is taken along to Mr Mainwaring's house in 'The King was in his Counting House' as an uninvited guest. It's just as well Elizabeth didn't make it downstairs in time to attend the function because she certainly wouldn't have approved. Walker is still dating her when the Americans arrive in 'My British Buddy', so he takes her along to the darts match at The Red Lion, although he probably wishes he hadn't because she's chatted up by the Yanks.

SHODSKI, CAPTAIN
In 'Don't Fence Me In' Shodski is a member of the Free Polish Forces and in charge of the guards looking after the 60 Italian POWs at a nearby camp. By the time the Walmington Home Guard arrive to relieve his men, Shodski has already left so he's never actually seen.

SHOESMITH, CAPTAIN
Shoesmith is a non-speaking character who attends the sherry party in 'My Brother and I', which is organised by the Home Guard officers in the district.

WORKING WITH HODGES

To be honest, I couldn't imagine anything more frustrating than working for Chief Warden Hodges, constantly placating him after one of his petty squabbles with his arch enemy, Captain Mainwaring. But for four episodes of the television series Stuart Sherwin played an assistant warden who had to do just that. Here Stuart shares his memories of appearing in *Dad's Army*.

'I always played an assistant ARP warden and was forever trying to calm him down after some particular brush he had with Captain Mainwaring and Co. One episode I remember particularly well was "Put That Light Out!" which saw some of the platoon marooned in a lighthouse and accidentally switching on the light. My part in the episode was to try and calm down Mr Hodges who was going mad with rage about the searchlight lighting up the entire coast. It was very funny and, I believe, was held up to be a perfect example of what a television comedy should be.

'I first met David Croft years previous when I had appeared in several episodes of a situation comedy he directed for Tyne Tees Television called *Under New Management*, about a pub where the landlady was played by Mollie Sugden. I was a neighbour who kept on complaining about the noise.

'My memories of *Dad's Army* are all happy ones. The regular members of the platoon were, of course, together all the time and so a newcomer in a particular episode could never be a part of the inner circle, so to speak, but you were always made welcome and if you were in more than one show, you were soon accepted. I was always amused by the way the regulars became the characters they were playing and vice versa. After rehearsals we all went to the pub for a drink and they were the same characters but in a different setting.

'I remember being in the pub after rehearsing an episode prior to the stage show going out on tour and John Laurie saying how he thought Arnold Ridley shouldn't be contemplating such a step – it was as if he was talking about Private Godfrey. A few minutes later I was talking to Arnold who was justifying going on the tour in typical Private Godfrey tones.

'My saddest memory is of touring in *Home At Seven*, the last play Arthur Lowe appeared in. We had completed the Wednesday matinée at the Alexandra Theatre, Birmingham, and Arthur went to his dressing room. When we came to do the evening show it was discovered he had collapsed. It was a dreadful time.

'What is very noticeable when you see a repeat on television are the long "takes" rather than the cuts and retakes you see today. All of the characters were originally stage actors whose vast experience made them able to cover any slight mistake, and more importantly still, not to let each other down. I think the series is a brilliant example of ensemble acting with all the characters complementing each other.'

STUART SHERWIN

SHOOTING PAINS

Recorded: Monday 20/5/68 (made in black and white)

Original transmission: Wednesday 11/9/68, 8.20–8.50pm

(This episode was originally planned for transmission on Wednesday 10 July at 8.20pm)

Original viewing figures: 9.7 million

Repeated: 21/2/69, 18/8/98, 28/6/99

CAST

Arthur Lowe . . . . .Captain Mainwaring
John Le Mesurier . . . . .Sergeant Wilson
Clive Dunn . . . . .Lance Corporal Jones
John Laurie . . . . .Private Frazer
James Beck . . . . .Private Walker
Arnold Ridley . . . . .Private Godfrey
Ian Lavender . . . . .Private Pike
Barbara Windsor . . . . .Laura La Plaz
Janet Davies . . . . .Mrs Pike
Caroline Dowdeswell . . . . .Janet King
Martin Wyldeck . . . . .Major Regan

Jimmy Perry . . . . .Charlie Cheeseman
Thérèse McMurray . . . . .Girl at the Window
Platoon: Hugh Hastings, Richard Jacques, David Seaforth, Jimmy Mac, Vic Taylor, Hugh Cecil, Chris Franks, Alec Coleman, Colin Bean

PRODUCTION TEAM

Script: Jimmy Perry and David Croft
Producer/Director: David Croft
Production Assistant: Harold Snoad
Studio Lighting: George Summers
Studio Sound: James Cole
Design: Alan Hunter-Craig and Paul Joel
Assistant Floor Manager: Evan King
Vision Mixer: Clive Doig
Costume Supervisor: George Ward
Make-Up Supervisor: Sandra Exelby
Marksmanship by Geoff Winship

The platoon is involved in target practice on Saturday. The previous week Mainwaring had been disappointed with the display, especially when they mistook the tyres on the Area Commander's staff car for the target. They even hit the spare! But Mainwaring's day is made when he learns that the platoon, being the first launched in the area, have been chosen to act as Guard of Honour for the Prime Minister's inspection of coastal defences.

The members of the platoon aren't keen to take part in the shooting practice because Major Regan will be there, and attend grudgingly.

'Shooting Pains'

Regan shows them how to use different weapons, but still classes the men as sloppy and in need of more practice.

Later, Regan tells Mainwaring he's asked the Eastgate platoon to be Guard of Honour because he was so disappointed with the Walmington men. However, as the Area Commander wanted to give them a second chance, they can redeem themselves, but only if they win a shooting contest between the two platoons. It's now left to Mainwaring to pick the three best shots for the contest.

'Shooting Pains'

To cheer themselves up, Walker suggests they go along to the Hippodrome Theatre where Charlie Cheeseman is top of the bill. That evening, one of the supporting acts is Laura La Plaz, who's a crack shot – so long as she's shooting between her legs or over her shoulder. Walker hatches a plan to help the platoon win the firing competition.

A heavily disguised Laura La Plaz is supposed to be the platoon's secret weapon, but when she's prevented from using her rather unorthodox shooting positions her accuracy goes haywire and it looks like the Eastgate platoon will win, but Frazer comes to the rescue.

SHORT, LIEUTENANT

(See 'Naval Officer, The'.)

SHOWING UP OF CORPORAL JONES, THE

Recorded: Monday 13/5/68 (made in black and white)

Original transmission: Wednesday 4/9/68, 8.20–8.50pm

(This episode was originally planned for transmission on Wednesday 3 July)

Original viewing figures: 8.8 million

Repeated: 14/2/69, 11/8/98, 18/8/98 (Wales), 11/7/99

CAST

Arthur Lowe . . . . .Captain Mainwaring
John Le Mesurier . . . . .Sergeant Wilson
Clive Dunn . . . . .Lance Corporal Jones
John Laurie . . . . .Private Frazer
James Beck . . . . .Private Walker
Arnold Ridley . . . . .Private Godfrey
Ian Lavender . . . . .Private Pike
Janet Davies . . . . .Mrs Pike
Martin Wyldeck . . . . .Major Regan
Patrick Waddington . . . . . . .Brigadier
Edward Sinclair . . . . .Caretaker
Thérèse McMurray . . . . .Girl at the Window
Platoon: Colin Bean, Hugh Hastings, Richard Jacques, Alec Coleman, Hugh Cecil, Vic Taylor, Jimmy Mac, Peter Whitaker, Chris Franks, David Seaforth
Training Sergeant: Charles Finch

PRODUCTION TEAM

Script: Jimmy Perry and David Croft
Producer/Director: David Croft
Production Assistant: Harold Snoad
Studio Lighting: George Summers

Studio Sound: James Cole
Design: Alan Hunter-Craig and Paul Joel
Assistant Floor Manager: Evan King
Vision Mixer: Clive Doig
Costume Supervisor: George Ward
Make-Up Supervisor: Sandra Exelby

Major Regan from Area HQ has been appointed to inspect training and battle drill in all Home Guard units in the area, and he decides to visit the Walmington platoon the night the men take over the patrol of the coastline from Stones' Amusement Arcade to the Jolly Roger Pier.

At 6pm, the Major arrives for the inspection. Everything proceeds to plan with plane spotting, map reading, first aid and unarmed combat, but Jones isn't performing too well: when his glasses steam up preventing him from charging with his bayonet, and he can't remember things, Regan tells Mainwaring the platoon has done well overall but Jones might have to go.

Later, a letter from GHQ arrives confirming Jones is over-age and must stand down. However, after considering his distinguished service record and Mainwaring's strong support, if Jones can complete the divisional assault course in 15 minutes he will be allowed to remain in the Home Guard.

Although Jones is 70 he's confident he can pass the rigorous test he's been set. That evening he tries out the assault course but two hours later he still hasn't finished! Then Walker has an idea. On the day of the test, the platoon help Jones with the aid of a ladder, doubles and other schemes, resulting in him completing the course in 13 minutes. Major Regan can't believe it, but there's nothing he can do.

Note: Caroline Dowdeswell was due to appear in this episode. The scene was cut, but she was still paid a fee.

SIEGFRIED LINE, THE
Before the outbreak of the Second World War this line of defence was built along Germany's western border. By 1944 the Allies were probing the line, and it wasn't long before they breached the fortifications in which Hitler had placed so much trust.

SIGNALLER, THE
(See 'Signals Private, The'.)

SIGNALS PRIVATE, THE
Played by Larry Martyn (TV); Michael Burlington (radio, although character called 'The Signaller')
In 'The Desperate Drive of Corporal Jones', the sandwich-munching signalman speaks to Jones on the phone during the divisional exercise to confirm Mainwaring and his men are in position.

SIGNATURE TUNE
People have often wondered whether the familiar 'Who Do You Think You Are Kidding, Mr Hitler?', which opened every episode, was a period recording; it was, in fact, recorded in February 1968, by the singer Bud Flanagan, who was paid £105.

While Jimmy Perry and Derek Taverner – who'd met in an army entertainment unit in India – were touring the country in a musical, *When You're Young*, back in 1967, Jimmy began telling Derek about his idea for *Dad's Army*, which was still at an embryonic stage. When it came to writing the theme tune, 'Who Do You Think You Are Kidding, Mr Hitler?', a title which was sparked by a wartime speech and, in particular, a quotation, Jimmy contacted Derek, who was doing a show in London, suggesting they worked on it together. While Jimmy wrote the lyrics and came up with the tune, Derek's main job was organising the music, putting it into a workable shape prior to recording.

During the process from writing to recording, changes inevitably occurred and at one point the verse was twice as long. Derek believes much of the credit regarding the tune's authentic sound lies with Flanagan, whose style of singing contributed greatly to this evocative number.

When it came to recording, Bud Flanagan was nearing the end of his life and it took over two hours before the job was complete. David Croft states: 'We were very lucky to get him. It turned out he'd never recorded a song that he hadn't actually sung before. We sent him the song and he turned up as planned for the recording session with the military band. Suddenly he realised that he didn't know the song. He was terribly apologetic about the whole thing, but in the end that signature tune was an accumulation of about eight takes pieced together.'

'Who Do You Think You Are Kidding, Mr Hitler?', sung by Bud Flanagan, was originally released as a record in 1969 on the Pye label, catalogue No 7N17854. It has been included in various compilations since, including the 'BBC Comedy Themes' LP in 1980, catalogue No REH387. This was also released as a cassette, catalogue No ZCR387.

The Band of the Coldstream Guards, conducted by their Director of Music, Major Trevor L Sharpe MBE, LRAM, ARCM, psm, played the tune which closed every episode of the nine series. The tune has been recorded by various other bands, including the Foden's Motorworks Band, conducted by Harry Mortimer, but the Coldstream Guards' version was recorded onto a BBC LP in 1978. The LP (catalogue No CN2956) contained the theme tunes from other popular shows such as *Dr Finlay's Casebook* and *Just a Minute*. It was issued for promotional purposes only.

SILVERA, CARMEN
Born: Toronto
Role: Mrs Gray (S4, episode 9: 'Mum's Army') (TV and radio)
Carmen, best known as Edith in BBC's hit comedy *'Allo, 'Allo*, appeared in the rather moving episode 'Mum's Army' as a woman who experiences a brief encounter with Mainwaring.

Although she's forged a successful career for herself in acting, Carmen originally wanted to be a dancer. Upon settling in England, she trained in ballet from the age of three. When evacuated to Montreal during the war she was given the opportunity to attend lessons with the Ballet Russe, later appearing in three of their shows.

When the war finished she returned to England and turned her attention to acting; she enrolled at LAMDA before beginning her career in rep. Carmen made her TV debut in *Z Cars* before landing the prominent role of Camilla Hope in BBC's 1960's drama *Compact*. Among her many TV credits are appearances in *New Scotland Yard*, *Doctor Who*, *Within These Walls* and *The Gentle Touch*. She's also been seen in *The Generation Game* and *What's My Line?*.

On stage, Carmen has appeared in many West End productions including *Waters of the Moon* with Ingrid Bergman, *Hobson's Choice* with Penelope Keith and *School for Wives* playing Georgette.

SIMMONDS, BRIAN
Prop man on numerous episodes (TV)
Brian was a child actor, appearing as an extra in several films, including *Oliver Twist*, *My Brother Jonathan* and *Great Expectations*. At 12 he left drama school and finished off his education before joining the merchant navy. He had a spell at British Rail and joined the Beeb as a relief prop man in 1964.

Eventually he was taken on full-time and worked on a number of hit shows, such as *Sykes*, *Some Mothers Do 'Ave 'Em*, *Last of the Summer Wine*, *Doctor Who*, *Dr Finlay's Casebook* and *See How They Run*.

Brian, whose responsibilities on *Dad's Army* would have included erecting and dressing the sets, left the BBC in 1984 and now works freelance.

SINCLAIR, DAVID (1934–1996)
Born: Ealham, Kent
Roles: GHQ Driver ('Command Decision'), German Airman ('The Enemy within the Gates'), 2nd ARP Warden ('The Menace from the Deep') (radio)
David trained at the Guildhall School and opted for a career in musical comedy instead of opera. He went on to appear in many West End musicals, including *Vanity Fair* and *My Fair Lady*, and toured America in two productions.

During the four decades David spent in the business, he worked in every medium, and even spent time doing cabaret on the Cunard and Canadian Pacific Lines, and two seasons with the Royal Shakespeare Company. But he was particularly active in radio, and was frequently heard on BBC radio.

Although he wasn't seen that often on television, David did appear in shows like *Randall & Hopkirk (Deceased)*, *… And Mother Makes Three*, *Out of the Unknown*, *Dead of Night* and provided the voice of the clerk in *Willows in Winter*. His last appearance was on *The World of Lee Evans*. David died of cancer, aged 62.

SINCLAIR, EDWARD (1914–1977)

Born: Manchester

Role: Maurice Yeatman, the Verger (49 TV episodes and *Christmas Night with the Stars* inserts; the film, the stage show and 11 radio episodes)

Edward was born into a theatrical family. His father was a stage actor, while his mother danced and sang. It's therefore not surprising that they introduced their son to the stage at an early age – he was six months old when he was carried on in *The Midnight Mail*.

When his father died, Edward was only 14. With two other children to support, his mother couldn't afford to let him attend drama school. If he couldn't train professionally, the next best

thing was to work on an amateur basis, and before the outbreak of war Edward had joined a local amateur company, the St Luke's Players. He worked with them for eight years before joining the Teddington Theatre Club in 1937, where he gained experience acting, producing and staging many productions, including *Busman's Honeymoon* and *The Admirable Crichton*. Edward loved every minute of it, and he began writing for the theatre club.

When he was called up, he joined the army's Oxford and Bucks Light Infantry and became involved with concert parties for the troops. A record of ill health – he suffered a severe bronchial condition as a baby – meant Edward was based in this country during hostilities. For the rest of his life, he was a bronchitic although he disguised the fact well.

When Edward was demobbed in 1945, he resumed his amateur acting career. Even though he enjoyed acting, he resisted the temptation to turn professional, realising the insecurity of the profession was incompatible with the responsibilities of a married man, who by this time was soon to become a father. His one desire was to support his family and the most

secure route was the one he knew: selling. From the age of 17, Edward had worked as a salesman, first selling men's clothing in a Kingston shop before moving to a high class store in London. But he was determined not to return to the outfitting industry, and although initially he found little work after being demobbed, he eventually joined a company selling hairdressing equipment.

Once his two sons, Peter and Keith, were in their teens and nearing the end of their education, Edward – then in his late forties – finally decided it was time to chance his luck in the precarious world of professional acting. He first started working in radio before offers for TV work came along, including the role of Barkis in the serial *David Copperfield*, *Z Cars*, *Special Branch* and *Dr Finlay's Casebook*. As well as the *Dad's Army* movie, he appeared as a taxi driver in the 1973 film, *No Sex Please, We're British*.

It's for his perfectly crafted performance as the Verger in *Dad's Army* that Edward is best remembered. He first appeared as the caretaker in the fifth episode, 'The Showing Up of Corporal Jones' and was then cast in the occasional episode, but it wasn't until the fifth season that he became a regular, by which time he was billed as the Verger. As the show progressed the number of lines allocated to Edward increased, and the role became the highlight of his career.

Just as the series finished he'd started receiv-

ing offers to play panto, and if he'd lived long enough his career would have prospered because of *Dad's Army*. Although he'd suffered bad health all his life, his death of a heart attack in 1977 came as a complete shock. He had been holidaying in Bournemouth with his wife, Gladys, and they decided to return home via Cheddar, Somerset, to spend time with their eldest son. On the final morning of their visit, Edward went indoors to start packing, suffered a massive heart attack and collapsed on the kitchen floor. Edward's devotion to his family meant that he started his acting comparatively late, and as a result was just reaching the peak of his career when he died.

TV credits include: *Compact* (three episodes), *Danger Man*, *The Paper Man* for Anglia, *Beggar My Neighbour*, *Hugh and I Spy*, *Rogues Gallery* for Granada, *Sunday Night Theatre*, *Crime and Punishment*, *Security Risk*, *The Frobisher Case* for Thames, *Dawson' Weekly*.

Theatre credits include: Joe in *All in Good Time* at the Richmond Theatre.

Film credits include: *Eye of the Devil* for MGM, *Bliss of Mrs Blossom*, *Take a Girl Like You*, *The Magic Christian*, *The Ski Wheelers* for the Children's Film Foundation, *Shirley's World*.

Commercials/commentaries include: Bournville, Oxo, commentary for Dutch documentary film, *Watney's Straight 8* and a national poster for BP.

```
       OH, DO BE PHILOSOPHICAL , IF YOU CAN.

                   Song and Lyrics
                        by
                   EDWARD SINCLAIR

       Verse

   Our philosophy, dear Vicar, is to fight
                             against the gloom,
   We must try and look as happy as can be.
   Let us 'keep the home fires burning'
   Without a thought of doom
   Our philosophy at Walmington-on-Sea.
   The 'Home Guard' may be trying,
   But they don't care a jot -
   Captain Mainwaring and his stalwart Company,
   'Cos he smiles, and says 'We'e British'
   We'll defend this 'Blessed Plot'
   That a grand phil-os-o-phy - -


       Chorus

   So, do be philo - philo - sophical,
   Oh, do be philo - sophical if you can
   When everybody's glum and the hens won't lay,
   The cow's on strike, there's no eggs to-day.
   Oh, do be philo - philo - sophical,
   Oh, do be philo - sophical if you can,
   For if you are a Briton, and you think you
                             look a wreck,
   Or if the cat is having kittens on the upper deck,
   Or if you fall downstairs one day and break
                             your blinkin' neck!
   Try to be philo-sophical, philo - philo - sophical,
   OH, DO BE PHILO - SOPHICAL IF YOU CAN.

                  ( Plus extra chorus )
```

SINGER, CAMPBELL (1909–1976)

Roles: Major General Menzies (S5, episode 6: 'If the Cap Fits…'), Sir Charles McAllister (S8, episode 3: 'Is There Honey Still For Tea?') (TV)

Campbell was a busy character actor on both stage and screen. He was also a published author. His television work includes playing Henry Burroughs in *The Newcomers*, a bailiff in *Rising Damp*, a porter in *The Persuaders*, several characters in *Doctor Who*, and Colonel Segur in *Danger Man*. On the big screen he was seen in over 50 pictures, such as *Take My Life*, *Operation Diamond* as Bert, *The Blue Lamp* as the station sergeant, *Someone at the Door*, *Cage of Gold* as a policeman, *Pool of London*, *The Man with the Twisted Lip*, *Lady in the Fog*, *The Yellow Balloon* playing Potter, *Home at Seven* as Inspector Hemmingway, *Emergency Call*, *The Titfield Thunderbolt*, *Street Corner*, *Conflict of Wings* as Flight Sergeant Campbell and *The Square Peg* as Sergeant Loder.

SIRLOVEKIN, PRIVATE

Not seen in sitcom, Sirlovekin is a member of the Walmington Home Guard. Jones calls his name in 'Absent Friends'.

SIX BELLS, THE

The Walmington Home Guard visit this country pub while dressed in German uniforms during the episode, 'Ring Dem Bells'. Mr Palethorpe is the landlord, and is assisted behind the bar by the tall blonde barmaid, Doris, who's sent to warn the villagers that the enemy has arrived when they understandably mistake the Walmington platoon for Germans. Some of the platoon return to the pub (situated five miles from Walmington, just off the Dymchurch road) in 'Wake-Up Walmington' dressed as fifth columnists, frightening away a couple of drinkers in the process.

SMALE, ELEANOR

Role: Mrs Prosser (S3, episode 9: 'War Dance' and S4, episode 9: 'Mum's Army') (TV)

Eleanor's other TV appearances included the BBC's 1969 series, *The Doctors*, playing a patient.

SMALL BOY, THE

The small boy is seen in 'The Recruit'. (See 'Hamish'.)

SMALL MAN, THE

Played by Leon Cortez (TV)

The small man appears in 'Man Hunt' as an angry husband of one of the women Mainwaring asks to show her knickers.

SMEE, ANTHONY

Role: Cricketer G C Egan ('The Cricket Match') (radio)

As well as working on radio, Anthony has appeared in television and films. His small-screen credits include playing a pressman in an episode of *Ripping Yarns*, Wenslow in a 1981 episode of *Bergerac*, *Alas Smith and Jones*, *Heartbeat* as Rod Dundas, and a superintendent in 1993's *Framed*. His film work includes playing an interrogation officer in the 1996 picture, *The English Patient*.

SMITH GUN

The Walmington platoon's Smith gun is seen in 'We Know Our Onions' when they take it along to a weekend efficiency test, run by Captain Ramsey. At its birth in 1940, the original Smith gun was rejected by the military, but after minor changes to the design, it became an official Home Guard weapon in 1941. The gun's favourable size and weight meant it was easily transported behind a small vehicle, and was therefore ideal for the Home Guard.

SMITH, MAJOR

Played by Alan Haines (TV); Jack Watson (radio)

In 'Battle School' Major Smith runs the training school which Mainwaring and his men attend for an exercise in guerilla warfare.

SNAGGE, JOHN (1904–1996)

It was John's voice that introduced each of the 67 *Dad's Army* radio episodes. Upon joining the BBC in 1928, he became one of the Corporation's best known announcers, particularly during the war years. He also commentated on the annual university boat race between 1931 and 1980. He retired in 1981 after just completing a long-running series, *John Snagge's London*, for BBC Radio London.

SNETTLEFOLD

This town is mentioned several times in 'The Royal Train'. When Mainwaring and his men are stuck in the train unable to stop, they fear arriving at Snettlefold station and ploughing into the back of another train. Thanks to the bravery of Mainwaring and Jones, matters are quickly brought under control before this happens.

SNOAD, HAROLD

Production assistant: S1; S2, episodes 1, 2, 3; S3, episode 1; S3, episodes 4, 5, 6, 7, 8, 9, 10, 12, 13, 14; S4, episodes 1, 3, 4 & 6; director: S2, episodes 4, 5 & 6; S3, episode 3; S3, episode 11; S4, episodes 2 & 5

Born in London in 1935, Harold Snoad became interested in the theatre as a boy. During the war his father, who was in the army, was stationed in Bath, and the Snoad family were regular visitors to the city's Theatre Royal. They moved to Eastbourne when Harold was 12 and he became hooked on the world of entertainment. While talking to the manager at the local theatre Harold expressed an interest in working backstage and before long was spending all his school holidays helping out on various productions. At 14, he began receiving a wage packet from the theatre.

A keen member of his school's dramatic society, he left Eastbourne College and attended drama school in Brighton. Upon graduating he spent his national service in the RAF, where he gained experience directing several plays.

For the last six months of his time in uniform he was stationed at Brighton's recruiting centre, where the commanding officer asked him to devise an entry for the RAF's annual window display competition. It was the early 1950s and the successful panel game, *What's My Line?*, had begun. Harold came up with an idea for a display based round the theme: 'What's My Line? What's Your Line? There are a 101 lines in the RAF!'. Wanting to obtain large photographs of the panellists from the BBC, Harold contacted Gilbert Harding, who happened to live in Brighton, and was invited to Harding's house where the TV panellist listened to Harold's idea and agreed to help.

The Brighton recruiting office won the competition and when Harold told Gilbert Harding, the subject of Harold's intention to return to theatre acting upon demob came up. Harding suggested he tried joining the TV industry. Harold took his advice and joined the BBC as a floor assistant in 1957. His long career with the Beeb saw him become one of the country's youngest TV producer/directors at the age of 30.

He has worked with many of the industry's 'greats', including Ronnie Barker and Dick Emery for eight years. Among the shows he's directed and produced are *Ever Decreasing Circles*, *Don't Wait Up*, *Oh, Brother!*, *Sykes and a Big, Big Show*, *Them*, *His Lordship Entertains*, *Casanova '73*, *Are You Being Served?*, *The Dick Emery Show*, *Rings on their Fingers*, *Legacy of Murder*, *Partners*, *The Further Adventures of Lucky Jim*, *Tears Before Bedtime*, *Hilary*, *Brush Strokes* and *Keeping Up Appearances*.

He has also directed a feature film (a Ray Cooney farce) and apart from his various writing credits, he and Michael Knowles also wrote the radio series *Where There's a Will*, *It Sticks Out Half a Mile* and adapted the *Dad's Army* television series for radio. He has also written a book, *Directing Situation Comedy*.

Since retiring from the BBC, Harold – who also does public speaking – has concentrated on freelance producing and directing, including going back to his old love, the theatre.

SNOEK

When Mainwaring eats at the British Restaurant in Walmington during the episode 'The Honourable Man', he finds snoek on the menu, but quickly gives it the cold-shoulder. During wartime, snoek (a large fish resembling the barracuda) appeared on menus and in shops around Britain. Frowned upon by many people, it was just one of many products the Ministry of Food introduced to the home market; it came in various guises, including pasties and paste.

SNUGGLY, MR

Pike takes his teddy bear, Mr Snuggly, along to the explosives course in 'Fallen Idol'.

SOLDIER, THE

Played by Neville Hughes (TV)

Just before the first parade of Walmington's LDV comes to an end in 'The Man and the Hour', a soldier arrives with a supply of armbands and pepper: the first step towards moulding the men into a lethal fighting force, or so Mainwaring would have us think.

SOLDIER, THE

Played by Gordon Peters (TV)

This soldier arrives with his colleague, Burt, at the end of 'Command Decision', to deliver the rifles the Walmington Home Guard have been desperately waiting for. He frustrates Mainwaring by requiring his signature on duplicate forms before releasing the rifles.

SOLDIER, THE

Played by Larry Martyn (TV)

When Walker is briefly at the infantry training barracks in 'The Loneliness of the Long-Distance Walker', he sits down in the mess hall beside two soldiers. Larry Martyn's character eats one of Walker's corned beef fritters, and with a mouthful of food, splashes Walker as he talks.

SOLDIER, THE

Played by Jeffrey Holland (TV)

In 'Wake-Up Walmington' the soldier drives a lorry which is stopped by Mainwaring and his men. The platoon speak with foreign accents in order to appear suspicious, but fail when the soldier, oblivious to their attempt at being fifth columnists, drives off claiming all foreigners are barmy.

SOLDIERS, THE

Played by John Leeson and Jonathan Holt (TV)

In 'Sons of the Sea' Mainwaring and his men think they've drifted across the Channel in their rowing boat. Unaware that they're back on home soil, they see the two soldiers.

SOLDIER'S FAREWELL, A

Recorded: Friday 2/6/72

Original transmission: Friday 20/10/72, 8.30–9.00pm

Original viewing figures: 17.7 million

Repeated: 14/7/73, 14/11/92, 28/1/93 (Wales), 27/7/96, 2/5/00

CAST

Arthur Lowe	Captain Mainwaring
John Le Mesurier	Sergeant Wilson
Clive Dunn	Lance Corporal Jones
John Laurie	Private Frazer
James Beck	Private Walker
Arnold Ridley	Private Godfrey
Ian Lavender	Private Pike
Bill Pertwee	ARP Warden
Frank Williams	Vicar
Robert Gillespie	Charles Boyer
Joan Savage	Greta Garbo
Joy Allen	Clippie
Colin Bean	Private Sponge

Platoon: Desmond Cullum-Jones, Michael Moore, Hugh Hastings, Leslie Noyes, George Hancock, Freddie White, Hugh Cecil, Freddie Wiles

Extras on Bus: Elizabeth Cullum-Jones, Linda Carroll, Doris Kitts, Hugh Elton, Fred Davies

PRODUCTION TEAM

Script: Jimmy Perry and David Croft
Producer/Director: David Croft
Production Assistant: Gordon Pert
Film Cameraman: Stewart A. Farnell
Film Sound Recordist: Ron Blight
Film Editor: Bill Harris
Studio Lighting: Howard King
Studio Sound: Michael McCarthy
Design: Paul Joel
Assistant Floor Manager: Peter Fitton
Vision Mixer: Dave Hanks
Costume Supervisor: Susan Wheal
Make-Up Supervisor: Cynthia Goodwin
Visual Effects: Peter Day

'A Soldier's Farewell'

The platoon spend an evening at the pictures watching Charles Boyer and Greta Garbo (played by Robert Gillespie and Joan Savage) in *Marie Walewska*. When the final frame is shown and the national anthem plays, there's a stampede to get out and Mainwaring, who's nearly crushed in the charge, is the only one who remains. On the way home on the bus, Mainwaring tells his men how disgusted he is, and that he feels their discipline has gone to pot. Another stampede follows when the bus arrives at Walmington and Hodges declares it's closing time in five minutes.

On parade next day, Mainwaring revisits the incident and gives his men a dressing-down. To make the punishment fit the crime, he plays the national anthem on a gramophone, and orders the men to attention, but playing the German national anthem by mistake doesn't go down well. The platoon isn't to be dismissed until the national anthem has played six times. To prevent them standing there too long, Jones speeds up the gramophone.

Before the end of the evening's parade, Walker brings in Mainwaring's order of cheddar cheese, as well as two bottles of milk stout for Wilson. Mainwaring was planning a toasted cheese supper with his wife, but when he phones and tells her he might have a little surprise for her tonight, she abruptly drops the receiver.

It looks like the supper is off until Wilson suggests they feast themselves on the cheese, bread and two bottles of milk stout. Just as they're about to prepare their evening treat, Jones comes in. When he's told there's only enough supper for two, he tells them he'll have to eat the kidneys he's got with him. Partial to a bit of kidney, Mainwaring and Wilson find a way of stretching the supper.

That night, Mainwaring can't sleep and regrets eating the cheese; it was far too rich. He takes indigestion tablets and ends up dreaming he's Napoleon and, amongst other things, sharing a toasted cheese supper with someone who looks remarkably like the clippie on the bus.

SOMETHING NASTY IN THE VAULT

Originally titled 'Don't Let Go'

Recorded: Sunday 15/6/69

Original transmission: Thursday 9/10/69, 7.30–8.00pm

Original viewing figures: 11.1 million

Repeated: 18/4/70, 16/3/71, 15/10/82, 17/10/89,
21/2/90 (N Ireland), 19/12/92, 4/2/93 (Wales),
13/1/96, 4/4/96 (Wales), 11/9/99

CAST

Arthur Lowe . . . . .Captain Mainwaring
John Le Mesurier . . . . .Sergeant Wilson
Clive Dunn . . . . .Lance Corporal Jones
John Laurie . . . . .Private Frazer
James Beck . . . . .Private Walker
Arnold Ridley . . . . .Private Godfrey
Ian Lavender . . . . .Private Pike
Janet Davies . . . . .Mrs Pike
Bill Pertwee . . . . .ARP Warden
Robert Dorning . . . . .Bank Inspector
Norman Mitchell . . . . .Captain Rogers
Yvonne Armitage . . . . .Girl Clerk in Bank
Christine Cole . . . . .ATS Girl
Eve Dewhurst . . . . .Old Lady in Bank
Platoon: Colin Bean, Frank Godfrey, Desmond
Cullum-Jones

PRODUCTION TEAM

Script: Jimmy Perry and David Croft
Producer/Director: David Croft
Production Assistant: Harold Snoad
Studio Lighting: Howard King
Studio Sound: Michael McCarthy
Design: Paul Joel
Assistant Floor Manager: Bill Harman
Vision Mixer: Dave Hanks
Costume Supervisor: Odette Barrow
Make-Up Supervisor: Jan Harrison
Special Effects: Peter Day

Walker tries paying in a £5 note at the bank, but
Pike thinks it's a fake and informs Mainwaring.
What no one realises is that the bank inspector is
standing in the queue, and he's far from pleased
when he hears Walker claim it came from the
bank!

Mr West, from head office, tells Mainwaring
his monthly report is becoming irregular, but
their meeting is suddenly interrupted by an air
raid; when they return two hours later they discover the bank has taken a direct hit. Mainwaring and Wilson fall through the floor and end up
cradling an unexploded German bomb, so Mr
West rushes off to get help. Mr Jones arrives and
is shocked to find Mainwaring and Wilson still
holding the bomb. He clears the bank, runs back
to his shop to call bomb disposal, and then summons help from the rest of the platoon.

When Captain Rogers from bomb disposal
arrives he takes charge. The first problem he
faces is getting into the strong room which won't
be easy because Wilson and Mainwaring have
the only two sets of keys. With the help of a fish-

'Sons of the Sea'

ing rod a set is retrieved and he manages to get
in, only to discover the bomb is a 'trembler' and
has to head back to HQ to pick up more tools.

In the meantime, the platoon rig up a piece of
equipment to lift the bomb. Their ingenuity pays
off and they escape from danger. While celebrating in the pub afterwards, Mr West shows the
bank's appreciation by paying for their drinks
with a £10 note – which turns out to be a dud.

SONS OF THE SEA

Recorded: Friday 5/12/69

Original transmission: Thursday 11/12/69,
7.30–8.00pm

Original viewing figures: 13.3 million

Repeated: 1/8/70, 10/12/82, 17/10/92, 11/3/93
(Wales), 6/6/94, 10/6/94 (Scotland), 27/1/96, 29/2/96
(Wales)

CAST

Arthur Lowe . . . . .Captain Mainwaring
John Le Mesurier . . . . .Sergeant Wilson
Clive Dunn . . . . .Lance Corporal Jones
John Laurie . . . . .Private Frazer
James Beck . . . . .Private Walker
Arnold Ridley . . . . .Private Godfrey
Ian Lavender . . . . .Private Pike
Michael Bilton . . . . .Mr Maxwell
Ralph Ball . . . . .Man on Station
John Leeson . . . . .1st Soldier
Jonathan Holt . . . . .2nd Soldier
Platoon: Desmond Cullum-Jones as Private Desmond

PRODUCTION TEAM

Script: Jimmy Perry and David Croft
Producer/Director: David Croft
Production Assistant: Harold Snoad
Film Cameraman: James Balfour
Film Editor: Bob Rymer
Studio Lighting: Howard King
Studio Sound: Michael McCarthy
Design: Ray London
Assistant Floor Manager: Bill Harman
Vision Mixer: Dave Hanks
Costume Supervisor: Michael Burdle
Make-Up Supervisor: Cecile Hay-Arthur

Mr Maxwell, a solicitor, informs Mr Mainwaring
of the death of Mr Johnson. He had no relatives,
and when he died his only possessions were the
clothes he stood up in and a boat, *The Naughty
Jane*. The bank account was overdrawn by £33
12s 6d, therefore the boat becomes the property
of the bank, but instead of selling it to offset the

MEMORIES OF A SOUND RECORDIST

One of the film sound recordists who worked on the TV series was John Gatland, who was responsible for series six and seven. Here he remembers those days in Norfolk.

'My career with the BBC started in 1955 when I joined London Recording Unit at 200 Oxford Street as a technical operator. I soon learnt that the main aim every day was for the shift to deliver the best product possible. Everyone wanted to share their knowledge and experience with me, so that I could contribute to this aim, and this set my standards for the future.

'I moved to television in 1958 and, after a period working at Lime Grove Studios as a telecine operator, I joined the BBC Film Unit at Ealing Film Studios in 1961 where I was pleasantly surprised to be reunited with many old friends from Sound Radio.

'As an assistant sound recordist, my first few years included filming *Maigret*, a highly memorable experience, and filming nearly every night on *Z Cars* throughout one of our harshest winters. We all still wanted the best product possible.

'The many problems that I and my fellow recordists had to solve included avoiding any sound that didn't match what the camera saw, and – even more difficult – the sound that did not exist at the time portrayed. *Dr Finlay's Casebook*, *Culloden* and, of course, *Dad's Army* were set before jet aircraft and Japanese motorbikes arrived on the scene! Being in the sound crew, making everyone wait until the intrusive sound had gone, meant you weren't the most popular person on the crew.

'In 1973 I had the good fortune to become one of the *Dad's Army* film crew and went off to Norfolk on location. Thetford and its surroundings were very pleasant – most definitely *Dad's Army* countryside. David Croft and his team gently controlled the cast, knowing how to get the best from them, which in turn allowed us, the film crew, to get the results David wanted. Everyone knew that there were professionals both sides of the camera. Sound crew problems were either solved or a suitable compromise found. I can't remember a "bad" day. Team work always won through. In one episode we even had our own full-size train set to play with – something that guaranteed a good deal of chuckling all round!

'Most evenings we congregated at The Bell Hotel where the cast and their families always stayed, meeting in the bar before dinner. Jimmy Beck, a man of great goodwill and generosity, always made sure you had a drink on arrival. He allowed me to repay his generosity only twice. He left a very noticeable gap when he died.

'Working with a cast of craftsmen, sometimes using the art of tact and diplomacy and achieving a superb result at the end, left me always looking forward to the next time.

'Having been involved when the original cast were still in fine fettle, 25 years later, I'm still very proud to be able to say: "I did *Dad's Army*".'

JOHN GATLAND

---

overdraft, Mainwaring plans using it for river patrols.

Some of the platoon christen the boat on the local river, but when fog descends the men get lost and instead of sailing down the river, drift out into the Channel. When Jones hears voices from the shore, Mainwaring and his men row to the shoreline, only to hear what they think are German voices. Believing they've drifted across the Channel, they plan to creep ashore and escape back to Blighty. Little do they know that they've been in British waters all the time, and the voices belong to French/Canadian pilots, whose squadron is celebrating shooting down their 50th Nazi plane.

Hiding in a railway wagon, they wake to find the train is on the move but it's a relieved group of men who unexpectedly pull up at Eastbourne railway station.

SOUND RECORDIST (ON THE LOCATIONS)

During the nine series of the TV series, five film sound recordists were employed. Their job entailed recording the sound whilst filming scenes on location; an entirely different team was responsible for studio recording.

SOUTHGATE

A town along the coast from Walmington, Southgate has its own Home Guard unit. They attend the weekend exercise in 'Room at the Bottom' during which Wilson is in temporary charge and leads his men into an ambush.

SPECIAL CONSTABLE, THE

Played by Felix Bowness (TV)
In 'Ring Dem Bells' the bumbling, cowardly special constable is called to The Six Bells pub when

---

Doris, the barmaid, reports a bunch of Germans are drinking there. After questioning Mainwaring, the special constable calls the superintendent at the Eastbourne police station.

SPIERS, BOB

Assistant floor manager: 'Battle of the Giants'; production assistant on eight episodes: S6, episodes 6 & 7; S7; director on five episodes: S9, episodes 1–5
At 13, Glaswegian Bob Spiers moved to London where he completed his education. Thanks to an inspirational drama teacher, he left school and started amateur acting. He performed at various venues around the capital including the Royal Court. During this period he also directed his first play, which transferred to the Arts' Club in Soho.

While his evenings were spent acting, he worked for an audience research company by day. In 1970 he joined the Beeb to work in their audience research department, maintaining his interest in amateur dramatics for the 18 months that he was there. He then transferred to the position of assistant floor manager and was later promoted to production manager. Later still, he turned his hand to directing, beginning with outside dance routines for *Seaside Special*. The first comedy he directed was a series of *It Ain't Half Hot, Mum*, before going on to direct many productions including *Are You Being Served?* and its Australian offshoot, the second series of *Fawlty Towers* and *The Goodies*.

Bob left the BBC in 1980 and now works freelance. In recent years he's worked on various projects, including four series of Channel 4's *The Comic Strip Presents…*, *Absolutely Fabulous* and a movie for Disney.

SPITFIRE FUND

During the war years, donations flooded in to help towards the cost of making Spitfires. The idea was conceived when a Jamaican newspaper sent a cheque for £20,000 to fund the building of a bomber. When this generosity and that of other organisations and individuals was publicised, donations from all over Britain and the Commonwealth arrived. Spitfires were valued at £5,000, and communities everywhere organised events to raise money. By 1941, over 13 million pounds had been collected, and the BBC began providing a list of recent donations at the close of the news broadcasts.

In *Dad's Army*, the first we hear of Walmington's Spitfire Fund is in the episode 'Command Decision' by which time 39s 4d has been collected. By 'Operation Kilt' the total stands at £4 7s 6d. In 'The Big Parade' a new Spitfire Fund is being launched with a parade involving the Home Guard and all the civil defence units. By the time 'The Godiva Affair' comes along, the town of Walmington is just £2,000 short of its target and, to help raise more cash, a whole week of special events is organised, culminating in a procession on the Saturday afternoon, during which the platoon partake in morris dancing.

SPIV

The term is often given to men who make their living through unethical dealings, especially those whose manner of dress is termed flashy. Joe Walker is frequently described as a spiv, partly because of his knack of obtaining rationed and scarce products via the black market.

SPONGE, PRIVATE
Played by Colin Bean (TV and film)

A sheep farmer by trade, Private Sponge remains something of a mystery. We learn very little

for active service this time around, a fact that bemuses him. If his services aren't wanted by the regulars, he's determined to make his mark in the Home Guard.

In 'Command Decision' he visits Mainwaring in the bank and suggests he take control of the Walmington platoon, even though he claims the Eastgate Home Guard are desperate for his expertise. When Square fails to usurp Mainwaring, he joins the Eastgate platoon and starts an unhealthy rivalry between the platoons which raises its head frequently during the sitcom's run.

In two episodes Square, with his handlebar moustache, carries the title 'Corporal-Colonel'.

DIRECTING THE FINAL SERIES

'I have nothing but fond memories of *Dad's Army*, but by the time the last series came around we had a few walking wounded. Arnold Ridley had his leg in plaster so had to be shipped up to Norfolk in a limousine which had sufficient leg room, while John Le Mesurier wasn't well because he was recovering from an awful bout of hepatitis caught whilst abroad. Olive Mercer had had shingles and was wearing a patch over her eye, and Arthur, due to his narcolepsy, kept dozing off – usually when David Croft was giving him notes. No one fully understood the extent of his condition at the time. Ian Lavender and Clive Dunn were OK, and so was John Laurie, who was getting very old but remained a fantastic actor. But I remember filming a scene and David turning to me and saying: "I've just got a feeling this is the last series!" We were shooting around things like Olive's patch and Arnold's leg, so we just knew this was the end.

'Filming at the military training ground in Norfolk was often eventful. It was an active army range and sometimes we'd be having breakfast when suddenly soldiers with guns would emerge from the bushes and have a free cup of tea before vanishing into the bushes again. There was also one occasion when we were given half an hour to move location because jets were coming in for an air strike. But the army were always cooperative, and the space gave us the chance to do some crazy things.

'The very last show, "Never Too Old", which David directed, was extremely moving; I was a relative newcomer but I'd still been around long enough to feel part of the team. It was the end of a very special era.'

BOB SPIERS

---

about him during the life of the sitcom, other than the fact he is a loyal member of Mainwaring's platoon. The original script for the episode 'War Dance', had planned for Sponge to bring his wife along, but this never happened and viewers were deprived of seeing his beloved.

SQUARE, CAPTAIN
Played by Geoffrey Lumsden (TV and radio)

There was no love lost between Captain Mainwaring and this old warhorse, whose brusque manner led to many arguments. Originally carrying the rank of colonel, earned during a war career that included serving four years (1915–1919) with Lawrence of Arabia in the desert, no one can doubt Square's military ability, especially as he won the DSO and commanded guerillas for a time. However, Square, who lives at Marsham Hall, is a little over the hill

When veterans of the Great War rushed to join the Home Guard during the Second World War, they weren't able to retain their ranks, so an agreement was reached whereby their old rank was preceded by their new title. Square was later promoted to captain of the Eastgate platoon.

When he's not working with his men at Eastgate, much of Square's time is taken up presiding over the local magistrates court.

ST CLAIR, JEAN
Role: Miss Meadows (S3, episode 1: 'The Armoured Might of Lance Corporal Jones') (TV)

Among Jean's other television credits are appearances in *Crown Court* (1982), *The Saint*, *Dick and the Duchess* and *All the Year Round*. On the big screen she's been seen in several films, including *Doctor at Large*, *Dentist in the*

Chair, *Carry On Doctor* as Mrs Smith and *The Great St Trinian's Train Robbery*, playing the music mistress.

STAFF CAPTAIN, THE
Played by Michael Knowles (film)

During the organising of the exercise attended by Mainwaring and his platoon, the Staff Captain reports to General Fullard.

STAGE SHOW

The stage show was presented by Bernard Delfont and Richard M Mills (for Bernard Delfont Organisation Ltd) and Duncan C Weldon and Louis I Michaels (for Triumph Theatre Productions Ltd).

Venues

Forum Theatre, Billingham: Thursday 4 September 1975 – Saturday 20 September 1975

The Shaftesbury Theatre, London: Thursday 2 October 1975 – February 1976

Opera House, Manchester: Tuesday 23 March – Saturday 10 April 1976

Theatre Royal, Nottingham: Monday 12 April 1976 – Saturday 1 May 1976

Alhambra Theatre, Bradford: Monday 3 May 1976 – Saturday 15 May 1976

Birmingham Hippodrome: Monday 17 May 1976 – Saturday 22 May 1976

Pavilion Theatre, Bournemouth: Monday 24 May 1976 – Saturday 5 June 1976

Winter Gardens, Blackpool: Monday 7 June – Saturday 19 June 1976

Theatre Royal, Newcastle-upon-Tyne: Tuesday 22 June – Saturday 3 July 1976

Richmond Theatre, Surrey: Monday 12 July 1976 – Saturday 24 July 1976

Theatre Royal, Brighton: Monday 26 July 1976 – 21 August 1976

Theatre Royal, Bath: Monday 23 August 1976 – Saturday 4 September 1976

Credits

Written by Jimmy Perry and David Croft

Directed by David Croft and Jimmy Perry

Staged by Roger Redfarn

Designed by Terry Parsons

Musical Director: Ed Coleman

Choreography by Sheila O'Neill

Lighting by Robert Ornbo

Costumes by Mary Husband

Sound by David Collison

Orchestrations by Don Savage, Dennis Wilson and Ed Coleman

Vocal Arrangements by Ed Coleman

Musical Associate to Jimmy Perry and David Croft: Jo Stewart

Company Manager: Peter Bevis (Billingham, The Shaftesbury, Manchester, Nottingham and Bradford); Tony Cundell (elsewhere)

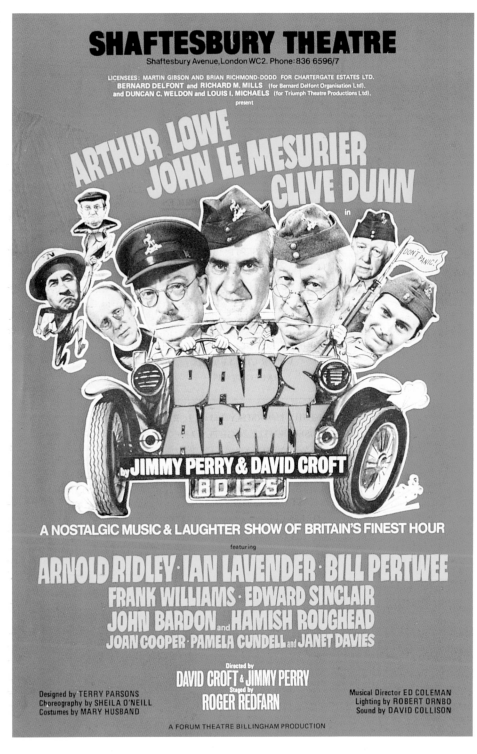

Watches by Timex Corporation

Binoculars by Dixons Photographic Ltd

Paper bags by Progressive Supplies (Paper) Ltd, London

Sharpening Steel by Scanlon Bros, London

Spectacles by C W Dixie Ltd

Prop costumes by Malcolm Waldock

Head-dresses by Pat Dawson and Mark Embleton

South American costumes executed by Natasha Kornitoff

Fur coats by Richard Catermole

Chesney Allen hats by Moss Bros

Chesney Allen suits by Carnaby Cavern

Tights by Elbeo

Miner's helmet and lamp supplied by The National Coal Board

Poster transparencies by courtesy of Trustees of the Imperial War Museum

Shirts executed by Katy Stevens

Pens by W A Shaeffer, Pen Company

Furniture by Old Times Furniture Co Ltd

CAST LIST
THE PLATOON

Captain Mainwaring .... Arthur Lowe

Sergeant Wilson .... John Le Mesurier

Lance Corporal Jones ...... Clive Dunn (Billingham, The Shaftesbury, Manchester, Nottingham, Bradford, Birmingham and Bournemouth); Jack Haig (elsewhere)

Private Godfrey .... Arnold Ridley

Private Pike .... Ian Lavender

Private Frazer .... Hamish Roughead (character only appeared at Billingham and The Shaftesbury)

Private Staines .... Michael Bevis (character first seen at the Opera House, Manchester)

Private Walker .... John Bardon (at Billingham and Shaftesbury); Jeffrey Holland (elsewhere)

Private Meadow .... Graham Hamilton (the character only appeared at Billingham and The Shaftesbury)

Private Woods .... Eric Longworth (the character only appeared at Billingham and The Shaftesbury)

Private Maple .... Norman MacLeod (the character only appeared at Billingham and The Shaftesbury)

Chief ARP Warden Hodges .. Bill Pertwee

Rev Timothy Farthing ..... Frank Williams

Mr Yeatman (Verger) ...... Edward Sinclair

Mrs Pike .... Janet Davies (Billingham and The Shaftesbury); Bernice Adams (elsewhere)

Mrs Holdane Hart (WVS) .. Joan Cooper

Mrs Fox .... Pamela Cundell (at Billingham and The Shaftesbury); Peggy Ashby (elsewhere)

General Von Seltz .... Bill Pertwee

German Inventor .... Jeffrey Holland

BBC Announcer .... Michael Bevis

Dolly (Godfrey's sister) .... Joan Cooper

Newspaper boy .... Ronnie Grainge

Hermann Goering .... David Wheldon Williams

Raymond .... Graham Hamilton (character only appeared at Billingham)

Stage Manager: Max Chowen

Deputy Stage Manager: Teena Steel (Billingham, The Shaftesbury, Manchester, Nottingham and Bradford); Trevor Ritchie (elsewhere)

Assistant Stage Managers: Ruth Halliday, Kevin Hubbard, Vivien Pearman and Gina Batt

Technical Assistant Stage Manager: Stephen Ward (later on in the tour Ward also took over responsibility for sound operation)

Assistant to Mary Husband: Ron Lucas

Assistant Wardrobe Mistress: Helen Pritchard

Wardrobe Master: David Morgan

Assistant: Roy Lovegrove

Sound Operator: Laurie Blackmore

Assistant to Robert Ornbo: Spike Gaden

Press Representative: Reg Williams

Lighting and sound equipment by Theatre Projects Services

Costumes by Bermans Nathans

Wigs by Simonwigs

The Town Clerk ....Eric Longworth
(character only appeared at Billingham and The Shaftesbury)

British Restaurant Lady ....Pamela Cundell
(character only appeared at Billingham and The Shaftesbury)

Dave (songwriter) ....John Bardon (Billingham
and The Shaftesbury); Ronnie Grainge (elsewhere)

Jim (songwriter) ....Jeffrey Holland (Billingham
and The Shaftesbury); Michael Bevis (elsewhere)

Carmen Caramba ....Bernice Adams

General Gordon ....Michael Bevis (Billingham);

John Conroy (elsewhere)
(character appeared at Billingham, Manchester, Nottingham, Bradford,
Birmingham, Bournemouth and Newcastle)

General Wolsey ....Norman MacLeod (Billingham
and Shaftesbury); Bill Pearson (elsewhere)
(character appeared at Billingham, Manchester, Nottingham, Bradford,
Birmingham, Bournemouth and Newcastle)

Dervishes ....Barrie Stevens,
Ronnie Grainge and Kevin Hubbard
(characters only appeared at Billingham)

Britannia ....Peggy Ann Jones (Billingham);
Peggy Ashby (elsewhere)
(character appeared at Billingham, Manchester, Nottingham, Bradford,
Birmingham, Bournemouth and Newcastle)

Soldier ....Graham Hamilton
(character only appeared at Billingham)

Izzy Bonn ....David Wheldon Williams
(character only appeared at Billingham)

The Andrews Sisters ......Bernice Adams,
Debbie Blackett and June Shand (at Billingham and The
Shaftesbury); Bernice Adams, Pauline Stork and Marsha
Harris (elsewhere)

Man on the Beach ....Graham Hamilton
(Billingham and The Shaftesbury) Bill Pearson (elsewhere)

Happidrome Announcer ....Eric Longworth (The
Shaftesbury); Bill Pearson (elsewhere)
(character first appeared at The Shaftesbury)

Mr Lovejoy ....Arthur Lowe
(character first appeared at The Shaftesbury)

Ramsbottom ....Michael Bevis
(character first appeared at The Shaftesbury)

Enoch ....Ian Lavender
(character first appeared at The Shaftesbury)

Max Miller ....Bill Pertwee
(character first appeared at The Shaftesbury)

Gert and Daisy ....Joan Cooper
andPamela Cundell (The Shaftesbury);
Joan Cooper and Peggy Ashby (elsewhere)
(characters first appeared at The Shaftesbury)

Robb Wilton ....Arthur Lowe
(character first appeared at The Shaftesbury)

Flanagan and Allen ....Arthur Lowe
and John Le Mesurier (characters first appeared at
The Shaftesbury)

Girls on the Beach ....Bernice Adams,
Debbie Blackett and June Shand (The Shaftesbury);
Elizabeth Suggars and Marianne Parnell (elsewhere)
(characters first appeared at The Shaftesbury)

THE HOME FRONT COMPANY

The following people appeared in the Company at some
point during the show's lifetime: Bernice Adams,
Michael Bevis, Debbie Blackett, Ronnie Grainge,
Graham Hamilton, Jeffrey Holland, Vivien Pearman,
Peggy Ann Jones, Eric Longworth, Norman MacLeod,
Kevin Hubbard, June Shand, Michele Summers,
Barrie Stevens, Jan Todd, David Wheldon Williams,
Alan Woodhouse, Peggy Ashby, Gina Batt, John Conroy,
Marsha Harris, Marianne Parnell, Bill Pearson,
Pauline Stork, Elizabeth Suggars

STANDBYS

For Arthur Lowe ....Eric Longworth
For John Le Mesurier .....Michael Bevis
For Clive Dunn ....Norman MacLeod

THE SCENES

When the show opened at the Forum Theatre in
Billingham, the programme consisted of the
following scenes:

ACT ONE

Scene 1   Who Do You Think You Are Kidding,
          Mr Hitler?
Scene 2   Put that Light Out!
Scene 3   When Can I Have a Banana Again?
Scene 4   Command Post
Scene 5   Carry On on the Home Front
          Butcher's Shop
          British Restaurant
Scene 6   Cliff Top
          Don't Panic
Scene 7   Battle of Britain
Scene 8   The Choir
Interval

ACT TWO

Scene 9   The Song We Would Rather Forget
          Rumour
Scene 10 Unarmed Combat
Scene 11 Tin Pan Alley
Scene 12 Too Late
          Rumour
Scene 13 A Nightingale Sang in Berkeley Square
Scene 14 The Floral Dance
Scene 15 Radio Personalities of 1941
Scene 16 The Beach
Scene 17 Finale

By the time the production opened in the West
End at the Shaftesbury Theatre, the programme
had altered to the following schedule:

ACT ONE

Scene 1   Who Do You Think You Are Kidding,
          Mr Hitler?
Scene 2   Put That Light Out!
Scene 3   Carry On on the Home Front
          British Restaurant
          Jones' Butcher's Shop
Scene 4   Command Post
Scene 5   Private Pike's Dream
Scene 6   Lance Corporal Jones Stands Guard
Scene 7   Lords of the Air
Scene 8   Choir Practice
Interval

ACT TWO

Scene 1   The Song We Would Rather Forget
Scene 2   Unarmed Combat
Scene 3   Tin Pan Alley Goes to War
Scene 4   Morris Dance
Scene 5   A Nightingale Sang in Berkeley Square
Scene 6   Radio Personalities of 1940
Scene 7   The Beach
Scene 8   Finale

When the show went out on tour after finishing
at The Shaftesbury Theatre in London, the programme was altered slightly, but remained constant thereafter. The third scene in Act One
became Carry On on the Home Front – Tackling
a Nazi Tank, while an extra scene, Too Late,
which was originally used at Billingham, was
reintroduced.

Other alterations to the programme and content were made early on, while the show was still
establishing itself, as David Croft explains. 'Like
all first attempts, we had a lot of cuts and modifications to make; it was quite a worrying time, it
always is, until you get it right. Unlike television
episodes where you're doing a different one each
week, the stage show is with you for some time,
so you have to get it right.'

Further cuts took place when it came to
London, partly because they had to reduce the
timing slightly, but also because Bernard Delfont, who financed the production, didn't think
certain items were up to scratch.

When the stage show opened at Billingham's
Forum Theatre, prior to going to London, it
received a glowing review by one of the local
papers, *The Hartlepool Mail*. Writing on 9 September 1975, Kevin Eason classed the musical
version as 'hilarious'. He termed the production
a 'British-Hollywood musical', and added: 'The
special bond of affection between the cast and
audience helped each item spark along.'

The Thetford Music and Drama Society
became the first amateur company to perform
the stage musical. In 1981, the society completed a nine-night run, six at Thetford's
Carnegie Room and three at the Theatre
Royal, Bury St Edmunds. The production was
directed by Fred Calvert, and kicked off with a
gala evening on Monday 11 May, with proceeds being split between two local charities.
The society then moved to the nearby Theatre
Royal between 20 and 22 May.

STAINTON, MICHAEL (c 1935–)

Born: Halifax

Role: Frenchy (S9, episode 1: 'Wake-Up Walmington')
(TV)

Michael spent the early years of his career on
stage, appearing at various rep companies and
theatres around the country, but the lion's share
of his work recently has been on television. In
1997, he played Edgar Sturgeon in *Dalziel and
Pascoe*, while two years earlier he was seen as

George in *Prime Suspect*. Other productions include *Jekyll and Hyde*, *Fellow Traveller*, *Only Fools and Horses* and six series of *Metal Mickey*, playing the father. He's played several policemen during his career, including one for an episode of *Juliet Bravo*, back in 1980.

STANLEY, MR

Not seen or heard in the sitcom, Mr Stanley is one of the OAPs who attends the dinner in the episode 'Turkey Dinner'.

STARK, GRAHAM (1922–)

Role: Private Walker ('The Showing Up of Corporal Jones', 'The Loneliness of the Long-Distance Walker', 'Sorry, Wrong Number' and 'The Bullet is Not for Firing') (radio)

Among Graham's many television credits are appearances in *Boon*, playing Charlie Luce, *Dramarama* as Simpkins, *Out of the Unknown* playing Morrey, and *Martin Chuzzlewit* as Nadgett. His many film credits, meanwhile, include *Curse of the Pink Panther*, *Superman III*, *Trail of the Pink Panther*, *The Prisoner of Zenda*, *There Goes the Bride*, *The Revenge of the Pink Panther*, *Casino Royale*, *The Plank*, *Alfie*, *A Pair of Briefs* and *Dentist on the Job*.

STATION MASTER, THE

Played by William Moore (TV); Stuart Sherwin (radio)

The station master in the episode 'The Royal Train', has the privilege of being in charge when King George VI passes through.

STEVENS, BARRIE

Roles: Member of the Home Front Company and a Dervish (stage show)

Barrie began his career as a dancer, before spending five years in Holland where he acted and had his own children's programme. He also worked with a theatre group. Barrie returned to Britain and toured the cabaret circuit before appearing in the *Dad's Army* stage show.

STEWART, CAPTAIN

Played by Michael Knowles (TV and radio)

Public school-educated Captain Stewart appeared in 'Round and Round Went the Great Big Wheel' and was tasked with telling the Eastgate, Dymwhich and Walmington Home Guard units what their special duties were.

STEWART, WALLY

Frazer talks about Wally, a friend, in 'Don't Forget the Diver', but he is never seen. They both went to the South Seas diving for pearls and Wally lost his life after a giant squid attacked him. Although Frazer was able to save him, he was pulled up from the depths too quickly and died of the bends. Frazer gave his friend's diving suit to his mother, but as she didn't want it he bought it from her for ten bob.

'A Stripe for Frazer'

STONE'S AMUSEMENT ARCADE

The amusement arcade marks one of the coastline boundaries which Mainwaring and his men are tasked with patrolling. It's mentioned frequently during the series.

STOTHART, JOHN

Film editor on four episodes (TV): S8, episodes 1, 3, 4 & 6

John was always interested in working within the film/TV industry and joined the University of Strathclyde's television department in 1966. After two years, he was recruited by Yorkshire TV, before moving on to the BBC as a trainee assistant editor, at the end of 1968.

Although he worked on a number of shows, including *Horizon* and *Panorama*, John mainly worked on drama productions. He left the BBC in 1998, and now works as a freelance editor.

STRIPE FOR FRAZER, A

Recorded: Friday 15/11/68 (made in black and white)

Original transmission: Saturday 29/3/69, 7.00–7.30pm

(This episode was originally planned for transmission on 27 January at 7.30pm)

Original viewing figures: 11.3 million

Repeated: 5/9/69

CAST

Arthur Lowe . . . . .Captain Mainwaring
John Le Mesurier . . . . .Sergeant Wilson
Clive Dunn . . . . .Lance Corporal Jones
John Laurie . . . . .Private Frazer
James Beck . . . . .Private Walker
Arnold Ridley . . . . .Private Godfrey
Ian Lavender . . . . .Private Pike
Geoffrey Lumsden . . . . .Corporal-Colonel Square
John Ringham . . . . .Captain Bailey
Gordon Peters . . . . .Policeman
Edward Sinclair . . . . .Caretaker
Platoon: Colin Bean, Richard Jacques, Frank Godfrey, Alec Coleman, Hugh Cecil, Jimmy Mac, Desmond Cullum-Jones, Vic Taylor, David Seaforth, Richard Kitteridge

PRODUCTION TEAM

Script: Jimmy Perry and David Croft
Producer: David Croft
Production Assistant: Clive Doig
Director: Harold Snoad
Studio Lighting: Dennis Channon
Studio Sound: Buster Cole
Design: Paul Joel
Assistant Floor Manager: Tony George
Vision Mixer: Dave Hanks
Costume Supervisor: Marjorie Lewis
Make-Up Supervisor: Sheila Cassidy

At the church hall Captain Bailey arrives from the Assistant Adjutant Quartermaster General with news that Mainwaring can promote a member of the platoon to the rank of corporal. With Jones a lance corporal, Wilson assumes he'll get the extra stripe, but Mainwaring feels the fairest way would be to make someone else up to lance corporal and see who shows the best potential. Mainwaring decides Frazer is the man, against Wilson's better judgement.

The lance corporals are keen to impress Mainwaring but the newly acquired power goes to Frazer's head. Mainwaring is shocked when, upon asking Frazer how the previous night's patrol went, he hands him several charge sheets. Pike is accused of deserting his post, Godfrey of cowardice in the face of the enemy and Walker of mutiny. Jones is not happy and Mainwaring and Wilson know they can't do anything with the charges, particularly as they are only the Home Guard. Mainwaring speaks to all the accused and hears their side of the story before adjourning the case until he takes legal advice. He tells Wilson he didn't believe Frazer could stir up so much trouble.

Corporal-Colonel Square, who's training the platoon in guerilla warfare, enters the office, sees the charge sheets on the desk and points out that they're incorrectly completed, a good enough reason for Mainwaring to class them invalid. But when Square puts Frazer on a fizzer, he storms off to get his boat hook!

STRONG, ADELE (1904–1990)

Born: London
Role: Lady with the Umbrella (S8, episode 1: 'Ring Dem Bells') (TV)

Adele studied at RADA and started her career as a comedienne on the stage. Later, with her husband, she formed a popular comedy double-act and toured the country. Adele also worked in reps and theatres, including long runs at Richmond and Watford. Towards the end of her career she started being offered small parts on television and in films, including *Crossroads*, Thames' *Six Days of Justice*, *Britannia Hospital*, *Smashing Time* and *O Lucky Man* (the last two both directed by Lindsay Anderson). Adele was still working when she was in her eighties.

STUNTMEN

During the course of the programme, stuntmen were occasionally used for the more daring escapades, which is hardly surprising, bearing in mind that most of the platoon certainly weren't spring chickens.

Phil Basey, who's now retired from running a motor engineering business, owns the motorbike Sergeant Wilson used in 'The Honourable Man'. Basey also doubled as Wilson during the episode, especially when film sequences demanded the rider drove the bike off the road and into ditches in the village of Honington.

Professional stuntmen were also used. London-born Johnny Scripps (1927–1989) was periodically employed to stand in for Arthur Lowe whenever a scene involved Captain Mainwaring in some precarious act, most famously in the barrage balloon fiasco in 'The Day the Balloon Went Up'. The man hanging from the end

of the rope when the balloon is out of control is Johnny Scripps, who began making a living out of extra work back in the 1950s. In the 1960s, he appeared in many movies, such as *Lawrence of Arabia* and *Goldfinger*. His work on TV included episodes of *The Adventures of Black Beauty* and *The Invisible Man*, playing the bandaged man himself.

Upon leaving school, Johnny – who also appeared in 'Don't Forget the Diver' and 'Boots, Boots, Boots' – served in the army before returning to civvy street and undertaking various jobs. His love for horses saw him work as a groom for over a decade before he moved into the film and TV industry, where he was regularly employed as an extra or stuntman. When he wasn't appearing on the screen, he frequently worked in the circus performing bareback horse-riding acts.

After spending three decades in the business, work eventually dried up and he became a driver for a car company until his death from cancer in 1989.

Other stuntmen employed during the series included Jim Dowdall and Derek Ware, who doubled for Ian Lavender and Clive Dunn respectively during the episode 'Number Engaged'. In 'Knights of Madness' three stuntmen were engaged: William Sully and Derek Ware doubled as Arthur Lowe, while Jimmy Lodge replaced Bill Pertwee during the battle scenes at the grand finale. In 'The Desperate Drive of Corporal Jones' a car scene required the services of two stuntmen, Billy Hughes and Leslie Conrad, while Tom Atkins helped out during the episode, 'The King was in his Counting House'.

SUGDEN, MOLLIE (1922–)

Born: Keighley
Role: Mrs Fox ('Mum's Army', 'The Godiva Affair' and 'My British Buddy') (radio)

Not long after Mollie left school the Second World War broke out and before she could start her acting career, she helped the war effort by working in a Keighley munitions factory making shells for the navy. When enough shells had been made, some two thousand women, including Mollie, were made redundant, giving her the opportunity to attend drama school.

She graduated from the Guildhall School of Drama and began an eight-year stint in rep, beginning at Accrington, then Oldham. Radio work followed and later television. Among her television credits are roles in the 1960s sitcom, *Hugh and I*, directed by David Croft. She also appeared in *The Liver Birds*, *Doctor in Charge*, *For the Love of Ada*, *My Wife Next Door*, *That's My Boy*, *Come Back, Mrs Noah* and *My Husband and I*. She's probably best remembered for her performance as Mrs Slocombe in David Croft and Jeremy Lloyd's *Are You Being Served?*.

Mollie is married to actor William Moore.

SUMMERS, GEORGE

Lighting supervisor on 17 episodes (TV): S1; S2, episodes 1, 2, 4 & 6; S4, episodes 7–13

George joined the BBC in 1938 as a junior engineer. During the war he was at the Daventry transmitter involved with secret homing devices for aircraft. He returned to the Beeb in 1946, and was quickly promoted to Senior Television Engineer, Technical Operations Manager and then Technical Manager 1.

The programmes he worked on prior to his retirement in 1976 included *Happy Ever After* and *The Dick Emery Show*.

SUMMERS, MICHELE

Born: Chingford
Role: Member of the Home Front Company (stage show)

Michele's first professional appearance involved singing on *The Black and White Minstrel Show*. Her career has encompassed all mediums, including pantomime and cabaret. She was also a contestant on the TV talent show *New Faces*.

SUSPECT, THE

Played by Patrick Tull (TV)

An Austrian ornithologist who has come over to England after reading that a rare bird was spotted in the area, this character asks Hodges the way to Downsend Woods in 'Man Hunt' and is eventually suspected of being a German.

SWALLOW BANK

George Mainwaring, Arthur Wilson, Frank Pike, Janet King and Digby (who never featured in any of the cast lists but was referred to in the original 'Battle School' script) were all employed at the Walmington-on-Sea branch of Swallow Bank. A dark-haired, unnamed, female clerk is also seen in 'Something Nasty in the Vault'.

Various bank inspectors and head office officials are seen, or heard of, from time to time, and viewers get the chance to see inside both the Walmington bank and another branch. When

By day, Mainwaring was in charge
at the Swallow Bank in Walmington.

Wilson gets promoted – albeit briefly – in 'A
Wilson (Manager)?', he is handed managership of
the Eastgate branch and the six members of staff,
including Mr Boyle, the aged chief clerk. Sadly,
Wilson's acquaintance with the pleasures of managing his own branch, after being firmly under
Mainwaring's thumb for so long, is short-lived
because the building is demolished during an air
raid, and head office, deciding not to rebuild,
transfer all business to the Hastings branch.

Although we never find out how extensive the
Swallow Bank branch network is, the fact that
Wilson was employed at the Weston-super-Mare
branch before he moved to Walmington suggests
that it's a nationwide chain. Not dissimilar to
other banks of that era, the Walmington branch's
décor is staid and traditional. Frank Pike and
Janet King work busily behind the obligatory
security screens, and near their work stations is
the manager's office, with half-panelled walls
and a hefty wooden desk. From his office
window, Mainwaring can scan the High Street
from Stead and Simpson's to Timothy Whites.

SWAN, CAPTAIN
Played by Robert Mill (TV); Fraser Kerr (radio)
In the closing scenes of 'A Man of Action', Captain Swan arrives at the church hall in Walmington to burst Mainwaring's bubble. Power and
authority have gone to Mainwaring's head as he
declares martial law, but he's stopped firmly in
his tracks when Swan, from the regular army,
arrives on the scene to take charge until the gas
and water supplies, as well as the phone lines are
restored to working order.

SWANN, MR
Played by Ronnie Brody (TV)
Mr Swann owns the grocer's shop in Walmington and appears in 'High Finance'. He wants to
speak confidentially to Mr Mainwaring, but is
continually brushed off. In the end, he embar-
rasses Mainwaring in front of a crowd of people
when he says Mrs Mainwaring hasn't paid the
grocery bill for six months, and £49 17s 6d is
owed.

SYLVIA
Played by Jean Gilpin (TV)
Sylvia, who's in the ATS, is Hodges' niece who
arrives in Walmington during the episode 'The
Making of Private Pike'. She fancies some fun
while she's on leave and pushes Pikey into taking
her to the pictures at Eastgate in Mainwaring's
new staff car. The evening doesn't go as Sylvia
had planned, with Pikey more interested in
sucking his thumb than putting his arm around
her. On the way home, the car runs out of petrol.
Completely fed up with Frank, she throws abuse
at him, describing him as soppy and retarded!

TASKER, BILL

Role: Fred (S8, episode 6: 'The Face on the Poster') (TV)

Bill, who died in 1992, appeared in numerous TV shows, including Thames' *Bill Brand* in 1976.

TAVERNER, DEREK

Co-wrote the music for the programme's theme tune, 'Who Do You Think You Are Kidding, Mr Hitler?' Born in Cambridge, Derek left school and became a cinema organist before joining the army. He spent some time in India, where he transferred to the entertainment unit and met Jimmy Perry.

Even as a boy, he was determined to pursue a music career, and all the musical lessons back in Cambridge paid dividends when upon demob he embarked on a path that quickly saw him conducting musicals (including numerous tours for John Hanson), pantomimes and reviews. He has also helped write various signature tunes, including one for *It Ain't Half Hot, Mum*.

After more than four decades in the profession, Derek retired from the business in 1995.

TAYLOR, DIANE

Producer's assistant on six episodes: S7

Born in Pendlebury, Diane left school at 18 and completed a secretarial course. She joined the BBC in 1969, working initially in radio. She later transferred to Television Centre and worked on *Twenty-Four Hours* before training to become a producer's assistant in 1973. During the five years spent as part of David Croft's team, she worked on shows including *Are You Being Served?*, *It Ain't Half Hot, Mum* and *Hi-De-Hi!*. She shared her *Dad's Army* job with Jennie Birkett.

Diane left the Beeb in 1979, joined Thames as a producer's assistant a year later, then became news director at LWT. In 1983 she left and has worked as a freelance PA ever since.

TAYLOR, JAMES

Role: Artillery Officer (S5, episode 5: 'The Desperate Drive of Corporal Jones') (TV)

James Taylor's other work includes playing a Polish officer in *Colditz* (1972), Mr Taylor in an episode of *Fawlty Towers* (1979), *Suez 1956* for

the BBC (1979), *Hale and Pace*, Mr Durham in Granada's *The Grand* and Cyril Sopwith in an episode of *Hetty Wainthropp Investigates*. On the big screen he's appeared in several films such as 1970's *Games That Lovers Play*.

TAYLOR, LAURIE

Studio sound supervisor on six episodes (TV): S9

Born in Wrexham, Laurie joined the BBC straight from school at the age of 18. As a technical operator, based in London, his early work included spells on shows such as *Juke Box Jury*, *Z Cars* and *Dixon of Dock Green*. He was promoted to sound supervisor in 1970 and worked on many of the top programmes of the day, like *The Generation Game*, *The Good Life* and *The Onedin Line*. More recent credits include *Hi-De-Hi!*, *Don't Wait Up* and *Keeping Up Appearances*. Laurie still works for the BBC, and recently finished *Dinner Ladies*, *Never Mind the Buzzcocks*, *Blankety Blank* and *The Clarkson Show*.

TAYLOR, VIC (1924–1972)

Born: Northampton

Role: Member of the platoon's back row in 37 episodes: S1; S2, not episode 4; S3, episodes 1–4, 6–9, 11, 12; S4; 'Battle of the Giants'; S5, episodes 1 & 4 (TV)

As soon as Vic left school he joined the army, and during the Second World War served abroad. Upon demob he worked as a builder's labourer before taking up stunt work in his early twenties. He later turned to modelling and crowd work, making a decent living from commercials and mail order catalogue assignments, receiving copious fan mail in the process. His face appeared on boxes of Paxo stuffing for years, and he was the first milkman advertising products for the Milk Marketing Board. In his thirties he moved into extra work on TV, appearing in shows like *Z Cars*, but he always continued modelling. Vic was a regular member of the platoon until his death from cancer at the age of 48.

TED

Does occasional work for Walker. Not seen in the TV episode, 'Getting the Bird', but Walker tells Jones he had to pay him ten bob for topping the pigeons.

TELEPHONE NUMBERS

During *Dad's Army* we get to know various phone numbers of people living in and around Walmington.

Walmington 92: Captain Mainwaring's home
Walmington 252: Jones' butcher's shop (4871 in the film)
Walmington 302: Aunt Elsie's home (Godfrey's relation)
Walmington 333 (later changed to 382): church hall
Walmington 633: Old Flour Mill, just outside Walmington-on-Sea
Walmington 991: Plaza Cinema
Eastgate 166 (later changed to 2468): GHQ
Eastgate 247: Captain Square

TELEPHONE OPERATOR, THE

Played by Avril Angers (TV)

In 'The Lion has 'Phones' Jones speaks to the operator when he's trying to contact GHQ. A muddle with the phone numbers finds him talking to a cashier at Walmington's Plaza Cinema. The same operator, who's called Freda, is seen in 'Put That Light Out!'. When Mainwaring tries getting the phone line in the lighthouse reconnected, she doesn't want to take responsibility, and as her supervisor has gone home, it looks as if she won't agree to help. But Walker, who's on first name terms with the operator, persuades her to connect the line.

TELEVISION SERIES

Between 31 July 1968 and 13 November 1977, 80 episodes of *Dad's Army* were transmitted by the BBC. In addition to the nine series and three Christmas Specials, various sketches were recorded for the small screen, including four which formed part of the perennial *Christmas Night with the Stars* in 1968, 1969, 1970 and 1972.

TEST, THE

(The working title for this episode was 'The Cricket Match')

Recorded: Friday 20/11/70

Original transmission: Friday 27/11/70, 8.00–8.30pm

Original viewing figures: 16 million

Repeated: 1/8/71, 5/12/92, 10/12/92 (Wales), 6/7/96

CAST

Arthur Lowe . . . . Captain Mainwaring
John Le Mesurier . . . . Sergeant Wilson
Clive Dunn . . . . Lance Corporal Jones
John Laurie . . . . Private Frazer
James Beck . . . . Private Walker
Arnold Ridley . . . . Private Godfrey
Ian Lavender . . . . Private Pike
Bill Pertwee . . . . ARP Warden
Frank Williams . . . . Vicar
Edward Sinclair . . . . Verger
Don Estelle . . . . Gerald
Harold Bennett . . . . Mr Blewitt
Freddie Trueman . . . . E C Egan
(special appearance)
Platoon: Colin Bean, Hugh Hastings, Vic Taylor, Hugh Cecil, Desmond Cullum-Jones, Leslie Noyes, Freddie White, George Hancock, Frank Godfrey, Freddie Wiles

PRODUCTION TEAM

Script: Jimmy Perry and David Croft
Producer/Director: David Croft
Production Assistant: Phil Bishop
Film Cameraman: Stewart Farnell
Film Sound Recordist: Les Collins
Film Editor: Bob Rymer
Studio Lighting: George Summers
Studio Sound: Michael McCarthy
Design: Paul Joel
Assistant Floor Manager: Roger Singleton-Turner
Vision Mixer: Dave Hanks
Costume Supervisor: George Ward
Make-Up Supervisor: Cynthia Goodwin

Mainwaring receives a letter from Hodges inviting the Home Guard to a game of cricket. The platoon is excited about accepting the challenge, and Mainwaring confirms, as expected, that he'll be captain.

Just before the game, Hodges greets E C Egan, who's playing for Hodges' team. To make every-

'The Test'

thing legal, he's signed up as a warden just before the start. Egan is a professional cricketer, and Hodges is out to win, even if a bit of subterfuge is involved.

When Godfrey turns up in his bowls hat, Frazer in his undertaking clothes, and Pike has no alternative but to wear a pair of Mainwaring's flannels, prospects don't look good for the team. When Mainwaring loses the toss, and is put in to field, his motley crew head towards the wicket. Gerald and Hodges open the batting for the wardens and smash Mainwaring's bowling attempts all over the field, including 24 off one ball; he gets so worked up over the incident, the Verger books him – even though it's cricket!

Hodges declares at 152–4, leaving Mainwaring's men three hours to reach the score. Mainwaring opens the batting with Wilson, but the jewel in Hodge's crown, Mr Egan, pulls his shoulder during the first over and retires hurt.

Mainwaring's team now has a chance and heads steadily towards the required total, with Wilson scoring 81. By the time the last man, Godfrey, heads towards the wicket only five runs are needed for victory, and he surprises everyone by clocking up the winning runs with a six.

THINGS THAT GO BUMP IN THE NIGHT

Recorded: Sunday 15/7/73

Original transmission: Wednesday 5/12/73, 6.50–7.20pm

Original viewing figures: 12.2 million

Repeated: 30/5/74, 9/4/91, 11/12/93, 18/12/93 (Wales), 24/5/97, 22/2/98 (Scotland), 31/5/98 (Scotland)

CAST

Arthur Lowe . . . . Captain Mainwaring
John Le Mesurier . . . . Sergeant Wilson
Clive Dunn . . . . Lance Corporal Jones

John Laurie . . . . Private Frazer
James Beck . . . . Private Walker
Arnold Ridley . . . . Private Godfrey
Ian Lavender . . . . Private Pike
Jonathan Cecil . . . . Captain Cadbury
Colin Bean . . . . Private Sponge
Platoon: George Hancock (Private Hancock) and Desmond Cullum-Jones (Private Desmond)

PRODUCTION TEAM

Script: Jimmy Perry and David Croft
Producer/Director: David Croft
Production Assistants: Gordon Pert and Bob Spiers
Film Cameraman: James Balfour
Film Sound Recordist: John Gatland
Film Editor: Bill Harris
Studio Lighting: Howard King
Studio Sound: Michael McCarthy
Design: Paul Joel
Assistant Floor Manager: Peter Fitton
Vision Mixer: Dave Hanks
Costume Supervisor: Susan Wheal
Make-Up Supervisor: Ann Ailes

The platoon fetch up at a deserted country house, or so they think. While out driving at night in a torrential storm, they find themselves lost with petrol running low. They stop at an old house, where Mainwaring suggests spending the night. When they find the door open they go in and explore the place. The sound of distant howling gives Frazer's claim that there's something amiss with the house a little credence. Although the house seems empty, a fire still burning makes Frazer enquire why the occupants left.

Mainwaring tells the men they'll bed down for the night: while he opts for a bed of his own, he expects the rest of the platoon either to share with Wilson, or sleep on the settee. Jones, helpful

'Things That Go Bump in the Night'

as ever, doesn't like the idea of Mainwaring sleeping in a damp bed and his plan to warm it up ends in failure when the bed catches fire before being drenched in water, leaving the Captain no alternative but to share the overcrowded bed.

When footsteps are heard climbing the stairs everyone is worried, but it turns out to be Captain Cadbury, who explains that the howling dogs are nothing to worry about because it's a dog training school; the house is used to train tracker dogs for the war office, but as things are a little slack at the moment, the Captain gave his men the weekend off.

The dogs are used to track down German parachutists, but they're only half-trained at present. They can track things down well enough, but they're liable to attack as the platoon discover the following day, when Pike, who ends up being dressed as a German, and Mainwaring find themselves being chased across the countryside by a pack of very hungry dogs.

Note: James Beck is seen in the location shots but not the studio recording, by which time he'd been taken ill. During the location shots a pack of bloodhounds chase Mainwaring and his men across the countryside. The hounds were supplied by a woman from Surrey, and were kennelled six miles from Thetford in Norfolk, during the filming. Mr and Mrs Barber, who looked after them, also let the BBC use their own dog, the one who jumps up at the tree. He was encouraged to do this by a member of the production team climbing up the tree with a piece of meat.

THOMAS, JENNY

Role: Violet Gibbons (S3, episode 9: 'War Dance') (TV)
Jenny played Pikey's fiancée, Violet, who's serving in the ATS, but used to work in a fish and chip shop. Their engagement is announced at the dance but is short lived.

THOMAS, RACHEL (1905–1995)

Born: Alltwen, near Swansea
Role: Mother Superior (S7, episode 3: 'Gorilla Warfare') (TV)
Rachel, who had always been involved in amateur dramatics and had taken part at the eisteddfod, was a primary school teacher for ten years before giving up the profession to marry in 1931. She moved to Cardiff with her husband, also a teacher, and began radio work after being spotted reading a lesson during a chapel service.

Her big break came when she played a mother in the 1939 film *The Proud Valley*, with Paul Robeson. She was seen playing small parts in several films during the 1940s, including *Undercover*, *Halfway House* as a housekeeper, *The Captive Heart* and *The Valley of Song*, She was also seen in *Sky West* and *Crooked*, with John Mills and Hayley Mills, and *Under Milk Wood* (she was also in the original radio productions).

Rachel's career contained the occasional excursion into theatre, such as *Gaslight* in Vienna. She also appeared in many television shows, including *Choir Practice* (her debut), *Z Cars*, *Dixon of Dock Green*, *Churchill's People* and *Owen MD*. She worked on a soap for S4C for over 20 years until her death aged 89.

THOMAS, TALFRYN (1922–1982)

Born: Swansea
Roles: Mr Cheeseman (S6, episode 2: 'My British Buddy'; S7, episode 2: 'A Man of Action'), Private Cheeseman (S7, episodes 3, 4, 5, 6) (TV)
Son of a butcher, Talfryn grew up in Swansea and upon leaving school trained as an instrument mechanic, working in the local weights and measures office. He also joined a local amateur dramatic society, the Landore Players, but didn't pursue acting professionally until he had served in the RAF during the war.

Having returned to his role as an instrument mechanic, he then decided to make acting his career. After training at RADA and working in provincial theatre he moved into TV, playing roles such as a garage mechanic in 'The Bodysnatchers', an episode of *The Champions*, Fiery Frederick in *The Avengers*, Tom Price in BBC's sci-fi series, *The Survivors* (1975–1977), and *Coronation Street*. He also teamed up with Ken Dodd for numerous radio and TV shows.

Talfryn appeared in a handful of films, including *Under Milk Wood* as Mr Pugh. His character in *Dad's Army* became a regular for the seventh season after Jimmy Beck's death. His last TV appearance was in *Hi-De-Hi!*. Talfryn died at the age of 60, after a heart attack.

THORNTON, FRANK (1921–)

Born: London
Roles: Captain Rogers ('Something Nasty in the Vault'), BBC Producer ('Ten Seconds From Now') (radio)
Frank had always wanted to be an actor, but upon leaving school he spent two years in an insurance office. When a colleague left to pursue an acting career, Frank enrolled for evening drama classes. When he was invited to become a day student for the second year, Frank managed to persuade his father to finance his studies.

Shortly after, the Second World War saw him evacuated with the drama school until he secured his first job, touring four plays in Ireland. Three years later he joined the RAF. When he was demobbed in 1947, Frank was lucky to be offered a job in rep and the occasional small part in films like *Radio Cab Murder*.

His busy career has included over 50 films, such as *Portrait of Alison*, *A Flea in Her Ear*, and cameo roles in *Carry On Screaming*, *The Big Job*, *The Early Bird*, *Crooks and Coronets* and *The Three Musketeers*. On TV he's best remembered for playing Captain Peacock in *Are You Being Served?* and more recently Truly in *Last of the Summer Wine*. He's also appeared in *Grace and Favour*, *Love Thy Neighbour*, *The Upper Hand*, *The Tommy Cooper Show* and *Steptoe and Son*.

THORNTON, SYLVIA

Make-up artist on 20 episodes: S7, S8, S9, 'My Brother and I' & 'The Love of Three Oranges'
Born in London, Sylvia qualified as a hairdresser and worked in a salon in London's Notting Hill, before joining the BBC in the mid-1960s. After the three-month training course, she moved into the make-up department and completed a further 21 months' on-the-job training. As an assistant, she worked on numerous productions, including *Henry VIII*. She was promoted to make-up artist and worked on many shows, such as *Bar Mitzvah Boy* in 1976, and six years later *Nancy Astor*, which earnt her a BAFTA. Sylvia was still employed by the BBC when she died of cancer in 1991.

TICKET COLLECTOR, THE

Played by Sue Bishop (TV)

The ticket collector works at Walmington rail-way station and is seen in 'The Royal Train' when the king's train speeds through the station without stopping.

TILVERN, ALAN (1920–)

Born: London

Roles: Captain Rodrigues (S3, episode 2: 'Battle School'), US Colonel (S6, episode 2: 'My British Buddy') (TV); Captain Rodrigues and Captain Ramsay (radio)

As his first job, Alan worked in the local market before starting his entertainment career as an amateur in variety. At the local boys' club he wrote, performed and directed. Turning professional in his twenties, his first two assignments were three months at Manchester Rep and a year at Oldham. After various theatre tours he moved into TV and was regularly employed. Because of his aptitude for accents he was often cast as foreign characters, particularly Americans and Russians.

His film credits include: *The Black Rose*, *Superman*, *Chase a Crooked Shadow*, *Desert Mice*, *Shadow of Fear* and *Hot Enough for June*. On TV he's appeared in *Espionage*, *Maigret* and *No Hiding Place*. Alan is also a qualified BBC director, and has directed on TV. Recent work has mainly been on the radio.

TIME ON MY HANDS

Recorded: Friday 8/12/72

Original transmission: Friday 29/12/72, 8.30–9.00pm

Original viewing figures: 16.6 million

Repeated: 18/4/74, 10/7/81, 3/8/81 (Wales), 7/11/89, 9/8/90 (N Ireland), 3/9/93, 14/2/97

CAST

Arthur Lowe . . . . Captain Mainwaring
John Le Mesurier . . . . Sergeant Wilson
Clive Dunn . . . . Lance Corporal Jones
John Laurie . . . . Private Frazer
James Beck . . . . Private Walker
Arnold Ridley . . . . Private Godfrey
Ian Lavender . . . . Private Pike
Bill Pertwee . . . . ARP Warden
Frank Williams . . . . Vicar
Edward Sinclair . . . . Verger
Harold Bennett . . . . Mr Blewitt
Colin Bean . . . . Private Sponge
Joan Cooper . . . . Miss Fortescue
Eric Longworth . . . . Mr Gordon (Town Clerk)
Christopher Sandford . . . . . . German Pilot
Platoon: Desmond Cullum-Jones, Freddie Wiles, Hugh Hastings, Freddie White, Hugh Cecil, George Hancock, Evan Ross, Leslie Noyes, Michael Moore
Extra in Tea Rooms: May Grimmer

PRODUCTION TEAM

Script: Jimmy Perry and David Croft
Producer/Director: David Croft
Production Assistant: Gordon Pert

Film Cameraman: James Balfour
Film Sound Recordist: Les Collins
Film Editor: Bill Harris
Studio Lighting: Howard King
Studio Sound: John Delany
Design: Paul Joel
Assistant Floor Manager: Peter Fitton
Vision Mixer: Dave Hanks
Costume Supervisor: Susan Wheal
Make-Up Supervisor: Anna Chesterman
Visual Effects: Tony Harding

Mainwaring and Wilson are enjoying their morning cup of coffee and Rich Tea biscuits at the Marigold Tea Rooms when Pike rushes in, hands them rifles and says the police have phoned: a Nazi pilot has bailed out and is hanging from the town hall clock.

The men of the Home Guard congregate at the town hall and try to work out how they'll capture the German. They consider different ways of pulling him in, including taking the minute hand off the clock, which has not worked since 1939. Inside the clock tower, a mishap sees Jones trapping everyone inside the tower.

Eventually they pull the German in and, while Jones guards him, Mainwaring writes a note, stuffs it in a bottle and drops it onto the road below asking for help to get down. But he doesn't hold out much hope of receiving aid from Hodges and the others below, so everyone racks their brains for a solution to their predicament. Although Walker's idea puts Jones in a precarious situation, Wilson's plan – based on a fairy story – comes up trumps.

TIVOLI CINEMA

The Tivoli Cinema in Walmington, where Edith Parish works as an usherette, is mentioned in 'Mum's Army'.

TODD, JAN

Born: Kingston, Surrey

Role: Member of the Home Front Company (stage show)

Jan started dancing as a girl and went on to appear in cabaret, including many seasons travelling the world aboard a cruise ship. She also appeared on the stage in many West End assignments.

TOMLINSON, FRED (1927–)

Born: Rawtenstall

Role: Member of the Choir (S3, episode 4: 'The Bullet is Not for Firing') (TV)

Together with Kate Forge, Eilidh McNab, Andrew Daye and Arthur Lewis, Fred Tomlinson sang in the choir during the episode 'The Bullet is Not for Firing'. All were professional singers and formed part of The Fred Tomlinson Singers. Fred ran his own company, supplying singers to stage and TV productions, as well as writing music for other performers to sing.

He had followed in his brothers' footsteps and become a chorister at Manchester Cathedral just before the war, where he learned to read music and sing. When war broke out he was evacuated to Thornton, near Blackpool for a year, before being seconded to King's College, Cambridge, as a chorister for two years.

When the war ended, it took a while before Fred began his career as a singer, partly because he had to complete his national service in the army, which involved teaching apprentices mathematics and spending two years in the Far East. Returning to civvy street, he was finally given his first break when he joined the famous Mitchell Singers, where he met Kate Forge, Eilidh McNab and Welshmen Andrew Daye and Arthur Lewis, who are now both dead. As part of The Mitchell Singers, they sang on various radio and television productions.

Eventually Fred Tomlinson decided to branch out on his own, and employed Forge, McNab, Daye and Lewis on numerous occasions. He arranged, organised and wrote songs for various artists, and was even involved in the famous lumberjack song in *Monty Python*. He also worked on *The Two Ronnies* for many years before his retirement from the business at the age of 72.

TOMMY ATKINS

A term used to describe a typical private in the British army. It is used occasionally in the sitcom, particularly by Mainwaring, for example in the episode 'Turkey Dinner'.

TOMMY GUN, THE

An American machine gun invented by General John Thompson in 1918. The gun was used extensively throughout the Second World War.

TOWN, CY (1931–)

Born: Newport, Shropshire

Roles: Mess Steward (S6, episode 4: 'We Know Our Onions'), Soldier at the church hall reception ('My Brother and I') (TV)

After leaving school, Cy worked in the office of an engineering firm, before moving on to Staffordshire County Council for six months. He completed his national service in the RAF after which he returned to office work, this time spending ten years in the accounts department of a London-based packaging company.

Throughout the years working in admin, Cy spent his evenings with various amateur dramatic companies, and when he moved to London he answered an advert in *The Stage* and joined a concert party which performed in working men's clubs and local parks.

By the time he decided to try his luck at acting full-time, Cy was office manager at a firm involved in packing and despatching advertising material. He was signed up by an agent and during his interview was offered a commercial, his first professional job.

His television work has been confined mostly to small parts, but he was always in demand. If he wasn't acting, Cy was content doing crowd work. His television credits include *Steptoe and Son*, *The Brothers*, *The Two Ronnies*, *Crown Prosecutor*, *Moonbase 3*, *Reeves and Mortimer*, *The Bill*, *EastEnders*, *Minder* and *Love Hurts*. Cy also worked as a Dalek operator for 20 years, and appeared in several films.

Cy retired from the profession in 1997 and lives in Kent.

TRAVELL, ALAN

Born: Newport

Role: Burt (S1, episode 3: 'Command Decision') (TV)
After leaving school, Alan joined the City Literary Institute in London's Drury Lane. Upon graduating from drama school in 1968, he was soon being cast in small parts on television, often playing policemen and villains in shows such as *Softly, Softly*. As well as other small-screen appearances, including a soldier in *Doctor Who*, Alan did a season on stage with Joan Littlewood at Stratford, and appeared in background scenes on film, but his career was largely spent working in TV.

Work began to dry up when Alan moved out of London, and when his wife died, he gave up the profession to look after his family. Nowadays he runs amateur drama groups near his home in Hampshire.

TREACHER, BILL (1937–)

Born: London

Role: 1st Sailor (S3, episode 10: 'Menace from the Deep') (TV)
Upon completing his national service, Bill worked as a steward for the P&O Line, sailing the world while he saved enough money to get through drama school. He eventually trained at the Webber Douglas Academy, before embarking on a busy career covering all parts of the profession. For four years (1965–1969) he was heard as Sidney, the milkman, in *The Dales*, while on television he's probably best known as Arthur Fowler in *EastEnders*, a part he played for ten years. Other appearances on the box include the black and white days of *Z Cars* and *Dixon of Dock Green*, *The Dick Emery Show*, *Bless This House*, *Angels*, *Sweet Sixteen*, *Bergerac* and Chadwick in the 1985 series, *The Bright Side*.

TRUEMAN, FREDDIE (1931–)

Born: Stainton

Role: E C Egan (S4, episode 10: 'The Test') (TV)
Freddie trained as a bricklayer before turning to cricket. A Yorkshire player for 19 years (1949–1968), he played in 67 test matches for England and took 307 wickets. In his county career he took over 2000 wickets. Since retiring from the game he's become a popular writer and commentator on the game.

TULL, PATRICK (1941–)

Born: Bexhill-on-Sea

Role: Suspect (S3, episode 12: 'Man Hunt') (TV)
Patrick, whose uncle was Desmond Llewelyn of 'Q' fame left school and joined LAMDA in 1959. He graduated two years later and spent six months as an ASM at the Nottingham Playhouse, before working in reps all over the country, including Sidmouth, Cromer and Salisbury.

His television career began at the age of 24 with a role in *Z Cars*, followed by *No Hiding Place* and other productions. As well as helping to provide the voices of the Krotons in an early episode of *Doctor Who*, Patrick has appeared in several films, including Flight Lieutenant Templeton in 1969's *Mosquito Squadron*, Cecil in *Parting Glances* and Jerry the bartender in the 1996 picture *Sleepers*.

Patrick, who had appeared on Broadway in the mid-1960s, moved to the States in 1973 and nowadays concentrates mainly on voice-overs and recorded books.

TURKEY DINNER

Recorded: Sunday 10/11/74

Original transmission: Monday 23/12/74, 8.00–8.30pm

(This episode was originally planned for transmission on 6 December)

Original viewing figures: 15.8 million

Repeated: 19/6/75, 23/4/91, 25/12/93, 21/12/95 (Wales), 23/12/95, 23/12/98

CAST

Arthur Lowe	Captain Mainwaring
John Le Mesurier	Sergeant Wilson
Clive Dunn	Lance Corporal Jones
John Laurie	Private Frazer
Arnold Ridley	Private Godfrey
Ian Lavender	Private Pike
Bill Pertwee	Chief Warden Hodges
Talfryn Thomas	Private Cheeseman
Frank Williams	Vicar
Edward Sinclair	Verger
Harold Bennett	Mr Bluett
Pamela Cundell	Mrs Fox
Janet Davies	Mrs Pike
Olive Mercer	Mrs Yeatman
Dave Butler	Farmhand

Platoon: Colin Bean, George Hancock, Evan Ross, Leslie Noyes, Michael Moore, Freddie White, Freddie Wiles, Hugh Cecil, Roger Bourne, Desmond Cullum-Jones

OAPs: Heather Graham, Daphne Day, Nellie Griffiths, Doris Littlewood, Constance Myers, Wynn McCloud, Vera Walden, Coralie Wilson, Gilly Flower, Eileen Matthews, Ruby Buchanan, Margi Young, Merrell Hobson, Charles Adey Gray, Vernon Drake, Walter Goodman, David Jay Graham, Frank Littlewood, Jimmy Mac, John Tucker

Walk-on (Land Girl at Turkey Farm): Jill Hope

PRODUCTION TEAM

Script: Jimmy Perry and David Croft
Producer/Director: David Croft
Production Assistant: Bob Spiers
Film Cameraman: Len Newson
Film Sound Recordist: John Gatland
Film Editor: Bill Harris
Studio Lighting: Howard King
Studio Sound: Michael McCarthy
Design: Bryan Ellis
Assistant Floor Managers: Anne Ogden and Sue Bennett-Urwin
Vision Mixer: Dave Hanks
Costume Supervisor: Susan Wheal
Make-Up Artist: Sylvia Thornton

At the church hall, Jones tells Captain Mainwaring about an incident while on patrol the previous evening. Being a cold night, he took his lads for a quick drink in The Horse and Groom. Afterwards, Cheeseman started shivering, so they popped in to The King's Head for a couple of pints. Next stop was The Goat and Compasses. After that, Godfrey started singing rau-

'Turkey Dinner'

cously – to everyone's surprise – so Jones took him inside The Red Lion to sober up, while the others enjoyed further drinks.

Before the night was out, Jones had shot a turkey. Mainwaring realises there's only one place the turkey could have come from: the North Berrington Turkey Farm. He therefore decides they must apologise to the owner, Mr Boggis, and pay for the bird.

Mr Boggis has gone to market and his brainless labourer is unwilling to accept any money and not prepared to accept ownership of the bird, even though it's the only turkey farm in the district. Undecided what to do with the turkey, Jones' section suggest giving a turkey dinner to the OAPs of Walmington; Mainwaring thinks it's a capital idea, and sets up a committee to organise the meal.

The turkey feast runs smoothly. Mainwaring, dressed in his dinner suit and dickey bow, prepares to leave for a Rotary dinner, but not before Pike tips gravy all over his white shirt. Blotting paper and white enamel paint lead to bigger headaches, so a sling is the only option to disguise the mishap, but there's a final problem facing Mainwaring.

'Turkey Dinner'

TURKEY DINNER GENERAL PURPOSES COMMITTEE

When the Walmington Home Guard find a dead turkey on their hands, they decide to throw a special dinner for the town's OAPs. As ever, Mainwaring thinks the event calls for a committee to be formed, ensuring that everything runs smoothly. Electing himself as chairman, he delegates the actual setting up of the meeting to Wilson. Jones, Hodges, Mrs Pike, Frazer, Mr Blewitt, Mrs Fox, Mr and Mrs Yeatman, Private Cheeseman and Pikey are all part of the committee. After voting, Mrs Fox is assigned the job of cooking the turkey, narrowly beating Mrs Pike to the task, who agrees to make the stuffing. Mrs

Cheeseman will make the gravy, while all the other jobs are dished out.

TURNER, CAPTAIN

Played by John Ringham and Timothy Bateson (radio)
Captain Turner appeared in two radio episodes. In 'Room at the Bottom', he had to deliver the news that Mainwaring was being demoted. In the TV version, the character was called Captain Bailey. In 'No Spring for Frazer', Turner was based at GHQ and Mainwaring reports the missing spring to him.

TURNER, STEVE

Production assistant on two episodes (TV): S3, episodes 10: 'Menace from the Deep' and 11: 'Branded'

TWELVETREES, MISS

Played by Natalie Kent (TV)
Miss Twelvetrees owns a small shop in Walmington's High Street, which is rented out to Frazer. The £10 per month rent she receives is donated to the local orphanage. She's interviewed by Mr Mainwaring in 'High Finance' in connection with Jones' financial problems.

TWO AND A HALF FEATHERS, THE

Recorded: Friday 6/11/70

Original transmission: Friday 13/11/70, 8.00–8.30pm

Original viewing figures: 15.6 million

Repeated: 18/7/71, 24/2/85, 28/11/92, 3/12/92 (Wales), 20/1/96

CAST

Arthur Lowe . . . . Captain Mainwaring
John Le Mesurier . . . . Sergeant Wilson
Clive Dunn . . . . Lance Corporal Jones
John Laurie . . . . Private Frazer
James Beck . . . . Private Walker
Arnold Ridley . . . . Private Godfrey
Ian Lavender . . . . Private Pike

Bill Pertwee . . . . ARP Warden
John Cater . . . . Private Clarke
Wendy Richard . . . . Edith
Queenie Watts . . . . Edna
Gilda Perry . . . . Doreen
Linda James . . . . Betty
Parnell McGarry . . . . Elizabeth
John Ash . . . . Raymond
Platoon: Colin Bean, Hugh Hastings, Vic Taylor
Customers: Charles Fisher, Reg Turner, Pat Donogue, Eddie Connor, Harry Douglas, Clifford Hemsley, Carrie Lambert, Rosa Gold, Pat Orr, Tessa Landers
Elderly Cashier: Margaret Boht
Washer Upper: Barbara Shackleton

PRODUCTION TEAM

Script: Jimmy Perry and David Croft
Producer/Director: David Croft
Production Assistant: Phil Bishop
Film Cameraman: Stewart Farnell
Film Sound Recordist: Les Collins
Film Editor: Bob Rymer
Studio Lighting: George Summers
Studio Sound: Michael McCarthy
Design: Paul Joel
Assistant Floor Manager: Roger Singleton-Turner
Vision Mixer: Dave Hanks
Costume Supervisor: George Ward
Make-Up Supervisor: Cynthia Goodwin
Visual Effects: Peter Day

Mainwaring and Wilson are having their lunch at the British Restaurant, where the menu is fairly limited. While they have a small portion of toad in the hole, Walker has a steak. Jones comes in to say he's off to London, it's the 42nd annual reunion for the veterans of the Battle of Omdurman.

On parade, Frazer brings along a new recruit, George Clarke, whom he met at The Anchor pub the other night. Clarke was in the Warwickshire regiment, the same as Jones. When Jones and Clarke meet the following evening, Clarke shows instant dislike for the local butcher.

After having a few drinks with Frazer, Clarke starts spreading rumours about Jones, who, meanwhile, receives two and a half feathers with letters saying he's a coward, and shouldn't have left his friend in the desert.

Mainwaring is determined to get to the bottom of the matter. Clarke believes it was a native who rescued him after Jones left him in the desert to die. Jones then tells his version of the story. He volunteered to go out and get help when his party were in trouble, Clarke went with him, but they were captured by two dervishes. After scaring the dervishes off, Jones rescued an unconscious Clarke and joined up with a relief column. When Mainwaring decides to confront Clarke, they find he's skipped town.

U-BOAT

Undersea boats (or U-boats), the German submarines, were first used in the Great War. They were very effective during the Second World War, sinking millions of tons of Allied ships, mainly in the all-important merchant supply routes of the Atlantic. The Armistice terms of 1918 required Germany to surrender all its U-boats, and the nation was forbidden to possess any in the future, but in 1935 Hitler virtually brushed the ruling aside as he built up his military arsenal. During the early months of the Second World War, Germany inflicted heavy casualties on the British Navy, even though the German fleet numbered just 57. During the war, over 1162 U-boats were built, of which 785 were destroyed.

U-BOAT CAPTAIN

Played by Philip Madoc (TV and radio)
Together with seven members of his crew, the arrogant German captain in 'The Deadly Attachment' finds himself being guarded by the Walmington Home Guard, after their submarine sinks and they drift in a rubber dinghy for two days. Even though he only made one appearance, the captain was one of the most memorable characters in the sitcom. He is called Captain Muller in the radio version.

ULMAN, ERNST (1914–1977)

Born: Vienna
Role: Sigmund Murphy (S2, episode 6: 'Under Fire') (TV)
Ernst played a detective in the 1944 film, *Hotel Reserve*, and a German sergeant in 1961's *Invasion Quartet*. On TV he was seen in shows such as *The Saint*, *Espionage* and *Aggy* in 1956.

UNDER FIRE

Recorded: Wednesday 27/11/68 (made in black and white)

Original transmission: Saturday 5/4/69, 7.00–7.30pm

(This episode was originally planned for transmission on 3 February at 7.30pm)

Original viewing figures: 11.6 million

Repeated: 29/8/69

CAST

Arthur Lowe	Captain Mainwaring
John Le Mesurier	Sergeant Wilson
Clive Dunn	Lance Corporal Jones
John Laurie	Private Frazer
James Beck	Private Walker
Arnold Ridley	Private Godfrey
Ian Lavender	Private Pike
Janet Davies	Mrs Pike
Geoffrey Lumsden	Corporal-Colonel Square
John Ringham	Captain Bailey
Queenie Watts	Mrs Keen
Gladys Dawson	Mrs Witt
Ernst Ulman	Sigmund Murphy
Bill Pertwee	ARP Warden
June Petersen	Woman

Platoon: Colin Bean, Richard Jacques, Frank Godfrey, Alec Coleman, Hugh Cecil, Jimmy Mac, Desmond Cullum-Jones, Vic Taylor, David Seaforth, Richard Kitteridge

PRODUCTION TEAM

Script: Jimmy Perry and David Croft
Producer: David Croft
Production Assistant: Clive Doig
Director: Harold Snoad
Studio Lighting: George Summers
Studio Sound: James Cole
Design: Paul Joel
Assistant Floor Manager: Tony George
Vision Mixer: Bruce Milliard
Costume Supervisor: Marjorie Lewis
Make-Up Supervisor: Sheila Cassidy

Wilson and Mainwaring arrive at the church hall in their pyjamas and change into their uniforms, shocking Corporal-Colonel Square who turns up to help with the morning's exercise. Captain Bailey arrives and tells Mainwaring the docks further along the coast took a pasting the previous night, as the Germans are using large numbers of incendiary bombs. All HG units are therefore to put maximum strength on duty to tackle them; Mainwaring assures Bailey that the unit will be fully prepared by the time the sirens blow: spotters will be posted on the church tower and the rest of the men will act as a mobile force.

That night, while Frazer and Godfrey are on the roof of the church tower on guard, they spot a light flashing from a house on the corner of Mortimer Street, near where the bomb dropped the previous night. They inform Mainwaring who initially plans on phoning the police, but Square convinces him he has got authority to act, and so he decides to investigate.

Mainwaring and his men arrive at Mortimer Street and establish the top flat where the light was seen is occupied by a man called Murphy, an Austrian who's been living in England for 25 years and is now a naturalised citizen. The other occupants of the house, Mrs Keen and Mrs Witt, both appear, claiming he's a spy. Even the woman opposite joins the argument claiming he was signalling last night.

They arrest Murphy and take him to the church hall, but have their work cut out: as well as guarding Murphy, incendiaries are landing everywhere and one crashes through the church hall roof. After a lot of flapping and chaos, Mrs Pike arrives and very calmly extinguishes the fire with a sand bag. Before the evening is out, Hodges confirms Mr Murphy isn't a spy, he was married to his aunt.

UNDERDOWN, EDWARD (1908–1989)

Role: Major-General Holland (S5, episode 12: 'Round and Round Went the Great Big Wheel') (TV)
Edward, who was also a successful jockey for a time, first appeared on stage in 1932, before moving into films and television later in his career. His early movies included *Wings of the Morning*, *The Drum*, *The October Man* and *Man on the Run*, but he completed over 30 more pictures before *Tarka the Otter* in 1978.

His numerous roles on television included an appearance in ITV's cult series, *Man in a Suitcase*.

UNIFORMS

The photos and captions on the following page detail how the uniforms worn by members of the Home Guard and the air raid wardens evolved during the war years. Jimmy Perry and David Croft, as well as the costume designers working on *Dad's Army*, did their utmost to

1 Although some units were issued with denim uniforms while still officially known as LDV, denims were eventually phased in for everybody. This style of kit was retained, in most cases, until the end of 1941, when serge battle dress was introduced.

2 This khaki band, like the LDV band before it, was worn on the upper right arm. They were largely withdrawn when the Home Guard adopted shoulder titles and regimental flashes, although some were retained by each unit and worn by denim-clad decontamination and cleaning units.

3 Field service caps were issued in only one size and carried the local regiment's insignia. In Kent, where the fictitious town of Walmington-on-Sea was situated, two badges existed: one for the Royal West Kent Regiment, which Mainwaring's men adopted, and one for the East Kent Regiment, whose insignia the Eastgate platoon and the Colonel (played by Robert Raglan) wore.

1 Between the autumn of 1940 and the end of 1941, the denim uniforms were replaced by the warmer serge battle dress for officers and privates. While privates fastened their battle dress to the neck, officers left their tunic open to show off a shirt and tie worn underneath.

2 While privates retained the forage cap, officers were eventually issued with peaked caps, again bearing the insignia of the local regiment.

3 While black leather boots were worn by the privates, the platoon officer would wear brown boots or shoes; if he chose the latter, he would discard his webbing gaiters.

4 Officers would wear a webbing belt and holster (usually containing a Webley revolver) and small ammunition pouch to match.

1 When it came to the fourth series of *Dad's Army*, the sleeves of the platoon's uniforms were displaying a new 'CP1' badge. Costume designer Barbara Kronig was responsible for this addition; instead of using the badge to signify the unit's location in the normal fashion, she used 'CP' to indicate 'Croft and Perry'.

2 The Home Guard shoulder title superseded the armband and was worn by all ranks.

3 The badges of rank were introduced in 1941 and became identical to that of the regular army. As it applied to the Walmington platoon, Captain Mainwaring wore three gilt stars on each shoulder, Sergeant Wilson had three worsted chevrons while Lance Corporal Jones one worsted chevron. The chevrons were worn on the upper arm of both the battle dress blouse and greatcoat.

1 Two specially commissioned pouches were worn. They were shorter than those used by the regular army. When *Dad's Army* started in 1968, the pouches couldn't be found so binocular cases were used instead.

2 Home Guard units initially suffered from a dearth of weapons: rifles used were often American P14s or Springfield 17s, originally used during the First World War. The latter had the disadvantage of not taking standard issue .303 ammunition. The rifle that eventually became the standard Home Guard weapon by late 1941 was the Lee-Enfield SMLE Mk IIIs.

ensure the uniforms used in the sitcom were as accurate as possible, although inevitably they were dependant on finding sufficient supplies.

HOME GUARD

The LDV (Local Defence Volunteers) was renamed the Home Guard in July 1940. Kitting out the Walmington-on-Sea platoon, just like the real Home Guard, was a slow job, with items of kit arriving in dribs and drabs, like the field service caps being delivered in 'The Enemy Within the Gates' but jackets not arriving until 'The Showing Up of Corporal Jones'.

Initially members of the LDV dressed in civilian clothes, with their only form of identity being an armband worn on their right sleeve. Heartening news arrived in June 1940 when full details were announced of the kit and equipment each member would receive. Unfortunately shortages in the regular army delayed supplies reaching Home Guard units. Even by the time the LDV had become the Home Guard very little had arrived.

AIR RAID WARDENS

The wardens began by wearing civvies with a silver lapel badge bearing the inscription, 'ARP'. They also wore ARP armbands. Eventually, just like the Home Guard, serge uniforms were issued, although those designed for the wardens were black.

Black helmets were also worn, while chief wardens were given white hats. Another feature of their serge uniforms were shoulder titles with ARP displayed in gold lettering. Much of the time wardens were seen wearing navy blue overalls with a maroon ARP breast badge.

UNINVITED GUESTS

Recorded: Friday 4/12/70

(The *Christmas Night with the Stars* insert was recorded the same evening)

Original transmission: Friday 11/12/70, 8.00–8.30pm

Original viewing figures: 13.1 million

Repeated: 22/8/71, 15/1/91, 6/11/93, 28/11/93 (Wales), 21/9/96, 3/11/96 (Wales)

CAST

Arthur Lowe	Captain Mainwaring
John Le Mesurier	Sergeant Wilson
Clive Dunn	Lance Corporal Jones
John Laurie	Private Frazer
James Beck	Private Walker
Arnold Ridley	Private Godfrey
Ian Lavender	Private Pike
Bill Pertwee	ARP Warden
Frank Williams	Vicar
Edward Sinclair	Verger
Rose Hill	Mrs Cole
Don Estelle	Gerald

Platoon: Colin Bean, Hugh Hastings, Vic Taylor, Desmond Cullum-Jones, Freddie Wiles, George Hancock, Leslie Noyes, Freddie White, Hugh Cecil, Frank Godfrey ARP Wardens: Anthony Lang, Bill Lodge, Clifford Hemsley, Dolly Brennan, Kim McAllen, Jean Reaves

PRODUCTION TEAM

Script: Jimmy Perry and David Croft
Producer/Director: David Croft
Production Assistant: Phil Bishop
Studio Lighting: George Summers
Studio Sound: Michael McCarthy
Design: Paul Joel
Assistant Floor Manager: Roger Singleton-Turner
Vision Mixer: Clive Doig
Costume Supervisor: George Ward
Make-Up Supervisor: Cynthia Goodwin
Visual Effects: Peter Day

When Hodges' air raid headquarters are bombed he's granted permission to use the Vicar's office: the problem is Mainwaring uses it too. When Jones sends Hodges fleeing, Mainwaring thinks he's sorted the problem, until the Vicar becomes involved.

Mainwaring refers his case to Area HQ, the civil defence bigwigs and the secretary of the council – a fellow Rotarian – giving them a piece of his mind. It's decided the wardens will be out of his hair as soon as possible, but until then Mainwaring will do his best to ignore them, which will be difficult, especially when the wardens start barging Mainwaring's men out of the way while on parade.

When the air raid sirens sound Mainwaring, Hodges and his assistant have to share the office and the telephone, causing all sorts of problems. The phone doesn't stop ringing, and all the calls are for the ARP, which annoys Mainwaring. When there's a call to report a chimney on fire next to the church it takes a second before they realise the blaze is in the church hall. The fire was caused by Gerald who lit the stove with one of Walker's fire-lighters. Too embarrassed to call the fire brigade, the Home Guard and ARP wardens try dowsing the fire themselves by going out on the roof. After much fussing about, Wilson saves the day by pouring salt on the fire, but Mainwaring, Hodges and the Verger get stuck and with a storm approaching, there is no option but to call the fire brigade.

UNITED MEAT SUPPLY

As mentioned in 'High Finance', Jones buys all his meat supplies from a company called the United Meat Supply.

US SERGEANT, THE

Played by Blain Fairman (TV); Michael Middleton (radio)

The sergeant arrives with the rest of the Americans in 'My British Buddy'.

USHER, THE

Played by Toby Perkins (TV)

The usher works in the magistrates court and is on duty when Mainwaring's case is heard in 'A Brush with the Law'.

VAN DRIVER, THE
Played by Barry Linehan (TV)

When the Walmington Home Guard and Hodges are roaming the countryside pretending to be fifth columnists in 'Wake-Up Walmington', a van driver pulls up and recognises them. He also spots Hodges and takes the opportunity to hit him because last time he visited the warden's shop, he was short-changed.

VAN DRIVER, THE
Played by Felix Bowness (TV)

When the Walmington Home Guard are trying to release a bomb which has become tangled in an important stretch of phone wires during the episode 'Number Engaged', the van driver has his load of furniture requisitioned in order to build a tower. The Home Guard's attempts are in vain because the tower collapses.

VAN NORDE, FRANZ
Role: Nazi Co-pilot (film)

Franz has now left the acting profession in Britain and is living in Holland.

VEHICLES

ANR 490 a green and black lorry bearing the company name L P Miller and Son. It was driven by Felix Bowness and carried furniture, which Mainwaring requisitioned in the episode 'Number Engaged', in order to build a tower on which it was hoped some fool would climb and release the bomb stuck in the telephone wires.

ATO 574 a motorbike and sidecar Hodges, Mainwaring and Pike use in the episode, 'Round and Round Went the Great Big Wheel', to lure the out-of-control wheel to the aerodrome. They borrow it from someone in exchange for some petrol coupons.

BMG 443 the Mayor's black Rolls Royce seen in 'The Captain's Car'. It is also seen in *To the Manor Born*.

BUC 852 a 1935, two-ton Ford box van, 3445 cc, which was used as Jones' butcher's van. It was donated to the Walmington Home Guard platoon in 'The Armoured Might of Lance Corporal Jones' and became a crucial component in Mainwaring's fighting force. Used extensively by the platoon, it was a trusty old warhorse, rarely letting the men down.

Frank Holland, who worked as assistant property master at the BBC for a time, spotted Jones' van when it was nothing more than an old, dilapidated van standing unwanted in a street in Streatham, London, long before *Dad's Army* was screened. Frank contacted Fred Willmington, who owned a company that loaned vehicles to the BBC, about the vehicle, which had been in the street for months. Willmington contacted the police, and after enquiries into its ownership had been conducted, he was allowed to claim the vehicle.

Considerable time and money were spent restoring the van, so when the BBC were on the look-out for a vehicle to use as Jones' butcher's van, Willmington felt confident about allowing the BBC to inspect it. Designer Paul Joel visited Willmington's site in Kingsbury and decided it fitted the bill, but that holes would need to be cut into the side, and part of the roof needed altering. Joel drew up the plans and Willmington's company converted the van accordingly.

Whenever the BBC didn't want the van for filming, it remained in its *Dad's Army* livery, but false sides were constructed which slotted into channelling on the vehicle, meaning it could be used as a normal vehicle.

Once the sitcom had ended, the van – which Fred Willmington drove to Brighton and back when he entered it for the annual Historic Commercial Vehicle Club run – was sold to a Ford dealer in Finchley, London; it took pride of place in their showroom. It was eventually sold at auction on 26 November 1990, to The Patrick Motor Museum in Birmingham, where it's currently displayed. The museum contains 86 vehicles, the oldest dating back to 1903. Although the museum no longer opens daily, pre-arranged visits for parties can be organised by calling 01527 857799.

The van remains in excellent condition and has been used in recent years for the Make a Wish Foundation at Silverstone, where it's driven around the racing track. A different van was used in the film.

CF 3440 a traction engine, known as Bertha, which was seen in 'All is Safely Gathered In'. Built by a Thetford company back in 1909, this general purpose traction engine spent all its working life threshing and on general farm duties. It was restored by Gerald Dixon of Sudbury in the 1950s, before being acquired by Alan Bloom for his collection in 1961, at a cost of £160. The machine is now kept at the Bressingham Steam Museum.

CT 6907 an Aveling steamroller was used in 'Museum Piece'. Now located at Holcot, Northampton.

DX 9547 a blue and cream coach used by the OAPs for their annual party in the episode 'Everybody's Trucking' was a Guilford AS6 with a 20-seat front entrance. Nowadays it's located at a secure undercover location in Northamptonshire, where it's looked after by the British Bus Preservation Group. The vehicle is now in need of renovation.

EU 2657 a little black Austin 7 Walker arrives during the episode 'The Desperate Drive of Corporal Jones'.

GJ 789 Frazer's black hearse used in 'Is There Honey Still For Tea?'. This 1930s Rolls Royce is now owned privately in Haywards Heath.

GLA 719 is Lady Maltby's 1939 Wraith Rolls Royce in 'The Captain's Car'. Now located in Leicestershire.

JJ 1813 a black Hillman Minx saloon appeared in the foreground during 'Time On My Hands'. It's now privately owned by someone in Ipswich.

JL 2323 a fire engine used in the episode 'Brain versus Brawn'. This 1934 Merryweather Leyland engine, which originated from Spalding, Lincolnshire, is now housed at the Bressingham Steam Museum. Named Robert Donnington, after the chairman of the Spalding Urban District Council, the fire appliance became part of the National Fire Service during the war. Afterwards, it passed to the Holland County Fire Brigade. Maintained in full working order by Kevin Kiddell of the Norfolk Fire Service, it is regularly used for weddings and fêtes, usually arriving under its own steam.

JYB 54 Hodges' BSA motorbike and sidecar are seen in the episodes 'Gorilla Warfare' and 'Everybody's Trucking'.

KJ 5595 the black staff car in which the Russian dignitary arrives during 'The Honourable Man'. Now white in colour, it is a 1929 Lanchester Landaulet.

M4 672973 a military two-seater Austin 8 staff car used in 'The Making of Private Pike'.

NF 3226 a red car used by the Colonel in 'The Desperate Drive of Corporal Jones'. It is a Vauxhall 14/40 and was destroyed during the making of the film.

PMP 782 the 1939 Bedford 19cwt green truck used as Hodges' greengrocer's lorry, was owned by the late Jack Mulley who lived in Ixworth, Suffolk, and ran a coach company, Mulley's Motorways. The vehicle remains in good condition and was last used in a rally back in 1990.

The lorry's first owner was the air ministry, who bought it from new and used it during the war. In October 1945 it was transferred to the Ministry of Supply, and was later sold to a private individual at Bury St Edmunds in December 1945. Jack Mulley later acquired the vehicle.

PW 1714 an eight-ton steam roller, called Boxer, which was used in the episode 'Everybody's Trucking'. It was built in 1923 by Charles Burnell and Sons of Thetford. It was formerly owned by a road-mending contractors before ending up in a scrap dealers in West Dereham, Norfolk. It was rescued by Alan Bloom in 1962 and restored. It can also be seen at the Bressingham Steam Museum.

RAF 7121 a motorbike used by an RAF officer at the end of the episode 'The Day the Balloon Went Up'. He arrives to congratulate Mainwaring's men upon rescuing the stray balloon, only for them to salute, releasing the balloon in the process.

UR 6962 is a Star lorry. Appeared in 'Time On My Hands' and 'Brain Versus Brawn'. Jack Mulley, who owned the vehicle, is seen in the driver's seat in both episodes.

VC 002 a black Austin 7 Hodges, the Verger and a RSPCA official use to bring a needle to inject the gorilla in 'Gorilla Warfare'. The vehicle was later spotted parked in the street in the episode 'The Face on the Poster'.

34YY02 an army lorry used in 'Number Engaged'. When Mainwaring's men arrive to take guard of the telephone wires, the regular troops depart in this vehicle.

558007 an army lorry driven by a soldier, played by Jeffrey Holland, in 'Wake Up Walmington'.

agricultural elevator seen in 'All is Safely Gathered In', this Marshall-made piece of machinery, is now owned by the Bressingham Steam Museum.

motorbike used by Wilson in 'The Honourable Man', until he ends up in a ditch, is owned by Phil Basey, the man who doubled for Le Mesurier during the filming. It's a 1941 Matchless and was originally owned by the War Department; when Basey left the army he acquired the bike which was then in pieces.

motorbike used by the production assistant when he arrives in 'Ring Dem Bells' to tell Mainwaring and his men that filming for the training picture has been cancelled.

saddle tank steam engine appears in the episode, 'The Royal Train', and is now located at Northampton and Lamport Station, Chapel Brampton, Northampton.

threshing machine was utilised in 'All is Safely Gathered In'. This was a 1940's Marshall 54 inch all-steel drum, originally owned by Sydney Hoskins of Fersfield, Norfolk.

Wellerhaus organ used in 'Everybody's Trucking', this organ is now at the Thursford Collection, Thursford, near Fakenham, Norfolk.

VEHICLES USED IN THE FILM

BPL 73 this 1934 Shelvoke and Drewry dustcart is now at Copthorne, Surrey, where it forms part of a collection displayed by the Southern Counties Historic Vehicles Preservation Trust.

FLT 159 the BSA motorbike and sidecar used by the AA.

KR 9378 Jones' van was a 1930's Ford, which was housed in a private museum in Reading until it was sold at a recent auction to a man from Lincolnshire.

OU 5264 a steam roller, now owned by a man in Andover.

RV 676 Bert King, played by the late Fred Griffiths, collected the Vicar's bells in this lorry. The Bedford lorry's home was the backyard of a Vauxhall car dealer for some time, but it's now residing at Castle Rising, Norfolk.

SMK 483 Hodges' motorbike.

77RA29 General Fullard's staff car had a military registration. A Humber seven-seater, it is now located at History on Wheels, Eton Wick, Berkshire.

VERGER, THE
See 'Yeatman, Maurice'.

VERNON, GABOR
Roles: Russian (S6, episode 5: 'The Honourable Man'), Polish Officer (S8, episode 6: 'The Face on the Poster') (TV)

Hungarian-born Gabor Vernon, who died in 1985, appeared in TV shows such as *The Professionals* as an ambassador, *Jason King*, *Whoops Apocalypse!* as a Politburo member, *Hazell*, *Quest of Eagles*, *Airline*, *The Brief*, *Mind Your Language*, *Colditz*, *Borderline* and the 1978 mini-series, *Holocaust* as Rabbi Samuel. On the big screen, his appearances included *Dracula* in 1979, *The Falls* in 1980, a jeweller in *Lady Jane* six years later, and two James Bond movies: *Live and Let Die* and *Octopussy*.

VICAR, THE
See 'Farthing, Timothy'.

VIDEO CASSETTES
As one would expect, the release of *Dad's Army* episodes on video has been popular. Two companies have marketed cassettes: the BBC, of course, and Britannia, who released a special 'Collectors' Edition' in conjunction with the Beeb.

BBC Releases
(listed in volume of sales as at December 1999)

1   'The Very Best of Dad's Army' (Catalogue No V5120 / release date: 31.12.93 / Sales: 46,631). Episodes included: 'The Day the Balloon Went Up', 'Sons of the Sea', 'The Two and a Half Feathers', 'Asleep in the Deep' and 'The Deadly Attachment'.

2   'The Very Best of Dad's Army, Volume 2' (Catalogue No V5396 / release date: 31.12.93 / Sales: 41,526). Episodes included: 'No Spring for Frazer', 'Mum's Army', 'Menace from the Deep', 'When Did You Last See Your Money?' and 'The Honourable Man'.

3   'Asleep in the Deep' (Catalogue No V4089 / release date: 7.10.87 / deletion date: 7.9.94 / Sales: 36,204). Episodes included: 'Asleep in the Deep', 'The Deadly Attachment' and 'Don't Forget the Diver'.

4   'Knights of Madness' (Catalogue No V5643 / release date: 8.8.95 / Sales: 23,561). Episodes included: 'Knights of Madness', 'The Making of Private Pike' and 'The Miser's Hoard'.

5   'The Enemy Within the Gates' (Catalogue No V4992 / release date: 5.7.93 / deletion date: 21.8.98 / Sales: 17,527). Episodes included: 'The Enemy Within the Gates', 'The Showing Up of Lance Corporal Jones' and 'Shooting Pains'.

6   'Round and Round Went the Great Big Wheel' (Catalogue No V5932 / release date: 8.10.96 / Sales: 17,492). Episodes included: 'Round and Round Went the Great Big Wheel', 'Time On My Hands' and 'We Know Our Onions'.

7   'The Armoured Might of Lance Corporal Jones' (Catalogue No V5857 / release date: 1.5.96 / Sales:

17,380). Episodes included: 'The Armoured Might of Lance Corporal Jones', 'Something Nasty in the Vault' and 'The Lion has 'Phones'.

8   'A Brush With the Law' (Catalogue No V5372 / release date: 1.7.94 / Sales: 14,164). Episodes included: 'A Brush with the Law', 'Brain versus Brawn' and 'Keep Young and Beautiful'.

9   'Sergeant Wilson's Little Secret' (Catalogue No V6162 / release date: 1.9.97 / Sales: 13,053). Episodes included: 'Sergeant Wilson's Little Secret', 'Things That Go Bump in the Night' and 'Everybody's Trucking'.

10   'Room at the Bottom' (Catalogue No V5967 / release date: 3.3.97 / Sales: 12,078). Episodes included: 'Room at the Bottom', 'War Dance' and 'Getting the Bird'.

11   'Mum's Army' (Catalogue No V4490 / release date: 3.6.91 / deletion date: 12.10.94 / Sales: 11,901). Episodes included: 'Mum's Army', 'The Armoured Might of Lance Corporal Jones' and 'Put That Light Out!'

12   'The Recruit' (Catalogue No V5572 / release date: 17.3.95 / Sales: 8908). Episodes included: 'The Recruit', 'A Man of Action' and 'The Captain's Car'.

13   'My British Buddy' (Catalogue No V5442 / release date: 12.1.95 / Sales: 8485). Episodes included: 'My British Buddy', 'The Royal Train' and 'All is Safely Gathered In'.

14   'The Deadly Attachment' (Catalogue No V4400 / release date: 9.90 / Sales: 7335). Episodes included: 'The Deadly Attachment', 'If the Cap Fits…' and 'The Honourable Man'.

15   'Turkey Dinner' (Catalogue No V658 / release date: 7.9.97 / Sales: 7040). Episodes included: 'Turkey Dinner', 'Ring Dem Bells' and 'When You've Got to Go'.

16   'The Man and the Hour' (Catalogue No V4892 / release date: 2.93 / Sales: 6624). Episodes included: 'The Man and the Hour', 'Museum Piece' and 'Command Decision'.

17   'Uninvited Guests' (Catalogue No V4764 / release date: 31.12.93 / Sales: 5894). Episodes included: 'Uninvited Guests', 'The Desperate Drive of Corporal Jones' and 'The King was in his Counting House'.

18   'The Day the Balloon Went Up' (Catalogue No V4088 / release date: 31.12.93 / Sales: 5316). Episodes included: 'The Day the Balloon Went Up', 'Sons of the Sea' and 'Don't Forget the Diver'.

19   'The Big Parade' (Catalogue No V6266 / release date: 6.7.98 / Sales: 5179). Episodes included: 'The Big Parade', 'Gorilla Warfare' and 'The Godiva Affair'.

20   'The Two and a Half Feathers' (Catalogue No V4320 / release date: 6.90 / Sales: 4961). Episodes included: 'The Two and a Half Feathers', 'The Test' and 'Fallen Idol'.

21   'Is There Honey Still For Tea?' (Catalogue No V6711 / release date: 1.2.99 / Sales: 4859). Episodes included: 'Is There Honey Still For Tea?', 'Come In Your Time is Up' and 'High Finance'.

22   'Man Hunt' (Catalogue No V4661 / release date: 8.95 / Sales: 4856). Episodes included: 'Man Hunt', 'Sgt – Save My Boy!' and 'Don't Fence Me In'.

23   'The Face on the Poster' (Catalogue No V6715 / release date: 7.6.99 / Sales: 4109). Episodes included: 'The Face on the Poster', 'My Brother and I', 'The Love of Three Oranges'.

24   'No Spring for Frazer' (Catalogue No V4763 / release

date: 6.92 / Sales: 3631). Episodes included: 'No Spring for Frazer', 'Absent Friends' and 'A Wilson (Manager)?'

25 'Wake-Up, Walmington' (Catalogue No V6810 / release date: 6.9.99 / Sales: 3467). Episodes included: 'Wake-Up, Walmington', 'Number Engaged' and 'Never Too Old'.

26 'When Did You Last See Your Money?' (Catalogue No V4660 / release date: 8.91 / Sales: 3368). Episodes included: 'When Did You Last See Your Money?', 'Battle School' and 'Branded'.

27 'Big Guns' (Catalogue No V4489 / release date: 6.91 / Sales: 3168). Episodes included: 'Big Guns', 'Menace From The Deep' and 'The Bullet is Not for Firing'.

Britannia Music Company Ltd have also released a collection of specially packaged videos. To date, 23 volumes have been released, covering all the episodes, with the exception of series one and two. Their volumes contain the following episodes:

Volume 1: 'The Armoured Might of Lance Corporal Jones', 'Battle School' and 'The Lion has 'Phones'.

Volume 2: 'The Bullet is Not for Firing', 'Something Nasty in the Vault' and 'Room at the Bottom'.

Volume 3: 'Big Guns', 'The Day the Balloon Went Up' and 'War Dance'.

Volume 4: 'Menace from the Deep', 'Branded' and 'Man Hunt'.

Volume 5: 'No Spring for Frazer', 'Sons of the Sea' and 'The Big Parade'.

Volume 6: 'Don't Forget the Diver', 'Boots, Boots, Boots' and 'Sgt – Save My Boy!'.

Volume 7: 'Don't Fence Me In', 'Absent Friends' and 'Put That Light Out!'.

Volume 8: 'The Two and a Half Feathers', 'Mum's Army' and 'The Test'.

Volume 9: 'A Wilson (Manager)?', 'Uninvited Guests' and 'Fallen Idol'.

Volume 10: 'Battle of the Giants', 'Asleep in the Deep' and 'Keep Young and Beautiful'.

Volume 11: 'A Soldier's Farewell', 'Getting the Bird' and 'The Desperate Drive of Corporal Jones'.

Volume 12: 'If the Cap Fits…', 'The King was in his Counting House' and 'All is Safely Gathered In'.

Volume 13: 'When Did You Last See Your Money?', 'Brain versus Brawn' and 'A Brush with the Law'.

Volume 14: 'Round and Round Went the Great Big Wheel', 'Time On My Hands' and 'The Deadly Attachment'.

Volume 15: 'My British Buddy', 'The Royal Train' and 'We Know Our Onions'.

Volume 16: 'The Honourable Man', 'Things That Go Bump in the Night' and 'The Recruit'.

Volume 17: 'Everybody's Trucking', 'A Man of Action' and 'Gorilla Warfare'.

Volume 18: 'The Godiva Affair', 'The Captain's Car' and 'Turkey Dinner'.

Volume 19: 'Ring Dem Bells', 'When You've Got to Go' and 'Is There Honey Still For Tea?'.

Volume 20: 'Come In, Your Time is Up', 'High Finance' and 'The Face On the Poster'.

Volume 21: 'My Brother and I', 'The Love of Three Oranges' and 'Wake-Up, Walmington'.

Volume 22: 'The Making of Private Pike', 'Knights of Madness' and 'The Miser's Hoard'.

Volume 23: 'Number Engaged' and 'Never Too Old'.

In 1999, Virgin also released a collection of 20 videos containing the BBC episodes. The set cost £139.99.

VISUAL EFFECTS TEAM

The BBC's visual effects department was often called upon by David Croft and his team to help on the making of *Dad's Army*. During the show's nine series run on television, seven people from the department were assigned to Perry and Croft's show: John Friedlander, Ron Oates, Len Hutton, Tony Harding, Jim Ward, Martin Gutteridge and Peter Day. Peter worked on 20 episodes (more often than any of his col-

leagues) and shares his memories of those enjoyable days.

VLADISLOVSKI, MR
Played by Gabor Vernon (TV); Fraser Kerr (radio)
The Russian worker, a hero of the Soviet Union where his team have made 5723 tanks, visits Walmington-on-Sea in 'The Honourable Man'. He's given a wooden key during a ceremony to signify being offered the freedom of the town, but turns around and criticises all the local dignitaries, classing them as bourgeois middle class.

VOLUNTEER, THE
Played by Richard Davies (radio)
Mr Brown is the man who volunteered to take part in a civil defence exercise, which involves him being carried on a stretcher. The character was called 'The Old Man' in the TV episode. He is heard in the radio episode, 'The Armoured Might of Lance Corporal Jones'.

MEMORIES OF DAD'S ARMY

'When I joined the BBC in 1958, there were just four of us in Visual Effects – then known as Visual Aids. I worked initially on school programmes, mainly making demonstration models, before moving on to light entertainment shows.

'One of the early episodes I remember was "Battle School", which required the platoon to go through smoke and explosions. Safety was essential, and I sat hidden from the camera with a firing box, but with a good view of the actors, so I could fire smoke and explosions a safe distance in front of the advancing platoon. David Croft and Jimmy Perry liked the sequence so much, that it was used at the end of every episode thereafter.

'I remember another occasion when we were about to film outside a row of eight cottages, when one owner stood at his door refusing to go inside, until persuaded with a £5 note. The next day, when we arrived to film, there were eight occupants standing at their doorways refusing to go in – a rather expensive day's filming!

'If any effect was called for, a yellow requirement form was sent to the department, outlining the effect. I would then attend a planning meeting, which included Design, Make-up, Costume, Props, etc, to discuss how the effect could be achieved, and the job was then costed. For one episode I had to produce about 50 "dead" pigeons, which Walker had hidden in the organ at a church parade. The organ made strange noises, and on cue

the congregation was showered with pigeons – made out of polystyrene with feathers stuck in them – and feathers; timing was all important in such cases. In the same episode, a pigeon appears behind Mainwaring while he's sitting in the church hall office: it was a glove puppet that I was operating.

'Another episode required a barn to be shelled. Our gallant platoon was on a scheme and had spent the night in a barn. Unfortunately they got the map reference wrong and should have been in a different place. They realised their mistake just in time as explosions rent the air. I mainly used Brocks fireworks and theatre maroons, and smoke of all colours; in this case, it was an eight inch maroon with a two pound bag of cement on top – a most effective visual bang!

'Most explosions were electronically fired, using a firing box and battery pack, with either push buttons or a rotary switch for rapid fire, when a turn of machine gun bullets was required.

'In another episode, "Asleep in the Deep", the platoon was trapped in a flooded cellar with rising water, and one of the actors (Bill Pertwee) had to paddle across the flooded room in an old water tank to reach a safety hatch – a very unstable boat! The set was built in the studio, and for safety reasons, I and an assistant, both wearing wet suits, sat in the tank out of camera shot, ready for a quick rescue if necessary. They were great times.'

PETER DAY

WAAF SERGEANT
Played by Jennifer Browne (TV)
When Mainwaring phones to report the stray barrage balloon in 'The Day the Balloon Went Up', the WAAF Sergeant takes his call in the operations room.

WADDINGTON, PATRICK (1900–1987)
Born: York
Role: Brigadier (S1, episode 5: 'The Showing Up of Corporal Jones', S2, episode 3: 'The Loneliness of the Long-Distance Walker') (TV)
Busy playing leading and, later, character roles on stage and screen, Patrick Waddington appeared in over 20 films, with early offerings being 1946's *Journey Together,* playing Flight Lieutenant Mander, and *School for Secrets* as Group Captain Aspinall the same year. Other pictures he appeared in include *It's Not Cricket* as Valentine Christmas, *A Night to Remember, The Moonraker* and *The Wooden Horse* playing a senior British officer. Among his many TV jobs was playing a NATO General in an episode of *Department S,* back in 1969.

WADE, KEN
Role: Member of the platoon's back row in three episodes (S4, episode 1: 'The Big Parade', episode 3: 'Boot, Boots, Boots' and episode 5: 'Don't Fence Me In') (TV)

WAITRESS, THE
Played by Melita Manger (TV); Mollie Sugden (radio)
A sarcastic waitress who works at Ann's Pantry, she serves Mainwaring when he meets Mrs Gray in 'Mum's Army'.

WAITRESS, THE
Played by Rosemary Faith (TV)
Working in the Marigold Tea Rooms in Walmington, she serves Mainwaring and Mrs Fox when they meet in the episode 'The Godiva Affair', and finds it all highly amusing. Mainwaring arranges to see Mrs Fox as a favour to Corporal Jones, who's starting to think her attentions are being drawn elsewhere – namely towards Mr Gordon, the town clerk.

'Wake-Up Walmington'

WAKE-UP WALMINGTON
Recorded: Friday 8/7/77
Original transmission: Sunday 2/10/77, 8.10–8.40pm
Original viewing figures: 10.2 million
Repeated: 11/9/78, 31/7/79, 19/12/89, 25/12/91, 30/10/93, 5/12/93 (Wales), 20/9/94 (N Ireland), 5/4/97

CAST
Arthur Lowe . . . . .Captain Mainwaring
John Le Mesurier . . . . .Sergeant Wilson
Clive Dunn . . . . .Lance Corporal Jones
John Laurie . . . . .Private Frazer
Arnold Ridley . . . . .Private Godfrey
Ian Lavender . . . . .Private Pike
Bill Pertwee . . . . .Chief Warden Hodges
Frank Williams . . . . .Vicar
Edward Sinclair . . . . .Verger
Geoffrey Lumsden . . . . . . .Captain Square
Sam Kydd . . . . .Yokel
Harold Bennett . . . . .Mr Bluett
Robert Raglan . . . . .Colonel
Charles Hill . . . . .Perkins, the Butler
Jeffrey Holland . . . . .Soldier
Barry Linehan . . . . .Van Driver
Colin Bean . . . . .Private Sponge
Alister Williamson . . . . .Bert, a Man at the Pub
Michael Stainton . . . . .Frenchy, a Man at the Pub
Platoon: Desmond Cullum-Jones, Freddie White, Jimmy Mac, Michael Moore, Roger Bourne, Freddie Wiles, George Hancock, Hugh Cecil, Evan Ross, Vernon Drake
Extras: (Fat Man) William Sully, (2nd Yokel) Percy Hay-Green

PRODUCTION TEAM
Script: Jimmy Perry and David Croft
Producer: David Croft
Production Assistant: Gordon Elsbury
Director: Bob Spiers
Film Cameraman: Peter Chapman
Film Sound Recordist: Graham Bedwell

Film Editor: John Dunstan
Studio Lighting: Howard King
Studio Sound: Laurie Taylor
Design: Tim Gleeson
Assistant Floor Manager: Susan Belbin
Vision Mixer: Angela Beveridge
Costume Designer: Mary Husband
Make-Up Artist: Sylvia Thornton
Visual Effects: Martin Gutteridge

While Mainwaring and Wilson are in the church hall chatting, a disgruntled Hodges comes in annoyed about finding Mr Bluett using a stirrup pump to spray his greenfly. When Mr Bluett follows him in and demands the pump back before telling Hodges how much he hates him, the warden gets upset and proclaims no one is taking the war seriously.

Morale is low in the platoon, and Frazer claims the Home Guard are being called the geriatric fusiliers around town. To shake the town out of its complacency, they decide to roam the countryside dressed up as fifth columnists and Mainwaring invites Hodges to join his team in a rare show of respect between the old rivals.

After clearing the scheme with GHQ, 'Operation Wake Up' is launched. The men rendezvous at the old flour mill just outside town. At first light, they march but no one seems to take any notice, even though they try looking suspicious and furtive. Back at the church hall office on Sunday morning, Captain Square turns up wanting Mainwaring, just as the police at Dymchurch call saying a fifth columnist has been spotted. Square sets off in pursuit in Jones' van with his men and the Verger.

At the old flour mill, just as they are about to march on the gasworks, Square and his men storm the building and can't believe it when the so-called fifth columnists are none other than Mainwaring and his men.

WALKER, APRIL (1943–)
Born: Milborne Port
Role: Judy, a Land Girl (S5, episode 8: 'All is Safely Gathered In') (TV)

April was educated at a convent in Sherborne and a girls' school at St Audries', Somerset. She initially wanted to be a dancer, but realising she was too tall, joined RADA in 1960 and pursued an acting career. Upon graduating she joined a weekly rep company in Chesterfield where she became the ASM and juvenile lead. The six-month stint gave her the perfect grounding as she moved on to spend nine months understudying Diana Rigg at the RSC.

Her TV career began in earnest during the 1970s when she appeared in numerous shows, such as *The Two Ronnies* (she appeared in many of their sketches for over 20 years), *The Morecambe and Wise Show*, *Sykes*, *The Onedin Line*, *Yes, Minister*, *Terry and June*, *Fawlty Towers*, *The Dick Emery Show* and the 1977 mini-series, *Anna*

Karenina, playing a character called Paula. At this time, April was also busy appearing in television commercials, including one for Typhoo Tea which involved a ten-day trip to Sri Lanka.

Theatre has dominated her career since the 1980s and she has appeared in the West End in *Key for Two* and *Present Laughter*. Among the other productions she's worked on is a tour of *Brief Encounter* with Hayley Mills.

WALKER, PRIVATE JOE
Played by Jimmy Beck (TV, film and seven radio episodes), John Bardon (stage) and Graham Stark/Larry Martyn (radio)
Address: c/o 1B, Slope Alley (just off the High Street), Walmington-on-Sea

Joe (Joseph) Walker, who runs a stall on Saturdays at the local market, is a wholesale supplier. He started his business just after war broke out:

realising shortages of every day items were inevitable, he grasped an opportunity to make money, and if his bank balance is anything to go by – it stood at £1,542 in 'The Two and a Half Feathers' – he's doing well.

A black marketeer who used to smuggle brandy from France before the war, Joe regularly supplies goodies to the rest of the platoon. He trades in everything from women's silks to cricket balls, and although he's not afraid to exploit a situation for his own benefit, he's also kindhearted and occasionally makes scooters for children in Eastgate Hospital. He shows other altruistic qualities: when Godfrey's cold-shouldered by everyone after admitting he was a conscientious objector during the Great War, Walker is the only one among the ranks who openly reveals sympathy.

Many people wondered why Joe wasn't serving in the regular army, but his allergy to corned beef put paid to that. When he received his call-up papers in 'The Loneliness of the Long-Distance Walker', he was shocked because he'd

recorded his occupation as a banana salesman and supplier of illuminated signs in the hope it would be classed a reserved occupation. He appealed, but to no avail, and spent a few days at an artillery training base, only to be discharged because of his corned beef allergy. His swift return to the streets of Walmington was welcomed by members of the Home Guard, who could, once again, enjoy the benefits of his black market dealings.

Joe's business address is in Slope Alley, where he rents a couple of old garages at the bottom of Sid Newman's yard, but he's known to have other stores dotted around the area, where he keeps his essential supplies, including a large shed just outside Walmington.

WALLER, SERGEANT
Played by Stanley McGeagh (TV)
A sergeant in the Coldstream Guards, Waller appears in 'The Lion has 'Phones' accompanying Lieutenant Hope Bruce to the reservoir where an enemy plane has crashed.

WALMINGTON-ON-SEA
If you were looking for a little peace and tranquillity by the sea, Walmington has all you could want from a seaside town. Time seems to stands still in this sleepy little resort, and not just because the town hall clock stopped at ten past three in 1939.

Situated 20 miles along the coast from Dover, and on an estuary, it's a haven for retired couples, released from the shackles of urban life.

There isn't any major industry, so unemployment could be a problem, but it has all the trappings one would expect of a seaside resort: a pier, an arcade and a myriad of quaint, little tea rooms and cafés where locals and day-trippers could idle away an hour watching the world go by. If it's shops visitors are looking for, they could spend time strolling down the High Street, Alexandra Parade or West Street. If it's lunchtime, a light snack can be bought in the Marigold Tea Rooms or Ann's Pantry, but if something more substantial is required, without spending a fortune, the British Restaurant may be the place to go.

For day-trippers the town has all the essentials, and there is also a weekly market, where Joe Walker can be seen earning a few quid on his stall. With time to spare, a walk in the town's park would be recommended, with its ample supply of colourful flowers in spring and summer time. During the holiday season one can collect a deckchair, relax in front of the bandstand and listen to a brass band. The bandstand is a rare example of Victorian ironwork, erected to commemorate Queen Victoria's visit to Walmington in 1891, when Jones formed part of the guard of honour. During the war years, Mainwaring applied to have the bandstand demolished because it stood in the firing line of the naval gun he acquired in 'Big Guns'; his request was declined after a delegation from the town council witnessed a disastrous Home Guard demonstration on how to operate the gun.

WALMINGTON-ON-SEA ATHLETIC CLUB
When their usual representative, Jim Cutforth, can't attend the Walmington Rotarian dinner in 'Brain versus Brawn', Jones replaces him. The local club is only mentioned in this episode.

WALMINGTON-ON-SEA COTTAGE HOSPITAL
This is the hospital where Captain Mainwaring has his ingrowing toenail operation during 'The Recruit'.

WALMINGTON-ON-SEA STREET MAP
Through the 80 scripts written for television, we come to know quite a lot about the characters of George Mainwaring, Arthur Wilson, Frank Pike et al. We start to understand and notice their foibles, strengths and unsavoury habits, establishing a picture of them as if they were real human beings. This insight into their fictitious lifestyles makes one curious about the little seaside town in which their lives unfold. We all know the place doesn't exist, but for the 30 minutes of escapism provided by the likes of Mainwaring and his motley crew, it's natural that we want to find out more about Walmington-on-Sea. And that's where Paul Carpenter's superb street plan comes to the fore. As a founder member of the DAAS (Dad's Army Appreciation Society), Paul has painstakingly researched the town of Walmington and created its own street plan. By listening to all the radio episodes and watching the film and TV instalments, he has extracted every reference, including names of streets and shops and constructed a town plan with over 100 reference points. So now if Captain Mainwaring, during a briefing session at the church hall, mentions marching to Stones' Amusement Arcade, we can get our bearings with just a quick glance at Paul's map – a must for all fans of the sitcom.

Paul used Chalfont St Giles – the town used for the *Dad's Army* movie – and Weymouth, a Dorset coastal resort as models for his street plan: he studied maps and visited both to get a feel for the layout of the real towns before setting to work producing a map of Walmington. After allocating all the names mentioned in the numerous episodes, Paul had to create a few himself to cover any remaining roads and to work around some inconsistencies in the scripts. The map took a year to complete.

(Further details regarding the map can be obtained by writing to Paul Carpenter, c/o DAAS, 8 Sinodun Road, Wallingford, Oxon OX10 8AA, enclosing an sae.)

WAR DANCE
Recorded: Thursday 30/10/69

Original transmission: Thursday 6/11/69, 7.30–8.00pm

Original viewing figures: 12.6 million

Repeated: 30/5/70, 26/9/92, 1/6/96, 27/6/00

CAST
Arthur Lowe . . . . .Captain Mainwaring
John Le Mesurier . . . . .Sergeant Wilson
Clive Dunn . . . . .Lance Corporal Jones
John Laurie . . . . .Private Frazer
James Beck . . . . .Private Walker
Arnold Ridley . . . . .Private Godfrey
Ian Lavender . . . . .Private Pike
Frank Williams . . . . .Vicar
Edward Sinclair . . . . .Verger
Janet Davies . . . . .Mrs Pike
Nan Braunton . . . . .Miss Godfrey
Sally Douglas . . . . .Blodwen
The Graham Twins
(Vicki and Cathy) . . . . .Doris and Dora
Olive Mercer . . . . .Mrs Yeatman
Hugh Hastings . . . . .Pianist
Eleanor Smale . . . . .Mrs Prosser
Jenny Thomas . . . . .Violet Gibbons
Platoon: Desmond Cullum-Jones, Vic Taylor, Freddie Wiles, George Hancock, Martin Dunn, Freddie White, Arthur McGuire, Leslie Noyes, Roger Bourne
Drummer: Michael Pullen
Saxophone Player: Jack Whiteford
Home Guard Girlfriends: Joanna Lawrence, Julie Castell, Lela Ford, Mary Stewart, Mary Maxstead, Constance Carling, Cherokee Burton

PRODUCTION TEAM
Script: Jimmy Perry and David Croft
Producer/Director: David Croft
Production Assistant: Harold Snoad
Studio Lighting: Howard King
Studio Sound: Michael McCarthy
Design: Richard Hunt
Assistant Floor Manager: Bill Harman
Vision Mixer: Dave Hanks
Costume Supervisor: Michael Burdle

Mainwaring has organised a platoon dance but he's surprised when Pike, who's approaching 19, tells him he wants to invite an ATS girl, who used to work in a fish and chip shop before joining up. Mainwaring doesn't think she's the right girl for Pike (considering his future with the bank), so he asks Wilson to talk to the boy.

'Operation Dance' is launched to organise the do. Drink will be provided by the golf club, food by Godfrey, while Jones and Mrs Mainwaring will take responsibility for the sausage rolls. Music is down to Hastings, a platoon member who can play the piano, and Walker will arrange to get a band from the RAF holding station at Godalston.

Wilson struggles to find the right words when he holds a private chat with Pike, who claims he loves Violet Gibbons and plans announcing his engagement during the dance. Wilson knows how upset his mother will be, so in desperation asks Walker to talk to him. As Pikey can be stubborn, Walker agrees to talk to Violet, whom he used to know, but it doesn't do any good.

At the dance, Mainwaring arrives sporting a nasty black eye. His wife burnt the sausage rolls so he gave her a good dressing-down, although it looks like Mrs Mainwaring took umbrage at being reprimanded. Mr and Mrs Yeatman are first to arrive, Walker turns up with the attractive twins, Doris and Dora, Frazer with Miss Blodwen, while Jones partners Mrs Prosser. The dance starts and the gum-chewing, blonde-haired Miss Gibbons arrives with Pike who is still intent on announcing his engagement. Wilson tries keeping Mrs Pike busy, but when Frank climbs on stage and breaks the news, Mrs Pike faints. She need not have worried however because the engagement is one of the shortest in history.

WARD, DERVIS
Role: AA Man (film)

Dervis, who died in 1996, appeared in a number of films and TV shows, dating back to the 1950s. On the big screen he played a mechanic in the 1956 picture, *Time Without Pity*, and Allegan in *Timeslip* the same year. Before the decade was out he'd played, among other things, a jailer in *Ben Hur*, and appeared in *The Long Haul*, and *Gideon's Day*. Other films he worked on include *The World of Suzie Wong*, *The Loneliness of the Long-Distance Runner*, *Deadlier than the Male*, *To Sir, With Love* and *Crossed Swords* in 1978.

WARD, GEORGE
Costume designer on 13 episodes (T): S1; S4, episodes 7, 8, 9, 10, 11, 12, 13

George left school just as war broke out, and spent four years (1943–1947) serving in the navy. After demob, he worked in an accountancy office for a while before applying for a job in the mid-1950s at the library at BBC Radio. He later transferred to become a dresser in the costume department before moving on to costume design. In this capacity he worked on numerous productions, including four years on *Warship*, and *Bar Mitzvah Boy* in 1976. After a long career with the Beeb, encompassing light entertainment and drama, George took early retirement in 1985 and now enjoys life in Kent.

WARD, JIM
Visual effects designer on two episodes: S7, 'Everybody's Trucking' and 'Gorilla Warfare'

Born in 1934, Jim's first job was as a printing and developing assistant in London's Portman Press Photographers. At 18 he joined the Royal Army Service Corps as a driver and served overseas. Upon returning to civvy street in 1955 he joined Metafilm before moving on to the Beeb in 1961, initially as a property maker and armourer. Jim transferred to the visual effects department in

EXPLORE WALMINGTON-ON-SEA WITH THE AID OF THIS TOWN PLAN

1	Swallow Bank
2	Jones' Butcher's Shop
3	Hodges' Greengrocer's
4	Frazer Funeral Director's
5	Stead & Simpson
6	Timothy Whites
7	The British Restaurant
8	The Fish and Chip Restaurant
9	Ann's Pantry
10	Marigold Tea Rooms
11	The Dutch Oven
12	Woolworths
13	Marks & Spencer
14	Frazer's Funeral Workshop
15	Elliott's Radio Store
16	Carter Patterson's
17	Dairies
18	Barber's/Hairdresser's
19	H E Drury Funeral Director's
20	Off-licence
21	Newsagent's
22	Newman's Bakery
23	Frazer's Shop
24	Co-op
25	Stones' Amusement Arcade
26	Novelty Rock Emporium
27	Girl Guide Hut
28	Embassy Cinema
29	Beach and Souvenir Shop
30	Charlie's Café
31	Swann's Greengrocer's
32	Free Polish Club
33	Seaman's Mission
34	Police Station
35	Town Hall
36	Magistrates Court
37	Godfrey's Cottage
38	ARP Post
39	St Aldhelm's Church
40	St Aldhelm's Church Hall
41	Milk Bar
42	St Matthew's Church
43	Harris Orphans' Holiday Home Hut
44	Sea-scout Hut
45	Darby and Joan Hut
46	Salvation Army Hall

47	Tivoli Cinema
48	Sweet Shop
49	Bugden Printers
50	Cottage Hospital
51	Sedgewick's Shoe Shop
52	Chemists
53	G A Taylor's Fishmonger's
54	Nolan's Draper's
55	Methodist Chapel
56	Cunningham's Jeweller's
57	Harris Orphanage
58	Dry Cleaner's
59	Jolly Roger Ice Cream Parlour
60	McCeavedy's Surgery
61	Maxwell Solicitors
62	Vicarage
63	Victoria and Albert Memorial Rose Gardens
64	Ladies' Health and Beauty Club
65	Electricity Sub-station
66	Jubilee Hall
67	Holiday Information Centre
68	British Legion Hall
69	Walker's Shed
70	Trustee Savings Bank
71	Stationer and Bookshop
72	Newman's Car Accessories
73	Florist
74	Taxi Garage and Rank
75	Walker's Shop
76	Gill's the Tailors
77	Petrol Station
78	Schools
79	Primrose Anne Laundry
80	Palmer's Stores
81	Adams' Music Shop
82	Sainsbury's
83	Plaza Cinema
84	Harrison Hairdresser's
85	Fire Station
86	Town Museum
87	Peabody Museum
88	Peabody Rooms
89	Health Centre and Clinic
90	Tennis Club
91	Italian POW Camp

92	Library
93	Jubilee Gardens
94	The Clifftop Hotel

PUBLIC HOUSES

101	The Anchor
102	The Bell
103	The Black Lion
104	The Dog and Partridge
105	The Feathers
106	The Fox
107	The Fox and Pheasant
108	The Goat and Compasses
109	The Hare and Hounds
110	The Horse and Groom
111	The Horse and Hounds
112	The King's Head
113	The Marquis of Granby
114	The Red Lion
115	The Six Bells

Numbers 95 to 100 have been left blank so that further locations can be added at a later point if necessary.

There is only one reference to Walmington found in the UK: a road named Walmington Fold in Woodside Park, London N12, on an estate built in the early part of this century.

The possible location of the town on the south coast is open to debate, but the small town of Littlestone-on-Sea, about 20 miles from Dover, with its proximity to Dymchurch must surely be where Jimmy Perry envisaged the home of Britain's most loved Home Guard platoon, Walmington-on-Sea's No 1 Platoon 'B' Company.

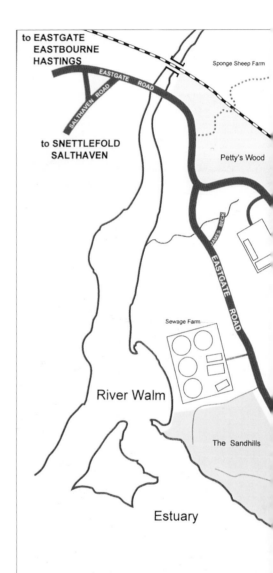

© Paul Carpenter 1996   redrawn & revised 01.03.99

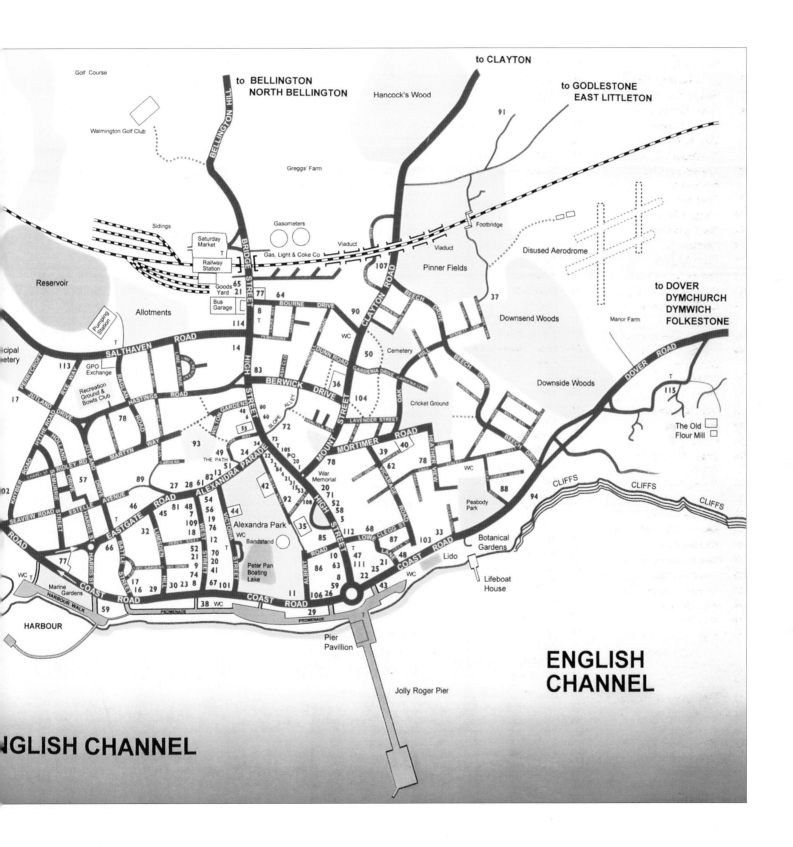

1963 and was promoted to effects designer three years later. Shows he worked on include *The Onedin Line*, *Softly, Softly*, *The Regiment* and *Doctor Who*.

WARDEN, MAY

Role: Mrs Dowding (S3, episode 4: 'The Bullet is Not for Firing') (TV)

May, who died in 1978, appeared in various radio and TV productions, such as the 1969 series *Ours is a Nice House* playing Gran, and the occasional film, including 1979's *It Shouldn't Happen to a Vet* playing Mrs Tompkins.

WATSON, JACK (1915–1999)

Born: London

Roles: Captain Ogilvy, Major Smith, Major Regan, a Sergeant, two Brigadiers, Sergeant Gregory, Captain Reed and Colonel Schultz (in eight radio episodes)

Jack started his career working alongside his father, comedian Nosmo King, before working extensively on the variety circuit for 15 years until he turned to straight acting after a part in *Z Cars*. He built up a long list of credits, especially on television. He played Bill Gregory in *Coronation Street*, a farmer in *All Creatures Great and Small*, Arthur Milne in *Love and Reason* and Vernon in *Common as Muck*. Other shows he appeared in include *The Troubleshooters*, *Upstairs Downstairs*, *The Onedin Line*, *Juliet Bravo* and *Minder*.

He made over 50 films, including *Time to Remember*, *Out of the Fog*, *The Night Caller* and *From Beyond the Grave*.

WATSON, KENNETH

Born: London

Role: RAF Officer (S3, episode 8: 'The Day the Balloon Went Up') (TV)

Kenneth, who began acting in his school's Shakespeare society, won a scholarship to RADA before beginning his career in rep theatre. After spending four years at Wolverhampton, he worked at Aberdeen and Edinburgh, where he was spotted and offered a part in *Emergency – Ward 10*, playing a guileful Scottish doctor who contracted polio.

Extensive TV work included a spell in *The Brothers*, *Take the High Road*, *Emmerdale Farm* and a running part in *Coronation Street*, playing Ralph Lancaster. During his career Kenneth played numerous uniformed characters, especially policemen in shows like *Dixon of Dock Green*, *Softly, Softly*, *Crown Court* and *Wycliffe*. He passed away in 1999.

WATTS, QUEENIE (1920–1980)

Roles: Mrs Keen (S2, episode 6: 'Under Fire'), Mrs Peters (S3, episode 1: 'The Armoured Might of Lance Corporal Jones') and Edna (S4, episode 8: 'The Two and a Half Feathers') (TV)

Queenie Watts spent a great deal of her career as a comedy actress on TV, but she still found time to make over a dozen films, including *Half a Six-pence*, back in 1967, *Up the Junction*, playing Mrs Hardy, *On the Buses*, *Alfie*, *Poor Cow*, *Sparrows Can't Sing*, *Steptoe and Son*, *Come Play with Me* as a café girl, and *Waterloo Sunset*. On the small screen her many credits include an appearance in *George and Mildred* and playing Lily Briggs in four series of LWT's sitcom, *Romany Jones* and the sequel, *Yus My Dear*.

WE KNOW OUR ONIONS

Recorded: Friday 15/6/73

Original transmission: Wednesday 21/11/73, 6.50–7.20pm

Original viewing figures: 11.6 million

(A strike prevented most of the studio scenes being recorded at the required time, so the majority of scenes originally scheduled for the studio had to be shot on location at Preston Barracks, Brighton)

Repeated: 16/5/74, 19/3/91, 27/11/93, 16/1/94 (Wales), 22/2/97, 23/2/97 (Wales), 20/6/00 (just 16 minutes transmitted on BBC1 due to power failure at TV Centre)

CAST

Arthur Lowe	Captain Mainwaring
John Le Mesurier	Sergeant Wilson
Clive Dunn	Lance Corporal Jones
John Laurie	Private Frazer
James Beck	Private Walker
Arnold Ridley	Private Godfrey
Ian Lavender	Private Pike
Fulton Mackay	Captain Ramsey
Bill Pertwee	Chief Warden Hodges
Edward Sinclair	Verger
Alex McAvoy	Sergeant
Pamela Manson	NAAFI Girl
Cy Town	Mess Steward

Platoon: Colin Bean, Desmond Cullum-Jones, George Hancock, Michael Moore, Leslie Noyes, Freddie White, Freddie Wiles, William Gossling, Evan Ross, Roger Bourne

Extras: (Soldiers) Compton Colson, Jack Blades, Clive Porter, Harry Wilkes, Mervin Evans, Sid Smith, Nelson Bishop, David Langley, John Kerridge, Tony Maxey

PRODUCTION TEAM

Script: Jimmy Perry and David Croft
Producer/Director: David Croft
Production Assistant: Gordon Pert
Film Cameraman: James Balfour
Film Sound Recordist: John Gatland
Film Editor: Bob Rymer
Studio Lighting: Howard King
Studio Sound: Michael McCarthy
Design: Paul Joel
Assistant Floor Manager: Peter Fitton
Vision Mixer: Dave Hanks
Costume Supervisor: Susan Wheal
Make-Up Supervisor: Ann Ailes
Visual Effects: Peter Day

The platoon is off on a weekend Home Guard efficiency test, taking with them the Smith gun, for which Godfrey's sister, Dolly, has made a floral cover. Mainwaring is keen to make an early start but when he opens the van door, hundreds of onions pour out. Walker had borrowed Jones' vehicle to transport onions to Hodges but he hadn't managed to deliver them yet.

Eventually they set off with the onions still in the back, and while they await their instructor at the camp, Mainwaring tells his men that if they pass the test with flying colours they'll be rated a 12-star platoon.

It's not long before Captain Ramsey and his sergeant, who are running the tests, arrive and the day begins. The first test involves Jones, Wilson and Mainwaring being forced to answer questions from Ramsay who plays a Gestapo officer. Next, Mainwaring is given the difficult choice of deciding who he'd throw out of a balloon in an emergency and, after excluding himself from the reckoning because he's much too valuable, he opts for poor old Godfrey. The following exercise involves using basic equipment to climb an electrified fence; they have 30 minutes but a dearth of ideas sees Captain Ramsay giving up on them at midnight!

Next morning the platoon is disappointed to find they've only been awarded one out of eight stars so far. The final test involves firing three dummy bombs at Ramsay's advancing troop of soldiers. As it's a soft bore gun, Mainwaring decides to use the onions as ammunition. He buys a pound's worth from Hodges, who's arrived to collect his produce, and the onions turn out to be lethal. At the close of play, Mainwaring's platoon head home with their heads held high because they're a 12-star unit.

WEST, HILARY

David Croft's assistant on 14 episodes: S8; S9; 'My Brother and I' and 'The Love Of Three Oranges'

Hilary began her BBC career in the finance department back in 1968, before moving into TV production as a secretary. After working as a production assistant on all genres of programme, she eventually transferred to light entertainment, initially working with Harold Snoad on *Seven of One* in 1973. Hilary now works as a freelance vision mixer, and for some time has worked on *EastEnders*.

WEST, MR

Played by Blake Butler and Robert Dorning (TV); Fraser Kerr and John Barron (radio)

Mr West only appeared in two scenes as the pompous, bespectacled senior bank official in 'A Wilson (Manager)?'. Based at Swallow Bank's head office, he breaks the news to Mainwaring that Wilson has been promoted to manager of the Eastgate branch. West also dedicates time to showing Wilson the ropes – something of a 'privilege', remarks Mainwaring, sarcastically. The next time we hear from Mr West is a telephone call he makes to Mainwaring, informing him that Wilson will be returning to Walmington after the Eastgate branch is demolished in an air raid, resulting in existing business being transferred to Hastings.

Note: Another Mr West, a bank inspector from Head Office, appeared in the earlier episode 'Something Nasty in the Vault'. It's unclear whether these characters were the same person. In 'Something Nasty …', Mr West, played by Robert Dorning, has a meeting with Mainwaring and moans because the monthly report is becoming irregular. From the original script, it would appear they are the same character because Robert Dorning was originally pencilled in for playing the character in 'A Wilson (Manager)?'

WEST, MRS
Not seen in the series, Mrs West is referred to by the Vicar in 'Getting the Bird'. She was the organist at St Aldhelm's Church in Walmington, but since her death the congregation has sung unaccompanied.

WEST PROMENADE
An area of Walmington mentioned in 'The Face on the Poster', where for years Sidney Blewitt ran a photographic concession, selling snaps to tourists.

WHEAL, SUSAN
Costume designer (TV): series 5, 6 and 7

WHELDON WILLIAMS, DAVID
Roles: Member of the Home Front Company, Izzy Bonn and Hermann Goering (stage show)
David made his London stage debut back in 1959, and has gone on to work in over 30 West End musicals. He has also recorded albums and appeared as the photographer in *Half a Sixpence*, and in *Funny Girl* and *Cabaret*.

WHEN DID YOU LAST SEE YOUR MONEY?
Recorded: Friday 10/11/72

Original transmission: Friday 1/12/72, 8.30–9.00pm

Original viewing figures: 16 million

Repeated: 25/8/73, 14/11/89, 16/8/90 (N Ireland), 18/9/93, 31/1/97

CAST
Arthur Lowe . . . . .Captain Mainwaring
John Le Mesurier . . . . .Sergeant Wilson
Clive Dunn . . . . .Lance Corporal Jones
John Laurie . . . . .Private Frazer
James Beck . . . . .Private Walker
Arnold Ridley . . . . .Private Godfrey
Ian Lavender . . . . .Private Pike
Bill Pertwee . . . . .ARP Warden
Frank Williams . . . . .Vicar
Edward Sinclair . . . . .Verger
Harold Bennett . . . . .Mr Blewitt
Tony Hughes . . . . .Mr Billings

Platoon: Colin Bean, Michael Moore, Freddie White, George Hancock, Hugh Cecil, Desmond Cullum-Jones, Freddie Wiles, Evan Ross, Leslie Noyes, Hugh Hastings
Extra: Miss Binns
Customer in Bank: Wendy Johnson

PRODUCTION TEAM
Script: Jimmy Perry and David Croft
Producer/Director: David Croft
Production Assistant: Gordon Pert
Studio Lighting: Howard King
Studio Sound: John Delany
Design: Paul Joel
Assistant Floor Manager: Peter Fitton
Vision Mixer: Dave Hanks
Costume Supervisor: Susan Wheal
Make-Up Supervisor: Anna Chesterman

The bank is open as usual, although it's still badly damaged as a result of the recent bomb. Working conditions aren't much fun: with rain dripping through the roof, Mainwaring has to work with an umbrella up. Jones calls in to deposit his takings and says he's got £500 to pay in, which the local shopkeepers have collected for the new servicemen's canteen in Walmington. He's wrapped it up like half a pound of sausages and when he hands it over to Pike, it turns out to be just that. Jones faints with shock.

On parade that evening Jones is in a right state because he still hasn't found the money. Frazer thinks he's gone senile and is incapable of carrying on as corporal. While sections two and three are on patrol, the rest of the men try helping Jones to remember where he put the money. He recalls everything that happened since Mr Billings came round with the cash. By the middle of the night everyone is still at the church hall,

but Jones still can't remember; he's so desperate he accepts Frazer's suggestion, resorts to hypnosis and it's discovered that a chicken taken to Mr Blewitt may have the money stuffed inside it.

At 2.30am everyone goes round to Mr Blewitt's house and asks to examine the chicken delivered for his golden wedding anniversary. When the old man enquires whether they've got a search warrant, Mainwaring demands in the name of the King to examine the chicken.

After ripping the bird apart, the money isn't found, so it looks like Jones will have to spend his life savings. At the bank, he's just about to withdraw the money when Mr Billings arrives and says the pack of sausages he bought from Jones the other day contained an unexpected surprise: £500!

WHEN YOU'VE GOT TO GO
Recorded: Friday 6/6/75

Original transmission: Friday 12/9/75, 8.00–8.30pm

Original viewing figures: 12.6 million

Repeated: 1/5/76, 28/5/91, 10/12/94, 22/12/94 (Wales), 19/4/97

CAST
Arthur Lowe . . . . .Captain Mainwaring
John Le Mesurier . . . . .Sergeant Wilson
Clive Dunn . . . . .Lance Corporal Jones
John Laurie . . . . .Private Frazer
Arnold Ridley . . . . .Private Godfrey
Ian Lavender . . . . .Private Pike
Bill Pertwee . . . . .Chief Warden Hodges
Frank Williams . . . . .Vicar
Edward Sinclair . . . . .Verger
Janet Davies . . . . .Mrs Pike
Eric Longworth . . . . .Town Clerk
Freddie Earlle . . . . .Italian Sergeant

'When You've Got to Go'

Tim Barrett . . . . .Doctor
Colin Bean . . . . .Private Sponge
Frankie Holmes . . . . .Fish fryer
Platoon: George Hancock, Michael Moore, Desmond
Cullum-Jones, Freddie White, Evan Ross, Leslie Noyes,
Roger Bourne, Freddie Wiles, Hugh Cecil

PRODUCTION TEAM
Script: Jimmy Perry and David Croft
Producer/Director: David Croft
Production Assistant: Jo Austin
Studio Lighting: Howard King
Studio Sound: Alan Machin
Design: Robert Berk
Assistant Floor Manager: Anne Ogden
Vision Mixer: Angela Beveridge
Costume Designer: Mary Husband
Make-Up Artist: Sylvia Thornton

Frank's got his call up papers, but with his bad chest, Mrs Pike thinks it's a waste of time, especially as he's got to miss a whole day of work for a silly medical. But she's in hysterics when he returns home and proclaims he's been passed A1. She doesn't want her son joining up, but Frank's excited at the prospect of joining the RAF.

To mark the occasion of Pike's departure from the platoon, Frazer suggests starting a collection – with the caveat of the maximum contribution being six pence. Godfrey suggests buying a penknife, but Wilson's suggestion of a celebratory fish and chip supper is preferred.

Meanwhile, the church hall is the venue for a blood donoring session for the next two days. The town clerk wants a big turnout and asks Mainwaring whether the platoon can help. With 20 people in the platoon he confidently promises 50 pints, but when he hears the wardens are donating the same, Mainwaring rather foolishly suggests 100 pints. With nine men ineligible for various reasons however, Mainwaring starts worrying. Hopes of beating the wardens look bleak, and when Wilson pulls out due to anaemia it seems as if the challenge is lost. Just when he's given up hope, Jones turns up with 80 Italian prisoners from the nearby POW Camp, and 17 nuns to save his captain's blushes.

Later at the fish and chip supper, with raspberryade to wash down the soggy chips, Pikey tells everyone the RAF won't have him because he has been identified as having an extremely rare blood group and is therefore too high a risk. He hadn't told anyone because he didn't want to miss his farewell supper.

WHITAKER, COLIN
Freelance animator involved in creating the opening credits
After school Colin joined a display studio in Leeds, while studying part-time at art school. He became interested in animation and headed south to a job at Howarth and Bachelor Films in Stroud, Gloucestershire.

Having married and started a family, Colin moved to an animation company in Boreham Wood, before turning freelance in 1964. His skills were soon in demand, and he worked regularly for the BBC, producing the animation for opening titles and programme inserts, starting off with *The Black and White Minstrel Show*. Other programmes for which he filmed the opening titles include *Harry Worth*.

Colin has now retired from the profession and concentrates on restoring and selling antiques, for a while owning two shops in London.

WHITAKER, PETER (1921–)
Born: London
Role: Member of the platoon's back row in five episodes (S1, episodes 1–5) (TV)
Peter left school at 16 and became a salesman at Simpson's department store in London, a job he kept until war broke out. As a member of the territorial army, he was called up and served until demob in 1946. He then gained a grant and secured a place at London's College of Music, graduating four years later. As a trained singer,

he found work in musicals, and sang at the Palladium, as well as touring as one of the George Mitchell Singers. In addition to stage work, he was busy filming commercials.

In the late 1950s he started doing walk-on work for TV, appearing in, among other shows, an episode of *Upstairs, Downstairs*. Peter continued working until suffering a heart attack, after which he decided to retire from the profession and move to Hove, where he currently resides.

WHITE, FREDDIE
Role: Member of the platoon's back row in 51 episodes (S3, episodes 8, 9, 11, 12; S4, episodes 1–3, 6, 9–13; 'Battle of the Giants'; S5, episodes 1–9, 11, 12, 13; S6, episodes 1–5 & 7; S7; S8, episodes 1–2, 4–6; 'My Brother and I'; 'The Love of Three Oranges'; S9) (TV); (Film)

Freddie was a farmer before the Second World War – during which he served as an officer in the army – and became involved in the hotel business afterwards. When a heart attack forced his retirement from the hotel trade, he worked for the local authorities transporting people back and forth from hospital, before developing his thespian interests and appearing on TV as a walk-on.

WHITEHALL, JOHN
Role: Member of the Choir ('The Bullet is Not for Firing') (radio)

WIG MAKER, THE
Played by Michael Burlington (radio)
When Mainwaring orders a toupee in the radio episode 'Keep Young and Beautiful', he speaks to the wig maker on the phone. The character isn't used in the TV version.

WILDE, MARJORIE
Role: Lady Magistrate (S5, episode 11: 'A Brush with the Law') (TV)
Marjorie played the magistrate who sat alongside Captain Square in the courtroom when Mainwaring was charged with showing a light during the blackout. She died in 1988.

WILES, FREDDIE (1905–1983)
Born: London
Role: Member of the platoon's back row in 57 episodes (S3, episodes 1–4, 6–9, 11, 12; S4, episodes 1–3, 5, 6, 9–13; S5; S6, episodes 1–5 & 7; S7, episodes 3–6; S8, episodes 1–2, 4–6; 'My Brother and I'; 'The Love of Three Oranges'; S9) (TV); (Film)
Freddie worked in a confectionery factory before becoming a sales rep for an asphalt company either side of the war. He'd always fancied acting, so upon retiring from industry he registered with an agency and started appearing as an extra on TV. Freddie joined *Dad's Army* when a fellow platoon member left through illness. In one episode he doubled up as Clive Dunn and drove Jones' van. His other TV credits included *The Benny Hill Show* and *Are You Being Served?*, but his last job was in a chocolate cake commercial in Rome. He died at the age of 78.

WILKINSON, GENERAL
(See 'Peppery Old Gent, The'.)

WILLIAM THE FOURTH, THE
Wilson and Pike visit this Walmington pub while searching for Frazer, who misses a parade in 'The Miser's Hoard'.

WILLIAMS, FRANK (1931–)
Born: London
Role: Reverend Timothy Farthing (39 TV episodes and *Christmas Night with the Stars* inserts, the film, the stage show and 14 radio episodes)

Frank's first taste of acting was at a North London grammar school, where he completed his education. But he had always been interested in theatrics, and as a small boy used to force all his friends into taking part in concerts and plays he'd written.

Upon leaving school, he sought to pursue his dream of becoming an actor. Frank had wanted to attend a children's drama school but his father insisted that he complete his education first. Once Frank had left school with his Higher School Certificate, still set on becoming an actor, his father gave him his support.

In 1951 Frank joined London's Gateway Theatre as a student ASM, which afforded him the chance to take on small roles in various productions, including Shakespeare, and a debut playing two parts in *The Insect Play*.

His TV break was in 1952's *The Call Up*, a dramatised documentary concerning conscripts going through national service training, followed three years later by *Those Who Dare*, about the building of the first open Borstal, with Frank playing the unlikely role of a Borstal boy. His first major part on TV was during the same year in the play *The Queen Came By*, with Thora Hird.

Frank was first seen on the big screen in the 1956 British Lion production, *The Extra Day*, and he has gone on to make over 30 films. But it's the TV series, *The Army Game*, which made his face familiar to the public. After playing several small parts, including a psychiatrist interviewing Bernard Bresslaw, he became a regular as Captain Pocket in some 70 episodes. His success in the role led to several TV plays for one of BBC's best known directors, Rudolph Cartier, including a production of *Anna Karenina* in 1961, with Sean Connery and Claire Bloom.

In 1957, Frank worked at The Palace Theatre, Watford, which was run by Jimmy and Gilda Perry at the time. He had two of his own plays produced there and became chairman of the Patrons' Club, forming a strong friendship with Jimmy that was to reap benefits a decade later with the arrival of *Dad's Army*, by which time he'd appeared in two episodes of *Hugh and I* for David Croft.

When he wasn't appearing in *Dad's Army*, Frank continued making the occasional film and appearing on stage, including three plays at The English Theatre, Vienna, where he played straight roles. Although he hasn't been seen much on TV since playing Timothy Farthing, he has appeared in a few programmes, like *Hi-De-Hi!*, *Bergerac* and *You Rang, M'Lord?* playing the Bishop.

His film career, meanwhile, includes several pictures with Norman Wisdom, such as *The Square Peg* and *A Stitch in Time*.

Often cast in comedy roles, Frank did complete a long run in *A Midsummer Night's Dream*, directed by Jonathan Miller, a couple of years ago. He's also a regular in panto, and a playwright. Over the past few years, there have been successful productions of four of his thrillers.

TV credits include: *The Grove Family, The Appleyards, The Golden Entry, Destination Downing Street, Motive for Murder, Skipper's Ticket, Emergency – Ward 10, The Common Room, The Assassin, The Frog, Tommy Cooper Show, Our House, Citizen James, Maigret, Compact, No Hiding Place, Here's Harry, Z Cars, The Handyman, Badger's Bend, The Worker, The Survivors, Adam Adamant Lives!, Love Story, Harry Worth, The Further Adventures of Lucky Jim, All Gas and Gaiters, Journey into the Unknown, The Troubleshooters, The Gnomes of Dulwich, The Worker, The Dick Emery Show, Monty Python's Flying Circus, The Morecambe and Wise Show, The Rock Follies, The Fosters, The Two Ronnies, First Among Equals, House of Cards*.

Theatre credits include: *His Excellency, The Substitute, How the Other Half Loves, Ghosts, The Editor Regrets, Stage Struck, Murder By Appointment*.

Film credits include: *Shield of Faith, The One That Got Away, Jazzboat, Inn For Trouble, The Bulldog Breed, The Dock Brief, Hide and Seek, Champagne Flight, The Yellow Rolls Royce, The Deadly Affair, Countdown to Danger, Robbery, The Headline Hunters, Smokey Joe's Revenge, The Ruttles, The Revenge of the Pink Panther, The Human Factor, The Island of Gloom*.

Radio credits include: *The Clitheroe Kid, Radio Tarbuck, All Gas and Gaiters, Pause for Thought, Christian Focus, The Government Inspector*.

WILLIAMS, PETER (1915–)
Born: New Orleans, USA
Role: Colonel ('A Question of Reference')
(radio)

Peter was just a few months old when his family moved to England. After completing his education he spent two years teaching in a private school in Cheshire, before joining RADA at 22. Upon graduating he worked in many reps, including Sunderland, Lowestoft and Northampton, before spending five years in the army during the Second World War.

He was demobbed as a Major and returned to the theatre, where he has spent much of his career, including the 1951 season at Stratford and many West End productions.

His screen career began in the 1950s and early films include *The Straw Man, The Ladykillers, Footsteps in the Fog, Dunkirk, Private's Progress, The Man Who Never Was, The Man Who Knew Too Much, The Bridge on the River Kwai, Two a Penny* and the lead in *Two-Letter Alibi*. His many television appearances, meanwhile, include two years as a detective in *Shadow Squad*, and *Barnaby Rudge, Blake's 7* and *Warship*.

Peter retired from the acting profession in the early 1980s and is enjoying his retirement in Bexhill-on-Sea.

WILLIAMS, SERGEANT
Williams takes the Walmington Home Guard for grenade practice at the School of Explosives in the TV episode 'Fallen Idol', but is not actually seen on screen.

WILLIAMSON, ALISTER (1919–1999)
Born: Australia
Role: Bert (S9, episode 1: 'Wake-Up Walmington')
(TV)

Alister came to England in his thirties. He'd already established himself as an opera singer before leaving Australia, but felt he needed to move to further his career. Upon his arrival he worked as a singer, making his first appearance in panto at Oxford. He became involved in musical comedies and also stage production, before television work started to come his way, including a spell in *Coronation Street* as a night-club owner. Other TV work included *Upstairs Downstairs, The Fenn Street Gang, Market in Honey Lane, George and Mildred, The Avengers* and *A Woman of Substance*, one of his last shows. He also made the occasional film, such as *Crooks in Cloisters* in 1963. Alister died of pneumonia.

WILSON, SERGEANT ARTHUR
Played by John Le Mesurier (all mediums)
Arthur Wilson fought overseas during the First World War as a sergeant, serving at places like Mons, Passchendale and Gallipoli. After training at Catterick, he was later promoted to officer.

In many ways, Wilson, who was frequently likened to Jack Buchanan, was stagnating in Walmington. To further his life and career, he needed to escape the constraints imposed by Mainwaring, who permanently kept Wilson in his shadow at the bank and the Home Guard. Just when it looked as if he'd finally broken free thanks to his promotion to manager at the Eastgate branch of Swallow Bank, a German bomb flattened the building. With no bank to manage, Wilson found himself back at Walmington as chief clerk, bugging his superior once again with his languid, self-effacing style.

What irked Wilson nearly as much as losing the chance to manage his own branch was finding out that if it hadn't been for Mainwaring, he would have been promoted years ago. Eventually Wilson steps up the management ladder by becoming manager at Frambourne-on-Sea, along the coast from Walmington.

Although his torpid, lackadaisical approach to life drives Mainwaring to despair, Wilson is far more capable than he's allowed to demonstrate. A mild-mannered man, his father worked in the City and the family enjoyed all the trappings associated with affluence, including employing a nanny to help with the raising of Arthur when he was a boy.

Throughout the series, Wilson's relationship with Mavis Pike – whom he's known for years – is examined; although we never learn if Frank is Wilson's offspring, we do discover he fathered a beautiful daughter, who serves in the Wrens, and was married for a time. Now his girl has grown up, he doesn't see much of her, but is proud to know that he was able to send her to a decent school.

In his leisure time, Wilson enjoys being captain of the town's cricket team, or playing a round of golf at the local club, which he was invited to join, much to Mainwaring's disgust, when he inherited the title 'The Honourable'. But he's not a particularly practical man when it comes to household duties, with Mrs Pike admitting that he can't even use a tin-opener!

Serretta, who played Wilson's daughter in the sitcom, made her TV debut in *A Class By Himself* playing a similar role. Other than a break to bring up her family, she has continued acting and has been seen in many TV shows, including *The Bill*, *Jeeves and Wooster*, a regular role as Stella Jordan in *London Bridge*, *The Upper Hand* as Diana, Susan Simms in *Dempsey and Makepeace*, *Space 1999*, *Warship* and *Shades of Green*.

On stage Serretta, who's also a qualified aerobics teacher, has appeared in national tours of *Death of a Salesman*, *House of Mirth*, *I'm Dreaming the Hardest*, in which she played Marilyn Monroe, *The Night They Raided Minsky's*, *Boeing Boeing* and *Oh, What a Lovely War!*. Other stage performances include *On Golden Pond* at

the London suburb of Shoreditch where her father was a bus conductor and her mother a dressmaker. As soon as she appeared in a dance school production as a girl, she knew she wanted to act. After studying at the Ada Foster acting school she was given her big break by producer Joan Littlewood in the production, *Fings Ain't What They Used To Be*, before appearing in Littlewood's version of *Oh, What a Lovely War!*, touring America.

Her film debut was as a schoolgirl in 1954's comedy, *The Belles of St Trinians*, but it was appearing in 1963's *Sparrows Can't Sing*, that she was spotted by Peter Rogers and recruited for the *Carry On* series. Her TV career has included appearances in *The Rag Trade* and *Up Pompeii!*.

WINGS FOR VICTORY

In 'Knights of Madness', the town clerk mentions that the climax of Walmington's 'Wings for Victory' week will include a performance by the Sea Scouts' Drum and Bugle Band, a keep-fit display by the ladies' netball team, a display of morris dancing and a grand finale involving the Home Guard and the wardens.

'Wings for Victory' was one of the many National Savings campaigns introduced by the government during the Second World War. Launched in March 1943, it was hoped the scheme would help raise £150 million for building bombers, with people being encouraged to purchase savings stamps.

WINOGRODZKI, CAPTAIN
Played by Carl Jaffé (TV and radio)

Captain Winogrodzki is from the Polish Free Forces, attached to GHQ. In 'The Enemy Within the Gates' he enters the church hall and interrupts Mainwaring's parade asking to see their weapons, before being placed under arrest because Wilson is suspicious of his foreign accent. Eventually it's discovered that he's genuine and he tells the platoon that GHQ is concerned that members of the Home Guard could shoot British pilots by mistake, if they see a lone pilot bailing out of a plane. Therefore, a £10 bounty is offered for every German pilot captured alive.

WILSON, SERRETTA
Born: Virginia, USA

Role: Wren (S5, episode 4: 'Getting the Bird') (TV)

Serretta was living in Africa before moving to England in the mid-1960s to study drama in London. Upon finishing her three-year course she went on to train as a dancer. After earning her Equity card she appeared in the occasional film, including the horror movies *Psychomania* playing a victim, *Tower of Evil* as Mae and *Sweeney 2*, as well as numerous theatre and TV productions.

Chester and a spell in Hong Kong playing Ella in *The Bed Before Yesterday*.

She's also appeared in commercials, including My Little Pony, Kwik Fit, Quick Brew and British Telecom, and done a great many voice-overs.

WINDSOR, BARBARA (1937–)
Born: London

Role: Laura La Plaz (S1, episode 6: 'Shooting Pains') (TV)

Star of nine *Carry On* films, and also a regular in *EastEnders* as Peggy Butcher, Barbara grew up in

WINTERGREEN, MR
Played by Jeffrey Gardiner (TV); Michael Knowles (radio)

In 'A Brush With the Law', Mr Wintergreen is the prosecuting barrister when Mainwaring finds himself in court after a light is found burning at the church hall.

WINTERS, COLONEL
Played by Fraser Kerr (radio)

In the radio episode 'The Deadly Attachment', Colonel Winters replaces the part played by Robert Raglan (Colonel Pritchard) in the TV version. He informs Mainwaring about the German sailors they'll have to guard.

WIPER, PRIVATE

Although he never appeared in the sitcom, Private Wiper, who also owns a shop in Walmington, is a member of the platoon. His name is mentioned by Wilson while talking to Mainwaring and Major Regan in 'The Showing Up of Corporal Jones'.

WIRELESS OPERATOR, THE

Played by John Clegg (TV)

The radio operator tries to control the wheel in 'Round and Round Went the Great Big Wheel' but fails dismally.

WITHERS, MILDRED

A telephone operator who works at the Walmington-on-Sea exchange, Mildred is mentioned in the radio episode, 'Put That Light Out!'. She is a friend of Sergeant Wilson, and attended the same pottery class as him.

WITT, MRS

Played by Gladys Dawson (TV)

Mrs Witt is a little old lady who has a flat in the same building as the suspected spy, Mr Murphy, and Mrs Keen in 'Under Fire'. A light is seen flashing from the building during the blackout.

WITTERSHAM PLATOON

(Film only)

This Home Guard platoon attend the weekend camp and are assigned the task of attacking the enemy (a detachment of Royal Marines) on the right flank.

WOMAN

Played by June Petersen (TV)

This character lives opposite Mr Murphy in Walmington's Mortimer Street, and when Mainwaring investigates whether Murphy is a spy in 'Under Fire', she comes across to tell Mainwaring that she thinks he's a Nazi because he was signalling the previous evening.

WOMEN'S VOLUNTARY SERVICE (WVS)

Founded in 1938, WVS members worked for local authorities or the government on national projects, as well as providing voluntary welfare services. During the war years, members were often seen helping in centres for the homeless, as well as running tea stalls and helping the emergency services tick over. They also maintained the census of residents, so vital to air raid wardens, distributed clothing and carried out other such essential duties.

In 'Sgt Wilson's Little Secret', it's the WVS that writes to Mrs Pike asking if she'll provide a home for an evacuee. In 'The Honourable Man', the WVS is represented by Mrs Fox at the General Purposes Meeting to decide who should co-ordinate the visit of the Russian worker.

WOOD, LIEUTENANT

Played by Robin Parkinson (TV)

Wood dresses up as a gorilla in 'Gorilla Warfare', and is suspected by Mainwaring of being a counter agent.

WOODBURN, ERIC

Role: George Jones, the Museum Caretaker (S1, episode 2: 'Museum Piece') (TV and radio)

Eric was a Scottish character actor who was associated with the Windmill Theatre for some years. He appeared on stage, television and films, making over 30 pictures, including 1936's *Digging for Gold*, *Interrupted Rehearsal*, *You're Only Young Twice*, *The Kidnappers*, *The Maggie*, *Geordie*, *Naked Fury*, *The Bridal Path*, *The Dock Brief* and *The Amorous Prawn*. He died in 1982.

WOODHOUSE, ALAN

Born: Leicester

Role: Member of the Home Front Company (stage show)

Alan trained for five years at the Guildhall School and went on to work extensively for the Royal Opera at Covent Garden. He made his first commercial stage appearance in *Dad's Army*.

WOODS, PRIVATE

A platoon member, Woods, along with Private Meadows, was ordered by Mainwaring to prevent anyone entering the church hall while the rest of the men practised their dance for the forthcoming procession to help raise money for the Spitfire fund in 'The Godiva Affair'.

WREN, THE

Played by Serretta Wilson (TV); Diana Bishop (radio)

The mysterious Wren who arrives in Walmington in 'Getting the Bird' and is spotted cuddling up to Arthur Wilson turns out to be his daughter, whom he sees infrequently since the break-up of his marriage.

WYLDECK, MARTIN (1914–1988)

Born: Birmingham

Role: Major Regan (S1, episodes 5: 'The Showing Up of Corporal Jones' and 6: 'Shooting Pains') (TV)

Martin's father was a Reuters correspondent and the family moved to Innsbruck shortly after he was born. Educated in Austria until the age of 11, Martin returned to England after his father's death to finish his education.

He started training as an electrician but it wasn't long before he'd decided he wanted to go on the stage, joining Colchester Rep until war broke out. He served in Burma with the army for four years before returning to Colchester.

He was gradually offered work on TV, had his own series with Eleanor Summerfield, *My Wife's Sister*, and appeared in many other shows including *Suez 1956*. A versatile actor, Martin appeared in over 30 films from 1948 including *Street Corner*, *The Frightened City* (playing a security officer), *Carry On Sergeant* (playing Mr Sage, Bob Monkhouse's father) and *Tiffany Jones*.

Martin died at the age of 74, after he'd just been offered a film role. His son is a director and his daughter an actress.

YATES, MR

Not seen in the series, Mr Yates is referred to in 'All is Safely Gathered In'. He owns Grove Farm, which is near Mrs Prentice's property, and had promised to help thresh her wheat, but when he started falling behind with his own work, he had to withdraw his offer.

YEATMAN, ANTHEA

Played by Olive Mercer (TV)

The fierce Mrs Yeatman, who's married to Maurice, certainly wears the trousers in the Yeatman household. If she ever managed a smile, they would put the flags out in Walmington because it would be classed a major event in the town's history. Inimical, stern, and overbearing, Anthea – who runs the local netball team – can't be an easy woman to live with, which is why the Verger, to quote Frazer, walks around with a face like a sour prune.

Note: Also referred to as Tracey and Beryl during the life of the series, Anthea Yeatman was called Mrs Harman in the early scripts, but this was changed before her episodes were even recorded.

YEATMAN, MAURICE

Played by Edward Sinclair (TV and radio)

The snitching Verger of St Aldhelm's, who began life as a caretaker, is always running to the Vicar or Hodges spreading rumours or telling tales in order to keep in their good books. He's not to be trusted, which is why Jones often asks why he takes the church collection home to count, or to The Red Lion, where Mr Yeatman claims the landlord helps him.

The Verger, a twin and skipper of the Sea Scouts, is one of those unfortunate characters in *Dad's Army* who must have suffered an identity complex because his christian name altered from time to time. This was because character profiles weren't recorded in the sort of detail that television companies keep today. Mr Yeatman found himself being announced as Henry, as opposed to Maurice, in 'War Dance'.

Note: In early scripts for the programme the Verger was called Mr Harman, but his name changed before any scenes were recorded.

YELDAN, MR

An ARP warden who patrols the area around Walmington's Kyber Road, Mr Yeldan never appears but is mentioned in 'Uninvited Guests'.

YOKEL, THE

Played by Sam Kydd (TV)

The yokel was drinking outside The Six Bells in 'Wake-Up Walmington' when Mainwaring and some of his men arrived dressed as fifth columnists. He becomes suspicious, runs into the pub and calls the police at Dymchurch, although this isn't actually seen during the episode.

YOUNG CHARLIE

Not seen in the sitcom, Young Charlie occasionally works for Walker doing odd jobs. He is mentioned by Joe in the Marigold Tea Rooms during the episode, 'Time On My Hands'.

SELECTED SCRIPTS

Reproducing the entire scripts of the sitcom would obviously be a separate project, but this section of the book focuses on a collection of scripts selected for particular reasons.

The 'Cut Scenes' will be of interest to fans of *Dad's Army* because they are the scenes and part-scenes that were cut before recording. Unseen by the viewing public, everything that suffered under the editor's knife is included, and makes interesting reading.

The 'American Version' is another piece of *Dad's Army* history which has not been seen by any fan. When Perry and Croft were discussing the possibility of their sitcom travelling across the pond, they wrote this script for any interested parties. As it turned out, a production company acquired the rights to create a US version of the show but commissioned another writer to produce a different script, *The Rear Guard*, which is also reproduced here.

When Jimmy Beck became ill, the cast was on the verge of losing one of its most popular members. In order to keep the show rolling, Jimmy Perry and David Croft had to rewrite the script for the episode 'The Recruit', ensuring any lines for Private Walker were re-allocated. Here you can read the original script for the episode, including all the lines intended for Jimmy Beck.

Finally, one aspect of *Dad's Army* often forgotten, particularly by TV schedulers who have little use for anything lasting less than 30 minutes, is the four sketches originally transmitted as part of the *Christmas Night with the Stars*, that British institution which brought entertainment to millions of viewers on Christmas night not too many years ago. For those people who haven't seen the sketches they should make interesting reading.

CUT SCENES

Every television programme is given pre-scribed timings and must not overrun. If a script is too long when it comes to the actual recording, the director must decide where cuts can be made to bring it within the required duration. Writing a script that runs exactly to time is nigh impossible, and it's only when it's brought into the studio to be rehearsed that the writer/s and the director know whether extra minutes of screen time need to be writ-ten, or whether scenes have to be cut.

Occasionally scripts are altered for other reasons than timing: when the words are brought to life in the studio, or out on location, it's a chance for the director to evaluate how the script will transfer to the screen. A particu-lar scene might not work, or may need extend-ing to grasp that extra ounce of humour.

In this section of the book, I have studied every script from the television series, together with the final draft of the movie script, to iden-tify where scenes in the scripts have been deleted or altered and, therefore, not transmit-ted. Odd words or phrases were often altered by the actors, and there were too many exam-ples to list in the book. Instead, I have concen-trated on the more significant differences between the script and the final recording. Although there are many interesting examples that follow, when considering 80 television episodes were recorded, it's remarkable just how little was altered: a reflection of the quality of the writing.

SERIES 1, EPISODE 1
THE MAN AND THE HOUR

The first difference, although minor, seen between the original script and the final recording is when Mainwaring and Wilson are in the office at the bank, discussing Mrs Hoskins calling her sister from the phone box nearby. In the recording, Wilson says she's phoning her sister in Thetford, while the script says Colchester.

A whole scene was cut from this episode because it was running approximately seven minutes over the required time. Perry and Croft intended using the fire brigade as another essential service needing to use the church hall, causing more aggravation and pain for Mainwaring. However, losing the scene put paid to that and the firemen were never seen again, although Gordon Peters reappeared in several other roles.

The edited scene would have appeared just after Mainwaring had inspected the men, with Bracewell asking whether they'll be long because he's taking his wife out for her birthday. A large fireman entered the hall at this point.

FIREMAN You gonna be long?

MAINWARING Why?

FIREMAN I've got a fire-fighting demonstration 'ere in ten minutes.

MAINWARING I'm trying to hold a parade.

FIREMAN Don't worry about me, just carry on as if I wasn't 'ere. I'll just lay out my hoses and ladders.

MAINWARING (**Trying to carry on.**) Now, I asked you all to bring your gas masks and I'm pleased to see that none of you have forgotten. Now as you know, Jerry hasn't used gas yet, but it's well on the cards that he may do so.

(**Fireman is unrolling a length of hose – it is about three feet in the air – the other person holding it is out of shot.**)

FIREMAN Excuse me, please.

(**Wilson and Mainwaring step over the hose, fireman addresses the front rank.**)

Excuse me, gentlemen.

(**They all step over the hose except Jones, the lance corporal who is a bit short. The others help him.**)

MAINWARING Make no mistake about it, gentlemen, nothing will come between us and our resolve to fight the…

(**The fireman backs by with a ladder.**)

FIREMAN Excuse me. (**Mainwaring and Wilson dodge under it.**) Excuse me, gents. (**The ranks step over it.**) We'll just go and get the rest of the stuff. (**He goes.**)

MAINWARING Don't leave it there – bring it back over the top.

(**The front rank lift the ladder above their heads, Frazer is next to Jones; as he lifts the ladder up, Jones, who is holding it, goes up in the air.**)

MAINWARING Let him down.

(**They drop the ladder. Jones has his arms above his head. The ladder slips down, he is caught between the rungs.**)

MAINWARING Get it up.

(**They raise it in the air. Jones is now pedalling in mid air.**)

MAINWARING Wilson! Wilson! Get underneath him.

(**Wilson does so. Jones now has his leg around Wilson's shoulders. The phone bell starts to ring. The fireman comes backing into the picture with another ladder.**)

MAINWARING How many more ladders are you going to bring in?

FIREMAN Don't you worry about us, sir – just you carry on. (**To Wilson, who still has Jones on his shoulders.**) Hold this will you?

(**He gives him the end of his ladder. The phone bell is still ringing. The picture is now thus: the first ladder is being held over their heads by the front rank and Jones is jammed in between the rungs. Wilson is holding the second ladder about waist height, the other end is being held by someone out of picture. Mainwaring is trapped behind the second ladder. The fireman enters with a third ladder. The phone is still ringing.**)

FIREMAN (**To Mainwaring**) Nice of you to give us a hand but you needn't have bothered, we can manage.

MAINWARING (**Livid**) That's alright – don't mention it.

FIREMAN By the way, aren't you going to answer your phone?

(**Mainwaring starts to fight his way through the ladders to the office.**)

INTERIOR OF OFFICE

(**Mainwaring staggers through the door, he picks up the phone from the desk; through the open door all is confusion and ladders. In the background can be heard shouts of: 'Get it up', 'Down a bit', 'Who do you think you're shoving?', etc.**)

MAINWARING Mainwaring here.

VOICE Oh, it's the G2HQ Eastern Command, how are things going?

MAINWARING Fine, sir. (**There are shouts in the background.**)

VOICE Started training already, I hear. By jove! Those men sound keen.

(**A ladder starts to come slowly into the room. Mainwaring doesn't see it. He has his back to the door.**)

VOICE It's the good old yeoman stock that does it, y'know, in times of crisis, they always rise to the occasion.

(**Mainwaring is goosed by the ladder.**)

MAINWARING Ye-es! (**The ladder is now pinning him to the desk.**)

VOICE You'll soon lick the men into shape. It's just a question of starting off with both feet planted firmly on the bottom of the ladder.

Fade

The next scene which immediately followed the fire-man's scene was also cut in order to reduce the over-all running time of the episode. In it we discover that Miss King, often only seen in cameo roles, played a role in designing the uniforms, even if it was only a small part.

(**Fade up Mainwaring's office. The calendar now shows May 21st. Mainwaring is at the desk. Mrs Pike is opposite and is just about to leave.**)

MAINWARING Well, I'm sure that will be alright, Mrs Pike, and if you have any other queries, no doubt my chief clerk will be able to answer them for you.

MRS PIKE I'm sure he will, Mr Mainwaring.

(**As she goes, Miss King pokes her head round the door.**)

MISS KING GHQ's on the phone, Mr Mainwaring. You can expect your first delivery of weapons tonight.

MAINWARING Excellent, Miss King. Have you finished the uniforms?

MISS KING Yes, sir. They look very smart.

MAINWARING Good. Pike, Wilson. (**Pike and Wilson

enter.) It's nearly time for the parade and we've good news, Wilson. Weapons are being rushed to us from GHQ and Miss King has finished the uniforms.

MISS KING Here they are, sir.

(She hands Mainwaring three arm bands with LDV painted on. An armband with three stripes and a fifth armband with 'Capt' written on it. They put the LDV armbands on the left arm and their sergeant and captain on the right.)

MAINWARING Very smart, Miss King. We owe you a debt of gratitude.

MISS KING I'm sorry the 'T"s a bit blodgy.

WILSON Not to worry, I've already had a cup of tea, Miss King.

(Miss King points to the 'T' on Capt.)

MAINWARING Never mind, they'll serve very well, Miss King. They give us military status and protection under the Geneva convention. We can no longer be looked on as Guerillas.

MISS KING I never did look on you as one of those, Sir.

MAINWARING Come along, Pike – the arms!

(Pike hands three pikes from the cupboard, they take one each. Mainwaring looks at the pikes, the three armbands and the three of them.)

MAINWARING Well, um – I don't think we'll march to our headquarters – we'll proceed independently.

WILSON Very good, sir. Independently – quick march.

(They march out of the office.)

Fade.

SERIES 1, EPISODE 2
MUSEUM PIECE

After the introductory newsreel scenes, the recorded TV episode cuts to Mainwaring's office at the bank, where Miss King, who's doing some filing, and Pike talk briefly about the manager being late, before Mr Wilson enters and says: 'Good morning'.

However, the original script contained a more extensive scene between King and Pike.

CUT TO MAINWARING'S OFFICE

(Janet King is taking down the blackout screen, to reveal the paper-taped windows. The radio is playing a current hit and she is whistling to it. Frank Pike enters carrying papers.)

FRANK Here's Mr Mainwaring's *Times*. And here's the one he reads. (He hands her *The Daily Mirror*. She looks at it.)

JANET Coo. It doesn't look too good, does it.

(CS of daily paper headline announcing the falling back of allied troops.)

FRANK My Mum hears that General Gort's letting 'em advance a bit so as to extend their lines of communication.

JANET What's the point of that?

FRANK Well, my Mum heard that when the time's right he'll get 'em – right in the soft underbelly.

JANET Sounds awful. Here, the Manager's late isn't he?

FRANK We were out on manoeuvres all yesterday. Perhaps it was too much for them.

JANET You're just like a lot of kids playing soldiers.

FRANK (In north country voice) Let me tell you, it's thanks to the LDV that you can walk home in safety at nights.

JANET I wish you'd get uniforms. Then I'd know whether I'm being followed by one of you lot or Jack the Ripper.

(The door opens, enter Wilson.)

SERIES 1, EPISODE 3
COMMAND DECISION

In this episode, there are no major cuts, but a joke was deleted involving Miss King, who was the victim of several cuts as far as her scenes were concerned during the first series.

While Mainwaring and Wilson are sat in the office at the bank discussing the dearth of currants in the buns they're eating during a coffee break, Wilson opens his and discovers plenty of fruit, which doesn't please Mainwaring. Soon Captain Square arrives at the bank and is introduced by Miss King.

MAINWARING'S OFFICE AT THE BANK

(There is a knock on the door and Janet enters.)

MAINWARING What is it, Miss King?

JANET Colonel Square to see you, sir.

Following two lines cut

MAINWARING Colonel Square. What's he look like?

JANET (Giggling) Sort of round looking, sir.

(She gives Mainwaring a card.)

SERIES 1, EPISODE 4
THE ENEMY WITHIN THE GATES

After the introductory newsreel scenes we move to Mainwaring's office at the bank. When Pike tells Mainwaring some of the uniforms have arrived, it's Wilson who brings through the equipment. The original script showed Miss King helping as well, but her involvement was reduced when it came to filming.

SERIES 1, EPISODE 5
THE SHOWING UP OF CORPORAL JONES

In the early scenes there are chunks of lines cut involving Mainwaring. The first instance is at the beginning of the scene when Mainwaring inspects the troops after previously sending them home to sew buttons on their jackets. Before Jones enters the church hall office to tell Mainwaring the men are ready for inspection, there was a little conversation between the captain and his sergeant.

(Side room of hall. Wilson and Mainwaring are putting on their jackets.)

MAINWARING There we are. Elizabeth was equal to the emergency. What do you think of those?

(He indicates three tin stars on each shoulder cut out of food tins.)

WILSON Very good, sir. (He looks closer.) A baked bean tin, sir?

MAINWARING That's right.

WILSON I thought so.

MAINWARING (Flicking at one of the stars.) Quite the little Sherlock Holmes today, aren't we?

(Jones enters.)

Returns to scene as per recorded episode

More deleted lines involving Mainwaring occurred

while he was inspecting the platoon; Godfrey tells Mainwaring that dress studs were all he could find at the spur of the moment. In the transmitted episode, Mainwaring walks off, but the original script had Mainwaring questioning Godfrey further.

MAINWARING Have you no buttons at home?

GODFREY Yes. Quite a selection.

MAINWARING You were in a gents' outfitters, weren't you? Surely you can sew them on yourself?

GODFREY Yes, sir. It wasn't that. I couldn't see to thread a needle.

MAINWARING Come round to my house tomorrow morning. I'm sure my good lady will be able to help.

At the end of the inspection the men fall out to check their weapons before heading out on patrol, while Wilson and Mainwaring go into the church hall office to examine their weapons and equipment. In the recorded episode it isn't long before Mrs Pike comes rushing in, but the original script contained a short sketch involving Mainwaring and Wilson discussing their sandwiches, prior to Mrs Pike's entrance.

(Mainwaring to Wilson as they go into office.)

MAINWARING (To Wilson) I think we'd do well to check our own weapons. (He comes to the desk.) Now let me see. Waterbottle, gas-mask, knife, knuckle-duster, bicycle chain, cosh, sandwiches. I wonder what Elizabeth has put in them? (He lifts up the sandwiches and peels one back.) Oh, dear. Snoek again. I hope she's put some pickle in them, ah good. Mango chutney made with carrots. I wonder what's for pudding? (He opens a packet.) Strawberry jam, made with carrots. After eating that lot I shall be able to see in the dark all right. What sort of sandwiches have you got, Wilson?

WILSON Cold roast beef with military pickle.

MAINWARING That's my favourite. Do you know there hasn't been any in the shops since war started. I wonder why you can't get military pickle now?

WILSON It's a Navy issue, sir.

MAINWARING Then how did you get it? Don't tell me – Walker?

WILSON Yes, sir.

MAINWARING I don't know what we'd do without him you know, Wilson. That reminds me. He's promised me half a dozen eggs tonight and a bar of milk chocolate.

WILSON Milk chocolate, sir. How much?

MAINWARING Half a pound block, and wrapped in silver paper.

WILSON Would you consider swapping one beef sandwich for six squares of chocolate?

MAINWARING Four.

WILSON Five squares.

MAINWARING Done.

Scene returns to recorded piece with Mrs Pike entering the church hall office

There is a complete scene cut from this episode, which included Miss King. When it was transmitted it was the only episode from the first series that didn't contain Janet. Straight after the church hall scene when Major Regan congratulates Mainwaring and his men on how well they've done, the edited scene, set at the bank, involved Mainwaring telling Miss King how pretty she is!

DAY

(**Mainwaring's office in the bank. Janet King is stacking the mail on Mainwaring's desk. The radio is playing a bright tune. It finishes.**)

ANNOUNCER This is the BBC Home Service and Forces Programme. In your garden today, here is Mr Middleton.

(**Recording of Mr Middleton. The door opens suddenly and Mainwaring comes in.**)

MAINWARING How many times have I told you that the wireless is for news, and emergency bulletins only.

(**Janet quickly turns the radio off.**)

JANET Yes, I'm sorry, sir. I keep forgetting. I was having music while I was working.

MAINWARING Well, I think I can forgive you just this once. (**He hums a little tune as he hangs up his hat and umbrella and sits on his desk.**)

JANET Thank you, sir. Is everything all right, sir?

MAINWARING Well, I don't see why it shouldn't be, do you? (**He gives a little chuckle.**) Has anybody ever told you, Miss King, that you're a very pretty girl?

JANET (**Backing towards the door.**) No, sir. I mean, yes sir. Thank you very much, sir. (**She quickly opens the door and goes.**)

(**Cut to the other side of the door, outside office. Janet stands with a puzzled look on her face. Wilson comes into the picture whistling softly to himself.**)

WILSON (**Very cheerfully**) Good morning, Miss King.

(**He taps on the door and there's a cheerful 'Come In' from Mainwaring. Wilson opens the door and goes in. Janet frowns and puts her ear to the door. Laughter comes from inside. Pike comes into picture and creeps up behind her.**)

PIKE Careless talk costs lives.

JANET (**Turning to him.**) What's up with everyone this morning?

PIKE Victory. That's what's up. We had an inspection by GHQ last night and they thought we were very good.

JANET Oh. I thought it was something important.

Returns to recorded scene

SERIES 1, EPISODE 6
SHOOTING PAINS

There are two main differences in this episode between the original script and what was actually transmitted.

First, when the platoon are on parade in the early scenes and Mainwaring asks anyone to step forward if they can't make the following weekend's shooting practice, to be attended by the unpopular Major Regan, everyone takes a pace forward. After Mainwaring walks along the front row and hears their excuses, he returns alongside Wilson. In the original script, but missing from the recorded episode, was an incentive Mainwaring arranged to improve the attendance at the weekend's shoot.

MAINWARING Oh yes, in order to give the shoot a competitive spirit, Mr Fountain, the Director of the Fountain Brewery, is giving me a keg of bitter to be awarded to the best shot. Right, Platoon attention.

The keg of beer influences the editing of further scenes before the studio recording. At the shooting range when Jones, Walker, Pike and Frazer arrive at the target pits, the phone rings and Jones rushes over to answer it. A scene was cut from the script at this point before Jones answers the phone.

(**Two large army targets worked by counterweights. When one is pulled down the other is exposed to fire. On the top of one is a large hook for hanging dummies. Private Walker is alone. He has set up the barrel of beer and is filling his water bottle from it. L/Cpl Jones and Privates Frazer and Pike come into the picture.**)

JONES Oh there you are. Got the beer I see.

WALKER Yeah, come on get stuck in.

PIKE Do you think we ought to drink the beer, Mr Walker? After all, it was supposed to be for the best shot.

WALKER That's all right, lad, you're bound to win. So we might as well drink now.

(**They all crowd round to fill their water bottles, except Jones.**)

JONES 'ere, wait a minute, what do you think you're doing? Flouting my authority like that. It's up to me to say if we're going to drink the beer or not. Now stand back.

(**They all do so.**)

FRAZER Well are we going to drink it, Corp?

JONES (**Filling his bottle.**) Yes.

PIKE The Major sounds in a cheerful mood, Mr Jones.

JONES 'E's up to something, you mark my words. I wouldn't trust him as far as I could throw him, Toffee-nosed twit.

Here the original script links to the actual recorded scene with Jones telling Pike to wave the flag every time a shot misses the target. In the script, when Major Regan comes down to the target pits himself because he can't believe he's missed the target, the keg is hidden inside a sandbag.

In between the recorded scenes when the platoon finish at the shooting range with Walker saying: 'Blimey, talk about tear around the dotted line', and Mrs Pike pours tea for the returning platoon back at the church hall, a whole scene was cut involving Wilson and a dejected Mainwaring, who feels he's let the platoon down because his own attempts at shooting were disappointing; as captain of the unit, he feels he hasn't set a very good example.

(**Low angle shot of Mainwaring and Wilson. We can only see them from the waist up. They might be sitting on a horse. In fact they are sitting on a farm gate. It is drizzling with rain. Mainwaring has his right hand stuck in his tunic like Napoleon with his greatcoat draped across his shoulders. Wilson, also has his coat draped over his shoulders. Muffled drums. They are both very miserable. Camera pans around. There is a track at the edge of the field. Straggling along it are the men of the platoon. They are spread out in single file with the look of a retreating army. As they pass Mainwaring they glance up with the misery of defeat on their faces. Bringing up the rear is the cart pulled by Walker and Pike with Frazer and Jones hanging on it. In the cart is the dummy, looking pretty shot up. Pan back to Mainwaring and Wilson. We see that they are sitting on a gate.**)

MAINWARING I can't bear to see the men looking at me like that, Wilson.

WILSON You weren't the only one, sir, it's not really our fault we've never had the ammunition to practise with before.

MAINWARING But to be shown up like that in front of the men, it was terrible, I feel I can never face them again.

WILSON But they didn't do any better, sir.

MAINWARING That's not the point, Wilson. As their Commanding Officer I should be able to set a good example.

WILSON Well come on sir, better get back.

(**They slip down from the fence and tag on behind the cart. As they go the rain pours down and the wheel of the cart starts to squeak.**)

In the later televised scene Major Regan waltzes into the church hall to tell Mainwaring that he's got to compete against the Eastgate platoon at a shooting competition; the original script found Regan talking to Wilson because Mainwaring had gone home after the debacle at the range.

A scene involving Walker and Barbara Windsor's character, Laura La Plaz, also got the chop. When Walker leaves his Hippodrome seat telling Mrs Pike he's nipping out for a minute, the recording moves straight to the church hall with Wilson telling Mainwaring that Walker has an idea for winning the shooting competition, missing out the following scene.

(**Laura's dressing room. The room is empty. Door opens. Walker pokes his head round the door, sees the room is empty and dodges in. Laura's act is just finishing. Applause and music in background. Walker looks around. Crosses to dressing table. A look of disgust comes on his face. He picks up a newspaper, rolls it up and brings it down with a quick whack on the dressing table. He looks a little closer and picks up a false eyelash.**)

WALKER I thought it was a spider.

(**The door opens and Laura comes in.**)

WALKER (**In his best Spanish.**) Bunos Notches, Senorita.

LAURA (**In Cockney.**) It's alright, I speak English. How the hell did you get past the doorkeeper?

WALKER He's a friend of mine. I come round here every Saturday night.

LAURA Oh you do, do you? Well whatever it is you've got to sell, I'm not interested.

WALKER (**Opening his case.**) 'ere what do you think of these?

LAURA (**Weakening**) How much?

WALKER Listen. If you're interested in a little proposition of mine, I'll let you have them for nothing.

LAURA And if you're not out of here in two minutes I'll have you thrown out.

WALKER No, it's nothing like that.

LAURA What do you mean?

WALKER It's very simple. There's nothing to it. This is what I want you to do. Now tomorrow afternoon…

The scene ends at this point, but Walker obviously goes on to explain that he wants Laura to take part in the shooting competition.

In the final scene Frazer wins the shooting competition for the Walmington platoon, but it's Laura La Plaz who's the jewel in the crown in the original script, winning the day for Mainwaring and his men against the East Littleton platoon, not the Eastgate platoon as in the TV episode.

DAY. TARGET PITS.

(Major and Walker are both looking up at target. Major has a clipboard in his hand. The East Littleton team has just fired their last shot.)

MAJOR Well, there's no getting away from it, those chaps from East Littleton are pretty good. Your lot will have to do damn well to beat that.

WALKER You look like a sporting gentleman, Major. Would you like a little bet on the side?

MAJOR Well, if you like. Ten shillings.

WALKER How about ten quid?

MAJOR That's a bit steep isn't it?… Oh very well.

DAY. RIFLE RANGE.

(The first platoon is in two lines. Laura is in the middle of Frazer and Pike in the front row. They are running on the spot.)

MAINWARING Platoon halt! The three contestants six paces forward march.

(Frazer and Pike each put an arm under Laura, lift her in the air and take six paces forward.)

MAINWARING Prepare to fire.

(They all lie down and get ready to fire. Laura has great difficulty. Close-up of Wilson and Mainwaring who has field glasses.)

WILSON Pte Frazer, 5 rounds rapid fire!

(Frazer fires 5 rapid shots.)

MAINWARING (Looking through glasses.) Not bad. He got 3 on the target.

WILSON Pte Pike, 5 rounds rapid fire!

(5 rapid shots.)

MAINWARING That's a bit better, but we're still a long way behind.

TARGET PITS.

MAJOR Well, your Polish chappie will have to do damn well if you're going to win. (They both look up at the target. Five shots ring out. Walker pulls down target. There are 5 bullet holes right in the centre.)

WALKER That's ten quid you owe me, Major. (Major livid hands him the money.)

SERIES 2, EPISODE 4
SGT WILSON'S LITTLE SECRET

There is one major difference between the original script and the recorded version of this episode from the second series. Wilson overhears Mrs Pike talking to Frank about accepting an evacuee, and gets the wrong end of the stick believing Mavis is having his child. After confiding in Mainwaring, Wilson is reminded that he must do the decent thing and wed Mrs Pike. In the TV episode the next scene shows Wilson knocking at Mrs Pike's door, at which point Walker appears on the scene cracking jokes.

In the original script it wasn't Walker who spotted Wilson, but a policeman.

SCENE 7: THE FRONT DOOR OF MRS PIKE'S HOUSE.

(Wilson comes into the picture, he gives a furtive look round and rings the door bell. Silence. He rings the bell again. There is the sound of a window opening above his head.)

MRS PIKE'S VOICE Who's that?

WILSON (Stepping back and looking up) It's me, Mavis. I must speak to you at once.

MRS PIKE What on earth do you want at this time of night?

WILSON It's only ten o'clock, I must see you at once.

MRS PIKE Really, what will the neighbours think. All right I'll come down.

(She closes the window.)

(There is dead silence, Wilson waits. Suddenly a figure comes out of the darkness. It's a policeman.)

PC May I see your identity card, sir?

WILSON (Turns startled) What?

PC Oh, it's you, Mr Wilson, sorry. I saw a figure in the dark so I thought I'd better check up.

WILSON Oh.

PC On some sort of night exercise are you, sir?

WILSON Yes, that's right.

PC That's funny I haven't seen any more of your chaps about.

WILSON Well I'm sort of on my own, you see.

(The letterbox opens and Mrs Pike calls through.)

MRS PIKE Arthur, darling, are you still there?

WILSON (With side glance at PC) Yes, I'm still here, Mavis.

MRS PIKE Good job you arrived when you did, I've only just got undressed.

(The PC gives Wilson a look. Wilson looks desperate.)

MRS PIKE Another five minutes and I should have been in bed and asleep.

WILSON Mavis, please. (He gives the PC a desperate look.)

PC Well I'll be pushing along then, Mr Wilson. It's rotten being up all night on duty, don't you think? Still that's war. Good night, sir. (He goes.)

WILSON Why on earth don't you open the door, Mavis?

MRS PIKE I can't. I've taken the blackout down, besides I've got my mother staying with me for a few days, what would she think?

WILSON But I want to talk to you.

MRS PIKE Well you can talk through the letterbox.

The scene continues to a conclusion in accordance with the TV episode.

SERIES 3, EPISODE 1
THE ARMOURED MIGHT OF LANCE CORPORAL JONES

The only significant difference between the original script and the recorded episode is the manner adopted by Mainwaring when Hodges, the newly promoted chief warden, arrives on the scene. We've come to expect immediate friction whenever these two meet, but in the original script Mainwaring holds back from his normal hostile treatment of the warden because he doesn't want to lose his custom from the bank.

WARDEN Now I've had instructions that we're supposed to cooperate. So I'll tell you once. I want this hall every Wednesday evening for an ARP lecture. Got it?

MAINWARING But I have a parade in the hall every Wednesday evening.

WARDEN Well you'll just have to parade out here in the yard, won't you, or shall we discuss moving my account?

MAINWARING Now look here. Can't we talk this over in a reasonable manner?

Mainwaring's concern over losing an obviously valuable bank account resurfaces later. When Hodges is trying to conduct a lecture inside the church hall and Mainwaring's men are making too much noise in the church yard, Hodges confronts Mainwaring, asking him whether they're playing cowboys and Indians.

MAINWARING Now look here. This has gone far enough. I know we're supposed to cooperate with you ARP chaps, but I find your highhandedness just a little too much to bear. Any more from you, and I shall stop you using our hall altogether.

WARDEN Which account do you want me to move first, my business account or my private account?

WILSON Steady, sir. We don't want to lose his business you know.

SERIES 3, EPISODE 2
BATTLE SCHOOL

The opening scene in the railway carriage, with the platoon heading off to weekend camp, is considerably different from what was originally penned. In the TV episode the train brakes heavily for the first time and shortly afterwards Godfrey states how he hopes they arrive soon because he requires the toilet. In the script several lines were written between that point and when Godfrey recites the poem, 'The Owl and the Pussycat'.

SCENE 2: INTERNAL. RAILWAY COACH. DAY.

(The right-hand side of the coach: at the far end in the corner is Wilson – next to him Mainwaring – next Frazer smoking large drop pipe, he is knitting socks – next Godfrey reading The Tailor and Cutter. The left-hand side: at the far end is Pike, he is reading a copy of The Hotspur and he is sucking his thumb. Next to him is Jones and then Walker – they are both playing crib on Walker's supply suitcase. Next Pte Sponge who is reading a HG Handbook. The train suddenly comes to a violent halt. Everyone is thrown about.)

WALKER (Picking up his cards off the floor) Blimey, gimme your cards, Jonesey. (He takes Jones' cards and shuffles the pack.) We'd better start again.

JONES That's not fair, I was winning.

WALKER Well I can't help it if the train keeps jerking to a halt, can I?

JONES Why is it the cards never fall on the floor when you're winning?

WALKER Oh stop moaning and get on with the game.

MAINWARING (To Wilson) It's too bad the way this train keeps stopping and starting. (Looking at watch) What time are we due at the weekend battle school?

WILSON Sixteen hundred hours, sir.

MAINWARING What?

WILSON Four o'clock.

MAINWARING I know, Wilson, I know. Fat lot of good it was getting off early from the bank – and then having to spend most of the day in a railway train. There's only Miss King and that old fool Digby left to attend to everything – and you know what a busy day Friday is.

Besides, if I'd known the journey was going to take all this time I'd have brought something to eat – I'm starving.

(Great puffs of smoke are being blown in Mainwaring's face. Mainwaring points to 'No Smoking' sign on window.)

MAINWARING Can't you read, Frazer?

FRAZER Aye, sir, I can.

MAINWARING Well why don't you put that filthy pipe out.

FRAZER There's a war on, sir.

MAINWARING What's that go to do with it?

FRAZER Well you don't take any notice of pre-war notices in wartime. (Pointing to advert above the seat.) That one says: 'Eat Parker's Pork Pies', but I'm not doing it, am I?

(Close-up of advert – with a picture of a delicious cut pork pie. Close-up of Mainwaring licking his lips.)

WILSON It does look rather delicious, don't you think, sir?

(Mainwaring gives him a glare and his eyes travel to the next advert. It is a picture of a large block of milk chocolate. Caption reads: 'Fry's Milk Chocolate… Four pence a quarter-pound block.' Close-up of Mainwaring. Cut to third advert. Picture of a cut salmon on a plate surrounded by cucumber. Caption reads: 'Sloane's Salmon… ninepence a tin… expensive, but well worth the extra.')

MAINWARING They should take all these old pre-war advertisements down, you know, Wilson – you can't get any of it… it's very bad for the morale.

WILSON Oh, I don't know, sir. It reminds us of what we're fighting for. Besides, we'll be able to get it all again after the war.

MAINWARING Well let's hope they reduce the price. A tin of salmon nine pence! It's absurd.

(He looks across at Pike who is reading *The Hotspur*. It has a lurid picture on the cover.)

MAINWARING Oh, do take your thumb out of your mouth, boy.

PIKE I'm sorry, sir – this story's so exciting. It's all about a bunch of soldiers who are trapped for weeks without food, they're all starving… so they decide to draw lots to see which one of them they're going to eat.

WILSON I say, that's an awfully good idea. Which one of them loses?

PIKE The Captain.

MAINWARING I've never heard such rubbish. You know I think it's disgraceful the way the whole platoon has been squeezed into two compartments. Being an officer I should have travelled first class.

PIKE (Getting his pack down from the rack.) I think I'll have my dinner now. (Handing Wilson a packet of sandwiches.) Here's yours, Uncle Arthur.

WILSON How nice… thank you, Frank.

(Pike unwraps his sandwiches and starts to eat. Mainwaring licks his lips.)

MAINWARING I think it's only right that you should share those sandwiches, Pike.

PIKE I'm sorry, Mr Mainwaring… my Mum said I was to eat them all myself. She says I'm a growing boy and I need to keep my strength up.

MAINWARING I can't help that, you're on active service now. Divide them out at once. Come on, Wilson, share yours out.

(The sandwiches are handed round.)

WALKER Blimey, I'm starving.

JONES If I'd known we were going to be all this time in the train, I'd have brought some of those sausages you like, Mr Mainwaring.

(They each get one small sandwich which is quickly eaten.)

JONES Where is this place, we're going to, sir?

WALKER Yes, come on, sir, tell us where this battle school is.

MAINWARING I'm afraid I can't do that, Walker… I'm under sealed orders… and I can't open them until we get out of the train.

FRAZER Aye, that's all very well, but how do we know where to get off?

MAINWARING Don't worry about that, Frazer, the guard will tell us.

GODFREY Well, I hope we get there soon.

MAINWARING Why?

GODFREY Well, it's a bit awkward… I mean with no corridor on the train… I don't think I can hold out much longer.

MAINWARING Well, you'll just have to control yourself… this is war, Godfrey… we're on active service, you know.

WALKER What you need is something to take your mind off it. Now how about a little flutter, gentlemen? I've got three cards here… two Kings and a Queen… all you've got to do is spot the Lady. (He turns the cards face downward and quickly moves them about.) Come on, Mr Godfrey. How about a tanner's worth?

GODFREY Very well. (He points to card.) That one.

WALKER (Turning the card up… it's a King.) Sorry, you lose.

(Godfrey hands him sixpence.)

WALKER Another go?

GODFREY No, thank you.

SPONGE I'll have a tanner's worth.

(Walker moves the cards quickly round. Cut to close-up of Frazer's eyes…they move like a hawk's.)

WALKER There you go then, Spongey.

SPONGE That one. (He points to card… Walker turns it up… a King.)

WALKER You lose, mate.

(Sponge hands him sixpence.)

JONES I'll have a go, Joe.

WALKER Right you're on, Jonesey.

(He quickly moves the cards. Close-up of Frazer's eyes.)

JONES That one.

(Walker turns the card up… a King.)

WALKER Better luck next time, mate. Anyone else? What about you, Mr Mainwaring?

MAINWARING Certainly not!

WALKER What about you, Pikey?

PIKE My Mum doesn't allow me to gamble.

FRAZER I'd like to try, Joe.

WALKER All right, Taff, what you want to bet, ha'penny?

(They all laugh.)

FRAZER No, a pound.

WALKER Ey! Oh all right then, let's see your money.

(Frazer puts down a pound. Walker moves cards. Close-up of Frazer's eyes.)

FRAZER That one.

WALKER You sure you want that one?

FRAZER Eye, I'm sure… turn it up, man.

WALKER Yes… er… well, all right then.

(Walker turns the card up… a Queen.)

FRAZER A pound, Joe.

WALKER Yes, well of course… I mean, I haven't got it on me now, have I.

FRAZER (Reaching across and grabbing Walker by his lapels.) A pound, Joe.

WALKER Well, if you insist. (He gives him a pound.)

SERIES 3, EPISODE 3
THE LION HAS 'PHONES

In the introductory scenes we see the platoon holding sheets of corrugated iron. The first interior shot in the church hall sees Mainwaring saying: 'A first-class exercise in the art of camouflage' and 'The subject of my lecture today is communication'; between these lines a scene was cut involving the men piling their pieces of camouflage in the corner of the church hall.

SCENE 5: CHURCH HALL. DAY.

(The platoon all file into the hall. They still have the pieces of corrugated iron attached to them. They form in three ranks and mark time. There is a terrible clatter.)

WILSON Platoon… halt. (He winces) Left turn. (Clatter) Stand at ease. (Clatter) Oh, do try not to make so much noise.

MAINWARING: A good morning's work, men. A first-class exercise in the art of camouflage. Now, on the command, move, I want you to pile your pieces of corrugated iron in the corner and fall in again. Move!

(They all pile the tin in the corner of the hall.)

WILSON Oh, do try to be a little quieter.

MAINWARING How can they pile corrugated iron quietly, Wilson?

WALKER (To Mainwaring) Can I have a word with you, sir?

MAINWARING Yes, what is it, Walker?

WALKER (Pressing a pound note into his hand.) An oncer be all right for you, sir?

MAINWARING What are you talking about, Walker?

WALKER You don't want those old bits of tin, do you?

MAINWARING Those bits of tin are government property, Walker.

WALKER (Handing him a ten shilling note.) Thirty bob, then?

MAINWARING (Giving him back the money.) Get back in your place, Walker.

WALKER Well, I only asked.

(The men have all fallen in again. Pike still has his piece of iron in front of him – we can just see his head.)

MAINWARING Why haven't you got rid of your tin, Pike?

PIKE Well, sir, it's a bit awkward. I feel so ashamed.

MAINWARING Why?

PIKE I haven't got my uniform on – my Mum's washing it.

MAINWARING Good heavens, do you mean to say that you've…

PIKE Oh, no, sir. I'm not naked. I've got my clothes on.

MAINWARING All right, all right. (He draws Wilson on one side.) Wilson, have a word with Mrs Pike, will you? This isn't the first time it's happened. We can't have young Pike coming on parade without his uniform.

WILSON It's no use me talking to her, sir, she's obsessed with cleanliness.

MAINWARING Houseproud, is she?

WILSON Many a time she's had my uniform off my back before I could say 'knife'.

MAINWARING Really? All right, men, on the command 'fall out' I want you to gather round the board for a lecture. Fall out!

The script reaches the point where Mainwaring gives a lecture

When some of the men are waiting at the edge of the reservoir, keeping an eye on the Germans, Pike's white scarf is waved in the TV episode, but the script refers to Pike's shirt, not scarf. Also, scene 16 of the original script was never recorded; it showed Hodges arriving at the reservoir before the regular army.

SCENE 16: EDGE OF RESERVOIR. NIGHT.

(**Mainwaring and Wilson are lying side by side. Jones and the warden crawl into picture. The firing from the plane has stopped.**)

MAINWARING Where have you been, Jones?

JONES Sorry, sir… I had a bit of a job getting through to GHQ. They're on the way now.

WARDEN He said they were firing at you.

MAINWARING That's right.

WARDEN Well they look peaceful enough to me. I think I'd better take charge… this is an ARP matter.

MAINWARING How dare you!

WARDEN Look, mate, don't try to teach me my job. A lot of fuss about nothing… they wouldn't dare shoot at me, I'm a civilian. (**He stands up and shouts.**) All right, you lot, out you come. (**There is a burst of fire and he goes flat on his face.**) Right, I'll leave you to it. (**He starts to crawl away.**)

MAINWARING Come back… we need every man we can get.

WARDEN Section 6, paragraph 3 of the regulations states: 'No ARP personnel will take part in any combat duties…' I'm off. (**He goes.**)

SERIES 3, EPISODE 4
THE BULLET IS NOT FOR FIRING

After patrolling the Walmington coastline all night, the men of the Home Guard are shattered and desperate for a hot cup of tea. But Mainwaring is a hard taskmaster and orders them to clean their rifles before a drink. In the final recording this scene is reduced slightly, with the edited lines showing Jones having trouble with his rifle.

FRAZER You don't call what you do a day's work?

WALKER That whiskey you get every week don't fall off a lorry of its own accord you know, it has to be pushed.

JONES It comes very hard when you have to work with the brain like I do.

WALKER Come off it, Jonesey. All you have to do is give a couple of good wallops with your chopper and keep your fingers out of the way.

JONES That's all you know, Joe. You want to try it some time. Here I am with a long roll of boned rib. 'I'll have three books' she says. That's three one and eights at two and two a pound. Now where do you slice it, that's the point, where do you slice it?

WALKER Go on, do what you always do, give 'em short weight and put your hand on the scales.

JONES That's liable that is liable.

WALKER (**Indicating the pull through and the barrel.**) Go on, bung it in the hole.

(**Jones makes a few attempts to put the pull through into the foresight end.**)

JONES You shouldn't make charges you can't substan…

substan… substanti… these barrels are smaller than what they used to be, aren't they?

WALKER It goes in the other end you silly old sirloin slicer.

(**Cut to Frazer, he is trying to pour hot water down the barrel. The fire bucket stands below to receive the water. He misses.**)

FRAZER That's a damn silly arrangement. Have yer no got a funnel?

GODFREY May I help?

FRAZER What makes you think you'd do any better?

GODFREY Well I get quite a lot of practice. You see I have to fill my sisters' hot water bottles every night.

FRAZER All right. I'll hold and you pour.

PIKE That's right, Mr Godfrey, you be mother.

(**Cut to Jones and Walker. Jones is struggling to pull through the pull through.**)

WALKER What's the matter, Jonesey?

JONES It's a bit stuck, Joe.

WALKER What have you got on the end? One of your old night-shirts?

(**Cut**)

SERIES 3, EPISODE 5
SOMETHING NASTY IN THE VAULT

The whole of the first scene in the original script was never transmitted. It involved Mainwaring and Wilson shaving after being out on patrol all night.

SCENE 1: MANAGER'S OFFICE. BANK. DAY.

(**Mainwaring is sitting at his desk writing – the calendar shows 14 May 1941 – there is a knock on the door.**)

MAINWARING Come in. (**Pike enters with a tray and two cups.**) Thank you, Pike – I hope it's nice and hot?

PIKE Yes, sir. (**He goes.**)

(**Mainwaring takes his jacket and collar and tie off. The door opens, Wilson enters.**)

MAINWARING It's all ready, Wilson.

WILSON Good.

(**He also takes his coat and collar and tie off – he draws a chair up to the desk and sits opposite Mainwaring. Mainwaring takes two rolled up towels out of the drawer and hands one to Wilson.**)

WILSON Thank you, sir.

(**They both unroll the towels – inside are their shaving things and two small mirrors – they prop the mirrors in front of them – Mainwaring has a shaving brush – Wilson a tube of brushless shaving cream.**)

MAINWARING What's that, Wilson?

WILSON It's Jiffy-Shave, sir. You don't need a brush.

MAINWARING I've no time for these new fangled inventions. If you want a really good lather, you've got to use a brush and soap.

(**Wilson squeezes the tube on his fingers and puts the shaving cream on his face, He gets a good lather. Mainwaring is still rubbing at his shaving stick and gets a rotten lather.**)

MAINWARING These all night patrol duties are all very well, Wilson, but I would like to shave in my own bathroom just for once.

WILSON Don't you think we could relax just a little?

MAINWARING Relax? Of course we can't relax. Now that it's spring again, Hitler could be across the channel and at our throats any minute.

WILSON You mean he's only been waiting for the spring to er… spring?

MAINWARING I suppose you could say that – yes. (**His razor blade is very blunt; as he draws it across his face he winces – it makes a scratching noise.**)

WILSON This shortage of razor blades is a terrible nuisance – I don't think I'm going to get many more shaves out of this one. Yours sounds a bit blunt too, sir.

MAINWARING Nonsense. Do you realise I've had 56 shaves out of this blade, Wilson. With a war on you just have to improvise – watch! (**He slips the blade out of the razor and strokes it on the side of his hand.**) That should do the trick, as sharp as a…

WILSON A razor, sir?

MAINWARING Quite. (**He slips the blade into the razor and starts to shave – it makes an even worse scratching sound.**) There you are – it works perfectly. (**He winces.**) Nevertheless, I think I shall have to ask Walker for some more blades.

WILSON Ah yes, sir, what would we do without Walker?

MAINWARING What would we do without any members of the platoon, Wilson? They are all part of a close-knit integral unit. By the way, do you realise what the date is? (**He taps calendar.**) It's exactly a year since we first heard that stirring call from Anthony Eden for Local Defence Volunteers.

WILSON So it is.

MAINWARING Exactly a year, Wilson, since we stood in this office, ready to fight to the last man – exactly a year since I was appointed leader of the platoon.

WILSON If I remember rightly, sir, you appointed yourself leader.

MAINWARING Why must you always spoil everything, Wilson? Anyhow, I appointed you sergeant, didn't I?

WILSON Well, there wasn't really anyone else, was there, sir?

MAINWARING Be that as it may – quite a lot of water has passed under the bridge since then. (**He knocks the cup of water onto his lap.**)

WILSON (**Offering him his towel.**) Would you like to borrow my towel, sir?

MAINWARING (**Snapping**) Thank you, I'll use my own.

The second scene starts with Jones entering the bank and speaking to Pike.

The script of the final scene, in which the platoon sit in The Rose and Crown pub celebrating, is different from what was televised. Mrs Pike has just rushed in proclaiming how brave Wilson and Mainwaring are.

(**Captain Rogers comes in and puts the fuse from the bomb on the bar.**)

ROGERS I was right after all. All that time you were holding a trembler.

MAINWARING A what, sir?

ROGERS When that bomb went through the concrete ceiling of the strongroom, the shock broke the wiring in the fuse and turned it into a trembler fuse. By keeping it horizontal you stopped it from going off. If you had tipped it by as much as a few inches, the whole lot would have gone up. The bank should be very grateful to you two. You certainly saved their bacon.

(**West comes in.**)

WEST There you are, Mainwaring. I've been looking for you everywhere. What do you think you're doing, drinking intoxicating liquor in a public house in the middle of the afternoon?

MAINWARING It's quite all right, sir. They don't close for another ten minutes.

WEST I think your behaviour today has been absolutely disgraceful. I shall put in a full report about this to Head Office.

(They all burst our laughing at him.)

SERIES 3, EPISODE 6
ROOM AT THE BOTTOM

Scene eight in the original script never appeared in the final televised episode.

SCENE 8: OFFICE. CHURCH HALL. DAY.

(Mainwaring and Wilson are standing facing each other. Mainwaring is dressed as a private.)

WILSON But you can't do it, sir, you just can't do it. You can't go on parade as a private.

MAINWARING Of course I'm going to do it. Don't you see – if I left the platoon now, it would only confirm what a lot of people have been saying.

WILSON What's that, sir?

MAINWARING That I'm only in the Home Guard for the glory I can get out of it as an officer.

WILSON I never said that, sir.

MAINWARING You may not have said it, Wilson, but it's been in your mind many a time. Anyhow, you're in charge of the platoon until a new officer takes over, so you can wear your beret again if you want to.

WILSON There's not much point really, sir. All the fun's gone out of it.

MAINWARING Forbidden fruit's are always sweeter, Wilson. You should know that.

WILSON Not always, sir. (He puts the beret on.)

MAINWARING And you don't have to keep calling me sir any more.

WILSON I can't get out of the habit, sir. Look, are you sure you want to go on with it?

MAINWARING The defence of this town must come first. This country needs every able bodied man it can get. And no man can be an island unto himself. All right Wilson out you go, fall the men in.

WILSON Oh really, sir, this is awfully embarrassing.

MAINWARING That's an order, Wilson.

WILSON I beg your pardon, sir?

MAINWARING I'm sorry, Wilson – force of habit.

SERIES 3, EPISODE 7
BIG GUNS

In the fourth scene, Mainwaring is seen writing at his desk in the church hall office when Pike and Jones arrive with the camouflage netting for the platoon's new naval gun. At that point, Mr Rees, the town clerk, arrives to watch the Walmington Home Guard's demonstration to try and convince the town council that it's essential the bandstand is dismantled in the park nearby because it's in the gun's line of fire. A section of dialogue involving Mainwaring and Wilson was cut from this scene.

JONES Private Pike is helping me sir.

(Pike sneezes.)

PIKE Blimey, it isn't half dusty.

MAINWARING Never mind, Pike, get it out of here and over the gun, spread it well out and hold it down with sandbags. Off you go.

(Jones and Pike struggle off with the net. Mainwaring goes to the door.)

MAINWARING Sergeant Wilson.

WILSON Yes, sir.

MAINWARING Town clerk is due here in a few minutes, call in the gun team and we'll give them a last minute practice.

WILSON I don't think that would be very wise, sir. They're pretty well all in after their practice at sunrise. Frazer's a bit dickey after his anti-tetanus inoculation.

MAINWARING Why did he have to have that today of all days?

WILSON Well, the hospital were rather insistent when we told them that he'd caught his forefinger in the breech block.

MAINWARING Well surely he can lay the gun with one hand?

WILSON Then Godfrey's lying down on the hassocks in the vestry.

MAINWARING What in heaven's name is the matter with him?

WILSON Well, I thought he looked a bit peaky, sir, so I told him to take forty winks.

MAINWARING Sergeant Wilson, do I have to remind you that the merciless Nazi dogs are about to leap snarling at our throats. We don't stop the war just because Godfrey is feeling a bit peaky.

WILSON Perhaps it would have been wiser to have trained a younger crew.

MAINWARING Oh no, younger men must be used to thrust out with fast patrols in the armoured car. The older men can handle the gun.

WILSON Yes, but will all those snarling dogs wait till Jones finds his bifocals?

(There is a knock on the outer door.)

SERIES 3, EPISODE 11
BRANDED

The moving scene in which Jones' section takes a well-earned cuppa while out on patrol and Private Godfrey walks into the hut was cut slightly.

JONES No, they're not black – they're the same colour as you, Pikey.

WALKER You mean they're green.

JONES Look, let me get on with the story, Joe. They've got hawk-like faces – with hook noses – and cruel beady eyes.

WALKER (Pointing to Frazer) Like old Taff 'ere.

JONES Come to think of it – he does look like a Pathan.

FRAZER Don't talk rubbish – I'm Highlander born and bred.

WALKER Perhaps his father had a bicycle.

JONES Anyhow – there we was surrounded by hundreds of Pathans – it was freezing cold and there were icicles hanging all around the side of the fort – and these Pathans kept charging at us – as fast as we shot 'em more took their place – in the end we'd got no more bullets left – so what did we do…?

WALKER You broke off the icicles and used them for bullets.

JONES 'ere… how did you know that, Joe?

WALKER I'm a mind reader.

PIKE But, Mr Jones, if you fired the icicles – surely the heat of the rifle must have melted them.

JONES Ah, but you see – when they travelled through the cold air…

WALKER They froze again.

JONES That's right – how did you guess, Joe? Anyhow, hence the expression 'Keep your powder dry'.

FRAZER That's nothing – I can remember in the last war during the Battle of Jutland – I was down below when we were struck by a torpedo. The water was rushing in so I had to act quickly. I tore off my jacket, shoved it in the hole – that wasn't enough – then I tore off my shirt and my underwear and shoved them in the hole… still no good… so I tore off my socks and shoved them in the hole – and that did the trick.

JONES & WALKER Hence the expression 'Put a sock in it'.

(They both roar with laughter.)

FRAZER Ah, you stupid idiots!

(Godfrey comes in.)

GODFREY Am I too late to make the tea?

PIKE Yes – I made it, Mr Godfrey – we didn't think you were coming.

FRAZER All of a sudden there's a very nasty smell in here – come on it's time to get back on patrol.

SERIES 3, EPISODE 14
SONS OF THE SEA

The first scene in this episode is slightly different to the original script.

SCENE 3: INSIDE MAINWARING'S OFFICE IN THE BANK. DAY.

(Mainwaring is standing in front of the window with his back to the camera. Mr Maxwell, a solicitor, is sitting in front of Mainwaring's desk. He is a small man in his early fifties.)

MAXWELL Well, Mr Mainwaring, I'm afraid it looks as if you've been left holding the baby.

(Mainwaring turns – he is holding a bundle in his arms.)

MAINWARING It does indeed, Mr Maxwell. (He unwraps the bundle – the Lewis gun is inside it – he sets it up on top of the sandbags.) You don't mind if I set up this Lewis gun while we're talking, do you?

MAXWELL Not at all.

MAINWARING It's my first job every morning – just in case of a sudden attack, you know.

MAXWELL Quite. Now to return to the problem of the late Mr Johnson. As you know, he had no relatives.

MAINWARING (Pressing buzzer.) Just a minute – I'll get my chief clerk in – he was familiar with his affairs.

MAXWELL The point is, when Mr Johnson died the only possessions he had in the world were the clothes he stood up in – and his boat, The Naughty Jane . It will have to be sold, of course – but it may not be easy – after all not many people will want to buy a boat in wartime.

(There is a knock on the door.)

MAINWARING Come in.

(Wilson enters.)

WILSON Good morning, sir.

MAINWARING Morning, Wilson. You know Mr Maxwell.

(They both nod.) I'm afraid we've got a bit of a problem here – we're discussing Mr Johnson's affairs. As you know, he died last week – unfortunately his account was overdrawn to the extent of £32 12s 6d.

WILSON Yes, sir – very awkward.

MAINWARING The only thing he left of any value was this – er… *Naughty Jane*, and we're trying to think of a way to raise some money with her.

MAXWELL After all she's getting a bit old now, but there's still plenty of life in her. And I don't think we ought to forget that she gave the town a lot of pleasure before the war.

MAINWARING Quite.

MAXWELL Of course, she's been neglected a bit lately – but after all, Mr Johnson was 88 when he died – and at his age he couldn't do very much for her.

MAINWARING Mind you – if things were normal, we could put her to work to bring some money in. But of course it's not allowed in wartime.

WILSON I'm awfully sorry, sir – but I can't quite follow all this.

MAINWARING Mr Johnson's boat, Wilson. He used to run pleasure trips with it round the lighthouse before the war.

MAXWELL (**Rising.**) Well, I'll be off now, Mr Mainwaring. I'll leave you my account, just in case you do manage to sell the boat and there's any money left over after paying off the overdraft. (**He hands Mainwaring an envelope.**) Well, good-day, gentlemen. (**He goes.**)

Later, when the men are in the church hall practising how to row a boat, two pages of script were not recorded.

SCENE 4: SECTION OF THE CHURCH HALL. DAY.

(**Frazer is setting up some chairs and benches to represent a boat. He is very happy and is humming to himself. Walker and Jones enter. They are all in their civilian clothes.**)

WALKER Hullo, Taff – what's going on?

FRAZER You'll know soon enough when Mr Mainwaring comes.

JONES I'd shut my shop, and I was going to have a nice afternoon in the garden.

WALKER What about me? I had to leave my brother in charge of my stall in the market.

JONES What's the matter – don't you trust him?

WALKER Of course I trust him – it's the feller with him I'm worried about.

JONES Oh, what's he do?

WALKER He's the probation officer.

(**Pike and Godfrey enter. Godfrey is wearing white flannels, blazer and Panama hat.**)

JONES Hullo, Mr Godfrey, you're looking very smart.

GODFREY Oh, thank you, how nice – as a matter of fact it was going to be my afternoon for some bowls.

WALKER Well, you won't be disappointed, Mr Mainwaring's got a new idea.

PIKE He was very excited in the bank yesterday. I think it's something to do with boats.

JONES Boats!

(**Mainwaring and Wilson enter with Sponge who is carrying four brooms.**)

MAINWARING Good afternoon, men – thank you for coming. All right, Sponge, put those brooms in the corner.

SPONGE Yes, Mr Mainwaring.

(**He puts the brooms down.**)

WILSON Shall I fall the men in, sir?

MAINWARING No, Wilson – this is quite an informal meeting. Now pay attention, men. Yesterday the winds of

fortune delivered a powerful weapon into my hands in the shape of a boat. Used properly this could give us additional striking power. Now what I want to do is to try this boat out this evening, on the river, under actual combat conditions. So this afternoon I want to work out some sort of drill – so that when we get on the river we know what we're doing. There might be people watching, and we don't want to make fools of ourselves in public, do we?

SERIES 4, EPISODE 1
THE BIG PARADE

Mainwaring wants a platoon mascot for the impending parade and while the men are gathered in the church hall, they discuss various options. Before Walker suggests asking Sponge, who's a farmer, for help, various ideas are bandied about, none of which appeared in the final recording.

JONES Permission to speak, sir. In bygone days, ships of the line used to have a figurehead as a mascot – a painted lady.

MAINWARING I was referring to something alive.

WALKER Well, couldn't we have a live painted lady?

WILSON Do be quiet, Walker.

PIKE I've got a white mouse, sir. What about that as a mascot?

MAINWARING Oh, don't be stupid, boy, you can't have a white mouse leading the parade. Besides, you'd never get the collar round its neck.

FRAZER Wait a minute, sir – what we want is a symbol of power and aggression. What about a golden eagle?

MAINWARING Have you got a golden eagle?

FRAZER Ai, sir – stuffed in a glass case.

JONES If it comes to that, sir. There's a stuffed fish in a glass case in the bar at The Anchor.

MAINWARING Oh no – no – we couldn't possibly lead the parade holding up a stuffed animal in a glass case. We must have something alive.

GODFREY I've got a very large cat, sir, the only trouble is that it's not very aggressive.

WALKER You could feed it the stuffed fish – that would make it aggressive.

MAINWARING I shan't tell you again, Walker. I appreciate your suggestion, Godfrey – but we'd never get a cat to march along smartly. (**Wilson sniggers**) What are you laughing at, Wilson?

WILSON I was just thinking, sir. (**Sniggers**) Perhaps the cat would follow Pike's white mouse.

PIKE I'm not having that Uncle Arthur, it might eat it.

MAINWARING Wilson! (**He draws him aside**) This is a serious discussion and as a sergeant you're supposed to set an example.

WILSON With everyone making all these stupid suggestions, I didn't think one more would hurt.

MAINWARING They may seem stupid to you, Wilson, but this is a democratic open discussion. I invited them to kick ideas around.

WILSON Really, sir, cats and white mice and stuffed birds – it's absurd.

MAINWARING Oh no, it's not. Don't you understand their minds are flexible, not rigid and unbending like Nazis. If we're going to win this war, we must be ready to suck up new ideas like blotting paper and examine them from every angle before we discard them.

WILSON But you must admit, sir – they're all talking rubbish.

MAINWARING (**Eyes narrowing**) That's quite enough of that Colonel Blimp talk, Wilson. You've been doing far too much of it lately. We've got to give them time – you'll see, the next suggestion will be a sensible one. (**He turns to the men**) Now are there any more ideas for a mascot? (**Pause**) All right then, let us consider the platoon motto, 'What we have we hold'. Now does that stimulate any ideas? Hmm? (**He rocks on his heels and slowly looks down the ranks**) 'What we have we hold'.

WALKER What about borrowing the sign from outside Sam Isaac's pawnbroker's shop?

(**Pause**)

MAINWARING (**Coldly**) Walker, if you make one more stupid remark, I shall order you off the parade.

At this point, a ram is suggested as a mascot.

Later in the episode, Mainwaring dismisses the platoon and confirms they'll meet up the following evening and march to Sponge's farm. While the TV episode cuts to a new scene with Frazer and some men hiding beneath a tree, several lines were cut from the script which found Walker up to his black market tricks.

(**Walker draws Jones on one side.**)

WALKER 'ere Jonesey, I've got an idea.

JONES What?

WALKER If we catch that ram, after we've used it in the parade, we can kill it – you can sell it in your shop, then we'll share the money 50/50.

JONES We can't do that, they'll wonder what's happened to it.

WALKER No, they won't if we're in charge of it, we'll say we lost it.

JONES But I'm not allowed to sell black market meat – I could go to prison.

WALKER Look, mate. Where is that ram doing the best for the war effort? Marching along all ponced up in a parade, or being eaten?

JONES I don't know, you're getting me confused, anyhow I couldn't kill a little animal.

WALKER What are you talking about? You're a butcher, you're cutting 'em up all day long.

JONES Yeah, but that's different – I don't know any of them personally. Anyhow, what about Private Sponge, it's his ram?

(**They both look at Sponge who is talking to Pike.**)

WALKER Look at him: does he look as if he goes short of food? Believe me, these farmers get plenty of meat. Look, mate, if we do this we shall not only be making some money, but you'll be able to let your lady friend have a bit on the side.

(**Jones stares at Walker. Opens his mouth to speak. Walker pats his cheek.**)

SERIES 4, EPISODE 2
DON'T FORGET THE DIVER

The TV episode shows a scene where the men are sat in the church hall discussing how they can beat Captain Square's Eastgate platoon in the forthcoming exercise. While Jones suggests digging a tunnel, Wilson refers to a play by Shakespeare. In the original script, Wilson's scene is extended.

MAINWARING Now, how are we going to tackle this? Let's try and take some examples from history. You'd better make notes, Wilson.

(**The Verger appears from the back dusting and listening.**)

WILSON Yes, sir.

PIKE What about King Alfred burning the cakes?

MAINWARING What bearing has that got on our problem?

PIKE I dunno, sir – you said you wanted examples from history.

MAINWARING Examples of people trying to get inside places, you stupid boy.

WILSON I've got an idea, sir – listen to this. 'As I did stand my watch upon the hill, I look'd toward Birnam, and anon, methought the wood began to move'.

MAINWARING What's all that rubbish?

WILSON Shakespeare – *Macbeth*, Act 5, Scene 4.

MAINWARING Are you trying to be funny, Wilson?

WILSON 'Let me endure your wrath, if't be not so. Within this three mile may you see it coming. I say a moving grove.'

GODFREY That's awfully good, Mr Wilson.

WILSON Do you think so? Thank you very much.

FRAZER (**Turning to Godfrey**) I don't agree at all – he should have given it more attack like this. (**Giving his all**) 'Within this three mile you see it coming. I say – a moving grove.'

WILSON (**Coldly**) And if I may say, I thought that was rather hammy.

GODFREY I quite agree. I prefer the more gentle approach myself.

FRAZER Rubbish, I hate wishy-washy acting.

MAINWARING (**Losing his patience**) Wilson, I know that you and Frazer are leading lights in the local Amateur Dramatics Society – but if you don't mind we'll return to the subject of how to get inside that mill.

WILSON I've got an idea, sir – in one of Shakespeare's plays – I can't quite remember which one it was, one of the characters dressed his army up as bushes so that they could move across the open ground – in order to attack the castle.

PAUSE

MAINWARING Yes, hmmm – yes – I'm beginning to see what you're getting at now, Wilson.

WILSON I'm so glad, sir.

MAINWARING Dressed them up as bushes eh, hmm! I must admit that is quite a good idea… (**He breaks off as he sees the Verger dusting.**) How much longer are you going to be dusting, Verger?

VERGER I don't know, I've got to keep the place clean. The state you leave it in after every parade is a disgrace.

MAINWARING If I have any more of that sort of talk – I shall report you to the Vicar.

VERGER You can report me as much as you like, I've got my job to do.

MAINWARING Well, you'll just have to do it some other time – and you're getting on my nerves creeping about the place with that miserable look on your face.

SERIES 4, EPISODE 4
SGT – SAVE MY BOY!

A couple of scenes were cut from the original script. They showed Mainwaring and Wilson slowly making their way through the minefield to rescue Pike, who is entangled in barbed wire.

SCENE 12: THE BEACH.

(**Mainwaring is prodding and easing forward.**)

MAINWARING Right, Jones.

WALKER Mr Mainwaring!

MAINWARING Yes Walker, we're here.

(**Cut to**)

SCENE 13: BEACH NEAR THE HUT.

WALKER Where the hell's these flags I'm supposed to follow?

FRAZER They're clearly marked.

WALKER Well I can't see 'em.

SCENE 14: THE BEACH (CENTRE).

MAINWARING I must say the orphans left a good supply of those flags.

JONES There weren't many, sir, but with great ingenuity I've been using them twice.

MAINWARING What do you mean?

JONES I shouldn't have done that, should I, sir?

FRAZER The old fool, he's taken out the markers behind us.

WILSON Really, Jones… that is a most awfully tiresome thing to have done.

MAINWARING Stay where you are, Walker! Frazer, prod your way back to Walker and mark the route with little heaps of sand.

JONES I would like to volunteer to do that, sir. I would like to volunteer to prod my way back to Walker and mark the route with little heaps of sand.

MAINWARING No, Jones, Frazer is going. We must press on. Shine the light, Frazer.

(**Mainwaring prods on in silence.**)

JONES I expect Private Pike is getting a bit anxious.

MAINWARING Yes, I expect he is.

(**Suddenly Jones yells at the top of his voice.**)

JONES (**Shouting**) Don't panic, Private Pike!

MAINWARING Jones!

WILSON Really, Jones, my nerves won't stand it.

JONES I was just giving Private Pike a word of advice and encouragement, sir.

MAINWARING Well don't. Just shut up!

(**Mainwaring prods again, he strikes something.**)

MAINWARING Hello, there's something there alright.

WILSON (**Also finding an obstruction.**) And here.

MAINWARING The damn things must be closer together than Frazer thought.

WILSON It could be a stone, I suppose.

MAINWARING Let's clear this one and have a look. Maybe we can lift it. (**He starts to clear the sand.**)

JONES: Be very careful, sir. Some of these things have booby trap devices to trap boobys.

SERIES 4, EPISODE 5
DON'T FENCE ME IN

Mainwaring and his men are standing outside the Italian POW camp, failing to attract anyone's attention. Before Wilson spots an Italian prisoner coming out of a hut, Walker cracks a joke about Frazer and a kilt. This section of the script was never filmed.

WILSON Walker – please.

FRAZER Look, sir, let me climb over the wire – it's not very high.

PIKE I shouldn't do that, Mr Frazer – it could be electrified – and you might get a shock.

WALKER If he was to climb over that wire wearing his kilt we'd all get a shock.

(**Frazer gives him a glare.**)

WILSON (**Pointing.**) Look, sir – there's someone coming out of that hut.

(**A dirty, scruffy looking POW comes out of one of the huts and slouches across the parade ground with his hands in his pockets.**)

MAINWARING (**Shouting**) Hey you.

SERIES 4, EPISODE 7
PUT THAT LIGHT OUT!

The televised scene in which Hodges enters the church hall office and finds Mainwaring and Wilson there, is shorter than in the original script.

SCENE 3: MAINWARING'S OFFICE.

(**He is preparing a schedule.**)

MAINWARING Right, so we'll revise Platoon into Contact and on Wednesday Platoon into Attack.

WILSON Isn't it about time we did Platoon in Retreat?

MAINWARING We're not going to do any retreating.

(**Enter the warden.**)

WARDEN Ah, glad I caught you. (**To Wilson.**) And you.

MAINWARING We're very busy Mr Hodges, what is it?

WARDEN I'll tell you what it is. (**He takes out a note book.**) For the last two weeks I've been having serious reports from my warden on this street. You've shown lights from this hall on 27 separate occasions. That's three more than 17 Pembroke Gardens and they turned out to be enemy aliens.

MAINWARING No, I'm sorry. I can't accept that at all.

WARDEN Look, it's all down here. On the night before last you opened and shut this door here so many times that my man lost count.

WILSON That's when Jones had been cooking sausages, sir, and the pan caught fire and you were trying to get rid of the smoke before the Vicar came in, so you opened and shut the door to make a sort of draught.

MAINWARING Yes, all right, Wilson.

WARDEN There you are – convicted out of your own mouth. Well, I'm not putting up with this any longer. One more infringement from your premises and I'm having you up before the magistrate.

MAINWARING I think you're being very high-handed about this… er… very trivial affair and what's more you have no authority over the military.

WARDEN Military! That's a laugh for a start. Now look here, Mainwaring. Do you think you can strut around here like Lord Muck? Well, you can't. (**He shakes his finger in Mainwaring's face.**) I'm in charge of this sector and I'm warning you.

MAINWARING Put your finger down and leave my headquarters.

WARDEN I'm going but you've had your last chance. (**He moves to the door.**) One more flash out of you and you'll have a policeman feeling your collar.

(**He goes.**)

MAINWARING What a common man he is.

WILSON All the same, I think we should be a little more careful until he cools off.

MAINWARING Oh there's no need for us to worry about him.

WILSON Well, I daresay he could bring some sort of prosecution.

MAINWARING I doubt it. The Chief Constable is a member of the Bridge Club you know. That reminds me, I must take you along there some time. You do like a game of bridge, I suppose?

WILSON No, not very much.

SERIES 4, EPISODE 8
THE TWO AND A HALF FEATHERS

Several scenes were cut from the final recording. When rumours spread around Walmington-on-Sea about Jones being a coward, we see Frazer on the phone discussing the matter with a friend, Walker chatting with his his girlfriend, Edith, and then Mainwaring in his air raid shelter. Walker and Mainwaring's scenes were reduced in the recording, while scenes involving Godfrey talking to one of his sisters, and Frank Pike having a chat with Wilson, were cut altogether.

SCENE 7: TINY SECTION OF GODFREY'S COTTAGE. NIGHT.

(Close-up of Godfrey sitting in armchair with large tortoise-shell cat on his knee. He is talking to his sister, Dolly, who is out of picture.)

GODFREY You see, Dolly, there's this awful rumour going around about Mr Jones. (A hand comes into picture with a cup of tea. Godfrey takes it.) Thank you, dear. I just can't believe that Mr Jones would run away and leave this man in the desert to die; I mean I've known him for such a long time, and after all he has won all those medals, and he couldn't have won them if he was a coward could he, Dolly? I mean he couldn't… could he?

(Cut)

SCENE 9: INTERIOR. SITTING ROOM, PIKE'S HOUSE. DAY.

(Wilson and Pike are sitting on the sofa together. They are both in uniform. Wilson is reading the paper, he is very much on edge. Pike is listening to the wireless, *Happidrome* is on. We hear a few seconds of it, then we hear Enoch's voice saying, 'Let me tell you.')

PIKE There he goes again: 'Let me tell you.' I love that Enoch don't you, Uncle Arthur?

WILSON (Rustling the paper) What?

PIKE That girl Jean in the bank thinks I'm just like him. Have you heard me do my impersonation of him?

WILSON No, I haven't.

PIKE (Right in his ear) 'Let me tell you.'

WILSON Oh, really, Frank. (He reaches up and turns the radio off.)

PIKE What did you want to do that for, Uncle Arthur – that's my favourite programme.

WILSON (Wilson lights a cigarette) I'm sorry, Frank, it was getting on my nerves.

PIKE What's the matter, don't you feel well?

WILSON It's this business with Jones, all these rumours flying about, the atmosphere on parade tonight was terrible.

PIKE Do you think it's true that Mr Jones left this chap in the desert to die?

WILSON I don't know, Frank. I just don't know. (He gets up) I'm going home.

PIKE Mum won't like that, she's just getting the supper.

WILSON Tell her I want to be alone.

PIKE I can do an impersonation of Greta Garbo too – would you like to hear it?

WILSON No, I wouldn't. (He goes.)

(Frank turns the radio on again and settles down on the sofa.)

SCENE 10: INTERNAL. AIR RAID SHELTER. NIGHT.

MAINWARING Two o'clock – (He croons softly to the outline above) Elizabeth are you awake?

ELIZABETH Mmmmmmmmmmmm.

MAINWARING You know, dear, I really think it would be better if we slept in the house when there wasn't a raid on – this shelter is very damp.

ELIZABETH Mmmmmmmmmmmm.

MAINWARING I just can't sleep – I think I'll read for a while. (He picks up a small home guard manual – props himself up on his elbow and starts to read – Elizabeth turns in her sleep – her outline changes and knocks him back on his pillow.) I think you'd be much more comfortable if I slept on the top bunk, dear.

ELIZABETH Mmmmmmmmmmmm.

MAINWARING I just can't get this Jones business out of my mind. The whole platoon is falling to pieces. You know how I used to look forward to going on duty every evening – the comradeship – the cheerful banter – the wonderful feeling of us all being banded together for a common purpose – now it's all turned to ashes in my mouth. I mean I had Jones in the office, I said to him why don't you deny this rumour that you left this chap Clarke in the desert to die. And he refused to say anything. Why? That's what I want to know – why won't he speak? (He is fiddling with a safety pin that is holding together the top of his pyjama jacket – it comes undone.) I wish you'd sew this button on for me, Elizabeth, I keep telling you about it – it's very uncomfortable. (He is now holding the safety pin open.) Elizabeth are you listening? (There is a loud snore from Elizabeth, she shifts in the bunk. Mainwaring looks up at the huge outline just above him – he looks at the safety pin in his hand – looks up at the outline – thinks better of it.) Good night, dear.

During the episode, Jones receives some hate mail, claiming there is no room in Walmington for a coward. Although in the televised episode we never discover who wrote these malicious letters, the original script reveals one of the writers to be the frail Mrs Prosser, one of Jones's best friends throughout the sitcom, and someone you would have expected to support the aged butcher in his hour of need.

JONES All these years I've carried the photograph and some letters from her – I found in Private Clarke's wallet. (He pulls out a package of letters.) Now at last I can burn them.

MAINWARING: I'm sorry, Jones.

JONES (He pulls out the other letters.) I can also burn these white feathers, sir.

FRAZER Well, speaking for the platoon Jonesy – I'm sure it was none of us who sent them.

JONES I know who one of them was.

FRAZER Oh who?

JONES Mrs Prosser (He takes a piece of notepaper out of one of the envelopes and sniffs it.) I'd know her lavender scented notepaper anywhere.

GODFREY Oh dear – I thought you and Mrs Prosser were friends.

JONES So we were, but I'll tell you one thing, in future she'll have to go somewhere else for her bits of kidney.

MAINWARING Well, now I'm going to deal with Private Clarke.

WILSON I think he slipped out a few minutes ago, sir.

MAINWARING Well why didn't you stop him? He's not going to get away with this – come on, Wilson.

(Mainwaring makes for the door followed by Wilson, Jones, Walker, Frazer, Pike and Godfrey.)

SERIES 4, EPISODE 10
THE TEST

The Verger was one of life's creeps, especially as far as the Vicar was concerned. But a little scene that didn't make the recording saw Mr Yeatman lose his temper with the Vicar.

SCENE 4: OUTSIDE THE PAVILION.

(The umpires are walking out to the wicket.)

VERGER It looks as if the good Lord has sent us a nice day for it.

VICAR Yes, hasn't he indeed. Er, are you in a hurry to get away after the match, Mr Yeatman?

VERGER Not particularly, sir.

VICAR In that case I think you ought to remove your bicycle clips.

(The verger does so hobbling along beside the vicar.)

VERGER I'm sorry if my appearance is a bit of an embarrassment to you, sir.

VICAR I didn't mean it to sound like that, Mr Yeatman.

VERGER I always try my best to perform the humble tasks that have been sent down to me from on high to purge my soul.

VICAR And very well you do them.

VERGER: But if you don't like the way I go on, sir, I think I ought to warn you that I've had a very interesting offer from the Vicar of St Mary's.

(He moves to his wicket leaving the Vicar worried.)

SERIES 4, EPISODE 11
A WILSON (MANAGER)?

Two scenes in the script were never recorded in the TV episode.

SCENE 9: INTERIOR. CHURCH HALL. DAY.

(Jones is standing at the blackboard. Frazer, Walker, Godfrey and the rest of the platoon are gathered around.)

JONES Right now, pay attention – Mr Mainwaring will not be with us tonight as he has a lot of work to do at the bank – so I shall be taking tonight's lecture which deals with tactics. (Points to diagram on board.) Now can anyone tell me what that is?

WALKER Three bits of Turkish delight.

JONES No it is not it is… (Pike enters in his bank clothes.) Hurry up, Private Pike, you're late – and why aren't you wearing your uniform?

PIKE I can't stop, Mr Jones, I'm helping Mr Mainwaring at the bank – he sent me down with a message.

JONES What is it?

PIKE He is expecting a very important call from GHQ.

JONES Right ho.

PIKE As soon as you've taken the message send someone over to the bank with it straight away. You won't forget will you?

JONES Of course not.

PIKE I must get back. (**He goes.**)

JONES Now where was I? Oh yes – now this is an Impi.

GODFREY Oh you mean a sort of little elf?

JONES No, Mr Godfrey – an Impi is a Zulu army.

WALKER Blimey, don't tell me you fought the Zulus as well?

JONES No, I did not, but I happen to be a student of military tactics.

FRAZER But we're not fighting Zulus – this is 1941, we're fighting Nazis.

JONES We should not disdain ourselves so that we cannot learn from the past, Private Frazer – now the Zulus always attacked in the formation of a fighting bull – the horns the head and the chest: the horns encircled the enemy first, the head smashed at the front, and the chest surged through the enemy and linked up with the horns. Now what lesson can we learn from that?

WALKER It's a lot of bull.

JONES One more remark like that, Joe, and I shall… (**The phone rings.**) I wonder who that is giving us a ring?

WALKER Perhaps it's a ring for the bull's nose.

FRAZER It must be the call Mr Mainwaring's expecting from GHQ.

JONES Right, Private Godfrey answer the phone and take the message. (**Godfrey goes into the office.**) Now the king of the Zulus was called Cetewayo and he…

GODFREY (**Poking his head round the door.**) Excuse me, Mr Jones, I can't find the phone.

JONES What are you talking about… Oh right, Frazer, Walker come with me, the rest of you men stay here.

(**Jones rushes in followed by Walker and Frazer.**)

(**Cut to**)

SCENE 10: INTERIOR. OFFICE. CHURCH HALL. DAY.

(**Jones come in with Walker and Frazer. All the time the phone is ringing.**)

WALKER (**Holding the end of the phone wire.**) Some fool's locked the phone in the drawer of the desk.

JONES I did it for security.

FRAZER What are you talking about security?

JONES Well, a fifth columnist could have come in here and phoned up Hitler.

WALKER Have you gone completely potty? And who put this ruddy great bar and padlock on?

(**The three right hand drawers of the desk have an iron bar running down the length of them secured by a large padlock.**)

JONES I didn't think the locks were strong enough.

WALKER Quick, give us the key.

(**Jones tries to open the top left hand drawer.**)

FRAZER What are you doing? The phone's not in there.

JONES No, but the key is.

FRAZER Well hurry up and open it.

JONES I can't. I've just remembered I've left the key in my shop.

WALKER Oh come out of it.

(**He picks up a paper knife, pushes Jones out of the way and**

opens it. Jones pulls the drawer right out and puts it on top of the desk – it is full of papers. He frantically throws them all over the place looking for the key.)

JONES (**Holding up the key.**) I've got it.

WALKER Quick, give it to me.

JONES No it's the key for this drawer – that's where the key to the padlock is.

(**Jones opens the bottom left hand drawer, pulls it out and puts it on the desk, it is full of papers, he pulls them out.**)

JONES Don't panic, Don't panic – I'll find it.

(**The phone stops ringing.**)

GODFREY It's all right, Mr Jones. It's stopped ringing.

FRAZER That message could have been an invasion stand-by – you've really done it now.

(**The phone starts again.**)

JONES (**Throwing a whole lot of papers in the air.**) Whoa – it's not here – it's not here. (**He tips the drawer up**) Right grab your rifles – we'll have to shoot the lock off – stand back. (**He picks up his rifle and shoots at the lock twice – the bullets ricochet round the room. They all dive for cover.**)

FRAZER You damn fool, those ricochet bullets could have killed us.

JONES There's only one thing for it – we'll smash our way in – I'll go in from the top and you go in from the side.

(**Jones jumps up on the desk and starts to smash the top of the desk with his rifle butt. Walker and Frazer start to smash at the back. By now the rest of the platoon are gathered in the doorway, the Verger pushes his way through. He stares open-mouthed at them smashing the desk up.**)

VERGER Vandals, hooligans, they've gone mad – I must tell the Vicar. (**He rushes to the back door shouting.**) Vicar, Vicar, Help – they've all gone mad.

(**The desk by now is in ruins.**)

WALKER (**Pulling out the phone.**) All right, I've got it.

JONES (**Grabbing it.**) 'ere give it to me – Lieutenant Corporal Jones here.

(**He stops and lowers the phone.**)

WALKER What's the matter?

JONES Wrong number.

A later scene, which finds Frank Pike and Mr Mainwaring sitting in a shelter, is changed slightly in recording.

SCENE 13: INTERIOR. AIR RAID SHELTER. DAY.

(**Mainwaring and Pike are sitting side by side.**)

MAINWARING Confounded nuisance this air raid – we're far enough behind with our work as it is.

PIKE I'm afraid I'm not doing very well as Chief Clerk, Mr Mainwaring.

MAINWARING It's not your fault you haven't got the experience, Pike – you're doing the best you can.

PIKE I wish Uncle Arthur was still with us.

MAINWARING Mmmm…

PIKE I never realised how important he was.

MAINWARING No one is indispensable, Pike.

PIKE We certainly miss him in the platoon – I don't think Mr Jones is as good a Sergeant as he was. How much did the Vicar say the new desk was going to cost?

MAINWARING Ten pounds.

PIKE Uncle Arthur wouldn't have locked the phone away like that.

MAINWARING Look, I don't want to discuss it any more.

PIKE All the same, I hope Uncle Arthur is all right.

MAINWARING Don't worry, the devil looks after his own. They haven't had a single bomb drop on Eastgate yet.

CHRISTMAS SPECIAL
BATTLE OF THE GIANTS

In the early scenes of the episode, prior to Captain Square arriving, the script contained a telephone conversation between Mainwaring and his wife, Elizabeth.

(**Pike has just damaged Mainwaring's hat with his bayonet. The phone rings. Wilson picks it up.**)

MAINWARING (**Shouting**) You did that with your bayonet?

WILSON (**On the phone**) Oh hullo – how awfully nice to hear your voice. Yes, of course. (**To Mainwaring**) It's your wife, sir.

MAINWARING I shall stop the money for this out of your wages, Pike.

WILSON Your wife, sir.

MAINWARING What… (**He crosses to Wilson, takes the phone and puts his hand over the mouthpiece.**) Tell her I'm not here, Wilson.

WILSON She heard you shouting, sir.

MAINWARING Oh really. (**Into the phone.**) Er – hello Elizabeth – yes dear, yes dear – I know, dear, but the fact is I just couldn't stand sleeping with you any longer. (**Look from Wilson.**) Down in the shelter – but we haven't had any air raids for months, dear, and it's so uncomfortable down there – no, no, dear, I didn't deliberately wait until you'd gone out to move the bedding from the shelter. (**Mainwaring turns and sees Pike grinning in the doorway.**) Don't stand there gawping boy – get out. (**Pike goes.**) No… no… not you dear… what? But I can't come and move the bedding back into the shelter now – I shan't be dismissing the parade for another hour . . . what?… oh I see you want to go to bed early. Yes … yes… very well Elizabeth… goodbye, dear. (**He hangs up.**) I've got to go Wilson – you'll have to dismiss the parade. (**He picks up his old hat and crosses to the door.**)

WILSON I wouldn't take it too much to heart, sir – marriage is an institution in which one has to give and take you know.

MAINWARING I'll see you at the bank in the morning, Wilson – Good night.

Later, five scenes were cut from the final recording.

SCENE 28: TELECINE. EXTERIOR. ROAD. DAY.

(**Jones' van comes along the road and stops – Mainwaring jumps down followed by Frazer and Wilson.**)

FRAZER Why have you stopped, sir? We're well ahead of them.

MAINWARING And we're going to be even further ahead of them – look. Wilson, you see all those sheep in that field?

WILSON Yes, sir.

MAINWARING (**Pointing**) I want you to take Frazer and the rest of the men and drive all those sheep out of that bottom gate so that they fill the road behind us – I'd like to see Square get through that lot.

(**Cut to**)

SCENE 29: TELECINE. EXTERIOR. ROAD. DAY.

(The Sergeant is closing the bonnet.)

SERGEANT It seems to be all right now, sir.

(Square is at the wheel – he revs up.)

SQUARE Well done, well done, come on get in, they can't be very far ahead of us.

(The Sergeant and Pte get in and the van roars off.)

(Cut to)

SCENE 30: TELECINE. EXTERIOR. ROAD. DAY.

(Mainwaring, Wilson, Pike, Frazer, Godfrey and Sponge are standing singly by the van – the whole road is full of sheep.)

MAINWARING (Shouting across to Wilson.) I distinctly told you to drive them out of the lower gate, Wilson.

WILSON I couldn't help it, sir – they insisted on coming out of the upper gate.

MAINWARING Well there's one consolation – Square won't be able to get through this lot, either.

(Cut to shot of road – we see Jones' van completely surrounded by sheep. Square's van appears – turns off into an opening into a field behind the sheep and comes out of another opening in front. It stops.)

(Cut to close-up of Square leaning out of cab and shouting back to Mainwaring.)

SQUARE The biter bit, eh, Mainwaring – har, har, har.

(He drives off.)

(Cut back to shot of road. The Warden's bike comes up and does exactly the same as Square's van.)

(Cut to close-up of Warden shouting back at Mainwaring.)

WARDEN What's the matter, Mainwaring? Why are you looking so sheepish? (He drives off.)

(Cut to close-up of Mainwaring purple with rage.)

SCENE 31: TELECINE. EXTERIOR. ROAD. DAY.

(Very long shot of Square's van passing followed by warden on bike.)

SCENE 32: TELECINE. EXTERIOR. ROAD. DAY.

(Different shot of Jones' van passing.)

SCENE 33: TELECINE. EXTERIOR. ROAD. DAY.

(We see Square's van coming from one direction and Jones' van from another. As Square's van reaches crossroads, Jones' van crosses in front. Both vans stop.)

MAINWARING They're going the other way, we'll turn round.

SQUARE They're going the other way, we'll turn round.

(Jones' van backs across. Square's van backs across.)

SERIES 5, EPISODE 3
A SOLDIER'S FAREWELL

In the scene where Sergeant Wilson and Captain Mainwaring decide to indulge in a toasted cheese supper, it's not long before Jones enters the church hall office with some kidneys and joins the little party. In the script, Frank Pike was due to make an appearance, before Jones, to try and get Wilson to come home. This scene was never televised.

(There is a knock at the door – Pike comes in.)

PIKE Excuse me, Mr Mainwaring. (Whispering to Wilson) Are you coming, Uncle Arthur?

WILSON Where to?

PIKE Home of course. Mum will have supper ready for us.

WILSON You'll have to go without me – I'm having a toasted cheese supper with Captain Mainwaring.

PIKE Mum will be furious – you're not going to eat all that cheese are you, Mr Mainwaring?

MAINWARING Yes, why not?

PIKE You'll have terrible dreams. Perhaps I ought to stay and help you eat it.

MAINWARING I'm sorry, Pike – there's only enough for two.

PIKE (Whispering to Wilson) What am I going to tell mum?

WILSON (Whispering) Tell her Captain Mainwaring needs my comradeship.

PIKE What's that mean?

WILSON Look – just go Frank.

PIKE Well, goodnight. Don't say I didn't warn you about the dreaming. (He goes out the back door.)

MAINWARING Right, you make the toast, Wilson. I'll cut up the cheese. (There is a knock at the door.) Oh really – come in. (Jones enters.)

JONES Well, I'm just off – oh – that's a nice bit of cheese – you going to have a snack are you?

MAINWARING There's only enough for two, Jones.

JONES (Taking out parcel) That's a pity – I shall have to eat these kidneys myself.

WILSON What kidneys?

JONES (Opening parcel) I was taking these home for my supper.

SERIES 5, EPISODE 6
IF THE CAP FITS...

One scene was cut slightly when it came to recording the episode.

SCENE 1: INTERIOR. SIDE OFFICE. DAY.

(Wilson is looking through a sheaf of papers – Mainwaring is standing by him. Jones is sorting through a box of lantern slides. The Verger is hovering round the slides.)

MAINWARING Now listen, Wilson, I want you to read those notes out in a loud clear voice – do you understand?

WILSON Yes, sir – a loud clear voice.

MAINWARING I don't want any mumbling.

WILSON Do I ever mumble, sir?

(Mainwaring reacts.)

MAINWARING Haven't you finished sorting out those slides yet, Jones?

JONES Not quite, sir – shan't be a tick. I'm very excited, we've never had a lecture like this before, that's what I like about you, Captain Mainwaring, you're always trying out new modern scientific methods.

MAINWARING I try to keep abreast with the times, Jones.

JONES There's no doubt about it – the magic lantern is a wonderful invention.

WILSON Yes, it's only been going a hundred years.

MAINWARING I don't want any of that sort of talk, Wilson.

JONES Permission to speak, sir – I do not like the Verger creeping around me when I'm trying to sort out my slides.

(The Verger is poking at the slides.)

MAINWARING Do stop creeping around Jones when he's trying to get his slides sorted out, Verger.

VERGER I beg your pardon, Mr Mainwaring, I am not creeping.

JONES Yes you are, you're the biggest creeper I've ever met – you're a trouble maker and a creeper.

VERGER You're the trouble maker – I am just here on the instructions of the Vicar – to keep an eye on his apparatus – and see that you don't abuse it when you use it.

JONES I won't abuse it, when I use it.

VERGER And I'm going to see that you don't abuse it, when you use it.

SERIES 6, EPISODE 1
THE DEADLY ATTACHMENT

This popular episode finds the Walmington platoon looking after some German sailors. A short scene involving Walker grasping the opportunity to earn a few quid never made it to the final recording.

WILSON I wonder if he's got any to spare, I'm right out of them.

MAINWARING This isn't a cocktail party, Wilson, did you prime those grenades?

PIKE Well, Mr Mainwaring we…

WILSON I think I can honestly say, sir, that all the grenades now have detonators in them.

MAINWARING Good, Pike get the Tommy gun.

PIKE Yes, Mr Mainwaring.

(He goes into the office. Jones comes over to Mainwaring and Wilson.)

JONES The prisoners are now in a huddle in the middle of the hall, sir.

MAINWARING Thank you, Jones.

(Cut to tight close-up of Walker talking to one of the sailors.)

WALKER 'ere listen, tell your mates that I am in the market for purchasing Nazi daggers, swastikas, badges, signed pictures of Hitler or similar souvenirs. I'll give you a good price. (The sailor shakes his head.) Oh blimey you don't speak English do you? Look Nazi daggers, see daggers. (He makes a stabbing motion at the sailor who jumps back.)

CAPTAIN (Crossing to Walker.) Get away from my men at once.

WALKER Don't start on me, mate.

MAINWARING Come over here, Walker.

(Walker crosses to Mainwaring, Wilson and Jones who are standing in a tight group away from the prisoners.) How dare you fraternise with the enemy.

WALKER I was only asking them if there was anything they needed.

Later in the episode, Jones has to endure the uncomfortable experience of having a bomb pushed down his trousers, a scene originally intended for Mainwaring. When Arthur Lowe refused to take his part in the original script, Jimmy Perry and David Croft had little option but to rewrite the scene.

MAINWARING You won't get away with this, we're bound to be spotted going through the town.

CAPTAIN No one will interfere, Captain, because you will be escorting us with empty rifles.

MAINWARING And how are you going to make us do that?

(Wilson returns with a Mills bomb and a piece of string.)

CAPTAIN Very simply. (He hands the revolver to one of the

sailors who holds it against Hodges' neck, he takes the bomb and string from Wilson.) Is it primed?

WILSON Oh yes.

CAPTAIN (**Unscrewing the baseplug.**) You don't mind if I make sure?

WILSON By all means.

CAPTAIN (**Looking in the bomb.**) Good. (**He screws back the baseplug.**) Take off your belt and undo the back of your tunic.

MAINWARING Now look here.

CAPTAIN Do as I say. (**He ties the end of the string to the ring of the pin. Mainwaring takes off his belt and unbuttons the back of his blouse.**) You will march in front of me. (**He puts the bomb in the waistband of Mainwaring's trousers.**) One false move, and I will pull the string. (**He buttons up the back of Mainwaring's blouse.**) Seven seconds will give me plenty of time to get clear but I think it is not enough time for you to unbutton your tunic.

MAINWARING You unspeakable swine.

FRAZER A terrible way to die.

JONES Permission to speak, sir, let me have the bomb in my trousers, let me have it.

MAINWARING Quiet, Jones. How can you hope to beat us? You see the sort of men we breed in this country?

CAPTAIN Yes, rather stupid ones.

MAINWARING You can sneer, but you've forgotten one thing, Captain.

CAPTAIN What is that?

MAINWARING The Royal Navy, you've got to cross twenty-five miles of water. You'll never make it.

CAPTAIN I think we will, because all of you will be on the boat with us. (**Points to Godfrey.**) We shall leave the old man behind to tell them. Your Navy won't fire on their own people.

(*Out in the street the men march along until they see the Colonel.*)

JONES Yes sir, yes sir, platoon by the right, quick march.

COLONEL Wait a minute. Halt! (**They halt.**) You know I'm surprised at you Mainwaring, you're usually so smartly turned out, you've got a great lump of string hanging down your back.

MAINWARING Where?

COLONEL Here.

(*He pulls the string and holds it up. We see the pin on the end of the string.*)

MAINWARING Oh no!

(*Everyone except the Colonel, Jones, Wilson, and Pike dive for cover and flatten themselves against the wall.*)

JONES Mr Mainwaring's got a bomb in his trousers, don't panic! Don't panic!

MAINWARING Get it out, Jones.

(*He starts to unbutton the back of his blouse. Close up of Hodges holding the Verger who has his fingers in his ears.*)

JONES I'll get it, sir. I'll get it.

(*Close up of Godfrey. Jones puts his hand in the back of Mainwaring's blouse.*)

JONES It's slipped down, Mr Mainwaring!

(*He thrusts his arm down the back of Mainwaring's trousers.*)

MAINWARING Save yourself, Jones.

(*Wilson crosses to Colonel.*)

WILSON I wonder if I might borrow your revolver, sir?

(*Mainwaring and Jones are dancing in the road.*)

JONES Don't panic, sir, don't panic.

COLONEL What the hell's going on?

WILSON I'll explain later. (**Waves revolver at prisoner.**) All you German chaps, would you mind just getting up against the wall, with your hands up, please.

(*The prisoners obey.*)

MAINWARING Jones, wait a minute, it should have gone off by now.

(*They both stop.*)

JONES So it should, you're safe, sir, you're safe.

(*Mainwaring limps over to Wilson, Jones still has his arm down his trousers.*)

MAINWARING I thought you said you'd primed those grenades.

WILSON I did sir, with dummies.

MAINWARING Why is it you will never… you've saved my life, Wilson.

WILSON Now perhaps you'll agree with me, that it's awfully dangerous to keep them primed.

MAINWARING (**To Jones**) Take your arm out of my trousers, Jones.

(*Credits*)

SERIES 6, EPISODE 4
WE KNOW OUR ONIONS

In the second scene, we see Jones, who had gone into the church hall to find Walker, take a phone call from Hodges. However, the original script had Walker speaking to the warden.

SCENE 2: STUDIO. SIDE OFFICE. DAY.
(*Walker is on the phone to Hodges.*)

HODGES Now listen to me, mate, I've had enough of your excuses, I want my onions, do you hear me?

WALKER Look, I'm sorry I couldn't bring them round sooner, but I had to wait for them to be dug up.

HODGES Listen, if I don't get those onions today, they'll have to dig you up.

WALKER Don't get so excited.

HODGES Excited! I gave you fifty quid in oncers for a half a ton of onions, you said you'd bring them round to my shop yesterday. Where are they?

WALKER They're in Jones's van.

HODGES Well bring them round.

WALKER I can't, we're going away for the weekend.

HODGES Going away for the weekend!

WALKER Yes, on a Home Guard efficiency test.

HODGES I'm coming round there now, and if I don't get my onions, there won't be anything left of you to test. (**He hangs up.**)

WALKER Temper, temper.

(*Jones comes in.*)

JONES Hurry up, Joe, Captain Mainwaring wants the key to the van.

WALKER Blimey, I hope he likes onions.

SERIES 6, EPISODE 5
THE HONOURABLE MAN

During this episode, Sergeant Wilson is ordered to ride a motorbike, against his better judgement. He turns out to be a danger to everyone as he careers across the roads, drives along the verge and down ditches. He also causes the Vicar, who's happily going about his business on a quiet country lane, to fall off his bike, a scene that was more extensive in the original script.

MAINWARING Right, get him on.

(*Wilson climbs on to the bike.*)

MAINWARING You've time for a good one-hour spin before you need to get ready for the ceremony.

WILSON Wouldn't ten minutes be enough?

JONES Now remember – squeeze the clutch with your left hand, kick upwards on to the gear with your right foot, like this. Rev up with your right hand by doing this sort of motion, and then let out the clutch with your left hand, like you were squeezing a lemon.

(*Wilson revs up and shoots off. They watch him go.*)

GODFREY Do you think I should follow on a bicycle with this? (**He holds up the red cross bag.**)

MAINWARING No, it's time he learnt to fend for himself.

(*Cut to long-shot of Wilson zig-zagging along a country road, then the Vicar cycling along a road. Wilson draws alongside.*)

WILSON (**Shouting.**) Excuse me. You don't happen to know how to stop these things, do you?

VICAR Well, as a matter of fact, many years ago, when I was quite a youth…

WILSON (**Drawing away.**) Too late.

(*The Vicar looks surprised.*)

VICAR Sorry if I was boring you.

(*Cut to long-shot of Wilson heading across fields.*)

(*Long shot of road, a staff car – preferably an army Humber – is progressing. Wilson comes out of the farm gate, turns into the same direction as the car and then goes into a ditch.*)

(*The driver stops and gets out to help him, closely followed by the Russian and his interpreter.*)

SERIES 6, EPISODE 6
THINGS THAT GO BUMP IN THE NIGHT

When Jimmy Perry and David Croft wrote the script for this episode little did they know that Jimmy Beck would be too ill to record the studio shots, so some of his dialogue was given to Private Sponge. There was also one complete scene not recorded.

SCENE 3: TELECINE. EXTERIOR. COUNTRY ROAD. NIGHT.

(*Walker and Frazer come round the back of the van. Above them is a tarpaulin about eight feet square. It is supported at each corner by Sponge, Hastings, Desmond and Pike. They have their bayonets on their rifles and these are stuck through the tarpaulin. They shuffle round to the door of the cab.*)

WALKER Right, Mr Mainwaring, you can get out. Come on Jonesy – get down.

(*Jones gets down.*)

JONES It's all right, Mr Mainwaring, you won't get wet, Joe has rigged up a great big cantaloupe. Come on sir, I'll help you down. Hold it steady, Pikey.

PIKE I am holding it steady.

JONES No you're not, you're jogging it, it's dripping on Mr Mainwaring, don't get any drips on the officer.

(*He paws Mainwaring.*)

MAINWARING Stop mauling me about, Jones.

JONES I must protect your welfare, sir, I will not have you having pneumonia.

MAINWARING Get down, Wilson.

WILSON Just coming, sir, isn't this nice? How awfully clever of you, Walker.

(They are all standing in a tight bunch.)

JONES Now, if we all walk in a line close together we won't get wet. You get in the front, Sarge, that will stop the drips going on Mr Mainwaring. (He pushes Wilson into position.) And you get behind him, sir, and put your arms around his waist. (He pushes Mainwaring.)

MAINWARING Now, just a minute, Jones, I am in command here, and I give the orders.

JONES I assure you, sir, I have no intention of usurping your officership, but I must keep you dry.

WILSON Better do as he says, sir, after all we don't want to get wet. I don't mind you putting your arms round my waist.

JONES Right, Joe, you get behind Mr Mainwaring, Jock, you put your arms around Joe. (He pushes them about.)

FRAZER I don't like this very much.

JONES And I'll put my arms around you. (He gets behind Frazer.)

FRAZER Now I'm certain I don't like it.

JONES Are we all ready? And don't forget to keep in step. By the left quick march. Left right, left right…

(They all shuffle forward.)

WILSON I feel rather like the Emperor of China in Aladdin.

WALKER I feel like I'm at a Jewish wedding.

MAINWARING Just a minute.

JONES Halt. Are you getting drips on you, sir? I told you not to joggle it, Pike.

PIKE I'm not joggling it.

MAINWARING Where's Godfrey?

FRAZER He's in the back of the van, sleeping like a baby.

MAINWARING We'd better go and get him.

JONES Right, sir. By the left quick march, left right, left right, left right wheel, right wheel.

(They shuffle round in a crocodile towards the back of the van. Walker makes a noise like a railway train.)

MAINWARING That will do, Walker.

SERIES 7, EPISODE 4
THE GODIVA AFFAIR

It was rare for back row members of the platoon to be involved in a particular scene, but George Hancock was written into the first scene of this episode, even though by the time the programme hit the TV screens, it had been cut.

SCENE 1: INTERIOR. SIDE OFFICE. DAY.

(Mainwaring is talking to Private Hancock, who has a rifle and a fixed bayonet.)

MAINWARING Right, Hancock, you are to stay on guard outside this door and let no one through, understand?

HANCOCK Right, sir, let no one through.

MAINWARING Maximum security, is that clear? Maximum security.

HANCOCK Yes, Captain Mainwaring, maximum security.

(Mainwaring goes through the door into the hall.)

Later on, when we see Frank Pike on the phone to Mr Cheeseman, a scene involving Mrs Pike was also cut.

SCENE 6: INTERIOR. TELEPHONE BOX. NIGHT.

(Cheeseman is on the phone, he is in civilian clothes.)

CHEESEMAN Hullo, Hullo, listen Pikey, I've got to speak to you, it's very important, boyo.

SCENE 7: INTERIOR. FRANK'S HOUSE. NIGHT.

(Pike is on the other end of the line, he is in his pyjamas and dressing gown.)

PIKE What do you want to ring me up at this time of night? Mum's furious.

(Mrs Pike comes into the picture.)

MRS PIKE Who's that on the phone, Frank, it's not a girl is it?

PIKE No Mum, it's Mr Cheeseman.

MRS PIKE How dare he ring you up in the middle of the night, tell him to go away.

PIKE It's only ten o'clock, Mum.

MRS PIKE I don't care, you should be in bed, and don't forget to clean your teeth.

(She goes.)

PIKE Mum says I've got to go to bed.

CHEESEMAN Wait a minute, I just want a bit of information. What time does Mainwaring go for his morning coffee?

SERIES 8, EPISODE 1
RING DEM BELLS

Wilson's predilection for sarcasm and his dry sense of humour saw him grasping every possible opportunity to dent Captain Mainwaring's pomposity. In the televised episode we see Mainwaring staring at himself in the mirror considering which is his best side. When Wilson enters the church hall his opinion is sought, although his true opinions were never recorded.

WILSON Well, sir, your nose does look a little red from this side, turn the other way. (Mainwaring turns.) Yes, it looks a bit red from this side as well; I don't think you've got a best side.

SERIES 8, EPISODE 5
HIGH FINANCE

The recorded scene in which Frazer states that Lance Corporal Jones is doomed if he lets Mainwaring and the bank study his company's accounts is shorter than what was originally written.

FRAZER Are you mad? Letting Mainwaring poke his nose into your affairs, once that bank's got their hands on you, they'll squeeze you and squeeze you, you're doomed, doomed.

GODFREY I don't agree. Mr Mainwaring would be the first person I'd go to if I were in trouble.

FRAZER He wouldn't have been in trouble if it hadn't been for Mainwaring. He's a vulture, you should have come to me for help, Jonesy.

JONES Will you lend me fifty quid then?

FRAZER Well er… you know the old saying – lend money and you lose a friend, and you're a very dear friend of mine, Jonesy.

GODFREY I wish I could help, but I've just lent some money to somebody else.

JONES Well if I go on like this, I'll end up in Carey Street.

PIKE Perhaps they haven't got any butcher's shops there, Mr Jones.

Later on, to try and resolve Jones' dire financial position, Mainwaring reviews the possessions and tools he could sell to raise some money.

MAINWARING Good point, Frazer, we'll buy it off him, put down nine pounds Wilson. What's next?

WILSON The chopping blocks.

MAINWARING Ah yes, the chopping blocks.

FRAZER We could cut them up and sell them for firewood, that should bring in about three pounds.

JONES 'ere, just a minute.

MAINWARING Quiet, Jones, put down three pounds, Wilson. Next.

WILSON The scales.

MAINWARING Two pounds. What's next?

WILSON That's all, sir, it comes to fourteen pounds.

MAINWARING Well that's not too bad, if we sell all your assets, we could pay off nearly a third of your debt.

JONES But if I do that, I shan't have any business left.

MAINWARING (Sharply) I'm trying to help Jones, I'm speaking as your friend.

JONES You don't sound very friendly.

MAINWARING Well what do you suggest?

JONES I don't know, I just can't bring myself to squeeze those poor little orphans.

MAINWARING What are you talking about?

CHRISTMAS SPECIAL
THE LOVE OF THREE ORANGES

Part of a scene was cut which involved the Verger and Vicar rushing into the hall, with Mr Yeatman complaining about the state of the floor.

MAINWARING (To the rest.) All the same a good turn out. In the event of snow we shall merge into the landscape.

PIKE Mr Mainwaring, what happens if it snows and we've left our disguise back home?

JONES Permission to speak, sir. I think we should have power to go up to a house and knock on the door and say 'I hereby requisition your sheets' – and I think you should give us a certificate of authority.

MAINWARING No, I don't think that would be a very good idea, Jones.

PIKE Here – Mr Frazer knows when it is going to snow, don't you Mr Frazer – his joints creak, don't they?

FRAZER Aye – the bones creak and groan like old ships' timbers.

PIKE Well when he hears his bones he could ring us up.

FRAZER Who's going to pay for the call?

(Enter the Vicar and the Verger.)

VERGER Look at that floor – just look at it. Three hours I spent on that – back breaking…

VICAR Never mind that Mr Yeatman. Captain Mainwaring, can I have a word with you?

MAINWARING Can't you see I'm busy?

VICAR We're all busy in our different ways, Captain Mainwaring. I just wanted to give you plenty of notice that you can't have the hall Saturday fortnight.

MAINWARING What do you mean? I may need it for a vital military purpose.

Later on, when the bazaar is taking place in the church hall, Mainwaring walks around visiting all the stalls. One small scene that was deleted saw Mainwaring leave Godfrey's stand and stop at Mrs Pike's stall before moving on to Frazer.

DOLLY Perhaps Mr Wilson would like to try some?

WILSON Oh how nice, thank you. (**He takes a mouthful, rolls it round his mouth and swallows.**)

MAINWARING What's all that palaver for?

WILSON That's the correct way to taste wine. Frenchmen always do it like that. One should, of course, spit it out.

MAINWARING We don't want any of those dirty foreign habits here, Wilson. (**They pass on to the jumble stall.**) You've got a lot of stuff there, Mrs Pike.

MRS PIKE Yes, Mr Mainwaring, people have been very generous.

(**Mainwaring points to a pink rowing cap.**)

MAINWARING Is that a man's cap?

MRS PIKE Yes, pretty isn't it? (**She picks it up.**)

MAINWARING What on earth sort of man would wear a nancy thing like that?

MRS PIKE Arthur gave it to me.

MAINWARING Is that your cap, Wilson?

WILSON Yes, I won it for rowing.

MAINWARING They gave you a pink cap for a manly sport like rowing?

WILSON It's quite common in public schools to wear pink caps.

MAINWARING Extraordinary. (**He passes on to Frazer's stall**) Silhouettes eh, that's quite a novelty, Frazer.

SERIES 9, EPISODE 2
THE MAKING OF PRIVATE PIKE

This episode introduces us to Hodges' niece, Sylvia, who's serving with the ATS. If the recording had stuck rigidly to the script, Sylvia would have made her entrance earlier, arriving at the church hall office at the same time as the Vicar, Verger and Hodges.

MAINWARING Now listen, half that keyhole is military property and I'm not having putty put in it.

HODGES You've got to Napoleon – it's regulations.

MAINWARING Who made them?

HODGES I did. It's been scientifically proved by experts that a thin shaft of light no thicker than a pencil shining through a keyhole can be seen by an enemy plane a thousand feet up. (**He sees Wilson smiling at his niece.**) Here – stop ogling that girl.

WILSON I wasn't 'ogling her' as you put it.

HODGES Oh yes you was. You've got a leering grin on your face. (**To Mainwaring**) Can't you keep your men under control, Napoleon?

WILSON I was simply smiling in a friendly welcoming fashion.

HODGES Well in my book that's ogling.

MAINWARING If you had any manners at all you'd introduce us.

HODGES Oh, this is my niece, Sylvia, she's got a spot of leave.

MAINWARING Ah – this is Corporal Jones, Sergeant Wilson you've already met. (**There's a honking car horn off.**) What on earth's that?

(**Pike rushes into the office.**)

PIKE Captain Mainwaring, sorry to interrupt, but the Colonel has just driven into the yard.

JONES The Colonel's just driven into the yard, Mr Mainwaring – turn out the guard.

SERIES 9, EPISODE 5
NUMBER ENGAGED

The first scene was altered when it came to recording in the studio. In the script we find Pike drawing on the black board.

MAINWARING (**Continued**)… the fact that we are all packed in here like sardines, but it's Warden Hodges' turn to use the hall tonight and I'm afraid there is nothing I can do about it. Now what I have to show you is top secret. Uncover the board, Wilson.

WILSON Right, sir. (**He reaches for the blanket.**)

MAINWARING Just a minute, hold it. (**He crosses to the door and opens it, then crosses to the other door and looks out.**) All clear, right, carry on Sergeant. (**Wilson takes the blanket off the black board. On it is drawn an aerial view of a line of telegraph poles.**)

WILSON There, isn't that nice?

MAINWARING All right, Wilson. Now, can anybody tell me what that is?

GODFREY Are you going to write a song, sir?

JONES That's a good idea, a platoon song. We had one out in the Sudan you know.

MAINWARING All right, Jones.

JONES (**Singing**) Oh Lord Kitchener, he may look very odd but in spite of what they say, I don't think he really is a…

MAINWARING Jones, please.

JONES Sorry, sir, I got carried away.

WILSON For goodness sake tell them, sir.

MAINWARING Patience, Wilson, let them try and work it out for themselves. Anybody else?

PIKE I think I know, Mr Mainwaring, can I borrow the chalk, please? (**He takes the chalk and crosses to the board and starts to draw. He stands right in front.**)

GODFREY I hope that boy's not drawing something questionable.

JONES Close your eyes, Mr Godfrey, I'll tell you if it's all right to look.

(**Pike steps back. He has drawn some cows looking over the wires with mountains in the background.**)

PIKE There you are, that's what I think it is, Mr Mainwaring.

WILSON That's rather good, Frank.

MAINWARING This isn't a game, boy, go and sit down at once.

PIKE Well I like that, you asked us to…

MAINWARING Another word out of you and I shall send you home. Now this is an aerial view of a line of telegraph poles. You see the wires running along there? Now these telephone wires are used for …

FRAZER Making telephone calls.

MAINWARING Making telephone… carrying highly important secret messages.

(**The door opens and Hodges and the Verger enter. They cross to a cupboard behind the desk.**)

HODGES Excuse me, Napoleon, I'm giving a lecture on gas attacks and I want my rattles and whistles.

MAINWARING Quick, cover the board, Wilson.

(**Wilson does so. Hodges takes the rattles and whistles out of the cupboard.**)

HODGES Don't worry about me. Just carry on.

MAINWARING What I am telling my men is top secret.

HODGES Then why don't you take 'em on the roof. Right, we'll just get this lot sorted out.

MAINWARING (**Crossing to Hodges**) Now look here, Hodges –

(**Hodges tries one of the rattles in Mainwaring's face**)

HODGES That's all right. (**He hands it to the Verger and tries another.**) That's all right. (**He tries a third.**) That's no good. (**He throws it back in the cupboard and tries the next one.**) That's OK – try the whistles.

VERGER Yes, Mr Hodges. (**He starts to blow the whistles.**)

MAINWARING I'll give you exactly ten seconds to get out of this office.

HODGES I'm not going until I've tested all my rattles and whistles.

MAINWARING We'll see about that. Jones, clear them out.

JONES Yes, sir, yes sir. (**He draws his bayonet.**) Come on out.

HODGES You flippin' hooligans.

VERGER His reverence is going to hear about this.

(**The door closes behind them.**)

WILSON What a dreadful common man he is, sir.

MAINWARING Unfortunately, in times of war, there are certain pompous men who just love to put on a uniform and strut about giving orders. We've all met one.

FRAZER Ai, we have indeed.

MAINWARING Uncover the board, Wilson. (**Wilson does so.**) Now the secret messages that are carried along these wires are…

HODGES Gas! Gas! Gas!

(**Rattles noise**)

MAINWARING Just a minute. (**He strides to the door and opens it.**) Hodges! (**He goes through and closes it. Pause. The door opens. Mainwaring comes back, he crosses to the board.**) That's the last we shall here of him. Now as I was…

HODGES All clear, all clear!

(**Whistles noise.**)

WILSON I'll go this time, sir. (**He crosses to the door, goes out. Pause. He returns.**)

MAINWARING I hope you were diplomatic, Wilson.

WILSON Oh yes, I told him if he didn't shut up, I'd hit him.

PIKE (**To Jones**) Uncle Arthur's ever so good. Mum says when he's roused he's like a tiger.

MAINWARING This is it men. Now a highly secret invasion warning device has been set up on the coast not far from here. It's purpose is to detect enemy boats and landing craft long before they reach the shore, and so give us the vital time we need to prepare our defences. All the information is carried to GHQ along these wires which are patrolled day and night by regular troops. Now, next weekend we shall take over the two mile stretch in our area for twenty-four hours. I don't have to stress the responsibility of this vital task. If anything should happen to those wires, it could alter the whole course of the war. Now let us consider what could happen to put these wires out of action.

WILSON You're not going to start guessing games again are you, sir?

MAINWARING I'm trying to make them use their brains. You'd better make a note of all the points that are raised.

JONES Permission to speak, sir. Birds could perch on the wires and bring them down.

MAINWARING I don't think there is a bird in the British Isles heavy enough to do that.

JONES What about an ostrich?

MAINWARING An ostrich? I don't quite follow you.

JONES I look at it this way, sir, supposing there is an air raid on London Zoo and one of the ostriches gets out. And he says, 'I think I'll have a day at the seaside,' and he runs and runs and runs – they run ever so fast. And when he gets here he gives a high leap, lands on the wire and it crashes down.

MAINWARING I think you're going into the realms of fantasy now, Jones.

JONES It's a possibility, sir.

PIKE Mr Mainwaring, bulls.

MAINWARING I beg your pardon?

PIKE A silly farmer could leave a gate open, a bull could get out, lean against the pole and bring it down.

MAINWARING (In despair) Anything else?

FRAZER Don't forget, Captain Mainwaring, there's always the unseen enemy.

MAINWARING The unseen enemy?

FRAZER Yes, worms – they could bring the wires down.

MAINWARING How?

FRAZER By eating the bottom of the pole. Even while we're sitting here, they're gnawing away at everything, gnawing away until in the end it's us. It's all worms in the end, did you hear what I said? Worms! Worms!

WILSON (Reading) Up till now, sir, we've had an ostrich, a bull and some worms.

MAINWARING All right, Wilson, I heard. I should have thought it was obvious to you all that the danger we have to guard against is Nazi paratroopers cutting the wires. I think we can disregard anything else.

GODFREY All the same one can't be too careful, sir.

MAINWARING Have you thought of something else, Godfrey?

GODFREY Yes.

MAINWARING What?

GODFREY My sister Dolly read in the newspaper that they cut open the stomach of a dead ostrich and found six gold sovereigns inside in perfect condition. (Mainwaring blows hard.) If it had been pound notes, they would have been digested. Money was money in those days.

JONES I quite agree, Mr Godfrey. I always said it was a pity we went off the gold standard.

(The door opens and the Vicar enters, followed by Hodges and the Verger.)

VICAR Sorry to bother you, Mr Mainwaring, I just want to finalise the arrangements for the Church Parade on Sunday.

MAINWARING I'm sorry, Vicar, we shall have to cancel it. Next Sunday we shall be on top secret duties.

HODGES They're only guarding some old telephone wires.

MAINWARING That's classified information, how did you know that?

HODGES See this white hat mate? Chief ARP Warden, that's how I know, so put that in your pipe and smoke it.

WILSON (Crosses to Hodges.) You know what I said to you outside the door just now. Well it still applies.

MAINWARING Believe me, Vicar, we're all very upset that we can't come to church.

VICAR Well I'll come out to you, we'll have a simple service in the open air.

MAINWARING Oh.

VERGER But we haven't got any transport your reverence.

VICAR Oh dear, I forgot that.

MAINWARING What a pity.

HODGES Don't worry, Vicar, I'll take you out.

SERIES 9, EPISODE 6
NEVER TOO OLD

During this episode Mr Mainwaring is invited around to see Mrs Fox, who asks him to give her away at her wedding. Whilst he's at the flat, waiting for her to finish dressing, she asks him to zip her up, a short scene that was never recorded.

MAINWARING Oh no – I couldn't really. Somebody might come in.

MRS FOX We'll lock the door.

MAINWARING That would be worse.

MRS FOX Anyway, you're practically a father to me now. It's not a very big one. (She turns to show the zip.)

MAINWARING Oh – very well. (He does it.) Now I really must go. I'll come back when the rest are expected.

MRS PIKE Cooee – are you there?

MRS FOX Come in, Mrs Pike.

(Mrs Pike enters.)

MRS PIKE Come in, Arthur, come in Frank. Take your hat off, Frank, where are your manners?

THE FILM

Although I have only been able to trace a copy of the final draft of the film script, there were still several scenes cut or altered between this draft and the filming of the picture.

SCENE 1: EXTERIOR. THE FRENCH COAST. 1940. DAY.
HIGH ANGLE SHOT FROM HELICOPTER.

A car is seen moving swiftly along the coast road.

(Cut to)

CLOSE SHOT OF CAR.

A Nazi pennant is flying on the bonnet. It is an open staff car. Inside are three high ranking German officers. The car is being driven by a very short orderly in a steel helmet. The car screeches to a halt at the edge of the cliff. The orderly jumps out and opens the door. The three officers get out with much slamming of doors… heavy, sinister German music.

They stride to the edge of the cliff. One of the officers, a very large fat man, is a general. He snaps his fingers, the orderly hands him a pair of field glasses. The general looks through them.

(Cut to)

VIEW THROUGH GLASSES OF THE ENGLISH COAST.

SCENE 2: EXTERIOR. THE ENGLISH COAST. DAY.
VIEW THROUGH GLASSES OF HIGH CLIFFS.

The glasses pan up and we see a small wooden hut on the top of the cliff. The focus is changed on the glasses, bringing the hut into close-up. Notice on hut reads: GENTS.

Private Godfrey, a man in his seventies, comes out. He is dressed in Home Guard uniform. He looks straight towards the glasses, gives a little start and picks up his pike (a carving knife tied to a broomstick) which is leaning against the hut. He assumes a defiant position for a moment.

VOICE Hurry up, Godfrey.

Godfrey hurries along the cliff top and joins a group. The field glasses focus on the group. It is composed of a tableau as follows:

CAPTAIN MAINWARING is centre. He is sitting on camp stool with his greatcoat draped round his shoulders à la Napoleon. Standing on his right IS SERGEANT WILSON holding a shotgun. On his left, LANCE CORPORAL JONES holding an assegai. Behind him PRIVATE PIKE holding a pole with a tattered Union Jack fluttering bravely in the breeze. Next to him is PRIVATE FRAZER holding an old-fashioned rifle. And next to him is PRIVATE WALKER holding a pike. And next to him PRIVATE GODFREY also holding a pike. The rest of the platoon are gathered around in various defiant positions holding pitchforks, old swords and a few rifles.

The titles 'DAD'S ARMY' bang in under the tableau. At the same time we hear the signature tune: 'Who Do You Think You Are Kidding, Mr Hitler'.

The field glasses focus into a close up of the main characters and their names come in underneath:

ARTHUR LOWE Captain Mainwaring

JOHN LE MESURIER Sergeant Wilson

Etc Etc Etc

SCENE 3: EXTERIOR. THE FRENCH COAST. DAY.

The Nazi General hands the glasses back to the orderly. They all stride back to the car and get in.

GENERAL (to other Nazi officer) The rules of war clearly state that when you lose, you surrender. Why are those British fools still fighting?

ORDERLY (turning round in the driving seat) Perhaps they have not read the rules, Herr General.

FIVE SHORT SCENES OF THE MEN'S ATTEMPTS TO ARM THEMSELVES.

SCENE 25: EXTERIOR. PARK WAR MEMORIAL. DAY.

A group of life-sized 18th-century soldiers are crouched round a cannon. PAN to reveal Jones, Frazer and Pike crouched behind a bush.

(Cut to)

Park keeper picking up papers on a spiked stick. He looks up. CLOSE UP of keeper looking amazed.

KEEPER Blimey!

Cut back to War memorial. The cannon is missing.

(Cut to)

SCENE 26: EXTERIOR. A GARDEN. DAY.

An old man is cutting a hedge with a sickle. As he draws his hand back another hand comes through the hedge and takes the sickle. The old man brings his hand down in a cutting stroke without the sickle.

SCENE 27: EXTERIOR. OUTSIDE A THEATRE. DAY.

CLOSE UP of poster outside which reads: THIS WEEK THE EVERGREEN ROMANTIC MUSICAL 'THE BRIGAND KING'.

SCENE 28: INTERIOR. STAGE OF THEATRE. DAY.

The scene is a mountain hideout. The Brigand King is singing. A queue of Brigands are lining up with their back to the camera.

BRIGAND KING Give me the men who will fight to be free
Give me the men who will march close to me
Give me your word that you'll fight to the end
Here are the guns that will prove I'm your friend.

As he sings, the Brigand King is handing out old-fashioned Arab rifles to the line of men. As the second man takes his he turns and we see underneath the head-dress that it's Walker. He quickly nips into the wings.

(Cut to)

SCENE 29: INTERIOR. A MUSEUM. DAY.

A guide is standing in front of a suit of armour which is holding a sword.

GUIDE (**Pointing to the sword**) And that Ladies and Gentleman is the actual sword that Queen Elizabeth used to dub Sir Charles. Now we'll just move along to the next exhibit.

The suit of armour walks away.

SCENE 108

MAJOR GENERAL (**Shouting**) Salute, man!

JONES Platoon hup!

The platoon all drop the rope and salute. There is a creaking sound as the centre section of the bridge breaks away. High angle shot as the section floats downstream with the Major General on his horse. Jones and the platoon run up to Mainwaring and Wilson – they gesture wildly and run along the bank.

SCENE 109: EXTERIOR. SMALL BOAT HOUSE. DAY.

A few motor boats are moored by the bank. The platoon run into the picture.

MAINWARING (**Pointing to the boat.**) Get in, Wilson.

WILSON But, sir.

MAINWARING Don't argue – get in.

Wilson jumps in the boat – Mainwaring follows.

WILSON But, sir, in wartime all boats are immobilised.

Mainwaring starts the motor – it roars to life.

MAINWARING Rubbish – this isn't immobilised.

(Cut to)

High angle shot – the boat roars out into the river – goes round and round in circles and makes straight for the opposite bank.

(Cut to)

Motor boat stuck in rushes

WILSON You see, sir, I was right.

MAINWARING Oh shut up – come on!

They both jump out of the boat and run along the bank.

(Cut)

CLOSING SCENE. EXTERIOR. CLIFF TOP. DAY.

GODFREY As a matter of fact I heard a scratching sound last night – I thought it was a mouse – of course it could have been a Nazi.

MAINWARING Well anyhow, there will be no weekends off. We shall be ready for them whenever they come – spring – summer – autumn – or winter – over the sea – out of the sky – or…

JONES Or up between our legs, sir.

MAINWARING (**Glaring at Jones**) How ever they come, we shall be ready for them. Here we are and here we stay.

GODFREY I wonder if I might be excused for a moment.

MAINWARING Certainly not.

The camera very slowly starts to track up and away from them. From here on the voices become more and more remote.

PIKE Perhaps they've got a secret weapon to freeze the sea. Then they could walk over the water like Moses.

WALKER Moses didn't walk over the water.

PIKE Well somebody did.

JONES If they're going to freeze the sea, couldn't we get a lot of gas fires, connect them along the seashore, and that would unfreeze it.

FRAZER I've never heard anything so stupid in all my life.

GODFREY When our garden path freezes, we always put salt on it.

The camera is still tracking up and away.

WALKER The sea is full of salt already.

JONES Permission to speak, sir – I think I can hear a burrowing sound.

MAINWARING Don't be absurd, Jones. (**Pause**) Hang on in – just a minute, I can hear something. Perhaps we'd better make sure – Wilson put your ear to the ground – I'll keep you covered. (**He draws his revolver.**)

WILSON Really, sir – that's impossible.

MAINWARING Do as you're told.

(Wilson gets down and puts his ear to the ground.)

Can you hear anything?

WILSON I can't quite make it out, sir.

MAINWARING What! (**He gets down and puts his ear to the ground.**) I can hear something.

By now, Jones and Walker have their ears to the ground.

WALKER There's nothing there, Mr Mainwaring.

JONES There is, you know.

MAINWARING What? (**To Pike**) Stop shuffling your feet boy – I'm trying to listen.

The camera is now very high up. We can see the cliffs – sea – and the small group of figures with their ears to the ground. We hear a voice.

VOICE The Nazis didn't invade that year, or the next – or the year after that – in the end we invaded them… by the way, we won.

(End)

DAD'S ARMY:
THE AMERICAN VERSION

This is the script Jimmy Perry and David Croft wrote when they attempted to sell the *Dad's Army* format to the United States. It was based on 'The Man and the Hour' and was set in Tulls Point, a small fictitious coastal town in Maine, USA. The script soon attracted interest from American production companies, but eventually Herman Rush negotiated an agreement securing the rights, although he commissioned another script for the pilot episode.

BY JIMMY PERRY AND DAVID CROFT

Dad's Army is the most popular BBC comedy show ever to be shown on British television. It has a regular weekly audience of 17 million out of a total UK population of 56 million. To date 65 half-hour episodes have been shown since it first started in 1968. It has won the Writers Guild of Great Britain Award for the best comedy script three times (1969, 1971, 1972); The Variety Club of Great Britain Award for best TV comedy show; The Society of Film and Television Arts Award; The Ivor Novello Award and numerous others. It has been sold to 16 countries including Sweden, Holland (voted the most popular comedy show on Dutch TV), Belgium, Denmark, Yugoslavia, Australia and New Zealand. In 1970 it was made into a feature film by Columbia Pictures.

Dad's Army is about the Home Guard, a citizen army which was raised in 1940 after Dunkirk to defend England against the menace of Nazi paratroops, and it is set in a small town on the south coast of England. The authors, Jimmy Perry and David Croft, have re-written the first episode for the American market. The scene is set in the USA just after Pearl Harbor.

LOCATION: Tulls Point is a small town on the coast of Maine in the early spring of 1942, a few months after Pearl Harbor.

CHARACTERS

Cornelius Bishop President of Tulls Bank. A short, fat, bald-headed, pompous man in his mid-fifties (Gail Gordon type).

Arthur Wilson Vice President of the Bank. An acid-faced man, a life failure, also in his mid-fifties (Clifton Webb type).

Frank Pike A spotty-faced high school boy of 17 who works as a teller at the bank in his spare time and during school vacations.

Jack Jones Owner of the town's butcher's shop. An old veteran in his late sixties who served with General Pershing against Pancho Villa in Mexico and in France in 1917 (Gabby Hayes type).

Jethro Muldoon The town's undertaker. A tall thin cadaverous character with flowing white hair and wild eyes about the same age as Jones. He is a fanatical teetotaller and prohibitionist (John Carridine type).

Nick Azzeretti A smart slick wheeler dealer in his thirties. Owner of the local pool room with connections in the black market.

Charles Godfrey A gentle old bachelor, who lives with his two spinster sisters (Edward Everett Horton type).

Bill Hodges Owner of Hodges' Diner. A rude, aggressive bull-necked man in his early forties. He is Chief Air Raid Warden.

NOTE: In the British production of *Dad's Army*, extensive use is made of the original songs and music of the 1940s, also reference to the radio shows and movies of the period.

SCENE 1: OPENING TITLES

Montage of newsreel shots early 1942: Nazi submarines, Nazi planes, US troops marching, Roosevelt making speech, GIs giving thumbs up sign. 'March of Time' commentary and urgent up tempo music.

SCENE 2: EXTERIOR. SMALL NEW ENGLAND TOWN. DAY.

Music changes to 'Bing Crosby Hot' of 1942. Close-up (CU) of banner stretched across main street which reads: War Bond Week.

Cut to shot of bank. Name reads – Tulls Bank.

A car of the period is parked in front of the bank.

SCENE 3: INTERIOR. BANK. DAY.

CU of door leading to President's office. Sign on door reads: 'Cornelius P Bishop, President'. Hand knocks on the door.

VOICE Come in.

Hand goes down to knob, opens the door and goes in.

SCENE 4: INTERIOR. BISHOP'S OFFICE AT THE BANK. DAY.

Bishop is sitting at his desk, Wilson is standing, Pike comes into the room.

PIKE I've checked everything, I'm just off home, Mr Bishop.

BISHOP Hold on a minute, boy, don't be in such a hurry, you know when I was your age banks didn't close at one o'clock on Saturdays, we had to work all day.

PIKE Yes, Mr Bishop.

BISHOP You young people of today don't know what hard work is. When I was a youngster we really had to work. Yes, sir.

PIKE Will that be all, Mr Bishop?

BISHOP No, I just want to check the final arrangements for this afternoon. What do you think of this, Wilson? (**He opens his desk drawer, takes out an 18th-century wig and puts it on his bald head.**)

WILSON So you finally came round to it at last and bought yourself a toupee. It looks good in front, but round the back, well I don't know what it looks like.

PIKE I do. It looks just like my Aunt Mabel.

BISHOP You stupid boy, it's a man's wig.

WILSON You'll have a hard job convincing people of that sir, may I suggest a visit to the barber's shop.

BISHOP This is not a toupee, Wilson, I thought I'd wear my costume for the rehearsal. I want to get the feel of it.

WILSON Must we rehearse again this afternoon, sir?

BISHOP See here, Wilson, you weren't born in this town, so it doesn't mean so much to you. But let me tell you this, we have been carrying out this ceremony every year here at Tulls Point for the past 150 years and what could be a better start to the War Bond Drive. (**He points to an open coal fire in the grate.**) Why do you think I have an old fashioned coal fire, Wilson?

WILSON Because you're cold, sir?

BISHOP Cold, how can I be cold with two radiators in here? Tradition, Wilson, tradition. It's what this whole town is built on. And this boy, Pike, should consider it a great honour that he has been chosen to play the part of our own Thomas Tull, the founder of this town.

PIKE Gee wiz, Mr Bishop, I really do appreciate it, it's just that I am so nervous.

BISHOP Don't worry, boy, you only have to say one line – 'The British are coming'.

WILSON I thought it was Paul Revere who said that?

BISHOP Don't believe everything you read in the history books, Wilson. Paul Revere was nothing more than a publicity hound.

WILSON I never knew that, sir.

BISHOP Believe me, the first person to say it was Thomas Tull, Paul Revere stole the idea, and got all the headlines because of his fancy name. Right boy, you put the telescope to your eye and say 'The British are coming'. Try it.

PIKE The British are coming!

WILSON Excuse me, sir, in this war the British are fighting on our side, they're our allies.

BISHOP I don't want any of that sort of talk, Wilson. Besides in time of war one cannot afford to be choosey about one's bedfellows.

PIKE Gosh, does that mean they're coming over here to sleep with us, Mr Bishop?

BISHOP You stupid boy, say the line again.

PIKE The British are coming!

BISHOP Then I make a speech. (**He takes up heroic pose.**) 'Citizens, lock up your women and stand to your arms.'

PIKE Why did they have to lock up their women, Mr Bishop?

BISHOP Well I er… that is er…

PIKE I don't see why they had to lock their women up, I

can't believe that these red coats would be afraid of a lot of silly girls.

(Bishop draws Wilson aside and whispers to him.)

BISHOP You know, Wilson, you're going to have to have a very serious heart to heart talk with that boy sometime.

SCENE 5: EXTERIOR. CLIFF TOP. DAY.

Establishing shot of statue of Thomas Tull in heroic posture. Pan to three solitary figures huddled under umbrellas. It is pouring with rain. Bishop is wearing the full colonial period costume.

BISHOP What do you know, Wilson, a little shower of rain and no one turns up.

WILSON Well you can't hardly blame them for not wanting to get wet, sir.

BISHOP Don't they realise how important this rehearsal is? Whatever happened to that good old Yankee get up and go? I tell you this town needs shaking up.

PIKE Shall we go home, Mr Bishop?

BISHOP Go home! That's defeatist talk, boy, we came here to rehearse and we're going to rehearse. Get on with it.

PIKE Just as you say, Mr Bishop.

(Pike puts the telescope to his eye and looks out to sea. He lowers it again and blinks his eyes.)

PIKE (continued) Gee wiz, gee…(He puts the telescope to his eye.)

BISHOP Get on with it, boy.

(Cut to view through telescope. We see a Nazi submarine with a swastika on it. This can be a stock shot with a blue filter.)

BISHOP Say the line.

PIKE I er… I er… .

BISHOP Say – the British are coming.

PIKE The er… The Nazis are coming.

BISHOP What's got into you boy, it's not the Nazis it's the British.

PIKE No it isn't it's the Nazis

BISHOP You know your trouble boy? You see too many movies.

(Bishop puts the telescope to his eye. Cut to view through telescope. The submarine crew are manning the gun. Bishop lowers the telescope and does a take.)

BISHOP Oh no! Take cover.

(They all throw themselves on the ground. Cut to close up of the three bodies as they react. There is the sound of a shell and a loud bang.)

SCENE 6: INTERIOR. BISHOP'S OFFICE AT THE BANK. DAY.

(CU of head of the statue of Thomas Tull lying on the desk. Pull back to reveal Bishop on the phone. Pike is standing beside him.)

BISHOP Hullo! Hullo! Long distance. I want the Capital Building in Portland. (Wilson enters.) Did you get on to the coastguard, Wilson?

WILSON Yes, sir, I told them where we spotted the submarine and they said they'd check it out.

BISHOP They said they'd … (Into phone) Hello, let me speak to the Governor, it's urgent… he's what … playing golf, well the Deputy Governor then… gone fishing. Look I want to get a message to the Governor, it's important. A Nazi submarine has shelled our town and… what did you say? Hullo! Hullo! They've hung up.

WILSON What did they say?

BISHOP Who are you kidding. I tell you Wilson it's Pearl Harbor all over again. The enemy are on our doorstep, the Governor's playing golf and the coastguards are checking it out. This town is defenceless, a gang of Nazis could land in the night, disguised as nuns, hide in the church over the road, and no one would be any the wiser.

WILSON I think they would, it's a Baptist chapel.

PIKE What about the National Guard, Mr Bishop?

BISHOP That's no good, the nearest armoury is over a hundred miles away. (He points to the head on the table.) Thomas Tull must be turning in his grave. He wouldn't take this lying down.

WILSON He hasn't got much choice, he's been dead for 150 years.

BISHOP That's just the sort of smart remark I expect … wait a minute. Thomas Tull founded the militia to defend this town against the British.

WILSON We all know that, sir.

BISHOP If Thomas Tull can do it, why can't I?

PIKE Do what, Mr Bishop?

BISHOP Form a militia, a citizen army, butchers, bakers, candlestick makers, minute men, ready to defend their homes at a minute's notice.

WILSON But I don't think you're allowed to do that, sir.

BISHOP Allow! Allow! This is America, Wilson, our homes are being threatened.

WILSON It's 1942, not 1776.

BISHOP Times haven't changed. I've got the same red Yankee blood in my veins as my forefathers. There's no one more suited to take command than me. In the last war I served in France as a Captain during the whole of 1919.

WILSON But the war ended in 1918.

BISHOP I don't want any of that sort of talk. I shall take command, you can be my second in command.

WILSON Thank you, sir.

BISHOP Now, the first thing we've got to do is to assemble all citizens on the common.

WILSON But it's raining, sir.

BISHOP What… Yeah, I forgot. I know, we'll assemble in the old Fire House. It hasn't been used since we built the new one.

WILSON What about the Fire Chief?

BISHOP He won't mind, we're both Rotarians you know. Now Pike I want you to tell everyone to report to the old Fire House.

PIKE Gee wiz, Mr Bishop, I'm not very…

BISHOP Don't prevaricate, boy, now you'll need a megaphone. Let me see… ah yes. (He crosses to the fireplace, picks up the funnel-shaped coal hod and empties it, he kicks out the bottom.) You will learn, Wilson, that in times like these, improvisation is the keynote to success. (Bishop hands the hod to Pike.) This is your megaphone, boy. Now I want you to get on your bicycle, and ride around the town with the message – 'All able bodied citizens report to the Old Fire House in one hour.' Try that.

(Pike starts to put the megaphone to his face but Bishop snatches it away.)

BISHOP I'd better show you. (His voice booms out.) All able bodied citizens report to the Old Fire House in one hour. (He lowers the megaphone to his face, he has a large black ring around his face.) How was that?

WILSON Swell, I don't know how you do it.

BISHOP History repeats itself, Wilson. Times of Evil always bring great men to the fore. Andrew Jackson, General Grant.

PIKE Al Johnson.

SCENE 7: INTERIOR. THE OLD FIRE HOUSE. DAY.

A large crowd of various men are all talking at once. Wilson is speaking to them.

WILSON Thank you for coming, Gentlemen. The Commander will see you as soon as he arrives. (He goes into a small office marked 'Fire Chief' and closes the door. Bishop comes into the picture and pushes his way through the crowd towards the office. Jethro Muldoon dressed in black clothes with top hat and crepe band stops him.)

MULDOON Hold on brother, hold on.

BISHOP Kindly allow me to pass.

MULDOON Get to the end of the line. We are waiting for the Commander.

BISHOP I am the Commander.

(He pushes his way through, opens the door and goes into the office.)

MULDOON Did you hear that, brothers, he's the Commander, I tell you the hour of judgement is at hand. We're doomed, doomed!

SCENE 8: INTERIOR. OFFICE. DAY.

Wilson and pike are standing by a battered old roll-top desk. Bishop comes in.

WILSON There you are, sir, did you get the enrolment forms?

BISHOP These will have to do.

(He throws some papers on the desk.)

PIKE Gee, Mr Bishop, these are application forms for a bank loan.

BISHOP Don't fuss boy, right, Wilson, get the first man in.

(Wilson goes to the door and opens it.)

WILSON Would you mind stepping this way, please.

BISHOP Hold it, Wilson, now see here, I intend to mould those men out there into an aggressive fighting unit, and I'm not going to get very far if you invite them to step this way in that Lavender Boston accent. Bark it out, bark it out.

WILSON (Barking) Would you mind stepping this way, please!

(Jack Jones enters, he is dressed in a straw hat and striped butcher's apron and a long steel knife sharpener dangling from his waist. He is doing his own commands.)

JONES Left right, left right, halt. (He salutes Bishop.) Howdy, Mr Bishop, Howdy, Mr Wilson, young Frank.

BISHOP Ah, Mr Jones, the butcher.

JONES Yes sir, that's me. Purveyor of the best quality meat and game, families waited on daily.

WILSON Don't you think Mr Jones is a little old, sir?

JONES Old, not a bit of it, just let me get at them Nazis. I'll show 'em. (He gestures with his sharpener.) They don't like it up 'em, they don't like it up 'em.

BISHOP That's the sort of fighting talk I like to hear, it's keenness that counts, Wilson, not age.

JONES You've said it, Cap'n, I'm keen as mustard.

BISHOP Any previous military experience?

JONES Now you're talking, Cap'n. I served with General Pershing against Pancho Villa in Mexico, there was plenty of action there. Them bandits used to come charging at you shouting Viva! Viva! waving their great long machetes. Zip you right open. Soon showed if you got any guts or not. (He makes a ripping noise. CU of Wilson looking sick.) I was with the General again in

1917 in France, what a man that General Pershing was. Jones, he used to say, give 'em the old cold steel, them Bosch don't like it up 'em.

BISHOP We need men like you, Jones, sign here. (**He points to the form.**)

JONES Sure thing, Cap'n. (**He signs the table.**)

BISHOP Why have you signed the table?

JONES Don't worry, Cap'n, the old eyes may not be as sharp as they were, but I can still give 'em the old cold steel, they don't like it…

BISHOP Thank you, Jones, that will be all.

(**Jones pushes a parcel across the desk.**)

JONES By the way, Cap'n, brought you a couple of pounds of steak, compliments of the house. Just one more thing, what about my stripes?

BISHOP Your stripes?

JONES Sure, I was a Corporal in the last shindig, I can keep 'em can't I?

BISHOP I'm afraid not, Jones.

JONES In that case, I'll take the steak. (**He picks it up.**)

BISHOP Hold it, Jones, I'll think about it. It could be that your past military experience will stand us in very good steak! … stead. That will be all.

JONES Thank you, Cap'n. (**He salutes and marches out.**) Left right, left right.

(**He passes Nick Azzeretti in the doorway. Nick slides into the office, he is dressed in a dark double-breasted chalk-striped suit, black shirt, white tie and white Fedora hat.**)

NICK Hi, gents.

BISHOP Name.

NICK My card. (**He hands his card to Bishop.**)

WILSON Surely you know Mr Azzeretti, sir, he keeps the pool room down the street.

NICK That's me, Nick Azzeretti.

BISHOP For your information, Wilson, I do not frequent billiard parlours. You're a young man, Mr Azzeretti, you should be due for the draft pretty soon.

NICK No chance, I'm what do you call it – essential occupation. I supply essential supplies.

BISHOP What?

NICK Anything that's short, you name it, I get it. Gasolene, tyres, meat, sugar.

BISHOP Black Market!

NICK Don't say that, it's an ugly word. I look at it this way, I'm helping the war effort, by cutting corners and getting rid of Government red tape.

BISHOP Any military experience?

NICK I've got a girlfriend in the WACS.

BISHOP Sign here, please.

(**Nick signs.**)

NICK By the way, how about some silk stockings for the wife, you can't get them anywhere these days.

BISHOP Certainly not.

NICK Well the lady friend then.

BISHOP How dare you! I haven't got a lady friend.

NICK I can soon fix that for you, how about…

BISHOP That will be all, Mr Azzeretti.

NICK OK, OK, OK.

(**He goes. Jethro Muldoon rushes in.**)

MULDOON How much longer are you going to keep me waiting?

(**Chief Air Raid Warden Hodges pushes his way into the office.**)

HODGES Who's in charge here?

BISHOP I am, why?

HODGES Clear these premises at once.

BISHOP Have you gone out of your mind? Don't you realise, history is taking place here?

HODGES Listen, pal, in five minutes an ARP lecture is taking place here.

BISHOP How dare you call me, pal, I am enrolling men here to defend the town. I have requisitioned this Fire House for military purposes.

HODGES You're too late, pal, it's been requisitioned by the Civil Defence.

BISHOP For the last time, stop calling me pal.

HODGES (**Pointing to the door**) I want those guys out of there in five minutes. (**Pointing a finger at Bishop**) Get out. (**He goes.**)

WILSON What a vulgar man that Air Raid Warden is.

BISHOP Did you notice his fingernails, they were filthy.

WILSON He keeps a diner on the outskirts of town.

BISHOP That place is an eyesore, it's a disgrace to the community. I'm going to bring it up at City Hall and get it shifted.

WILSON What are we going to do, sir, we've only enrolled three?

BISHOP We shall just have to dispense with formalities, that's all. (**He crosses to door.**) Pike.

PIKE Yes, Mr Bishop.

BISHOP Get them all in here.

PIKE Gee there's an awful lot of them, Mr Bishop.

BISHOP Out of my way, boy. (**Shouts**) Right, in here, all of you at the double.

(**They all swarm into the room, Bishop and Wilson are backed into a corner. The men pour into the small room until it is jammed tight. Bishop is pinned into the corner. Muldoon's face is pressed very close to his. Bishop starts his 'call to arms' speech.**) Men, today you have answered your country's call, and we are here to defend our homes and loved ones from a brutal enemy. I know you will not shrink from that duty.

(**The men's faces are pressed close, hanging on his every word. Bishop notices a small boy about 12 staring right up into his face.**)

BISHOP Go away, boy.

BOY No, I want to fight those nasty Nazis.

BISHOP Don't be absurd, you're far too young.

MULDOON Get on with it, brother, the hour of judgement is close at hand.

BISHOP We are fighting a brutal enemy, but we are a free nation, and we have one invaluable weapon in our armoury: ingenuity and improvisation.

MULDOON That's two.

BISHOP Now I want you to go to your homes, arm yourselves with what ever you can, and be back here at six o'clock. That's er… twelve… thirteen…

WILSON Eighteen hundred hours, sir.

BISHOP (**Glaring at Wilson**) I know, Wilson. Be back here at eighteen hundred hours. From tonight, whatever the odds, we can look the enemy squarely in the face and say – come on Hitler we're ready for you.

BOY You've got a great long hair growing out of your nose.

FADE…

SCENE 9: INTERIOR. FIRE HOUSE. EVENING.

The men are lined up in two ranks. Jones wearing a World War I uniform: Buster Brown belt, broad brimmed hat, gaiters etc and Corporal stripes. He is carrying an old Winchester rifle. Charles Godfrey is wearing an old fashioned tuxedo, and carrying a golf club. Pike has a broom with a large knife tied to the top. Nick Azzeretti with fancy sporting rifle, Jethro Muldoon with huge duck gun, the rest of the men are carrying various different weapons.

WILSON Squad attention. (**He salutes Bishop**) Men all ready for inspection, sir.

(**Bishop starts to inspect the men. He stops in front of Jones.**)

BISHOP Very smart, Jones.

JONES Thank'ee, Cap'n, I kept my stripes on, OK?

BISHOP Well er…

JONES I'll send two more pounds of my best steak round to the bank first thing in the morning.

BISHOP Thank you, Jones. (**Points to the rifle.**) That's a handy weapon, the old Winchester '73.

JONES There's only one trouble, Cap'n, you can't fix a bayonet on it, when are we going to get proper rifles and bayonets, we got to have bayonets. They don't like it up 'em…

BISHOP All in due course, Jones. (**He stops in front of Pike, and points to the broom.**) What's this supposed to be?

PIKE You said if we hadn't got anything else, we were to fix a carving knife to a broom handle.

BISHOP I didn't mean you to keep the broom on it you stupid boy.

PIKE Gee wiz, well you should have said.

BISHOP I don't want any insubordination either. Take his name, Wilson.

WILSON (**To Pike**) Name?

PIKE Oh really, Uncle Arthur, you both know my name.

BISHOP Wilson. (**He draws Wilson on one side.**) Why does he call you uncle?

WILSON Well, sir, I've known his mother for a number of years now, she's a widow.

BISHOP Really.

WILSON I often go round to her home, for a meal and that sort of thing.

BISHOP What sort of thing?

WILSON Well er… (**He trails off.**)

(**Bishop gives him a glare and passes on, he stops in front of Godfrey.**)

BISHOP (**Sarcastically**) You needn't have bothered to dress. It's not formal.

GODFREY To tell the truth, it's my sister Dolly's birthday, and we're giving a little dinner party tonight. I'd ask you along too but we haven't really been introduced have we?

BISHOP (**Acid**) No we haven't.

WILSON We'll soon settle that, may I introduce Mr Bishop, this is Mr Charles Godfrey, he lives with his two sisters and…

BISHOP Hold it, Wilson. (**He draws Wilson to the side.**) What do you think you're doing?

WILSON I thought he might ask me too.

(**Bishop gives Wilson a glare and turns back to Godfrey.**)

BISHOP (**Points to golf club**) What's that for?

GODFREY Well, when you said bring a weapon, I looked around my home, and do you know, this was all I could find.

BISHOP That's no darn good.

GODFREY You're right, I should have brought a number nine iron, much heavier.

(Bishop and Wilson move on. Nick nudges Godfrey.)

NICK (Whispering) Sister's birthday today, huh?

GODFREY Yes.

NICK You got her a nice present?

GODFREY Well no, to tell the truth, with all this confusion I just have not had the time.

(Nick unbuttons his suit and swings the coat back, pinned inside are a row of watches.)

NICK Anything you fancy here?

GODFREY Oh my, what lovely watches.

NICK (Unhooks watch.) How about this? Fifteen jewelled, solid 18 carat gold, waterproof, shock proof, you can't get 'em anywhere these days, 25 dollars and it's yours.

GODFREY Oh my, how very kind, thank you. (He gives him the money and takes the watch.)

NICK I don't suppose by any chance I could interest you in a watch (Muldoon gives him a glare.) I guess not.

(Bishop addresses his men.)

BISHOP Splendid turn out, splendid. If in one hour we can achieve this formidable fighting potential, think what we shall be able to do with two weeks' training.

(Hodges enters with two firemen.)

HODGES You gonna be long, pal?

BISHOP What's it got to do with you?

HODGES I gave these guys permission to hold a fire-fighting practice in here, OK buster, bring 'em in.

(The firemen unroll a length of hose, it is about three feet in the air.)

BISHOP Look, I am holding a parade in here.

FIREMAN Pardon me.

(Bishop and Wilson step over the hose.)

FIREMAN Pardon me.

(The front rank step over the hose.)

BISHOP See here, Hodges, I've had…

(Fireman backs by with ladder.)

FIREMAN Pardon me.

(Bishop and Wilson dodge under it.)

FIREMAN Pardon me.

(The front rank steps over it.)

BISHOP Don't leave it there, bring it over the top.

(The front rank lift the ladder above their heads, two tall men are each side of Jones. As they lift, Jones who is holding the ladder goes up with it. The phone in the office starts to ring.)

BISHOP Let him down.

(They drop the ladder, Jones has his arms above his head. The ladder slips down, he is caught between the rungs. The phone is still ringing all the time. More hoses and ladders are being brought in.)

BISHOP (To Pike) Answer the phone, boy. (Pike goes into the office.) Get it up! Get it up!

(They raise the ladder, Jones is now pedalling in mid air.)

BISHOP Wilson, get underneath him.

(Wilson does so. Jones now has his leg round Wilson's shoulders.)

PIKE (From the office door) You're wanted on the phone, Mr Bishop.

(Bishop fights his way through the ladders and hoses to the office.)

BISHOP Take charge, Wilson.

WILSON (Who is nearly being throttled by Jones's legs) Yes, sir.

SCENE 10: INTERIOR. OFFICE. EVENING.

Bishop staggers in to the office and takes the phone from Pike. The Governor is on the line.

GOVERNOR Well done, Bishop, thanks to your information, the coastguard caught that submarine.

BISHOP That's good news, sir.

GOVERNOR And that's the spirit that's going to win this war, Bishop. Under the emergency powers invested in me, I give you full permission to raise your militia.

BISHOP Thank you, sir.

GOVERNOR From today your force will be known as the Tulls Point Volunteers, I'm making arrangements for you to get weapons and uniforms from the National Guard. One more thing – you will retain your old rank as Captain.

BISHOP Thank you, sir.

GOVERNOR Carry on, Captain Bishop. (He hangs up.)

BISHOP Captain Bishop.

(He crosses to the door and opens it.)

SCENE 11: INTERIOR. FIRE HOUSE. EVENING.

The place is in chaos, ladders and hoses everywhere. Bishop strides through the door.

BISHOP Good news, men, from today we shall be known as the Tulls Point Volunteers. A short time ago we were a disorganised rabble, and now look at us. We have an unbreakable fighting spirit and a bulldog tenacity that makes us hang on as long as there's breath in our body. You don't get that with dictators or jackboots, you get that by being American. So come on Adolf, we're ready for you.

(The men cheer, music, shots of members of the platoon advancing with great determination. This is superimposed over archive shots of massed Nazi tanks, planes, troops.)

CAPTIONS ROLL

THE REAR GUARD

After acquiring the rights to produce an American version of *Dad's Army*, Herman Rush, the producer, commissioned Arthur Julian to pen a script based on the British episode 'The Deadly Attachment'. This is the script.

PROLOGUE

Much has been written about those gallant soldiers of World War Two who met and defeated the enemy. But there were those who stayed behind to defend our shores. They were the men of the Civil Defence to whom this show is dedicated.

ACT ONE, SCENE 1: INTERIOR. CHURCH OFFICE OF THE VOLUNTEER CIVILIAN DEFENCE CORP HEADQUARTERS. DAY.

Captain Nick Rosatti is on the phone. Max Raskin is changing from his civilian garb into uniform.

ROSATTI (Into phone) Right… Right…Right… Right…! Right…! Right. (Hangs up phone.)

RASKIN Who were you talking to – General Eisenhower?

ROSATTI You're close – my wife. Hey, Raskin, turn that radio off and go out and call the men to attention, will ya?

RASKIN Why don't you call them to attention, Rosatti? You're already buttoned up.

ROSATTI Because I'm the Commanding Officer.

RASKIN So are your lips painted on?

ROSATTI Raskin, you are the Sergeant – I am the Captain.

RASKIN To the Civilian Defence you're a captain – but to a captain are you a captain?

ROSATTI Raskin! You're out of uniform.

RASKIN In the garment district, this is the uniform.

(Takes off the Fedora and puts on an overseas cap, then exits.)

(Cut to)

INTERIOR. CHURCH HALL. DAY.

Rosatti enters. The unit is standing casually in two rows.

RASKIN Attention! All right men, dress it up… Dress it up! Shoulders back… Come on. Come on. Look smart!

CRAWFORD Look smart? How do you look smart in this uniform?

RASKIN Again with the uniforms, Crawford?

CRAWFORD Raskin, I'm a professional actor. I'm used to being dressed in the proper wardrobe. These uniforms are from the wrong war.

RASKIN So, you're a professional actor. Act like it's from the right war!

FOSTER I ain't ashamed of these khakis. In World War I, I marched all across France in this uniform.

RASKIN Don't you think it's time you had it cleaned?

ROSATTI All right now, look men, the army ain't got enough uniforms to go around for real soldiers. So we're just going to have to make do.

KRUPINSKI I think somebody already made do on Kirby's uniform.

ROSATTI Now – as you men know, Father Fitzgerald is doing his part for the war effort by allowing us to use this hall in the church – except on Fridays when they play bingo. So I don't want anybody throwing cigar butts down the john … even if you're Catholic.

(Marsha Wilson enters.)

MARSHA Oh, Captain Rosatti.

(Platoon reacts.)

RASKIN Come on, come on…Ten-shun!

ROSATTI What is this? (Walks down the line, looking at the platoon.) You guys are supposed to be at attention. Let's snap to it! Shoulders back. (Stops in front of Marsha) Not you, Marsha, don't make it any worse.

MARSHA Mr Wagner, the new volunteer is here.

ROSATTI Oh good! Send him in. Now you guys, look sharp for the new man. He's a war veteran.

(Bert Wagner walks in.)

WAGNER Bert Wagner reporting for duty, sir. (He salutes.)

RASKIN That's by you a war veteran?

ROSATTI This uniform looks like it's from the Spanish-American war.

CRAWFORD He's two wars behind.

WAGNER I rode up San Juan Hill with Teddy Roosevelt. Charge! (Pulls out handle, the sword remains in the case. Marsha pokes head out of office door.)

MARSHA Oh, Mr Rosatti, you're wanted on the phone. Frank Sanicola from the fishing pier. He says it's urgent.

ROSATTI OK, thanks Marsha. Raskin take over. (He exits to the office.)

RASKIN All right, Wagner, stand in formation with the other men.

WAGNER Can I sit down for a minute, I walked all the way up here from the bus stop.

RASKIN The bus stops right in front of the church.

WAGNER That's right.

(Cut to)

INTERIOR. OFFICE. DAY.

Rosatti is on phone. Note: following is a two-way conversation and we intercut to Sanicola.

ROSATTI (Into phone) Yeah, Rosatti speaking.

SANICOLA (Into phone) Rosatti, this is Frank Sanicola down at the harbour.

ROSATTI Yeah, Frank.

SANICOLA Hey look. We just came back from a fishing trip and we picked up a German U-boat Captain and five members of his crew.

ROSATTI No!

SANICOLA Yeah… Their submarine was sunk and they were drifting in a rubber dinghy.

ROSATTI All right, Sanicola. Keep 'em covered. I'll be down to get 'em.

SANICOLA Right.

ROSATTI … and save me two pounds of flounder.

(He hangs up and dashes out of the office.)

(Cut to)

ROSATTI Men, Frank Sanicola's fishing boat just picked up a German U-boat crew.

RASKIN What?

ROSATTI Yeah, and we're going down to the harbour to get them.

(Platoon hubub)

RASKIN Hold it! Hold it! Why us? Why not the army?

ROSATTI We'll call the army later. They're 85 miles away… We are the only ones who can handle them Nazis.

CRAWFORD I'm not supposed to handle Nazis… I'm 4-F.

ROSATTI We are operating as a fighting unit – we are fighting men.

RASKIN (Points to Wagner) Shhh. One of your fighting men is taking his nap.

ROSATTI All right, you guys, line up outside. Crawford, Henderson – while we're gone I want you to put detonators in all the hand grenades.

RASKIN Rosatti, you're out of your mind.

ROSATTI What's the problem? There's only six of them Germans and 12 of us. We got 'em outnumbered two to one.

RASKIN Can we get better odds?

(They notice Wagner.)

ROSATTI (As they lift him) Charge!

WAGNER Charge! Wha… Wha…

ROSATTI & RASKIN Hut, two, three, four…

(They exit.)

INTERIOR. OFFICE. NIGHT.

Marsha, Crawford and Bobby.

MARSHA Well, I'm going to be leaving now.

CRAWFORD Marsha, if you're going out with another man, I'm going to throw myself on this hand grenade.

MARSHA Don, I told you I'm on the night shift at the aircraft plant this week.

BOBBY Gee! That's terrific. Are there lots of women working at your aircraft plant?

MARSHA I'm the only woman on the night shift.

CRAWFORD She keeps the morale up.

MARSHA I try to… But last month there was a 50 percent rise in accidents and nobody knows the reason why.

CRAWFORD I can give you two reasons.

MARSHA (Crosses US) I'd better be going. So long.

BOBBY Keep 'em flying!

(Crawford looks at Bobby. Marsha exits.)

CRAWFORD Bobby, bring that box of detonators over here.

BOBBY This box says 'Dummy Detonators – for training purposes only.'

CRAWFORD Bobby, this outfit isn't trained to handle live hand grenades.

BOBBY But we've all seen war pictures… Gary Cooper just pulls the pin out with his teeth and throws it.

CRAWFORD Bobby, nobody in this unit has his own teeth. We'd be throwing hand grenades with dentures.

BOBBY Captain Rosatti said.

CRAWFORD Look, kid, I don't want to be the first 4-F to win the Purple Heart.

ACT TWO, SCENE TWO

INTERIOR. CHURCH HALL. NIGHT.

(OS we hear Raskin.)

RASKIN (OS) Left, right, left, right…

(Raskin and Rosatti enter, followed by the platoon which has the Germans.)

Hurry before it starts to rain …Left, right, left, right… Platoon, halt. At ease men. Not you, you Nazis!

ROSATTI They can take their hands down, Raskin.

RASKIN I knew an Italian would be soft on the Germans.

ROSATTI I was born in Bayonne, New Jersey. I ain't no Italian, I'm an American.

RASKIN You can take the boy out of olive oil but you can't take the olive oil out of the boy.

ROSATTI Krupinski, go get the machine gun and set it up on the stage so you got a clear sweep of this entire hall.

KRUPINSKI Right, sir.

ROSATTI Foster, go get a ladder.

FOSTER Right, sir.

(He exits.)

ROSATTI Wagner!

(Wagner jumps up.)

WAGNER Charge! Wha… wha…

ROSATTI Never mind. Raskin, I want you to get the prisoners in a tight group in the middle of the hall.

(Wagner motions to the Germans.)

RASKIN Achtung! In the middle of the hall.

WAGNER Achtung – in the middle of the hall.

RASKIN Mach Schnell!

(Crosses, subdues and seats Wagner. Crawford and Bobby come out of the office.)

BOBBY Wow, real Germans. Just like in the movies – that one looks like Erich von Stroheim.

ROSATTI Did you put the detonators in the hand grenades?

BOBBY Captain Rosatti, sir.

CRAWFORD I can honestly say, sir, that all the grenades now have detonators in them.

(Krupinski enters carrying a machine gun. He crosses to the stage.)

ROSATTI All right, men, the army's going to pick these guys up in a few minutes and in the meantime, we've got to have maximum security.

WAGNER Captain… Captain…

ROSATTI What is it, Wagner?

WAGNER If you want maximum security, cut the buttons off their pants.

ROSATTI What for?

WAGNER They can't run very far with their pants down around their ankles.

GERMAN CAPTAIN You wouldn't dare do anything of the sort. The Geneva Convention clearly states that prisoners of war will not be put into degrading positions.

WAGNER One more word and I'll put this in a degrading position.

GERMAN CAPTAIN And don't threaten me, you silly old fool, and call me 'sir'.

WAGNER Charge! Why, you –

(Raskin subdues him.)

ROSATTI That's all right, Wagner. You get back in the middle and you speak only when you are spoken to.

GERMAN CAPTAIN I'm warning you too, Captain.

(Foster enters carrying a ladder.)

ROSATTI Foster, bring that ladder over here, Henderson get up there with your gun so that you've got a clear sweep of the entire hall.

BOBBY But Captain Rosatti…

ROSATTI I gotta go call Colonel Walsh.

BOBBY But Captain Rosatti…

(Bobby starts up the ladder as Rosatti crosses to the office door.)

SFX Clap of thunder.

BOBBY Mr Raskin, you know I'm afraid of heights.

RASKIN This is war, kid.

BOBBY But I brought a note from my mother.

RASKIN I brought a note from my mother – get up the ladder!

(Cut to)

INTERIOR. OFFICE. NIGHT.

ROSATTI (On phone) Yes sir… yes sir. We got 'em all right here.

COLONEL WALSH (On phone) You and your group are holding German prisoners?

ROSATTI Yes sir, Colonel. That's right.

COLONEL WALSH Now look, Rosatti, don't do anything foolish… just stay right there.

SFX Loud clap of thunder.

ROSATTI Colonel, could you speak up just a little bit? I can't hear you with all that thunder.

COLONEL WALSH Listen carefully, Rosatti… the bridge is washed out and I won't be able to send my men over 'til tomorrow morning.

ROSATTI You mean you want us to keep the prisoners all night?

COLONEL WALSH Yeah, give them a blanket each, bed them down and give them something to eat.

ROSATTI But, but, sir we're in a church – all we can do is scrape up a few wafers.

COLONEL WALSH Send out for some sandwiches.

ROSATTI Oh, yes, sir. Should I put them all on one, or is that separate cheques?

COLONEL WALSH The army will reimburse you, Rosatti. Goodbye. (The Colonel hangs up, stands and turns to a map of Long Island.) The first captured Germans on American soil and they wind up with those Civilian Defence yoyos on Long Island.

(Cut to)

WAGNER I really think you ought to cut the buttons off their pants, that's what Teddy would do. (Brandishes sword.)

ROSATTI Yeah, yeah, OK Wagner. I gotta talk to these prisoners. (Rosatti crosses to the prisoners.) All right, prisoners, attention!

(The prisoners come smartly to attention.)

(To Raskin) I gotta say they're pretty well-disciplined.

RASKIN That's not discipline. They're just a country full of robots led by a lunatic who looks like Charlie Chaplin!

(German Captain takes out a notebook and writes.)

GERMAN CAPTAIN I'm making a note of your insults, Sergeant. Your name will go on the list, and when we win the war, you will be brought to account.

RASKIN You can put down whatever you want, but you're not going to win this war.

GERMAN CAPTAIN Oh yes we are…

RASKIN Oh no you're not…

GERMAN CAPTAIN Oh yes we are…

RASKIN Oh no …

BOBBY (Sings) Adolf Hitler is a jerk
He's nothing but a Nazi
He thinks that he will win the war…

(The German Captain looks at him.)

He's not so hotsy totsy.

GERMAN CAPTAIN Your name will also go on the list. What is it?

ROSATTI Don't tell him, Henderson.

GERMAN CAPTAIN Henderson … Thank you, Captain.

ROSATTI You know what you can do with that list.

GERMAN CAPTAIN Tsk, Tsk, Tsk, Captain Rosatti, I was trying to keep you off but you asked for it. Rosatti. Is that two 'T's or one 'T'?

BOBBY Two 'T's. Mr Raskin… (He starts down the ladder.) Can I tell the German Captain I was only joking?

RASKIN Get up there!

ROSATTI Come down here!

RASKIN See? You think you got trouble?

ROSATTI Henderson. We gotta get some sandwiches for the prisoners. Go over to my cousin Mario's restaurant.

RASKIN Hold it… You can't feed them from your cousin Mario's restaurant. I ate there last week.

ROSATTI So?

RASKIN Under the Geneva Convention you cannot give the prisoners cruel and inhuman punishment.

BOBBY Why don't I go to Greenblatt's kosher delicatessen on the corner?

RASKIN For the Germans?

GERMAN CAPTAIN The kosher deli will be fine.

ROSATTI All right, get six salami sandwiches.

GERMAN CAPTAIN I would like corned beef.

ROSATTI All right. One corned beef…

GERMAN CAPTAIN Lean.

ROSATTI …and five salami sandwiches.

GERMAN CAPTAIN Just a minute. (He says something in German to his crew, Raskin and Rosatti react.) Make that three corned beef, two salamis and a tongue sandwich.

BOBBY Three corned beef, two salamis and a tongue.

GERMAN CAPTAIN Hold the mustard on the corned beef.

ROSATTI Henderson, go back to the original order – six salami sandwiches.

RASKIN On white bread, with mayonnaise… the hell with the Geneva Convention.

(The German Captain takes out his notebook.)

END OF ACT ONE

ACT TWO, SCENE ONE

INTERIOR. CHURCH HALL. NIGHT.

Germans are finishing sandwiches. Platoon casually guarding them. As one German rises platoon rises ready to attack. He drops remainder of sandwich in bag. Platoon relaxes.

WAGNER Captain Rosatti.

ROSATTI Yes, Wagner.

WAGNER May I leave the room?

ROSATTI You've already gone four times in the last hour.

RASKIN Not bad for a man of 70.

ROSATTI I want you to stick to your post.

(Wagner counts. Father Fitzgerald enters with Mr Muldoon.)

MULDOON See what I mean, father? I told you you can't keep prisoners in a church.

RASKIN Let Father Fitzgerald decide that.

MULDOON I am the custodian of this church and I say throw the blockheads out and they can take their prisoners along with them.

FATHER FITZGERALD Now, Mr Muldoon…

MULDOON You shouldn't have been permitted to use this hall in the first place.

FATHER FITZGERALD Mr Muldoon, we've all got to do our part for the war effort.

(The German Captain suddenly clutches his stomach and groans.)

MULDOON What's the matter with him?

GERMAN CAPTAIN I feel sick. (He groans and slips to the floor.) It must have been the kosher salami.

MULDOON Anybody would get sick eating kosher salami in church.

ROSATTI Stay away from that prisoner.

FATHER FITZGERALD You can't just leave him lying there.

ROSATTI I don't trust him, Father. Look sharp, Henderson. Watch him like a hawk… Krupinski, keep him covered. Crawford, over here… Raskin, draw your side arm. I'm going in. (Rosatti crosses to German Captain) The whole thing looks pretty fishy to me.

MULDOON What are you afraid of, he's unarmed.

(Rosatti kneels down over the Captain.)

ROSATTI Yeah well, he seems to be breathing pretty good. (Suddenly the German grabs Rosatti's revolver out of his holster, gets his arm around Muldoon's neck and points it at him.)

GERMAN CAPTAIN All right, nobody moves! (In German) Get the machine gun!

KRUPINSKI You'll never get this! (Krupinski backs away and trips. The machine gun goes off and all hell breaks loose.)

ACT TWO, SCENE TWO

INTERIOR. CHURCH OFFICE. NIGHT.

The German Captain is holding a gun on Muldoon. Father Fitzgerald and the other German Sailors watch.

(Cut to)

INTERIOR. CHURCH HALL. NIGHT.

Rosatti, Raskin and Company are facing the office door. Krupinski is behind the machine gun. Foster and Bobby are standing beside Krupinski with their rifles. Wagner is dozing in his chair.

RASKIN That troublemaker Muldoon. It's all his fault. He got us into this.

ROSATTI It won't be long now – they're bound to crack. We're holding all the trump cards.

(The office door opens a few inches. They all cock their rifles. A hand comes out of the door and waves a white handkerchief.)

Hold your fire, men. All right, c'mon on out.

(Father Fitzgerald comes hurrying out.)

Are they ready to surrender, Father?

FATHER FITZGERALD Well, I've got a message from the Captain. He wants you to take him and his men back to the fishing boat so they can make a rendezvous with another U-boat.

ROSATTI He's out of his mind.

FATHER FITZGERALD If you don't agree to his terms, he's going to blow Mr Muldoon's head off.

RASKIN That's the first good news we've had all day.

FATHER FITZGERALD We must be charitable, Mr Raskin.

BOBBY But if they get back to Germany, they'll get another U-boat and start sinking our ships again.

CRAWFORD The kid is right. It's Muldoon's life against thousands.

ROSATTI Boy, that's a tough decision to make.

RASKIN Yeah. But I say let bygones be bygones and we'll send flowers to his funeral.

FATHER FITZGERALD Well, Mr Rosatti?

INTERIOR. OFFICE. NIGHT.

Muldoon is sitting at the desk. The Captain is sitting beside him with gun still on him. Father enters.

GERMAN CAPTAIN Well?

FATHER FITZGERALD He's thinking it over.

GERMAN CAPTAIN I give him until dawn.

MULDOON Father, what do you think my chances are?

FATHER FITZGERALD: I'll light a candle for you…

(Cut to)

INTERIOR. CHURCH HALL. DAY.

Raskin crosses DS from window to Rosatti, ducking under Bobby's poised rifle.

RASKIN Rosatti, Rosatti, it's morning already.

ROSATTI If only we could get that gun away from him.

CRAWFORD Wait a minute. What are we worried about? If this group is marching through town with a bunch of German prisoners it's going to attract some attention and somebody is bound to call the army.

BOBBY That's brilliant, Mr Crawford.

CRAWFORD Of course.

ROSATTI OK, that's worth taking a chance. **(He shouts at the office)** All right you Germans in there, we're ready to listen to your terms. **(To Raskin)** Even if they get on the boat, the coastguard will probably get them before they've cleared the harbour.

(The office door opens. The German Captain, with Muldoon at gunpoint, comes out. The priest and sailors follow.)

GERMAN CAPTAIN I'm glad to see you've come to your senses, Captain. **(In German to the sailors)** Get the machine gun and cover them. Drop your rifles. Unload the rifles. **(Sailors unload the rifles.)** Captain Rosatti, you will put your men into formation.

ROSATTI All right men, line up… Wagner!

WAGNER Charge!

(Raskin once again subdues him and gets him in line.)

ROSATTI You won't get away with this. We're bound to attract attention marching through town without rifles.

GERMAN CAPTAIN No one will interfere because you will be escorting us with empty rifles.

ROSATTI You've thought of everything, haven't you?

GERMAN CAPTAIN I certainly have. Take off your jacket and unbutton the belt.

ROSATTI Now just a minute…

GERMAN CAPTAIN Do as I say. **(Rosatti starts to unbutton his jacket.)** I have taken the liberty of borrowing one of your hand grenades, which you were kind enough to already have primed.

CRAWFORD That's right, I primed them all myself.

RASKIN What are you going to do? What are you going to do with the hand grenade?

GERMAN CAPTAIN I'm going to put it down his pants.

ROSATTI Oh no!

GERMAN CAPTAIN You will march in front of me. One false move and I pull the string.

RASKIN What a way to go.

WAGNER **(Steps forward)** Wait a minute, Captain Rosatti. You are our leader. Put the grenade in my pants.

ROSATTI Thanks, Wagner. Thank you. You see the kind of man this country produces?

GERMAN CAPTAIN Ya. Stupid ones. Raus!

RASKIN You think you are so smart. You'll be picked up by the United States Coastguard before you clear the harbour.

ROSATTI He's right. You'll never get away.

GERMAN CAPTAIN I think we will, because all of your men will be coming with us. We shall leave behind the priest and dumkopf to tell them. Your Navy will not fire on their people. Put on the belt. You, freckle face, open the door. Captain Rosatti, I present you back with your own empty gun. When we get to Germany you will all be my prisoners… and then we shall examine the list.

BOBBY Captain Rosatti. Captain Rosatti. What are we going to do? Colonel Walsh is coming.

ROSATTI Your game is up.

GERMAN CAPTAIN You will bluff your way through.

RASKIN Oh no he won't.

KRUPINSKI Please, Raskin, he'll pull the string!

ROSATTI Forward march and bluff! **(As they march out of the church)** … two, three, four, hut, two, three, four…

FATHER FITZGERALD I'll pray for you boys – as soon as I get my hands untied.

(Cut to)

EXTERIOR. CHURCH COURTYARD. DAY.

(The platoon marches in from the church.)

COLONEL WALSH Rosatti?

ROSATTI Platoon, halt!

COLONEL WALSH Where are you taking the prisoners?

ROSATTI Well, you see, Colonel.

RASKIN Captain Rosatti thought it would be a good idea if we gave them some exercise. They've been cooped up in a submarine for weeks.

COLONEL WALSH Uh-huh. I just stopped by to tell you the escort for the prisoners is on the way.

ROSATTI Forward… march.

COLONEL WALSH Rosatti.

ROSATTI Halt!

COLONEL WALSH I'm surprised at you. You're usually spit and polish. You've got a big piece of string hanging down your back.

ROSATTI Where?

COLONEL WALSH Here. **(He pulls the string.)**

ROSATTI Oh no!

(Everyone except the Colonel, Crawford and Bobby dive for cover.)

RASKIN Rosatti's got a grenade in his pants.

ROSATTI Somebody help me get it out!

RASKIN I'm going in.

(He is frantically trying to unbutton the jacket. Raskin crosses to Rosatti, pulls his jacket up and sticks his hand in the back of his pants.)

ROSATTI Save yourself, Raskin!

(Crawford crosses to Colonel.)

CRAWFORD May I have your gun, Colonel?

(Raskin and Rosatti are jumping around.)

COLONEL WALSH What is going on?

CRAWFORD I'll explain later.

(The Colonel hands him the gun. Crawford points it at the prisoners.)

All right, Nazi Germans. Get up over here in one group. Raus. Mach schnell, mach schnell!

(The prisoners obey.)

ROSATTI Wait a minute, Raskin, it should have gone off by now.

(They both stop. Rosatti crosses to Crawford. Raskin follows, his arm still down the back of his pants.)

CRAWFORD I thought you said you primed those grenades.

CRAWFORD I did sir, with dummies.

ROSATTI Crawford, why can't you ever obey orders?

CRAWFORD Just lucky, I guess.

ROSATTI Raskin …

RASKIN Yes.

ROSATTI Take your hand out of my pants.

END OF ACT TWO

TAG

INTERIOR. CHURCH OFFICE. DAY.

(Raskin is putting on his civilian clothes with his overseas cap still on his head. Marsha is at the typewriter. Rosatti, still in uniform, is standing next to her with a sheet of paper. Crawford, in civilian clothes, is combing his hair at the mirror.)

ROSATTI Hey, Crawford, when you finish with your comb, give it to Marsha… she can grease the typewriter with it.

(Bobby in civilian clothes, rushes in holding an envelope.)

BOBBY Captain Rosatti, Captain Rosatti, here's an envelope marked urgent from Colonel Walsh.

ROSATTI I'll bet it's a commendation. Read it, Raskin. **(Raskin takes the envelope from Bobby.)** Gee, I hope Colonel Walsh didn't just single me out… the whole unit deserves a medal.

CRAWFORD What's the Colonel say?

RASKIN Says 'the German U-boat Captain has one request – he wants to know the name of the kosher deli.'

(They react.)

THE END

THE RECRUIT

Jimmy Beck became ill after 'The Recruit' was written, but before the episode was recorded. The script therefore had to be rewritten in order to reallocate lines that were intended for Walker. The likeable spiv, so brilliantly played by Beck, would never be seen again. For the first time, the original script of this episode is published.

SCENE 1: A PRIVATE WARD, WALMINGTON COTTAGE HOSPITAL.

Mainwaring is in the only bed, with a small cage under the bedclothes over his feet.

He is reading the paper. A young nurse enters.

NURSE How are they feeling now, Mr Mainwaring?

MAINWARING They're throbbing from time to time but I'm just grinning and bearing it.

NURSE Well we've got some visitors to cheer you up.

MAINWARING Not Mrs Mainwaring?

NURSE No – it's two gentlemen. (**She calls through the door**) You can come in, he's quite respectable.

(**Jones puts his head round the door. He is in his civilian clothes.**)

JONES Can I do you now, sir?

MAINWARING Come in, Jones.

(**Jones enters, Wilson follows, he is in his bank suit.**)
Hello, Wilson.

NURSE You can stay till the bell goes.

WILSON (**To her**) Thank you. It was very sweet of you to show us the way.

NURSE That's quite alright, sir.

WILSON And that uniform does suit you most awfully well.

NURSE Thank you, sir.

MAINWARING Thank you, nurse.

WILSON It's that belt – it makes your waist look absolutely tiny.

MAINWARING That'll be all, nurse.

(**The nurse goes.**)

They have work to do, Wilson – tending to the sick. They've no time to stand around listening to all that Ronald Colman stuff.

JONES I brought these for you, sir. (**He presents a small, tissue covered basket, tied with ribbon.**)

MAINWARING That's very kind of you. Make yourself at home.

(**Wilson sits on the only chair, Jones sits on the bed and gets up suddenly. Mainwaring removes a revolver from under the pillow.**)

JONES Hitler's not going to catch you bending is he, Mr Mainwaring?

MAINWARING Quite right, Jones. I have to hide it from Matron of course. (**He has opened the package.**) Great Scott – grapes. I haven't seen them since 1939. (**He takes one and eats it.**)

JONES Well they're not real grapes, sir. We impersonated them out of electric light flex and shaved gooseberries.

MAINWARING (**Who has just bitten a gooseberry and got the sour taste.**) I see what you mean.

JONES The gooseberry fur give us a bit of bother and then Mr Frazer found a bit of very fine glasspaper what he finished his ten guinea coffins with and that seemed to answer.

MAINWARING Well it was very thoughtful of you, Jones. As a matter of fact I have received some fruit from Mrs Mainwaring.

(**Wilson picks up an apple from the side table, to which is attached a label.**)

WILSON Is this it, sir?

MAINWARING Yes that's right.

WILSON (**Reading**) 'Get well soon' – Isn't that nice.

JONES There's something on the back.

WILSON (**Turns over the label.**) 'The Anderson shelter is leaking again.'

MAINWARING It'll have to wait until I get back, I'm afraid.

WILSON How is the operation?

MAINWARING Ah. I wanted to talk to you about that – in private. I wonder if you'd mind popping out of the room for a moment, Jones.

JONES Who, me sir?

MAINWARING Yes, Jones. I have something rather personal to say to Sergeant Wilson.

JONES Of course, sir. (**Jones goes to the door and they wait for him.**) I shall be just outside, not quite in earshot.

MAINWARING Thank you, Jones.

(**Jones goes and closes the door.**)

Now, Wilson, I asked Jones to pop out because I thought you ought to see my feet.

WILSON (**After some thought**) Why?

MAINWARING I think you should understand the full implications of this whole affair. (**Mainwaring throws off the blanket and takes his feet out of the cage to reveal two bandaged big toes.**)

WILSON My, my.

MAINWARING Now it's my contention, Wilson, that this is due entirely to active service.

WILSON What? Ingrowing toenails?

MAINWARING There's no doubt about it at all. It's those long hours on duty – they'll never be the same again you know.

WILSON Are you going to try for a disablement pension?

MAINWARING Oh no, nothing like that – but mark my words, it's all that standing about that's done it.

WILSON You do an awful lot of sitting about as well – have you had any trouble there?

MAINWARING You have a very coarse streak, Wilson. You got it at public school I suppose.

WILSON I'm sorry, sir.

MAINWARING I'm simply alerting you to my condition so that you can be on guard against it yourself and on behalf of our troops.

WILSON I'll watch it very carefully.

(**Mainwaring puts his feet back under the cage.**)

MAINWARING I shall never mention it again. Come in, Jones.

(**Jones enters.**)

JONES I didn't hear a word, sir.

MAINWARING (**Tapping the newspaper**) I'm glad to see our lads are doing so well in the desert. Those Eyeties are no match for Tommy Atkins, eh, Jones?

JONES That's because we've been going in with the cold steel a lot, sir. Those wops are not used to it you know, sir. Well some people never get used to it. I mean it stands to reason – when you get a great big Grenadier Guardsman going wher-er wher-er up you like that, very few take kindly to it.

MAINWARING Yes alright, Jones. How's the platoon, Wilson?

WILSON Oh they're getting along swimmingly.

MAINWARING Really.

WILSON We miss you of course.

MAINWARING Yes, you're bound to. Unfortunately it looks as if I shall be stuck here for another four days.

JONES Well don't you fret yourself, Mr Mainwaring. Mr Wilson here is making us carry on as if your invisible presence was with us like a guiding star, only he don't go in for so much bull.

MAINWARING I'm not in favour of bull, Jones, as anyone will tell you. The thing is – are you maintaining discipline?

WILSON Oh yes, sir – I am keeping discipline really rather well – in my own style.

MAINWARING I sincerely hope you are. There's only one way to run an Army, Wilson, you must have obedience – instant, unthinking obedience.

CUT TO

SCENE 2: SIDE OFFICE.

Walker, Frazer, Godfrey. Pike and Jones are sitting round the desk, where Wilson is sitting in Mainwaring's seat. They're all talking at once.

WILSON Please. Please – one at a time.

WALKER I'm sorry, Arthur, but if you ask my opinion you've done the wrong thing.

WILSON Oh dear. Now you've given me a headache.

WALKER I'm sorry but I just don't agree with having vicars in the army. It don't mix – it's like oil and vinegar.

GODFREY It makes very good salad dressing.

WILSON What does?

GODFREY Oil and vinegar – as long as you put the oil in first or is it the vinegar?

WALKER Look, I'm not talking about salad dressing. I'm simply saying that when Arthur here let the Vicar and the Verger join the platoon – he dropped one.

WILSON But Joe, what else could I do? (**He picks up a newspaper.**) The story's all here – lots of clergymen have joined.

FRAZER Mark my words, that verger's a Jonah. He's a face like a sour prune.

GODFREY If Mr Mainwaring had been here I'm sure it wouldn't have happened.

WILSON Well he isn't here – and he won't be here for another three days. I just wish you wouldn't all go on at me so.

PIKE I think Uncle Arthur did right. Vicar's are a good thing sometimes. Look at Spencer Tracy – James Cagney was going to the chair and Spencer Tracy told him to behave like a coward so the dead-end kids wouldn't think he was a hero – and in the end he went shouting and screaming and carrying on something awful – so he died all yellow.

WALKER That was Charlie Chan.

JONES We had a Padre when I was with Lord Kitchener. He was a hard man Kitchener was and he did a lot of cursing and swearing and the Padre was forever begging him to turn from his evil habits. Anyway, the night before the Battle of Omdurman, he lined us all up and gave Kitchener and the rest of us a drum head service. Well next day, just before the battle was due to start Kitchener grabbed hold of his binoculars and there on the horizon he saw forty thousand Dervishes chasing towards us. 'Oh my God,' he says and the Padre was all smiles cos he thought he'd done a good job on him.

WILSON Well it's no good going on and on about it – it's done.

GODFREY (Looking at watch) And it's nearly half past.

WILSON There you are you see. You really are very naughty all of you. You've kept me chatting here and we should be on parade or something. Now come along all of you.

(Enter the Vicar in Home Guard uniform with dog collar underneath. They start to move towards the hall.)

SCENE 3: CHURCH HALL.

VICAR Sorry I'm late – the confirmation class went on and on and on. Have I missed anything?

WILSON No – we're just going on parade now.

VICAR Oh how very exciting.

(The Verger enters in uniform with his usual flat hat. He carries the Vicar's belt.)

VERGER You left your belt in the vestry, your Reverence.

VICAR Oh dear, clumsy me.

WILSON Well if you're both ready I think we can start.

VICAR Oh goody goody.

(Wilson moves into the hall, Vicar turns to the Verger.)

VICAR Private Yeatman – hat.

(The Verger substitutes a forage cap for his cap.)

WILSON (In hall) Now just stand at the end here and try to follow the others and we'll see how we get on.

(Wilson takes up position camera right. Reading right to left they are lined up Jones, Pike, Walker, Godfrey, Frazer, Vicar, Verger. Pike carries a violin case.)

WILSON Squad. Squad shun.

(Jones, the Vicar and the Verger are late.)

Stand at ease.

(The same thing happens.)

That wasn't awfully good. You see the general idea is to try to do it all together. Now let's try again. Squad shun.

(There is some improvement.)

WILSON Stand at ease. That was quite a lot better.

(Mainwaring has entered from the rear door. He comes between Wilson and the platoon. He walks on two sticks and he wears a pair of canvas gym shoes with the toes cut off.)

MAINWARING Oh no it wasn't. It was an absolute shambles.

WALKER Blimey! Hopalong Cassidy.

WILSON We didn't expect you for another three days.

MAINWARING Obviously. Beds were needed for some urgent cases so I discharged myself and by the look of things it's just as well.

JONES Good to see you firmly in the saddle again, sir.

MAINWARING Thank you, Jones.

JONES Even if you are a bit doddery on your pins.

MAINWARING I think I'd better inspect the men, Wilson.

WILSON Yes sir. Squad…

MAINWARING Wilson.

WILSON Squad…

MAINWARING Wilson – stand further away from my feet.

WILSON I'm sorry, sir. Squad shun.

MAINWARING (Moving to Jones) Very smart as usual, Jones.

JONES Thank you, sir. I always try to be smart and very alert, sir. Even though I'm talking to you now, my eyes are darting everywhere, hither and thither in case there should be a lurking danger and if I detect one little bit of peril I'm on to it before you can say wher-er-er. (He grabs Pike by the throat.)

PIKE Aaaah. Let go.

JONES What's your game then – what's you game? You moved.

MAINWARING Put him down, Jones.

JONES He moved and I detected him.

PIKE Please, Mr Mainwaring, can I stand next to someone else?

MAINWARING Stay where you are, Pike. (He sees the violin case.) What's that?

PIKE It's a violin case, Mr Mainwaring.

MAINWARING A violin case. How dare you come on parade carrying a violin. Take this man's name, Sergeant. (He turns to Wilson) Would you please keep away from my feet.

PIKE Mr Mainwaring, I'm not carrying a violin inside it. I'm carrying a Tommy gun like Edward G Robinson did in Scarface. I can whip it out in a second.

MAINWARING Did you know about this, Wilson?

PIKE (Whipping out the Tommy gun while Mainwaring is looking towards Wilson.) A-a-a-a-a-a-a-a-a-a-a.

MAINWARING Pike! My feet!

PIKE I'm sorry, Mr Mainwaring.

WALKER Here, I'll tell you what – I think I can lay my hands on a wheelchair, Mr Mainwaring. Sergeant Wilson could push you up and down like Lionel Barrymore in Dr Kildare.

MAINWARING That won't be necessary thank you, Walker. (To Pike) Don't bring that on parade any more and you'd both better see me in the office after parade. (He is about to pass Walker and then he sees a small earring in Walker's right ear.) Just a minute. What's that Walker, in the lobe of your ear?

WALKER It's an earring, Mr Mainwaring.

MAINWARING Get it off. What do you think you are – Carmen Miranda?

WALKER Well it's the only way I can get into the camp to see this gypsy bird, see.

MAINWARING Ah – I might have known that there was some girl at the bottom of it.

WALKER It's not her I'm after. It's her Dad. He's got the clothes pegs see and they need them for the war effort at the ATS camp.

MAINWARING I've never heard such nonsense.

WALKER It's the truth. They hung out the washing last Thursday with no clothes pegs – a gust of wind blew, and there was khaki knickers all the way to Eastgate.

MAINWARING That'll do, Walker. See me afterwards in the office.

WILSON There's going to be quite a queue isn't there?

MAINWARING That's quite enough from you, Wilson – and keep away from my feet. (He turns to Godfrey.)

GODFREY Good evening.

MAINWARING (Seeing a small piece of white paper in Godfrey's hat band) Godfrey – there's a small piece of white paper in your hatband.

GODFREY Yes, sir. It's for the sun.

MAINWARING The sun?

GODFREY Yes – I have a rather sensitive nose and since Sergeant Wilson wouldn't let me wear my Panama hat on parade, I thought this was the next best thing. (He places the piece of paper over his nose and secures it in position with a pair of sunglasses.)

MAINWARING (Turning to Wilson) Words fail me!

WILSON Perhaps he'd better see you in the office.

MAINWARING At least you look normal, Frazer.

FRAZER Thank you, sir. The wee moose will be gone from my pocket by the morrow.

MAINWARING The what?

FRAZER The wee moose. (He puts his hand into the top pocket of his jacket and takes out a small mouse.) I didna want to leave her alone. Her bairns are due.

MAINWARING A pregnant mouse, nose shields, earrings, violins – I'm away for a few short hours and you allow the whole unit to crumble before your eyes, Wilson. (He turns and sees the Vicar.) What's this?

VICAR I've joined your happy band.

VERGER Where his Reverence goes – I go.

MAINWARING If this is your idea of a joke, Wilson, it's a very bad one.

WILSON They asked to join and I saw no reason to stop them.

MAINWARING All three of you had better follow me. (They march into the side office.) Now – what's all this tomfoolery?

VERGER Don't call his Reverence a Tom Fool.

WILSON Look, it's all in the paper.

MAINWARING I've read all that rubbish.

WILSON Well they asked to join – so I signed them up.

VICAR It was a spontaneous thing – I'm rather like that you know. I've been wrestling with my conscience for some time.

VERGER It's been agony. He was wrestling night and day – I can vouch for that.

VICAR Thank you, Mr Yeatman. Finally I asked myself – could I stand by and watch my wife being raped by a Nazi? No I said to myself, I couldn't.

MAINWARING But you're not married.

VICAR I have a very vivid imagination. So with the example of all those other clergy before my eyes, I knew that my place was at your side.

MAINWARING I don't want you at my side.

WILSON I'm afraid it's too late to do anything now.

MAINWARING Are these the papers?

WILSON I think so.

MAINWARING Well I'll show you if it's too late or not. (He is about to tear them.)

VERGER Don't you dare destroy his Reverence's particulars.

WILSON It won't help very much anyway, they're duplicates.

MAINWARING Very well, if that's the way the land lies – soldiers you are and soldiers you will be. You'll both parade tonight with Jones' patrol and we'll show you what army life is all about. And we won't spare you, I promise you that. You'll find no pulpit to lean on here.

(Cut to)

SCENE 4: EXTERIOR. COMMAND POST.

This is a sandbagged hut, about 15' x 10'. It's set at the entrance to a factory or gas works. Jones leads the section on, including the Vicar and the Verger. The air raid siren is just finishing.

JONES Left – right – left – right – Halt. Private Pike, Private Vicar and Private Verger stand fast, the remainder into the guard room. Fall out.

(They do so.)

(To Vicar, Verger and Pike) You'd better put your tin hats on in case a bomb drops. Now then, Private Vicar, Private Pike and myself are going to demonstrate to you the correct proceedings for military soldiers guarding things on sentry. First of all, you will be on the look out for parachutists, saboteurs and enemies of the realm. When you see any of these approaching your person you will challenge them in the aforesaid manner. Show them, Private Pike.

PIKE Halt – Who goes there?

JONES That was very good. You do it just like that.

PIKE Can I go in now cos it's chilly and I haven't got my muffler.

JONES You don't want to bother about mufflers, lad, you're a soldier now. **(He sneezes.)** There is a nip in the air, isn't there. Never mind – we won't be half a tick. Now Private Vicar, you do what Private Pike just done.

VICAR Halt – Who goes there?

JONES Yes, well you want to say it a bit more fierce, like you was a rough, devil-may-care, brutal sort of person.

VERGER I thought he did it very well.

JONES I'm not asking you – silence in the ranks.

VERGER I'm not frightened of you, you know. You don't impress me at all.

VICAR Be quiet, Mr Yeatman.

JONES If he starts making trouble he'll be on a fizzer under Section 40 – that's Conduct to the Military Discipline Prejudice.

PIKE Can we do the next bit?

JONES Yeah yeah – what's next?

PIKE On being challenged with 'Halt – Who goes there?', the parachutist or saboteur says 'Friend' whereupon you shout – 'Advance Friend and be recognised'.

JONES Yeah – well go on and do that.

VICAR Advance Friend and be recognised.

JONES Yes, but you mustn't say it so friendly. You're asking them if they're friendly but you don't want to be friendly yourself.

VICAR Supposing he advances and I don't recognise him.

VERGER Well if you didn't know him, he'd know you. Everyone knows his Reverence – and respects him.

JONES Well there's a lot more to it, but you'll pick it up as you go along. If you have any bother you send for the Guard Commander – that's me – and if I have any trouble or if anyone shoots you or anything like that, I say 'Turn out the Guard' and we'll all come and give you a hand.

SCENE 5: INSIDE THE COMMAND POST.

Walker is handing out packets of razor blades.

WALKER Come on – I've only got four more packets left. Two bob a packet of five – last chance for a clean shave.

FRAZER Two bob! It's daylight robbery.

WALKER Listen – they cost me one and nine.

(Jones enters.)

JONES What you got there, Joe?

WALKER Razor blades – two bob for a packet of five. You can't afford to miss it.

JONES I'll have a couple.

GODFREY I tried sharpening the last one on the inside of a tumbler – I cut my finger rather badly.

FRAZER I've a piece of frosted glass saved from my grandfather's hearse that hones them a fair treat. I'm still using the blade I bought when the pound fell in 1932.

WALKER Right – now you've got the blades you'll need razor's to fit them. Here you are – three bob each.

JONES What are you talking about? I've got a razor.

WALKER Ah – but it won't fit these blades. They're Wardonia and you need a special razor. Three bob each – best brown Bakelite. **(Holds up safety razors.)**

(Cut to)

SCENE 6: EXTERIOR. COMMAND POST.

VERGER Your Reverence – somebody is making an approach.

VICAR Where?

VERGER Over there. I can just see something through the murk.

VICAR Oh dear. Will you do it or will I?

VERGER Don't worry yourself, sir. I'll take care of it. Halt – who goes there?

SMALL BOY What did you say?

VERGER I said – Halt – who goes there.

SMALL BOY Adolf.

VICAR What did he say?

VERGER I think he said Adolf.

VICAR Did you say Adolf?

SMALL BOY That's right.

VICAR Adolf who?

SMALL BOY Adolf Hitler.

VERGER I think it's a cheeky young boy, sir, and he's having us on.

VICAR Come here little boy.

(The boy approaches.)

If you don't behave properly you'll be in serious trouble for disobeying army orders.

SMALL BOY Go on – you're not proper soldiers. You're an old vicar and he's your old verger. I'm not taking any notice of you.

VICAR I'll give you one more chance. Say it again, Mr Yeatman.

VERGER Halt – who goes there?

SMALL BOY Adolf Hitler.

VICAR We'd better send for Mr Jones.

VERGER I could clip his ear for him.

VICAR No – no violence. We'll send for Mr Jones. Turn out the Guard, turn out the Guard!

(Cut to)

SCENE 7: INTERIOR. COMMAND POST.

JONES Come on lads. The Vicar's in trouble. Turn out the guard, turn out the guard.

(Cut to)

SCENE 8: EXTERIOR. COMMAND POST.

The Verger has hold of the boy. The section rushes out.

JONES Where are they? Where's the enemy? Fix the bayonets.

VICAR Mr Jones. I said 'Halt – Who goes there?' – just as you told me – and he positively refuses to say 'Friend'.

JONES Who does?

VICAR This little boy.

WALKER Blimey – have you turned us out for him?

VICAR He's supposed to say 'Friend' – you said so yourself.

JONES I know him – he's a cheeky little monkey. He runs into my shop when it's full of people and shouts 'Sainsbury's'.

PIKE Yeah, and he runs into our bank and shouts 'National Provincial'.

SMALL BOY You can't do anything about it – you're not proper soldiers.

JONES Oh – aren't we? I'll show you. Bring him inside.

VERGER You heard what the Corporal said. Get inside. **(He swipes him one.)**

SMALL BOY Here – he hit me. You're not supposed to do that – it's against the Geneva Convention.

VERGER Yes – and so's that. **(He swipes him again.)**

(Cut to)

SCENE 9: INTERIOR. COMMAND POST.

JONES You come in here, young feller-me-lad.

SMALL BOY He hit me, the great big bully. I'll tell my uncle on you.

WALKER Now listen, sonny – if you don't use your loaf and behave yourself, you'll be handed over to the coppers.

JONES That's right – for not compiling with lawful army things what we're telling you to do.

(Mainwaring enters.)

MAINWARING What's going on here? Why is nobody on guard?

JONES We've detained a suspect, sir, and we're just interrogating him.

MAINWARING A suspect! Where is he?

JONES There. **(He points to the boy.)**

WILSON He doesn't look very suspicious to me.

VICAR He said his name was Adolf Hitler.

MAINWARING I shouldn't set too much store by that if I were you, Vicar. Go away little boy and in future don't be cheeky.

SMALL BOY He hit me. I want an apology.

MAINWARING Just run along or my sergeant'll put his belt across your backside.

WILSON Who, me?

SMALL BOY So that's how it is, is it? Assault, battery and threats and foul language. My uncle will have the law on you.

MAINWARING See him off, Wilson.

WILSON I wish you'd stop talking to me as if I was a Labrador.

VERGER Go on you little perisher. (**He chases the boy off.**)

SMALL BOY I'll tell my uncle. I'll tell my uncle.

MAINWARING Right, in case there is any follow-up to this incident, I want a full report from you all as soon as Sponge's section relieves you.

SCENE 10: SMALL WARDEN'S POST.

The warden and the assistant warden are listening to the boy recounting the incident.

SMALL BOY Anyway uncle, I was just having a little joke with them when this great big Home Guard fetched me one across the earhole.

WARDEN Go on. Go on, Wilfred.

SMALL BOY Then he did it again and then they all set on me.

WARDEN Pushing and shoving and punching?

SMALL BOY That's right. Then the Officer with the sour old face –

WARDEN You mean Mainwaring?

SMALL BOY That's him – he told his Sergeant to give me a whipping so I ran away in terror.

WARDEN If there's one thing that makes my blood boil, it's cruelty to innocent children.

SMALL BOY They was cruel – very cruel.

WARDEN You come with me. I'll settle Mainwaring's hash.

SMALL BOY Are you going to hit him and punch him?

WARDEN Well, we'll see what happens.

(**Cut to**)

SCENE 11: CHURCH HALL

Wilson is sitting at a table writing. The section are lined up.

FRAZER He was a young monkey – he deserved a skelping.

MAINWARING Well if you've got it all down, Wilson, I'll sign it and then you can put it on the file, but if I'm any judge of these sort of things, we'll hear no more about it.

(**Enter Warden.**)

WARDEN Right, Mainwaring, get your jacket off and come outside.

MAINWARING What are you talking about? How dare you come barging in here like that.

WARDEN Come in here, Wilfred. (**Little boy enters.**) Now just you repeat what you told me.

SMALL BOY (**Pointing at the Verger**) That's the one – he hit me time and time again. (**Points at Jones**) And he pointed a bayonet at me, and that fat pompous one said 'Just run along or my Sergeant will put his belt across your backside.'

WARDEN Just about your mark, isn't it Mainwaring? Bullying little boys. (**Squaring up**) Now have a go at someone your own size. Come on try hitting me.

MAINWARING Hold my glasses, Wilson.

JONES Don't you tangle with him, Mr Mainwaring, not in your crippled state. Let me do it for you.

WALKER Here, hold my rifle, Pikey, while I just hang one on him.

WARDEN Oh that's sporting, that is. Nine of you against one.

PIKE It's only eight, I'm not feeling very well.

WARDEN Well, that settles it. I'm bringing in charges. I'm having you all up in court. You'll hear a few home truths there.

SMALL BOY They're a laughing stock, aren't they, Uncle?

WARDEN Course they are.

SMALL BOY Playing at soldiers – that's all they do.

WARDEN That's right – playing at soldiers.

SMALL BOY (**Pointing at Jones**) And his sausages are all bread.

JONES They're not all bread – you can't get the meat.

WARDEN Go on – tell them, tell them.

SMALL BOY You should hear me and my mates laugh when you go on church parade. (**Points to Godfrey**) His hobbling around with his Red Cross handbag.

WARDEN That's it – tell them, tell them.

SMALL BOY They're almost as funny as the wardens.

WARDEN That's right, almost as funny as – what did you say?

SMALL BOY (**Carried away**) You with your white hat and your flat nose – your left right, left right – halt.

WARDEN You cheeky little whipper-snapper – you wait till I get my hands on you. (**Starts to chase him out.**) I'll give you flat nose.

(**The platoon laugh and jeer.**)

WALKER Lend him your belt, Sarge.

WILSON I haven't even got a belt.

MAINWARING Well that's probably the end of that. But I think one thing is very clear. If you Vicar, and you Verger, had dealt with this in the proper military manner in the first place – this incident would not have occurred.

VICAR Oh I see, it's all my fault, is it?

VERGER It's his Reverence's fault, is it?

VICAR Well, as far as I'm concerned, it just goes to show how very silly the whole thing is. I'm just fed up to the teeth with the lot of you. (**Crosses to Mainwaring.**) You can keep your silly gun. (**Hands each item to Mainwaring.**) And your silly hat, and your silly tunic.

(**Moves to the door.**)

VERGER What about the silly trousers?

VICAR I'll send those round in the morning. Come along, Mr Yeatman.

(**Warden dashes back in.**)

WARDEN Here – come on, quick – there's a stick of incendiaries dropped across the High Street. We'll have the whole town on fire in a minute.

MAINWARING Right – get the sand buckets. Walker – stirrup pump – Pike – two buckets of water – move all of you.

(**They all dash for the various items. Wilson bumps into Mainwaring.**)

WILSON Sorry sir – did I tread on your feet?

MAINWARING Oh, don't worry about that – there's a war on.

ROLL CREDITS

CHRISTMAS NIGHT WITH THE STARS

With specially written sketches entertaining millions of viewers, *Christmas Night with the Stars* became a British institution. Jimmy Perry and David Croft wrote four sketches for the annual Christmas day show, all of which are reproduced here.

THE FIRST SKETCH WAS UNTITLED (1968)

SCENE 1: SIDE OFFICE. CHRISTMAS MORNING. DAY.

(Mainwaring is sitting at his desk, Wilson enters, salutes.)

WILSON Merry Christmas, sir.

MAINWARING Merry Christmas, Wilson. Are the men all ready for inspection?

WILSON Yes sir, but I must say they weren't too keen about parading on Christmas Day.

MAINWARING I know it's a bit much, Wilson, but we can't afford to take any chances. If the Hun wants to invade, he won't let the fact that it's Christmas stop him. It doesn't mean the same to them you know.

WILSON Really, sir, I always thought Santa Claus was a German.

MAINWARING We don't want any of that filthy Nazi propaganda here, Wilson.

WILSON Sorry, sir. Oh, by the way, as it's Christmas I took the liberty of telling the men that they could parade in their civilian clothes.

MAINWARING Well you'd no right to do anything of the sort, Wilson.

(They both go into the hall.)

WILSON Platoon, attention. **(The platoon come to attention, Wilson salutes Mainwaring.)** Platoon ready for inspection, sir.

MAINWARING **(Returning salute)** Thank you, Sergeant. **(He does a take)** What do you mean ready for inspection, Wilson? The front rank's missing.

WILSON What? Oh sorry, sir, you know I thought it looked a bit odd.

(Glare from Mainwaring. Jones hurries in. He is wearing his bayonet. His rifle is in his hand. His respirator and helmet are slung. He is dressed as Father Christmas.)

JONES Sorry I'm late, sir.

MAINWARING Why on earth are you dressed like that, Jones?

JONES Well, sir, Sergeant Wilson said we could parade in our civvies this morning.

MAINWARING You could hardly describe that outfit as civvies, Jones.

JONES Ah! That's just the point, sir, it is this morning; you see after the parade I'm going round to the Darby and Joan club. I give 'em each a bit of suet and a few sausages, I do it every year; after all we've got to look after our old people you know, sir. I mean we've all got to grow old some day.

MAINWARING I appreciate that, Jones.

JONES Then when they've had their dinner I give them a bit of a turn.

MAINWARING Really.

JONES Yes, I recite 'Christmas Day in the Workhouse', with actions.

MAINWARING Supposing a Nazi paratrooper walked in, in the middle of it?

JONES Well I'd just have to change the actions. They don't like it up 'em you know, sir, they don't like…

WILSON All right, Jones, fall in.

(Godfrey hurries in, he is also dressed as Father Christmas.)

GODFREY I hope you'll excuse me being dressed like this, sir, but you see over the holidays I've been obliging in the toy department at Palmer's stores in the High Street.

MAINWARING But you're not working this morning are you?

GODFREY Well no, sir, but you see just before closing time last night, I went to wash my hands and unfortunately I got locked in.

JONES Couldn't you get out up the chimney?

MAINWARING That will do, Jones, all right fall in, Godfrey. **(He takes Wilson to one side, they both have their backs to the platoon. Walker, Frazer and Pike come in, they are all dressed as Father Christmas. They quietly take their places.)** Now you see what can happen when you let discipline slip.

WILSON Well I've said I'm sorry, sir. What more do you want?

MAINWARING It's all very well to say that Wilson but what would it look like if they all turned up as Father Christmas?

(Mainwaring turns and sees the whole line of Father Christmases. There is a pause. Mainwaring pulls himself to his full height and goes straight to Frazer.) What's the meaning of this, Frazer?

FRAZER I'm going from house to house collecting saucepans for Spitfires, sir.

MAINWARING There's no need to be dressed like that is there?

FRAZER Well you see it promotes good will, sir, not only that, sometimes they give me a drink as well.

MAINWARING **(To Wilson)** I find that very difficult to swallow, Wilson.

FRAZER I don't, sir.

MAINWARING **(Moving to Pike)** What's your excuse, Pike?

PIKE I'm helping Mr Jones, sir.

MAINWARING **(Moving on to Walker)** And I suppose you're helping Jones as well, Walker?

WALKER No, sir, I'm helping myself, I mean I'm delivering essential supplies in me sack.

MAINWARING What essential supplies?

WALKER Chocolate, soap, hair grips, razor blades, knicker elastic – you name it, I've got it. That's why I'm dressed as Father Christmas. A copper tried it on this morning and a crowd of kids nearly lynched him.

MAINWARING Pay attention, men, I expect a lot of you have noticed that telegraph pole over there, and are wondering what I intend to do with it.

(Platoon laugh.) Now GHQ have come up with a very original idea. The object of the exercise is that we are to use these poles for PT to make us work as a team, make us pull together, and to co-ordinate our eyes, limbs and muscles. Now on the command 'Move', the front rank will fall in behind the pole over there, the centre and rear ranks will bring in the other two poles which are in the yard. Right move!

(The front rank fall in behind the pole. The other two ranks run out.) Astride the pole. Jump. Astride, Godfrey. On the end. One, I want you to bend down pick up the pole and bring it in to the centre of the hall. One!

(They all pick up the pole. Jones has a bit of difficulty.) Get it up higher, Jones, come on higher!

JONES I can't get it any higher, I'm joined at the top.

MAINWARING Right, quick march.

(They march into the centre of the room with the pole.) Halt!

FRAZER Thank goodness I'm not wearing ma kilt.

MAINWARING Now where are the instructions, Wilson?

WILSON Here they are, sir. **(Hands them to him.)**

(Mainwaring starts to look through them.)

PIKE Look, while you're finding your place, do you think we could put this down – it's heavy.

MAINWARING I can't understand why you're making all this fuss. What's the matter with you?

JONES They don't like it up 'em you know, sir, they don't like…

WILSON That will do, Jones.

MAINWARING Now on the command 'Down', you… put it down then I want you all to sit crossed-legged behind your poles.

JONES Cobblers!

MAINWARING I beg your pardon, Jones.

JONES You mean you want us to sit like a lot of cobblers, sir, with our legs crossed.

MAINWARING Right move.

WILSON Now sit behind your pole with your legs crossed, mind how you go, Godfrey, give him a hand, Pike.

(They all sit crossed-legged behind pole.)

MAINWARING On the command 'One' I want you to pick up the pole in your arms. 'One'!

(They pick up the pole.) On 'Two' straighten out your legs. 'Two!'

(They straighten out their legs.) And on 'Three' lie slowly back. 'Three!', right ready one, two, three.

(They all fall back.) Now grasping the pole tightly I want you to straighten up and lie back ten times. Go!

(Nothing happens.) Now come on put your backs into it. Come on, Frazer.

FRAZER Why aren't you doing it or is this for other ranks only?

(Mainwaring hands the instructions to Wilson.)

MAINWARING We don't want any of that sort of talk, Frazer. I suppose I shall have to set an example as usual. **(He gets down behind the pole next to Jones.)** Now come on. 'Up.'

(Still nothing happens.) Come on, Wilson, get on their end.

WILSON But I'm holding the instructions, sir.

MAINWARING Do as you're told at once.

(Wilson gets down on the other end of the pole.) Right 'up'.

(They slowly rise.) Down!

(They sink back.) Up!

(They slowly come up again. The telephone starts to ring in the office.) Answer the phone, Wilson.

(Wilson gets up and goes into the office.) Now hold it men, hold it.

(The line starts to quiver, Wilson comes back in.) I'd better come. I expect it's for me. (He gets up from behind the pole.) All right, men, carry on. (He goes into the office followed by Wilson. The line falls back and they are all flat on their backs trapped under the pole.)

(Cut to)

SCENE 3: SIDE OFFICE.

Mainwaring and Wilson come into office. Mainwaring picks up phone.

MAINWARING Captain Mainwaring here… Happy Christmas to you sir… No the men didn't mind parading today… Yes, they're all as keen as mustard…

(The Verger comes into the office.)

WILSON What is it, Verger?

VERGER Here, there's a telegraph pole lying on the floor next door. And there's five dead Father Christmases under it.

WILSON Yes we know.

MAINWARING Thank you, sir. Goodbye. (He hangs up.) Nice chap that Major you know, Wilson.

WILSON Yes, awfully nice, sir.

(They both cross back into the hall followed by the Verger. The other two ranks come back into the hall carrying their poles which are cut up into short lengths.)

MAINWARING What on earth's happened to our poles?

VERGER I'm sorry I didn't know you wanted them, I'd started to cut them up for firewood. They make nice Yule logs, don't you think?

MAINWARING How dare you interfere with Army property, I shall report you to the Vicar.

VERGER He was the one who suggested it.

MAINWARING (Icy) All right, fall the men in, Sergeant. I wish to speak to them.

WILSON Come along fall in, three ranks. Platoon attention! (He salutes Mainwaring who returns it.)

MAINWARING Thank you, Sergeant. I'm proud of you chaps – very proud. You didn't want to turn out today, but you knuckled down just the same. Well that's the spirit that's going to get Jerry on the run. We're going to win this war, and when we do, we're going to make an end of violence and bloodshed. We're going to build a brave new world. Then we'll have real Christmases again – just like they used to be – with our children or maybe even our grandchildren at our feet. And they'll look up at us and they'll say: 'Thank you, Dad'.

JONES Or thank you, Grandad.

MAINWARING That's right, Jones. Mark my words – 'Thank you' they'll say – and our chests will swell with pride – and all this will have been worth while. Right – dismiss – and Merry Christmas.

JONES Three cheers for the Captain.

(They all cheer and shake Mainwaring's hand.)

RESISTING THE AGGRESSOR DOWN THE AGES (1969)

SCENE 1: CHURCH HALL. SIDE OFFICE. EVENING.

It is empty.

MAINWARING All right, Sergeant – fall the men out for a smoke.

(The door opens. Mainwaring enters. He is dressed as John Bull.)

MAINWARING (Calling through door) Wilson!

(Sergeant Wilson enters – he is dressed as Napoleon.)

MAINWARING Now look, Wilson, how do you think that we're ever going to win this war, if you can't speak with a French accent?

WILSON Perhaps you should be Napoleon and I should be John Bull, sir.

MAINWARING Oh no – you've got the wrong sort of face altogether for John Bull. After all, Napoleon was a Corsican and you've got those dark swarthy dago looks. Then there was all that business with Josephine. Oh no, you're much more the type. Now you must try and get the accent right – that's why I've brought you in here. I don't want to show you up in front of the men.

WILSON Thank you very much, sir.

MAINWARING Now try it again.

WILSON (In a terrible French accent) England will be crushed never to rise again.

MAINWARING No, no. It just won't do, Wilson. I've got an idea – think of Charles Boyer. After all you must have seen him in that film with Greta Garbo.

WILSON No, I didn't see him in that one but I saw him in *The Garden of Allah* with Marlene Dietrich.

MAINWARING Well that's the same sort of thing, it's all foreign. Can't you remember something he said in that?

WILSON Well er… he said, 'Come with me to the Casbah'.

MAINWARING He said what?

WILSON 'Come with me to the Casbah.'

MAINWARING You know you did that quite well, Wilson.

WILSON Oh thank you, sir, there's only one snag – he didn't say 'England shall be crushed never to rise again.'

MAINWARING I know that – think of 'Come with me to the Casbah' and say 'England shall be crushed never to rise again.'

WILSON 'England shall be crushed never to rise again.' Oh really, sir. I don't see how all this is going to help the war effort.

MAINWARING Can't you see by performing this pageant all over the town during war weapons week, we shall not only be raising money for the war effort – but we shall also be putting over a powerful bit of propaganda – and the propaganda, Wilson, is the keynote of modern warfare. Now come on, let's get on with the rehearsal.

(Cut to)

SCENE 2: CHURCH HALL. EVENING.

The hall is draped lengthways with blankets with a large Union Jack in the centre. In front is an oval plaque. It is four feet high and is the centre of the royal coat of arms without the lion and the unicorn. It is painted with the four divisions. Beside it is a dinner gong and about six feet to stage left is a beer box. The pageant is played facing the studio audience.

MAINWARING (Shouting) All right, we're ready to start. Jones. Walker.

(They both come from behind the blankets. Jones is dressed à la farmer Giles with white smock, felt hat, etc. He is carrying a pitch fork. Walker is dressed in a coloured frock coat, beaver hat, etc (Victorian 1845). He is carrying a small pair of justice scales.)

WALKER 'ere, Mr Mainwaring, I don't half feel funny in this outfit. I feel like one of those.

JONES One of those what, Joe?

MAINWARING That will do, Walker, just take your place and you Jones.

(They take their places each side of the plaque.)

MAINWARING Are you all ready behind there, we're going to start?

(Muttered voices from behind the blankets.)

JONES Permission to speak, sir.

MAINWARING Not now, Jones, I'm going to do the prologue.

JONES Joe and I have written a little something extra. It's a sort of prologue to the prologue. I think you'll like it, sir.

MAINWARING Oh very well.

JONES & WALKER (In unison) Ladies and Gentlemen. Walmington-on-Sea Home Guard present 'Resisting the Aggressor Down the Ages'.

WALKER Written by Captain Mainwaring.

JONES Produced by Captain Mainwaring.

WALKER And performed by members of the Walmington-on-Sea Home Guard by permission of their Commanding Officer, Captain George Mainwaring.

JONES The part of John Bull, played by Captain Mainwaring. (To Mainwaring) How's that, sir?

MAINWARING Excellent, Jones. (He clears his throat.) I am John Bull the fighting spirit of England.

WALKER I didn't know John Bull wore glasses?

MAINWARING Walker. I am John Bull – the fighting spirit of England.

FRAZER (Poking his head over the top of the blanket) What about Scotland?

MAINWARING Oh… er… I am John Bull the fighting spirit of England, Scotland and er… Wales and Ireland.

WALKER And the Isle of Wight.

MAINWARING Now all the youth of England are on fire. And silken, dalliance in the wardrobe lies. Now thrive the armourers, and honour's thought reigns solely in the breast of every man.

(After Mainwaring has spoken the first two lines.)

WALKER 'ere, Jonesey. Mr Mainwaring writes nice stuff don't he?

JONES Yes, it's good ain't it, Joe?

MAINWARING They sell the pasture now to buy the horse.

(He stops and points dramatically to Walker and Jones.)

JONES I am the spirit of agriculture.

WALKER And I am the spirit of commerce.

JONES & WALKER And we are the people who have put the Great in Britain.

FRAZER Illiterate rubbish.

MAINWARING (Well away) Down through the ages many tyrants have cast their greedy, beady foreign eyes, on England's green and pleasant lands – 55 BC. Julius Caesar. (There is a pause) Hurry up, Godfrey. (There is the sound of a flush and Godfrey hurries on and stands on the beer box – he is dressed as Caesar.)

GODFREY I'm sorry, sir.

MAINWARING Oh get on with it.

GODFREY (Feebly) England shall be crushed never to rise again.

MAINWARING That's no good, Godfrey, you've got to be far more aggressive.

GODFREY Don't forget Julius Caesar was an intellectual, sir.

MAINWARING Look, who's producing this? Just do as I tell you and point your finger at them.

GODFREY (**Pointing**) England shall be crushed – never to rise again.

JONES Those rotten Romans shall not pass.

MAINWARING I didn't write rotten Romans, I wrote raiding Romans, Jones.

JONES Sorry, sir. Those raiding Romans shall not pass. Those raiding Romans did not pass.

WALKER They went misere.

(**Wilson comes from behind the blankets.**)

WILSON Excuse me, sir – what time do you think you'll get to Napoleon?

MAINWARING How on earth do I know, Wilson, we've got two thousand years of history before we get to you.

WILSON Oh, Lord. (**He goes.**)

MAINWARING All right, Godfrey, you've been beaten – take up a cowered position. (**Godfrey gets down off the box and cowers.**) One thousand years have passed.

(**Jones bangs the gong ten times.**)

JONES That's one bang for every hundred years, sir.

MAINWARING Excellent, Jones. 1066! William the Conqueror!

(**Frazer leaps on to the box – he is dressed as a Norman.**)

FRAZER (**Giving his all**) England shall be crushed, never to rise again.

JONES Those nasty Normans shall not pass.

MAINWARING I didn't write nasty Normans – I wrote nefarious Normans.

JONES I know sir – but I could not get my tongue round such a word.

MAINWARING Oh all right.

JONES Those nasty Normans shall not pass. Those nasty Normans did not pass.

MAINWARING Right, Frazer – get off the box and cower.

FRAZER I'm not cowering for anybody.

(**Wilson enters.**)

WILSON Excuse me, sir. I don't think that this is historically accurate. Both Julius Caesar and William the Conqueror won.

MAINWARING We don't want any of that sort of talk, Wilson. Anyhow from now on they all lost.

(**Wilson goes.**)

FRAZER (**Muttering**) Illiterate that's what he is – illiterate.

(**Mainwaring notices for the first time that Frazer is wearing the nose protector of his Norman helmet over his left eye.**)

MAINWARING Frazer – why are you wearing your helmet with the nose protector over your eye?

FRAZER Because I canna get it over my nose, that's why.

(**He stands beside Godfrey.**)

MAINWARING Oh… er. Five hundred years have passed.

(**Jones bangs the gong five times.**)

MAINWARING 1588 – King Philip of Spain.

(**Pike enters and jumps on the box, he is dressed as a Spanish toreador.**)

Pike, what on earth are you doing dressed like that? You look like Eddie Cantor in *The Kid from Spain*.

PIKE This was the costume I was given. What's wrong with it? It's Spanish isn't it?

MAINWARING Oh never mind, get on with it.

PIKE England shall be crushed, never to rise again.

JONES Those sadistic Spaniards shall not pass.

MAINWARING Why must you keep changing everything, Jones? I wrote those spurious Spaniards.

WALKER I made him change it, Mr Mainwaring. Every time he said spurious Spaniards, I got soaked through.

MAINWARING I don't care, that's what I wrote and that's what I want.

JONES Sorry, sir. Those spurious Spaniards shall not pass. Those spurious Spaniards did not pass.

(**Pike jumps down and cowers by Frazer.**)

MAINWARING Two hundred and twenty-seven years pass.

(**Jones bangs the gong twice and says 'twenty-seven'.**)

MAINWARING 1815 – Napoleon Bonaparte.

(**Cut to close up of Wilson waiting.**)

WILSON (**Muttering to himself**) Come with me to the Casbah. Come with me to the Casbah. England shall be crushed never to rise again.

MAINWARING Come on, Wilson.

(**Wilson jumps on the box.**)

WILSON Er… Come with me and be crushed in the Casbah.

MAINWARING Wilson!

WILSON Oh… England shall be crushed never to rise again.

JONES Those… French shall not pass. Those… French did not pass.

MAINWARING Why have you changed it again, Jones?

JONES I'm sorry, Mr Mainwaring. I'm not going to say what you wrote.

WILSON Shall I do the cower bit now, sir?

MAINWARING Yes get on with it.

(**Wilson gets down and cowers beside Pike.**)

MAINWARING Over two thousand years many men of guile have fought to get their hands on this sceptred Isle. They tried but they did not succeed. Because they were up against This! Happy! Breed!

(**They all line up and sing 'Land of Hope and Glory' Frazer muttering 'rubbish', etc. Suddenly the sirens go.**)

MAINWARING All right, men, fall in.

WILSON Hadn't we better change into our uniforms first, sir?

MAINWARING There's no time for that, Wilson. Right men get your steel helmets, masks and rifles.

(Cut to)

SCENE 3: SIDE OFFICE. EVENING.

The door opens and the ARP warden comes in pushing a German Pilot. There are two other wardens with him.

WARDEN Now look, mate, don't get stroppy with me. There's an alert on. I can't waste any time looking after you.

(The German spits on the church floor.)

That's nice, that is – spitting on Church property. (**He pushes him towards the door leading to main hall.**) I'm handing you over to Captain Mainwaring. (**They go into the main hall.**)

(Cut to)

SCENE 4: MAIN HALL. EVENING.

WARDEN We caught this German Pilot, Mr Mainwaring, and… blimey. (**He's seen the tableau.**) What's going on here?

MAINWARING Never mind that, what happened?

WARDEN He's just bailed out by parachute. He's giving us a lot of trouble, it took three of us to get him here.

MAINWARING Damn cheek. (**He crosses to German.**) Now look here my man, just watch your step. Any more trouble out of you and we shall lock you down in the cellar. Now what have you got to say for yourself?

PILOT England shall be crushed never to rise again. Heil, Hitler.

(**Jones who still has his pitchfork sticks him in the backside.**)

JONES Those flippin' Nazis shall not pass. Those flippin' Nazis shall not pass. You see they don't like it up 'em you know, sir. They just don't like it.

THE CORNISH FLORAL DANCE (1970)

SCENE 1: INTERIOR. CHURCH HALL. DAY.

The platoon are standing in a semicircle. At one end are four lady ARP wardens. Sgt Wilson is sitting at the piano. Suddenly from the office we hear the voices of Mainwaring and the Warden shouting at each other. There is a pause – it goes quiet.

MAINWARING No – No – No certainly not. I've never heard of anything so outrageous in all my life.

HODGES Why should you be in charge of the choir any more than me – what do you know about music?

JONES Did you hear what they said, Sergeant?

FRAZER I should think the whole of Walmington-on-Sea heard it.

WALKER If you ask me, those poor wounded soldiers have got enough troubles without having us to sing to them.

(Cut to)

SCENE 2: INTERIOR. SIDE OFFICE. DAY.

Mainwaring and the Warden are facing each other across the desk.

MAINWARING Now, look here, Mr Hodges. For the last time I'm telling you that this choir is my idea – and I'm conducting it.

HODGES Look! You asked for some ladies – I brought some along – so why can't I conduct?

MAINWARING Because most of the choir come from my platoon – they're all men.

HODGES I've only got your word for that, mate.

MAINWARING (Holding himself in check) Now look, this is the season of peace and goodwill – so we'll settle it peacefully – we'll toss for it. (He produces a coin.) Heads – I conduct the choir – tails – you conduct it.

HODGES Oh, all right.

(Mainwaring tosses the coin – it comes down heads.)

MAINWARING Heads! I conduct the choir.

HODGES Best out of three.

SCENE 3: INTERNAL. CHURCH HALL. DAY.

(Mainwaring and Hodges come through the door.)

MAINWARING Right, Mr Hodges, take your place, please.

(Hodges gives them all a glare and takes his place amongst them, next to Jones.)

MAINWARING Right now, gentlemen, as quite a number of the soldiers we're going to sing to are from the Duke of Cornwall's Light Infantry, I have chosen the Floral Dance to open the concert. Mr Hodges.

HODGES Yes.

MAINWARING I don't think it's necessary to wear your steel helmet to sing in.

(Hodges gives him a glare and takes it off.)

PIKE (Whispering to Godfrey) I've never seen him without his helmet before – I always thought he hadn't got a top to his head.

MAINWARING Right now, gentlemen. Most of you know the tune – it's very simple. The first bit's nearly all on one note like this. (He las the first few bars.) Right, Wilson, just play the tune through for them in single notes.

(Wilson plays the first few notes, nothing happens.)

WILSON I'm afraid the note's broken, sir.

MAINWARING Well, play the next note.

WILSON That's not the right one.

MAINWARING All right then, play one like it.

WILSON There isn't one like it in this part of the keyboard.

MAINWARING Don't try and blind me with science, Wilson.

WILSON I can manage it an octave lower, sir.

JONES Permission to speak, sir. It's too low. I think the ladies are having a little trouble.

MAINWARING It's too low, Wilson.

WILSON All right, sir, I'll go up a bit.

MAINWARING Good – ready – one – two

(Wilson plays it two octaves higher. They sing it right up to 'Quaint Old Cornish Town'.)

JONES Mr Mainwaring – it's too high. The men are having a bit of trouble.

MAINWARING It's far to high, Wilson. We don't want the one below or the one up there – we want the one in the middle.

WARDEN I can't stand any more of this – I'll give it to you.

(He sings it through up to 'Cornish Town') How's that?

JONES That's the wrong key!

WARDEN What are you talking about? I've got perfect pitch.

JONES No it's – Far…Far… Far…

PIKE Actually it's higher Mr Jones. Far… Far… Far…

GODFREY No it should be lower – Far… Far… Far…

WALKER You're all wrong – it's Far… Far… etc.

(They are all Faring and Laring together.)

MAINWARING (Shouting) Quiet!

(Godfrey continues.)

FRAZER It's a lot of Peewely weely rubbish. Up in the Highlands we sing without a piano – only the wind in the heather to give us the key. (He gives a high pitched cry of the sound of the wind and then sings.) Speed bonny boat like a bird on a wing, over the sea to Skye. (Pause) It's the wind you see, the wind.

WALKER Well don't just stand there, go and take some bicarbonate of soda.

MAINWARING That will do, Walker.

GODFREY Couldn't we recite it, sir. The words are rather pretty.

WARDEN Oh get on with it do.

WILSON I think I've found out the trouble, sir – there's something blocking the note. (He reaches inside the piano and pulls out half a bottle of whisky.) It's a bottle of whisky.

MAINWARING Walker! Does that belong to you?

WALKER Yes it does.

MAINWARING (To Walker) How dare you use the Vicar's piano for illegal purposes.

WALKER I'm sorry but…

MAINWARING Take this bottle at once, Walker. I don't want to see it again.

WALKER Please yourselves – it's your Christmas present.

MAINWARING What?

WARDEN Oh, do get on with it.

MAINWARING Right. Now we'll take it from the beginning. We want someone for the solo – 'Borne from afar on the gentle breeze'.

JONES I should like to volunteer to be the one 'borne from afar on the gentle breeze'.

MAINWARING Oh very well – all ready? One… two…

(They sing the first six bars properly – when they reach the word 'town' they hold the note for the next two bars and the girls harmonise.)

JONES (Coming in two bars too soon) Borne from afar on a gentle breeze.

MAINWARING (Stopping him) Jones! Jones! (The rest stop – Jones still carries on.) Stop him someone.

WARDEN Hey – Hey! (He touches Jones.) Hey!

JONES Whoa – er. (He grabs the Warden by the throat.) Oh I'm sorry.

MAINWARING You came in too soon, Jones. Try it again. From 'into the sweet and scented air' One – two…

(They all sing, the girls harmonise.)

JONES (Coming in two beats too soon) Borne from afar…

MAINWARING Jones!

JONES I'm sorry, sir, I was borne too soon again.

WALKER A sort of premature birth.

MAINWARING This time we'll count for you Jones. Its 2–3–4–5–6–7–8 in. From the same place. One – two…

(They all sing from 'into the sweet and scented air'. They break off on the word Cornish and count while the girls harmonise.)

JONES 2–3–4–5–6–7–8 in (Jones gives a start and comes in.)

JONES Borne from afar on the gentle breeze. Joining the murmur of the summer seas, distant tones of an old world dance, played by the village band perchance. In the calm air came floating down.

MAINWARING Thank you, Wilson. Not bad – not bad at all – now we'll take the next bit. 'I thought I could hear the curious tone of the cornet, clarinet and big trombone. Fiddle, cello, big bass drum, bassoon, flute and euphonium.' I think we'll split this up. Godfrey, you take the cornet and clarinet.

GODFREY Cornet and clarinet – yes, sir.

MAINWARING Frazer – big trombone.

FRAZER Right.

MAINWARING Pike, you take the fiddle and cello. (Wilson starts to giggle.) What are you laughing at, Wilson?

WILSON Well, I was just thinking, wouldn't it be better if Walker was on the fiddle?

(He laughs – the rest of the platoon stares at him in stony silence.)

MAINWARING Yes well, we'll get on shall we? Walker, you take the big base drum.

WALKER Right ho.

MAINWARING Jones – bassoon and flute. Mmmm we're one short. There's no one to do the euphonium.

WALKER Why don't we split it up, Mr Mainwaring? Jonesey can be the 'U'. I'll be the 'Phone' and Pikey can be the 'bum'.

MAINWARING One more remark out of you, Walker, and I shall ask you to leave.

WARDEN Oh get on with it – I'll be the euphonium.

MAINWARING Thank you, Mr Hodges. Right are you ready? (Wilson starts.) Don't anticipate me, Wilson – watch my stick. Ready – one – two…

JONES I thought I could hear the curious tone,

GODFREY Of the cornet, clarinet,

FRAZER And the big trombone ai!

MAINWARING Just a minute. There's no 'ai' after trombone, Frazer.

FRAZER I know there isn't – I just put it in, it gives it a bit of guts. Washed out English tune.

MAINWARING We'll do without it if you don't mind.

FRAZER It won't be so good. (**Frazer mutters to himself.**)

MAINWARING From the beginning once more. Wilson – watch my stick. One – two –

JONES I thought I could hear the curious tone.

GODFREY Of the cornet, clarinet,

FRAZER And big trombone.

PIKE Fiddle, Cello.

WALKER Big base drum.

JONES Bassoon, flute.

WARDEN And euphonium.

JONES (**Trancy**) Far away as in a trance. (**Fast**) I heard the sound of the floral dance.

MAINWARING Excellent – excellent. Now, we'll go straight through to the end. Pike, you take the solo. I've marked it for you. Slowly and dreamily.

PIKE Yes, Mr Mainwaring. Slowly and dreamily.

MAINWARING Are you ready? (**Wilson starts.**) Wilson, don't anticipate me, Wilson. Watch my stick. (**To Pike**) From there. One – two…

PIKE I felt so lonely standing there, and I could only stand and stare, for I had no boy girl with me.

MAINWARING (**Stopping him**) Stop! Stop! Why are you singing, for I had no boy girl?

PIKE That's what it says here, Mr Mainwaring. For I had no boy girl with me.

MAINWARING If you are a boy, you've a girl, and if you're a girl you've a boy, you stupid boy.

PIKE What am I then?

WALKER We're all beginning to wonder.

MAINWARING You sing you're a boy. Now once again – one – two…

PIKE For I had no boy.

(**They all sing right through, each singing his solo – working up to the big finish.**)

ALL Then suddenly hast'ning down the lane,

A figure I knew I saw quite plain,

With outstretched hands I rushed along,

And carried her into that merry throng,

And fiddle and all went dancing down.

We danced to the band with the curious tone.

GODFREY Of the cornet, clarinet.

FRAZER And big trombone – ai!

PIKE Fiddle, Cello.

WALKER Big base drum.

JONES Bassoon, flute.

WARDEN And euphonium.

ALL Each one making the most of his chance,

Altogether in the floral dance,

Dancing here, prancing there,

Jigging jogging ev'ry where,

Up and down and round the town,

Hurrah – for the Cornish floral dance.

BROADCAST TO THE EMPIRE (1972)

SCENE 1: INTERIOR. SIDE OFFICE. DAY.

On the desk is a mass of radio equipment, wires are strung across the room. An engineer is sitting at the desk with earphones on. The door opens, Pike comes in, crosses to the desk and takes the phone off the hook.

PIKE (**To engineer**) Mr Mainwaring says he doesn't want the phone to ring during the broadcast.

(**The engineer gives him the thumbs up sign, Pike returns it. There is a loud knocking on the outside door, Pike crosses and unlocks it. Hodges pushes his way in.**) Happy Christmas, Mr Hodges.

HODGES And the same to you, what's going on?

PIKE You can't come in, you mustn't make noises.

HODGES (**Pointing to wires**) What's all this? A new secret weapon Napoleon's trying out. Why was the door locked?

PIKE Don't you read the *Radio Times*?

HODGES I haven't got time to read that rubbish, there's a war on.

PIKE We're taking part in the lunch time programme, *To Absent Friends*. Soldiers all round the British Empire send their greetings.

HODGES Since when have you lot been soldiers? Why wasn't I told?

PIKE Security, we had to keep it a secret. We're doing the bit where it says: 'Greetings from a Home Guard Unit somewhere on the South Coast of England'. We're on just before the King's speech.

HODGES Blimey, as if he hasn't got enough to put up with. I'm not going to miss this, I'll go and listen to it on the Verger's wireless. I bet you lot make a mess of it. (**He goes.**)

SCENE 2: INTERIOR. CHURCH HALL. DAY.

The hall is covered in radio equipment. Mainwaring, Wilson, Jones, Frazer, Walker and Godfrey are standing round a microphone, beside them is a large loudspeaker, and a red signal bulb on a stand. An engineer is sitting at the equipment with earphones on. Pike joins the group.

PIKE I've taken the phone off the hook, Mr Mainwaring.

MAINWARING Good, we don't want any interruptions. (**To engineer**) Are we through to the producer in London yet, engineer?

(**Engineer turns.**)

Are we through to the producer in London?

(**Engineer gives thumbs up.**)

Good.

(**They all give thumbs up.**)

PRODUCER Good morning, everyone, my name is Willerby Troughton-Maxwell, and I am your producer. Now this broadcast will be heard all over the empire, and your section will come just before His Majesty the King's speech.

MAINWARING (**To Wilson**) Do you hear that, Wilson, just before the King's speech, what an honour.

WILSON Yes, sir, awfully good.

PRODUCER Are your men all ready, Captain Mainwaring?

MAINWARING (**Into the loudspeaker**) Yes, all ready.

PRODUCER Would you mind speaking into the microphone, please.

JONES This is the microphone, Mr Mainwaring. (**He taps and blows into the mike three times.**)

ENGINEER Arrah! (**He snatches his earphones off.**)

PRODUCER Don't do that!

MAINWARING Yes, don't do that, Jones.

PRODUCER Now I'd like to try a voice test. Will someone speak, please.

MAINWARING Go on, Wilson.

WILSON What shall I say?

MAINWARING Don't ask me, ask him. (**Points to speaker.**)

WILSON (**Into speaker**) What shall I say?

JONES Speak into here, Mr Wilson.

ENGINEER Arrah! (**Snatches off earphones.**)

PRODUCER I told you not to do that.

MAINWARING Don't do that, Jones.

WILSON (**Into mike**) What shall I say?

PRODUCER Oh anything you like. Try a nursery rhyme.

WALKER There was a young lady from Buckingham.

MAINWARING Walker! Get on with it, Wilson.

WILSON Very well. Lavender blue, dilly, dilly. Lavender green. I'll be your King, dilly, dilly. If you'll be my Queen.

PRODUCER That was awfully good.

WILSON Oh, thank you.

PRODUCER You really have an excellent microphone voice. Have you ever done any of this sort of thing before?

WILSON Well I played the White Rabbit, in *Alice in Wonderland* at school.

PRODUCER Really! So did I. What school were you at?

WILSON As a matter of fact, I went to…

MAINWARING Can we get on, please.

GODFREY Excuse me, sir, I don't speak until page seven, do you think I could possibly…

MAINWARING Certainly not, Godfrey.

PRODUCER One more voice test please.

JONES I should like to volunteer to be one more voice test, sir. (**Sings**) Any old iron, any old iron. Any, any, any old iron.

WALKER & JONES Oh, I wouldn't give you twopence for your old watch chain. Old iron, old iron.

JONES (**Solo**) Diddle, diddle, dum, dum. Diddle, diddle, dum, dum. Pom, tiddley, om pom. Pom, pom. (**He taps the mike twice.**)

ENGINEER Arrah! (**Snatches off earphones.**)

FRAZER Poem. Robbie Burns. What then poor beastie. Thou' maun live, daimon' icker in a thrieve is a sma' request. I'll get a blessing with a lave, and never miss't. Was that nice and clear?

MAINWARING Thank you, Frazer.

PRODUCER Let's start on the script please, and I want you to read the lines in perfectly normal natural voices.

MAINWARING Hullo soldiers of the Empire. I am a Home Guard commander in charge of a platoon somewhere on the south coast of England.

WILSON And I am the Sergeant. I'm second in command.

JONES And I am the Lieutenant Corporal. I'm third in command.

PRODUCER Just a minute could the officer speak a little more clearly, please?

MAINWARING What's the matter? Can't you understand what I'm saying?

PRODUCER Well the fact is, you don't sound very much like an officer. Try and make your voice a little more officerish.

MAINWARING (**Giving the speaker a glare**) Our HQ is perched on top of a windswept cliff looking out across the angry sea.

PRODUCER Just a minute, engineer.

ENGINEER (**Crossing to the mike**) Yes, sir.

PRODUCER I shall want the sound effects in here.

ENGINEER I'm afraid that's going to be a bit difficult, sir.

PRODUCER Why?

ENGINEER I had a phone call from the sound effects chaps about half an hour ago, their van's broke down. I don't think they're going to make it.

PRODUCER But this is absurd, I must have the wind and water. Captain Mainwaring, couldn't some of your men simulate them somehow?

JONES Permission to speak, sir. I should like to volunteer to simulate the surging surf sound of the sea. (**He makes sea noises.**)

PIKE Mr Mainwaring, could I do the seagulls?

WALKER Mr Mainwaring, shall I make wind, sir?

MAINWARING Another remark like that, Walker, and I shall order you to leave the broadcast.

PRODUCER Start again please with the sound effects.

MAINWARING Our HQ is perched on top of a windswept cliff, looking across the angry sea.

(**Pike and Jones push Mainwaring out of the way and do the gulls and the sea. Mainwaring pushes his way back.**)

While you are eating your Christmas dinner, we are guarding hearth and home, from the ever present threat across the Channel. I decide that we don't just sit here, it's time for us to go out on patrol. I speak to my Sergeant. It's time for us to go out on patrol.

WILSON Cor blimey, sir, so it is, and it ain't half cold an all. (**Mainwaring reacts.**)

MAINWARING Corporal it's time for us to go out on patrol.

JONES Men it's time for us to go out on patrol.

MAINWARING The men now realise that it is time for them to go out on patrol. Who wrote this rubbish?

PRODUCER I did!

WILSON (**Covering the mike**) Be careful what you say he can hear every word.

JONES Come on, lads, we're going on patrol.

MAINWARING And in less time than it takes to tell, the men are marching along the cliff top, in the teeth of the biting wind. Suddenly one of them points and speaks.

WALKER What's that, Corp'?

JONES What's what?

WALKER Look there's an object floating in the water.

WILSON S'truth there is an' all.

FRAZER Och ai, the mons right the noo, och ai.

MAINWARING Said Jock, our Scottish Private. All eyes peered out sea.

JONES What can it be, what can it be, Sarge?

WILSON Cor blimey, stone the crows, it looks suspicious an' all. Look I don't want to be awkward or difficult, but this doesn't seem awfully good English to me.

PRODUCER It's not supposed to be good English, it's supposed to be cockney.

WILSON But I don't speak with a cockney accent.

PRODUCER I naturally assumed that being a Sergeant you would.

WILSON Well I don't.

PRODUCER Oh dear, look I know what, how would it be if the Sergeant played the part of the Officer and the Officer played the part of the Sergeant. I think that would sound more natural.

MAINWARING Young man, I am the Officer, and he is the Sergeant and it's staying that way.

PIKE Mr Mainwaring, I haven't got anything to say. Is it because I speak common like you.

MAINWARING Just carry on being a seagull, Pike. And try and make your voice more seagully. All right, Jones.

JONES What can it be, what can it be, Sarge?

WILSON Cor blimey, stone the crows, it looks suspicious an' all.

GODFREY I've got an idea, sir, if you keep me covered, I'll shin down the cliff, dodge between those boulders, crawl under the barbed wire, and out along the jetty where I can get a closer dekko. Then I'll quickly nip back and give you the griff, won't take two shakes of a lamb's tail.

WILSON Right, scarper down and take a quick butchers.

GODFREY I'm off.

WILSON Cor blimey, sir, look at him go an' all.

FRAZER Och ai, he's like a wee mountain goat.

MAINWARING I decided to take no chances, tell the men to get under cover, Sergeant.

WILSON Right guvnor, 'ere corp, tell the men to get their flippin' 'eads down.

MAINWARING Come on, Jones, it's you.

JONES What page is it? Tikayetye BO.

MAINWARING Tikayetye BO – tikkiti boo.

JONES Tikkiti bo, Sarge, you heard what the Sarge said, take cover.

MAINWARING The men moved like a smooth well-oiled machine. Suddenly above the sound of the surf, we heard the faint cry of Godfrey's voice.

GODFREY All clear.

MAINWARING We heaved a deep sigh of relief.

(**They all sigh.**)

It was a false alarm, but it could have been a Nazi submarine. So give us a thought as you are tucking into your Christmas dinners. Think of us the men of Britain's Home Guard, who are on constant watch day and night. Simple men, shop keepers, factory workers, butchers, bakers…

FRAZER And undertakers. James Frazer, 91, High Street, Walmington. Reasonable prices, sympathetic attention.

MAINWARING Frazer! … men from all walks of life. We seek no reward, only to do our duty, content in the knowledge, that our children, and our children's children, will grow up to be free men, and women…

WALKER And children. (**Mainwaring reacts.**)

SCENE 3: EXTERIOR. BROADCASTING HOUSE. DAY.
Stock shot of BBC, 1941. Over the picture we hear the start of the Christmas Day broadcast 1941. *To Absent Friends.*

SCENE 4: INTERIOR. CHURCH HALL. DAY.

JONES They're a bit late, Mr Mainwaring.

MAINWARING Yes, I can't understand it, look at the time, we should have been on the air ages ago. (**To engineer**) What's happening?

ENGINEER I can't quite make it out, nothing's come through, but don't worry, I'm just waiting for the standby light, should be through at any minute.

MAINWARING Stand by everyone, and when I get to my final speech, just give me plenty of room. I enjoy doing that speech you know, Wilson.

WILSON Yes, sir, it is rather moving.

MAINWARING Gives me a warm glow, right here.
(**Taps his chest.**)

PIKE Just think, Mr Mainwaring, you'll be the last one to speak before the King, do you think he'll be listening?

MAINWARING Oh yes, and the Queen and Princess Elizabeth and Princess Margaret Rose.

(**Hodges bursts in singing. They all ssshh him.**)

HODGES What happened to you lot?

MAINWARING Be quiet, we're just about to go on the air.

HODGES It's all over, I've just been listening to the King's speech. *Old Mother Riley's Christmas Party* is on now.

MAINWARING Old Mother…

PRODUCER Awfully sorry, chaps, Hong Kong over ran. Had to cut you out. We couldn't keep His Majesty waiting.

MAINWARING (**Quietly**) There's something I want to say and I want you to listen very carefully. Are you listening?

PRODUCER Yes, I'm here.

(**Mainwaring blows and bangs the mike three times.**)

A LEGEND BEGINS

Everyone involved in the location shooting for the very first series back in 1968 was sent a copy of Harold Snoad's filming schedule, informing them of all the arrangements. This detailed memo makes interesting reading and provides an insight into just how much is involved in arranging such an event.

```
        "DAD'S
        ARMY"

(by Jimmy Perry & David Croft)



        FILMING

        SCHEDULE

          and

        general

        arrangements


          AT

    THETFORD, NORFOLK

          and

    surrounding areas


    TRAVELLING APRIL 1st.
    FILMING APRIL 2nd.-6th.
```

```
                                                            Page 1
        WHO'S WHO !                     AND WHERE THEY'RE STAYING

DAVID CROFT          Producer/S'writer      Bell Hotel
HAROLD SNOAD         Production Asst.        Bell Hotel
EVELYN LUCAS         Producers Asst          Bell Hotel
EVAN KING            Asst.Floor Manager      Bell Hotel
JIMMY PERRY          Scriptwriter            Bell Hotel

SANDRA EXELBY        Make Up Supervisor      Bell Hotel (also make-up
MARGARET MACKINNON   Make Up Asst.           Bell Hotel          room)
GEORGE WARD          Costume Supervisor      Bell Hotel
ALAN HATCHMAN        Wardrobe Asst.          Bell Hotel
PAUL JOEL            Designer                Bell Hotel

MAX SAMMETT          Cameraman               Making own arrangements
TERRY CHAPMAN        Asst.Cameraman          Making own arrangements
Unknown at present   Grips                   Anchor Hotel
BILL WILD            Sound Recordist         Anchor Hotel
JOHN TELLICK         Asst.Recordist          Anchor Hotel

JACK LEMMOX          Armourer                Central Hotel
                     Visual Effects          Anchor Hotel
LES BLAKE            Prop man                Central Hotel
STEPHEN PHILLIPS     Prop man                Central Hotel
Unknown at present   Prop van Driver         Central Hotel
Unknown at present   Make Up van Driver      Central Hotel
JACK WRIGHT          Motor Cyclist           Anchor Hotel(Mon.nt.only)


A ROOM HAS BEEN BOOKED AT THE BELL HOTEL AS A JOINT PRODUCTION
OFFICE AND WARDROBE
        ARTISTES

ARTHUR LOWE          Capt.Mainwaring         Bell Hotel (from Tues.nt.)
JOHN LE MESURIER     Sgt.Wilson              Bell Hotel
CLIVE DUNN           L/Cpl.Jones             Bell Hotel
JOHN LAURIE          Pte.Fraser              Bell Hotel
JAMES BECK           Pte.Walker              Bell Hotel
ARNOLD RIDLEY        Pte.Godfrey             Bell Hotel
IAN LAVENDER         Pte.Pike                Bell Hotel

RICHARD JACQUES      )                       Bell Hotel
HUGH HASTINGS        ) Members of L.D.V.     Bell Hotel
COLIN BEAN           )                       Bell Hotel

GEOFFREY LUMSDEN     Colonel Square          Bell Hotel (Thurs.nt.only)
THERESE MCMURRAY     Woman in house          Bell Hotel (Wed.nt.only)
LEON CORTEZ          Henry,the Milkman       Anchor Hotel (Wed.nt.only)
CHARLES HILL         The Butler              Anchor Hotel (Wed/Thurs.
                                                     nts.only)
                     George (at Museum)      Bell Hotel (Wed.nt.only)

CHRIS FRANKS         )                       )
DAVID SEAFORTH       )                       )
ALEC COLEMAN         )                       ) Anchor Hotel
HUGH CECIL           ) Additional L.D.V.     ) (Tues.nt.only)
VIC TAYLOR           ) personnel             )
JIMMY MAC            )                       )
PETER WHITTAKER      )                       )
8 RIDERS                                     Anchor Hotel (Thurs.nt.only)

Addresses of hotels   Bell Hotel,      Anchor Hotel,    Central Htl.
                      King Street,     Bridge Street,   Market Place
                      Thetford,Norfolk Thetford,Norfolk Thetford,Nfk.
                      (Thetford 2055)  (Thetford 3329)  (Thet'd 2259)
```

TRAVEL ARRANGEMENTS   Page 2

This refers to Artistes and staff who are not able to travel down
to Thetford on the coach leaving T.V.C. (Main Reception) at 3.0 p.m.
on the 1st.April and returning to London on the 6th.

Monday, 1st.April

By car (after evening recording)   Clive Dunn
By car   John Le Mesurier

Tuesday, 2nd.April

By train (Dep.Liv.St.8.36   Arthur Lowe
         Arr.Thetford 11.05)   Chris Franks
                                    David Seaforth
                                    Alec Coleman
                                    Hugh Cecil
                                    Vic Taylor
                                    Jimmy Mac
                                    Peter Whittaker

Retrning to London   Jack Wright

Wednesday, 3rd.April

By train (Dep.10.36 Liv.St.   Therese McMurray
         Arr.Thetford 13.02)   Leon Cortez

         (Dep.22.44 Liv.St.   Charles Hill
         Arr.Thetford 01.20(Thurs.)

Returning to London   7 additional LDV members
                                     who came down on Tuesday

Thursday,4th.April

By train (late afternoon ?)   Geoffrey Lumsden
By road ("   "   )   Horses & Riders
Returning to London   Therese McMurray
                                     Leon Cortez

Friday,5th.April

Returning to London   Charles Hill
                                     Geoffrey Lumsden

Returning to Kent ?   8 Horses and Riders

_____

TRAIN TIMES THETFORD TO LONDON

Dep. 07.22, 08.52, 10.31, 12.39, 14.40, 16.57, 19.02, 23.57.

All the times mentioned on this page are believe to be correct
but it is suggested that they should be checked nearer the dates
in question. It is normally necessary to change at either Ely or
Cambridge. Trains also leave from Kings Cross.

MONDAY,1st.APRIL   Page 3

A.M.   Load Prop van

P.M.   Coach departs from Main Reception at Television
            Centre at 3.0 p.m. for Thetford

NOTE

IT WILL BE SEEN FROM THE FOLLOWING PAGES
THAT A COACH LEAVES THE BELL HOTEL, THETFORD
AT 9.0 A.M. DAILY (EXCEPT WEDNESDAY) TO
TAKES ARTISTES AND STAFF TO OUR VARIOUS
LOCATIONS.   THIS VEHICLE WILL ALWAYS BE
AVAILABLE FOR BOARDING UP TO FIFTEEN MINUTES
EARLIER.   AS WE HAVE A VERY TIGHT FILMING SCHEDULE
IT IS EVERYONES OWN RESPONSIBILITY TO SEE
THAT THEY ARE ON BOARD READY TO GO AT 9.0 a.m.
IT CAN TAKE UP VALUABLE FILMING TIME SCOURING
THREE DIFFERENT HOTEL FOR STAFF OR L.D.V. PERSONNEL
WHO HAVE GONE A.W.O.L. (OR WORSE STILL - DESERTED !)

ARTISTES SHOULD BE CHANGED INTO COSTUME AS ONLY
THE VERY MINIMUM OF CHANGES WILL BE COMPLETED
ACTUALLY ON LOCATION

TUESDAY, 2nd.APRIL   Page 4

LOCATION   STANFORD PRACTICAL TRAINING AREA

How to get there   Take A134 out of Thetford (signposted Mundford)
                   and after approx. 5½ miles turn Right (B 1108)to
                   West Tofts. Rendezvous on road outside Army
                   camp which is on the right hand side of the road

TIME   COACH LEAVES BELL HOTEL AT 8.45 a.m.
                   (other vehicles to rendezvous at Army camp at
                                                        9.0 a.m.

FILMING DETAILS

Show	Page	Action	Artistes	Costume
2	2	Map business	Jones Jack Wright	1914/18 uniform Dispatch rider
4	1	Flamethrower	Jones/Pike	Wing suits plus armbands
4	1	Tank routine	Jones	Wing suit plus armband
1	2	Stakes in ground	Frazer	Naval pullover, flannels,etc.
3	1	Road block (was trench business)	Frazer Dispatch rider Godfrey	Naval pullover, flannels etc. Tweed suit (both plus a'bands
2	1	Parade inspection	Mainwaring Wilson Jones Walker,Fraser,Pike Godfrey 10 add. L.D.V.	Tweed suit,cap Tweed or check suit.Pk.-pie hat 14/18 uniform Working suits Assorted suits
1-6	crds	Extended order marching (4 different versions to be shot)	7 principals 10 add.L.D.V.	4 different sets 1)working suits 2)above(+ furniture) 3)battledress + denim 4)L.D.V.uniforms
1	2	Signpost business	Jones Jack Wright (Dispatch rider)	Tweed w/coat, striped shirt, trilby,L.D.V. band + 1 stripe uniform

NOTES 1) Location Caterers will be in attendance for lunch
       2) Coach will leave location at approx.11.30 and pick up
          Arthur Lowe at the Bell Hotel and Chris Franks,David
          Seaforth,Alec Coleman,Hugh Cecil,Vic Taylor,Jimmy Mac,
          and Peter Whittaker from the Anchor Hotel at 12 noon.
          Thse Artistes should have arrived at Thetford by train at
          11.05. and by 12 noon be changed into costume. The coach
          will bring them back to the location.
       3) AS THE NAME OF THE LOCATION IMPLIES THIS AREA IS A MILITARY
          BATTLE AREA. BECAUSE OF THIS AND THE PRESENCE OF ASSORTED
          SHELLS WHICH THE ARMY FIRE ON 68 DIFFERENT RANGES OVER THE
          AREA ARTISTES AND STAFF MUST NOT WANDER OFF OR COME AND GO
          AS MIGHT NORMALLY HAPPEN. THIS POINT CANNOT BE OVER-
                                                        EMPHASISED

WEDNESDAY,3rd.APRIL   Page 5

FIRST LOCATION   THE NORVIC ROOM,ANCHOR HOTEL,THETFORD

TIME   FILMING STARTS AT 11 a.m. (Lighting will be rigged prior
         to this and make up and costuming completed)

Show	Page	Action	Artistes	Costume
1	a	Re-union dinner	Mainwaring Godfrey,Walker, Fraser,Pike, Richard Jacques, Colin Bean + Peter Whittaker as Head Waiter	Assorted Dinner Suits Tails

AFTER LUNCH which will be taken in Thetford according to individual
                                                        requirements
LOCATION a nearby road - Newtown

| 2 | 25 | Milk float procession | 7 main characters
Henry(milkman) | working suits |

LOCATION (Mr.& Mrs.Ringer) 59 Newtown

| 5 | 1 | Digging for Victory | Jones,Frazer,Godfrey | Working suits, Armbands,tin helmets |

LOCATION (Mr.& Mrs.Gray) 60 Newtown

| 5 | 1 | Window box gag | Mainwaring,Wilson
Therese McMurray | Working suits (steel helmets with nets) |

AND AFTER DARK

| 6 | | Back garden & key business | Walker,Richard
Jacques,Colin Bean
Therese McMurray | Battledress denims + s.hel. |

THURSDAY, 4th. APRIL Page 6

FIRST LOCATION   ON ROAD OUTSIDE FENGATE FARM, WEETING, NR. BRANDON

How to get there   Take B.1107 out of Thetford (signposted Brandon)
and follow this to Brandon turning Right onto
the B.1106 to Weeting. There is an un-numbered
road on the left just as you enter the village
and about a mile down the road is Fengate Farm
(reached by a rough track which is a fork on the
left)

TIME   COACH LEAVES BELL HOTEL AT 8.45 a.m.
(Other vehicles to rendezvous at first location
at 9.0 a.m.)(NOTE Reserve of garden roller to
be taken in coach. PROP VAN to proceed straight
to Oxburgh Hall dropping off garden roller, rope
etc. at second location on the way)

FILMING DETAILS AT FIRST LOCATION

Show	Page	Action	Artistes	Costume
2	2	Steamroller gag (end of)	Richard Jacques, Hugh Hastings, Colin Bean	See beginning of gag at 2nd. location

SECOND LOCATION   GRASSED PIT ON RIGHT HAND SIDE OF ROAD
BETWEEN SWAFFAM AND OXBURGH

How to get there from first location   Go back to B.1106, turn
right and then left. This will join up with
the A.1065. Follow this to Swaffam. In the
village of Swaffam turn left
About a mile after a rifle range(to be seen on
the right) there is a white gate alongside the
grassed pit.

2	2	Steamroller gag (start of)	Mainwaring Wilson Jones 4 other main characters Richard Jacques Hugh Hastings Colin Bean	Tweed coat, cap Tweed/check suit 14/18 uniform Working suits Working suits (all with LDV armbands)

THIRD LOCATION   OXBURGH HALL, OXBURGH
How to get there from second location   Continue on same road to
village of Oxburgh.
PARKING   On sandy road opposite main entrance to Hall

3	4	Museum sequence	7 main characters R.Jacques, C.Bean H.Hastings George	as Milk Float procession yesterday
		Scuffle gag	Jones	Working suit with LDV armband
3	4	Hitler at door of Oxburgh Hall	Mainwaring Butler	Working suit with LDV armband

NOTES   Location Caterers will be in attendance at Oxburgh Hall for lunch
Prop van to collect garden roller etc. from second lunch
location on way back to Thetford

FRIDAY, 5th. APRIL Page 7

LOCATION   STANFORD PRACTICAL TRAINING AREA (Rendezvous on
B.1108 just before the right hand private road
which leads to the actual camp)

NOTE   THE SAME SAFETY REGULATIONS AS MENTIONED ON TUESDAY'S
SCHEDULE MUST APPLY AT THIS LOCATION

TIME   COACH LEAVES BELL HOTEL AT 8.45 a.m.
(Other vehicles to rendezvous (as above) at 9 a.m.

Show	Page	Action	Artistes	Costume
3	41	Scene with horses	7 main characters R.Jacques, C.Bean H.Hastings Butler Colonel Square 8 riders	Working suits with LDV a'bands
5	69	Assault course	Walker Pike R.Jacques, C.Bean H.Hastings	Jeff/George denims, white ho. as above - with ordinary helmet as for Pike

Note   Location Caterers will be in attendance for lunch

SATURDAY, 6th. APRIL Page 8

FIRST LOCATION   IN THETFORD (but exact details to follow)

TIME   FILMING TO START AT 9 a.m.

Show	Page	Action	Artistes	Costume
3	2	Business with railings	7 main chars. R.Jacques, C.Bean, H.Hastings	All in working suits with LDV armbands

SECOND LOCATION   STANFORD PRACTICAL TRAINING AREA (Rendezvous
as yesterday)

2	3	Crossing the river	Jones Walker	14/18 uniform and Long Johns Working suit or sports coat & fl'n's (gets wet !)
6		Bayonet fighting	Frazer, Jones Pike	LDV uniforms and armbands
6		Marching with small handcart	7 main characters R.Jacques, C.Bean, H.Hastings	All in LDV uniform with armbands, for'ge caps and steel helmets

ANYTHING NOT COMPLETED WHICH WOULD BE POSSIBLE ON THIS
LOCATION

It should be possible to take lunch (possibly rather late) in
Thetford before returning to London

FILMING CONTACTS and
PHONE NUMBERS   Page 9

Stanford Practical Training Area	Colonel Pleasbey-Thompson (Thetford 3224)
Steam Roller	Mr.Parrot, Fengate Farm, Weeting, Nr. Brandon (Brandon 317)
Location Caterers	Roff's (Bury St.Edmunds 3419)
Milk Float	Mr.A.Manning (Watton 460)
Oxburgh Hall	Custodian Mr.Hart, Stable Cottages, Oxburgh (Gooderstone 258)
	National Trust Area Agent Mr.Corbin (Aylsham 312)
59 Newtown, Thetford	Mr.& Mrs.Ringer (no 'phone)
60 Newtown, Thetford	Mr.& Mrs.Gray (no 'phone)
Bell Hotel	Manager Mr.Burnley (Thetford 2055)
Anchor Hotel	Manageress Mrs.Bishop (Thetford 3329)
Central Hotel	Proprietor Mr.Talbot (Thetford 2250)
Thetford Railway Station	Thetford 2243
Thetford Police Station	Thetford 2223

TECHNICAL REQUIREMENTS

35 mm. sync.shooting. 10/1 zoom (Silent shooting at times)
2 LOUDHAILERS , Lights (as ordered by Cameraman)(with 300ft.
leads)on 3rd.April and 4th.April. Their first meeting with
us will be at 9.30 a.m. at the Anchor Hotel, Thetford on the 3rd.

Small dolly for tracking indoors plus facilities to enable
filming from roof of camera car and possibly from roof of
Dormerbil (which I believe the Grips will be driving)

NOTE   This schedule was compiled and laboriously typed by
Harold Snoad (the slowest one finger typist in captivity)
and Miss Evelyn Lucas wishes it to be known that she
dis-associates herself from its content, layout or any
tyrogpaphikal errors.

WALMINGTON PHOTO GALLERY

This is one of my favourite sections of the book. My aim was to produce a photo montage representing moments in the lives of some of the main performers who appeared in *Dad's Army*. Thanks either to the actors themselves, or relatives of deceased members of the cast, I have been able to obtain photographs from their own family albums, most of which have never been published before. Although, in some cases, I had more photos than I could possibly use in the book, I feel that those selected in this chapter provide a glimpse of the subjects' lives away from Walmington.

ARTHUR LOWE

1 Arthur with his pony, Daisy.

2–4 Arthur with his wife, Joan Cooper, who made several appearances in *Dad's Army*.

5 An early character shot.

JOHN LE MESURIER

1 John, aged three.

2 Appearing in *Strife* at Croydon Rep.

3 In *Winter Sunshine*, John played a blind man.

4 With his wife, Joan, at home.

5 John watches the world go by from his garden.

CLIVE DUNN

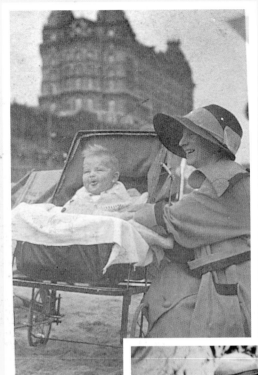

1 Clive and his mother at Scarborough in 1920.

2 Clive with his mother, Connie, on Llandudno pier in 1935.

3 Clive, ready to perform, in 1948.

4 Clive during his army days, in 1942.

IAN LAVENDER

1 A young Ian in Llandudno in 1956.

2 Ian made his TV debut in *Flowers at My Feet* in 1968.

3 Ian marries Michele.

4 Playing Mother Goose in a 1996 panto.

5 As Noel Coward in *Noel and Gertie* in 1999.

JOHN LAURIE

1 Between 1916 and 1917, John served in the 2nd battalion of the Honourable Artillery Company.

2 Playing Dr James Garsten in the 1947 film *Mine Own Executioner.*

3 During a break from filming 1950's *Pandora and the Flying Dutchman*, John signs autographs on Pendine Sands.

4 Outside a Stratford-on-Avon hotel in 1928, John shows off his car.

5 Getting married in 1928.

JIMMY BECK

1 Jimmy Beck, aged six.

2 Jimmy at home with his wife, Kay.

3 Jimmy, in his twenties, takes a walk with his friend.

4 During national service Jimmy (back row, 2nd left) was a PT instructor.

5 An early shot.

ARNOLD RIDLEY

I Arnold as
a young man.

2 Out on location.

3 The face of Private
Godfrey.

4 Off on a trip.

5 Arnold relaxes
in the garden.

FRANK WILLIAMS

1 Frank, aged one.

2 Aged 16, with his parents and pet dog, in 1948.

3 Playing in the garden.

4 Frank made his name playing Captain Pocket in *The Army Game* (1960–1961).

5 Frank is his early thirties.

EDWARD SINCLAIR

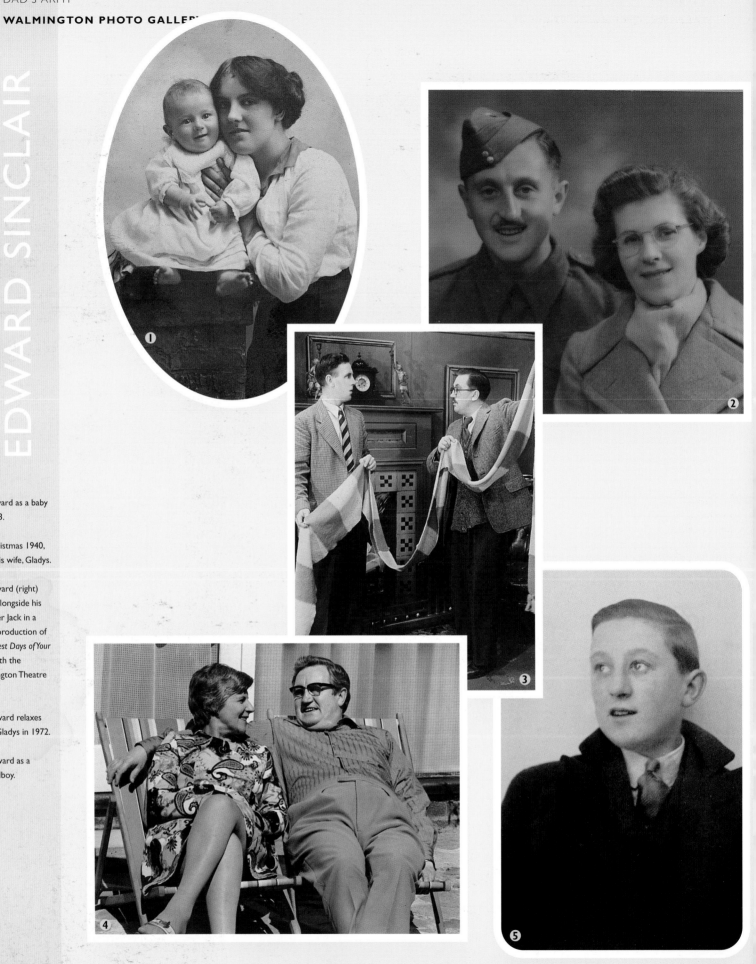

1 Edward as a baby in 1913.

2 Christmas 1940, with his wife, Gladys.

3 Edward (right) plays alongside his brother Jack in a 1951 production of *Happiest Days of Your Life* with the Teddington Theatre Club.

4 Edward relaxes with Gladys in 1972.

5 Edward as a schoolboy.

BILL PERTWEE

1 Bill, aged five, in his garden at Hereford, in 1931.

2 A mid-1970s film appearance.

3 Bill appearing in a 1950s radio broadcast of *Workers' Playtime*.

4 Bill with his wife, Marion, and their son, in 1966.

5 Bill, aged 21.

JANET DAVIES

1–3 Janet with her
son, Andrew.

4 Cast of *The Love
Match* in the mid-
1950s.

5 With Arthur Askey.

ERIC LONGWORTH

1 Eric as a boy.

2 A perfect character pose.

3 Eric in a 1948 production of *Clutterbuck* at Oldham.

4 Appearing at Northampton in a 1978 production of *Hobson's Choice*.

5 Eric on leave in Kashmir, 1943.

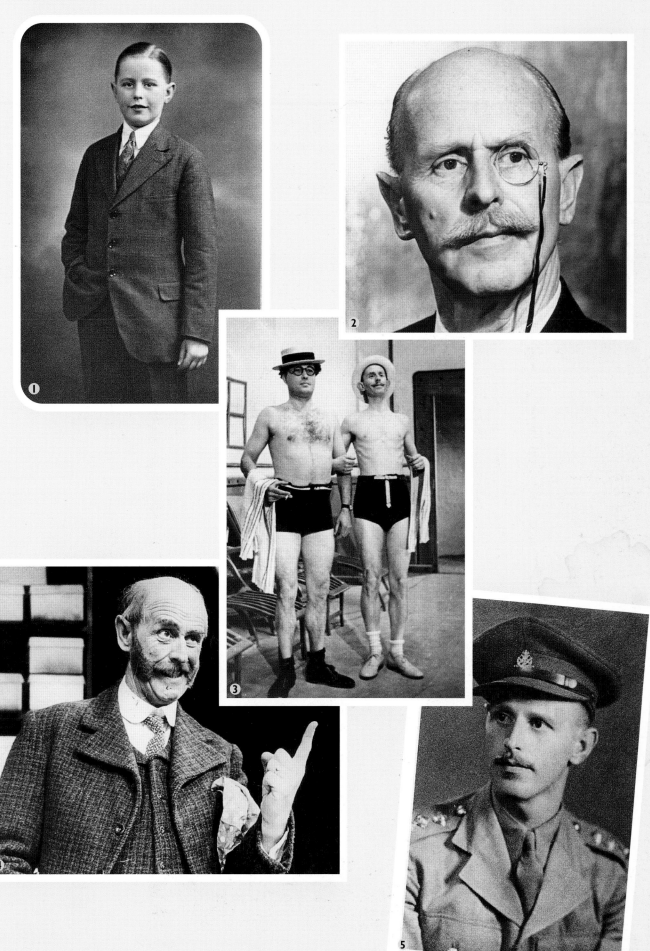

PAMELA CUNDELL

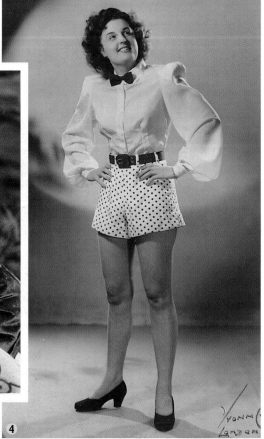

1 A portrait from 1950.

2 Entertaining an audience in 1948.

3 & 4 Pamela has played varied roles during a busy career.

ROBERT RAGLAN

1 Robert as a boy.

2 Robert
(3rd from left)
serving in the army.

3 A young actor.

4 Robert (centre)
playing George
in *The Young Idea*.

5 Playing a
character part.

GEOFFREY LUMSDEN

1 Geoffrey as
a little boy in 1917.

2 Growing up.

3 Relaxing in 1949.

4 Geoffrey (1st left)
in *The Happy Man* at
the Salisbury
Playhouse, 1958.

5 Getting married
in 1947.

HAROLD BENNETT

1 Harold as
a young boy.

2 Harold posing
for a publicity still.

3 Serving in the
army during the First
World War.

4 A portrait.

5 Enjoying a day
out fishing.

AND FINALLY...

The final word has nearly been penned. A lot of effort and time has gone into writing this book, but that's a pleasure when it involves your favourite sitcom. One of the joys of completing this project has been smiling at life in Walmington-on-Sea, sharing a moment with the likes of pompous Captain Mainwaring and his nonchalant sergeant, Arthur Wilson.

There are so many special moments in *Dad's Army* that picking favourite scenes and episodes is an almost impossible task. It's a tough job but I thought I'd do my best and share with you examples of what I regard as among Perry and Croft's finest achievements in respect of this sitcom.

People question whether writers of television shows use their scripts to convey inner meanings and statements on life when half the time they are simply trying to produce a straightforward, funny script. That said, intentionally or not, Jimmy Perry and David Croft delivered a multitude of scripts that as well as being outstandingly humorous, tackled and explored some of the social issues facing Britain during the war years. When it comes to selecting favourite episodes, my choice contains instalments which mixed laughter with a touch of pathos. 'Branded', which comes out top of the pile, broaches the controversial subject of conscientious objecting, a delicate matter carefully examined by Perry and Croft. In fact when the episode was first shown, many viewers who could appreciate the tension and hurt such an issue could cause, wrote in to congratulate the writers on how they handled the episode. The poignant scene when Godfrey is cold-shouldered and left alone in the patrol hut to munch away at his upside-down cakes almost brings a tear to the eye.

Next on my list of favourites is 'Mum's Army', a brilliant parody of that classic movie *Brief Encounter*. This episode exposes the vulnerability of the bravehearted Captain Mainwaring, who lets his emotions get the better of him when he becomes besotted by the charms of Walmington's newest resident, Mrs Gray. Mainwaring's home life brings him nothing but misery, so when someone comes along who epitomises what a perfect wife should be, he gets swept along and declares that he'll do anything for her, even if that means giving up the bank. I feel sorry for the Captain in this instalment, bound to a life from which he so desperately wants to free himself.

My third choice is 'My Brother and I', which introduces the black sheep of the Mainwaring family: the drunken brother Barry, who's lost his way in life and resorts to the bottle to see him through. I like this episode for all the obvious reasons, including the solid acting and wonderful script, but it also spotlights the adage: 'Life is what you make it', exemplified beautifully by the Mainwaring brothers.

I find it impossible to choose a favourite scene, there are so many; but I'd like to mention some of those I particularly enjoy and could watch incessantly, laughing every time. In 'Mum's Army' we find Mainwaring sharing a table with Mrs Gray in Ann's Pantry. The scene in which he ends up explaining to most of his platoon, who just happen to be frequenting the café that morning, that he pops in from time to time, is extremely funny. Mainwaring appears in another classic scene in 'A Wilson (Manager)?'. He hasn't been at his desk long when he receives a series of infuriating phone calls, resulting in him asking the Vicar sarcastically whether Wilson's been made Archbishop of Canterbury – great viewing.

'Fallen Idol' in which Mainwaring gets drunk while on an exercise, includes the gloriously funny moment when the Captain swivels around the tent pole, mistaking it for revolving doors. The so-called party, which Mainwaring throws in his house during 'The King was in his Counting House', is an enjoyable scene, as is the time members of the platoon push Barry Mainwaring into a cupboard to keep him out of harm's way in 'My Brother and I'. One of the things I liked about Arthur Lowe's portrayal of Captain Mainwaring was the little idiosyncrasies he injected into the character: perfectly timed pauses, glares, a rub of his red rotund face or a little puff, seen when he's on the phone to Godfrey, who's got confused in 'Wake-Up Walmington'. And no selection of golden moments from the *Dad's Army* legend would be complete without the touching closing scene in the final episode, 'Never Too Old', when the actors toast the Home Guard.

What would we have done without the delights of *Dad's Army*?

FALL-OUT

'We had been going for eight years. During this time we had made 74 programmes, created a West End stage show followed by a national tour and also we had made a feature film. We had lost Jimmy Beck who played Walker and missed him sorely. Arnold Ridley (Godfrey) and John Laurie (Frazer) were getting distinctly frail while John Le Mesurier was looking positively ill. On location in the middle of the Stanford Battle Area during the shooting of "Number Engaged" I remember ordering all the lights to be assembled and switched on to make him a six-foot square Riviera to warm him up a bit. These facts, coupled with the feeling Jimmy and I had that we had squeezed all the best juice out of the *Dad's Army* orange, made me reluctantly come to the conclusion that it was time to end the much-loved series.

'The show had become very popular but I don't think any of us realised that it was to become a television legend and be voted the best comedy series of all time – not that this would have altered my decision. "Leave them wanting more" is an excellent show business motto.

'The last recording was a very emotional experience for us all. The production gallery was unusually quiet during the recording and a truckload of lumps were in a lot of throats. Just before the end I remember sadly thinking that poor old John Le Mesurier would probably never work again. In fact he made a good recovery, worked a lot and I used him myself in *Hi-De-Hi!*, a year or two later, so I was very wrong. But it was a sad evening. We had all enjoyed a glorious run of success and to stop, albeit at the top, was a wrench. And as they assembled for the last shot and raised their tea mugs to join Arthur's toast, "To Britain's Home Guard", there wasn't a dry eye in the studio.'

DAVID CROFT

BIBLIOGRAPHY

The following publications have proved useful sources of information whilst writing my book.

Calder, Angus, *The People's War – Britain 1939–1945*, Jonathan Cape Ltd, 1969, ISBN 0712652841

Donovan, Paul, *The Radio Companion*, HarperCollins, 1992, ISBN 0586090126

Hayward, Anthony, *Who's Who on Television*, Boxtree, 1996, ISBN 075221067X

The Macmillan Encyclopedia, Macmillan, 1999, ISBN 0333725220

Mercer, Derrik (ed), *Chronicle of the Second World War*, Chronicle Communications Ltd, 1990, ISBN 1872031374

Lee, Min (ed), *British Biographies – The 20th Century*, Chambers, 1993, ISBN 0550160450

Minns, Raynes, *Bombers and Mash*, Virago, 1999, ISBN 1860497942

Palmer, Scott, *British Film Actors' Credits, 1895–1987*, St James Press, 1988, ISBN 1558621660

Vahimagi, Tise, *British Television*, Oxford University Press, 1994, ISBN 0198183364

Webber, Richard, *Dad's Army – A Celebration*, Virgin Publishing, 1999, ISBN 0753503077

Dad's Army Handbook, DAAS, 1999, fully revised and extended by Tony Pritchard and Paul Carpenter, adapted from *Dad's Army, A Guide to Television, Film, Radio and Stage*, originally compiled, researched and produced by David Hamilton, Alan Hayes and Alys Hayes

The theatre programmes from the tour of the stage version of *Dad's Army* were very useful as was the following website: www.imdb.com.